Live Theory

LIVE THEORY

The Aronowitz Reader

Edited by Peter Bratsis, Bruno Gullì,
Kristin Lawler, and Michael Pelias

With a Foreword by Cornel West

ERIS

ERIS

86–90 Paul Street   265 Riverside Dr.
London, EC2A 4NE   New York, 10025

Distributed by Columbia University Press,
New York, NY, and London, England

Designed by Alex Stavrakas

ISBN 9781999798154

eris.press

Contents

LIVE THEORY

CORNEL WEST

Foreword

It is really difficult for me to talk about Stanley because he was such a special person in my life. We knew each other for forty-five years and would meet weekly at Tom's Restaurant or a pizza place. And Stanley was just so fundamentally committed to the life of the mind. I don't think there's been a greater intellectual who was in love with working-class people and culture in the history of the American empire. He was somebody who would uplift you. Now he's twenty years older than me. So he was a kind of uncle. But he always treated me as an equal. And that's very, very rare anywhere in the world, let alone in New York City. I just loved him so very, very dearly, just like he loved me. And I respected him so very, very deeply. Just like he respected me; we were brothers to the bone. Forty-five years. I would have taken a bullet for him, and he would have taken a bullet for me.

When I think of brother Stanley I got to think of what the Greeks said about Socrates. They call him *atopos*. Unsubsumable, unclassifiable: no label, no category could begin to describe his richness, his complexity, his depth, his scope, his breadth, his personality. He was as unique and singular as they come. And yet, at the same time, he was so down to earth. He was in love with those Sly Stone called "everyday people." Poor and working people sat at the very center of his sense of who he was, not just as a thinker, but as a human being. I would say, unequivocally, that

9

Stanley Aronowitz was the greatest organic intellectual of his generation. And if Antonio Gramsci had not invented that term, we would have had to invent it in order to begin to account for who Stanley Aronowitz was, what his calling was, what his vocation was, in the midst of an American empire—in the midst of a predatory capitalist civilization. You could argue, in fact, that he's one of the greatest organic intellectuals in the history of the country. And again, by organic intellectual what I mean is somebody whose commitment to the life of the mind is absolute. And somebody's commitment to the empowerment of poor and working people—absolute. And someone's commitment to finding joy in that intellectual vocation, and in that political engagement—absolute.

It's like Hans-Georg Gadamer. Never used just one note when it came to reflecting—just like a jazz musician. So disciplined, so voracious, reading over and over again, and then taking off and soaring like an eagle. And self-taught—*False Promises* was before his dissertation. We don't have examples of that in the history of American intellectual life. With one exception: St Clair Drake wrote *Black Metropolis* in 1945 and wrote a dissertation in 1952. *Black Metropolis* is still a classic to this day. And I believe that *False Promises* remains a classic and that it puts to shame so many of these highly formalized academicized scholars who gain access to unbelievable privileges and opportunities and who still have so little to say when it comes to serious intellectual substance, let alone to having any political courage. When the history is written of the rise and fall of the American empire and we tease out those intellectuals who were fundamentally committed to telling the truth, standing up for justice, being concerned, pursuing justice at any costs, Aronowitz is going to be one of the few.

Stanley Aronowitz has to be understood, always, as tied to a quest for truth. He followed Adorno in those early moments of *Negative Dialectics* where he says that the condition of truth is allowing suffering to speak. Aronowitz's commitment was to a quest for beauty. Truth is inseparable from beauty, but not identical with it. Here we'll see his fundamental preoccupation not just with culture, but with music. With Beethoven. *Roll over Beethoven* was the name of one of his books. Shostakovich's Symphony Ten he'd hear over and over again. He was a jazz man to the core of his being. He was not just hanging out at Birdland, not just hanging out at Smalls Paradise in Harlem, as we did; he was someone who took jazz seriously as a way of understanding reality, catastrophe, crisis—as a way of generating sustenance, resilience, resistance, the quest for truth, the quest for beauty and yes, the quest for goodness too. The quest for goodness too: the ethical, the moral, inseparable from the beautiful and the truthful. Scientific truth, existential truth: all of that was part and parcel of brother Stanley's *Weltanschauung*, of his overarching worldview.

And in an interesting kind of way, over the forty-five years we had many, many discussions about a variety of different issues, and we would have wonderful fights over religion. He knew about my own revolutionary Christian sensibility. And Stanley was one of the most religiously secular intellectuals that I knew. He was somebody who could put himself in the skin of persons who were still tied to a certain kind of God talk, a certain kind of faith talk. That's what allowed him to be organic to the black freedom struggle. That's what allowed him to be assigned by Bayard Rustin and A. Philip Randolph to be the person to bring the trade union movement into the March on Washington in 1963, when he was only twenty-nine years old. It was the same Stanley that could go into a black church—and I've seen him do it over and over again—and move black folk at the deepest level of their souls because he emptied himself. He gave of himself rhetorically and existentially and connected with them in their church, even given his secular sensibility coming out of the Jewish side of the Bronx—that rich secular Jewish tradition that Stanley was fundamentally shaped by and grounded in.

But his roots, as rich as they were, were broad. They connected him with the routes that he took. He was a cosmopolitan and an internationalist, a globalist to his heart even as he was a localist, even as he was grounded in everyday struggle, even as he was grounded in grassroots organizing his whole life. Where do you begin talking about brother Stanley? I think of T. S. Eliot's raid on the ineffable: language fails, words will fall short; even given this magnificent day, Stanley is too much. He reminds me of Henry Adams's Dynamo. That's brother Stanley: volcanic energy. You think of Keats's fundamental question: energy or despair, Keats says in one of those wonderful poems. Stanley's energy, vitality, vibrancy: all the way live, always engaged, and yet on intimate terms with the darkness. On intimate terms with the underside, the night side—that wonderful line of Tennessee Williams's in *The Night of the Iguana*: the "unlighted side" of the human condition. Stanley Aronowitz, my dear brother Stanley, always connected to the unlighted side—to the suffering and the misery of working people, not just in the American empire but in every corner of the globe: Africa, the Caribbean, Latin America, Asia, Europe, indigenous peoples across national borders. Unlighted condition, underside, and yet always looking for a way out.

He was a walking *paideia*, to use the Greek term for deep education (rather than cheap schooling). That's why my dear brother Henry Giroux who, probably knew Stanley intellectually better than most, made the juxtaposition: *against* schooling, and *for* deep *paideia*, deep *Bildung*, deep education. Suspicious of narrow information and truncated skill acquisition, and much more concerned with the transformative process by which we engage in critical thinking, critical pedagogy has everything to do with the formation of attention. Attending to the things that matter, separating them from the superficial levels that too often constitute the source of our attention. Life, death, sorrow, agony, anguish, justice, dread, despair, disappointment, family, community, civic affiliation. How do we mobilize whatever intellectual, moral, spiritual, political resources we can in order to live well—which is to say, live with moral and spiritual excellence, with what the Greeks called *arete*. Stanley exemplified a moral and spiritual and political excellence. Excellence is understood here as a virtue, and virtue, you understand, is a verb, as well as a disposition of behavior.

Stanley was always in motion, like Curtis Mayfield: always keeping on pushing, always moving. He's full of attempts to connect to the kenosis, to the emptying, in the sense that he was always pure: always pouring out what was inside of him, but always connecting it to others so as to enable and to empower them. And I am a living example. I will always fall short of my dear brother Stanley's example. When I conceive of my own work, given my own formation, it's so often over against not just the forty-five years of Stanley's examples, but also those very, very deep and intimate conversations over pizza every Friday night (from 1979 until I made my way to New England), as well as the conversations that would take place around *Social Text*—the journal with Fredric Jameson,

Anders Stephanson, Sonia Sayers that would meet every two weeks. And then Stanley's lectures at Columbia and NYU on *Science as Power*, and his attempt to engage in such profound connections regarding scientific rationality, and how it's under the aegis of capital in its relation to the university—as a site for professional managerial production, as a knowledge factory that has its own narrow, disciplinary divisions of knowledge, and disciplines that make it very, very difficult for the kind of intellectual work that Stanley was interested in. Why?

Because that kind of specialization, professionalization, fragmentation, and differentiation makes it very hard for Stanley to transmit to the younger generation what he was about in terms of synoptic vision, synthetic analysis, synecdochic imagination—synecdoche of course being the rhetorical trope that has to do with the relation of parts and wholes, and with the ways in which parts are interdependent and intertwine. Interrelated, and yet the whole is always more than the sum of the parts. And when that synoptic vision, synthetic analysis, and synecdochic imagination are put in the service of a radical imagination, and when radical democracy is put in the service of a militant activism, conformity is shattered, complacency is shattered, complicity is shattered, and, most importantly, what his hero C. Wright Mills called moral cowardliness in the academy is shattered. And it's no accident that Stanley's next to last book was on one of his own heroes, the iconoclastic, idiosyncratic sociologist at Columbia, riding his motorcycle, with his hat on, from Texas: C. Wright Mills. Dead at forty-five, but lived at least two lifetimes in terms of the scope of his production. Stanley was very much influenced by that C. Wright Mills, who, in his classic of 1959, *The Sociological Imagination*, had his critique of abstract empiricism, of abstract theory that had very little to do with the lived experience of suffering and struggling, poor and working people.

I think Stanley's text of 1981 really requires a serious rereading: *The Crisis in Historical Materialism: Class, Politics, and Culture in Marxist Theory*. We've yet to really catch up with that text. It's one of the most important texts in the history of the American left, in the history of American Marxist theory. I remember writing a review of it in the January 1982 issue of the *Village Voice*. And I started off saying it's a book that's in a class of its own. It is pioneering in its theoretical formulations, it is

13

powerful in its philosophical interrogations, it is penetrating in its social analysis, historical analysis, and it is provocative in its prescription for political action.

Because what Stanley was doing there was writing at a time in which the left was wrestling with the French occupation of its mind, in which Derrida and Foucault and Deleuze and Lyotard and other persons highly suspicious of any notion of totality—any notion of synecdochic ways of thinking—were becoming hegemonic. And Fred Jameson on the one hand (so deeply tied to Lukács), and Stanley Aronowitz on the other (also deeply tied to Lukács), were trying to recover some notion of totality—not as an ontological notion, not at all. They were following Adorno; it's a heuristic. But it's a lens through which you still have a sense of the whole, even as our universities, as knowledge factories, were becoming places where any sense of what the forest looked like was called into question and where more and more people were concerned with just shining their little narrow nuts in the corner. So the students who come through have very little sense of what the relation is between personal and political, existential and economic, social and spiritual, what the relation is between the nation state and the capitalist economy and the civic sphere and everyday life. What the relation is between the personal problems that might lead one to go to the psychiatrist (on the one hand), and the structural and institutional crises (on the other), and how intertwined they are—the problematic again, in many ways, of C. Wright Mills and others.

Stanley Aronowitz was true to his vocation. He took seriously those two essays by Max Weber of 1917 and 1919: "Science as a Vocation" and "Politics as a Vocation." And whereas Weber divided the ethics of responsibility from the ethics of conviction, Stanley says: I am going to provide a line between social democratic reformism and dogmatic Leninism so that the left can understand that its sense of vocation is always already rooted in an ethics of conviction. But our ethics of responsibility will not be the compromise that Weber talked about; it will be itself a way of continually trying to subvert the ways in which we view the world, the ways in which we organize, and the ways in which we try to fit into narrow two-party politics, or into truncated electoral politics, or simply into an accommodating academy. So that this radical imagination that he has is rooted in vocation, but it is also immersed in an interpretation of the left tradition, in his sense of history.

Deep. And he, like myself, came from a very, very small sliver of the Marxist tradition—they are called council communists. We spent many, many, many, many evenings talking about Gorter, Pannekoek, talking about the great Rosa Luxemburg. In fact, I would argue, there's a sense in which brother Stanley Aronowitz is an American analog to the great Rosa Luxemburg—and there's no Rosa Luxemburg, there's nobody close to her in a variety of different ways. But trying to find ways in which the vanguardism of Lenin is called into question. So you go down with the sailors of Kronstadt—Soviets without Bolsheviks, workers' councils without professional revolutionaries. We want self-management, we want self-education of the workers, we want self-governance of the workers. We don't need this external vanguard who in their elitist way impose their will upon everyday people. Council communists. Like Muste's American Workers Party, like Paul Mattick—that small sliver. Stanley would spend much time in the journal *Root and Branch* in the 1960s—come back again in *Social Text*, come back again in *Situations*—trying to keep alive that council communist, radically democratic, all-the-way-down (but still revolutionary) orientation. We had many discussions, of course, with brother Michael Harrington and our dear sister Frances Fox Piven, and Richard Cloward, and Barbara Ehrenreich, and Manning Marable. Those were some wonderful, wonderful days. But it was a matter of somehow trying to keep the reformers under questioning, so they don't become comfortable with their reformism. And, at the same time, holding at arm's length any of the dogmatic vanguardists whose elitism was too often a sign of their arrogance vis-à-vis everyday people, vis-à-vis working people and poor people. And Stanley provided a grand example of inhabiting that space. And more and more we were beginning to talk about just revolutionary and radical democracy, but it's really a council communist tradition. And Stanley was very, very explicit about that. And of course this all had fascinating relations to the anarchist tradition—even C. Wright Mills would say, "deep down, I really am an anarchist." Bayard Rustin says, "of course I'm an anarchist." Hmm, interesting, interesting.

In that text, *The Crisis in Historical Materialism*, Stanley tries to take very seriously what he always, always viewed as a fundamental part of himself: the Black Freedom Movement. He's one of the rare vanilla left-ist intellectuals—vanilla Marxist intellectuals—who would not just spend time in the *context* of the Black Freedom Movement, but who would also spend time with the movement in his texts. How does white suprema-cy, how do the racist dynamics of a predatory capitalist civilization—the racist dynamics of a settler colonial experiment called the USA—how does that connect with radical thinking and radical politics? And, of course, sister Ellen Willis: one of the great, towering intellectuals wrestling with patriarchy and male supremacy in her own unique feminist way. You got this dynamic duo in the same household. I was blessed to spend a whole lot of time in that household. Very much so. In fact, they were both at my wedding that I had at Union Seminary. One of my contributions was that I had Stanley teaching at Union Theological Seminary in 1979. The first time you had such a towering Jewish secular figure teaching in the Chris-tian seminary, and the students loved him, they packed his classes. They packed his classes. And he would bring Ellen, with her own unique fem-inist formulations. So that Stanley's embracing of the social movements was tied to so-called "identity politics." If you read his book on the politics of identity, you'll see that it's still so much deeper than any of the neoliber-al conceptions of identity politics that you see these days, so much deeper than so many of the theorists these days. Because it's always tied to class, it's tied to empire, and it's tied to culture as a force in and over against the worst of what we see in capitalist civilization and in the imperial project that commenced when the Europeans arrived vis-à-vis indigenous peo-ple, dispossessing their land and subordinating their people.

So Stanley has this overarching view that connects the parts and the wholes, an analysis that is not just intersectional but also constitutive of a larger regime that is tied to profit maximizing. This is where Murray Bookchin plays an important role in his thinking: a domination of nature, a subordination of the environment or the non-human. And Stanley in 1981 has a whole section on the ecological catastrophe and its challenge to Marxist theory. So you got to rethink scientific rationality as a mode of dominating nature. Hence his coming up with: what forms of knowledge can be produced that allow us to view nature as a thou rather than an it (to invoke the language of our dear brother, Martin Buber)? Stanley Aronowitz was already raising those questions forty-three years ago, and look at the mess that we find ourselves in now. How do we cultivate the capacity of the species to avoid self-destruction? With the corporate greed running amok, with the inability to have democratic accountability of elites who are obsessed with money making, and who could actually undercut the possibility of life on the planet?

Brother Stanley was raising that question, which is part of the underside—the unlighted side—that Stan was on intimate terms with, even given his endless smile and what Du Bois would call his delicious chuckle. Stanley's laugh was a sublime activity. It could not but kindle inside of the soul of anyone who heard it something positive, something uplifting. And yet he knew in his vocation, in his calling, that everything was at stake. Everything: life on the planet, a decent life for the masses and for a majority of human beings on the planet. And for him, intellectually, artistically, the higher qualities of being human. And the higher qualities of being human, in this sense, made Stanley in some ways an old-school intellectual. He was very much tied to the Socratic legacy of Athens and to self-interrogation and self-examination as a mode of self-transformation.

Brother Stanley wrote a book in 1970 on the nature of fascism. It's called *Honor America: The Nature of Fascism, Historic Struggles Against It and a Strategy for Today*. Fifty-two years ago, because he knew, like Sinclair Lewis, that it *can* happen here. Yes, fascism is always already at work within the democratic—the so-called democratic—experiment: vis-à-vis indigenous peoples and slavery and Jim Crow and Jane Crow, as well as the vicious patriarchal subordination and ugly degradation of precious gays and lesbians, and of the non-binary. And so, for Stanley, right wing populism in the American empire can easily shade into a full-scale fascist project. So, when he saw Trump, he was not surprised. At all. And he thought the left had spent so much time talking about issues that were not deeply connected to capitalist processes, to class struggle, and to the militarism of the US empire in Africa (with Africom, as well as the 800 military bases around the world). And he also thought the left was too obsessed with critique and didn't talk as much about construction and alternatives.

That's why he ran for governor. He called me up: "Brother Cornel, I'm running for governor." "You running for governor? Good God Almighty, you've been running all your life. Now you running for governor? Oh, Lord." Green Party. Oh, that's brother Stanley. Indeed, that's brother Stanley: "why, we've got to provide some way of getting beyond this narrow view of: there is no alternative to the capitalist order. Margaret Thatcher was wrong; there's got to be an alternative." And people have to see it. They have to hear it in the language, hear it with the vision, hear it with the analysis. And it must be intellectuals who are articulating it within the context of movement—organic intellectuals.

I'm just touching the surface of the genius of my brother. By genius I don't mean some romantic notion of an isolated individual who has just unbelievable cognitive capacity. No, I mean it in a Russian sense. And Stanley was deeply Russian. I would push for Chekhov, he would push for Dostoevsky; we would fight over Dostoevsky vs. Chekhov for hour after hour after hour, but the Russians had a notion of geniality when they talked about genius. Largeness of mind. Largeness of soul. Largeness of heart, largeness of commitment, and, for Stanley, largeness of courage. He never sold out. He never became well-adjusted to injustice and well-adapted to indifference. He knew that indifference is the one trait that makes the very angels weep. He knew that indifference to evil is more insidious than evil itself.

He remained full of that style, that joy, that commitment, that vision, that engagement, that sense of being alive and being glad of being alive in such a hellish world. I would tell him all the time, I'd say: fella, when I grew up in the black church, from the Jackson side of Sacramento, we were told, if the kingdom of God is within you, then everywhere you go, you got to leave a little heaven behind. Brother Stanley left heaven behind in his own distinctive, secular Jewish way that we shall never forget. And so much of his heaven is in my heart, is in my soul. And I will never ever forget my brother Stanley's love for me and others. His service to me and others, and his intellectual commitment to trying to find a way out, given the kind of multi-level catastrophes in which we find ourselves.

MICHAEL PELIAS

Stanley Aronowitz's Living Singularity

"The True is the whole. But the whole is nothing other than
the essence consummating itself through its development..."
Hegel, *The Phenomenology of Spirit*

When a singularity is encountered, it is essential to understand its unique-
ness, its power, its active becoming in the world, and its contribution. Stanley Aronowitz was and remains the consummate labor intellectual in North
America. Ranging from his early journalistic pieces in the US *Guardian*,
alongside his organizational acumen and verve, to the publication of his
widely acclaimed and paradigm-shifting book *False Promises* in 1973, he
stayed the course of labor militancy and its variable ontology until his last
days in the August of 2021. His was a singularity forged in the heat of civil
rights and black power upheavals, in organizing campaigns from the shop
floor to the negotiating tables, and in long studies in philosophy, literature,
science, and the arts—especially film, and above all music. His intellectual
life was marked by his relevance to the rapidly changing times we occupy.

As a labor theorist, Aronowitz emphasized the limitations of collective
bargaining, which he baptized as "collective begging," and the concomitant class-compromised function of the 1935 National Labor Relations Act.
The latter was a sellout of labor militancy. He understood viscerally the
bosses and their functionaries (from the shop floor to the boardrooms), and
he understood the trap that so many labor unionists fall into—that is, the
drive for security at all costs, and the rush to contract in lieu of a transformation of the workplace and the creation of a new drive towards liberation
from tedious, repetitive, and spirit-breaking labor. His career of thinking

through what work is spanned over sixty years, and, unlike many academic labor specialists, Aronowitz brought learned lived experience to his work and teaching—experience that translated into a poignant and analytically superb account of the modern university and its division of labor.

But Stanley Aronowitz was much more than the premier labor intellectual of his generation. He was a transdisciplinary educator and writer. Not only was his range and scope impressive, but its quality was also remarkable. He had the ability to engage and interconnect well beyond the labor question. This collection of thirteen assembled essays represents some of the best of Aronowitz, and it demonstrates the singularity of his thought as it extended across the intellectual divide and its multiple disciplines. What is shown is a poignant grasp of the totality of interconnectedness of all things. Taking off from creative encounters with the necessity of the study of philosophy—while engaging with a moment in which, as a discipline, it lives on even as its actualization has not been realized—Aronowitz showed beyond his reflections on the labor question the need for the invention of new concepts. He understood that eros, as a guiding principle, is the core of the political fight. Unlike many of the orthodox Marxists of his generation, he accentuated the centrality of subjectivity and its relationship to agency. His encounters with Henri Lefebvre's works on everyday life, alongside his appropriation of Heidegger's being-in-the-world and his notion of care as vocation, penetrated his teaching and writing in what we could consider a break in his thought in the last two decades of the twentieth century. Never complacent or comfortable, Aronowitz moved with the *Zeitgeist* in a singular way and with an amazing bird's eye view of the long march that would be required from the streets, and of the journey and struggle that would be needed within the liberal institutions.

In Aronowitz's formation three significant twentieth century philosophical works loom large:

1. Georg Lukács's *History and Class Consciousness*, whose concepts of reification, alienation, and objectification play a significant role in his labor ontology,
2. Henri Lefebvre's *Critique of Everyday Life*, whose everyday-life storytelling of strikes, social movements, and class relations would be

amplified by much of Aronowitz's writings on popular culture, and

3. Theodor Adorno's *Negative Dialectics*, which pervades much of the open methodology of his work on film and music.

Behind all this is the consistent practice of reading Hegel's seventy-two propositions in the Preface to the *Phenomenology of Spirit*, which yielded a special interpretation of scientific cognition with the caveat that there is "no royal road to science." The essays in this volume consistently demonstrate the influence of the rigor of these seminal thinkers on Aronowitz, as well as the originality with which he deploys their thought in order to address the contemporary.

In the cultural and educational field, Stuart Hall and the Birmingham school opened a path for the development of Cultural Studies in the United States. Aronowitz was at the forefront of this movement, and the reader will encounter here a study of the dialogical imagination (much forgotten today)—a brilliant approach to the Dziga Vertov school of filmmaking in the 1920s Soviet Union and its conflict with Eisenstein's montage analytic. As a grand theorist who understood the limitations of the postmodern notion of "partial totality," he reminded us once again of the totality of involvements that would be necessary in order to build a pedagogy of liberation and a future politics of emancipation. Only through the rigors of theoretical critique and reevaluation is a sustained movement possible, and the works contained in this reader consistently remind us of this. Practice without theory is blind, just as theory without practice is useless.

This reader contains more than a sample of Aronowitz's seminal ideas. It more accurately demonstrates his totalizing mind at work—a mind in which the general interconnections between science, labor, culture, education, and, above all, the political nature of the disciplines interact as a unified field. Like Aristotle, Aronowitz understood politics as the master science, and his own organum reflects and refracts this consistently. He stood at the crossroads of theory and practice but never submitted to the dichotomy that plagues so much thought and research today. We invite you to engage a body of work that is more relevant than ever to the rapidly disintegrating and dysfunctional times in which we live. Aronowitz was one of the very few intellectuals of the New Left who did not "sell out" the power of ideas to transform life, and who viscerally shunned resignation and institutional recognition and acceptance.

In this vein, I would like to note four crucial theoretical works that exemplify his ongoing relevance, and to make a modest proposal for reading him substantively and dialectically. *False Promises* was the first of four major theoretical interventions. It still resonates today, especially given the recent American labor union upheaval. The work still raises fundamental questions concerning labor ontology—primarily the need to think life outside of the working day and exhausting labor processes. *The Crisis in Historical Materialism* opened a new debate on how to engage the politics of deconstruction, the ongoing schisms in Marxism, and other left tendencies that attempted to meet the right-wing reaction of the early 1980s. *Science as Power* brought to the foreground questions of how Technoscience dominates our lives and research heuristics. Despite some unevenness, this work is prescient in its anticipation of public policy failure and of the drive for power that marks our epoch. Finally, *How Class Works* reoriented the question of class struggle and class relations into a creative paradigm of class-as-movement that included feminist, black power, disability, and new labor struggles.

His legacy, as he desired, will involve a constant critical reevaluation of his work. He wanted to be remembered first as an educator and a writer, an organic intellectual par excellence who continued the good fight for a society of equality and freedom until the very end. His "live theory" will live as an "essence in development" in the strongest Hegelian sense, and it yields for us orientation in a time of great disorder and confusion. Stanley Aronowitz was a force who knew how to take it bigger, and his gift to us is only beginning to be mined for its infinite wealth of possibilities. We invite you to the journey through this remarkable body of work—interwoven and powerful in the grand spirit of the organic intellectual—and to take the risk of making it bigger and of doing so in a singular fashion to Aronowitz's own. He left us with a radical politics without a party, a war of position that never ends, and the arduous task of building an alternative on the left that thinks and acts beyond the practice of protest and resistance. Aronowitz's singularity was one that simultaneously transformed self and world.

PART ONE

PHILOSOPHY

CHAPTER ONE

The Necessity of Philosophy

The crisis of Marxism deepens, interest in Marxism explodes in America. A group of French philosophers declares the death of Marxism,[1] a British analytic philosopher of language defends Marx's theory of history, pronouncing it an infant science.[2] At the same time, André Gorz, standing somewhere between the two extremes, proclaims that Marxism is at once an indispensable way of looking at the social world but has "lost its prophetic value."[3] Throughout Latin America, radical theologians discover in Marxism an important way to liberate theology from its "other-worldly" predilections, but combining the teachings of the Christian church with the "scientific" teachings of historical materialism.[4] But those reared in the tradition of critical social theory—like Jürgen Habermas, whose Marxist roots were sunk into the eroded soil of postwar German social democracy—have decided that a reconstruction of historical materialism was needed.[5] Such a theory would, according to Habermas, recognize the moral and cognitive dimensions of social transformation where Marxism has refused such recognition; a new kind of historical materialism is necessary to insert a principle of *intersubjectivity* as an objective constituent of the historical process. Habermas seeks a secular ground for moral development and a spiritual ground for secular evolution.

Such is the debate in contemporary theory. Idealists grab for materialist legitimacy, materialists grope for a new terrain in which ethical considerations may be accorded a position of relative autonomy in the processes of historical transformation.

1. At the sociological level, the crisis of Marxism is rather easily explained. Among the underlying reasons for the current disorientation among socialist intellectuals who have adhered to the Marxist theory of history is the palpable failure of the proletariat in the most advanced countries of late capitalism to become the self-conscious agent of revolutionary change. Gorz's claim that Marxism has no prophetic value refers specifically to the expectation that the working class—as the most exploited class within capitalism—was at the same time its gravedigger. Those whose defection from Marxism is grounded in this historical failure hold that the working class has been hopelessly integrated into advanced capitalism by the development of new structures, such as the interventionist state, mass culture, and technological developments that succeed in mitigating—if not removing—economic crises and their consequences for the working class. In addition, the very strength of trade unions—which have produced agreements with employers that provide regular wage increases, codify working rules, and, in the political sphere, have successfully won benefits such as pensions and healthcare for all and protections against the economic impact of joblessness and old age—has stabilized capitalism, or at least has served to encapsulate workers' hopes within the capitalist system rather than outside it. To this tendency of recent theory, workers have become part of the system, even if militantly opposed to particular policies and governments.

2. The discovery, made sooner or later by most socialists of all ideological hues, that "socialism as it really exists"[6] is not only seriously flawed in comparison to the implied and explicit visions of its intellectual founders, but that the actual socialist regimes may be obstacles for achieving human freedom, rather than its bearers. To the extent that Marxism has promised that the condition for the achievement of a self-managed society is the abolition of private property in the means of material production, "really existing" socialism has served as a reminder that other conditions must be present before

equality of access to resources, workers' self-management, and conventional freedoms such as the right to dissent, may be secured.

In this connection, it will not do to argue that self-management can
only be effected under conditions of world socialism or, at the minimum, when the material conditions for its existence are assured. This
argument enabled many intellectuals and militants of the communist
movement to remain staunch supporters of the Soviet Union in the
years between the two great world wars. Many of them stayed in line
during the difficult early postwar period, when the Soviets successfully overcame the economic effects of the scourge left by Nazi destruction. But the failure of de-Stalinization after 1956 has distanced
several generations of intellectuals from the Soviets until, in the past
five years, even most Western communist parties have been forced to
remove themselves from the hegemony of the Soviet bloc or risk disintegration. Today, images of the Gulag no longer evoke as much as a
flutter of protest among most Western Marxists. (The only important
exception in this regard is a trickle of Trotskyists, whose defense of
the Soviet Union carefully separates the Soviet Union's record on human rights from its substantial economic achievement, particularly
the abolition of private ownership of the means of production.) The
work of Rudolph Bahro has solidified the perception that socialism
exists as an antidemocratic, bureaucratic, and anti-ecological system
that has lost touch with its emancipatory precepts. For self-proclaimed
post-Marxists, the truth of historical materialism lies not with the
libertarian hope of its founders, but with the crimes of its children.
For the "new philosophers" of France and their counterparts in other
Western societies, the metaphor of the Gulag defines socialism and
has been the determinate fate of historical materialism. After the fact
of "really existing" socialism, it became the task of those who were
interested in Marxism's burial to show that the logic of Marxism finds
its apogee in the labor camps and mental hospitals that sequester the
system's opponents.

3. Rising new nationalist movements in the Third World have based
themselves upon religious ideas rather than proclaiming some kind
of unique socialism. The confusion among Marxists regarding the

Islamic revolution is a powerful illustration of the current disarray. Marxists at first hailed the overthrow of the Shah of Iran by a mass movement dominated by leaders of religious persuasion, but—having discovered that they were as anti-socialist as they were anti-imperialist—began to hedge on their enthusiasm, retreating to a class analysis that ascribed the revolution to a "national bourgeoisie" unable to complete the revolution. To this day, they have failed to understand the specificity of Islam as a revolutionary, anti-imperialist (and anti-socialist) force. Here, religion is not merely an ideological prop to a class, but has become the form in which revolutionary society may be consolidated. Similarly, many dissident currents within the Soviet Union and other Eastern European countries have adopted religion as the symbolic expression of their rebellion. In both cases "class analysis"—although necessary to understand the course of political and social movement—is clearly insufficient to yield genuine understanding, because it subsumes the moral under economic and class dimensions. The rise of the Catholic and Protestant left defies time-honored images and conceptions of religion among Marxists. Although Marx himself comprehended religion as the sigh of the oppressed, Marxism has focused almost exclusively on its institutional manifestation, finding—often correctly—that organized religion was allied to established regimes, a faithful retainer of the status quo. In consequence, and with few exceptions, Marxism has been unable to grapple with the new currents within the world's religions without the handy tool of class analysis. Thus, on the whole, Marxism remains uncomprehending of Islam, of new currents in Catholic doctrine and of the partial eclipse of political conservatism among world protestants.

Although violations of human rights in Iran have occurred with depressing regularity since Ayatollah Khomeini consolidated his power in 1980, the spectacular death sentence he issued to Salman Rushdie in winter, 1989 underlines the political seriousness of Islamic fundamentalism as a world religion. We have learned by this event that Islam means to exercise power on a global scale and that religious ideas are not merely superstructural phenomena. That they have been intimately linked with power in the Arab world is not surprising, unless you are accustomed to the usual formulae of materialist orthodoxy. In this connection, it is interesting to note that journalists have observed that the threat came in a period when Khomeini's influence may have been waning in favor of a partial move toward secularization among Iran's ruling elite. Such observations are partial explanations but do not exhaust the issue. Modernists seem completely baffled by the resurgence of theocratic politics because they have accepted the evolutionist proposition according to which secularization is an inevitable victor in the war against superstition, that science and technology constitute a value system antithetical to Deism. Clearly, these hasty modernist conclusions have proven to be seriously flawed. While the tendency away from magic and religion accompanies industrial society, it is precisely because modernity has failed in crucial respects, especially spiritually, that anti-modernisms of the left and right are resurgent even as new modernist conquests are recorded in countries of the semi-periphery and the Eastern bloc.

4. The political and social programs of feminism and the ecology movement have evinced a wide spectrum of responses from socialist and communist parties and Marxist intellectuals. On the one hand, the Western left announces its support of women's rights, but practically and theoretically engages in subtle or blatant tactics of cooptation where appropriation is impossible. The Marxist left agrees that there should be abortion on demand, equal pay for comparable work, and full equality in the home between husbands and wives. But Marxism cannot unambiguously grant that the oppression of women is trans-historical, rooted in male domination as much as class domination. Furthermore, Marxism has historically hesitated before the demand for a sexual and social revolution to accompany the political changes socialists desire. Theoretically, Marxism seems bound to its conception of the priority of *class* over race, nationality, or sex as both a historical and epistemological category. Practically, the doctrine of the primacy of the proletariat as the basis of socialist transformation and movement prevents a bold alliance with the women's movement. Often the socialist left must be dragged kicking and screaming to support the practical demands of women or, equally often, drags its

feet in the wake of religiously motivated objections by workers, or of recalcitrance that stems from male privilege on the job and at home.

There are many within the socialist movement who recognize the social and historical roots of the crisis of historical materialism but hesitate to trace its elements to its theoretical dimensions. Instead, the crisis in Marxism is understood exclusively within the discourse of political strategy, where specific socialist and communist parties are found to be seriously "opportunist" in their practical and political application of Marxist theory. Or, the crisis is ascribed to a series of misunderstandings by his epigones of Marx's intentions and method. The stress on methodological clarification assumes that Marxism is a science of society and history but—because it is simultaneously an ideology[7]—lends itself to misconstructions. Thus Marxist philosophy, like contemporary analytic philosophy of science and language, is obliged to clear away misunderstandings by either linguistic analysis—so as to purify and universalize the discourse of Marxism—or to engage in conceptual clarification—in which the structure of Marx's thought is construed in a way that makes space for historical anomalies.

Nevertheless, Marxist scholarship has arisen in the past two decades to new levels of articulation and sophistication. Beyond unearthing new contributions from Marx and Marxism (notably the rediscovery of the *Grundrisse*, the discovery of the unpublished works of Gramsci, republication of Lukács's early works, and the Korsch revival), a plethora of Marx commentators have made serious efforts to rescue Marxism from the wounds inflicted upon it by history. Most notably, the main burden of this commentary has been concerned with overcoming what is commonly termed "vulgar" Marxism. Here the label "vulgar," although containing strong pejorative connotations, is meant to designate the set of interpretations dominant in the socialist movement, i.e. those advanced by Lenin, Trotsky and Stalin in the interwar period and its immediate aftermath.

The failure of proletarian revolution in the West, the deformations of "really existing" socialism, and the new issues raised by feminism, nationalism and the ecology movements—in short, the rise of cultural movements that appear to circumvent or challenge the traditional economist assumptions of historical Marxism—have given rise to a variety of "schools" of Marxist thought. Until World War II, those tendencies which tried to come to grips with theoretical problems (as opposed to resting content with making accusations that their political opponents were guilty of perfidy) evolved what may be called theories of *mediation* to account for the historical anomalies that plagued Marxism after Marx.

Theories of Mediation

The concept of mediation is, of course, extremely controversial in contemporary Marxist debates. The concept is derived from Hegel's distinction between *sense certainty* as a moment in the movement of consciousness and the *totality*, i.e. the identical subject-object, where the problem of knowledge which implies their alienation is overcome by a series of historical stages towards self-consciousness. According to Georg Lukács, the active mediation between consciousness and its object is historical praxis, not the activity of thought. But mediations are not one-sided; they are both movements of reification and emancipation from alienated labor. Lukács argued that the totality is not "the mechanical aggregate of individual historical events nor is it a transcendent heuristic principle opposed to the events of history" as the Kantians contended.[8] The totality is a "real historical power," the universal that exists in particular phenomena. Contrary to empiricism, which holds that only particulars have reality and that concepts of totality, the universal, and the like are categories of thought, Lukács insists upon the objectivity of the totality. "It should not be forgotten that immediacy and mediation are themselves aspects of a dialectical process and that every stage of existence (and of the mind that would understand it) has its own immediacy...in which when confronted by an immediately given object, we should respond just as immediately or receptively and therefore make no alteration to it, leaving it just as it presents itself." Mediation, according to Lukács, is the process whereby this immediacy gives way to the *"structural principles and the real tendencies of the objects themselves."*[9]

The proletariats' existence as immediacy presents itself as merely trade unionism, that is, the struggle for its reproduction within the capitalist order. But this existence is not the truth of the class as historical actor, according to Lukács. Through economic and political struggles, the *reified appearances of real relations* are revealed, transforming workers from a plethora of groups engaged in immediate struggles for a living wage into a self-conscious revolutionary class.

Lukács was giving theoretical expression to Lenin's theory of the party, which argued that without the mediation of scientific theory and strategic leadership the working class could not become a revolutionary force. Lenin's concept of the party as a scientifically guided vanguard of revolutionary intellectuals and advanced workers was the earliest theoretical recognition within the Marxist tradition of the incommensurability of the economic infrastructure and the ideological and political superstructure of capitalist society.[10] Contrary to the main body of Second International thought—which understood the party as an educational instrument and representative of workers' immediate interests at the level of the state, but failed to draw the consequences implied by the concept of representation of education for a theory of class formation—Lenin followed a suggestion by Kautsky and pointed to the one-sidedness of the proletariat's immediate existence.[11] Only the totalizing praxis of the party apparatus could rescue the proletariat from the swamp of reform. Alternatively, the prevalent theory of the great German Social Democratic Party held to the view that the workers' own organizations became revolutionary under conditions of capitalist crisis, and that the party was essentially one of its instruments, but by no means its leader.

The orthodoxy of the Second and Third Internationals found its roots in a specific "reading" of Marx and Engels. Put plainly, the "mode of production" of material life is understood as the determinant of the "immense superstructure" of capitalist institutions, including law and the state, education, ideology, and religion. This mode of production (consisting of the forces and relations of production) is influenced but not determined, in turn, by institutions to which it has given rise. However, despite Engels's famous caveat—that he and Marx stressed the primacy of economic relations and interests in the context of a determinate set of ideological struggles within the socialist and liberal movements with which both were involved, and which therefore should not be endowed with immutable status as truth—the Marxism of the Second and Third Internationals persisted in taking this metatheory literally: *determining, in every instance,* historical development.

Lenin succeeded in codifying as philosophical precept the one-to-one correspondence of base and superstructure by elevating this relation to an epistemological principle. Lenin applied the "correspondence" theory he "read" in Marx's of *Preface to the Contribution to the Critique of Political Economy* to the relation between thought and the external world. In a polemic against Ernst Mach and his Russian followers, Lenin attacked Kant's epistemology, which held that thought constituted the object of knowledge.[12] For Lenin, scientific knowledge was obtained by *reflection* of the actual processes it discovered in nature. Scientific law was an approximation of the external world but could not reproduce an exact "copy." Its relative truth was limited only by the level of development of the forces of production and scientific knowledge, that is, the degree to which humans acted upon nature in order to meet their needs. As the productive forces achieved greater mastery of nature, our ideas would more accurately correspond to their object, which was independent of the will of humans. Thus, ideas about the external world obtained by means of scientific—i.e. experimental and theoretical—investigation were the "superstructure" determined by the external world as "base." Similarly, the relations of production—the class consisting of the ruling capitalist class and the working class, the two great historical actors within capitalist society—determined the whole realm of ideology. Since in every epoch the ruling ideas of society as a whole are the ideas of the ruling class, political, philosophical, religious and other ideas are typically considered so many aspects of bourgeois ideology. Unless armed with Marxist theory, the working class is subject to these ideas (the immutability of human nature, "you can't fight city hall," the natural superiority of men over women) as much as the rulers in whose interest these ideas are promulgated. Marxism, the science of history and of revolutionary change, is like any science grounded in rigorous methodology, an approximation of the actual movement of history and society. Its dialectical "method" allows it to comprehend the apparently anomalous (i.e. "contradictory") nature of the social world, assuring that its generalizations are reflections of the "real" world.

For the purposes of this analysis, I do not propose to rescue Lenin from the charge of "vulgarity," since this term connotes nothing more than (*i*) the reflection theory of knowledge and (*ii*) a correspondence theory of truth grounded in the distinction between base and superstructure in which the latter is determined by the former, not only in the final instance, but in each of them. As has often been pointed out, such a strict determinism forced Lenin and Stalin to adopt an extreme voluntarism in political strategy. On the one hand, all elements of the superstructure were nothing but reflections of class relations and the degree of human mastery over nature. On the other hand, the party and the proletariat— armed with Marxist science that explained with precision the course of political and economic development—could overcome the deficiencies of the historical moment. Thus, despite formal adherence to a rather mechanistic view of historical materialism, Lenin evolved a theory of *mediation* between base and superstructure based on the concept of *scientific politics*. Whereas bourgeois political theory had consigned the realm of the political to the sphere of "art" or ethics, acknowledging only political economy as social science, Lenin insisted that questions of strategy and tactics belonged to the discourse of science. And, since science was the instrument of human mastery, an overcoming of once-feared natural forces, the transformation of politics from a practical art to one in which scientific reason prevailed multiplied human powers of historical change.

Lenin's recovery of the concept of politics as a science owes much to Machiavellian and Hobbesian notions that the state's rule over civil society must be grounded in more than ethical principles. Rather, it must be conceived as a rigorous and systematic inquiry. In contrast, the parties of the Second International had understood politics within capitalist society as the art of the possible, critically severed from history, whose movement could be discerned with precision on the basis of the "laws of motion" of capital discovered by Marx. For the Marxists of the Second International, the socialist practice of reform within the framework of the bourgeois state was essential for both the amelioration of the immediate conditions of the working class and for building socialist strength for the ultimate revolutionary conflict. But political strategy was otherwise disjoined

34

from the historical process and could not be considered a science. Even Rosa Luxemburg believed the party's role to consist principally in "calling out to the masses their tasks." The success of the revolution ultimately rested on the masses, not the party. It was the place of political economy to predict the moment and the circumstances under which the proletariat would be obliged to wage the final struggle for socialism. Thus, for the leaders of most socialist parties prior to World War I, politics within the bourgeois state remained a necessary, but subordinate, holding action. As early as his pamphlet *What Is To Be Done?* (1902), Lenin suggested that the question of the party could not be confined to its necessary educational function. In fact, in his polemic against spontaneity and its advocates, Lenin's precise argument rested on the significance of elevating political strategy to the level of military science. Forces would be deployed on the basis of a conception of the division of labor, i.e. specialization. On the other hand, Lenin calls for the end to fragmentation and the development of a plan of work to overcome it. Instead of leaving revolutionary activity to chance, he asks that the Social Democrats provide a systematic training program for their cadre.

The formation of an "all-Russian newspaper" is seen by Lenin as the core of the program, an institution able to unite all revolutionists in "common work," ending the fragmentation that had prevented the party from achieving unity of strategy and tactics. Standing at the center of Lenin's program is the elevation of theory to the status of "guide" to revolutionary activity. Instead of yielding to spontaneous trade unionism and the economic struggle of the working class, and running furiously to catch up with it, Lenin proposes to "replace this hodgepodge" with a party able to lead the struggle because its ideology has been transformed into scientific socialist strategy.

Thus, for Lenin, a theoretically based socialist strategy mediates between the spontaneous resistance of the workers against capital and the socialist revolution. The party is the only force able to overcome the wall separating the two. The party is the "advanced" contingent of the workers' movement precisely because it has made scientific theory the basis of its political activity. The specific scientific content of politics consists in situating the question of organization at the center of political discourse.

Once a sober assessment of the "objective" circumstances that condition political action has been made (the task of political economy), all theoretical questions merge with those of strategy and tactics. It would be an error to underestimate the departure Lenin's theory of politics represents from the main body of Marxist doctrine. Of course, Lenin does not believe that the party can replace either the proletariat or control the actions of the bourgeoisie. But given these boundaries, whose content may be discerned with precision, it is only by putting politics on a new—scientific—basis that socialist victory can be assured.

It is not that politics is somehow separated from the historical conditions within which it functions. Just as the categories of political economy were, for Marx, the foundation upon which a scientific socialist theory was erected, so Lenin wished to construct a theory of organization as a part of that foundation. The categories that comprise the theory are grounded in the dialectic between specialization and the totality. Its glue is discipline and centralization of command. These are the same categories as military organization. At the foundation is the understanding that the workers, by their own efforts, will not achieve political revolutionary consciousness. Capitalism—with its division of labor and the fragmentation that confines struggles to particular industries, sectors, and regions—does not, despite its breakdowns, create the conditions for revolution without the intervention of scientific consciousness as an objective historical mediation.

Toward "Crisis in Marxism" Theories

The contradictions of the socialist movements in the twentieth century were apparent to the generation of Marxist intellectuals who reached their majority in the aftermath of World War I. In this period world revolution appeared on the agenda of the socialist and workers' movements. The stunning success of the Bolshevik revolution in consolidating its power in Russia at first seemed to prefigure the spread of socialism to the most advanced capitalist countries of Europe, vindicating Lenin's notion of the party as mediator. Indeed, the Hungarian Soviet republic and the German revolution of 1918 were signs that Marxism, too, was destined for vindication as a scientific prophecy. However, world capitalism proved capable of staging a powerful counterattack against the proletariat, not only in the form counterrevolutions in Hungary, but also—with the aid of a section of the socialist movement—in Germany as well. Germany became the first in a long succession of capitalist regimes ruled by socialist parties. While the condition of the working classes improved considerably under social-democratic governments, neither the "dream of the whole man" or the self-management of society by the producers appeared closer to realization as a result of social-democratic rule in countries of Europe. Moreover, the reformist, socialist-led governments of the Weimar Republic and other European countries were unable to stave off inflation and economic crisis. With the founding of the Third (Communist) International, the promise of a really revolutionary socialism once again was made, only to degenerate into a Stalinist swamp in the late 1920s.

Before, as now, the working class proved unable to constitute itself as a class capable of social rule where its putative interests became those of society as a whole. Divided by the split in the socialist movement, weakened as much by mass culture as by mass unemployment, the workers were defeated and partially absorbed by fascism, or state capitalist parties. The crisis in Marxism first appeared in the context of the rise of fascism, because of all of the "objective conditions" appeared present for a revival of the revolutionary movement in the wake of capitalism's world economic crisis. For Marxists able to perceive the defeats of the fascist era beyond the categories of strategy and tactics (where leaders of socialist factions accused each other of perfidy, and implicitly suggested that the problems of revolutionary action were confined to issues of policy), the rise of fascism and the concomitant collapse of the workers' movement was a second occasion for examination of Marxism itself.

In the 1920s and 1930s several main left-wing tendencies which openly argued for a "crisis in Marxism" could be discerned. By far the most important theoretically was the work of those who, following some motifs of Lukács's *History and Class Consciousness*, stressed the failure of Marxism to take account of the importance of cultural mediations between the contradictions at the level of the economic base and the concrete consciousness of the proletariat. But where Lukács posited the distinction between actual and putative class consciousness, holding that the latter was an objective consequence of capital's logic of commodity production and the division of intellectual and manual labor, the major tenets of the Frankfurt School of critical theory refused his optimism.

The results of the historical tragedy of the European proletariat led Max Horkheimer and Theodor Adorno to the conclusion that there was no inevitability to revolutionary praxis, if by the term we mean the capacity of the working class to constitute itself through its political activity as a historical subject, one which sees itself not merely fighting for particular interests but for the interest of human emancipation. The Frankfurt School drew the consequences of Lukács's theory of consciousness that Lukács himself was unwilling to face because of his adherence to Lenin's concept of the party. Lukács found an explanation for the defeat of the postwar revolutions in the process of capitalist production, rather than relying exclusively on political explanations emanating from leaders of the labor and socialist movements. For Lukács, the central category showing why the workers failed to carry through the revolution lay in (*i*) reification, (*ii*) the division of labor, and (*iii*) capitalist rationality. While revolutionary praxis was inevitable because of the misery capital visited upon the workers, the underlying form by which capital ruled was impenetrable by ordinary consciousness without the mediation of theory. Lukács provided rigorous theoretical arguments for Lenin's dicta that trade union activity leads only to trade union—i.e. particularistic—consciousness, and that—owing to the structural incapacity of workers within capitalism to generate revolutionary consciousness on their own—socialist consciousness must be brought to the working class from the outside.

Lukács rendered the famous Marxist theory of the proletariat as the revolutionary subject problematic, but without drawing the logical conclusions from the theory of reification. In the end, he held to the classical Marxist view that the capitalist class, the degree of working-class organization, and socialist leadership were sufficient to produce revolutionary praxis, even as the conditions of the reproduction of capital thwarted such a development. Nevertheless, Marxism now had a theory which lent critical weight to the specificity of culture, understood as a moment in the unfolding of the commodity form. Marx's theory of fetishism, assiduously ignored by the theoreticians of the Second International, was understood as a structural category for explaining the persistence of capitalism in the wake of wars and depressions. Whereas Lenin had relied on the theory of imperialism with his "labor aristocracy" concept to understand the failure of the Second International to make "war on war" in 1914, Lukács argued the heretical proposition that the failure referred partially to the workers themselves because of capital's rationality. Together with the later-discovered Gramscian theory of "hegemony," Lukács's work revived considerations of ideology and culture within Marxist theory. But contrary to previous doctrine—which taught that ideology was merely "false consciousness," i.e. a body of beliefs and values held merely subjectively—Lukács advanced the heretical idea that ideology, rather than being conceived as an imposition from without, was produced as a moment of the lived experience of capitalism itself.[13] The key cultural and social property of commodity production is the "thingification" of social relations. While capital is a relation between that portion of the working day which labor produces for its own reproduction as labor power and the portion appropriated by the employer(s), this relation cannot become an object of knowledge in the immediate process of production. Following Simmel, whose *Philosophy of Money* already suggests the centrality of reification as a theoretical ground for the production of ideology, Lukács argued that the real object of knowledge, capitalist social relations, could not be known without the aid of *mediation*, i.e. theoretical construction. Like Hegel, Lukács insisted that sense perception could only yield knowledge of appearances, while real relations remained veiled in the objects of the commodity world.

"The historical knowledge of the proletariat begins with knowledge of the present, with the self-knowledge of its own social situation and with the elucidation of its necessity (i.e. its genesis)."[14] But only when the working class abolishes its own particular existence, i.e. is able to see itself as a world-historical actor, can the reified consciousness be overcome. And this requires "self-knowledge" which, in turn, presupposes a break in the process of commodity reproduction. For it is not in the "empirically given" that class consciousness may be constituted, but in the process by which the proletariat constitutes itself independently rather than remaining one of the constituents of capital.

Writing *History and Class Consciousness* in 1919–23, Lukács remained optimistic about the possibility of revolutionary praxis. However,
the rise of fascism, the degeneration of the Bolshevik revolution, and the
apparent ability of capital to overcome the deepest economic crisis in its
three hundred years convinced members of the Frankfurt School that
something had transpired to challenge the underlying prophetic value of
Marxism. For Adorno, Horkheimer, and Marcuse, it was not, at first, a
question of abandoning Marxism. Certainly, the absence of an analysis
of political economy in the corpus of much critical theory is not meant to
be a statement of its insignificance. On the contrary, Marx's categories of
value, surplus value, and the rate of profit, with later Marxist analyses of
imperialism and monopoly, were taken as the necessary presuppositions
of their social theory. But the categories of political economy were no
longer able to constitute a sufficient basis for social theory, nor were they
adequate to historical explanation. It was not enough to make historically specific the way in which the conditions of capitalist reproduction
produced a given level and character of political and social consciousness. Whereas Lukács was persuaded that Marx's *Capital* was not only a
critique of political economy but also a theory of consciousness that rendered unnecessary new categories to explain historical events, the critical
theory of the Frankfurt School remained unconvinced. For it was one
thing to argue that the postwar defeats were but temporary episodes in
the long march to human emancipation, where history's forward motion
was rechanneled into reform and consolidation; fascism, on the other
hand, was a regression the understanding of which could not rest merely
on the vicissitudes of commodity production and capital accumulation.

The Problem of Fascism

The theory of fascism offered by both the Communist International and
its orthodox Marxist adversaries such as the Trotskyists adhered to a
view of fascism as an exceptional development of monopoly capitalism.
Capitalism, in its crisis, could no longer tolerate democratic liberties
where labor and socialist movements were strong; even the elementary
rights of workers and members of the middle class to organize freely in
their own immediate interests were untenable. To overcome the crisis,

argued the orthodox Marxists, capital required a new form of state power. In Italy and Germany, the state was no mere watchman over capitalist property, but wielded both the club and the law to enforce the domination of capital. Fascism represented the merger of the giant corporation with the state. The "command" state came into being where capital required assistance from the legitimate authority of government to promote investment on a grand scale. No longer confined to rails and other means of communication, state investment and planning would now direct the very processes of capital accumulation, if necessary. The communists argued that fascism was a "terroristic dictatorship of the bourgeoisie" arising on the base of the disgruntled petty bourgeoise.[15] But its essential class character was not petty bourgeois; it was supported by the biggest financial and industrial capitalists, who now required emergency measures to save the system. Trotsky differed with the communists on historical and strategic questions but agreed with theoretical explanation for the rise of fascism. The working class was defeated not only by force, but by the splits among its leaders. Had the leadership of the working class been united, Trotsky argued, fascism would have been vanquished. He blamed both the social-democrats and the communists for this division, arguing that the sectarianism of the Communist International and the anti-communism of the socialists were largely responsible for the rise of Hitler to power.[16]

Critical theory offered a different way of seeing the rise of fascism. Fascism was no extraordinary development that contradicted the main drift of advanced capitalism. On the contrary, according to Max Horkheimer, fascism was a *logical* development from monopoly capitalism. The end of the market economy signaled the impossibility of sustaining an effective opposition to the authoritarian state. The burden of Horkheimer's analysis is to link capitalism's evolution, particularly the rise of monopolistic control over the market, to the appearance of fascism. Contrary to the main tendency of Marxist explanation, he insists that the authoritarian state is immanent in capitalist development, and that the modern era has brought the tendency toward state capitalism to fruition.[17] In the process, the state has finally integrated its own opposition—the working class and other exploited strata. Horkheimer argued that working class and its parties are inextricably linked to the state, mediated by bureaucracies which not only administer capital but also dominate the workers' movement through administration. *Administration* has become the critical mediation that throws into question the Marxist faith in historical progress. It is the synchronization of the system with its own putative negation that gives Horkheimer grounds for despair. Like Walter Benjamin,[18] Horkheimer abandons the Marxist doctrine of historical inevitability, because the working class is no longer fated to become the determinate, self-conscious negation of capitalism; rather, it may try to advance its own cause which, in 1940, is still understood by Horkheimer to be inherently democratic, if not necessarily revolutionary. Administration of persons and things is objectified in a large bureaucracy on the basis of principles of scientific rationality. This development is not only the property of state capitalism, but of state socialism as well. The workers are obliged to resist all authoritarian regimes, whether their own unions and parties orchestrate (in fact they appear to be virtually the same thing in Horkheimer's analysis), but the outcome has been rendered uncertain by the passing of the market economy which, in its own chaos, offered the space for resistance.

Lukács's historicization of Weber's notion of rational calculation as one of the defining features of capitalism constitutes the crucial intellectual foundation for Horkheimer's refusal to follow the Leninist theory of the party (i.e. mediation) which Lukács defended so well. Horkheimer shows that the concept of the party as the midwife of revolution is a metaphor inherited from the French Revolution. For Horkheimer, the party is no less an organ of administration than the state, and its midwifery "degrades the revolution to mere progress." Certainly, Robespierre and the Jacobins were agents of "progress" in comparison to the feudal regime that they replaced. By centralizing the means of administration and communication, they succeeded in exercising a revolutionary dictatorship on behalf of the bourgeoisie. Progress is not the object of the socialist struggle. It is workers' self-management of society, according to Horkheimer. But the "deduction of the capitalist phases from simple commodity production" has played a trick on Marxism. Marx and his followers expected that the contradictions of capitalism as it moved through its phases would create the conditions under which humans could achieve freedom. Horkheimer points out the irony that alongside this truth another, contradictory, truth has emerged: growing capitalist antagonisms have also produced conditions that lead to unfreedom. "With state capitalism those in power can strengthen their position even more" than in previous phases. The clear implication for Horkheimer is that socialism has become no more than a possibility for the future. Its essential precondition, an autonomous workers' movement, seemed a more distant shore in 1940 than in the nineteenth century.

The dialectical theory of the Frankfurt School leads to a conclusion neither Lukács nor Karl Korsch was able or willing to confront. Under conditions of total administration, self-managed socialism becomes an ethical ideal rather than a historical inevitability. Despite the distance between this formulation—Eduard Bernstein's—and critical theory, the political convergence is striking.[19] Lukács's explanation for the failure of the revolutionary project relied on the introduction of the theory of *mediations* into Marxism, in the hope that a comprehension of the specificity of culture stemming from the commodity form could lead to workers' self-knowledge. Horkheimer admonishes reification has not prevented the opposition from emerging in late capitalism. But the conjuncture of the merger of the state and capital with the rise of administration as a social form par excellence has rendered difficult if not impossible the task of sustaining systemic opposition.

For critical theory, the advanced capitalist tendency to total administration makes critical thought increasingly difficult as well. According to Horkheimer and Marcuse, critical reason had as its historical precondition a free market economy. The bourgeois revolution arises as a defense of the free market against feudal restrictions. Its demand for the autonomy of civil society in relation to the state finds an echo in the demand for the freedom of reason from the repressive apparatus of the Church. Horkheimer's analysis of the eclipse of reason in late capitalism is grounded in the tendencies of the bourgeois epoch itself.[20] Despite the ideology of freedom, the practice of capitalism is embodied not only in the free market of commodity exchange, but in the organization of production. Here, in the development of the productive forces, rationality consists in the subordination of nature to human (i.e. bourgeois) will, and concomitantly the domination of human nature by industrial organization. Time as well as space becomes subject to rational calculation. Just as nature (space) is now subsumed by production and is increasingly perceived as "raw materials" to be transformed by the labor process, so the labor process is rationalized according to the criterion of efficiency (maximum production in the least amount of time). Labor becomes a function of time, and time has no significance apart from its role in production. Thus technical rationality replaces both the spirituality of religion, now assigned to the margins of society, and the bourgeois belief that accorded to reason an autonomy not subject to the encroachments of state or civil society.

The passing of the free market is linked by the Frankfurt School to the domination of nature (science and technologically grounded machinery) and the subordination of the labor process to technique (administration, specialization of tasks). Monopoly capital is only the extension of the processes by which technical rationality replaces the autonomy of critical reason. Reason remains critical because its autonomy is insured by the anarchy of production and exchange. The unification of reason with nature not only produced the domination of nature by rational calculation, but the domination of reason by its instrumentalization. Marcuse and Adorno argued that, under these circumstances, art becomes the only truly subversive form of human activity, because it could not be rendered consistently useful for the domination of nature and humans. Its subversive character was guaranteed by its political and scientific impotence. Even when recruited as ideology, it reminded people of a reason which defied this-worldly rationality. For its rationality was not the same as the labor process but remained opposed to it.[21]

As capitalism develops, its own contradictions become so acute that it is obliged to abolish its specifically bourgeois presuppositions, especially the free market and the autonomy of thought. Now science becomes subordinate to the requirements of production for profit and is, in a large measure, transformed into technology. Consequently, for critical theory, the emancipatory content of bourgeois science has been subverted by its own logic. While scientifically based technology may be capable of liberating the masses from back-breaking labor, it does not bring social and spiritual emancipation. For technology has invaded reason itself. Reason is no longer subversive to the given order; it has become the condition of the reproduction of domination, both of nature and consequently of humans, by the prevailing social order. Thus, the condition of human emancipation, the autonomy of reason, no longer exists except in the margins of society—as art. Even philosophy has become a servant, insofar as it renounces its metaphysical roots and defines its mission as clearing the path for a science that can dispense with philosophy by showing that all philosophical questions are really issues within language, discourse, or communication.

The Necessity of Philosophy

One of the great contributions of the Frankfurt School to our understanding of advanced industrial societies is to show that the cause of human freedom cannot abolish philosophy until social praxis has succeeded in realizing it:

> Philosophy, which once seemed obsolete, lives because the moment to realize it was missed. The summary judgement that it had merely interpreted the world, that resignation in the face of reality had crippled it, in itself becomes a defeatism of reason after the attempt to change the world miscarried. Philosophy offers no place from which theory as such might be concretely convicted of the anachronisms it is suspected of, now as before.... Theory cannot prolong the moment its critique depended on. A practice indefinitely delayed is no longer the forum for appeals against self-satisfied speculation, it is mostly the pretext used by executive authorities to choke whatever critical thoughts the practical change would require.[22]

In these opening lines of his *Negative Dialectics*, Theodor Adorno indicts, in one stroke, a Marxism that believes itself free of the obligation of speculative—i.e. critical—reason. His argument rests not upon an immanent critique of Marx's powerful eleventh thesis on Feuerbach, but on a historical judgement. The proletariat which, owing to its praxis, abolishes the requirement of metatheory, for a philosophy that extends

45

beyond science (theory), has failed to measure up to the expectations of historical materialism. It retains a practice of opposition to this or that policy or program of the "executive authorities" and of capital itself, but—having refused to situate itself on the terrain of history—the proletariat and its organizations can no longer claim the moral authority with which to refuse an intellectual project that insists upon the critical examination of Marxism and its philosophical presuppositions.

For Adorno, departing (in the double sense) from Horkheimer's earlier hope that oppositional practice would realize philosophy, it was not enough to specify the triumph of total administration, to mourn the end of reason. The concrete totality of which Marx and Lukács had confidently spoken had been betrayed by history. The putative subject of history, the working class, may remain the most exploited class within modern society when measured by the categories of political economy, but its subsumption under the canons of technical rationality blocked self-knowledge. The proletariat discovered in the relatively luxuriant unfreedom of late capitalism a means by which its obligation to history could be avoided. The fundamental issues raised by both enlightenment and socialist thinkers had not been resolved by the ability of capitalism to deliver the goods, or by the workers' movement to achieve a version of the "good life" without revolutionary power. But it was beyond the categories of scientific thought to address issues that had belonged to metaphysics. Adorno's emblem, "philosophy lives," really meant that theory lives, and it was Adorno's task to challenge the fundamental concepts of Marxism in the light of the historical anomalies that befell humanity in the aftermath of World War I.

The "fundamental concepts" of which I speak include the most cherished categories of dialectical thought, of the capacity of history to settle all questions of morality and of ethics, of the sanctity of materialism as an epistemological stance. Adorno's departure from the Horkheimer of *The Authoritarian State* and from Marcuse's pessimistic *One Dimensional Man* consists in an exegesis on the historical judgement that "philosophy lives because the moment to realize it miscarried." For if historical materialism was no science—in the sense that it could abolish the need for speculation, including its moral dimension, but rested on the results of praxis—then the issue was what went wrong, why did history fail to live up to the prophetic vision? Adorno attempted to show that the very categories, the presuppositions from which Marxism springs, were misdirected. Thus, it is to his *Negative Dialectics* that I must turn, because it remains the most important attempt within Marxism to provide an immanent critique of the entire scaffolding of historical and dialectical materialism. Where Lukács, Horkheimer, Marcuse, and Korsch tried *within* the framework of historical materialism to account for the fragmentation and the refusal of the concrete totality to emerge in the twentieth century, Adorno proposes nothing less than the revival of the concept of philosophy and *its* categories. If this return to the Kantian problematic appears anachronistic to those reared in the Hegelian-Marxist traditions (even the recalcitrant Althusser held to the totality, albeit in a non-Hegelian form), it is only because historical materialism has become historicist, because dialectical thought has become formal in the wake of the triumph of technical rationality.

Adorno intends, by returning to a critical examination of philosophical problems, to found a materialist dialectics on new theoretical premises: "The call for the unity of theory and practice has irresistibly degraded theory to the servant's role, removing the very traits it should have brought to the unity."[23] The attempt to revive theoretical studies must begin with the goal of emancipatory practice, but for just that reason it requires an autonomy from all given practices as a provisional stance in order to finally find the basis of an alliance, not a unity, with practice. Adorno's purposes remain critical. In fact, his critique of the fate of the dialectic in both Hegelian and Marxist thought is precisely that "dogmatism and thought taboos" have robbed them of critical content. On the other side, those Marxists like Lenin—whose opposition to dogmatism was uncompromising—were led, nevertheless mistakenly, according to Adorno, to abandon philosophy's insistence that the object was constituted reflexively, and substituted a naive realism in its place. That is, Lenin's refusal of the rituals of epistemology in his *Materialism and Empirio-Criticism*—motivated by suspicion that philosophy served the interests of the status quo—disabled Marxism for half a century (save those who insisted on the importance of theory at the price of political isolation). What was taken by Marxism for theory was a dialectics that was little more than a version of formal logic, an Aristotelian logic of *identity*.

Adorno's program goes beyond Lukács and the Frankfurt School, anticipating recent French post-structuralist theory. First, he undertakes a fundamental examination of the Hegelian logic upon which contemporary Marxism rests. Despite the discovery by Hegel and the development by Marx that the logic of contradiction was objectively constituted and not merely a property of thought to be overcome by clearing logical confusions, the materialist presuppositions of this move are, in Adorno's view, undermined by the metaphysics of identity. Only a dialectics that insists on *difference* as the ineluctable feature of objective reality can form the basis of a new critical theory. "Its motion does not tend to the identity in the difference between each object and its concept; instead, it is suspicious of all identity. Its logic is one of disintegration of the prepared and objectified form of the concepts which the cognitive subject faces, primarily and directly. The identity of the subject is untruth."[24]

Adorno is constrained, therefore, to oppose two central concepts of the Hegelian dialectic which have been carried over into Marxism. Against Lukács he insists that "totality is to be opposed by convicting it of non-identity with itself." The recuperation of difference by a higher identical synthesis is "a primal form of ideology," for it destroys the negativity that difference implies.[25] We may discern in the passionate defense of negativity an attempt to preserve that which the concept of "negation of negativity" nullifies. Here, the anti-Stalinist as well as anti-bourgeois echoes sound in Adorno's polemic. For socialist states claim to have overcome the contradictory differences that are inevitably a mark of civil society, just as contemporary Marxist and some types of bourgeois ideology argue for the end of the dialectic in the realization of the categories of freedom and equality.[26] Secondly, against the later Hegel and Marxism Adorno refuses positivity, holding to the negative character of the dialectic. The negation of the play of difference is not, itself, to be overcome by historical change, reintegrating it into a new given. Difference is suppressed, not liberated, by its negation in a world marked by the domination of nature and humans. "Objectively, dialectics means to break the compulsion to achieve identity, and to break it by means of the energy stored up in that compulsion and congealed in its objectifications."[27]

For Adorno, the link between the Hegelian dialectic and formal logic consists in the shared goal of *identity*. Contradictions are to be overcome for the dialectic which, only under certain historical circumstances, lead to new contradictions. Adorno wishes to assert difference as a condition of arriving at truth and negativity as the condition of freedom. But this does not imply a return to Kant and British empiricism, only an argument for the persistence of the questions they raised, and which remained unresolved by Hegel. Adorno explicitly opposes the a priori subject, insisting that it is constituted by history, including natural history. Thus, unlike Lukács—whose *History and Class Consciousness* was, among other things, an argument for a conception of the dialectic in which the subject appears as one of its first terms and the object its other—Adorno argues that "The most enduring result of the Hegelian logic is that the individual is not flatly for himself, he is his otherness and linked with others." Thus, non-identity is not difference *between* two things (subject/object) but exists *within* each. This is, undoubtedly, the tribute modern dialectical thought must pay to Freud, for whom the psychic structure was unified but never identical with itself. Consciousness can never fully subsume itself as its object, since the unconscious remains outside its control. The self is fractured objectively; its unity is achieved as a process of repression and displacement, but its negativity is never overcome.

Non-identity and Difference

Both bourgeois and socialist theory have been forced to recognize non-identity, but in both cases, difference is historicized by being pronounced "fragmentation" or "atomism" by liberal thought, for which harmony of interests and classes remains the goal of theory and practice. The differences within physics between wave and particle theories of matter, the indeterminacy principle discovered by Heisenberg, Einstein's relativity theory, all are accommodations to the impossibility of arriving at a unified field theory, one in which the "anomaly" of difference for a theory which posits identity may be resolved without challenging the presuppositions of science itself. The invention of probability theory, the attempt to ascribe the contradictions of measurement to "subjective" error, or to incomplete or inadequate instruments, and Niels

Bohr's complementarity principle, all show the will to totality in modern science. This example of rationalization difference is reproduced in social science, for which the goal of prediction and control, presumed to have been achieved by physics and other "natural" sciences, is primary. Social science's preoccupation with the problem of "methodology" is a sign of the importance it attaches to perfecting quantitative procedures (cognitive instruments) that lead to the predetermined goal of prediction and the political imperative for social control. Contemporary social science is unable to accept difference, at least in its qualitative connotation. Its elevation of number to the status of the invariant language of social science and spatial relations to its framework is grounded in the logic of identity, for the historical and the qualitative imply difference. For, as Marx's critique of exchange value shows, only when the qualitative differences between two commodities and their process of production (always a qualitative activity) are abstracted or reduced to a common quantitative denominator can exchange take place. Thus, Adorno's critique of identity is also a critique of modern science as much as are the philosophies of Heidegger and Husserl, which—while purporting to be concerned with the play of difference—actually seek the identical in a new doctrine of being. Similarly, Marxism's adherence to the concept of a totality produced by the identity of the subject—humans—with the object—nature—prevented it from reconciling itself to the differences between the two. "The objectivity of historic life is that of natural history."[28] Praising Marx, Adorno quotes a passage from *Capital* where Marx places the limit upon consciousness, including human praxis. "Even if a society has found its natural law of motion, natural evolutionary processes can be neither skipped nor decreed out of existence."[29] Adorno finds this "social Darwinism" in Marx to be eminently critical, rather than regressive as in Herbert Spencer, because it recognizes the disjunction between human desire and its object, but at the same time understands that nature gives rise to the social process and becomes part of the social process as its "unconscious." Thus, Adorno relies on Marx to affirm his critique of Marxist voluntarism which, in the last instance, subsumes nature under history, social processes under conscious activity, otherness under identity.

Adorno's appeal to Marx for support for his dialectic of negativity is also an attack against contemporary Marxism's tendency to ontologize history as the ultimate ground of being: "When history becomes the basic ontological structure of things in being, if not the *qualitas occulta* of being itself, it is mutation as immutability copied from the religion of inescapable nature."[30] Dialectics recognized the "painful antithesis of nature and history." On the contrary, the ideal of the enlightenment and of contemporary Marxism to gloss over this opposition has led to a kind of "crypto-idealism" and, as Horkheimer and Adorno argued in the *Dialectic of the Enlightenment*, not to the realm of freedom but back to human domination. "The moment in which nature and history become commensurable with each other is the moment of passing." This cognition may be seen in Benjamin's *Origins of German Tragedy* for in tragedy history appears as writing and, in turn, is already inscribed with the countenance of nature which, according to Benjamin, "is really present as a ruin." The ruin of nature in "pictographs," its passing into history, is the hideous outcome of a scientifically based technical rationality, the moment when nature—once hypostatized by religion—is demystified and becomes an object without qualities "for us"(Engels).[31]

The Problem of Praxis

Marxism's glorification of the domination of nature prefigures a radical historicism for which nature has been relegated to the periphery of the social process and human praxis elevated to the sublime. Thus, does contemporary Marxism abolish the limits to human action, which would be the necessary concomitant of a theory of non-identity. Lukács developed his theory of the primacy of praxis in the context of a hegemonic Marxism which, in the zenith of the Second International, was afflicted with "naturalism" and thus became a necessary corrective to mechanistic determinism. His standpoint must be understood as an antimony to Kautsky's appropriation of natural history, in which praxis was merely the inevitable outcome of capitalist crisis. The crucial contribution of Adorno's theory of the negative dialectic is his assertion of the non-identity between nature and history, subject and object (subject as object). But Adorno cannot generate a theory of praxis, claiming that such a project would be premature in the wake of the subsumption of theory by practice in the twentieth century. There is no space for conscious praxis in Adorno's *Negative Dialectics*; this is the result not only of the historical assessment of Marxist voluntarism, but of its assignment of praxis to the theoretical. Adorno's praxis is, in the final sum, theoretical activity. The dialectic of non-identity, the careful argument for negativity as a transhistorical principle, is an argument for critical theory as the only possible praxis in a world in which history has become repressive.

Unlike much of contemporary Marxist theory, which blames Stalinism and the deformations of socialism "as it really exists" on purely historical aberrations or authoritarian dogmatism, Adorno's attempt to resuscitate philosophy simultaneously condemns the foundations of historical materialism. For Adorno, the causal determinism inherent in Marxism is no aberration of Marx's epigones. It is grounded in the outcome of Hegelian philosophy, to which Marx was heir. Historical materialism seeks not only the negation of the status quo, but the negation of the *negation*. For Adorno, this is nothing less than a call for the end to critical thought, for the suppression of reason, save that reason which is instrumental to the reproduction of the given: technical reason. The emancipatory goal of socialism is subverted by its own historical logic. As Marxism reads history, contradictions appear as a consequence of class-divided societies. The very principle of historical specification (Korsch)[32] which liberated nineteenth-century social theory from the metaphysics of the absolute spirit has become a fetter on critical theory, preventing it from performing its vital, if autonomous, function in relation to practice: the disintegration of the "prepared and objectified form of the concepts" so that the differences repressed within them may be released. Stalinist theory ascribes to historical determinations the objectivity of contradiction. Even if differences remain under socialism (cf. Mao's concept of non-antagonistic contradictions) these are to be conceived not as inherent in the nature of the social system. Difference is thus rendered harmless by the Marxist theory of socialist society. For if classes in the Marxist sense of the term disappear, the historical basis of contradiction also disintegrates.

Critical theory holds the principle of disintegrative reason as the absolute from which there is no appeal if the hope of human freedom is

to be kept alive. Thus, for Adorno, the very practice of human emancipation must promote theory as a permanent feature of its project. The
"realization" of philosophy can no longer be entrusted to the proletariat,
or to a Marxism whose adherence to the Hegelian dialectic impels it to
the liberal ideal of harmony. As Adorno develops his ruminations on the
fate of historical materialism and the dialectic, it is clear that he means
to understand that the moment is past when reason comes back to itself
and eliminates the object as otherness. Thus, nature's subordination to
man—bourgeois reason's ideal since the enlightenment, with the ability
of science to predict and control nature, including human nature—must
be abandoned as a misdirected adventure. But immanent to Adorno's
position is that there never was such a possibility in any case. The concept that the contradictory motion of history is a return to reason's identity with itself was only an archaic hope that could never be achieved.

Adorno's contribution is to suggest the lines by which the formalism
inherent in Hegelian dialectical reason may be broken. More, it offers
the germ of an entirely different movement of critical theory. Since it is
explicitly a theory in which concepts such as progress must be denied—
especially after Auschwitz (Adorno's metaphor for the triumph of unreason as the logical outcome of technical rationality—there is no question
of deriving a new historical subject which might, putatively to be sure,
be assigned the role of bearer or personification of the historical process.
For this reason, "Dialectics is the self-consciousness of the objective context of delusion; it does not mean to have escaped from that context. Its
objective goal is to break out of the context from within."[33] Yet thought
may transcend its object by means of a logic which grasps the "coercive
character of logic," embracing an absolute which is not identical with
itself or coming to rest as a totality.

While it was necessary for Adorno to do battle against the forms of
thought which have merged with the object to form a repressive totality
of domination, the absence of a philosophy of emancipatory praxis in
his work presupposed the priority of theory in the wake of a practice
which could do no other than serve the status quo. It was not that Adorno
privileged the theoretical reconstruction of the dialectic in some abstract

hierarchy of human activity in which mental labor was given a reified status. The point of his argument is against the subordination of theory to practice, a view held by those who wished to change the world without confronting the repressive totality in which thought is made an instrument of unfreedom. His project, to free the forms of thought from their instrumental rationalist premises, can only be welcomed—even if the history is thereby rendered disembodied.

It remains for us to find the bearers of a non-identical dialectic. We must begin to draw the implications of the revival of theory for a political praxis that itself remains non-identical with the theoretical underpinnings and the specific content of the historical material isms of the Second and Third Internationals, but we cannot be satisfied with the theory of mediation offered between the wars as a means to preserve Marxism. At the same time, the project of founding a praxis whose aim is to emancipate humanity from the conditions of social domination but which insists on theoretical grounds, must be considered profoundly Marxist in outlook, if not in doctrine.

Aspects of Theoretical Crisis

It may be useful to review the argument in the previous section before suggesting a new approach towards the reconstruction of historical materialism. The crisis of historical materialism which forms the specific theoretical content of Marxism was *detonated* by social and historical developments but cannot be confined to them. Certainly, the *refusal* by the proletariat in Western advanced capitalist countries to enter the historical arena after World War I as a subject in the Marxist sense could not have helped but produce the conditions leading to a comprehensive theoretical examination of the foundations of historical materialism. Similarly, the inability of the proletariat in "really existing" socialist countries to form a self-managed society in the wake of the triumph of communist bureaucracies (conjoined, of course, by two world wars) ignited a wave of anti-communism among Western left intellectuals and workers. The rise of religiously inspired nationalist revolutions in the Middle East, Ireland, and Third World countries raised serious questions concerning the Marxist expectation that the national revolution must pass into the socialist revolution. After three decades of nationalist rule in the Middle East and North Africa, new forms of state capitalism—ones not based upon advanced industrial development—may have consolidated a long period of rule. Finally, the rise of feminism and the significance of race in world politics raise serious issues concerning the adequacy of the Marxist penchant for reduction of social antagonisms to their class dimensions. Feminist and black-nationalist theories challenge the very core of Marxist theory of historical periodicity, as well as the historicist assumptions of many tendencies in contemporary historical materialism.

The movement of theory that has been called, erroneously, "Western Marxism" arose after World War I to explain some of these developments not by means of a "revision" of Marxism, but by returning to Marx himself, by reviving "orthodox" Marxism against its revisions by the leaders of the Second International. The crucial innovation—or to be more precise, discovery—of the postwar Marxists was the concept of *mediation* between the economic base and the superstructure of capitalist societies. The notion of mediation was drawn from no less an authoritative work in the Marxist literature than *Capital* itself. Lukács's contribution was to discover in the theory of commodity fetishism the source of capital's capacity to gain ideological hegemony over the proletariat. Ideology was seen not as false consciousness but as a moment in the reproduction of capital, a necessary rather than contingent feature of commodity production and class struggle. The unique contribution of the Frankfurt School was prompted by the rise of fascism which called into the question the *capacity* of the working class to transform society. Whereas Lukács adopted the Leninist theory of the party as educator, organizer, and demystifier of the commodity fetish and its consequences, Max Horkheimer and Theodor Adorno refused this solution. Rather, they found in Weber's sociology the notion that capitalism was a way in which the entire social world was subject to rational calculation and thus made relatively immune from fundamental social transformation. For them, the theory of bureaucracy was adequate to understand the role of the party as a purveyor of a new unfreedom, as well as one that could deepen Marx's and Lukács's theories of political and social consciousness. Further, they challenged the view that the domination of nature was a form of emancipation, and the ideas of progress and historical inevitability which pervaded Marxism. In his later years, Adorno attempted to codify these discoveries in a new and fundamental critique of the materialist dialectic, with a view to its reconceptualization. The theory of *Negative Dialectics* asserts the non-identical character of the objective world, the non-overcoming of contradictions, and the importance of the incommensurability of nature and the social world. Marxism remained, according to Adorno, ensconced in the categories of the Hegelian dialectic, in which the overcoming of the negative was the outcome of the contradictory historical process; Adorno insisted to the contrary that the survival of critical reason—the necessary condition for an emancipatory praxis—demanded that theory should not be subordinate to technical rationality. The critique of instrumental reason advanced by the Frankfurt School was at the same time a theory of the principal form of domination characteristic of late capitalist societies. According to Marcuse, the power of late capitalism consisted in the presentation of technology and science as the only acceptable rationality. The material basis of technology and science as prima facie evidence that capitalism is civilization rests on the integration of the relations of production by the productive forces. Marcuse's critique of technology exposes the ideological content of science by showing its instrumentalization in the service of domination. Thus, the burden of the Frankfurt School's argument is to show that technological rationality is a kind of unreason because it subverts the function of reason in history—human emancipation.

What is startling about this judgement is the degree to which it violates the eighteenth-century idea of progress that linked science and technology with human freedom. Marcuse showed that the subsumption of science and technology under capital resulted in their irrationality from the point of view of the goal of freedom. Whereas virtually all nineteenth-century thought was locked into the presuppositions of social evolutionism—which postulated the relationship between human mastery over nature as the condition of the emancipation of humans *from* nature—Marcuse and others argued that the transformation of nature by means of the ratio had deleterious consequences for social relations, and forms of thought as well. Accordingly, until science and technology could be freed from the bonds of instrumental reason, that is, until knowledge was separated from the commodity form in which it was subordinate to and became a kind of cultural capital, it would remain a form of ideology as well.

Despite the appearance of *One-Dimensional Man* as late as 1964, the Frankfurt School's theoretical life as a more or less coherent tendency *within* Marxism ends with World War II. In his later years, Horkheimer became a more or less unabashed champion of bourgeois liberalism. As we have seen, Adorno's rejection of the Hegelian-Marxist concept of the dialectic placed his work outside traditional historical materialism, although it may not be claimed that he was a post-Marxist in the contemporary sense since he was still grappling with the old categories, with the old problematic of human emancipation.

Habermas and Latter Critical Theory

Jürgen Habermas finally severed the relation of critical theory to Marxism by undertaking a fundamental reexamination of historical materialism. Habermas, too, departs in the double sense from critical theory's appropriation of Weberian "rational calculation." Where Marcuse, for example, borrowed from Weber in order to enrich the critique of capitalist rationality and, in effect, turned Weber around by showing the subversive possibilities of his thought (just as Marcuse's misreading of Freud pressed the conservative Freud into the service of emancipation), Habermas turns Marcuse around and returns to Weber.

Habermas asks that the critique of technical rationality be abandoned because Marxism's expectation that human emancipation may be achieved through the transformation of social labor controverts the evidence of biological and social evolution. In his criticism of Marcuse's critique of Weber, Habermas calls technical rationality merely the "rational-purposive" action necessary for the reproduction of the human species.[38] Marcuse's call for a new relationship with nature in which "repressive" mastery is replaced by one that is "liberating" is, for Habermas, a false project because it would imply the possibility of a new science and a new technology. Habermas argues that science and technology are forms of human knowledge that are rational because they serve human purposes, however instrumental to these purposes technology is rendered.

According to Habermas, Marcuse has failed to specify how human

knowledge may become liberating in the sphere of work, how our relations to nature may be transformed in accordance with the parameters of human survival. Having found that Marcuse lacks an empirical
basis for his claim to found an alternative science and technology in
which political domination does not circumscribe rationality, Habermas makes a crucial distinction that is to become the foundation of his
own reconstruction of social theory, the obliteration of historical materialism. According to Habermas, Marcuse's mistake was to confuse
two distinct realms of human action: work and interaction. The Marxist
belief that work relations could be transformed according to the canons
of emancipatory socialism miscarried because capital had already organized the labor process based upon the elevation of *knowledge* as the
principal productive force corresponding to human needs. This development is merely the logical outcome of biological and social evolution
that points to the development of "scientific-technical" progress as the
realization of human interests as a whole. The labor process was no
longer an issue for critical examination. Thus, science and technology
cannot be "ideological" if by the term we mean ideas, beliefs, and norms
which correspond to particular interests, that is, interests not shared by
society as a whole.

Work is redefined by Habermas as "rational-purposive action" governed by "technical rules based on empirical knowledge." These rules
imply predictions that may be correct or incorrect but, in any case,
cannot be verified normatively, that is, are subject only to the rational
calculation of alternative technical choices, not political criteria. This
type of discourse is context-free, i.e. outside of history focusing on prob-
lem-solving in the service of power over nature in order to develop the
productive forces. Following Weber, Habermas understands the state
as one of the primary forms by which rational-purposive action of this
kind is institutionalized. The state thus becomes a neutral instrument,
a sub-system along with the economy in the sphere of rational—i.e.
non-ideological—domination.

The inclusion of the state in the sphere of work rationality may, at first
glance, appear remarkable from the perspective of critical social theory.
But on closer examination Habermas is simply being consistent with his

first postulate, that any action that belongs in the sphere of the reproduction of the forces of production must be considered technical, i.e. outside the sphere of moral discourse. In modern industrial societies, the state acts as a force of capital accumulation, as an institution intervening in the development of the productive forces. Its planning functions, the system of law that governs contracts, its investments become types of problem solving. For Habermas, the state is no longer a repressive apparatus, a form of institutionalization of class domination, but primarily a technical apparatus instrumental to the domination of nature. Thus, he recreates a conception of the state closer to that of Hegel and Hobbes than to Marx. Emancipatory "politics" must now be confined to the sphere of interaction which, for Habermas, remains relatively undeveloped in the wake of the emphasis of industrial societies on perfecting their institutions of purposive rational action.

In his later work, Habermas is constrained to reintroduce the problematic of social domination into the productive sphere. The essays in *Communication and the Evolution of Society* and *Legitimation Crisis* recognize implicitly that the distinction between work and interaction is not nearly as absolute as was suggested in the earlier Marcuse critique. To the extent that in democratic societies the legitimacy of the state rests on the consent of the underlying population, normative structures remain an aspect of rational purposive action, at least to the extent that the accumulation functions of the state do not appear to have purely technical criteria. On a broader theoretical level, the essay "Reconstruction of Historical Materialism" tries to maintain the earlier distinction between technical and moral reason, and, at the same time, to establish a more solid foundation for their linkages. Perhaps the dualism of the earlier position appeared increasingly untenable in the wake of historical developments as well as theoretical critique, but it is clear that Habermas began to solve the antinomies of his earlier thought.

Habermas's solution—which owed much to the developmental psychology of Lawrence Kohlberg as well as to recent anthropology—was to assert that historical evolution owes as much to the efficacy of normative and cognitive structures as to structures of instrumental or strategic action. Thus, Habermas not only retains the split between work and interaction and argues for the independent development of the former, but precisely reverses Marx's theory of causality, which accords primacy in the processes of historical change to the changes in the infrastructure. Habermas adduces evidence from empirical sciences to demonstrate his thesis that it is the capacity of a society to generate learning mechanisms which accounts for its adaptation to conditions of natural as well as social development. Given the contradictions between productive forces and productive relations in the history of human societies, the ability of a culture to resolve these in the interest of its survival depends on the normative structures it has generated that permit the development of its learning mechanisms, rather than its relations of production, i.e. class relations. Those societies survive which can evolve institutions to codify mutual cooperation rather than competition. Hence, for Habermas organization becomes Marxism's missing link between infrastructure and superstructure. Organizational forms are the key linkage between communicative action (interaction) and instrumental, or productive action. While the rules governing each form of action are different (one depends on domination, the other on equality), it is the forms of interaction, transvalued into organization, which are primary for understanding societal evolution:

> The introduction of new forms of social integration—for example, the replacement of the kinship system with the state—requires knowledge of a moral-practical sort and not technically useful knowledge that can be implemented in rules of instrumental and practical action. It requires not an expansion of our control over external nature but knowledge that can be embodied in structures of interaction—in a word, an extension of the autonomy of society in relation to our own internal nature.[35]

For Habermas, the problem of modern, industrially-developed societies is that the "cognitive potential" of society has neglected moral development, pouring all knowledge into the "socialization of production"; this potential will not lead to evolutionary change until mechanisms of learning are developed that innovate new forms of social integration.

Habermas has not offered, of course, a new kind of historical materialism, but its determinate negation. Only unlike Adorno, for whom the negative as absolute constitutes the fundamental condition for social transformation, Habermas wishes to establish a world of harmonious relations, and not on the ground of a transformation of power relations. First, he regards the sphere of production to be free of internal antagonisms. The class struggle which, implicitly, presupposes hierarchy and scarcity as the basis for domination, exists as a vestige of earlier, exogenous conditions, but it neither constitutes the basis of historical change nor remains a vital element in the course of advanced industrial societies. For Habermas, as long as knowledge is the central productive force, the whole mode of production is subsumed under the categories of progressive rationality. The domination, therefore, is not subject to critical inquiry, and human domination must be strictly separated from social labor.

Second, it must be clear that the whole of Habermas's "reconstruction" rests on his rejection of the Frankfurt School theory of the domination of nature as the basis of human domination. The achievement of social integration—i.e. of social harmony—depends not on realigning our relations with exogenous conditions. Habermas views this relation as the greatest achievement of bourgeois society and claims it must be preserved by any new social order, since it is the universal pragmatics of reason. Social integration remains elusive because we have not succeeded in finding those normative structures upon which we may learn from our current crises. These normative structures must be "sought first on the psychological level," according to Habermas, since he has treated all "system problems" as "disturbances of the reproductive process of a society that is normatively fixed in its identity," and this "identity" is conceived as dysfunctional to its reproduction. Thus, finding a new identity for society is the condition for its survival as a reproductively efficient social system.[36]

Weberian theory has come full circle with Habermas. There is no critique of administration as in the Frankfurt School. The question of organization becomes primary for social reconstruction because this is the link between moral and instrumental action. But despite Habermas's claim to find, in moral categories, the key to systemic change, the objective is system maintenance. And why not? If capitalism has solved the problems of scarcity through its evolution of a system of instrumental/strategic action, i.e. a scientifically based labor process that "solves" the problem of nature's mastery over society better than any other, then our "problem" is no longer one of accumulation, of mastery over nature, but of the mastery of human social organization. Marx was wrong, according to Habermas, because he located the central problems of human societies in the labor process, assuming their normative structures would follow from social production and were conditioned by it. Once work and interaction have been severed, not only is the critique of the labor process nullified as a proper object of social knowledge, but moral development is, thereby, made possible without a fundamental change in the nature of production relations. Habermas's proposal for theory's task is to devise modes of interaction, including discourse, which can assist society as a whole to shift its cognitive resources to problems of ego identity, i.e. to the conditions upon which society defines itself morally and establishes, on the basis of this self-understanding, rules of action. Of course, interaction is not context-free and technical in character, since reflexive thought is the basis of distortion-free communication. That is, every speaker must, in order to communicate perfectly, (*i*) be aware of the degree to which his discourse is informed by interests and (*ii*) separate the two.[37] Thus Habermas ends up with an argument that wishes to make normative structures universal as rational-purposive action, by transforming the speech situation in accordance with canons of reflexivity. The aim is a rational society, one free of "negativity" (now understood as "disturbances" in the reproduction process of society, rather than contradictions). Socialism is, under this rubric, no longer the determinate negation of capitalism, but becomes a new ego-ideal, the normative structure of cooperation and undistorted communication—in short, the rational discourse needed to achieve new levels of social integration, appropriation and positivization of critical theory.

Like Eduard Bernstein's, Habermas's critique of historical materialism postulates that the working class has succeeded, not failed, insofar as it has attained most if not all of its demands within the framework of late capitalism. But the demands of the proletariat are no longer the demands of society as a whole. The new needs created by the success of the forces of production and the institutional framework of late capitalism are moral in nature. According to Habermas they address, for the first time, what is specifically human about our species. Our humanity consists not in the fact that we produce our means of subsistence; other primates also are required to engage in social production. Humanity is defined by our capacity for reflexive interaction through the invention of language. It is our requirement that whatever we do contains normative and cognitive structures that distinguish humans—by *learning* as a basis of social reproduction.

Of course, Habermas remains within the framework of Marxism insofar as he asks questions that concern processes of social transformation. His departures begin, however, with a precept shared by Marxist orthodoxy—the progressive character of instrumental reason, the irreversibility of science and technology as it has been developed by capital. But he has not succeeded in overcoming Marcuse's contention that a new science and technology, based upon a different relationship between humans and nature, is necessary for social emancipation. Written in 1968, Habermas's critique of Marcuse's theory of the ideological within contemporary science and technology may have been premature; it predated the emergence of the ecology movement and the environmentally oriented research of the 1970s, which were based upon a solid body of evidence arguing that the results of the forms of the domination of nature of modern industrial societies were inimical to human survival. From the experimental evidence of such investigators as Barry Commoner and others, the empirical criteria Habermas used to condemn Marcuse's insistence on the necessity of a new science seem, in retrospect, to have been vitiated by others. More importantly, Marcuse's argument appears prophetic in the light of recent history, particularly the nearly incontrovertible evidence of Three Mile Island, an event that has become an emblem of the dangers of nuclear power, and a signal that nuclear power, the apogee of knowledge as a productive force, may not conform to canons of rational-purposive action. Equally important, the hazards to the health and safety of both workers and communities produced by the substances used in the ordinary productive forces such as asbestos, polyvinyl chloride, and other hydrocarbons that are among the foundations of "rational-purposive action" have revealed contradiction between humans and nature at the level of the question concerning rationality.

However, the appeal of theory to empirical evidence may be a necessary, if not sufficient, condition for historical argument. More germane is Marx's insistence that humans are part of natural history, and Adorno's amendment that the unity of humans and nature is a contradictory process. On the one hand, as Habermas acknowledges, we are a stage in biological evolution. On the other hand, we are not able to claim that our productive forces are rational insofar as they ignore the autonomy of nature.

This is not an epistemological question, but a historical and structural issue. Habermas has ignored the thesis of the *Dialectic of the Enlightenment* that the domination of nature was grounded not only in the mastery required for the reproduction of the social order and of the species, but in the fear of the external environment humans have harbored in their social unconscious. This fear was historically allayed, according to Horkheimer and Adorno, by the instrumentalization of nature, its subsumption by a quantitatively based science and technology. The outcome of the relentless rampage of humans against nature, now conceived as pure alterity, was not only expressed in the production of an idealist philosophy that posited the autonomy of the spirit, but also in the destruction of the autonomy of reason, as a kind of dialectical revenge.

And here is Habermas, invoking the rationality of science and technology, of instrumental reason itself, as the threshold of the new holocaust, one that could easily make Auschwitz a historical dress rehearsal. The brutalization of spirit revealed in the Nazi concentration camp was reproduced by the United States in the napalm bombs and the "strategic hamlet" program in Vietnam, the more or less explicit triage practiced by Western powers against Bangladesh and India, and more recently, in the mass slaughters in Chile and Argentina. All of these are illustrations that social contradictions extend to the state, that the forces of production are also forces of destruction under the concrete social relations of late capitalism, that irrationality conquers on the foundation of technical reason.

This of course does not obviate the importance of Habermas's insistence upon the specificity of normative structures in the development of the mode of production. Habermas's contribution to critical theory has

been to underline the relative autonomy of the normative in human history. But in the final analysis we must reject his attempt to substitute moral and cognitive learning for class struggle. It is not only that his assessment of the degree to which the revolutionary need has been overcome by late capitalist organization is wrong. This is an empirical question, the answer to which depends to some extent on how one views the problems of war, ecological disaster, and the persistence of opposition within the labor process and in public life. Habermas could easily reply to the empirical arguments advanced here that these are merely "problems" subject to solution through rational calculation, a contention close to that advanced by Daniel Bell and other American theorists of post-industrial society.[38] American social theory does not posit that capitalism has succeeded in overcoming conflicts, even those based on class, only that these conflicts are subject to technical resolutions.

The major objection to Habermas's reconstruction of historical materialism must rest upon theoretical grounds. The issue is joined by Habermas's contention that science and technology are subject to merely technical criteria because they express a universal rationality, that is, their development corresponds to the general interest of society. Although in the later work Habermas attempts to ground his separation of work and interaction within social evolution rather than philosophically, it is evident that he misunderstands the relationship between work and interaction because he has accepted the dubious perspective that labor is nothing but instrumental to the domination of nature and related thereby instrumentally to human subsistence. For Habermas as well as virtually the entire Marxist tradition, work itself is not a need whose relation to the social structure has normative implications. By confining the normative to the sphere of interaction and the cognitive to the sphere of production, Habermas has reproduced the division between moral and instrumental reason that is inherent in the antinomies of bourgeois thought. His theory is but a mirror of a society in which the division between the spiritual and the material is accepted as part of the natural order. Habermas's theoretical construction accepts the division between intellectual and manual labor. His biologistic orientation towards the domination of nature simultaneously argues that "moral development" is the specifically human in nature but that production is fundamentally continuous with our animal nature.

In this respect, although Habermas's attack against the anthropomorphism of Marxism is warranted and constitutes a major corrective to its theoretical premises, he appears to deny the historical character of the production of needs. That is, even if social labor inheres in previous stages of evolution, it does not follow that work as such may be naturalized. For what has transpired in the late capitalist era is precisely that the satisfaction of human needs includes work, and this problematic contains a moral and ethical dimension. Workers no longer confine their demands to a decent wage, job security, and "pleasant" working conditions. The moral development of which Habermas speaks has historically extended to the quality of working life. Workers are beginning, by fits and starts, to need a working life which is marked by reflexivity and communicative action. Habermas's assignment of work to "rational-purposive"—i.e. instrumental—action corresponds to a version of socialist ethics in which the goal of labor apart from physical spheres is rich in interaction but where the labor process is subject only to "technical" rules. In this world of the work/leisure dichotomy, questions of production are devoid of moral content. Needless to say, such a theory becomes technocratic, reproducing the division between intellectual and manual labor which permeates capitalist production and its culture.

Of course, we are still in the throes of a debate in which the labor process has, for the first time since *Capital*, acquired a specific content for socialist theory and labor research. However, recent Marxist writing has focused exclusively on the degree to which the labor process is subject to the logic of capital, that is, it is still preoccupied with the modus operandi of the consequences of rationalization of and by science and the technology of production. Harry Braverman, André Gorz, and Serge Bologna, among others, have argued persuasively that the "technical" division of labor is both hierarchical and degrading.[39] The degradation of labor is only acceptable, of course, to those like Habermas, who would insist that this is a price worth paying for material abundance and that satisfactions should be sought elsewhere. On the other hand, if work itself has become a part of the moral as well as the political economy, then its intrinsic character is subject to scrutiny as a system of communication action. Further, returning to Habermas's own insistence upon an historical/empirical basis for the construction of social theory, the workers' protests common in all capitalist countries in the 1960s and 1970s were directed not against the traditional issue of wages as much as at questions of control and management. Strikes, sabotage, and other means of work disruption amounted to a refusal to work under degraded working conditions, that is, under conditions marked by a rationality that aims at reduction of working time required for the production of the commodity. The purposivity of "scientific" management consists in its attempt to delete from the labor process any activity not directed towards capital accumulation. The rationality of production under these conditions presupposes the primacy of organization over interaction in Habermas's sense of the term, interaction, which is necessarily reflexive, appears as a "disturbance" within the prevailing system of reproduction. Yet, from the point of view of those who disturb, reflexivity is a need and is objectively contradictory to capital's rationality, just as an ecologically sound environment appears as an "interest" of society as a whole against the particular rationality or logic of capital.

To offer a universal pragmatics without ideological presuppositions is itself a "primal ideology." It is only given to those for whom the achievement of the enlightenment, with its binary oppositions, can be regarded as a historically constituted but ontologically immutable ground. The appeal to social evolution must not be taken as irrefutable scientific evidence for a position which has become problematic, owing to the "action-critique" that refuses to exempt either science and technology or the labor process from the criterion of moral development. But it remains for us to constitute this critique on a theoretical terrain.

NOTES

1. Bernard-Henri Levy, *Barbarism with a Human Face* (New York: Harper and Row, 1978).

2. G. A. Cohen, *Karl Marx's Theory of History: A Defense* (Princeton: Princeton University Press, 1978).

3. Andre Gorz, *Ecology as Politics* (Boston: South End Press, 1980).

4. See especially Juan Luis Segundo, *The Liberation of Theology* (New York: Orbis Books, 1976).

5. Jürgen Habermas, "Reconstruction of Historical Materialism," in *Communication and the Evolution of Society* (Boston: Beacon Press, 1979).

6. The term was coined by Rudolph Bahro, *The Alternative in Eastern Europe* (London: New Left Books, 1978).

7. Louis Althusser, *For Marx* (New York: Vintage Books, 1970), 10–2. Althusser argues that some varieties of Marxism, particularly what he calls Marxist humanism are ideological because they have failed to constitute the object of social knowledge as society. By naming "man" as the subject/object of history, humanism, according to Althusser, has perpetuated the ideological forms of pre-Marxist—i.e. pre-scientific—discourse because it posits an a priori subject that stands outside history. In another place he asserts that politics as a practice is a form of ideology, even those political practices inspired by Marxism.

8. Georg Lukács, *History and Class Consciousness* (London: Merlin Press, 1971), 151–2.

9. Ibid. 155.

10. V.I. Lenin, "What is to Be Done," in *The Lenin Anthology*, ed. Robert C. Tucker (New York: W.W. Norton and Co., 1975).

11. Ibid. 27–8. Lenin quotes a long passage from Karl Kautsky's comment on the draft program of the Austrian Social-Democratic Party printed in *Neue Zeit*, 1901–2 (10/3), 79. In this remark able passage Kautsky asserts the fundamental principle that socialism as a scientific discourse arises "side by side" with the class struggle. Although they are both the effects of economic relationships, they are separate.

"The vehicle of science is not the proletariat but the bourgeois intelligentsia" according to Kautsky. "Thus, socialist consciousness is something introduced into the proletarian class struggle from without and not something that arose within it spontaneously." Lenin adopts this viewpoint without criticism and it becomes the basis of his critique of spontaneity within socialist ranks. Also Althusser's distinction between science and ideology originates in this conception, as does Gramsci's argument that every class seeking

68

social and political power must form intellectuals who articulate the class's claim to moral and intellectual leadership, i.e. hegemony, over society as a whole.

12. V. I. Lenin, *Materialism and Empirio-Criticism* (Moscow: Progress Publishers, 1967), especially ch. 2, sec. 4, "Does Objective Truth Exist?".

13. Despite Marxist-structuralism's accusation against Lukács of essentialism, I believe his concepts of hegemony and ideology are close to those of Gramsci and Althusser since all of them insist that ideology is an aspect of the structure of society rather than a property of incorrect ideas or "false consciousness." Lukács theory of mediation is a statement concerning the reality of appearances, that is, their objective existence. For Lukács, drawing from Marx's theory of fetishism of commodities, the origin of ideology is in the permutations of the commodity form.

14. Lukács, *History and Class Consciousness*, 159.

15. Georg Dimitrov, *The United Front Against Fascism*. This was the main report to the Seventh Congress of the Communist International, 1935.

16. Leon Trotsky, *What Next?* (New York: Pathfinder Press, 1973).

17. Max Horkheimer, "The Authoritarian State," *Telos*, 15 (Spring, 1973).

18. Walter Benjamin, "Theses on the Philosophy of History," in *Illuminations*, ed. Hannah Arendt, (New York: Shocken Books, 1969).

19. Eduard Bernstein, *Evolutionary Socialism* (New York: Shocken Books, 1961).

20. Max Horkheimer, *Eclipse of Reason* (New York: Seabury Press, 1974).

21. See for example Herbert Marcuse, *The Aesthetic Dimension* (Boston: Beacon Press, 1978).

22. Theodor Adorno, *Negative Dialectics* (New York: Seabury Press, 1973), 3.

23. Ibid. 143.

24. Ibid. 145.

25. Ibid. 147.

26. One finds this tendency in Mao's essay *On Contradiction*, where the distinction is drawn between antagonistic and non-antagonistic contradictions. The former are a property of capitalist societies while the latter tries to explain the persistence of difference within "really existing" socialist countries on the basis of a category that may not imply political struggle, that is, a struggle for power within society. Similarly, the communist parties of Eastern Europe have, until the Polish events of summer 1980, refused to acknowledge the structural differences between state and party, on the one side, and subaltern social classes on the other.

Since there could be no antagonism between the party of the working class and the class itself, any struggles between them were viewed as the consequence of outside interference from the capitalist powers whose agents infiltrate the workers' movement. A similar line was taken to explain the Hungarian Revolution of 1956 and the attempt to effect fundamental changes in the relations among party, state, and the workers in Czechoslovakia in 1968. Since the workers, by their own efforts, would never oppose the party, strikes, demonstrations, and other manifestations of opposition had to be the result of outside influences or the political "backwardness" of the workers.

27. Adorno, *Negative Dialectics*, 159.

28. Ibid. 354.

29. Ibid.

30. Ibid. 358.

31. Ibid. 359.

32. Karl Korsch, *Karl Marx* (New York: Russell and Russell, 1963), ch. 2.

33. Adorno, *Negative Dialectics*, 360.

34. Jürgen Habermas, "Technology and Science as 'Ideology'" in *Towards a Rational Society* (Boston: Beacon Press, 1970).

35. Jürgen Habermas, *Communication and the Evolution of Society*, 146.

36. Ibid. See especially the chapters on "Moral Development and Ego Identity" and "The Development of Normative Structures."

37. This is, of course, little more than Weber's project for a value-free "scientific" sociology. See "Science as a Vocation," in *From Max Weber*, ed. Hans Gerth and C. Wright Mills (New York: Oxford University Press, 1958).

38. Daniel Bell, *The Coming of Post-Industrial Society* (New York: Basic Books, 1973). See also S. M. Lipset, *Political Man* (New York: Anchor Books, 1962).

39. Harry Braverman, *Labor and Monopoly Capital* (New York: Monthly Review Press, 1974), and André Gorz (ed.), *Technical Division of Labor* (London: Harvester Press, 1976).

CHAPTER TWO

Marxism as a Positive Science

The virtue of Habermas's work is to remind us of the indissolubility of the Marxist framework. It is not possible to dissociate the theory of ideology from classes and class struggle, any more than science and technology can be regarded as either historically or logically independent of social relations. But that is exactly what Louis Althusser and his school have attempted to do.[1] Their assertion that Marxism is a science is specifically linked to the concept that in order to become a science, its theoretical system or discourse must separate itself from ideology. Althusser regards the critique of ideology as the first and crucial step in the development of science and claims that the early Marx may be partitioned from the late Marx on the basis of his critique of idealism. Althusser distinguishes science from ideology in three distinct features: (*i*) the object of knowledge is different in the two. The scientific object of knowledge, while different from the "real" world, is no longer informed by religious, abstract essences. In elaborating his claim that the early and late Marx may be differentiated on the basis of an epistemological break from the idealism of Hegel, Althusser argues that the condition for Marx's "theoretical revolution" was his constitution of a new object of knowledge. Marx moves from philosophical speculation to scientific practice when he discovers that society as a structure is the proper object of investigation, not the essence of humans.[2] (*ii*) But it cannot be said that science and ideology are separated by a Chinese wall; science emerges out of its critique of ideology and constitutes itself in and through this critique. For Althusser, scientific knowledge is marked by its mode of production of knowledges (the plural here refers to Althusser's insistence that the knowledge modes of production, e.g., chemistry, physics, Marxism, are distinct practices that make up science: the use of the singular is ideological because it connotes a totality that is more than the ensemble of material practices). This mode of production, according to Althusser, may be likened to the labor process. The specific object of knowledge for each science is the raw materials from which the theoretical means of production (the methods of science including theory, experiments, technique, etc.) derives a result. Althusser acknowledges that the historical relations ("both theoretical, ideological and social") form the context of scientific labor. But these historical relations are accorded no determinative weight in the mode of production of scientific knowledge. Althusser holds that scientific knowledge is "concerned with the real world through its specific mode of appropriation of the real world...the mechanism that insures it."[3] This mechanism, the process of the production of knowledge, enables us "the grasp of the concept." For, even though the object of knowledge and the real world are distinct, science can, in Althusser's view, appropriate the real object or the real world through both a critique of the ideological object and its ability to form a mechanism of knowledge.

At this point, it is necessary to caution against the apparent homology between Althusser's concern with the process of the production of knowledges, its theoretical conditions, so to speak, and traditional concerns of epistemological inquiry. For he distinguishes his approach not only from the school of Marxist humanism, according to which (in his account, at least) the a prioris of appearance and essence and of the abstract totality climax in an idealistic ideology that must be banished from Marxist science, but also from Husserl and his school which proceeds from the problem of whether knowledge is possible.[4] Althusser implicitly agrees with the view that knowledge and its mode of acquisition is the object of philosophical inquiry, but not the question of how a subject can know the object. For Althusser, this is the wrong question since it ignores the real progress of science, a mode of production that has already established the possibility of science free of ideological determinations by its grasp of the real world through its mechanism and its means of production.

(*iii*) Althusser places himself within one tendency within Marxist thought, a Marxism that makes a decisive break with reflection theory, according to which knowledge is "reflection" of the real world where ideas correspond to material processes as a matter of simple causality. Althusser recognizes that the mechanism of scientific practices yields only a "knowledge effect," from which theory must make inferences. Althusser's theory of truth retains the traditional notion of the existence of an external world "independent of the process of knowledge" but makes no claim for the correspondence of ideas derived from scientific practice with this world as some kind of reflection:

> We can say, then, that the mechanism of production of the knowledge effect lies in the mechanism which underlies in the action of the forms of order of the scientific discourse of the proof...in the fact these forms of order only show themselves as forms of the order of appearance of concepts in scientific discourse as a function of other forms, which without themselves being forms of order, are nevertheless the absent principle of the latter...the forms of order (forms of proof in scientific discourse) are the diachrony of a basic synchrony.... Synchrony represents the organizational structure of the concepts in thought—totality or system (or, as Marx puts it, 'synthesis'); diachrony the movement of succession of the concepts in the ordered discourse of proof.[5]

But proof is "not in the eating," in Engels's alimentary metaphor. The proof is found in the internal structure of science. The famous criterion of practice as the verification of a theory means the distinct scientific practice to which any specific discourse refers. For Althusser, the theoretical "practice" is self-contained by its own structural unity, a logical order that grasps the real "in thought" (although thought includes, even subsumes, the theory and technique of a specific scientific practice). There are no "guarantees" for scientific truth, except the norms of theoretical validity established by the scientific community.

Thus, we arrive at a convergence between the work of Thomas Kuhn, Charles Peirce, and Althusser. Kuhn locates scientific revolutions, defined as the replacement of an old paradigm by a new one, in the contradiction between the old paradigm and the anomalies of its experimental practice.[6] A shift to the new paradigm takes place, according to this theory, only when that paradigm is able to explain phenomena considered anomalous by the older one. The new paradigm that changes the substance of science may also entail new relationships both between science and nature, and within science itself. Yet, the norms of theoretical validity remain those accepted by the scientific community. Change is a process occurring within science; it takes place on the basis of the willingness of those whose work is "normal" with respect to existing scientific practices to accept the validity of the new paradigm. The scientist is already equipped with a series of concepts, a theoretical framework capable of grasping the real world in thought. Knowledge is not derived from observation but is only confirmed by it: there are no self-evident "facts." In the last analysis, Althusser implicitly follows Leibniz in his belief that the predicate of any true affirmative proposition lies, implicitly or explicitly, in its subject. This relation between subject and predicate resides in the "grounded connection" between the two or, in Althusser's terms, in their unity in structure. For Althusser has evolved a theory in which the forms of thought, the correspondence among the various elements, and the logical principle of order constitute the proof of theory. Here verification through practice, labeled by Althusser as rank empiricism, is subsumed by the logical principle of order. The "absent" link in Althusser is the relation of thought processes to nature.

This link is provided by the historical godfather of structuralism, Émile Durkheim. For Durkheim's major contribution to the legitimation of the social sciences was his insistence that they were continuous in their epistemology and methods with those of any other science: society as much as nature is "a structured and rational order, whose phenomena obey invariant laws and are determinate."[7] The critique of Durkheim's reliance on experience for obtaining truth from an Althusserian perspective refers back to the idea that theory requires no empirical basis for its propositions, but these propositions are true because they obey the same logical order as nature or society.

74

The notion of empirically grounded knowledge is always found in the realm of ideology. Thus politics, indeed, all the sciences whose subject is "man," must be ideological. According to Althusser, the subject of social science is social structure (the synchronic) and its ordered discourse which is prior to verification. Here, the reconstitution of the object of knowledge from "man" to "society" as a social fact irreducible to individuals, their subjectivity, their ideological relations to each other, and the social structure within which they live combines with the ordered discourse to constitute science itself. Thus, Althusser says that Marx constitutes the science of society as an object of knowledge through his critique of abstract "man," the object of the so-called human sciences, derived from Kantian premises that problematized the possibility of knowing anything outside human interaction.[8]

Althusser introduces a dualism in the study of the social world. There can be no science of social relations unless these are treated as a determinate ordered discourse, obeying definite laws already specified by the Althusserian canon that makes structures the true object of any science. Nevertheless, people do study interaction, social norms, and record their experiences of the social world unmediated by structural analysis. These studies are called ideology by Althusser and are defined pejoratively, although accorded the status of legitimate, ideological discourse—but not science. This is the sphere of "lived" experience or the "imaginary," which has an indirect relation to the real, imaginary because these inquiries are not theoretically grounded; they lack the apparatus of true knowledge and cannot grasp the real except as ideology.

Hence, class struggle, at the level of either trade union practice or practical revolutionary politics, can only be ideological since these practices arise from the lived experiences of workers. Science is somehow separate from the class struggle, even though class and class struggle may be the object of knowledge of scientific investigation provided they are viewed from the mechanism of structuralist analysis. In this mode, a priori, there are a finite set of categories, derived from the ideology critique from which the science has arisen, which form a grid through which reality is grasped, or appropriated. The progress of the scientific study of social structure, called the mode of production by Althusserians, takes place within the social context of lived experience, but this experience cannot have a decisive influence on the configuration of the science of society because it obeys a different set of rules.

In the end, Althusser claims that Marxist science, like any other science, can be value-neutral. It has overcome the "iron cage" of the imaginary within which all ideological discourse is imprisoned. Its language machine is capable of assimilating any raw material, chopping it up into discrete objects, ordering it according to logical principles, naming and mapping in advance, and "producing" knowledges that take on the aspect of a predicate of which the mechanism itself is the subject.

Althusser's metaphor of production and of the machine is not arbitrary. His Marxism turns out to be an almost conscious adaptation to the age of mechanical reproducibility, one in which the machine is both form and content, or, to be more exact, the form implies the content, which, however alien at the beginning, is produced as a reified object with no history. Althusser's attack on the search for origins as ideological is an attack against the effort to insist on the validity of knowledge before the Enlightenment, just as Copernican science criticized its forebears as mysticism. For, at base, Althusser is a rationalist: anything that refuses his mechanical idea grinder is labeled irrational, or ideology. A science of politics or of art is possible only on condition that these are treated as ideological discourses since they are premechanical.

Among other problems, the Althusserian theory of science seems incapable of finding the new features of social, economic, and political development since, in his own metaphoric analogy, these are part of the social unconscious, and he views the unconscious as the seat of the irrational, the structural root of all ideology. Following the metaphor, the process of acquiring scientific knowledge may be compared to the process by which the patient makes conscious irrational, unconscious desires and needs in order to control them. The congruence of Althusser's conception of science and the instrumentalization of reason that has been integrated harnesses the unconscious and makes it part of the conscious life, transforms it from alien nature to raw materials for the theory machine.

I do not believe that this comparison of Althusser's separation of science and ideology to the unbridgeable parts of the psychic structure in Freudian theory is farfetched.[9] Just as Freudian psychology has a side that seeks to subordinate anarchic, irrational human nature to rational-purposive action, so Althusser wishes to restrict ideology to certain spheres of human activity or, if possible, to progressively subordinate them to Marxist science, considered here sovereign because untrammeled by lived experience,

John Mepham has likened the relation of science and ideology to two different generative sets having a different matrix of internal relations.[10] Both are considered structured discourses that may be understood as separate languages. In Mepham's conception, "social life is structured like language" arranged on a semantic field that is, in the main, beyond the scientific comprehension of those who participate. Mepham: "The natural self-understood meanings encountered in social life form a text which we need to decipher to discover its true meaning."[11] The comparison with Freud's theory of dreams comes to mind. Just as the dream speaks a language different from that of the conscious life and defies literalization, so people in everyday life speak an unconscious language that can only be translated by means of other, more scientific categories. The structure of Freud's thought entailed a "generative set" of concepts through which the dream work could be deciphered. These were grounded in the mechanism of the psychic structure and certain processes that followed from the contradictions among its elements. Freudian-Lacanian psychoanalysis constitutes itself much like the Althusserian definition of science. The unconscious speaks a language whose meanings are hidden to ordinary comprehension. It can only reveal itself through slips of the tongue, jokes, gesture, and dreamwork, which must be transcoded into the language of science in order to be understood. The "real" is a set of relations constituted as a structured discourse that is invisible to ordinary cognition but presents itself in a "phenomenal form." Social life perceives this phenomenal form and translates perception into the structured discourse of ideology, which is constituted as a symbolic order, maintaining the real as opaque, that is, concealing its generative set of relations.

In Freud's theory, science as ordered-discourse-deciphering is necessary, but not sufficient, for cracking the hidden code of the unconscious. The unconscious constructs mechanisms of defense (condensation, displacement, linear causality, clues that lead to blind alleys), just as the real masks itself in cognition. Thus, the Althusserian attack against the possibility of gaining scientific knowledge through observation since the "data of experience" yield only the real in its phenomenal form. Science must treat the observed perception of things with skepticism, treating these data as ideology, the critique of which will constitute the first step in the development of science. The transformation of the data of experience into the raw material upon which the knowledge-producing machine will labor is the way Freud hoped to make the manifest text of the dream part of the process by which the latent text is revealed.

Althusser's theory of the relation of science and ideology is that ideology is not produced by erroneous or even class-bound beliefs or value systems. If this were so, ideology would disappear with the end of class society. But the Althusserian variety of Marxism insists that ideology is structured discourse of lived experience whose variance from the "real" is not subject to historical change. The particular phenomenal form of real relations will surely change with the transformation of capitalism into socialism. But the gap between real relations and phenomenal forms is transhistorical, that is, ideology as "lived experience" does not disappear with the new social order because its source is not the distorted values and beliefs of bourgeois society; it is not false consciousness. Ideology transcends one mode of production because it is a structure of relations between lived experience and the real.

Once again, we are reminded of Freud's remonstrance against the "naive" Marxist belief that the collective ownership and control of the means of material production will abolish all conflict, certainly all human contradictions.[12] Just as Freud posited the invariance over time of the contradiction between the pleasure principle and the reality principle (or, in the earlier form, the id and the superego), so Althusser holds to the eternity of the distinction between ordinary ideological discourse and scientific discourse, where the former is considered a generative set of concepts inscribed in everyday language and interaction.

Science arises from the critique of ideology in every society. The theory machine will always be necessary to prevent the phenomenal form of real relations from rendering all reality opaque. Here, then, is the inevitable privileging of science, the necessity of its separation from ideology, the heart of the concept of its transhistoricity. While Kuhn does not, in principle, exclude social and historical determination, or at least influence, of the process and structure of scientific knowledge (indeed, his analogy between scientific and political revolutions is explicitly drawn), he has brought none of these relations inside the process of scientific development. The implication of this exclusion from the discourse of Kuhn's investigation of the history of science is close to Althusser's attempt to separate science from ideology. Both would agree, to be sure, that historical, ideological, and social considerations are part of the context of science, but the insistence on the autonomy of normative practices such as criteria for validity, constitution of the scientific object, etc., tends to neutralize the ideological influence/determination of science itself.

Kuhn is, of course, much more critical of the category of scientific truth than Althusser, whose insistence on the discontinuous, with his categories of relative autonomy and of the primacy of structure, render his complex argument philosophically naive, in the last instance. Although he does not go as far as Paul Feyerabend[13] in claiming that the dominance of a scientific paradigm in any historical period is arbitrary, that it has no historical necessity, Kuhn does argue that scientific "progress" remains in the eye of the beholder.[14] But what puts Althusser and Kuhn in the same theoretical camp is the notion that the relative autonomy of the scientific community from the "laity and everyday life" is the foundation of the insularity of science from ideology.

In this respect, Kuhn's ascription of insularity to the separateness of science in social terms from everyday life, its institutional autonomy, has the virtue of leaving the door open for an empirical investigation of whether this assertion holds for contemporary science, if it ever did for earlier periods. I shall examine in this chapter the thesis that such autonomy of science from ideology could ever be successfully argued, at least up to the present. Althusser, on the other hand, in his desire to show the scientificity of Marxism, an antiempiricist and antipositivist science to be sure, has been constrained to hermetically seal both Marxism and other "scientific" practices from interaction with social, ideological, and historical relations that determine, in any measure, the content of scientific knowledge, except insofar as science emerges at the intersection of the epistemological break from ideology in terms of the constitution of the object of knowledge. But, for Althusser, the paradigms of science are debated, decisions arrived at, new theoretical norms agreed upon, entirely within the scientific community.

Consider the words of the philosopher of science Charles Sanders Peirce. Referring to the concept of truth, Peirce says:

> The opinion which is fated to be ultimately agreed to by all who investigate is what we mean by truth, and the object represented in this opinion is the real.[15]

Peirce was aware of the problem of the necessity of these opinions and the question whether it was possible to speak of infallible results of investigation. He viewed the object as independent of the processes of knowledge but remained fixed on the ideal of one necessary result of investigation by all those competent to conduct this work. For Peirce, as much as for Althusser, the mechanisms of science are the road to knowledge. It is their infallibility that must be relied on to yield truth. If these could be challenged, the relativity of scientific truth, its fallibility, and thus its ideological character would logically result.

Althusser has worked himself into a cul de sac on the road to asserting the scientificity of Marxism. Since he can only admit that Marxism may be an ideology from the point of view of the revolutionary movement but not in the rigorous terms in which scientific discourse is cast, and he rejects the reflection theory of knowledge and the correspondence theory of truth, he finds himself caught in a very un-Marxist idea, that is, the possibility that a sphere of social activity may be free of what he considers ideology to consist in—a structured asymmetric relation between humans and their objective world. In his conception, Althusser has posited a privileged mechanism that saves science from historical, political, and social determination. This mechanism is the category of structure or system of concepts that are ordered in a type of hierarchy where the succession of one concept by another has a specific form that is said to be scientific. The origins of these concepts are obscure, except insofar as we may trace their ideological roots, e.g., the development of modern chemistry from the phlogiston theory, or Galileo's radical critique of Ptolemic physics from within science. However, all true science adopts, according to Althusser, "an ordered discourse of proof" that enables it to grasp the real unmediated by social determinations.

In fact, Althusser finds the concept of mediation itself to be ideological since this is not a material concept. By its insertion into the process of the production of knowledge, it undermines the certainty of knowing and reintroduces the question about the problematic relation of science to its object. Thus, we find Althusser in the position, especially curious for a Marxist theorist, of asserting that the mechanisms of scientific knowledge are ideologically neutral. This implies that technique, the experimental method, and technology as such are neutral as well since, in Althusser's conception of the history of science, scientific knowledge gives rise to technology. Consequently, Althusser equates science and technology with the labor process as the sum of human relations to nature, constituted as material practices that are entwined with the structure of production. The forces of production, in Althusser's discourse, follow Marxist orthodoxy: they are (relatively) independent from and prior to the relations of production. When Althusser uses the metaphor of production processes to understand knowledge, it is not, in his own term, "innocent." The theoretical terminology anticipates the result: science and technology are free of ideology since the former is part of the base of society and the latter is part of its superstructure. The superstructure, according to Althusser, is relatively autonomous from the economic base and may have some influence upon it, but the forces of production, of which science and technology are important elements, are the materializations of society's grasp of the real world through a theoretical practice of which technique is a crucial part.

I have argued that the doctrine of the neutrality of technology is untenable. We must now demonstrate that the ideological neutrality of science is similarly untenable. Despite their antagonistic theoretical frameworks, both Habermas and Althusser deny that technology and science are ideology. But, where Habermas's argument rests on his conception of the permanence of reification after the universalization of the commodity by capitalism and has conflated reification with the new given of rationality,

Althusser has attacked the category of reification as such. For Althusser, science is a self-legitimating discourse whose ordering of proof, apparatus of theory, and method of discovery are unproblematic. His task is to show that Marxism is scientific because it orders its concepts in a structural unity that is homologous with other sciences—theoretical practices whose histories consist in the overturning of the ideological character of prior paradigms. So Marxism is now a social theory whose determinations are relatively independent of their social, historical, and ideological contexts, since science cannot refer to its origins or its context, but is ultimately self-justifying.

The importance of Althusser's contribution to the Marxist theory of ideology is his insistence that ideology is situated within the forms of social life rather than within the realm of ideas alone. However, the freeing of the concept of ideology from the label of "mere illusions" was originally suggested by Georg Lukács, who found the basis of ideology, not in Weberian values and beliefs, or the earlier Marxist idea of "false consciousness," but in the ordinary apprehension of the forms of appearance of things.[16] But Lukács's argument stems from his theory of reification within capitalist society. To the degree that, historically, the commodity becomes dominant in the process of production, relations among persons (the "real relations" within the capitalist mode of production) are enshrouded in a fog of mystification. Their form of appearance is relation between things, an exchange of equivalents that seem to be grounded in the intrinsic properties of objects rather than in social relations. In this conception, the source of ideology, which is universal among all those who live within the capitalist mode of production, is the commodity form. The opacity of the material world is not a property of perception, but a "natural" cognitive effect of the transformation of use value into exchange value, the process of production into the process of exchange and the subsumption of the labor process under capital.

For Lukács, class relations *mediate* these fundamental sources of the production of ideology by giving ideology a specific character. But the values, beliefs, etc., of a certain class are necessarily variants of bourgeois beliefs, not because of the imposition of these ideas by concrete persons who may be their bearers but because the configuration of commodity production subsumes the concrete into the abstract, both at the level of labor, where labor time as a unit of measurement replaces the specific kind of labor (weaving, carpentry, cooking, waiting on tables, etc.), and at the level of the commodity, where use value is subsumed under exchange value. Thus, we measure ourselves in terms of how much wages the sale of our labor power will bring. We are "worth a definite quantity of money." Mepham points out that the transformation of the value of labor power (the amount of socially necessary labor time embodied in the commodities necessary for the reproduction of the worker and her/his family) into wages is a prime example of how the form of appearance of real social relations leads to ideology. The worker believes that her/his wages represent the number of hours for which labor power has been sold. Thus, the ideological category the "value of labor," as if the exchange of a certain quantity of labor power for wages was an exchange of equivalents. In turn, this mystification hides the source of capitalist profits that now appear to originate in the marketplace, the risk factor in investment, or in the morality of individual enterprise. The form of appearance of the commodity, in this case labor, hides the source of profit, the difference between the value of the commodity and the value of labor power. Marx uses the terminological transformation to point to his distinction between appearance and reality. The value of labor power becomes wages; surplus value becomes profits; production becomes a series of market exchanges. It is not that the perception of the social reality is false, but that the reality has two forms: its appearances and its real relations.

Lukács locates the appearance/reality problematic within a definite historical stage of development: the capitalist mode of production. Althusser, on the other hand, transforms Lukács's insistence on the historicity of the category of ideology into a structural principle. That is, he posits the distance of humans from the real and the *opacity* of the real relations as transhistorical, since these relations are rooted not in the commodity form but in the structural distinction between the language of appearances and the language of reality. Since these languages are ordered discourses that obey their own inner laws, and are quite separate from each other, the deciphering task is finally cognitive rather than a social and historical problem. The consequence of formulating the problem of ideology in these terms is to establish science as the only possible means by which ideology may be overcome. There are, for Althusser, no circumstances that may render social relations transparent to lived experience. We are *always* destined to live our lives ideologically, regardless of the social system.

Thus, the ideological is *naturalized* by Althusser's structural binaries. On the one hand, he has abolished the myth of the "integrated civilizations" which was, for Lukács, the basis for his critique of late capitalist society. In Althusser's hands, the critique of ideology no longer relies on the assumption that transparent social relations may be experienced under any circumstances. Our relation to the real will always be problematic because of the incommensurability of the symbolic order as discourse with the real; only science, by constructing a mechanism of knowledge ordered in the manner of the real by the structural rather than empirical homology, may grasp the real. On the other hand, the implicit assertion of Althusser's theory of science is that the real is the rational; that is, modern scientific knowledge is an ordered discourse that holds the secret of the real, and its concept will only be overthrown from within its practices, its theory machine. Habermas really ends with a variety of "end of ideology" critique that was typical of American and British sociology in the late 1950s.[17] At that time, the prospects for capitalism appeared limitless; the working class appeared safely integrated into the apparatus by the rewards of technological development and trade union successes; and the system seemed amenable to an infinite series of technical adjustments to keep it going at high levels of production and consumption. Since the source for the production of traditional ideology was the reflection in our minds of the real class relations, as these relations took on the character of a reified totality, that is, as it could no longer be argued that society was irreparably divided against itself, only an act of will could restore that which was lost by the capacity of technocratic consciousness to subsume ideology within the processes of technical problem solving—the utopian element in all ideological production.

Althusser's fundamentally rationalist framework privileges theory as a series of practices that, taken together, constitute the "real." Science is constituted by its nonessentialist categories which are developed by the critique of ideology. Materialism is combined with the Kantian preoccupation with epistemology to produce a theory of knowledge whose referent, but only in the last instance, is the real world. However, in Althusser's version, the real world, like economic relations, has no *practical* significance; it is a postulate that remains unexamined in an otherwise methodological inquiry that focuses on the problem of theory-formation. In this sense, the concrete empirical object is always supposed as theory dependent and has little status in scientific inquiry.

In contrast, Galvano Della Volpe seeks to restore to the concrete object the position of both starting point and end of the process of knowledge, at the same time insisting on a critique of categories as necessary meta-science.[18] That is, Della Volpe agrees with Althusser that Marxism's scientificity depends on more than the correspondence of its propositions to an objective world; the work of constituting categories precedes specific scientific hypotheses. However, his purpose is to clear Marxism of its metaphysical, irrationalist baggage, in a word, to free Marx from Hegel. The key move will be to install formal logic, especially the principle of noncontradiction as a positive science. Della Volpe argues that judgment always entails identity and noncontradiction. Thus Hegelian dialectics is effectively removed from Marxism.

Marxist structuralism is neither dialectical in the Hegelian sense nor, strictly speaking, materialist. Rather, it adopts the position of the Kantian tradition. While distancing himself from Kant's essentialism, Lucio Colletti (who calls Della Volpe's *Logic as a Positive Science* "the most important work produced by European Marxism in the post-war era") still insists that "it is important to take epistemology as one's starting point in order to understand the genesis of the Marxist concept 'the social relations of production' in the very problems of classical philosophy."[19] According to Colletti, these problems are the relation of thought to its object, a relation which is, of course, always problematic for classical philosophy because of the nonidentity of thinking and being. Colletti shows that for Marx, the concept of work as simultaneously human beings' transformation of nature and themselves is the core of Marx's transformation of the Hegelian categories from idealism to materialism. But Colletti's main concern is not this, a point both unremarkable and unexceptionable in Marxist literature. More important is his implicit Kantian reading of the epistemological consequences of the labor process. Following Della Volpe's insistence on the continuity of the early and late Marx, Colletti reads the early Marx's *Economic and Philosophic Manuscript*, not as a derivative Feuerbachian text still mired in the Hegelian problematic (as Althusser claims), but as embryonic historical materialism, the key to Marx's theoretical revolution. But what is historical materialism? For Colletti, it is the doctrine according to which nature is "objectively sensuous," that is, ineluctably linked to "my own subjective sensitivity itself." The "object" nature does not take on significance, even if posited formally outside human consciousness, until it is appropriated through labor. And this appropriation is, at the same time, a cognitive act both of nature and of self. "There is no consciousness of the object without self-consciousness. What I see of the world is what my ideas predispose me to see. My relation to nature is conditioned by the level of social-historical development."[20]

There are many things to unpack from these sentences. First, there is Colletti's own framework of self-consciousness, of his focus on knowledge for the individual, which implies that the process of knowing is the subject of philosophical inquiry. With Engels, Colletti conceives the object always in the process of traversing the "in-itself" to the "for us" by means of the labor process. In this reprise, knowledge of nature is made possible not only because of the mediation of labor as equally historical and epistemological activity, but also because "man" is part of natural history, linked to nature by the totality of being, while admitting the heterogeneity of thought and being. Thus, Colletti with Della Volpe affirms that materialism always needs a concept of noncontradiction to establish the status of its epistemology. "Noncontradiction" becomes the "material determinacy" of thought, but only mediated by the social relations of production. For Colletti, consistent with both Marx and part of the Marxist tradition, these social relations are, first of all, relations with nature. Thus, "thought is not a self-contained entity of epistemology" but must necessarily complement the sciences of "man" as a "natural being," a being with imagination prior to labor.

Hence, labor is always purposive activity, with purposes that refer not only to the adaptation of humans to nature, but also to their mutual relations. Colletti's concept of social relations of production reveals the degree to which scientific knowledge is always mediated by social relations, although Colletti does not make this point explicit because, like Della Volpe, he stops with the explication of the logical structure of knowledge, a debt they both owe to Kant. Yet, in concert with Althusser, the efforts of Horkheimer and Adorno to show the ideological character of science are met with scorn. Science is nothing less than "higher achievements of human thought," which the authors of *Dialectic of the Enlightenment* subject to "nihilistic negation." The Frankfurt School has confused the romantic critique of the Enlightenment, a current ingrained in the phenomenology of Heidegger and Husserl, with the critique of capitalism. So, Colletti identifies himself, albeit implicitly, with the Marxist reverence of science as truth, a reverence that has marked philosophy as such since Bacon and, later, Kant. And it is quite reasonable, one would like to say "natural," for Colletti to dismiss the critique of science as an aspect of the domination of nature precisely because of his own Kantian framework for which the "respect" for nature as autonomous is a meaningless concept in light of his valorization of work as knowledge-producing activity. Since the theory of knowledge is the starting point of our comprehension of nature and social relations, Colletti falls into the hole of the radical separation of space and time, privileging, as do all structuralists, the former. Temporality becomes a purely intellectual category and history subordinate to epistemology. The fundamental relation between the priority of the problem of knowledge and ahistorical ideology becomes the basis of the structuralist attack against the Marxism of Lukács, the Frankfurt School, and Jean-Paul Sartre. What united these otherwise heterogeneous modes of thought is their conception of dialectical reason as nonidentical with scientific practice. Sartre makes this distinction most explicit: "Bachelard has shown clearly how modern physics is in itself a new rationalism: the only presupposition of the praxis of the natural sciences is an assertion of *unity* conceived as the perpetual unification of an increasingly real diversity. But the unity depends on human activity rather than on the diversity of phenomena. Moreover, it is neither a knowledge, nor a postulate, nor a Kantian a priori. It is action asserting itself within the undertaking"[21] in which the ends of the activity take precedence over means. For Sartre, the key distinction between scientific rationality and dialectical reason consists in the latter's situating itself in the world, rather than making the radical separation of subject and object which is a basic presupposition of modern scientific ideology. Sartre also attacks the substitution of analytic for historical reason which he accuses many of his contemporaries, notably Claude Lévi-Strauss, of having done. Here, Jonathan Ree defines analytical reason as "the form of reason appropriate to the external relations which are the object of the natural sciences,"[22] or, to put it another way, the rationalistic core of these sciences. Yet Colletti, who wishes to comprehend the object subjectively, argues for this concept of knowledge by defining activity as chiefly *appropriation*, in contrast to which Sartre maintains his earlier position of *Being and Nothingness* by locating human activity within the world. Colletti understands this as human self-production but through appropriation, thus reproducing the assumptions of scientific rationality. As the mediation between us and nature, the core concept of labor is made, like much of the Marxist tradition, into a neutral activity; and human purposes, which must always be ideological, are purged of their antagonisms.

In effect, Della Volpe and Colletti seek to provide a philosophical basis for Marxist science by bringing the propositions of Marxism into conformity with scientific method. Della Volpe argues for a conception of "matter" that is quite distinct from thought. Moreover, this matter is intelligible, unlike the presupposition in Althusserian thought that, following a more orthodox Kantianism, holds the reverse. But, as Martin Jay has remarked, Althusser's antipositivism treads dangerously close to idealism, despite his materialist intentions. Della Volpe veers toward positivism when he declares that experimental science would verify the basic propositions of Marxism or it could not claim the mantle of science. At this juncture in the argument, Della Volpe invokes Galilean science as the model to which Marx adheres, at least morally.[23]

The internal debate among anti-Hegelian Marxists fails to resolve the antinomy of idealism and positivism precisely because its starting point remains ensconced in the problem of knowledge. Since Althusser's rationalism is ultimately unacceptable to those who would insist on the

scientificity of Marxism in the usual sense of the term, it is only a short step to an unabashed positivism. And that is precisely what the recent spate of philosophical and social theoretical attempts to resolve the crisis in Marxism have done. Gerry Cohen, John Roemer, Jon Elster, and Erik Olin Wright[24] have insisted that Marxist categories and propositions concerning the social world be subjected to the same analytic scrutiny and empirical falsifiability which any assertion of normal natural science must suffer. Finding no empirical basis for a given category or proposition (the labor theory of value or surplus value, for example), Jon Elster takes up the basic axioms of "Marxian economics" as if they were those of positive science and concludes that while many of Marx's own discoveries remain valid, others do not. Especially important in Elster's *Making Sense of Marx* is his own acknowledgment that the validity of any set of propositions depends on their methodological assumptions, which must be justified by whether they can be demonstrated as "theorems that would otherwise be unsubstantiated postulates." In other words, the criterion of operationality governs the validity of the assumption of methodological individualism upon which neoclassical economics is based. Although Elster is careful to avoid the equation of "rational" economic "man" with this methodological theorem, arguing that individual action and belief rather than human nature is the starting point, Marx is faulted for his frequent, although never consistent, assumption of methodological "collectivism," which Elster equates with Hegelian essentialism.

As Elster explains, the labor theory of value makes the collectivist assumption of homogeneous labor. Elster argues that if it can be shown that labor is irreducibly heterogeneous, value theory in Marxist economics is inevitably undermined since the entire foundation of his hypothetic-deductive system depends on this assumption. Elster always assumes that the question is the scientificity of Marx's work, especially whether he is a social scientist in the contemporary, positive sense. Are the various elements of historical materialism and the political economy of capitalism demonstrable as rigorously empirical propositions? As Elster surveys Marx's work from his own analytic perspective, three closely related criticisms emerge: Marx employs metaphysical assumptions upon which empirical assertions are based; he is guilty of teleological thinking, in which intentionality is held as a presupposition of social action; and Marx stands condemned of functionalism, which is, of course, counter to the nominalist a priori of methodological individualism.

Of course, the key metaphysical assumption is dialectics, a Hegelian hangover which is the basis of methodological collectivism. On the other hand, Elster tries to save Marx from condemnation as just another metaphysical philosopher by examining his theories to show that when he adopts principles such as those inherent in the mechanical, positivist perspective, he produces much that is of scientific value.

Since this body of work draws its fundamental inspiration as well as core categories from concepts that are, to say the least, as contestable as those of Marx and Hegel, one would want Elster, Cohen, et al., to provide justification that would take account of the criticism leveled by, say, the Frankfurt School, against positivism. Instead, the criterion of operational, behavioral nonteleological science is invoked sui generis as if no debate exists within natural and social sciences concerning these issues. Elster shows that Marx is not methodologically consistent, but Gerry Cohen finds no such inconsistency. Instead, he chooses to justify, or, in his words, "defend" Marx's theory of history using the presuppositions and logical categories of analytic philosophy. Consequently, he tries to assert a technological determinist interpretation of historical materialism by showing that the forces of production are not part of the economic infrastructure but, on the contrary, determine them. Cohen has a substantive as well as a methodological theory of science. Science can in no way be an ideology since it is not part of the superstructure but is, for Marx, located in the productive forces insofar as the theory of history is concerned. (Cohen acknowledges that science is not totally subsumed by productive forces, but that portion of scientific discovery which contributes to the growth of the productive forces is.) It is instructive to examine Cohen's argument in some detail because it reveals precisely what the issues are in the effort to read Marx's theory of historical materialism as positive science.

One of Cohen's key objectives is to purge Marx-interpretation of its vague, ambiguous elements. He wants to employ the "standards of clarity and rigor which distinguishes twentieth century analytic philosophy" to this task, not only because of the mistakes of his followers but also because of the confusions in Marx's own language and sometimes his formulations of theory. In his pursuit of rigor, none of the distinctions Cohen wishes to make is more apposite than that between material relations of production and social relations of production. Quite apart from Cohen's claim that this distinction is crucial for understanding Marx's own technological determinism, an analysis of what he means by it will instruct us best concerning his defense of historical materialism. For, although Cohen performs much textual reading, particularly Marx's Preface, to show that he wanted to separate the forces from the relations of production, it is his own categorical separations that give force to the argument. Quoting Marx, he argues that:

> machinery is no more an economic category than the bullock that drags the plough. Machinery is merely a productive force.... The modern workshop which depends on the application of machinery is a social production relation, an economic category.[25]

Although Cohen acknowledges that the forces of production change over time, depending increasingly on scientific discovery and the application of the results to technology, and that productive relations may retard or advance this process, Cohen's point is that to confuse material relations of production with social relations of production violates the rules of logic. More particularly, the problem is the relation of form to content. Machinery is not capital, which is a social relation, until it enters exchange. Until then, it is only a means of material production, a use value. For Cohen (as for many in the orthodox tradition), machines are tools that help humans negotiate their relationship to nature. But since modern machinery is indirectly the product of scientific development and, according to Cohen, despite the fact that it shares the quality of being a mental activity with ideology ("science is not ideology"), machinery can be understood in its material substance as a thing, except under certain conditions. This means, we may infer, that whereas capitalism is responsible for setting social conditions that spur or retard material production and its preconditions such as science and technology, machinery is not a social relation.

Similarly, the relations that workers enter as they saw wood, for example, are material relations. The mode of cooperation between two workers has nothing to do with social relations of production until their product enters the marketplace. Unless we grant these distinctions, the weight of Cohen's argument for a technological determinist interpretation of historical materialism is seriously impaired. "History is the growth of human productive power, and forms of society rise and fall accordingly as they enable or impede that growth."[26]

Is machinery a thing, or are work relations merely a material relation that becomes social relations only under specific circumstances? The core of Cohen's methodological argument rests on the assertion of the ideological neutrality of science and technology, that machinery, for example, would be the same under different and even competing social systems that employ different economic structures. Presumably, the different systems using the same technology would or would not maximize its most effective impact, but the technology would not, in the last instance, be dependent on these different social systems with respect to its character as a material productive force.

If the socially neutral covering of science and technology is removed, the entire picture changes. We might find that machinery is not merely "machinery" in Cohen's sense, that its embeddedness in social relations of production extends to its core design as well as to its function. This would not obviate the statement that a worker operating a drill press makes a hole, but it must be pointed out that the drill press is a design that presupposes a division of labor marked by increasing specialization. This division of labor is not "technical" in the sense of being neutral with respect to class and other social relations of production. The single valence machine is the product of a long process in the class struggle and is *embodied social interest*. The object "drill press" is constituted by social relations of domination, and its material configuration is not outside these relations. Of course, in order to undertake this kind of analysis, one would have to set aside the analytic "rigor" that supposes an object can be identical only with itself and takes on a new form only when it enters a different context. For the object itself possesses a twofold character: material production contains its social character within its (non)identical material form.

This formulation entails that an economic and social system that includes its overt and covert ideological premises in all of its mental activity, including science, will be found embedded in its material relations of production, such as machinery, forms of cooperation in the labor process, and in the organization of work. In the case cited above, we no longer assume that the drill press, the computer, and laser technology are devoid of social/discursive premises. Thus, when the Soviet state chooses to replicate the Ford production process in its giant Kama truck plant, this technology transfer has social consequences because the production of trucks in Ford entails a division of labor, forms of specialization, and management control that are intimately linked to social domination.[27]

That the assembly line is a socially constituted technology should not be news to anyone who has perused the recent Marxist and non-Marxist literature on the labor process. But there is no evidence in *Karl Marx's Theory of History* either that Cohen has considered this literature or that he has taken it into account in his reading of Marx himself. Marx's own study of the labor process led him to understand the embeddedness of social relations in the material process of production. That he elided the question of science is, of course, consistent with a long tradition that is now in the process of being reexamined from many perspectives, including that of neo-Marxism.

One of the crucial concepts in the recent understandings of science and technology is the close link between professional engineering and the struggle waged by capital in the industrializing era to wrest control of the workplace from craftpersons. This is an instance of the power/knowledge fusion spoken about by sociologists of science such as Bruno Latour, historians such as Michel Foucault, and the philosopher Alfred Sohn-Rethel. That knowledge is bound up with power, and in the late nineteenth and twentieth centuries increasingly seeks this tie as a condition of its own growth, does not obviate the proposition that it is constituted through discourse/knowledge. These concatenations take place in the sphere of "pure" science as much as in technology insofar as concept and object are constructed and not merely "there" to be discovered.

For these propositions to hold, it is not necessary to show that Pasteur's discoveries of a serum for anthrax became de rigeur in agricultural practice because he successfully "marketed" his product within the scientific community, agricultural business, and the state (although Latour shows that this was the case). More to the point is the fact that by the eighteenth century, a nexus of cause and cure for disease was established, and that medical science incessantly sought explanations for the spread of disease that biochemical substances could thwart. Thus, the National Institutes for Health in the United States allocate large sums to scientists for the purpose of investigating how multiples of individuals may be cured of cancer by means of some medical procedure that arrests the growth of cancer cells in the individual body.

What counts, therefore, is that medical science has defined the object of inquiry as the individual who "has" the disease. Much research is devoted to discovery of why some people are susceptible and others relatively immune. Thus, the body becomes a material object upon which scientific efforts to oppose disease are focused. Is this choice "innocent" of the tradition of both medical science as well as philosophy? The question is whether the metaphysics of Descartes, Hobbes, Condorcet, and others bears at all on science in defining its object and its conceptual apparatus of inquiry.

This question is particularly apposite to biological and social sciences, but of course has relevance to physics as well. Even if scientists do not seek a fusion with large-scale pharmaceutical firms, regarding their work as pure discovery, their theory and practice are themselves formed by these discourses. For these reasons, the ontological distinctions made between material, social, and discursive relations are not tenable. Cohen's defense gives us only a rigor that ossifies the categories, and a clarity that obscures the relationships, particularly between thought and object.

There are other specific problematic aspects of Cohen's defense. One is the assertion that human nature is inherently rational; another is that "the historical situation of men is one of scarcity," which places work at the center of their life activity.[28] A third is that society does not replace one set of productive forces with inferior ones (this is stated as a "fact"). To elaborate:

a. The idea of rationality is identical with what I have called instrumental rationality, in this case, the ability of humans to identify and set

94

about to meet their needs and wants, to wrest from nature the required raw materials from which to fashion products of consumption.

b. Cohen's work contains no idea of the historicity of the category of scarcity.[29] There is no intimation that scarcity is not, in contemporary societies, a function of material scarcity in the sense of being separate from social relations, although scarcity manifests itself for Third World societies and individuals everywhere as a material phenomenon.

c. What is superior or inferior in Cohen's defense of the idea of "progress" in the development of the productive forces is almost exclusively linked to productivity and the scientific and technical conditions for it. There are, for example, no ecological mediations to progress in productivity, and no sense of the environmental impact of technologies that have revolutionized the workplace.

Most astounding is the statement that "when knowledge provides the opportunity of expanding productive power, they [humans] will take it, for not to do so would be irrational."[30] So, it turns out that what is real is rational; a society is to be evaluated by the degree to which it succeeds in expanding productive power. Even if a ruling class promotes this development, Cohen admits that this coincides with the general human interest.

Cohen has given us nineteenth-century evolutionary Marxism without the reservations that the ghastly consequences of development have generated, even among enthusiasts of science and technology. We would have expected that analytic rigor would have helped introduce these mediations into consideration of the primacy of the productive forces. That some of our key scientific and technological advances are bound up with the accretion of forces of destruction (not only military weapons but also chemicals, fuels, the mass automobile) seems to have escaped Cohen's understanding of rationality criteria. What Cohen has described accurately is the degree to which a specific conception of rationality may lead to a general celebration of the "scientific technological" revolution as the motor of history.

In sum, there are two points to be made about the new analytic Marxism: first, its relentless effort to purge the dialectic from Marx's discourse by demonstrating, even when not asserting explicitly, Della Volpe's insistence on the logical principle of noncontradiction as the central a priori of social theory. Second, in Cohen's work, the remarkable reassertion of unilinear causality and the idea of progress based, not so much on evolutionary theory, but on the formal logic of recent analytic philosophy for which two opposing concepts cannot occupy the same temporal space. This implies that concepts such as multiple determination, "overdetermination," etc., are simply metaphysical propositions. For Cohen, technological change is conceived in terms of autonomy from social determination—an objectivist, internalist account upon which rises forms of society. Absent is more than the Hegelian dialectic: also missing is any reference, except in derision, to social relations as the "material" framework within which scientific and technological change occurs. The primacy of the scientific technological revolution over social relations and the preeminence of history as the embodiment of "progressive reason" are also the twin pillars of Soviet discourse on science and technology. This is invoked not to show the convergence of the structuralist and analytic tendencies (in different ways) with Soviet Marxism, but to assert the unity of an orthodoxy based on scientific and technological determinism regardless of particular political tendency.[31]

Even if the Frankfurt School failed to complete its critique of modern science and technology by showing concretely how they were constituted as hegemonies and refused to specify what a new science might be, their singular contribution was to have shown the ideological underside of the scientific worldview. In contrast, Jürgen Habermas, as perhaps the major legatee of the Critical Theory tradition, abandoned the project by declaring that science and technology corresponded to the *general*, i.e. human, interest, notwithstanding its ideological features. His category "rational-purposive" action to describe science merely removed this sphere from the searchlight of ideology critique. Henceforth, theory became an inquiry into the condition for undistorted communication, a language game whose space was confined to the surplus. Now, in a major respect, this shift from the sphere of production to "interaction" followed the suggestion of Marcuse at the conclusion of *One Dimensional Man* that there was no longer a *practical* critique of technology since it had succeeded in completely dominating the contemporary social world.

Marcuse, in effect, calls for a politics of marginality, a new focus on the *remainder* where emancipation is possible precisely because of its trivi-alization by the forces of domination. But where Marcuse speaks of the Third World and art as fields of political contestation, Habermas tries to integrate traditional sociological and psychological theory, particularly functionalism, with the philosophy of language to discover the "human" interest per se. In this respect, his work moves away from the "Critical" tradition. Theory is no longer deconstructive, a means to critique the forms of social domination, but becomes an algorithm for establishing the harmonious community in which social distinctions no longer regu-late "higher" activity.

What unites this program with that of Marxist structuralism is not common purposes, but a common *will to scientificity* that is shared with the analytic school. The common category that spans these other-wise disparate discourses is the principle of noncontradiction, that is, the return to Kant and scientific philosophy. In these theories, science and technology are not regarded as forms of ideology because of their inescapable rationality, their universality, their correspondence with human interests taken in their totality. For analytic Marxism and the structuralists, the task is to integrate Marxism with science, to ruthless-ly expunge its metaphysical elements carried over from Hegel. While Habermas seems to have abandoned Marxism, at least for the most part, his dedication to universal and rationalistic principle is no less fervent. In fact, his program for undistorted communication varies from the sci-entific ideal insofar as it retains traces of hermeneutic interactionism, but his tendency is toward positivism.

As Marxism becomes dissociated from any possible critical, revolu-tionary social movements of the working class or others, its main ref-erent as a school of social thought is increasingly the universities and the intellectuals who inhabit them. Now the university is among the premier sites of scientific and technological inquiry. Far from being a pole of critical discourses opposed to prevailing political and econom-ic forces, major universities are today places of knowledge production, much of which is destined for the industrial workshop, health institu-tions, and military installations. Not only natural sciences but social

97

sciences as well have become crucial elements of national policies of all industrial and industrializing nations. The reasons, cited earlier, are that these discourses are understood as the central preconditions for both economic growth (capital accumulation) and political stability. In short, science and technology are not merely knowledges that contend in the "marketplace of ideas": they are inextricably bound with power. To employ a metaphor invented by Althusser to show the materiality of ideologies, science and technologies are *apparatuses of power*. Following from this, even Marxism is obliged, whether or not willingly, to accommodate to that power. In its most supine manifestations, Marxism becomes official knowledge, as in Eastern Europe and China; in Western countries, its relationship to mainstream science varies from enthusiastic integration, as with the analytic school and Italian structuralism, to reluctant, almost shamefaced collaboration, as in post-Frankfurt School social theory. Thus, in the 1940s, one of the paragons of Critical Theory, Adorno, directed a major study of the authoritarian personality and employed some of the characteristic techniques of the sociology of his time—the structured interview, "scales" of behavioral variation, and so on. Adorno, anxious to find both income and some academic status in the United States, understood that one of its main requirements was to do "normal" social science. I am not claiming that the value of this study is thereby diminished. The construction of the F scale, the measuring instrument to determine degrees to which individuals and groups correspond to characterological authoritarianism, may have been a useful innovation, and the interview material is often fascinating. Taken as a whole, one may learn a great deal about America and Americans from this study. The point is that the work is entirely uncharacteristic of Adorno's position, stated most sharply in his essays in the *Positivist Dispute in German Sociology*, that the presupposition of such empirical methods is that they are closely associated with the commercial and administrative interests from which they have emanated and have, at best, limited value.[32] The empirical methods most typically used in social research can only skim the surfaces and, contrary to their claim to objectivity, are nearly always bound by their own subjectively-wrought aims.

Adorno argues for metatheoretical presuppositions that are close to those of dialectical, speculative reason. The empirical is not defaced but is relegated to a contingent place in the pantheon of social inquiry. Faced with the overwhelming fact that the context for knowledge is inescapably linked to interest, the intellectual possesses few exits. Against her/his will, the intellectual becomes complicitous—this is the price one pays for space in the precincts of knowledge production.

To the extent that the avant-garde has passed into history, hastened by the closing of critical, marginal spaces, both physically and intellectually, artists and intellectuals typically turn to teaching to support their work. Their communities are dispersed by high rents brought on by the transformation of traditional cultural cities such as New York, London, and Paris into international financial and administrative centers. Consequently, alternative presses, art forms, and journals occupy an ever-shrinking space in cultural life. Thus, the university becomes a refuge, but it exacts a price that is calculable in terms of both the decline of the audience for critical discourse in recent years, in comparison to the nineteenth and first half of the twentieth centuries, and the pressure, now open, now covert, on intellectuals within the university to produce work that conforms to the ethical and formal precepts of modern scientific knowledge.

Within the university, the humanities, particularly literary criticism, have constituted an alternative cultural sphere precisely because of their marginal position with respect to the main aspects of technological and social policy (which are, for practical purposes, merged). But with the organization of national and international foundations, ministries, and professional organizations to support the arts and humanities, the chance of bureaucratization of these discourses grows, even as cultural apparatuses protest that their mission is to support, not direct, the arts and humanities.

Only the most myopic would claim that Marxism or any other nineteenth-century theoretical paradigm remains unaltered in the wake of criticism, both internal and external, and parallel developments in competing and complementary paradigms. Since social sciences are not marked by evolutionary development in which one paradigm displaces another, but characteristically retains their many systems, Marxism stands alongside others such as functionalism and empiricism. In different historical periods, Marxism is insurgent and in many Western countries becomes the semi-official social knowledge even where Marxist-oriented political parties do not enjoy state power.

Such was the case in France in the two decades immediately following the last world war, and in Austria and Germany in the 1920s and early 1930s. Today, in Great Britain, academic Marxism enjoys a degree of ascendancy it has never before experienced, despite the long-term decline of the Labour Party as a political and social force. But in nearly all instances, Marxism does not flourish (or wane) in some mythic pristine form. Its existence as a major paradigm depends, in the main, on the degree to which its axiomatic structure and its methodological framework (both technical and epistemological) conform with that of prevailing, normal science. Marxism adapts itself to other paradigms and adopts them as a condition of its own legitimacy within the academy. Far from constituting an alternative to "bourgeois" theory, it becomes a variety of this mode of theorizing.

I do not want to imply that, for these reasons, Marxism offers nothing to the accumulated treasure of social knowledge. Its insistence that capitalism is structured by class relations, that what we mean by the "economic" is entwined with class struggle, its powerful theories of ideology, its pathbreaking work on the nature of the state—particularly the capitalist state and its truly powerful historiography which, at times during the last twenty years has dominated the American as well as world discourse on history—are contributions that should not be demeaned, even in the course of a critique. But one cannot ignore the overwhelming evidence for a convergence thesis, that is, my claim that Marxism resembles more a normal social science, especially in its discourse on the epistemology and methodology of science and technology. For it is in this discursive space that Marxism must face the positivism of its own axiomatic structure, particularly its tendency to posit science and technology (forces of production) as knowledges and material relations that stand outside the matrix of social relations that can somehow be exempted from "ideology," even when self-critical. That contemporary Marxism exhibits this tendency is prepared, as we have seen, by Marx himself and especially

Engels. What has disappeared in the current conjuncture of theory with its institutionalization is Marxism's subversive side, its insistence on historical agency—that "history is made by men" and not by reassembled structures. For it is precisely the indeterminacy of social actors formed as social movements that ruins the technological theater in which causality is produced by purpose and organization. Social actors who play outside the rules of the political game, an event that is posited by Marxism as a consequence of the contradictions of accumulation and political struggle, have the capacity to belie forecasts by their own refusal.

But in scientific Marxism, the "actor" disappears or is made a dependent variable of the accumulation process. Just as Marx was constrained to acknowledge that although "men make their own history, they do not do so as they please," modern Marxism takes the cue and takes determination away from agents. This absence is due, in no small measure, to the project—flagrant since the late Marx—of removing ethics from social inquiry. Social science may study the role of moral precepts as a "mediation" of the determination by strict material causes of historical events but may not impute to them a crucial moment of independent determination. Ethics are always an efflux.

Recent work on social movements that wishes to restore to social theory its critical edge has insisted on the relative autonomy of the agents or the historical actors from the social situation within which they operate. Of course, such writers as Alain Touraine, Henri Lefebvre, and Fredy Perlman,[33] who examine the uprisings in France in May 1968, do not ignore or minimize the social structural constraints of "new" political activity. The issue is where the emphasis lies. For scientific Marxism, these constraints are what counts in the acquisition of social knowledge for they provide a measurable object in contrast to the movements that resist such rationality. Again, the issue is not one of scientific accuracy, but the standpoint from which inquiry is conducted. Does the "observer" intend to discover irregularities, want to find whether and how the reductions that inhere in structure are destroyed or circumvented? Or, in terms of Parsonian sociology, are we trying to find continuities in social life, a biological or even physical analogy to explain why and how movements are reintegrated by the social order?

These are important questions for social theory which bear on the distinction between critical or transformative scientific work and normal science which always takes the point of view of the established order, however insightful its findings. Of course, it is unrealistic to expect Marxism to place itself outside the prevailing order, given the conditions of its own existence as an important discourse of mainstream social science. Yet, it must be noted that most, if not all, radical theoretical and empirical investigations are conducted by those whose Marxist roots are revealed in the choice of the object as well as the referent of class relations, constituting a point of departure from which the claims of autonomy for social movements not rooted in these relations derive.

Post-Marxism cannot avoid class, ideology, and the state as crucial categories of social inquiry. What distinguishes its works is the way in which these are concatenated as relations and relations of relations. Even those who ostensibly owe little or nothing to the Marxist tradition must, when confronted with the question of the social relations of science, situate their own work in relation to the categories of ideology, power, and state. So, it is not so much the specific propositions of Marxism that account for its enduring influence as its categorical structure, which, like Kant's categories of judgment, appear to be the only possible framework from which "science" is done.

The contribution of Antonio Gramsci to the discussion of ideology begins to correct the limitations of recent Marxist theories. At the outset, it is important to recognize the similarity between the thinking of Gramsci and the structural conceptions of ideology advanced by Lukács and Althusser. Gramsci's polemic is directed against those who maintain that ideology is a mere "reflex" of the economic infrastructure, a distorted image in the minds of persons and groups of underlying processes that has no material effect. Gramsci also attacks the pejorative use of the concept of ideology by insisting that it is "necessary to a given structure" and is thus an element of power to the extent that "ideologies mobilize human masses," but also because they "create a terrain on which men move, acquire consciousness of their position, struggle, etc." For Gramsci, ideology is the form of which material forces is the content (of social structure), although this distinction between form and content has purely "didactic" value since each is, in his account, necessary and is inconceivable without the other.[34]

So Gramsci refuses the concept of ideology as error or false consciousness as merely superstructural (which effectively connotes its status as an epiphenomenon). At the same time, he situates the ideological in the processes of social life, in the sinews of politics and revolutionary action. But he also situates science within the same context:

> If it is true that man cannot be conceived of except as historically determined man—*i.e.* man who has developed, and who lives in certain conditions, in a particular social complex or totality of social relations, is it then possible to take sociology as meaning simply the study of these conditions and the laws which regulate their development? Since the will and initiative of men themselves cannot be left out of account, this notion must be false. The problem of what "science" itself is has to be posed. Is not science itself "political activity" and political thought, as much as it transforms men and makes them different from what they were before? If everything is "politics," then it is necessary—in order to avoid lapsing into a wearisome and tautological catalogue of platitudes—to distinguish by means of new concepts between on the one hand the politics which correspond to the science which is traditionally called "philosophy" and on the other between the politics which is called political science in the strict sense. If science is the "discovery" of formerly unknown reality, is this reality not conceived of in a certain sense as transcendent? And does the concept of science as "creation" not then mean that it too is "politics"? Everything depends on seeing whether the creation involved is "arbitrary," or whether it is rational—i.e. "useful" to men in that it enlarges their concept of life, and raised to a higher level develops life itself.[35]

Much of Gramsci's conception of science was developed in a polemic against Nikolai Bukharin's "popular manual" of Marxist "science" published in the Soviet Union in the 1920s. Here, Gramsci opposes Bukharin's repetition of the now orthodox view that science and ideology can be strictly opposed by showing that neither can the methodologies of the natural sciences be mechanically applied to the social sphere, nor can science itself be abstracted from the totality of social relations that produce it. For Gramsci, there is a distinction between ideology as the false conceptions of a few individuals, and ideology and science as different sides of the material forces of historical change. According to Gramsci, science is a form of politics, i.e. an ideology which "discovers" a formerly unknown reality, not as a discourse separate from the social and historical context that gives rise to it but as a function of that context.

Consistent with one list of Marxist theory of ideology, for Gramsci, every class that contends for political and social power generates its ideologies that compete for "hegemony" within civil society and the state. The dominant class establishes its reign over intellectuals, who contend for moral and intellectual leadership in society because no class may rule without the "spontaneous consent" given by the great masses to the general direction of social life given by the dominant social group. The social group does not gain ascendancy arbitrarily but dominates because of its position in production. While the proletariat cannot gain power or achieve hegemony over the producers of ideologies (the intellectuals) until the crisis of the existing order has loosened the hegemony of the bourgeoisie, it proposes its science against bourgeois science, whose adequacy may be measured by the degree to which it can "uncover" reality.

In the sense in which ideology with a small "i" is deeply political, its close relation with science, which is also political, is evident. Since, for Gramsci, science is a "praxis," that is, a set of material practices infused with the political ideologies of social classes, which seek political, social, and economic hegemony over other social classes, the idea of the neutrality of science is simply not in accordance with the conditions for the possibility of science as it actually exists.

Gramsci implies that the "truth" of science arises as an outcome of the material conditions, the complex of social relations that give rise to it and within which it functions. When Gramsci states that science "transforms" people and constitutes a form of "creation" itself, the "will and initiative" of scientific praxis, that is, the subjective teleological element, cannot be abstracted from either the process of knowledge, its production, or its results.[36] And, since sciences as much as ideologies mobilize masses, we are talking about a conception of science that does not require a special machine to legitimate itself, does not need to distinguish itself from ideology, except insofar as the neutrality of science is a type of ideology when, grasped by ruling groups, it becomes an aspect of their effort to gain the "spontaneous consent" of the masses.

According to Gramsci, the proletariat gives rise to an ideology that becomes scientific because it does not require a self-legitimating dogma to mask the coercive basis of the power of its apparatus over civil society. In this respect, Gramsci locates the possibility of a Marxist science that can "transcend" the opacity of social reality because its class praxis is "interested" in emancipatory discoveries. But this creative process of discovery may not be construed as non-ideological. Even if it arises as a critique of the dominant ideology, it is a type of political discourse, one that has a teleological element and is limited by its historical and social circumstances.

The theory of hegemony, according to which systems of ideas are produced by dominant social groups or groups seeking power whose object is to create a new terrain "on which men move" to mobilize masses to struggle or not, I call the *general* theory of ideology. Not only is ideology produced by the metonymic extrapolation from the forms of appearance of "real relations," which in Althusser's theory become materialized in social institutions that are self-reproductive (the famous concept of ideological state apparatuses—religion, education, trade unions, the family). It is also produced by the process by which the ruling class or the oppositional class in capitalist society gains hegemony over a group of intellectuals who generate a language, a cognitive apparatus of investigation and understanding which expresses its specific relation to the world and tends to reproduce it as "natural." The degree to which its language and apparatus successfully penetrate the material world of society and "nature" is an aspect of its collective relation to social life.

The binary structure of Althusser's thought—the "real" and the imaginary, appearance and real relations as *formal* oppositions, and science and ideology—is overcome in this conception by the common root of "science" and "ideology." Both terms refer to the material world. They are not chiefly distinguished by their ordered discourse (language), which, in any case, may be the same although their vocabularies may differ. For example, mathematical and other theoretical concepts may be, in fact, as political as a strike slogan, but expressed entirely in the discourse of "normal" science. So it is not the language or even the mechanism of knowledge that distinguishes science from ideology, for the mechanical metaphor for knowledge is, at the bottom, a bourgeois metaphor, one that arose from a system of ideas that had definite historical origins, and that succeeded in creating a terrain upon which social perception and social struggle were obliged to enter. That is, the "forms of appearance" in which the universe appeared to be a machine not only were created by the commodity but were entwined with the praxis of the rising bourgeoisie, its theory as much as its institutional matrix. The praxis of the bourgeoisie in the transition from feudalism to capitalism was linked to its ability to make the world a "universal marketplace," a metaphor for the subsumption of nature and humans under the laws of commodity production. Thus, scientific theory became an instrument of human domination over nature, and techniques the instrumentalization of science. The debate within the history of technology concerning the relations of science, technology, and craft-wrought invention has focused on the question of succession—i.e. which came first? Or, more exactly, did modern industrial technology arise out of sciences or the practice of craftpersons in production? Evidence has been adduced to support both theses,[37] but I believe that the argument may be subsumed by the priority of the domination of nature and humans by capital. Both technology and science were able to remain relatively autonomous while, at the same time, infused with the dominant ideology regarding nature within the bourgeois epoch, according to which (*i*) the "book of nature" was a text deciphered only by mathematics, and (*ii*) nature could be pictured as a machine.

NOTES

1. See especially Louis Althusser's *For Marx* (New York: Vintage Books, 1970).

2. Althusser, *Reading Capital* (London: New Left Books, 1970), 67.

3. Ibid. 4.

4. Ibid. 52–3.

5. Ibid. 67.

6. Thomas Kuhn, *The Structure of Scientific Revolutions* (Chicago: University of Chicago Press, 1967).

7. Émile Durkheim, *Rules of Sociological Method* (New York: Free Press, 1959), 27.

8. Althusser, *Reading Capital*.

9. See Althusser, "Freud and Lacan," in *Lenin and Philosophy* (London: New York Left Books, 1971).

10. John Mepham, "Theory of Ideology in Capital," *Working Papers in Cultural Studies* 66 (Autumn 1974).

11. Ibid. 107.

12. Sigmund Freud, *Civilization and Its Discontents* (New York: Norton, 1965).

13. Paul Feyerabend, *Against Method* (London: New Left Books, 1976).

14. Kuhn, *Structure of Scientific Revolutions*.

15. Charles S. Peirce, "The Fixation of Belief," in *Selected Writings of C. S. Peirce*, ed. Justin Buehler (New York: Dover Edition, 1955).

16. Georg Lukács, "Reification and the Consciousness of the Proletariat" in *History and Class Consciousness* (London: Merlin Books, 1971).

17. See Jürgen Habermas, *Knowledge and Human Interests* (Boston: Beacon Press, 1971), 62–3, where by insisting that Marx's mistake was to throw together "work and interaction," human sciences were merged with natural science. For Habermas, the critique of ideology consists in the effort to show that the methods of natural sciences are inappropriate for the human sciences since the latter have to do exclusively with communicative actions which are inherently self-reflexive, whereas the former are (appropriately) forms of instrumental actions. Since ideology refers to class relations and Habermas tries to show that these have been subsumed under the "general" interest entailed by production, ideology as a social category is no longer adequate to descriptions of the social world.

18. Galvano Delia Volpe, *Logic as a Positive Science* (London: New Left Books, 1980).

19. Colletti, *Marxism and Hegel* (London: Verso Books, 1973), 199, even though "Marxism is not an epistemology in any fundamental sense."

20. Ibid. 227.

21. Jean-Paul Sartre, *Critique of Dialectical Reason*, trans. Alan Sheridan-Smith (London: New Left Books, 1976), 20.

22. Jonathan Ree, "Glossary," in Sartre, *Critique of Dialectical Reason*, 827.

23. It is interesting to compare this aspiration with Brecht's, who "saw himself as a theoretical Galileo whose task was to bring drama into line with Einstein" (Ronald Hayman,

Brecht: A Biography (New York: Oxford University Press, 1983), 138). The Galilean model was a theater without motivation. Rather, "fate's no longer an integral power but more like a field of force" (ibid.; this quote is Brecht's own).

24. John Roemer, *Analytic Foundations of Marxian Economic Theory* (London and Boston: Cambridge University Press, 1981); Jon Elster, *Making Sense of Marx* (London and Boston: Cambridge University Press, 1985); Jon Elster, *Logic and Society* (New York: Wiley, 1978); Erik Olin Wright, *Classes* (London: New Left Books, 1985).

25. G. A. Cohen, *Karl Marx's Theory of History: A Defense* (London and New York: Cambridge University Press, 1978).

26. Ibid. 26.

27. I would also add: the production of trucks is not merely production of use values outside a specific social context. Their *mass production* as alternatives to trains or any other means of transport is not devoid of premises that are linked to economic and political decisions. In the same vein, roads are not roads; they are instances of historically situated social relations which imply a whole regime of *how* humans interact with nature.

28. Cohen, *Karl Marx's Theory of History*, 152.

29. Or, to be more precise, Cohen, echoing Marx, holds that scarcity is the a priori condition for history itself. For without the naked, shivering human production, growth would not occur. At the same time, the concept of scarcity itself is not really historicized. When scarcity is evoked as a political and ideological weapon in contemporary late capitalist societies, its historicity is never more evident.

30. Cohen, *Karl Marx's Theory of History*, 153.

31. Nevertheless, I do not contest that Cohen's is a plausible interpretation of Marx and the mainstream of the Marxist tradition, even if his citations from Marx himself are employed to buttress this interpretation. Missing, of course, is Marx's own ambiguity on many of the issues.

32. In the course of rendering a generally enthusiastic account of the research project that culminated in the book *The Authoritarian Personality*, Adorno acknowledges "we had to water our wine a bit. It seems to be the defect of every form of empirical sociology that it must choose between the reliability and the profundity of its findings. It is difficult for me to avoid the suspicion that the increasing precision of methods in empirical sociology, however impeccable the arguments for them might be, often restrains scientific productivity." Theodor Adorno, "A European Scholar in America," in *The Intellectual Migration*, ed. Donald Fleming and Bernard Barlyn (Cambridge, Mass: Harvard University Press, 1969), 366.

33. See Alain Touraine, *The May Movement* (New York: Random House, 1971); Henri Lefebvre, *The Explosion* (New York: Monthly Review Press, 1969); Fredy Perlman, *Student-Worker Committees* (pamphlet) (Detroit: Black and Red, 1968).

34. Antonio Gramsci, *Prison Notebooks* (New York: International Publishers, 1971), 376–7. One example, "the thesis which asserts that men become conscious of fundamental conflicts on the level of ideology is not psychological or moralistic in character, but structural and epistemological; and they form the habit of considering politics, and hence history, as a continuous marche de dupes, a competition in conjuring and sleight-of-hand." Page 164 also in his discussion of the relation of economic structures to ideology, 168–9.

35. Ibid. 244–5.

36. Ibid. 468, where Gramsci argues that all scientific theories "are superstructures." "According to the theory of praxis (Marxism), it is evident that it is not atomic theory that explains human history but the other way about, in other words, that atomic theory and all scientific hypotheses and opinions are superstructures." Compare this formulation to that of G. A. Cohen, for whom science is meaningful only to the extent that it is integrated with productive forces.

37. For the view of the autonomy of science from technology, see David Landes, *Unbounded Prometheus* (London: Cambridge University Press, 1969). Of course, Engels was a strong proponent of the view that science is a generalization from the practical problems generated by craft practices and economic circumstances, especially trade in the late Middle Ages. See B. Hessen, "The Social and Economic Roots of Newton's Principia," in *Science at the Crossroads* (London: Kniga, 1931).

PART TWO

LABOR

CHAPTER THREE

Marx, Braverman, and the Logic of Capital

Introduction

The power and scope of large-scale industry among advanced capitalist societies has made it increasingly difficult for us to imagine a different mode of material production. We are all convinced that artisanship in our epoch is merely a form of bourgeois ideology, whose effect, if not intention, is to foster illusions of mobility among workers, and to create an artificial hierarchy within the labor process. The few instances of handicraft which remain in our social world are considered to be so marginal that we have learned to take for granted the mechanization of the labor process and its consequences for the transformation of the content of labor.

Perhaps the most serious consequence of the obliteration of history by the totalizing force of industrialization has been the tendency of the population to regard the texture of the social world, especially the work world, as self-evident. Indeed, Marxism, after Marx, ratified that perception of the permanence of mechanical reproduction by accepting the development of the so-called "forces of production" as a part of the legacy of socialism. For the leaders of both the Second and Third Internationals, the development of science and technology were progressive and autonomous features of the capitalist mode of production.[1] The task of socialists, in their algebra of revolution, was to help transform the relations of production so that they would conform to the new forces of production generated by capitalism. The exploitation of labor by capital, personified by the subordination of workers under capitalists, would be ended by the workers' assumption of power over the means of production. In the process the whole of social life would be changed, since the relations of production, at least in the last instance, determined the character of everyday life and the relations of domination within social institutions (such as education, the family, and the political structures of societies).

In the new society, collective ownership of the means of production and workers' control over the state would result in the full development of science and technology, which were relatively fettered by capital. In consequence, labor would be freed from its subordination and from back-breaking routinized labor. In the conception of socialism of the orthodox Marxist traditions, the new society would undertake production cooperatively, for the use of its members rather than for the profit of the few. Individual enterprises would be merged into socialized units and the concentration of industrial means would be even greater than in the present. For both Kautsky and Lenin, the advent of monopoly capitalism crushed the small producers' handicrafts and small capitalists, but was a matter of complete indifference to the proletariat. At best, the concentration and centralization of capital made easier the transition to socialism since capital itself performed the task of socializing the forces of production in its own interest.[2]

The received truth of the socialist movement is that socialist revolution is made inevitable by three features of capitalist development. (*i*) The concentration of capital into ever larger units brings millions of proletarians into communication with each other and facilitates their class organization and consciousness. (*ii*) The contradiction between the forces of production (which develop up to a certain point independently of the social structure) and the capitalist relations of production which fetter them, is the most general cause of the capitalist crisis. (*iii*) The particular cause of the crisis, the contradiction between the social character of production and its private appropriation, manifested in the crisis of overproduction and unemployment, generates the objective conditions for social transformation, of which the mass organization and social consciousness of the workers are the subjective condition. Along with these features, Lenin, Stalin, and Trotsky stressed the absolute centrality of the party as the vanguard of the working class, its function as the general staff of revolution and as the guiding force in the transition from capitalism to socialism after the revolution.

We are in the midst of a major reevaluation of all of these propositions, largely as a result of the failure of socialist revolution to succeed in any capitalist country, except as nascent tendencies in western Europe, which however remain curiously underdeveloped (or overripe, as Trotsky put it) and the breakdown of state socialist regimes throughout the world. By now, most socialists are aware of the historical explanations for the retardation of social transformation in the West. These vary from the theory of the emergence of the labor aristocracy, both within the working class and the socialist movement, to the theory of imperialism which speaks to the displacement of the capitalist crisis by the exploitation of the Third World (that is, by the formation of capitalist world system), to cultural theories which, while acknowledging the centrality of political and economic integration, insist that the specificity of ideological and cultural domination must also be stressed. The mainstream of historical explanations insists that the corpus of Marx's work remains valid, that what they are doing is to "update" the theory to account for historical changes within the capitalist mode of production.

Others have argued that the problems with the Marxian theory of revolution lies in omissions and reductions within the basic theory of social development. Jürgen Habermas, Alvin Gouldner, Marshall Sahlins, Jean Baudrillard, and Pierre Bourdieu[3] have, each in his own way, argued a similar point: the dialectic of labor, according to which the relations of humans with nature form the character of social relations, is seriously flawed. In their view, Marx reduced the complexity of social relations and therefore of historical change to a single dimension, the labor process. Humans, according to this theory are not formed just by their labor, but are formed by their interaction as well, by noninstrumental relations of exchange among themselves. Marx errs, in their view, when he ascribes the self-formation of human societies in every epoch exclusively to the character of their relations of social production.

According to Baudrillard and Sahlins, relations of symbolic exchange are more significant in human history than commodity exchange or the production process, except under capitalism, when the commodity form becomes universal. For Baudrillard, Marx becomes a nineteenth-century thinker, perhaps that century's most important theorist. Beyond acknowledging his contribution to the theory of the origins and development of capitalism, then, Baudrillard and the other writers try to historicize Marx. They claim that his theory is valid for capitalism in its emergent phase, but is adequate neither for the advanced stage of capitalism nor for pre-capitalist modes of production. Baudrillard has gone so far as to repudiate the concept of mode of production, as itself determined by bourgeois ideology, according to which production is the center of the social universe.

This chapter will attempt to assess some of the problems raised in recent Marxist theory in the light of fundamental tendencies of Marx's own work which may have led both to the misconceptions characteristic of the orthodox Marxist view and to the inadequacies of the historical response, which tends to disregard the problems in Marx's theoretical formulations. On the other hand, I do not propose to treat in any detail the specific objections of post-Marxian theorists, whose conclusions in my view rest largely on the reductionism of orthodox readings of Marx.

However, I must locate the sources of some of the confusions prevalent in recent interpretations of Marx. It is my contention that much of the problem at the theoretical level resides in Marx's description of the underlying logic of capital, particularly its inherent tendency to "subsume" labor, science, and technology under its domination. By subsumption, Marx means the reduction of the autonomy of these forms of mental and manual labor to "moments" of capital. In turn the "form of appearance" of capital, given the universality of commodity, is autonomy. Thus, the relations of labor to capital in the process of material production are reversed. In material production, capital appears to labor as a passive object, since it has been materialized into raw materials, machinery, and buildings which are acted upon by the workers as preconditions for the production of commodities. Within the material production process, living labor is sovereign as a form of activity, an active subject, while capital, as the past, dead form of labor, already appropriated by the capitalist as surplus value, is merely the object upon which living labor operates.

The machines, raw materials, and buildings, however, do not *appear* to be a function of labor. Labor is increasingly subsumed as a factor of production whose guiding force is capital; labor appears to be a function of capital. Science and technology, which result from the work both of craftspersons and of independent scientists outside the production process, are also increasingly integrated by capital under its laws of accumulation. The social relation between capital and labor appears separate from the material relation. In the social relations of production, according to Marx, capital takes on the appearance of dominance even though in the materialization of these relations, living, purposive labor dominates capital since labor confronts capital as mere raw materials.

The "logic" of capital's self-expansion is its increasing subsumption of labor under its laws. This subsumption does not signify the destruction of labor as the crucial force animating the entire production process, but rather the appearance of the reduction of labor to just another "factor" of production, alongside the science and technology congealed in the machines. Capital also subsumes scientific investigation as one of its aspects, these appear as aspects external to the worker, as the property of capital, and appear to have been created by capital.

Capitalism is marked by the dominance of the social relation over the material relation and the appearance of the social relation as a material force.

The inner logic of capital consists precisely in its capacity to determine the character of labor, the object, method, and form of results of scientific investigation, and the subordination of all science to a technology for capital's expansion. In turn, science and technology are related to labor insofar as they are directed by capital towards labor's degradation. Of course, the use of science to segment, routinize, and otherwise deskill the labor force appears as a "natural" benefit owing to the claim that machine production relieves labor of onerous and arduous tasks and provides material plenty. Technologies of degradation appears as "progressive"—not only to capitalists and workers who have been subjected to their "inevitability," but also to those socialists who have come to regard the forces of production as independent of capital's rule, at least in part.

As Marx drew the consequences of the subsumption of labor, science, and technology under capital, the outward appearance of his writing is that this process so reduces culture, ideology, and politics to a function of capital that socialism appears to come to the working class "from the outside." Its ally, the forces of production—which are nothing but human knowledge materialized in machinery, the social organization of labor, and scientific invention, as well as human skills—also appears external to the existing relations of production.

It may be argued that the prevalence, in the first half of this century, of breakdown theories of capitalism's downfall, and the doctrine that the Third World has become, *in toto*, the modern proletariat (owing to the absolute power of capital among advanced industrial societies), are ascribable to the implicit reification of Marx's theory of subsumption.[4]

It may also be shown that the darkest analysis of the theorists of everyday life and cultural production, particularly the representatives of the Frankfurt School, were also animated by their belief in the absolute power of capital over all social relations. For Theodore Adorno and Herbert Marcuse, the advent of mass culture could only be understood as a function of the accumulation and expansion of capital into the farthest reaches of ordinary existence, of the invasion of the private sphere by the marketplace. In the felicitous phrase of Hans Magnus Enzensberger, the tendency of late capitalism is to "industrialize the mind," just as capitalism industrialized the production of goods during its rise. Human thinking becomes mechanized and the mind corresponds to the machine—a technicized, segmented, and degraded instrument that has lost its capacity for critical thought, especially its ability to imagine another way of life.[5]

The culture industry, for Henri Lefebvre, is responsible for more than the production of cultural commodities. It has colonized everyday life, transforming it into a "bureaucratic society of controlled consumption." The development of habitual consumption is no less pernicious than the habituation of the worker to routinized, degraded labor. If the Marxist theories of capital's logic have pointed to the narrowing of the universe (at the point of production) to the laws dictated by capital, "neo-Marxism" argues for a similarly relentless closing of the universe of critical discourse, one in which consciousness is bound by the requirements of technological domination. For those Marxists applying to everyday relations the logical principles of capital accumulation and the universalization of the commodity form, the culture of degradation may be regarded as the sufficient condition, and degraded labor the necessary condition, for the hegemony of capital.

Finally, we must mention recent developments in the Marxist theory of the state. Capital not only achieves hegemony over the labor process and the cultural domains, but its domination over political structures has become an essential component of its self-reproduction.

The two leading Marxist theories of the state[6] agree that one of the main characteristics of late capitalism is the transformation of the state from "watchman" of capital's interests and protector of property, into an aggressive "intervenor" in the accumulation process itself. From the point of view of capital's logic, the mobilization of the state as its adjunct capitalist is simply an extension of the categories of hegemony. Another crucial aspect of hegemonic relations between labor and capital is the formalization of a series of ideological apparatuses of the state. That is, bourgeois ideology no longer remains merely a series of values and beliefs about the eternal life of the capitalist system, but now produces a series of materializations, institutions that embody bourgeois ideology. Bourgeois ideology becomes a form of "lived experience." For Louis Althusser the state apparatuses are perhaps the main forms in which experience is lived.

This contribution to the Marxist theory of the state is complementary to Lefebvre's thesis about the bureaucratization of everyday life. For the soul of the state is the bureaucracy; and the ideological state apparatuses of schools, mass media, family, trade unions, and health institutions (to mention some key institutions) make it all but impossible for the individual to escape living the experience of bureaucratic domination, since all spaces of the everyday have been filled.

As capital incorporates and subordinates the state to its needs, it may be argued that the idea of the historical subject—of the relatively autonomous class of workers who are forced to labor under capital's domination in order to live but who do not share the rewards of bourgeois society—

has now been occluded from social experience. A socialism that arises from the internal contradictions of capital itself becomes increasingly problematic. Instead, recent Marxist theory of nearly all stripes has explained the fortunes of the revolutionary project in terms of Marx's description of capital's inexorable logic.

The inescapable conclusion from the drawing together of the three strands of contemporary Marxism—the degradation thesis, the notion of one-dimensionality, and the new functions of the state in capitalist society—is that we have come to the end of the inner dialectic of capitalism's development and decline. For the inference that may be drawn from these positions, when taken as part of a single theoretical system, is that capitalism is able to repress its contradictions, not because of this or that policy, but because its logic of integration and subsumption makes the concept of a "class in radical chains" absurd within the prevailing order.

I will now probe the heart of capital-logic, the doctrine of the subsumption of labor, science, and technology under capital. The first part of the paper will suggest some theses arising from Marx's analysis of the development of capitalism, particularly the transition from the artisanal to the industrialization stages of the labor process. Second, I will relate the historical dimension of the logic of capital to the structural dimension; that is, I will relate (a) the changes brought about by industrialization to (b) the emergence of the relative form of production of surplus value to centrality within the production process. The third part will deal with technology and science as forms of bourgeois ideology, corresponding to their subsumption by capital in the transition from manufacture (artisanship) to industry. Here, the attempt will be made to distinguish my reading of the approach Marx takes to the question of the social relations of science from orthodox Marxist views which adopt the traditional concept of the neutrality of these structures in order to argue for the revolutionary impact of the so-called forces of production.

Fourth, I shall suggest some empirical and theoretical contradictions in the logic of capital that may point to a view that the logic of subsumption is no more than a *tendency*. Just as the law of the tendency of the rate of profit to fall has its counteracting causes, the theses of degradation of labor, industrialization of culture, and state integration must be seen as theoretical and historical generalizations that are fought day to day by workers, popular movements, and individuals. My thesis here is that the configuration of capital—including the social organization of labor, the application of machine technologies to the production process, the production of ideology and culture (and therefore consciousness)—cannot be deduced from social "scientific" formulae according to which the entire social world appears to be a function of capital accumulation.

Instead, *I argue for the relative autonomy of labor, culture, and consciousness within the broad framework of Marxist theory of capitalist development.* That is, I take the aphorism "all history is the history of class struggle" seriously. If this is the case, then the doctrine of subsumption must not be taken as an empirical description; rather it is a powerful tendency that becomes an aspect of the mode of production, but is counteracted both by the historical cultures of the working class (which have their roots in precapitalist social formations as much as the culture that arises from the labor process itself), and by the formal and informal organization of the working class, which restrains the subsumption process and causes its retardation and deformation. That is, the general rule that capitalism "sweeps away all the idyllic relations" of past societies is empirically accurate as an impulse of capital accumulation—but it may not be taken to mean that class fragments of prior modes of production do not exert significant social influence, and even power, within advanced capitalism, any more than it may be taken as a description of the end of proletarian discourse never emerged within capitalism (nor could it emerge except incipiently), it does not follow that the concept of a working-class culture is completely overtaken by the laws of capitalist development.

I wish to caution the reader that in some of the first sections of this paper I will render an account of the central themes of the subsumption thesis from the point of view of an advocate. The reason for this strategy is that I believe it impossible to understand the full significance of a theory unless one renders it from the inside. This method is sometimes referred to as immanent critique; the critique consists in drawing out the implications of the thesis under examination in relentless manner in order to show its inner tendency.

In the case of the capital-logic or subsumption thesis, and its relation to Marx's corpus, let me say at the outset that I believe that Marx developed this side of his theory most fully; the oppositional side remained underdeveloped theoretically, both during his lifetime and among his epigones. With the notable exceptions of Lenin and Gramsci, who in different ways tried to suggest theoretical supplements that retained the possibility of a socialist revolution from inside capitalist social relations, all other Marxist theories of revolution after Marx relied on versions of the breakdown thesis. Thus this chapter should be seen as a contribution to the critique of Marx as well as Marxism *from the inside*.

I

Among the most significant developments in Marxist thought over the past decade was the rediscovery of the centrality of Capital's domination over the labor process for an understanding of the persistence of bourgeois hegemony in the twentieth century, especially in advanced capitalist countries. The work of Harry Braverman, Stephen Marglin, Kathy Stone, André Gorz, and others[7] has explored the dimensions of this domination, particularly in the historical emergence of what has been variously called "Taylorism" and (by Gramsci) "Fordism."[8] The specific discovery was already present in Marx, but was ignored since his death in many sectors of the socialist movement.

The key concept is this: the rise of modern industry, with the introduction of large-scale machine production and the concomitant employment of science and technology as key productive forces, was no neutral process. The modern factory is a capitalist factory; the consequence of the rationalization of the labor process, signified by the introduction of assembly-line methods of production, has been to degrade and dequalify labor. The fundamental mechanisms of this degradation are implied by the "technical" division of labor: the separation of mental from manual labor, or, as Braverman put it, the division of concept from execution, such that the worker is reduced to a detail operative under the supervision and direction of management, which (alongside science) has now been simultaneously to destroy the last vestiges of the old artisanal mode of production, subordinating skilled workers to the rule of capital, and to accelerate the emergence of collective labor; the working class is largely de-skilled, at the mercy of capital, and reduced in its functions to an aspect of capital. Contrary to both popular belief and the ideologies of contemporary capitalism, most work has become routinized, boring, and repetitive.

The reduction of human faculties to a single dimension, that of performing the same detailed operation over and over, is of course not confined to the factory. The same rationalization of tasks divested of their creative and autonomous function has permeated the office, many professions, and the service industries. The checker behind a supermarket counter performs no more conceptually challenging or socially "meaningful" labor than the automobile assembly line worker. Witness cash registers at Taco Time: the keys no longer have numerical faces, but rather each stands for one product—taco, burrito, chips, etc. The medical specialist (say, a resident in a large hospital) may enjoy higher income than the detail worker in a factory or office, but the *tendency* of her/his labor is toward narrower spheres of activity.

The full contours of the descriptive content of this discovery are too well known to be repeated here. What I attempt to explore here are the consequences of the issue of the degradation and subordination of labor to capital in modern capitalism for a Marxist theory of technology, science, and social consciousness.

My contention is that the theoretical underpinnings of the historical researchers of Braverman and others include five theses, as follows. (*i*) That science and technology perform specific functions within the framework of capitalist production such that their characteristics cannot be separated from the structure of bourgeois hegemony. Thus the distinction between forces and relations of production made by Marx in the famous *Preface* to the *Contribution to the Critique of Political Economy*[9] is not, even for Marx in *Capital*[10] a defensible position, except for analytic purposes. Not only do relations of production constrain the development of the forces of production, but they shape them in accordance with the subsumption of labor under capital.

(*ii*) That technology is not a socially neutral "thing" that can be extracted from its uses within the framework of capitalist production. Technology is rooted in the social and technical divisions of labor specific to the capitalist mode of production. Therefore it can be characterized as bourgeois technology or monopoly capitalist technology depending on the epoch under examination.

(*iii*) That capital not only subsumes labor under its rule but subsumes science as well. The implication, which Marx only hints at, is that the view that science is absolutely separate from ideology—upheld in some versions of Marxist theory, notably Althusser and some older versions of Marxism—is itself a type of bourgeois ideology.

The relations of humans with nature, including their labor as well as their scientific practice, is mediated by the force of the subsumption of all human activity under capital. Therefore, science is bourgeois science within the capitalist mode of production. This does not limit the "truth value" of science's discoveries. Just as the concepts of democracy, the individual, self-management and control, and freedom were developed by the rising bourgeois class (as an expression of its bid for moral and intellectual leadership in the transition from feudalism to capitalism) and are taken over and transformed by the working class and the socialist movement in our day, so the basic theoretical framework of modern science is an aspect of bourgeois hegemony, particularly its claims to find the "objective" laws of nature, the mechanical world picture that obeys the rules of bourgeois rationality, and to be able to know the world exclusively through the senses.

To the extent that praxis within the capitalist mode of production is the self-reflexivity of science, as well as of a technology that no longer functions (if it ever did) apart from the imperatives of capital's logic, the notion of the autonomy of science expresses nothing else but the desire of scientific labor for independence in the wake of its almost total permeation by capital's requirements.

(*iv*) That, therefore, the transfer of technology and science from one country to another, in the period of the transition from capitalism to socialism, is politically and ideologically significant. It may not be argued that technological transfer necessarily signifies the convergence of one society with another as many have claimed—since culture and social structure mediate the effect of these technologies—but the reverse is true.[11] That is, technology that is developed within the framework of bourgeois relations of production is nothing but the objectification of those relations, and would tend therefore to subvert the socialist intentions of a society that refused to recognize this formulation.

(*v*) That the theory upon which the concept of labor degradation is based contains the danger of an undialectical view of historical process, because its *tendency*, Marx's intentions notwithstanding, is to generate a closed system from which the only possible escape is its breakdown. That is, the basic direction of Marx's theory of the *"Results of the Immediate Process of Production,"*[12] in which Marx outlines his fundamental perspective on the emergence of developed capitalist society, is to close the spaces within which the working class may struggle for its emancipation, except under limited conditions that arise from the breakdown but are essentially outside the control of workers. The consequence of "capital logic theory," which has been given historical and contemporary specification in Braverman's work, is to raise the whole question to whether socialist revolution is theoretically possible.

II

The *"Results of the Immediate Process of Production"* was originally intended by Marx to be Part 7 of *Capital*. According to Ernest Mandel's introduction to the English translation of this section, which was included in a recent edition of Capital, Vol. I, as an appendix, the *"Results"* may have been conceived as a transition between Vol. I and Vol. II.

Whatever the reason that Marx failed to include the *"Results"* in the first volume, it may safely be said that this section constitutes much more than a summary of *Capital*. It constitutes nothing less than the foundation upon which Marx develops an argument that (*i*) the subsumption and subordination of labor under capital is the heart of the logic of the capitalist system, and (*ii*) modern capitalism tends toward the absolute, self-directed hegemony of capital as a social relation, rather than as a system where exploitation and domination are contingent features determined by the actions of capital's personifications, the employer class and the state. In a little less than 150 pages, Marx shows with relentless coherence the stages by which capital both sweeps away the old modes of production (which, during its rise, linger as fragments in the labor process), and establishes itself as a "mode of production sui generis" in all branches of industry and, by extension, in all forms of labor.[13] Let us examine the concept of subsumption in the two forms that Marx describes.

The core of Marx's argument is that the production of surplus value not only is a process that reveals the secret of capitalist profit, but also contains an inexorable logic of domination as well. It will be recalled that the earliest form of surplus value production is what he calls "absolute" surplus value; that is, surplus value consists in the prolongation of the working day so that the proportion of labor time required for the reproduction of the laborer and her family is reduced in relation to the amount of time spent working for the capitalist's surplus.

In early manufacture, the capitalist employs skilled labor inherited from the artisan mode of production. The assumption made is that capitalist domination is limited to the transformation of the independent artisan into a wage worker; the worker is separated from the "natural" conditions under which both labor and labor power remain the property of the producer. In this early stage, the capitalist merely succeeds in divesting labor of its ownership of the means of production, but leaves the labor process intact. In the manufacturing stage, the old artisanal mode of production remains, which implies that workers may still control the process of production, even if they have been divested by ownership of their means. Surplus value is extracted by an increment of the amount of socially necessary labor time required for the production of the commodity over that portion of labor time required for the reproduction of surplus value by the only possible means available, given the transitional stage at which the system functions in this historical period—that is, by increasing the working day.

Marx calls this the *formal* subsumption of labor under capital, because the only change (in comparison to the artisanal mode of production) is the appearance of wage labor, under which workers must sell their labor power rather than the commodities that they have produced. In effect, the formal subsumption of labor under capital signals the formation of a working class from those feudal and transitional classes that historically possessed the instruments of production as social private property. It also marks the first stage in the domination of capital over labor.

The purchase and sale of labor power is, for Marx, the hallmark of capitalist production as a whole, even though wage labor existed prior to the rise of capitalism as a system. Marx defines capital as nothing but "objectified" labor. Its existence as an autonomous "thing" appears self-evident because, as Marx points out, it is congealed in objects: the money, machinery, raw materials, and commodities that are consumed for subsistence.

It may be said that "things" are the form of appearance of social relations, which constitute the essence of capitalist society. Capital becomes the key social relation in the capitalist mode of production but appears as an autonomous force. Its existence is owed to the labor that produces it. Its power increases as it is able to reduce the time required for the reproduction of the laborer in comparison with the labor time appropriated by the capitalist.

But under the formal subsumption of labor under capital, only an extension of the working day can increase the size and power of capital. The workers constantly try both to reduce the length of the working day and to raise wages, and thus to increase the amount of labor time spent in their own reproduction in comparison to the surplus value extracted. It can be shown that the transformation of absolute surplus value into relative surplus value, as the central mode of exploitation under capital, is in part the outcome of the class struggle over the length of the working day as well as the falling rate of profit. In the United States, the eight-hour-day movement in the late nineteenth century, just like the earlier ten-hour-day struggles in Britain, was conducted by the skilled workers, who by virtue of their power in the production process, are able to limit their subsumption under capital. In addition, competition among capitals on a world scale generated the conditions for measures to increase relative surplus values.

For Marx, even the relatively limited *formal* subsumption of labor under capital introduces changes in the labor process. The capitalist directs the labor process more and more, as he attempts to get workers to intensify their labor by producing more in less time, to extend their working day, and to reduce the amount of "soldiering" on the job. (Marx calls this reduction "making the work more continuous and orderly."[14]) But "in themselves these changes do not affect the character of the actual labor process, the actual mode of working." What he calls a "specifically *capitalist mode of production* (large scale industry etc.)"[15] is characterized by the transformation of the labor process by capital.

In the period of the formal subsumption of labor within capitalist production, the extent of capitalist domination is mediated by the *relative* autonomy of the skilled workers. Even where they are not able to control the process of production completely, their power at the workplace is expressed by their possession both of tools, and of the knowledge (at the conceptual as well as the detail levels) of the labor process. Their ability to organize collectively against the power of capital to extract surplus value is enhanced by the fact that capital still *appears* as an external force, that is, as a force confined to supplying raw materials on one side of the production process, and disposing of the finished commodity on the other side, in the exchange relationship. The mercantile character of capital is expressed in that its function appears to be a matter of buying and selling.

At this moment in the historical process, capital is still personified by the capitalist; personal relations between employer and worker have not yet been abstracted. Although the employer may or may not appear at the workplace as a director, the function of supervision is determined by the boundaries established by handicraft. Typically, the journeyman produces the whole product or an entire section of the product. The craft is established by tradition as "multivalenced"; that is, the worker's *power* to labor contains, within its definition, qualifications that span several different skills. Work is performed by hand; more exactly, the hand is extended in its productive powers by tools whose efficacy has historically been measured, not so much by the ratio of labor time to surplus value (which demands that the commodity be of *average* quality, so that it may qualify as a use value), as by customs and rules that have their own laws not fully subordinate to exchange value. Because of this, tradition modifies and competes with capital's inner compulsion for absolute domination.

In the early stages of manufacturing the old guild system retains its influence over the production process. But commodities of a definite quality, produced by methods which, as Marx remarks, are controlled "not by tradition but by the Guild,"[16] are inimical to capital accumulation.

Since there are physical limits to the ability of the worker to endure the expansion of the working day, as well as customary limits to intensification of labor beyond the bounds of craft, the formal subsumption of labor under capital reaches its internal limits from the point of view of capital accumulation and capital's domination.

Now Marx introduces the concept of "real" subsumption of labor under capital, corresponding to the centrality of relative as opposed to absolute surplus value, to signify the initiative and intervention of the capitalist in the labor process. This intervention—marked by the introduction of machinery simultaneously to replace labor and to reduce the worker from multivalenced artisan to detail worker—results in the intensification of labor by reducing the amount of socially necessary time required for the production and reproduction of the worker, but without increasing the working day. Wages remain the same, but the volume of surplus is increased by means of (a) replacement of living labor with machinery, and (b) intensification of labor, in the form of speedups, stretchouts, or increased workloads.

The order and flow of the work is guaranteed by the domination of the machine over the worker. The machine appears to employ the worker, not the other way around. Marx calls this the confrontation of "objectified" dead labor with living labor. That is, past labor congealed in raw materials and machinery confronts the worker as an alien power that stands over him and appears as pure alterity (otherness). This otherness is the form of appearance of capital which Marx reveals to be nothing else than a definite quantity of labor time congealed in things.

By this process, skills are destroyed, and labor is made infinitely versatile, that is, able to move from job to job, industry to industry, and country to country without the barriers of tradition, craft, or even language (since the tendency of this specific capitalist mode of production is to produce labor as a universal and virtually mute function of the machine).

The contribution of Braverman, Marglin, and Stone consists in their rich historical descriptions of the forms of intervention of capitalist management in the twentieth century. They have characterized the entire function of management in terms of the task of reducing labor to an aspect of the organization of production according to the new logic of capital. This logic compels the capitalist constantly to reduce the part played by living labor in the production process.

This reduction takes two principal forms. On the one hand, the worker becomes a single-valenced detail in a highly rationalized specialization of tasks, in which it is no longer possible for labor to conceptualize the labor process; rather, these conceptual functions are systematically transferred to the managers. The function of the bosses, as Braverman and Marglin show, is to degrade labor beyond its reduction to a commodity. Capitalist rationalization is a means to remove the boundaries, set historically by working-class self-organization, culture, and skill traditions, upon the capacity of capital to become the tendency toward production for its own sake—that is, production as an end in itself (which under the formal subsumption of labor under capital is merely incipient—now becomes realized and dispensable to capitalist production, becomes in other words a compulsion.

On the other hand, the introduction of machinery "freeing" the laborer from the production process is viewed as an aspect of the fierce competition that ensues with the industrialization process. Machinery, however, does not simply replace living labor that performed the tasks of production. It simultaneously replaces labor and transforms the labor process in accordance with the rationalization and segmentation of labor. The new machines are forms of the social organization of labor introduced by management. That is, from the multivalenced character of the all-purpose lathe, for example, where the drill, the cutting tool, and the facing tool were combined in a single machine, production machine shops separate these tools into three machines. Further, the functions of design, of the setting up of the machine in accordance with a blueprint representing the design, and of the single operation performed by a single-valenced machine tool (say, the hole boring operation of the drill press), are segmented into three jobs, personified by three different workers.

Whereas in the old toolmakers' trade, designing the tools and parts, setting up the machine, and producing the parts were invested in a single craft, now the organization of machine-tool and metal-parts production has created an army of semi-skilled workers. Some of them are called craftspersons, such as designers, toolmakers and machinists, set-up men, and maintenance mechanics. But even these crafts have experienced considerable degradation in comparison to the period of manufacture, when a single "artisan" performed all of these functions, combining design and execution.

For Marx, the increasing scale of production made possible by machinery, and by capital's intervention in the labor process by its devalorizing labor, becomes identical with the mode of production. The production of relative surplus value—that is, the increase in the proportion of unpaid labor to living labor embodied in the commodity—is the sole purpose of production. The subsumption and subordination of science, technology, and human labor are merely facets of this compulsion toward extracting profits.

> It is not just the objective conditions of the process of production that appear at its [the real subsumption] result. The same thing is true also of its specific social character. The social relations and therefore the social position of the agents of production in relation to each other, i.e. the relations of production, are themselves produced: they are also constantly renewed as a result of this process.[17]

Thus the production of relative surplus value tends toward the absolute subordination of all consciousness purposive activity within its parameters. The worker has become a collective worker since the particularity of her/his labor has been dissolved by its transfer to the machine. As Marx notices in the *Grundrisse,*

> The specific mode of working here appears directly as becoming transferred from the worker to capital in the form of the machine, and his own labor capacity devalued thereby…[18]

Under the capitalist mode of production, the transformation of science consists in its subordination to the division of labor appropriate to the devalorization of labor and the domination of capital. Chemistry, mechanical engineering, and computer technology do not appear derivative of the division of labor. On the contrary. Scientific knowledge, which is nothing other than the formalization and commodification of the transfer of artisan skill, appears to determine the process of production. Actually, Marx shows the relations of science to industry to be mutually determining. Large-scale production is the condition for the transformation of "invention (into) business."[19] In turn, science and technology as forms of objectified labor now confront the living laborer as a form of capital's compulsion that appears inexorable and even beneficial.

III

Before considering the problems that arise from the theory of capital logic for the prospects for socialist transformation, I want to draw out the implications of this theory for understanding the production of ideology. Students of Marx have noted the distinction he made between (a) the essence of capitalist production that resides in the alienation of labor and its exploitation by capital, and (b) the *forms of appearance* that this exploitation takes. Marx's distinction forms the basis of his late theory of ideology.[20] The character of labor as objectified labor congealed in machinery strands opposed to living labor such that both capital and labor appear to possess a thing-like appearance rather than a social relation. The function of management, even its scientificity, is not perceived as an aspect of the function of capital's logic, but seems to possess a natural existence, insofar as the totalizing power of the real subsumption of labor mystifies the centrality of the labor process for human existence. Science and technology appear to be autonomous forces rather than the outcome of the struggle between capital (itself a form of congealed labor under specific historical conditions) and living labor. Living labor's own devalorization and degradation *appear* to be functions of the inadequacy of the worker himself, rather than an aspect of the inherent logic of capitalist production.

For Marx then, ideology does not consist principally of ruling ideas that are imposed upon the workers from above—e.g., a system of ethics and morality that are "reflections" of capitalist interests. This view of ideology, all too common among Marxists, tends to impute ideological domination to conscious intention. The Marxist theory of ideology begins with an understanding of the process by which the forms of appearance of a commodity, such as labor power, are materialized as practices having an existence independent of human activity. Ideology is rooted in (*i*) the invisibility of labor within the "thinghood" of the commodity, and (*ii*) the real subsumption of labor under capital such that labor can no longer conceive of its mental side and can only see itself as a detail of large-scale industrial production. Thus, production's degraded division of labor appears "technical" rather than a function of domination, "rational" from the point of view of capital, but "irrational" from the perspective of specific humanity of labor.

The capitalist as the personification of Capital is no more able to comprehend the essence of the social process within which he functions than is the worker. For Marx, the labor of supervision, or management, produces its ideologies of rationality, of what Braverman calls the "habituation of the worker"—e.g., industrial psychology and education, mass advertising and other forms of mass culture, and technologies of industrial production—not as conscious means to subordinate the worker to its concrete interests, but as compulsion over which the manager has no control.[21] The manager believes his function to be "necessary" from the point of view of the labor process as well as of the general interests of society. His activity of intervention to reduce labor to a detail appears as technical as that of the quality control engineer who insures that the commodity conforms to the requirement for average quality in order to qualify as a use value.

Thus ideologies that legitimate the rule of capital arise from the process of capitalist production, and are aspects of the production of relative surplus value, the dominant mode by which the real subsumption of labor under capital occurs. The forms of appearance are "real" insofar as capital overturns historical memory, not just as a process of consciousness repression (Henry Ford: "History is bunk."), but because social relations are always materialized in the forms of machines, raw materials, money, and consumer goods.

Among the most significant ideological productions of the logic of capital is the notion of the autonomy of science and technology. Braverman superbly demolishes the concept of technology's neutrality by showing that degradation of labor (a function of management within the detailed division of labor) is the presupposition of the so called scientific revolution of the twentieth century.[22] "Scientific management" as the crucial technology of monopoly capital cannot be separated from the rule of capital over labor, and can no more be ascribed to the technical division of labor than can the division of mental from manual labor be ascribed to differences among the innate capacities of persons. Historically, labor is devalorized both qualitatively and quantitatively by what Proudhon, referring to property, once called "theft."[23] Just as property is the theft of the labor of the immediate producer in the transition from feudalism to capitalism, so technology is the theft of the artisan's craft in the transition from the formal to the real subsumption of labor under capital.

Of course, the question of science as ideology is far more complex. The conception of science as a neutral form of knowledge is so deeply embedded in bourgeois culture that the assertion of its ideological character appears absurd. Since the so-called "Copernican Revolution" of the sixteenth and seventeenth centuries, during which what Dijksterhuis calls the "mechanization of the world picture" occurs,[24] the basic concepts of modern science appear self-evident. Even Marxists such as Louis Althusser take these concepts for granted, while at the same time acknowledging that ideology is a type of "lived experience" of bourgeois society rooted in material institutions such as the state, schools, trade unions, and art.

According to Althusser, Marxism is a science of society and history analogous to physics and chemistry. It is not the idea that scientific propositions are ultimately empirically verifiable that is at issue here, if by empirical we mean the correspondence of our ideas to a reality independent of our volition. For Althusser science is a body of knowledge, or, to be more precise, a theoretical practice, that is radically separated from ideology by virtue of its explicit or implicit self-detachment from ideology. This detachment is achieved by revealing its past to be ideological. Presumably modern physical sciences are genuine, scientific *sui generis*, because of their epistemological break from prior theories that were pseudo-scientific because they were permeated by idealism. This definition of science includes just two elements: first, the critical side, namely, the continuous critique of ideology which is, in every case, a material practice located inside the system of social relations; second, a system of concepts held together in contradictory unity according to the principles of the materialist dialectic. Naturally, Marxism for Althusser is not just a theory of society that possesses a scientific character—as opposed to those theories that are ideological because they are the lived experience of social relations, despite their appearance as science. Rather, Marxism is also a theory of theory, revealing the general laws of all scientific discourse.[25]

Althusser's claim stands in continuous relation with the claims of the history of science, except that he does not accept its positivist methodological premises. What is common to both his theory and bourgeois scientific philosophy is the assertion that science may avoid a mediated relationship with nature, that is, that the specific characteristic of scientific propositions may be related to the configuration of social relations within a given mode of production, not only with respect to their uses and transformation into bourgeois technology, but also with respect to the content of the propositions themselves.

But if Marx is correct concerning the subsumption of science as well as labor under Capital, then it should be possible to trace the ways in which scientific discovery is subsumed by capitalist social relations, not only with respect to the object of scientific investigation (and how much it is determined by the compulsions of capital to direct scientific practice toward modes of domination of nature that result in domination of labor), but also with respect to scientific methodologies and theoretical concepts. Dijksterhuis has shown, for instance, that the development of physical science is attributable in great measure to the "far reaching effect (of) the emergence of the conception of the world usually called mechanical or mechanistic."[26] The burden of his argument is that the mechanical world picture determined, as well as was determined by, the development of science. Of course no history of science, including Dijksterhuis's, has pointed to the degree to which the picture of the world as a giant machine (whose laws, subject to quantification by mathematical means, are verifiable (or falsifiable) by empirical observation and experiment) corresponded to the processes of capitalist rationalization of industry. But even if we admit that mechanization as a philosophical tenet need not correspond, as a precise reflection, to underlying economic relations, there can be no doubt that the bourgeois world outlook which preceded the development of modern industry presupposes capital's compulsion to subsume society and nature under its rule. The mechanization of the world picture is the ideological form of social domination insofar as capital claims that its epistemology is an immutable law of nature.

Even the claims of bourgeois science to empirical proof of the truth of its propositions rests on assumptions about ways of knowing the world that are already permeated with its ideology. The experimental method of knowledge enunciated so eloquently by Francis Bacon "forgets" that the scientist acts on the world, mediated by social class and ideology, in order to know it. All knowledge of the external world is conditioned, if not determined, by the fundamental premise of all labor, i.e. by the determination of all activity within the bourgeois mode of production by its instrumental character. Even if the scientist believes that knowledge is acquired for its own sake, capital imposes its forms, if not a specific content, on investigation. These forms are the general parameters of scientific discourse, according to which (a) the world is orderly and lawful; (b) all knowledge is subject in principle to mathematical reduction, such that quantity dominates over quality and, in the development of bourgeois philosophy, quality is regarded as belonging entirely to the subjective realm; (c) science is, if properly cleansed of its ideological remnants, capable of value-free inquiry; and (d) the world corresponds to the principles of classical mechanics.

Dijksterhuis disputes the theses of Franz Borkenau and Georg Simmel that the development of science in the fifteenth and sixteenth centuries owed a great deal to the early innovation within handicraft production of mechanical tools.[27] His argument rests on the apparent temporal discrepancy and geographical dispersal of scientific discovery in this period, a spread that does not appear to be influenced by technology. It seems to me that Marx's theory of the development of capitalism and the formation of capital transcends arguments whose veracity depends upon causal explanation. *For the thrust of Marx's argument is that the capitalist mode of production produces ideologies that seek to preserve a system of social relations, quite apart from the relation of any particular part of that complex to another. The question of determination between science*

and technology may be unanswerable at the level of causal discourse.
What is at stake in Marx's theory is the concept of the hegemony of the
specific system of social relations called capitalism over forms of thought
as well as over the fate of social classes within it.[28]

We may speak of the relative autonomy of science insofar as scientific discovery constitutes a moment of determination within a complex totality. One does not need a theory of correspondence to assert the dependence of science on capital if the propositions concerning the subsumption of science under capital are accepted as a historical phenomenon. The historical specificity of the universality of the commodity form, based upon the separation of labor from its natural conditions within the feudal mode of production, and the formation of a class of wage workers, creates the conditions for the domination of capital, if not of the capitalist class, over all forms of social life. The primacy of social relations over the forces of production is not to be construed as an invariant law of historical materialism. What it implies is the reversibility of the concept of a science that can stand apart from the system of social production, that is, as an autonomous sphere. For this reason, the merging of science and ideology under the rule of capital emancipates thought from the scientific ideology which declares its independence from social relations, and makes the project of scientific autonomy an aspect of socialist struggle.

The problem with recent treatments of the labor process within late capitalism is that the "scientific/technical revolution" is treated as conjunctural with the capitalist division of labor and the subsumption of technology under capital. The inner laws of science—its ideological presuppositions rooted in the relations of domination between predatory capital and nature, whose configuration expresses the relations of domination among humans—are left untouched.

Braverman repeats the error: "The old epoch of industry gave way to the new during the last decades of the nineteenth century primarily as a result of advance in four fields: electricity, steel, coal-petroleum and the internal combustion engine."[29] He goes on to describe how these innovations were recognized by the capitalist class as important "as means for furthering the accumulation of capital" but deals with the phenomenon of the incorporation of science into industry as the meeting of two relatively autonomous structures. One could argue that the chemical, electronic, and information revolutions were themselves subordinate features of the logic of domination. They did not merely conjoin with the emergence of large-scale industries that arose from the concentration and centralization of capital; rather, they appeared as the result of the separation of mental from manual labor and the "theft" of the conceptual functions that had been merged with execution within the artisanal mode of production. More specifically, they are expressions of the tendency of the "specifically capitalist mode of production" for continuity and order in the labor process.

The chemical, electrical, and information technologies arose out of scientific labor resting on the foundations of mathematical reduction of the materiality of the world to number. Whereas the older industrial revolution was based on pulleys, gears, and other machines that rested on the mechanical world picture and still entailed the confrontation between objectified labor and living labor at the level of sensuous experience (that is, it was a visible confrontation, even if mystified by the reification of social relations in their thinghood), the new scientific discoveries and technical processes were invisible. They abstracted labor as a use value to a much higher level, such that mental labor, not so much management as science, emerges as the primary productive force.

Thus the historical process whereby labor is degraded and the machine appears to possess skill as an inherent property is advanced to a new stage: capital now subsumes the mental laborer and presses the laboratory into its service. But this incorporation rests on the traditional insistence of bourgeois science that the world can be expressed in terms of numbers that stand in objective relations to each other according to definite logical processes.

When number becomes the language of science, its transformation into technique ensures the continuity of production, even if the worker refuses to be subordinate to the machine. Under the mechanical means of production, this refusal could be materialized as the refusal to work, as a disruption of production expressed as sabotage, slowdowns, and strikes. The new technologies are based upon scientific principles that are anti-mechanical. Whereas auto workers may still shut down the assembly line, revealing to them that the line is after all objectified labor and merely an extension of their own productive powers, the cracking plant or power generator, indeed the computer that can regulate machine production, appears to be autonomous with regard to human labor. Of course, as Marx pointed out in the *Grundrisse*, this form of appearance is essentially no different from the mechanical processes of production.[30] Now, however, mental labor, personified not by engineers and technicians but also by electronic controls, may operate the machines even if the manual workers refuse to perform the labor of watching and recording.

Automated production is not based upon the application of time and motion studies to human labor, as in the mechanical phase of production, since the tendency of these technologies is to make production continuous without the intervention of labor since all operations are regulated by electronic controls that simulate human activities numerically. Of course, the machine is still partially built by labor, including the labor of calculating the various frequency of numerical control devices corresponding to operations that were performed by manual labor. But the process of devalorization of living labor approaches, but never reaches, zero.

This tendency toward the absolute devalorization of labor time required for the production of commodities is still undeveloped in most sectors of American industry, but exists in almost all basic industries in theory. Marx spoke of abstract labor as the result of the separation of exchange value from use value, and of the quantification of labor as a function of time; now capital has found a way—via the development of scientific principles inherent in the paradigm of modern science itself— to create the abstract worker within the labor process. Under these circumstances, plants become smaller, employing fewer workers, whose productivity is virtually incommensurable with the mechanical phase of capitalist industry. At the same time, the centralization of capital, assisted by the new technology, results in a tendency toward the decentralization of industrial production. The need to be close to waterways, once the *sine qua non* of industrial location, has disappeared because neither power nor transportation depend on water. Under these circumstances, the new logic of subsumption makes possible the dissolution of the natural bonds of working-class solidarity which Marx found to be an unintended consequence of the centralization of capital in ever larger industrial units during the period mechanization.

IV

The emergence of science as a primary productive force under capital results in the further fragmentation of labor; that is, the relation between its objectified form and its living form appears even more alien. Even the function of management appears superfluous, since the logic of industrial production appears to reside within the self-correcting continuous flow operation of electronic or chemical processes that now conceal more than they reveal.

The trade union is already a dependent variable to the old industrial order, since it has been reduced to fighting to prevent the price of labor power from sinking below its value, and to maintain the position of a shrinking industrial labor force, while at the same time serving as a central instrument to discipline that force and make it a cooperative factor of production; now it is placed in an even more ambiguous position by the logic of capital. Now the union struggles to valorize capital, by acting as a counter-tendency against the compulsion of capital to deprive labor of "its direct form"; the subsumption of living labor under "self-activating objectified labor" generates a crisis of valorization of capital for the system as a whole, since unpaid labor is the only source of surplus value. One of the functions of trade unions becomes to safeguard capital against its own tendency to render the worker superfluous to itself within the labor process, since, at the level of exchange value, labor remains absolutely essential.

This contradiction in the character of workers' organization is not a product of the "class collaboration" of the union leaders, their misleadership, or even their bureaucratic character. Rather these characteristics of the unions are produced by the logic of subsumption. The unions' subordination to capital does not consist in their selling out, even though this is the appearance. The necessity for labor time to be present, as a regulator of exchange value preventing the surplus value within commodities from actually reaching zero, is expressed in trade union demands for minimum crews on various industrial operations, even on those that (because of high levels of technological development) reduce the worker to a watcher and tender of a machine that appears to produce commodities independent of the direct intervention of the worker.

Marx calls unions "insurance societies formed by the workers themselves for the protection of the value of their labor power."[31] In the earlier transitional artisan mode of production, in which the labor process was still under the control of the workers but the product had already been alienated by capital, workers' combinations prevented the extension of the working day beyond the bounds of human endurance, and thus produced the transformation between the formal subsumption of labor under capital and the real subsumption (in which objectified labor confronts living labor in an antagonistic relation and reduces the latter to a function of the machine). But the role of unions, in the period when "the workers' activity [is] reduced to a mere abstraction of activity [and] determined and regulated on all sides by the movement of machinery"[32] (i.e. modern industry), is reduced to protecting the value of a fragment of the value of the commodity. The workers can no longer through combined activity do more than accelerate or retard the transformation of the labor process into one wherein objectified labor rather than living labor dominates.

The results of the immediate process of production tend toward the elimination of living labor as a force of production and its replacement by the dead hand of objectified labor. The past dominates the present, and, insofar as Marx has charted a logical process that no longer admits of human intervention except in the period of the breakdown of capital's self-reproduction, capitalism becomes a system where the future is an extension of the present.

The idea of a scientific-technological "revolution" is a form of reification in Marx's schema of subsumption. Although mental and physical labor remain the basis of the entire productive system,

[the] science which compels the inanimate limbs of the machinery, by their construction, to act purposefully, as an automation, does not exist in the worker's consciousness, but rather acts upon him through the machine as an alien power, as the power of the machine itself... The

production process has ceased to be a labour process in the sense of a process laminated by labour as its governing unity. Labour appears, rather, merely as a conscious organ, scattered among the individual living workers as numerous points of the mechanical system; subsumed under the total process of machinery itself, as itself only a link in the system, whose living unity exists not in the living workers, but rather in the living [active] machinery, which confronts his individual insignificant doings as a mighty organism.[33]

If Marx is correct that the character of the labor process structurally prevents the workers from recognizing themselves as the motive force of the entire system, and that all institutions of society are subsumed by capital, including labor, then even the forms of workers' resistance are imprisoned within the boundaries set by capital itself. At least, the tendency toward the replacement of living labor by its objectified, mechanical form shrinks the power of the working class within the system; this does not happen as a function of its false consciousness; the "false consciousness" is itself produced by capital as an aspect of its inner logic. Nor is the material base of the loss of workers' power the perfidy of trade union or socialist leaders; rather it is the "scattering" of the workers among the giant machines of modern capitalism.

Anyone who has ever witnessed the operations of an oil refinery, a modern heavy chemical processing plant, a food processing plant, or a modern electronics facility cannot fail to understand the concrete specification of Marx's synthetic and prophetic vision of the inherent tendencies of the labor process. Here the worker is actually reduced to a watcher and tender, while scientific and technical employees, whose labor appears abstract to the workers since it is embodied (invisibly as it were) within the machine's parts, become the key productive force. But the form of appearance of this productive force has no personification, only an embodiment in the inanimate object which Marx says appears as the "active force." Since scientific and technological labor is analogously degraded to that of manual labor, its centrality to the labor process is no less hidden to itself than is the labor of manual workers subsumed in the autonomy of the machine.

The ominous consequence of this historical process—one in which even its historical character has no immediate existence to those who have become its objects, the workers and technical intelligentsia within the labor process—is nothing less than the tendency of capitalism to abolish the subject as an historical actor. For subjectivity or conscious-ness depends, not on the "scientific" understanding of the few intel-lectuals whose social formation and distance from the overwhelming power of capital's domination within the labor process allows for the possibility of critical analysis, but rather upon the contradictions of the social system that produce the necessary conditions for self-activity. This self-activity, within the framework of Marxist theory, may not be regard-ed as a phenomenon that arises from the depths of human volition; Marx had patience neither with doctrines that relied on innate characteristics of human nature to explain the possibility of revolutionary action, nor with those that relied on moral outrage. His theoretical premise is that subjectivity must have a material basis within the process of production, in the alienation of human labor from itself, which of course remains in existence between the two principal stages in the development of the labor process under capital's domination.

But the problem with the second stage of this process is that his the-ory only permits of two sources for the emergence of the proletariat's self-consciousness. The first (a conclusion to which Lenin and Lukács were irresistibly drawn by their analysis of capitalist production arising out of their reading of *Capital*) was that the working class, by its own efforts, could not achieve revolutionary consciousness; the recognition of its historical task must be brought to it from the outside, because of the occlusion of capitalism's essential processes by the appearance of its social relations in the form of thing-like relations.

It must be emphasized that the Leninist theory of the party is not a variety of "elitism," as many have argued; rather it is the inexorable result of the rigorous application of Marx's theory of capitalist develop-ment, particularly his analysis of the labor process, to problems of po-litical organization. It will not do to ascribe the notion of the structural limitation of worker's consciousness, as some have charged, to the petty bourgeois character of socialist leadership. According to this critique,

Leninism is the self-justification of a jacobinite tendency in the socialist movement. Whether or not the theory of reification that permeates
Marx's *Grundrisse* and *"Results,"* as well as the first chapter of *Capital*,
is defensible in the last analysis, it is a powerful description of the logic
of capital, one that has withstood a century of world history. Even in
a cursory reading, Lukács's *History and Class Consciousness* argues
persuasively for the theory of the Leninist party, on the basis of the repression of subjectivity by late capitalist society.

When Braverman warns that *Labor and Monopoly Capital* will make
"no attempt...to deal with the modern working class on the level of its
consciousness, organization or activities," even as he acknowledges the
importance of this line of inquiry, he may not have chosen this limitation,
as he says he has, because of the priority of the task of describing the
working class "in itself" before trying to find the basis of the formation
of the class "for itself." Rather, the "shape given to the working population by the capital accumulation process,"[34] the subject of the book, may
itself exclude the question of consciousness, if Marx's theory is rigorously followed, as Braverman attempts to do. For the result of the process is
the exclusion of contradictory processes of capitalist accumulation of a
kind that may reveal to the workers themselves the truth about the labor
process and the capitalist system as a whole.

The theory of the Leninist party becomes a perfectly reasonable deduction from the capital-logic argument, although even here a relentless
application of capital logic would preclude the appearance of those radical intellectuals who, at the turn of the century, were still formed by the
humanist tradition which capital was in the midst of extirpating from
public discourse. As André Gorz has shown,[35] following Marx's doctrine
of subsumption of all science under capital, the intellectual educated in
the philosophical and cultural traditions of classical Greek thought, Renaissance ideas, and the French Revolution has all but disappeared in the
modern world. The scientist no longer engages in "pure" research, but
"research directly or indirectly connected with the production process."
The traditional intellectual has given way to a "technical intelligentsia"; these strata "supervise, organize, control and command groups of
production workers,"[36] or, within universities and mass communication

media, generate and disseminate technocratic ideologies which function both to legitimate capitalist domination and to reproduce a labor force that regards its own subordination as a natural fact. The fundamental distinction between the traditional intellectual, and the technical intellectual devoted to the reproduction of appearances since he is tied to the logic of capital, makes the project of a revolutionary party problematic. For where can we expect the critical intellectuals to emerge from, if the proletariat has become merely a "conscious organ of the machine"? Clearly, the program of Lenin and Lukács relied on the transitional nature of eastern European societies, where traditional intellectuals still existed who could go over to the proletariat.

However, the technocratic character of the French and Italian communist parties may attest to the difficulties in the Leninist conception in advanced countries. These mass parties adhered to revolutionary ideologies albeit in a degraded form, but seem unable to develop an autocritique of their own practice—the only possibility of retarding, if not totally precluding, their integration within capital's political as well as economic hegemony. At the same time, the working class, which in the main supports socialist and communist parties in these countries, frequently shows its capacity for revolt, but seems unable to transcend the objective conditions of its fragmentation. At best the workers pursued the dual strategy of disrupting both the factory and the trade union bureaucracies that appear as their antagonists, and supporting their left parties at the polls, as the best chance to achieve amelioration of social grievances within the system.

Of course, these parties, which for the most part are identical with the trade unions (if not in function at least in personnel), reveal the contradictions within working-class practice. To draw a homology to the relation of the worker to the machine, the trade unions and left political parties are themselves personifications of capital, even as they represent the workers' immediate interests. The unions and the parties, as forms of objectified labor, confront their constituency in the form of bureaucracy, itself an alienated moment of capital. For it cannot be denied that workers form these organizations as their "insurance societies" against the reduction of their living standards, that is, support the left as organized labor's defensive instrument. But the parties have ceased to express the revolutionary intellectual's self-transformation into a catalyst of working-class activity. They have become the political sign of capital logic. This is the phenomenon often referred to as the "integration of the working class into late capitalism," when monopoly capital incorporates its own opposition as a feature of the system such that the workers are no longer in "radical chains." They are now, according to this view, both in and of capitalist society; and Marx's theory of the production of relative surplus value and its consequences becomes both the necessary and sufficient explanations for this historical development.

Recognizing the problem of late capitalist integration, one important political tendency in advanced capitalist countries, often defined as the extreme left, has attempted to find a way out by the relentless pursuit of the capitalist crisis. The underlying hope of those who look to the crisis as the sufficient condition for revolutionary action is the tendency of the capitalist system periodically to experience economic breakdown. According to Marx's theory of capitalist development, breakdown is only one of the possibilities arising from the higher organic composition of capital, that is, from the rising proportion of capital to living labor. Since living labor is the only source of surplus value, this historical replacement of humans by machinery within the labor process is only the qualitative expression of the drive of capital to subsume labor under itself, in order to facilitate the accumulation of capital on a continuous basis. Marx argues that this subsumption constitutes an internal contradiction in capital's logic of accumulation since it reduces the amount of socially necessary labor required for production of commodities and thus reduces the portion of surplus to congealed capital. But Marx was quick to point out "counteracting causes" of the tendency of the rate of profit to fall and of industrial production to be disrupted by this lower rate.[37]

Among these counteracting trends is (i) raising the intensity of labor by supplementing the production of relative surplus value with absolute surplus value extraction. The working day is lengthened in our epoch by both compulsory and voluntary overtime, which in such industries as auto are not the exception but during peak season have become the rule; and by the old-fashioned methods of speedup in "medium" technology industries, that is, in industries not yet characterized by continuous or automatic production, like auto assembly or steel, which have a relatively high level of mechanization but not yet a system of developed numerical control systems based on information processes. Among other counter-acting trends are the following:

(*ii*) One can cheapen the elements of constant capital; this is a relative category expressing the difference in the rate of growth of value of constant capital to the volume of total capital. As the volume of total capital is larger because of the productivity of labor, the decline of the rate of profit of each unit of production does not result in a significant halt or slowdown in industrial production or mass of profit.

(*iii*) Marx says that "relative overpopulation" is inseparably linked with "the development of the productivity of labor expressed as the falling rate of profit."[38] The large number of unemployed tend to depress wages in some branches of industry, retarding the subordination of labor to capital by reducing the pace of the introduction of labor-saving technologies that reduce the rate of profit. Lenin adapted this counter-acting cause to his theory of uneven development, according to which the masses in the least developed sectors of the capitalist world system would show the way to revolutionary change.[39] If Marx's theory is followed in its implication, one might infer that the possibility of revolution is either reduced or increased partially on the basis of the pace of subordination of labor under capital. At the same time, this phenomenon is internally contradictory to the doctrine of the inevitability of capitalist crisis, since unevenness is among the retardants of the crisis (seen in some versions of Marxist analysis to be the *sine qua non* of either revolution, radicalization of the working class, or both).

(*iv*) It may be argued that Marx's designation of "foreign trade" as a major deterrent to crisis was adapted in the twentieth century to the theory of imperialism, notably by Lenin, Hilferding, Luxemburg, and Bukharin. Capitalism may avoid breakdown by expanding its foreign trade so that, by competing with countries producing commodities under less developed conditions of production, it permits an enlargement of its own scale of production, thus cheapening the elements of production (such as raw materials and machinery) even as the mass of commodities produced is increased and the number of employed laborer is increased in absolute terms. Thus the rate of surplus value is raised, vitiating the tendency of the profit rate to fall.

(*v*) But the most significant of the counteracting causes of capitalist crisis is contained in the tendency of capital to subsume the state, its own opposition (labor), and science. This is the fundamental basis of the historical appearance of state capitalist planning in the twentieth century with its capacity to counteract the inherent crisis tendencies of the system. It is not that crisis has been permanently pre-empted by state intervention in the economy, the reduction of the working class to a function of capital, or the advent of modern imperialism as a counteracting tendency to crisis. Rather, the crisis is displaced by the enlargement of the state's function as employer of labor, by the arms economy, by the export of capital to other countries (who, owing to the law of uneven development are now burdened by capital's internal disruptions), by the phenomenon of "internal colonialism" expressed as the systematic exploitation of the countryside by the town within advanced capitalist countries, and by racist and sexist divisions of labor that constitute a "counteracting cause" insofar as they allow capital to contain the falling rate of profit by increasing the rate of exploitation among sectors of the "surplus population."

Thus the logic of subsumption, in which capital presses all social institutions into its service either as ideological or economic apparatuses, forms the core of what may be termed "managed" capitalism, which extends from the labor process to society as a whole. Management is a technological expression of the logic of domination, a means of creating a closed universe such that contradictions, far from disappearing take the form of the appearance of "social problems" subject to manipulation of social policy. In the wake of this displacement, a virtual army of social workers, educators, and other strata of the technical intelligentsia arise as the personification of the state—as personifications of the ideology adequate to an epoch of capitalism in which, in conformity with the degradation of labor, the social world is broken up into a series of "problems." Capital successfully transforms "alienation" into a social neurosis that becomes the property of an individual who is now called "deviant" from the social norm of integration and subordination.

Since World War II, "overpopulation" (i.e. unemployment and under-employment) has been disguised by the internationalization of the division of labor, which between 1880 and 1920 had functioned as an effective counteracting cause to the agrarian crisis by displacing redundant labor to the United States. Now, unemployment is absorbed by the most advanced countries, a result of the ability of capitalism to subject its own contradictions to its underlying logic of technical rationality so that they appear as phenomena subject to rational calculation and solution. When Marxists assert with confidence that these are not subject to such manipulations, but merely taken on a different appearance within the world system, the problem remains of the ideological form that effectively makes possible the reproduction of the system. Here the concept of ideology as a set of material practices is particularly relevant to understanding why the working classes view themselves as a function of capital. For it is capital which appears to send good things from above, to paraphrase Marx's description of the conditions for the formation of a "class."[40]

I will set aside, for the purposes of this argument, the questions of whether workers' organization constitutes the necessary condition for a revolutionary situation and whether, given this circumstance, the crisis becomes its sufficient condition. What I have attempted to show casts doubt upon the certainty *either* of the emergence of a revolutionary party within advanced capitalism, *or* of the economic crisis that may transform the workers from a function of capital of a world historical revolutionary force.

It has been remarked that *Capital*, despite its bulk and complexity, was an unfinished work and, as the very last pages of the third volume indicate, was meant to constitute a description only of the objective side of the capitalist order. The manuscript stops at the moment when Marx was preparing to derive a theory of class from the motion of capital. Presumably the theory of consciousness would have followed, or at least a more complete theory of revolution than is offered in the *Communist Manifesto*.

The problem is, however, not what Marx intended, but what his legacy is. The result of his analysis of the labor process, and of the accumulation of capital of which it is a part, has been to abolish the possibility for a theory of subjectivity. Braverman, Marglin, and others who have studied the degradation of labor following Marx's suggestions cannot find a solution for the problem of consciousness, not because they are "bad" Marxists, but because they have been faithful to the framework that he set out in his magisterial fragment. The results of degradation as Marx outlined it are not to destroy the empirical consciousness of particular groups of workers, to destroy their will to struggle against the results of the domination of capital. The problem is to locate the theoretical basis of the revolt such that its character transcends particularity without the decisive substitution of the party for the class since, as I have tried to show, the party is, as much as any institution within capital's hegemony, subject to its domination and becomes a function of it.

Lenin found the solution not so much in the theory of the party as in his law of uneven development. The counteracting cause of crisis became, for him, the space within which revolutionary politics was possible. That is even if the subordination of labor under capital is taken as an empirical truth within a limited historical frame, the progressive freeing of labor by capital, and its ruthless pursuit of markets by penetrating colonial and semicolonial countries, constitute the "Achilles heel" of the system. From this perspective, Braverman's modest hope that his work could "supplement" the work of Paul Baran and Paul Sweezy is more than that. It is the internal argument for why the working classes in the developed capitalist societies cannot be expected to attain revolutionary consciousness, and for why only the masses of those underdeveloped countries in which capital attempts to attenuate its own contradictions can provide the scene of social transformation. For the specification of degradation in the metropolitan countries of western Europe and the US can be understood only within the context of uneven development, which generates opposition to the system from the unexpected sources of peasant societies or the backward sectors of advanced countries. Braverman, then, lends his updating of Marx's analysis of capital logic to the doctrine according to which the center of world revolution has shifted to the so-called Third World.

This is not the place to show the historical tendency of these revolutions to become subsumed under capital, just as labor has become subsumed within advanced countries. The point is that Marx's theory of capital accumulation leads to the conclusion that its global character makes revolution a conjunctural phenomenon. There is no counter logic of revolutionary upheaval *within* the theory, since subjectivity itself, under the rule of capital, is afforded no autonomous space. Working-class praxis is at best disruptive of the reproduction process, which is simply restored by the rising investment in constant capital.

Of course, this dialectical relation—between (*a*) workers' struggle at the point of production against the formal and real subsumption of labor under capital, and (*b*) the tendency toward a rising organic composition of capital which, in the form of the falling rate of profit, becomes part of a "scissors" crisis of capitalism—is part of the story of the development of European neocapitalism since the end of World War II. In countries like France, Italy, and Great Britain, trade union struggles, combined with the political organization of the working class, have partially arrested the logic of capital (or, to be more exact, have shaped its development to a degree not anticipated by the category of subsumption). After the forward march of western European capitalism until 1955, workers' militancy successfully limited the capacity of capital to extract surplus value at the international rate, and simultaneously limited the power of capital to recoup its position by a shift to the underdeveloped world or by a new surge of introductions of labor-saving technologies. This is not to say that technological change and the international migration of capital were not the characteristic moves of capital. The point is that mass working-class and middle-strata mobilizations at both the extra-parliamentary and parliamentary levels were major forces in restricting the success of these strategies.

The political class struggle and the cultural struggle, at the point of production and in the spheres of social consumption, do constitute "counteracting" causes to the logic of capital. This is precisely the central significance of the movements for social, cultural, and political emancipation in the 1960s, both in the United States and in several countries of western Europe. In terms of the capital-logic argument, some of the emergence of neo-socialist (new left) and workers' movements in this period is explicable by the "law" of uneven development, according to which surplus populations generated by the international subsumption of labor under capital are not yet sufficiently fragmented by the subsumption (that is, they share a mode of life in which the bonds of social and cultural solidarity have not yet been sundered).

Another possibility is contained in the so-called new working class thesis advanced by several neo-Marxist theorists, including Gorz and Mallet, in the period during which the subsumption of science was underway in France in the 1960s. The core of the theory, which has now been severely and widely criticized, even by Gorz himself, remains compelling in the context of the problem of socialist praxis: scientific and technological labor is only partially subsumed under capital. The contradiction between the demands of capital for its degradation and the cultural and ideological traditions of autonomy and social responsibility constitute a basis for an oppositional practice by these groups.

Their recognition that the ideologies of emancipation embedded in scientific education and bourgeois culture are subverted by the technicization of all science, and by its subordination to the requirements of capital, generates political and cultural movements among some sections of the middle strata. This is not a result of some abstract oppositional moral assumptions, but rather is a result of the unevenness of relationship between the institutions of material production (in which the logic of subordination appears hegemonic) and the institutions of "social reproduction," in which capital logic is mediated by ideologies which, if not anti-capitalist in origin, become problematic from the point of view of capital's domination in its monopoly stage.

New ideologies, more consonant with the real subsumption phase corresponding to the rise of monopoly capital, are certainly in the process of being created. But these ideologies are by no means hegemonic, even against the old bourgeois morality of the eighteenth century that calls forth science as a liberating force against the evils of capital accumulation (e.g., poverty, back-breaking labor, and cultural deprivation). Many scientists and technicians in France and elsewhere joined students' and workers' revolts in the late 1960s participating in factory occupations, joining parties of the left in the 1970s and organizing ecology movements explicitly directed against the subordination of science under capital. It may even be argued that the crisis of European capital is due as much to the disaffection of sections of the middle strata, and the revolt against the logic of subsumption of labor under capital, as it is to the subordination of national European capital to international, US-based multi-national capital in this period.

V

The above illustrations are offered as an introduction to the conclusion that the theses adopted by Braverman and others who have applied Marx's capital-logic argument, may only be taken as *tendencies* within a broader social and historical context. On the other side are the counter-acting causes, among them the law of uneven development, the profound influence of ideological and cultural questions within capitalist societies, and of course the contradictions of the internationalization of capital.

The most serious error of much of modern Marxism was to fall into a kind of historical amnesia in the 1970s and 1980s. The rise of capital-logic theory is an important addition to Marxist theory if it is understood as an abstraction of one side of concrete historical processes which cannot be subsumed under its laws. For even though there is a tendency toward the technicization of all intelligence (a phenomenon well described by Herbert Marcuse in his seminal work, *One Dimensional Man*[41]), and a powerful tendency toward the limiting of all workers' struggles within the terms dictated by the real subsumption of labor under capital, there are also counteracting tendencies.

I wish to offer several theses about what it would be necessary to amplify in order to construct a theory of the capitalist totality adequate to the requirement explicit in Marx himself that the role of human praxis is central to any possible theory of social transformation.[42]

(*i*) Capital logic must not be taken as an *empirical* description of the process of capitalist development. Instead, it should be regarded as an *approximation* of one side of that process, the side suggested by the doctrine of the fetishism of commodities, in which capital *appears* to be an autonomous, internally-generating subject of history. Marx argues that the essence of capital is living labor and that the core of the labor process is the relationship of humans to nature and the social relations of production. The actualization of labor—which becomes the object of socialist revolution—is the emancipation of labor from its subsumption by capital. This objective can only be achieved by the assertion of workers' autonomy over production, freed from the domination of capital which (as Braverman and Marglin have shown) is mediated within modern capitalism by the function of "scientific management."

(*ii*) Since the possibility of the subsumption of labor under capital is implied by the detail laborer, whose central category is mental and manual division, a theory of social transformation must show that much of that division functions on the ideological level rather than as an empirical given, i.e. as a fact. Even the most degraded labor involves considerable mental operations. Execution is a type of conception and conception a kind of execution. The object of the assertion of an antinomy between mental and manual labor is to secure the habituation of the worker in order to reproduce herself/himself in as degraded a form as the objectivity of degradation produces. Yet part of the everyday life of the factory or office is the constant effort of workers to create a work culture that becomes the focus of resistance against the absolute domination of capital over the labor process.[43]

This culture of resistance must be first *theorized* as one of the results of the immediate process of production in order to be investigated. It is the moment, or aspect of the labor process that represents the workers' praxis. Among its manifestations are informal rules established by workers to govern the quantity of production; the frequent acts of sabotage that reduce productivity even in highly mechanized plants; the refusal to work, manifested as absenteeism and lateness, a big issue of the 1960s and early 1970s that was temporarily "solved" by the two recessions of 1974–5 and 1978–9; the refusal of workers to tolerate the results of the chemical and electronics revolution that tend to endanger life and limb (not only the coal strike of 1978 signifies this refusal, but so do the recent struggles of occupational health and safety regulations in various important industries including oil, asbestos, textiles, and chemicals); and rank-and-file struggles against bureaucratic and corrupt union officials in the name of democracy.

This slogan of democracy both reveals and conceals the depth of discontent at the workplace: it reveals that workers do not accept simply the "insurance society" functions of the union, but which the union to be the political representative of their *community* as well; it conceals the profound cultural base that already exists in the workplace. For if such a community in formation did not exist, how would the Sadlowski campaign be possible, or the wildcat strikes in coal, or the feminist movement among clerical workers? As Henri Lefebvre has remarked, referring to the May 1968 events in Paris, "events belie forecasts."[44] That is, the model of capitalist accumulation of the tendency toward subsumption and subordination has only limited predictive value. Time and again, confident forecasts of working-class embourgeoisement and capitalist integration have suffered in the wake of history. Unless one holds to a dialectical view of the labor process which accounts for resistance as more than spontaneity, Marxism becomes a sterile, deterministic doctrine which prefigures its own demise in the loom of historical change.

But the concept that work culture is intrinsic to the labor process, particularly to its collective character, cannot depend on scattered evidence that workers desire workplace democracy or resist degradation. The view that degraded labor is only one tendency of the specific capitalist labor process, even if it appears as the dominant historical tendency, depends on two separate arguments.

(a) The first argument consists of the dialectical theory of development, according to which the new stage of the labor process generated by the dominance of relative surplus value has contradictory aspects: on the one hand, degradation and de-skilling of labor; on the other hand, the reconstitution of the working class such that new skills are created within the general movement of degradation. That is, degradation presupposes the artisan as the standard of skilled labor because, in this form of work, mental and manual labor are united in a single craft. What the "degradation thesis" forgets, however, is that the loss of craft may not signal the end of skill. The reconstitution process entails the development of a "new" working class. The socialization of labor, its mutual dependence in the production process, makes united action easier. Putatively the formation of class consciousness is no longer a function of the struggle to maintain craft in the wake of capitalist rationalization; it now becomes the function of the collective character of labor.

The new "natural" conditions of labor are collective insofar as each worker may recognize herself/himself as a link in the chain of production without which the process cannot be reproduced. The collective powers of labor are not just a Marxist slogan. They are manifested every day in the forms of interaction among workers that reproduce work culture (for example, in the emergence of a world of social discourse that tries to maintain its autonomy from the eyes and ears of foremen and supervisors). As I have shown elsewhere,[45] this is manifested in work-sharing arrangements, or in saving finished pieces that are lent to others so that rates may be met by fellow workers having a hard day (because of machine breakdown, because they do not feel good, etc.).

The cooperation of workers in rolling mills and basic steel operations is by now legendary, especially in management circles. The work is performed by crews whose coordination is the essential condition of production and it is not managed by capital, except by the process of trying progressively to replace and segment labor by new processes that transfer skills to the machine. The US steel industry has failed to "modernize" not only because of the stupidity and greed of the owners, although this narrow-sightedness is certainly germane to the last twenty years of steel production. Rather, steelworkers were militant in protecting the older processes, which were grounded in their solidarity. Here the erosion of older skills was *not* replaced by mere degradation in the twentieth century.

As Charles Walker and Steve Packard[46] have shown in their respective studies (written more than twenty-five years apart) of the modern US steel corporation, the degree of worker autonomy even within mechanized operations is considerable. Workers have a culture sufficiently developed to make their role in the configuration of production significant. Listen to Packard:

One day a white crane man was assigned to a good crane that should have gone to a black... Black cranemen decided to sabotage production until this bullshit was straightened out. They had mild support from most white cranemen, who also thought the foreman was wrong.

Nothing can operate without the cranes bringing and taking steel, so blacks quietly stopped the whole mill. They kept the cranes in lowest gear and worked in super slow motion. Foremen soon began hatching out of their offices, looking around, rubbing their eyes in disbelief. It was like the whole building popped LSD or the air had turned into some kind of thick jelly: everything but the foremen moved at one-tenth of normal speed.[47]

Packard goes on to describe how "union sharpies swooped down" urging the men to "submit a grievance." He reports that after a couple of hours "the company backed down."

In Packard and Walker's descriptions of steel labor, the degree of "management" that is on the surface of the auto industry, or even a garment factory, is severely limited by the power of workers' cooperation. To be sure, "men don't usually talk about this stuff," according to Packard. "Communication is carried out through undercurrents and understandings" that are part of the workers' own unspoken cultural life within the mill. Occasionally, he reports, the right to "sluff off" by working less is a subject of wash-house graffiti.

Packard notes, "there is something revolutionary about the workers' controlling the pace of work in this way." At the same time he notes the "circles of soot-black hulking shapes sitting joyless, motionless around the salamanders."[48] Steel labor cannot be glorified beyond what it is— hard, dirty labor where autonomy is sought as a subversive activity. The culture that lurks beneath the surface is generated by the reconstitution of the labor as degraded.

But the workers have learned new skills; there is a "high rate of human interaction between all members of the crew either by word of mouth or by other means."[49] This report of Charles Walker, written in 1950 about a hot rolling mill, corresponds to Packard's description of life in a Gary, Indiana mill more than twenty-five years later. Even though considerable technological transformation has occurred in the steel industry in this period, it has not diminished the degree to which degradation is counteracted by the workers' own relationships. "This condition may be contrasted with certain jobs on the assembly line and with other types of work where layout and mechanical conditions often preclude such interaction during the working day."[50] In three major studies of steelworkers in America spanning a seventy-five-year period, the characteristic of a work culture remains throughout changing technical conditions.[51]

Crane operators are not de-skilled; many operations in modern steel-mills require collective rather than individual skills to manipulate machinery. While some rolling processes have been automated, a longtime struggle among steelworkers dating from the Homestead strike of 1892 has prevented capital from subsuming labor entirely by mechanization. The past twenty years have witnessed two major industry-wide strikes in steel and several stages of rank-and-file effort to make the United Steelworkers union responsive to the defense of a work culture that does control the pace of work under the older technologies. Unless the thesis of degradation is mediated dialectically by an understanding of work culture, it becomes a new orthodoxy, dogmatic and ideological, and prevents an understanding of how mass struggles are possible among workers.

Nor is the case of steel an exception to the general rule, of which the automobile assembly line may be considered paradigmatic. Close human interaction based on the persistence of "layout and mechanical conditions" have not succeeded in fragmenting and atomizing workers in mining, steel fabricating, and most labor-intensive industries such as textiles and clothing. The model of the assembly line is really an ideal for subsumption, not mainly because it de-skills, but because it separates labor during the working day and restricts its ability to act collectively to control the pace of work. What I wish to argue is that de-skilling is a historically relative category. Contemporary labor has, indeed, lost most of the old craft skills, but these have been replaced by new skills: workers today are obliged to be more inventive in their resistance. They can communicate by writing as much as by speech, thanks to the requirement that most workers be literate (and this requirement is more important in industries having continuous flow technologies than in mechanical trades).

Degradation has forced many workers to take their culture underground. Of course, this maneuver makes sociological and economic investigation harder, because it is not subject to the usual quantitative methods, such as survey research, interviews, or participant observation, except in unusual cases. For this reason, the nature of social investigation becomes significantly more complex to unearth these phenomena. The observer must, as Walker and Packard did, theorize the existence of culture in order to find it.

But just as the Ancient Order of Hibernians (the Molly Maguires) lit up the coalfields in the 1870s before formal union organization was well developed, the steel and longshore experiences[52] demonstrate the existence of two types of organization at the workplace (at least in the monopoly sectors where unionism is strong). The first is the formal organization of labor by management and by unions who are integrated into existing normative relations determined by capital's logic. Here I do not mean to reduce the trade unions entirely to functions of management, but rather to point out that the social organization of labor by capital defines the limits of trade union functions on a day-to-day level. The second is the self-organization of the workers into informal work groups (a term I learned from the excellent work of Stan Weir), which, although determined by layout and mechanical conditions as outer boundaries, have their elements of autonomy. That is, there are new "natural" conditions that countervail the imposition from above of conditions of labor. These conditions may be called "interactions," both spoken and gestural, personified and anonymous, written as graffiti and whispered as conspiracy.

Most sociologists and economists cannot grasp the significance of the play element in work culture, much less the existence of the culture itself. Since bourgeois training in sociology privileges the "scientific" mode of inquiry (read here, "positivist"), qualitative investigations are trivialized as so many forms of "poetry" or journalism. But is not the dialectic itself the "play" of oppositions, their mutual determination, rather than such rigid binaries as skill and de-skill? As workers lose many of their old skills to management, they acquire the new skills related to interaction.

(b) The second argument is the historical argument concerning the question of the uneven development of capital, both on a world scale and within the advanced capitalist countries themselves. The labor process varies within the same plant or industry as well, so that workers both acquire skills within the framework of technological change. The new skill of crane operation could be duplicated within the steel plant; workers now may bid for jobs as inspectors and other semi-clerical operations the character of which is not commensurable to the older processes, but not necessarily degraded, except by craft criteria. Older skills of heater and helpers on furnaces—while different from those performed in the iron foundries of the 1840s, or even in the Bessemer and early Open Hearth operation in the late nineteenth and early twentieth centuries, because of the introduction of new oxygen furnaces—are not comparable to automobile assembly work or assembly of television sets (although even here, the self-images of performing "donkey-work" ought not to obscure the significant degree to which mental and manual labor is combined in many operations, or the degree to which workers try to vary the labor by sub-rosa rotation schemes).

Moreover, many workers, perhaps a majority of those in manufacturing, are in labor-intensive industries in which older skills are still a significant component of the labor process. The tendency toward degradation is somewhat attenuated by the low capital-output ratio, the nature of the market for certain commodities, and the persistence of traditions among the workers. For every instance such as printing, where the old typesetting skills have become virtually extinct, mechanical processes in garment cutting have not succeeded in reducing the skill to a mere abstraction of capital.

Similarly, while the technology exists for replacing the meticulous machinist trade with numerically controlled lathes and milling machines, in which the programmer rather than the operator controls the process, it is also important to note that numerical controls have not yet dominated the machine tool industry, nor does their introduction signal absolute degradation except in comparison to a standard suggested by the old trade. Further, the introduction of numerical controls into machine tool plants has not meant that their use is by any means insured. Machine tool manufacturing plants have installed numerical controls devices that remain unemployed for various reasons: many toolmakers and machinists have claimed that their efficiency is debatable, and have either refused to work with them or have demonstrated their technological difficulties. The struggle over the use of numerical controls has not been won by management, and recent evidence points to a long-drawn-out fight. Similarly, recent technological changes in the steel industry are not of a qualitative nature; that is, many of them do not represent revolutionary new methods of production. Instead, many "improvements" are investments of mere replacement of worn-out equipment.

In sum, what lies behind much of the thesis of degradation is an anterior standard of craft, combined with a tendency toward overgeneralization that prevents investigators from making a concrete, historical study of the differences among industries, of the definition of skills and of the mediation of culture.

(c) Braverman's model of all capitalist production is the assembly line, exemplified by the ideology of Taylorism. But there is a substantial difference between the model of the reduction of work to a detail of capital accumulation, and its actual unfolding. Concrete investigations of types of work in advanced-, medium-, and low-technology industries would reveal that the work process is far more complex than the Taylorists would have liked.

Braverman, of course, understood the difference between the logic of degradation and its empirical reality. We must avoid the danger of taking the critique of Taylorism too literally. In the first place, the pace and direction of technological innovation is uneven for the economy as a whole, as well as for particular sectors. While upgrading is not the tendency of this innovation, its boundaries are determined by the struggle at the point of production as well as in the public sphere. For example, it took a compliant trade union to enable the steel industry to "modernize" its production, after twenty-five years of technological backwardness facilitated by the privileged position of US capital in the world market. Even though the Steelworkers union has agreed to a six-year contract without a strike, it is by no means inevitable that numerical controls will be widely introduced, that older plants will be shut down without resistance, and that strike activity will not disrupt production.

In this case, the logic of degradation is undeniable from the point of view of capital. But unless Marxists make *no* a priori theoretical assumptions about the results of the struggle, a concrete understanding of the situation is impossible. To be more general: any theoretical model must be mediated by the real relations of class struggle. In the final analysis, human praxis is not determined by its preconditions; only the boundaries of possibility are given in advance. But no situation points in a single direction: workers have choices, even within the framework of degraded labor, relative fragmentation, and the iron grip of bureaucratic unionism. These choices constitute the possibility for genuine contradictions, within the system, that may transcend it.

(d) The moment of praxis is relatively autonomous. That is, a theory of determination is only part of the "algebra of revolution." It is not a question of what workers or degraded members of the middle strata think, but of what they do. Could capital logic have predicted that Paris technicians and broadcasters would have seized communications media on behalf of the revolt during May–June 1968? Could the LIP strike against the shutdown of a watch factory have been predicted, or that workers would have resumed watch production on their own, rather than setting up a picket line as in bourgeois unionist practice? Of course, each of these circumstances may be considered "exceptional" because they have specific features, such as a large body of relatively skilled workers in each setting. Or American coal miners' struggles in the recent past could be explained as an exception, since they still have a living historical culture. Or Italian Fiat workers' struggles since the mid-1960s, or the Clyde shipyard workers' seizure of their workplace. What these events of the past decade show is that a Marxism shorn of a theory of culture, of everyday life, becomes a recipe rather than a living theory.

(e) The final point concerns the theory of ideology, to which I have already referred. Althusser's theory of ideology constitutes a valuable addition to the concept of ideology as the perception of the form of appearance of social relations. His notion of ideology as a set of material practices through which people live their experience of capitalist social relations enables us to understand the concept of mediation as a material force and to remove it from its ideal form. Mediations are inscribed in institutions which are the scenes of the social reproduction of capital, that is, in the ways in which labor is reproduced in the family, school, religion, and bourgeois trade unions. These are not just groups to which persons adhere in the same way that they wear clothes or own a television set. What we mean by experience is materialized within these institutions, and they are contradictory in their internal relations just as the point of production is formed out of the contradiction between labor and capital. These institutions are determined only in the last instance by the conditions of capitalist domination, but function relatively autonomously within the social process.

The class struggle, then, is conducted at the ideological level, as well as at the point of production (even within the realm of theory as a practice

and not merely as a "battle of ideas"). Since the process by which domination is legitimated and internalized depends upon the degree to which
institutional life, or what I will call everyday life, is experienced as rational, to that degree labor can be subsumed under capital. Thus, the point
of production is only one side of the social totality, even if it is a central
aspect of it. The displacement of the contradictions of the accumulation
process to the sphere of social consumption—by which I mean the totality
of relations inscribed ideologically within institutions but also experienced as language, interaction, and artistic culture—constitutes both an
integrating and oppositional feature of contemporary capitalism.

The descriptions by Baran and Sweezy, as well as Braverman in his
chapter "The Universal Marketplace,"[53] reveal the pitfalls of capital-logic
analysis because these phenomena are not grasped dialectically, but are
understood as mere functions of capital, subject to the same laws of subsumption. An alternative understanding would entail an examination
of the cultural contradictions of capitalism in order to locate the crisis
features of the system which are not typically manifested as a problem
of accumulation. Marxists have been mystified by the forms of appearance insofar as they have reduced all capitalist contradictions to their
economic dimension.

Another feature of ideology is Gramsci's concept of bourgeois hegemony, which is defined as the process by which capital secures the "spontaneous consent" of the masses to its "general direction of social life."[54]
Gramsci argues that this consent must be won through the mediation of
intellectuals who struggle for moral and intellectual leadership of society.
Their self-understanding, of course, is far from that of conscious agents
of the bourgeoisie. Rather, capital wins their consent by persuading them
that intellectual life is free of the rule of society, much less capital. An example of this form of appearance of autonomy is the slogan "art for art's
sake," or the notion of "pure science" that has no apparent functional
relation with production.

Gramsci theorizes the possibility that bourgeois hegemony may fail,
because consent of either the intellectuals or the masses cannot be won
under certain circumstances. Capital tries to confine intellectual functions to "the social necessities of production"[55] but the character of

bourgeois democratic society expands intellectual functions beyond this sphere. The sphere of social consumption, the production of ideologies, the unemployment of intellectuals, all subvert capital logic, which functions at best as a broad framework for cultural and intellectual discourse. Within this framework, oppositional ideologies contend for hegemony against the dominant ideology. For example, within the bourgeois university, Marxism may be said to be oppositional within the framework of bourgeois hegemony, so long as its theories and research is confined to the work of intellectuals. When the working class and middle strata call into existence their own intellectuals, or, to use Gramsci's terms, when they establish their hegemony over a group of intellectuals, Marxism and other revolutionary doctrines become "counter-hegemonic" in character. That is, as Marx remarked, theory becomes a material force "when it has gripped the masses." Gramsci's clarification is important here because of this reversal of the meaning of the process: theory becomes a revolutionary force when the masses have gripped the theoreticians against bourgeois hegemony. The signal contribution of Gramsci was to remind us that the level of struggle for "moral and intellectual" leadership is a sphere of class struggle, wherein this struggle, if conducted with determination, reduces the chance of the "spontaneous consent" capital seeks for its domination over labor.

NOTES

1. For an interesting convergence on the question of the autonomy of the forces of production compare Karl Kautsky, *Class Struggle*, especially part 4 (New York, 1971), with Joseph Stalin, *Dialectical and Historical Materialism*, first published as a section of his History of the CPSU (B) and subsequently reprinted in pamphlet form. In both treatments of the theory of social revolution, the concept of the irreconcilability of the forces of production and the capitalist relations of production is seen as the driving force for socialist transformation. However, the forces of production are viewed by both as subversive to capitalist relations because they have been socialized and represent the accumulation of human labor including its form as knowledge. In this perspective, capitalism fetters the productive forces which seek room to develop under a system of socialized property (Stalin referred to this process as the cunning of history, an adaptation of Hegel's concept of the cunning

of reason that, however repressed, becomes the unifying force of historical development).

2. See V.I. Lenin *Imperialism: The Highest State of Capitalism.*

3. Jürgen Habermas, *Knowledge and Human Interests* (Boston: Beacon Press, 1971); Alvin Gouldner, *Dialectic of Technology and Ideology* (New York: Seabury Press, 1976); Marshall Sahlins, *Culture and Practical Reason* (Chicago: University of Chicago Press, 1976); Pierre Bourdieu, *Outline of a Theory of Practice* (Cambridge: Cambridge University Press, 1977); Jean Baudrillard, *Mirror of Production* (St Louis: Telos Press, 1975).

4. It should be pointed out that Marx himself was not a subsumption theorist. Rather he regarded subsumption as a moment in the social process. To those who may object that the evidence for this thesis which has been called "capital-logic" by some European Marxist writers remains fragmentary, I would retort that all of Marx's writings after 1850 have a fragmentary character since his magnum opus *Capital* was never finished during his lifetime. Further, the theory of relative surplus value to which I will refer below contains the seed of the subsumption thesis insofar as the formula entails the assertion that enlarging the volume of surplus value becomes a function of reducing the laborer in comparison to the value of the commodity. In the period of machine production and especially the so-called third industrial revolution of recent times, the domination of capital is immeasurably enlarged by virtue of its capacity to subsume all the factors of production.

5. See Max Horkheimer and Theodore Adorno, *Dialectic of the Enlightenment* (New York: Seabury Press, 1972); and Herbert Marcuse, *One Dimensional Man* (Boston: Beacon Press, 1964); Hans Magnus Enzensberger, *The Consciousness Industry* (New York: Seabury Press, 1974), ch. 1; Henri Lefebvre, *Everyday Life in the Modern World* (New York: Harper and Row, 1971).

6. Among the most recent work in this area see especially Nicos Poulantzas, *Political Power and Social Classes* (London: New Left Books, 1974); and Ralph Miliband, *State in Capitalist Society* (New York: Pantheon Books). The Miliband-Poulantzas debate on certain points of the theory of the state does not obviate their essential agreement on its integrative functions. Following Louis Althusser, Poulantzas expands the concept of the state to include the family and trade unions. These "ideological apparatuses" of the state function to preserve the rule of capital by penetrating the spheres of working-class activity that were once autonomous. We cannot explore the theoretical underpinnings of this view here, but it suffices to point out that the Althusserians advance a mechanism of subsumption which is at once novel and depressing when they insist that ideology is a material practice. Since bourgeois ideas are hegemonic in capitalist society, their materialization within the public and private spheres of working-class life extends the rule of capital beyond the

workplace or the institutions of repression such as the police and courts. Miliband adopts the thesis of capitalist integration exemplified in the ability of the modern state to accommodate working-class demands for reform, even at the structural level, including the possibility that labor and socialist parties may manage the capitalist state.

7. Harry Braverman, *Labor and Monopoly Capital* (New York, Monthly Review Press, 1974); Stephen Marglin, "What Do Bosses Do?", in *The Division of Labor,* ed. André Gorz (London: Harvester Press, 1976); Kathy Stone, "Origin of Job Structures in the Steel Industry," *RRPE,* Summer, 1974; and André Gorz, "Technology, Technicians and the Class Struggle," in Gorz (ed.), op. cit.

8. Antonio Gramsci's "Americanism and Fordism," in *Selections from Prison Notebooks,* ed. Quintin Hoare and Geoffrey Nowell-Smith (New York: International Publishers, 1971).

9. Karl Marx, *Contribution to the Critique of Political Economy,* trans. N. Stone (Chicago: Charles Kerr Co., 1904).

10. All references are from the Penguin edition of *Capital* (London: 1976).

11. See Frederic Fleron (ed.), *Technology and Communist Culture* (New York: Praeger, 1977); particularly Andrew Feenberg's "Transition or Convergence: Communism and the Paradox of Development," where he argues that technology transfer does not automatically imply the convergence of capitalism and socialism because socialism has its cultural autonomy that mediates the ideological impact of technology.

12. In Marx, *Capital,* included as an appendix to the 1976 Penguin edition.

13. The basis of Marx's hostility to the political programs of anarchism and of the utopian socialists of his day, which in the Soviet-produced Foreign Languages Publishing House edition of *Selected Correspondence,* are termed "petty bourgeois," was his scorn for their belief in the concept of self-directed workers' cooperatives or councils within the framework of the industrial stage of capitalist production. In the 1840s Marx was particularly concerned to reduce the influence of Pierre Joseph Proudhon because he held that the demand to restore the artisanal mode of production when elements of producer control still existed was nothing but the pipe dream of a stratum of society that could only look backward rather than discover how socialism could arise from the conditions of capitalist development. The popularity of ideas of producer control over production, of cooperatives, and of anti-industrialism within the socialist movement was to plague Marx and Engels throughout their activity in the First International and after its demise in 1864. The problem was that Marx's critique of capitalism was grounded in the British case, which for most of the nineteenth century was an exception to the general pattern

of economic and social development. The fundamental strength of Proudhonism was in the Mediterranean countries and Latin America, where artisanship was very much alive and the predatory impact of imperialism that was destroying this mode of production was among the best recruiting grounds for revolutionary socialism, if not its Marxian variety. Of course, Marx did not oppose self-management as a socialist goal, but he believed that the struggle against capital had to be based upon the "mass" worker, i.e. on that growing portion of the working class for whom the artisanal mode was not even a living memory.

14. Marx, op. cit.

15. Ibid. 986.

16. Ibid. 1029–30.

17. Ibid. 1065.

18. Ibid.

19. Karl Marx, *Grundrisse* (London: Penguin Books, 1973).

20. Karl Marx, *Capital*, vol. i, sec. 4, and also "Results of the Immediate Process of Production," 1005–6.

21. Braverman, op. cit., chs. 6 and 13.

22. Ibid., ch. 4. But in his section on science and technology "as such" this insight is partially nullified by his failure to come to grips with science and technology as ideology. See chs. 7 and 8 especially for this point.

23. Unfortunately most Marxists read about Proudhon through Marx, especially his *Poverty of Philosophy*, a merciless attack against Proudhon's *Philosophy of Poverty* in which the concept of property as theft is enunciated. In fact, although Marx and Engels regarded some of Proudhon's doctrines as wrong-headed and even dangerous to the socialist movement, they adapted many of his ideas to their own, particularly the idea that communism was the free association of producers and that worker's self-management of production was a necessary condition of human emancipation. See the writings of Pierre Joseph Proudhon.

24. E.J. Dijksterhuis, *The Mechanization of the World Picture* (New York: Oxford University Press, 1961).

25. Louis Althusser, *For Marx*, trans. Ben Brewster (New York: Vintage Books, 1970).

26. Dijksterhuis, op. cit. 3.

27. Georg Simmel, *Philosophie Des Geldes* (Leipzig: 1900); Franz Borkenau, *Studies in the History of the Period of Manufacture* (in German) (Paris: 1934). Simmel's book, which has never been translated into English except fragments in several anthologies of his writings, must be rated as among the masterpieces of the theory of reification which

has influenced Lukács's *History and Class Consciousness*, and was itself an important addition to the critique of bourgeois culture, albeit from a non-Marxist, neo-Kantian perspective. I have not read Borkenau's book.

28. Marx, *Capital*, vol. i, ch. 1, especially sec. 4, "The Fetishism of Commodities." Also Georg Lukács's *History and Class Consciousness* (Boston: MIT Press, 1971); "Reification and the Consciousness of the Proletariat." The theory of appearances extends to the idea that science and technology may be forms of thought that enjoy a relation with nature unmediated by ideological forms is a result of the rise of the scientific world view during the renaissance according to which empirical verification of propositions about the world can be derived from experiment and the evidence of the senses, in the last instance. The power of Marx and Lukács is their insistence on a historical framework for all knowledge which, under the capitalist mode of production takes the form of ideological production as a mediation of and concomitant of science for reasons explained below.

29. Braverman, op. cit., 159. My objection to this formulation is that it tries to establish a causal relation between these advances and the new epoch of industry without comprehending not only the social conditions within which the advances were made, but also the ideological struggles that helped form scientific thought. However, Braverman understands the relation of scientific development to the development of technique following the work of David Landes in *The Unbound Prometheus* and thus breaks with the conventional view of the determination of social relations by the "forces of production," which in the Marxism of Kautsky, Plekhanov, and Stalin are the driving forces of history.

30. Marx, *Grundrisse*, 693.

31. Marx, *Capital*, 1066–71 (The Sale of Labour Power and Trade Unions).

32. Marx, *Grundrisse*, 693.

33. Ibid.

34. Braverman, op. cit. 26–7.

35. Gorz, op. cit.

36. Ibid. 162–3.

37. Marx, *Capital*, vol. iii, ch. 14.

38. Ibid. 277.

39. V. I. Lenin, *Imperialism: The Highest Stage of Capitalism*, in Selected Works, vol. v. Also in the same volume a more explicit application of the theory to the concept of the Right of Nations to Self-Determination which is included in part 4 as a series of theses called "The Socialist Revolution and the Right of Nations to Self-Determination." The content of the strategic argument between Lenin and the Bolsheviks and the German

social democrats whose chief spokesperson on this question was Rosa Luxemburg is too well known to be repeated here. Suffice it to say that for Lenin, the results of the export of capital, i.e. foreign trade in capital as well as commodities, were both to temporarily resolve the tendency within the advanced capitalist countries towards crisis and to provoke a political, economic, and cultural crisis within the colonial and semi-colonial countries owing to the constraints of capitalist domination on the native bourgeoisie and the brutal exploitation of wage labor within extractive industries of these countries.

40. Karl Marx, *The Eighteenth Brumaire of Louis Bonaparte*, in Karl Marx, *Surveys from Exile*, Political Writings, vol. ii, ed. David Fernbach (New York: Vintage Books, 1974). See especially part 7, p. 239, where Marx offers the only "definition" of class under capitalism in his work.

41. Herbert Marcuse, *One Dimensional Man* (Boston: Beacon Press, 1964). While Marcuse seems often too impressed by the degree to which technology has become a social force *sui generis*, his descriptions of the transformation of critical reason into instrumental technical thought in which among other things language as discourse is pressed into the service of domination, is an important concretization of the thesis of real subsumption.

42. For the Marx of *Economic and Philosophical Manuscripts* and *German Ideology*, praxis is the self-conscious political and social activity of humans directed towards purposive goals. Here determination by past praxis became the "conditions" of this activity in the present. But just as living labor cannot be entirely determined by its past, congealed form, so the social conditions in which classes in society confront their own future cannot circumscribe either the content or the form in which emancipatory practice occurs. There is a moment of indeterminacy in the collective action, that is, the transformation of what Sartre calls "seriality" into fusion, the process by which people take control of their own activity calls into existence new forms of social life, i.e. self-management.

43. For the most comprehensive treatment of the question of work culture, I have consulted the unpublished manuscript of Stan Weir on the work culture of Longshore industry of the US West Coast. Scheduled for publication by Free Press.

44. Henri Lefebvre, *The Explosion*, (New York: Monthly Review Press, 1969), 7.

45. See Stanley Aronowitz, *False Promises*, (New York: McGraw Hill, 1973), ch. 1.

46. Charles Walker, *Steeltown* (New Haven: Yale University Press, 1950); Steve Packard *Steelmill Blues* (San Pedro: Singlejack Books, 1978).

47. Packard, op. cit. 12–3.

48. Ibid. 14–6.

49. Walker, op. cit. 81–2.

169

50. Ibid., 83. Yet, the auto industry has produced more militancy in the past forty-five years than any other manufacturing sector. Even the "layout and mechanical conditions" of "pure" execution has not prevented the collective laborer from struggling against speedup. Not that the pace of the auto assembly line remains about where it was in 1955 except in Lordstown and a few other small-car plants.

51. They are David Brody, *Steelworkers in America* (Cambridge: Harvard University Press, 1960); John Fitch, *Steelworkers* (repr., New York: Arno Press, 1969); and William T. Hogan, *Economic History of the Iron and Steel Industry in the United States*, 5 vols. (Lexington, Mass.: D.D. Heath Co. 1971).

52. Weir, op. cit.

53. Braverman, op. cit., ch. 14. This is perhaps the weakest chapter of his book because of its failure to probe the specificity of cultural questions and its methodological functionalism.

54. Gramsci, op. cit. 12–3.

55. Ibid.

CHAPTER FOUR

Trade Unionism: Illusion and Reality

I

The configuration of strikes since 1967 is unprecedented in the history of American workers. The number of strikes as a whole, as well as rank-and-file rejections of proposed union settlements with employers, and wildcat actions has exceeded that in any similar period in the modern era.

The most notable feature of the present situation is that the unions are no longer in a position of leadership in workers' struggles; they are running desperately to catch up to their own membership. There are few instances in which the union heads have actually given militant voice to rank-and-file sentiment. In many cases, union sanctions for walkouts have followed the workers' own action. In others, the leadership has attempted to thwart membership initiative and, having failed, has supported a strike publicly while sabotaging it behind the scenes. For the most part, the national bureaucracies of the unions have sided with employers in trying to impose labor peace upon a rebellious membership. What is remarkable is that the rebellion has been largely successful despite enormous odds.

The unions are afraid to oppose the rank and file directly. Their opposition has taken the form of attempting to channel the broad range of rank-and-file grievances into bargaining demands which center, in the main, on wages and benefits, while the huge backlog of grievances on issues having to do with working conditions remains unsolved.

Rank-and-file militancy has occurred precisely because of the refusal of the unions to address themselves to the issues of speedup, health and safety, plant removal, increased workloads, technological change, and arbitrary discharges of union militants.

Wages have, of course, also been an enormously important factor in accounting for the rash of strikes. Since 1967, workers have suffered a pronounced deterioration in living standards. Despite substantial increases in many current settlements, real wages for the whole working class have declined annually, for there are few contracts which provide for cost-of-living increases in addition to the negotiated settlements. Even where C-o-L clauses have been incorporated into the contracts, there is usually a ceiling on the amount of increase to which the company is obligated. In many contracts, the first-year increase is equal to the cost of living increase as tabulated by the Bureau of Labor Statistics for the previous year. But the second- and third-year increases are usually not as great and during these years workers' real wages are diminished significantly.

Long-term contracts, which have become standard in American industry, have robbed the rank and file of considerable power to deal with their problems within the framework of collective bargaining. Workers have been forced to act outside of approved procedures because instinctively they know that the union has become an inadequate tool to conduct struggles, even where they have not yet perceived the union as an outright opponent to their interests.

For most workers, the trade union still remains the elementary organ of defense of their immediate economic interests. Despite the despicable performance of labor movement leadership during the past thirty years, and especially in the last two decades, blue- and white-collar workers regard their unions as their only weapons against the deterioration of working conditions and the rampant inflation responsible for recent declines in real wages.

In part, trade unions retain their legitimacy because no alternative to them exists. In part, workers join unions because the unions give the appearance of advancing workers' interests, since they must do so to some extent to gain their support. A national union bureaucracy can betray the workers' elementary demands for a considerable period of time without generating open opposition among the rank and file. Even when workers are aware of the close ties that exist between the union leaders and the employers, rebellion remains a difficult task for several crucial reasons.

First, in many cases, the union bureaucracy is far removed from the shop floor because membership is scattered over many plants or even industries. In unions like the United Steelworkers, only half the 1.2 million members are employed in the basic steel sector of the industry. The rest of the membership spans the nonferrous metals industry, steel fabricating plants, stone working, can companies, and even a few coal mines. Most of the membership is in large multiplant corporations that have successfully decentralized their operations so that no single plant or cluster of factories in a single geographic region is capable of affecting production decisively. The problem of diffusion is complicated by the recent trend of US corporations to expand their manufacturing operations abroad rather than within this country. In these circumstances, many workers, unable to communicate with workers in other plants of the same corporation since the union has centralized communications channels, feel powerless to improve their own conditions.

Second, the structure of collective bargaining enables the national union to transfer responsibility to the local leadership for failures of the union contract on working conditions issues, while claiming credit for substantial improvements in wages and benefits. This practice has been notable in the Auto Workers, the Rubber Workers, and others that have national contracts with large corporations.

Although the last decade has been studded with examples of rank-and-file uprisings against the least responsible of the labor bureaucrats, in nearly all cases, the new group of elected leaders has merely reproduced the conditions of the old regime. In the steel, rubber, electrical, government workers, and other important unions one can observe some differences in sensitivity to the rank and file among the newer leaders. They are more willing to conduct strike struggles and their political sophistication is greater. But these unions can hardly be called radical nor have they made sharp breaks from the predominant policies of the labor movement in the contemporary era.

Some radicals explain this phenomenon in a purely idealistic way. According to them, the weakness of the factional struggles within the unions over the past decade has been that they have been conducted without an ideological perspective that differs from the procapitalist bias of the prevailing leadership. The left has been largely irrelevant to them. Therefore, if the new leadership merely recapitulates "the same old crap" (Marx's words), radicals should blame their own failure to concentrate their political work within the working class. Presumably, a strong left could have altered the kind of leadership and the program of the rank-and-file movements.

There is undoubtedly some truth in these assertions. Yet the disturbing fact is that the communist left was very much a part of the trade union leadership for several decades prior to 1950; in some unions there are remnants of the left still in power. There is a tendency to explain the failure of the old communist left by reference to its "revisionist" policies. Such superficial explanations assume that if only the politics of radical labor organizers had been better, the whole picture would have been qualitatively different. This will be shown not to be the case.

If the trade union remains an elementary organ of struggle, it has also evolved into a force for integrating the workers into the corporate capitalist system. Inherent in the modern labor contract is the means both to insure some benefit to the workers and to provide a stable, disciplined labor force to the employer. The union assumes obligations as well as wins rights in the collective bargaining agreement.

Under contemporary monopolistic capitalism, these obligations include: (*i*) the promise not to strike, except under specific conditions, or at the termination of the contract, (*ii*) a bureaucratic and hierarchical grievance procedure consisting of many steps during which the control over the grievance is systematically removed from the shop floor and from workers' control, (*iii*) a system of management prerogatives wherein the union agrees to cede to the employer "the operation of the employer's facilities and the direction of the working forces, including the right to hire, suspend, or discharge for good cause and...to relieve employees from duties due to lack of work,"[1] and (*iv*) a "checkoff" of union dues as an automatic deduction from the workers' paychecks.

The last provision, incorporated into ninety-eight per cent of union contracts, treats union dues as another tax on workers' wages. It is a major barrier to close relations between union leaders and the rank and file. Workers have come to regard the checkoff as another insurance premium. Since they enjoy little participation in union affairs, except when they have an individual grievance or around contract time, the paying of dues in this manner—designed originally to protect the union's financial resources—has removed a major point of contact between workers and their full-time representatives. This procedure is in sharp contrast to former times when the shop steward or business agent was obliged to collect dues by hand. In that period, the dues collection process, however cumbersome for the officials, provided an opportunity for workers to voice their complaints as well as a block against the encroachment of bureaucracy.

The modern labor agreement is the principal instrument of the class collaboration between the trade unions and the corporations. It mirrors the bureaucratic and hierarchical structure of modern industry and the state. Its provisions are enforced not merely by law, but by the joint efforts of corporate and trade union bureaucracies. Even the most enlightened trade union leader cannot fail to play his part as an element in the mechanisms of domination over workers' rights to spontaneously struggle against speedup or *de facto* wage cuts, either in the form of a shift in the work process or by inflationary price increases.

The role of collective bargaining today is to provide a rigid institutional framework for the conduct of the class struggle. This struggle at the point of production has become regulated in the same way as have electric and telephone rates, prices of basic commodities, and foreign trade. The regulatory procedure in labor relations includes government intervention into collective bargaining, the routinization of all conflict between labor and the employer on the shop floor, and the placing of equal responsibility for observing plant rules upon management and the union.

The objective of this procedure is to control labor costs as a stable factor of production in order to permit rational investment decisions by the large corporations. The long-term contract insures that labor costs will be a known factor. It guarantees labor peace for a specified period of time. The agreement enables employers to avoid the disruption characteristic of stormier periods of labor history when workers' struggles were much more spontaneous, albeit more difficult.

An important element in the labor contract is that most of the day-to-day issues expressing the conflict between worker and employer over the basic question of the division of profit are not subject to strikes. In the automobile and electrical agreements as well as a few others, the union has the right to strike over speedup, safety issues, or a few other major questions. In the main, however, most complaints about working conditions and work assignments are adjusted in the final step of the grievance procedure by an "impartial" arbitrator selected by both the union and management. Even in industries where the strike weapon is a permitted option, the union leaders usually put severe pressure on the rank and file to choose the arbitration route since strikes disrupt the good relations between the union bureaucracy and management—good relations which are valued highly by liberal corporate officials and union leaders alike.

With few exceptions, particularly in textile and electrical corporations, employers regard labor leaders as their allies against the ignorant and undisciplined rank and file. This confidence has been built up over the past thirty-five years of industrial collective bargaining.

The trade unions have become an appendage of the corporations because they have taken their place as a vital institution in the corporate capitalist complex. If union leaders are compelled to sanction and often give at least verbal support to worker demands, it is most often because the union is a political institution whose membership selects officials. However, almost universally, the democratic foundations of the trade unions have been undermined.

The left understood that the old craft unions were essentially purveyors of labor power, controlling both the supply of skilled labor and its price. The most extreme expression of their monopoly was the terror and violence practiced by craft union leadership against the rank and file. Since the old unions were defined narrowly by their economic functions and by their conservative ideology, the assumption of the socialists and communists who helped build industrial unions which included the huge mass of unskilled and semiskilled workers was that these organizations would express broader political and social interests, if not radical ideologies.

On the whole, despite corruption and bureaucratic resistance to the exercise of membership control, many unions in the United States have retained the forms but not the content of democracy. It is possible to re-move union leaders and replace them, but it is not possible to transcend the institutional constraints of trade unionism itself.

Trade unions have fallen victim to the same disease as the broader electoral and legislative system. Just as the major power over the state has shifted from the legislative to the executive branch of government, power over union affairs has shifted from the rank and file to the cor-porate leaders, the trade union officials, and the government. Trade un-ions are regulated by the state both in their relations with employers and in their internal operations. Moreover, the problems of union leadership have been transformed from political and social issues to the routines of contract administration and internal bureaucratic procedures, such as union finances. The union leader is a business executive. His account-ability is not limited to the membership—it is extended to government agencies, arbitrators, courts of law, and other institutions which play a large role in regulating the union's operations.

The contradictory role of trade unions is played out at every contract negotiation in major industries. Over the past several years the chasm between the leadership and membership has never been more exposed. During this period, a rising number of contract settlements have been re-jected by the rank and file; in 1968, the proportion of rejection was nearly thirty per cent. In contract bargaining the rank and file has veto power, but no means of initiative. In the first place, many major industries have agreements which are negotiated at the national level. There is room for local bargaining over specific shop issues, but the main lines of economic settlements are determined by full-time officials of the company and the union. One reason for this concentration of power is the alleged techni-cal nature of collective bargaining in the modern era. Not only leaders and representatives of the local membership sit on the union's side of the bargaining table, but lawyers, insurance and pension experts, and sometimes even management consultants as well; the rank-and-file com-mittees tend to be relegated to advisory or window-dressing functions or simply play the role of bystander. The product of the charade that is characteristic of much of collective bargaining today is a mammoth document which reads more like a corporate contract or a mortgage agreement than anything else. In fact, it is a bill of sale.

The needs of the membership only partially justify the specialization of functions within the trade unions. Insurance and pension plans do require a certain expertise, but the overall guidance of the direction of worker-employer relationships has been centralized as a means of preventing the direct intervention of the rank and file. More, the domination of specialists within the collective bargaining process signals the removal of this process from the day-to-day concerns of the workers. The special language of the contract, its bulk and its purely administrative character put its interpretation beyond the grasp of the rank and file and help perpetuate the centrality of the professional expert in the union hierarchy.

In this connection, it is no accident that the elected union official has only limited power within the collective bargaining ritual (and, in a special sense, within the union itself). Few national union leaders make decisions either in direct consultation with the membership or with fellow elected officials. It is the hired expert who holds increased power in union affairs and who acts as a buffer for the union official between the corporate hierarchy and the restive rank and file. As in other institutions, experts have been used to rationalize the conservatism of the leadership in technical and legal terms, leaving officials free to remain politically viable by supporting the sentiments expressed by the membership while, at the same time, rejecting their proposed actions. The importance of the experts has grown with the legalization of collective bargaining, especially the management of labor conflict by the courts and the legislatures, with legislation, and restraining orders limiting strikes, picketing, and other traditional working-class weapons. In industries considered public utilities, such as the railroads, a strike is almost always countered by a court order enjoining the workers from taking direct action on the grounds that such action constitutes a violation of the national interest. The lawyer has become a key power broker between the workers, their unions, and the government. He is considered an indispensable operative in contemporary labor relations.

Some unions have promoted their house counsels from staff to officers. The secretary-treasurer of the Amalgamated Clothing Workers of America was formerly general counsel; its president began his career as counsel for the Detroit Joint Board of the union. The president of the United Packinghouse Workers was also its counsel for many years. But even without holding executive office the labor lawyer is placed in a position of both influence and ultimately of power within the organization by the increasing volume of government regulation of all types of trade union affairs. The same tendency can be observed within corporations where, together with financial experts, attorneys are replacing production men as the new men of power.

During the past decade in the auto, steel, rubber, and other basic manufacturing industries, the critical issues of working-class struggle have been those related to control over the workplace. The tremendous shifts in plant location, work methods, job definitions, and other problems associated with investment in new equipment, expansion, and the changing requirements of skills to operate new means of production, have found the union bureaucracies unprepared. The reasons for trade union impotence at the workplace go beyond ideology. They are built into the sinews of the collective bargaining process.

Many important industries have national contracts covering most monetary issues, including wages. In the electrical, auto, and steel industries, negotiations are conducted with individual companies, but in reality there is "pattern" bargaining. A single major producer is chosen by the union and corporations to determine wage and fringe benefit settlement for the rest of the industry. All other negotiations stall until the central settlement is reached.

National union leadership always poses wage demands as the most important negotiating issues. Problems such as technological changes, work assignments, job classifications, and pace of work are usually negotiated at the local level after the economic pack age has been settled. And by the time the local negotiations begin—often conducted between rank-and-file leaders and middle managers—the national union has lost interest in the contract. Its entire orientation is toward the narrowly defined "economic" side of the bargaining. Although many agreements stipulate that resumption of work will not take place before the resolution of local issues, the international representatives and top leaders of the union put enormous pressure on the membership to settle these issues as quickly as possible. It is at the plant level that most sellouts take place. The local feels abandoned, but resentment is diverted to the failure of the shop leadership rather than that of the top bureaucracy, because the national union has "delivered the goods" on wages and benefits.

For example, after every national auto settlement, a myriad of local walkouts are called over workplace issues. These strikes are short-lived and usually unsuccessful. In the main, in struggles against speedup, young workers and blacks are the spearhead. The impatience of the bureaucracy with this undisciplined action is usually expressed in long harangues to local leaders and the rank and file by international representatives who are employees of the national union. When persuasion fails, the rebellious local is sometimes put into receivership and an administrator is sent from the head office to take it over until order is restored.

Among radicals the conventional wisdom of today is to admit the conservative character of trade unions in the era of monopoly capitalism—their integration and subordination to the large corporations. At the same time, many radicals stress the important defensive role trade unions perform during the periods when growing capitalist instability forces employers to launch an offensive against workers' living standards and working conditions. Despite the conservative ideology of labor leaders and legal constraints upon them, rank-and-file pressure today is occasionally able to force unions to lead the fight against employer efforts to transfer to the working class the burdens of recessions or the dislocations of the labor force that occur during periods of technological change.

A recent illustration was provided by the 1969 national General Electric (GE) strike. The conjuncture of inflation, deteriorating working conditions, and the arrogant bargaining posture of the company produced the first unified strike in the electrical industry in twenty-three years. It does not matter that the leaders of the AFL-CIO unions representing most of the workers wanted neither the strike nor unity with the independent United Electrical Workers. Rank-and-file pressure within the largest AFL-CIO union in the industry, the International Union of Electrical Workers, was sufficient to threaten the hegemony of the leadership and reverse the timid collective bargaining strategies of past contract negotiations. Repeatedly rejecting offers by the unions for arbitration of outstanding issues, GE attempted to win a clear-cut victory in order to break the emerging solidarity of the workers and set a pattern for other industries. Its objective was a return to the old divide-and-conquer practice of a separate agreement with each union, but for a time it had little success in encouraging back-to-work movements.

Yet it would be a mistake to infer from the GE experience that temporary trade union militancy in response to employer opposition signals an end to class collaboration or the institutional constraints of collective bargaining on workers' autonomy. In fact, the GE strike points sharply to the persistence and dominance of these constraints. The call by the unions for arbitration and acceptance of the intervention of "neutral" political figures such as Senator Javits in a fact-finding investigation was an indication that the leadership lacked confidence in the ability of the workers to win their own struggle and sought to end the strike as soon as possible. The trade union movement, particularly the AFL-CIO with its tremendous financial resources and thirteen million members, could not effectively mobilize support for the boycott that had been called by AFL-CIO President George Meany to supplement the electrical workers' own efforts.

The weakness of the strike was not a lack of willingness to fight on the part of workers. Despite the past sellouts, and the paternalism and anti-communism used for years to split their ranks, GE workers exhibited tremendous courage and a capacity for organized struggle in defending their living standards. But, locked within the apparatus of bureaucratic unionism, the workers were unable to broaden the struggle beyond the quantitative economic terms framed by the leadership. The strike was settled on the basis of agreement on wages and the cost-of-living clause — with all other demands referred to arbitration and discussion.

In 1971, top union leaders reacted with militant rhetoric to President Nixon's announced wage freeze; in this case, they could not simply give outright support to government and corporate efforts to discipline the work force. Officials from all wings of organized labor attacked the freeze, declaring that it amounted to a windfall for big business. George Meany led the barrage of invective against the administration, threatening a rash of strikes if the freeze was maintained. Leonard Woodcock, the head of the million-and-a-half member United Auto Workers, declared that the union would cancel its contracts with auto-makers unless the freeze was rescinded or the government took steps to place severe enforceable restrictions on prices at the same time. Harry Bridges of the West Coast Longshoremen, the grand old man of labor's decimated independent "left-wing" unions, refused to end the coastwide strike currently in progress.

Behind the threats of mass strikes and scorn for the wage freeze demand, however, were factors more indicative of the real positions of the unions. In the first place, the unions would have risked another blow to their declining prestige among the rank and file if they had refused to protest the blatant inequality contained in the President's order. Second, Meany himself had been proposing a wage-price freeze since 1969. Union leaders were willing to suspend the strike weapon and demands for wage increases if the administration was prepared to impose similarly stringent controls over prices. In effect, they were prepared to accept another step in the direction of government regulation of labor relations if the corporations would agree to the principle of "equality of sacrifices." Third, unions had warmly cooperated with two previous freezes imposed by Democratic administrations during World War II and again during the Korean War. There was much suspicion that the unions would not have reacted so vocally to the order of a Democratic President. In the end, after much vacillation, top union leaders, even the "liberal" Woodcock, rejoined the board set up by President Nixon to implement the freeze.

Even during the 1950s union leaders were often forthright in their criticism of the big-business orientation of the Republican Eisenhower administration, particularly with respect to economic policies. But one must recall the feeble union response to the enactment of the Landrum-Griffin Act in 1959 to keep the infrequent evidence of rhetorical militancy in perspective. Although the bill to extend controls over labor's financial affairs was introduced by a Republican and a Southern Democrat, it had genuine bipartisan support, including the active backing of then Senator John F. Kennedy. Union lobbyists welcomed

Kennedy's participation in the formation of the legislation because they appreciated his efforts to moderate the extent of controls. Only the Teamsters Union and the handful of other independent unions really opposed the bill. For the most part, union leaders were unwilling to fight the legislation because they felt that it was inevitable. Moreover, they had been convinced by many of their loyal congressional supporters that outright rejection of the idea of reporting and disclosing union finances would merely provoke a movement for stronger requirements. The unions offered tepid opposition because they would not risk hurting Democratic chances in the 1960 elections.

Until the strike wave which began in 1967 in response to the decline of real wages, economic issues have not been sufficient to spur workers to undertake protracted strikes. For example, the 116-day steel strike in 1959 was fought over the right of the company to change work rules and institute technological changes without consulting the union. The two-year-long oil strikes that began in 1963 were conducted over the question of layoffs and job security in the wake of technological innovations. Most auto walkouts in recent years have been over speedup and other working-conditions issues. Even the lengthy GE strike was fought against the arbitrariness of the company; its attack was against working conditions as much as wages.

But the trade union structure has become less able to solve elementary defensive problems. Higher wages for organized workers since the end of World War II have been purchased at a high price. One result of the close ties between unions and corporations has been the enormous freedom enjoyed by capital in transferring the wage increases granted to workers in the shop to the shoulders of workers as consumers. Wage increases have been granted with relative ease under these circumstances in the largest corporations and the most monopolized industrial sectors.

Equally significant has been the gradual increase of constraints in the collective bargaining agreement on the workers' freedom to oppose management's imposition of higher production norms, labor-saving technologies, and policies of plant dispersal. (The last left millions of textile, steel, auto, shoe, and other workers stranded in the '40s and '50s.) The bureaucratization of grievance procedures has robbed shop stewards of their power to deal with management on the shop floor. The inability of workers to change their working conditions through the union has had two results: workers limit their union loyalty to the narrow context of wage struggles, and they go outside the union to solve their basic problems in the plant. Thus the wildcat strike has become a protest not only against the brutality of industrial management, but also against the limits imposed by unionism. The conditions pertaining to the role of trade unions during the rise of industrial capitalism in the United States no longer apply in the monopoly epoch.

II

A little more than fifty years ago, in 1919, the first national strike among unskilled workers in a mass production industry ended in defeat. Judge Elbert Gary, the last of the old barons of the steel industry, defeated the efforts of the 350,000 workers by the tenacity born of the immense resources of the US Steel Corporation, combined with the use of divisive propaganda to sever the fragile unity of skilled and unskilled workers, plain scabherding, and other more blatant forms of strikebreaking. Some old-timers and trade union historians claim that the real cause of the defeat lay in the old AFL style of organization by craft which dominated the strike even though the organizers of the strike were strong advocates of industrial unionism.

Although the strike was not successful, it was remarkable for the fact that workers stayed out for over three months to gain union recognition. Their chief demand was the right to bargain collectively with the giants of the steel industry. The employers agreed that they would unilaterally meet many of the other demands of the strikers, including a cut in the number of work hours—US Steel actually reduced the twelve-hour day to eight hours, with an accompanying twenty-five per cent increase the following year—but they would never deal with outside representatives of their employees. The open shop was a sacred principle of Judge Gary and his fellow steelmen. After the strike the union withered until the great industrial union movement fifteen years later.

However, the corporation heads of the steel industry and other mass production industries were by no means unified on the question of

collective bargaining. The older production men heading the large corporations were haunted by memories of the great Homestead Steel Strike
of 1892, the national strikes in mining and in railroads at the turn of the
century, and the development of the Socialist Party into an important
force in American politics. They were in genuine fear that a unionized
work force would lead to radical social change.

The kernel of their objections to unionization was not that unions would
elect more representatives to public office or even that they would provide
organized pressure for wage increases and more social benefits. Gary himself was one of the leading proponents of corporation-sponsored "welfare
capitalism," a phrase denoting the recognition by the corporations of their
obligation to make provisions for the nonwage needs of the workers. The
near monopoly position of the giant industries in the American economy
was already making them more receptive to economic demands.

The old robber barons who headed the major corporations were
afraid that unions would intrude on the prerogatives of management
and would represent a threat to corporate control of production and
the direction of the labor forces. But a newer group of corporation directors had made their appearance in American industry in about 1910.
They were not cut from the mold of the self-made man or the production manager. They were sales experts and financial wizards. Charles
Schwab, Gary's successor, was a professional fund raiser and administrative expert who had reorganized several faltering corporations prior
to his assumption of the position of chief executive officer of US Steel.
Similarly, Gerard Swope, the head of General Electric, had not been a
production manager before assuming leadership of the giant electrical
corporation. These men were interested in lower production costs and
uninterrupted production. They were keenly aware of the costs of the
long steel strike to industry.

As early as 1915, Swope was prepared to entertain the possibility of
dealing with labor organizations. He even went so far as to suggest to
Sam Gompers, the president of the AFL, that GE could be organized.
Swope, undoubtedly influenced by the mass strikes in mining and textiles and the garment trades during the previous five years, was looking
for ways to stabilize labor relations—to make labor a known cost factor

as well as to delimit the influence of unions in determining the pace of work and the direction of the work force. He was also impressed by the role of unions in disciplining the work force. In the same year, a member of the Employers' Association of the Chicago Men's Clothing Industry praised the leader of the Amalgamated Clothing Workers' Union, Sidney Hillman, who later would become a major force in the CIO. "We regard Sidney Hillman very highly," he said. "We believe him honest, high-minded and capable.... With Hillman dead or dethroned we would be in the hands of the old grafting pirates who would not enforce an agreement, who would foment shop strikes...."[2]

To be sure, most corporation leaders did not look to the AFL as the solution to the labor problem, even though Gompers had become a junior crony in the National Civic Federation—an early attempt to find a meeting ground between labor, management, and the public in the interest of advancing American capitalism. Instead, the main direction of their efforts was to establish employee representation plans.

Despite the reluctance of some sectors of industry (notably, the recalcitrant Judge Gary), the "works councils" or employee associations strengthened the belief of many corporate liberals that collective bargaining provided the best hope of retaining control over the labor force and dissipating the more radical elements in the unions.

During World War I, hundreds of company unions were ordered formed by government edict prompted by employers who were frightened by the chance that genuine unionism would challenge their power. In many cases, including the steel and packing industries, the union militants succeeded in taking over these organizations and the companies were forced into primitive collective bargaining under pressure of the government's resolve to insure continuous production of war materiel.

With the ranks of labor, however, the idea of collective bargaining itself was not a universally accepted strategic goal. Around the turn of the century, revolutionary syndicalism, a doctrine whose origins were to be found among workers in under-industrialized countries such as Spain and Italy, had begun to take root in America, even though the idea had been espoused by the Socialist Labor Party as early as the 1880s.

The spread of syndicalist ideas was remarkable among the native-born American miners as well as Italian shoe and textile workers and Jewish garment workers. Unlike the socialists, who believed that the struggle for liberation from capitalist oppression must be preceded by a prolonged period of reformist struggles, especially through collective bargaining and peaceful parliamentary activity, the syndicalists advocated the formation of revolutionary unions whose object was to capture power in the factories, smash the state since it attempted to protect property, and establish a society controlled directly by the producers.

In contrast the demands of AFL leaders, socialist and non-socialist, were by definition reformist, since they attempted to wrest concessions from employers without fundamentally changing power within the factory or in society. For the craft-minded AFL, the ability to win depended on the skill of the workers as much as on their degree of organization or their economic conditions. Where unskilled or semiskilled workers had flocked to the unions, as in the garment and mining industries, it was explained as aberration. The AFL leaders held that the skilled craftsmen in these industries, such as cutters and weighers, were the soul of the struggle. Without their support, union organization was out of the question. By themselves, unskilled workers could not carry through a successful battle, even if they could be organized—a doubtful prospect in any case.

Between 1905, the year of the formation of the Industrial Workers of the World (IWW), and the Depression of the 1930s, the syndicalist spirit continued to be an influence among American workers, even when the fortunes of the IWW were low. The IWW never succeeded in generating a national strike. Its most dramatic activities were confined to individual strikes in mass production industries. But it showed that unskilled workers were indeed capable of sustaining long strikes and were potentially, at least, a force to be reckoned with by both employers and reformist-minded unions.

The IWW abhorred collective bargaining. It believed that the uprising of a group of workers within a particular industry was produced by their grievances and could only end when the grievances were totally redressed. The employers could restore a wage cut, slow the pace of work, or grant other concessions, but the workers should decide independently whether to return to work or spread the struggle to other industries. The

IWW hoped for the general strike which would bring down the system of industrial slavery and capitalist governments. In any case, they refused to sign contracts guaranteeing labor peace. If the workers returned to their jobs, they reserved their right to strike at any time.

The IWW was more of a movement than an organization. Its bureaucracy was fairly loose, its organizers undisciplined. In many industries, such as the garment trades, IWW sympathizers belonged to the established union but agitated consistently for no compromises with employers, for the general strike, and for flash strikes over grievances.

The revolutionary ideology of the IWW infused its organizing tactics: it was prepared to employ any means necessary to achieve the goals of the class war. Yet even though in its propaganda it had contempt for legality, one of its most important achievements was its remarkable defense of civil liberties in Seattle, Paterson, and other places where local public officials attempted to limit its right to operate. For most of its colorful career, the staid guardians of the traditional craft unions remained adamantly opposed to its attempt to organize "dual unions," that is, organizations that competed actively with AFL affiliates in particular trades and industries. The IWW's lumber workers affiliate was in competition with the AFL carpenters union; its efforts among textile and metal workers were regarded as direct affronts to established crafts. The old union leaders regarded the IWW as "hoboes," "riffraff," and "vagabonds" who gave the legitimate labor movement a bad name. Even many trade unionists who were members of the Socialist Party held this view, although, it must be remembered, some socialists such as Eugene Debs were present at the founding convention of the IWW. Others, like members of the Brewery Workers and the Western Federation of Miners, which were led by confirmed Socialists, who at least believed in the radical reorganization of society, were unable to affiliate with the IWW over the long run, because they perceived that trade unionism was incompatible with political sectarianism. In the main the Socialists remained part of the traditional labor movement even if they were sympathetic to IWW strikes and gave material support in such instances as the Lawrence and Paterson textile struggles.

Sidney Hillman of the Amalgamated Clothing Workers (ACWA) and the leaders of the International Ladies Garment Workers Union (ILGWU) ruthlessly opposed the efforts of anarchists and syndicalists within their unions. The Amalgamated was particularly hostile to the idea of revolutionary unionism. By 1914 it had embarked on a course from which it was never to depart, when it proclaimed the era of permanent labor-management cooperation in the men's clothing industry as a result of its victory in the Hart Schaffner and Marx strike the same year. Industry-wide boards regulating piecework rates, establishing welfare programs, and consulting on industrial conditions were established on a bipartite basis.

However, the Amalgamated remained militant with respect to the unorganized sector of the industry. Indeed, the subsequent twenty years were marked by strikes and energetic organizing campaigns to consolidate union power. But the Socialist leaders of the union were clear about the separation of politics from economics. Socialism was a doctrine to be preached in the union publications and in educational programs; it had no place around the bargaining table. Although the Socialists who were active in the union disagreed with Gompers on many ideological issues, including the necessity for unions to get involved in the main stream of American politics (the ACWA supported Socialist candidates until 1936), their disagreements with the AFL president on trade union matters were limited to tactics. The Amalgamated was one of the first unions to become a sophisticated purveyor of business interests as the best insurance of its own members' welfare.

It is interesting to compare the role of Gompers during World War I with that of Hillman during World War II. Each became the labor spokesman within the government as well as the government spokesman within the ranks of labor. The presumed antagonism between industrial unionists and Socialists within the AFL on the one hand and the business-minded leadership of Sam Gompers and his successors on the other revolved around the methods rather than goals. The AFL had sponsored the steel strike of 1919 and given it direction. Its goals were fully consistent with AFL philosophy. The fact that the strike was lost may be a function of the incompetence and venality of the old type of craft organization which spent more energy jockeying for jurisdictional positions than working to win the strike. But its object, collective bargaining for unskilled as well as skilled workers, prefigured essentially the program of the CIO.

In 1919, employers had not yet accepted unions as an essential element of the industrial structure; it was not until the 1930s that they were willing to listen carefully to those who claimed that unions would be important allies in the quest for labor peace. The 1920s witnessed the near destruction of the most powerful of the industrial and craft unions and the end of the growth of unionism in some basic industries, such as steel and packing, where beachheads had been established during the war. The ten-year period following World War I brought a return to the prewar conditions of wage cuts, arbitrary firing of working-class militants, and attempts by conservative trade union leaders to make bargains with employers in order to insure the survival of the union and their own leadership within it. The prosperity of the 1920s had its reflection in rising wages, but it cannot be said that the trade union was instrumental in determining the wage level.

After the 1929 crash, most of the corporation leaders and their government allies were in confusion and disarray. Big business had no program to deal with the economic and social crisis beyond measures to transfer the burdens of shrinking employment, profits, and production to the workers, farmers, small businessmen, and other countries. Only a minority of those with power sought to prepare a broader program for economic revival.

The remnants of the AFL leadership were caught in the interstices of the big-business offensive and their own desire for institutional survival. They held tenaciously to a keyhole vision of the crisis. With their organizations reduced in numbers and their political influence at a low ebb, the stolid guardians of the "House of Labor" whined their litany of complaint but firmly rejected mass struggle. Only the ex-Socialist Sidney Hillman of the ACWA and the United Mine Workers' president, John L. Lewis, leaders of the two most important industrial unions in the Federation, were able to seize the opportunity presented by the rebellious mood of the workers.

The Amalgamated, the International Ladies Garment Workers Union, and the Miners were able to recover somewhat from the dismal union decline of the 1920s and to organize thousands of new members. But most craft unions shrank to skeletal size as building construction ground to a near-halt, industrial production declined nearly fifty per cent, and millions of skilled workers joined the ranks of the unemployed.

John L. Lewis and Sidney Hillman were old AFL men. Both believed in the strike only as an ultimate weapon to force employers to deal with unions over the bargaining table. Both opposed the radicals within their ranks until the radicals came over to their way of thinking. When the radicals proved loyal to trade union objectives, they were permitted to join the effort to organize workers in mass production industries into the CIO. In some cases, they were even permitted to lead unions, provided they represented no sharp departures *in practice* from the policies of the central organization. Autonomy was permitted to international unions on all matters not specifically covered by CIO policy. During the organizing upsurge of the early 1940s, left wingers who veered from CIO doctrine of support for Franklin Roosevelt's foreign policy were slapped on the wrist but not opposed frontally. Later, after the upsurge was spent, the left was unceremoniously removed.

In the 1930s, shorn of the genuine radical wing, which had been represented by the now-defunct IWW, the trade unions had moved rapidly to cement their alliance with both employers and the government. The union drive against General Motors in 1936–7 was militant because the company, still ensconced in the old ways, refused to recognize the union. A week after the sit-down strike at GM resulted in union recognition, Myron Taylor of US Steel concluded an agreement with John L. Lewis recognizing the Steelworkers Organizing Committee (SWOC) as bargaining agent for its employees. Between 1933 and 1937 the bulk of workers in basic industries were organized by the CIO or its rival AFL.

Perhaps it was indicative of the future direction of labor-management relations in the steel industry that US Steel's recognition of SWOC took place across a dinner table rather than across the picket line. From that time on the Steelworkers' organizing drive was to be conducted in a relatively mild way, compared to the battles of earlier years. There was only one major battle ahead—the strike of 1937, which was conducted against the so called "Little Steel" corporations. They were to prove more resistant to union organization. According to Walter Galenson, a leading historian of the CIO upsurge, the Republic, Bethlehem, and smaller steel companies refused to follow the example of US Steel for two main reasons: at the time of the union organizing campaign among the Little Steel producers, the "second depression" was already under way and steel, normally extremely sensitive to economic vicissitudes, was among the first to record the downward movement of the economy. Apart from economic conditions, the figure of Tom Girdler, the recalcitrant president of Republic Steel and a veteran union opponent, loomed large in the determination of other corporations to resist the SWOC organizing drive. Girdler had been plant manager of the Alaquippa works of the Jones & Laughlin Company before coming to Republic and, by all accounts, had greeted with terror the attempts to organize the huge works in 1934. Conditions had changed by 1937. Instead of a relatively isolated drive by a weak union, the steel industry was being challenged by a well-organized, coordinated effort aimed at all holdouts. Yet once again the use of terror through firings, shootings, and blacklisting succeeded in stemming the union tide.

There is no doubt that the steel companies were holding the whip hand in the 1937 strike. Despite the ability of the union to shut down a large number of mills, the economic conditions and the united front of employers slowed the organizing campaign seriously. It was not until 1941 that the first breakthrough was achieved among Little Steel companies, but this time it was through a representation election conducted by the National Labor Relations Board rather than through strike activity. By then the demand of the Roosevelt administration for uninterrupted war production, combined with an increasingly buoyant economy, helped turn the tables for the union. According to Galenson, "An important factor in the growth of the SWOC...was the assistance rendered by the National Labor Relations Board in a number of important decisions."[3] These included reinstatement of "a considerable number of strikers with back pay" after the ill-fated 1937 events, upholding the union's claim that some companies had engaged in unfair labor practices under the law by refusing to bargain in good faith with the union, and declaring that the "Bethlehem plan,"[4] an employee representation scheme to stave off union organization, was company dominated, another violation of the Labor Relations Act.

The SWOC leadership had learned an important lesson from the 1937 defeat: "the methods used in the early SWOC campaigns had become stale.... Early in 1940 there were no signs of anything like the hysterical enthusiasm of 1937. Consequently the organizing campaign against Bethlehem was settling down to a long-run educational program"[5] rather than mass strikes, which in the eyes of the SWOC leaders were ineffective against determined employer resistance. The Steelworkers and other CIO affiliates became more and more dependent on government assistance and peaceful methods. The remainder of the Little Steel companies were organized by representation elections rather than strikes and the use of legal means became a critical factor in determining victory or defeat in the overwhelming preponderance of unionization drives. For five years after the formation of SWOC, it was difficult for the membership to achieve a real voice in the affairs of the union, since most of the funds for the organizing drives came from the CIO. The leadership resisted forming an international union with a formal constitution and elected officers. Decisions regarding the disposition of dues, collective bargaining objectives, and political issues were made by the interim officers who had been appointed by John L. Lewis. As one delegate to a Wage and Policy convention ironically mused: "The Steelworkers Organizing Committee is a democracy. It is a democracy of steel workers and for steel workers but not by steel workers."[6]

The Steelworkers were to become almost unique among the CIO unions in the absolutism of its bureaucratic methods of operation, its lack of social vision, and its fervent anxiety to please the corporate heads of the industry. But, business unionism, which seemed so anachronistic in the early years of the CIO, became more common in the postwar era. The patterns of internal bureaucracy and close collaboration with the employers prefigured a unionism that was to become dominant later on.

Popular explanations for the rapid victory of industrial unionism rely heavily on the influence of the economic crisis. But this explanation is not good enough. The wave of union organization actually occurred during an economic upswing, not in the depth of the Depression. Between 1929, when there were two important textile strikes in the South, and 1933, the year of the mass strike among miners and the general strike in the garment trades, both union organization and strike struggles were at their ebb.

Beginning in 1933, the companies started to hire again. Most of the new workforce were young. Able to stand the swift assembly line pace, they were eminently employable and had been able to find work even in the depths of the Depression. For the entire period, even during the upswing, the hardest hit sections of the work force were the older workers, recently displaced agricultural workers, and minority group workers.

The new organizing upsurge began in 1933. By all accounts the spearheads of the drive in the shops were the young workers, and it was they who made the victories, helped to some extent by older veteran unionists who had spent much of the previous decades in small, often secret, union groups that rarely enjoyed company recognition. The younger workers were more militant because they had not experienced the dismal defeats suffered by the entire working class after World War I and were thus more optimistic about the chances of winning. They were not cowed by the employers to the same extent as older workers, for whom steady work had become a blessing after the lean years between 1929 and 1933, and they resented the attempts of corporations to exploit them by demanding more work for less pay and forcing them to endure speedup, stretchout, and other measures designed to increase profits.

Almost all of the most important plant leaders of the CIO organizing drive and a fair number of national CIO figures were under thirty-five. These were the workers for whom the Depression had not meant soup kitchens and breadlines. The preponderance of youth was particularly evident among the leadership of the auto and electrical workers. Few of the most important militants of the auto sitdown strikes of 1936–7 in Detroit, Cleveland, and Flint were over thirty. Organizers Richard Frankenstein, the Reuther brothers, Robert Travis, and most of the key rank-and-file activists were in their twenties or early thirties. In the electrical industry the picture was similar. James Carey was twenty-four years old when he assumed presidency of the United Electrical, Radio, and Machine Workers of America. As a worker in the Philco plant in Philadelphia, Carey had been twenty-one when, in 1933, he signed the first contract recognizing the in-plant union as collective bargaining agent for the company's workers. Julius Emspak, a union leader at the Schenectady plant of GE, and James Matles, the leader of a few locals of an independent machinists union that affiliated with UE, were equally youthful.

Strikes in the mid-'30s occurred as much because of speedup and the authoritarianism of management as they did because of declines in real wages, whether caused by wage cuts or price in creases engendered by the government's policies of providing investment incentives. Between 1933 and 1935, industry-wide strikes broke out in the mines and in the garment and textile industries; general strikes paralyzing San Francisco and Minneapolis arose from walkouts of workers in important transportation industries. Flash strikes broke out in auto, steel, electrical, and rubber plants, but these were local struggles and failed to encompass the whole industry until several years later.

In this recovery period of 1933–6, corporations and smaller employers felt particularly bold in putting pressure on workers, both because of the persistence of large-scale unemployment in the midst of the upturn and because of the protection afforded business by the government's policy of assuring high rates of profit through artificially stimulated prices.

The general strike in San Francisco, the Minneapolis Teamsters' strike, and the national textile strike of more than 300,000 workers, took place in 1934, a full year before the passage of the Wagner Act. The organization of these struggles occurred mainly outside the framework of the AFL or other branches of organized labor. Led by young workers, some of whom were communists, the strikes took place in part as a revolt against the conservative policies of the AFL unions who held formal jurisdiction in these industries. The unions—both the AFL and the short-lived communist variety—actually sought to thwart or channel these struggles. In most of the labor struggles of the '30s, the militants were defeated in the end. Suffused with uncompromising spirit, if not syndicalist ideology, they opposed settlements, refused to sign no-strike agreements, and became oppositionists even in the so-called left-wing unions.

If the necessary condition for the success of industrial unionism in the '30s was the revolt of young workers, this did not prove sufficient to determine the character of the labor movement or labor relations. There was a stronger force that was to be far more influential—the historical tendency within both employer and trade union ranks to formalize and regulate labor relations, which was to find fertile soil in the development of state capitalist forms during the New Deal period.

The economic expansion of modern capitalism depends upon the close integration of the state and the corporations. The same policies responsible for attempting to synchronize the activities of the government and of private corporations to guarantee recovery and sustain economic growth were responsible for developing the means to make labor a stable factor of production, that is, to make it possible to predict its price with a degree of accuracy sufficient to enable the undertaking of corporate and state planning. When corporate and government leaders understood the critical importance of coordinating their efforts in order to prevent disaster in the economic crisis of the early 1930s, they immediately recognized the importance of bringing unions into partnership. For if workers were to continue to struggle around their needs without regulation, the whole enterprise of state capitalist planning could be disrupted. From the point of view of the national economic and political leadership, the economic crisis was an emergency akin to war.

The first New Deal measures after the corporatists (whose national coordinator was Roosevelt) had ascended to power were not addressed to problems of hunger or disease. Rather, Congress was asked to delegate to the executive branch of government powers to restore the banks, stimulate investment, regulate wages, and increase prices. The National Recovery Act was the agency charged with the task of dealing with trade, of which labor relations were regarded as a dependent variable.

The first attempts at government regulation of labor relations were somewhat crude. Union representation on the industry boards responsible for setting wages and prices was too weak to influence the decisions of these bodies except in scattered instances, such as the clothing industry, where they had managed to preserve some of their pre-Depression strength. For the most part, the union leaders cooperated with Roosevelt's program of massive state intervention to save the tottering social and economic system, hoping for some crumbs from the corporate table. The reward for their cooperation was Section 7A of the National Recovery Act, which guaranteed the right of workers to join unions of their own choosing; in practice, this guarantee was neither legally enforced by the government nor capable of practical implementation by the unions, whose financial resources remained meager and whose moral stature among workers had been damaged by the degrading company unionism of the 1920s. In a few instances, the NRA provisions helped viable labor organizations to recruit new members. In the main, the workers in the mass production and transportation industries remained outside the traditional trade unions during the early years of the New Deal. It was no easy task to impose a partnership on the rank and file even if the discredited labor leadership was eager to be absorbed in the emerging state capitalist Roosevelt coalition.

In the first two years of the New Deal, prior to the 1935 Wagner Labor Relations Act (which established government machinery for regulating trade unions and was the first serious attempt to bring the class struggle under the aegis of government supervision), there had been the unprecedented outbreak of mass strikes in many important industries. In most cases the strikes had a spontaneous quality of reaction to immediate causes, although they were preceded by considerable agitation, partial walkouts, and organizational activity conducted by radical and labor organizers. Where unions captured leadership of these strikes and were able to direct them into acceptable collective bargaining channels, this was often accomplished after the strikes had already begun.

The Communist Party, the left wing of the Socialist Party, and other left-wing groups viewed the early New Deal with open hostility. In the radical view, the New Deal was created to achieve economic, social, and political stability in the interests of the continued domination of the country by the giant corporations, rather than in the interests of workers, black people, and farmers. The left denounced the NRA as an attack on workers' living standards. They described Section 7A as a chimera designed to lull the working class into false security.

Historically, there had been disagreements on the left over the application of the rule of law to trade unionism. The traditional IWW position, shared by many other radicals, was that workers should not seek union contracts, since they limited or prohibited the right to strike and narrowed the possibility of militant struggle against onerous working conditions. The CP, which dominated most of the radical movement after 1931, never took a clear-cut position on these questions of trade union practice. In 1936, when the party supported the Wagner Act and other state capitalist measures affecting workers, it did so without explaining or justifying its position.

In the period from the onset of the Depression in 1929 to 1935, the CP labor policy in this country had pursued two paths. The main thrust was to form independent, dual unions. But it also urged its members to "penetrate the fascist mass organizations like the AFL."[7] In cases where the leadership of established AFL unions was both powerful and so repressive that militants were barred from effective functioning as in the United Mine Workers, the CP formed dual "revolutionary unions." In other cases, as in the auto industry, CP militants were no weaker than their AFL counterparts. In these instances, the party leadership was often forced to acquiesce in the wishes of its own rank and file and countenance the formation of independent unions. In fields such as the electrical, food, and maritime industries, where there was barely the shell of an AFL affiliate, the CP helped form independent unions, sometimes under its own domination but sometimes in coalition with other independents.

Prior to 1935, the party wielded its two tactics in a flexible manner. Many of its leading trade union cadres were AFL stalwarts, especially those in the building trades. Even though the party policy was officially inclined toward dual unionism for much of the 1929–35 period, it allowed deviations from this line when the realities of the situation did not permit dual organization.

In the early days of the New Deal prior to the Wagner Act, industrial unionism was viewed by the AFL as a radical product, which it largely was, since most of the effective unionism during this period had taken place outside the AFL. It was John L. Lewis and Sidney Hillman who recognized that the New Deal, combined with the persistence of the economic crisis, presented a new opportunity for the rise of union organization among unskilled and semiskilled workers. They were acutely aware of unrest among these workers and vainly attempted to convince Gompers's successors of the necessity of establishing leadership over the new industrial union movement.

Both men were close to the Roosevelt administration and did not hesitate to use the prestige of the administration to assist recruiting drives within their own industrial jurisdictions. Hillman saw a rejuvenated labor movement as an important ally to Roosevelt's coalition. The evidence of his activity points to the distinctly political character of the Amalgamated's interest in helping to form a Committee for Industrial Organization within the AFL.

It was plain to Lewis and Hillman that unless the AFL acted decisively to control the developing mass upsurge among industrial workers, the left could pose a serious threat to conservative and liberal leaders of the unions and upset the emerging Roosevelt coalition. An ardent supporter of NRA section 7A, Lewis was convinced that workers would never join unions as long as they appeared to be radical and subversive. But, according to Saul Alinsky, Lewis's best biographer, the miners' president "could read the revolutionary handwriting on the walls of American industry" in the 1934 strikes.[8] After several years of futile appeals, Lewis finally convinced the AFL to set up the Committee to thwart the threat from the left, and insure that workers would be firmly ensconced within the AFL House of Labor.

The year 1935, however, brought a sharp reversal in CP policies. Instead of attempting to form independent, dual unions under their own leadership, the Communists were now committed to collaborate with the socialists and trade union leaders within the mainstream of political and trade union organizations. The Seventh World Congress of the Communist International of 1935 heard its General Secretary, Georgi Dimitrov, proclaim the end of the period when Communists would attack socialists and the bourgeoisie with merciless equanimity. Now the crucial task of the working class was to oppose fascism. The defense of liberal capitalism and civil liberties was the basic precondition of revolutionary action in the future. The Communist policy of branding socialist and liberal forces as "social fascists" had backfired severely in Germany and Italy. Now fascism was about to overthrow the Spanish Republic, was threatening to capture power in France, and was even bidding for a mass constituency in the United States. According to the new policy of the world Communist movement, the time had come to put aside sectarianism and join forces with all democratic organizations to prevent Hitler's drive for world domination. The Soviet regime made proposals at the League of Nations for collective security against Hitler. The new policy meant that the Communists were no longer to be found in the opposition to the liberal state and the social-democratic labor leaders.

Within the United States, Communists were obliged to abandon their virulent attacks on the Roosevelt administration and on the liberal wing of the AFL. The Trade Union Unity League (TUUL), the CP instrument in the labor movement, was dissolved, and militants were urged to merge with AFL unions in their industries. In many basic industries, the CP and TUUL organizations were transformed into nuclei for the CIO organizing drive. In his report to the 1936 convention of the party, CP General Secretary Earl Browder declared:

> The Committee for Industrial Organization has taken up the task of organizing all mass production industries in America in industrial unions. The success of this effort is a basic necessity upon which depends the future of the American labor movement in all other respects. The CP unconditionally pledges its full resources, moral and material, to the complete execution of this great project.[9]

The CP remained somewhat critical of Roosevelt, but supported his reelection in 1936. They also supported the state capitalist measures of his administration, including the National Labor Relations Act, which simultaneously widened government intervention into the collective bargaining process and protected the right of workers to join unions. The CP and most radicals never perceived the dangers inherent in greater government regulation of labor relations. They were dedicated and tireless organizers within the "center-left" coalitions led by Lewis that welcomed the enlarged government role in collective bargaining.

In 1935–6 CP trade unionists in New York, Michigan, Wisconsin, and elsewhere worked for the formation of local labor parties, patterning themselves after the Minnesota Farmer-Labor Party, which had succeeded in electing its candidate for governor, Floyd Olson, in 1934. The strategy underlying CP support of the Farmer-Labor Party movement was twofold: on the one hand, it would provide a mass base for the defeat of the ultra-right in American politics and mitigate its influence over liberal capitalists such as Roosevelt. On the other hand, it would represent the political expression of the developing trade union and farmers movement, providing at the same time a wider political base for Communist influence. The CP also attempted to influence the leaders of the newly emerging CIO, which was then regarded as the main force for worker organization.

Although CP leadership urged its rank and file to build the Communist Party as the mass party of the American working class, these appeals were subordinated to the main task of building "the people's front against fascism" and its core organization, the CIO. In effect, the party became a pressure group on the Democratic Party and the CIO. The Farmer-Labor parties, particularly the American Labor Party in New York State, which represented the political left-center coalition, were little more than another line on the voting machine to harness labor's support for the Democrats. In the tradition of the British Labour Party, the ALP had a dual structure. On the top were the leaders of the key industrial unions, particularly of the garment trades and transport workers. In the neighborhoods, the left-wing activists, members of the CP or on its periphery, or active rank-and-file trade unionists, performed social services for constituents, organized rent strikes, consumer protests, and election campaigns.

After 1937, the modest criticisms of Roosevelt and the CIO leaders still evident at the 8th CP Convention during the previous year all but disappeared. In the July 1937 issue of *The Communist*, the party's chief theoretical organ, its editor, Alexander Bittleman, vehemently defended both Roosevelt and Lewis. Against the charge that Lewis had become a "labor dictator with great power," Bittleman replied: "The crime of the CIO is not that it is a dictatorship but on the contrary that it is a progressive labor movement seeking to build itself up on the basis of inner union democracy as well as a force for democracy in the country."[10] He went on to say, "The CIO is already one of the chief fortresses of democracy, its brightest hope and promise of realization. That is the message Communists must spread widely among the masses."[11]

Roosevelt was defended by the Communists against those who

criticized his proposal to enlarge the Supreme Court from its traditional nine members in order to give his program more support. The CP was also critical of those left-wingers who blamed the administration for the shootings of steelworkers by Chicago police in May 1937 during a demonstration demanding union recognition from the Little Steel companies.

By 1939 Communists had become entrenched in the top echelons of several important CIO and, to a lesser extent, AFL organizations. At one point it was estimated that a third of the CIO membership belonged to unions euphemistically called "left-wing." In practice, they were mostly not under direct CP control but had top leaders and secondary officials who were close to or in the party. The "left-wing" unions included those of electrical workers, auto workers, West Coast longshoremen, maritime workers, transport workers, metal miners, packinghouse workers, furniture workers, distributive and department store workers, fur workers, office and professional workers, food and tobacco workers, and public workers.

Among AFL unions, Communists did not play leadership roles on national levels, but were important in local and district organizations of painters, carpenters, hotel and restaurant workers, railroad brotherhoods, and some others. In a remarkable article written for *The Communist* in November 1939, William Foster, twenty years earlier the secretary of the AFL committee directing the 1919 steel strike and now a leading American Communist, wrote an article on CP trade union policy of the preceding two decades. The article represented the perspective of a man who had long since renounced dual unionism. Foster's two key points were that Communists must now work for AFL-CIO unity, basing themselves on the tactic of pressuring the decent elements in both the Federation and the government, and that the CP should no longer maintain factions within the CIO. On the first point, Foster wrote:

> Roosevelt in his unity efforts reflects the desires of the great majority of New Dealers. Lewis speaks for the solid unity sentiment of the entire CIO Tobin expresses the unity will of a big majority of AFL members, and Whitney undoubtedly does the same for the bulk of railroad unionists.[12]

And on the second, he stated:

> The organizational forms of Communist trade union work have changed
> radically to correspond to the present period (of center left unity). Party
> members do not now participate in groupings or other organized activi-
> ties within the unions. The party also discountenances the formation of
> progressive groups, blocs, and caucuses in unions; it has liquidated its
> Communist factions, discontinued its shop papers, and is now modifying
> its system of industrial branches. Communists are policy making and
> administrating on an unknown scale...building the highest type of trade
> union leadership based on efficient service and democratic responsibility
> to the rank and file.[13]

Not only did the CP abandon dual unionism and subordinate its organizing thrust to the CIO under Lewis, it abandoned its own political identity.
Important trade union cadres became trade union bureaucrats for whom
an independent rank and file was anathema.

However, even as early as 1940, well before the so-called McCarthy
attacks, the left was used as a scapegoat by labor leaders. When some delegates to the 1940 Wage Policy convention held by the SWOC distributed
a leaflet calling for immediate action to draw up a constitution and hold a
convention to establish an international union, Philip Murray of the CIO
declared: "Now I am wondering, I am just wondering, if it is the business
of the Fascists or the Nazis or the Democrats or the Republicans or the
Communists to tell us what we are supposed to do in these conventions....
Anyone else outside who wants to help us that's all right as long as it's
constructive help...and cooperation—I welcome that, but I do not welcome and I do not want and I am not going to tolerate undue interference
with the work of this organization."[14] As president of the CIO, Murray had
learned to live in peace with Communists as long as they did not interfere
with the affairs of "his" union. But now his attitude had changed. The use
of the words "Fascist" and "Nazi" and the mention of the other two political parties before the CP were evidently a veil for the real attack against
what Murray and his associates believed was a CP campaign to push for a
formal union structure. Ironically, in contrast to many other CIO unions

where Communists had been prominent in the top leadership or influential among the middle levels of power, the CP had never gained a foothold in the Steelworkers' hierarchy. The left-wing activists that were elected to office were mainly to be found in large local unions in the Chicago area, and in a number of Little Steel locals around the country, particularly in Bethlehem's Baltimore and Buffalo plants.

During World War II, Communist trade unionists became indistinguishable from their liberal colleagues. Left-wing leaders of the new mass industrial unions in auto, electrical, and other basic industries put the objective of winning the war ahead of the workers' immediate interests and voluntarily gave up the right to strike. Communists joined their liberal allies and urged workers to abandon their traditional hostility to piecework schemes and incentive pay. In some industries where company efforts to introduce these methods of speedup had been the catalyst for union organization—packing, steel, and the electrical industries, for example—day-work systems gave way to incentive pay geared to productivity or even to outright piecework. In the auto industry, the assembly line was simply speeded up, while workers were asked to maintain their no-strike pledge and wage freeze.

Wildcat strikes were frequent in the auto industry, shipbuilding, and other areas of mass production during the war. In many cases, the deep resentment of the workers was corralled by opportunistic leaders like Walter Reuther, who used the occasion to attack the "center-left coalition" which led the UAW. After the war, Reuther easily defeated the Thomas-Addes leadership of the union which was supported by the CP.

When the USSR-US alliance was erased by the Cold War, the combination of rank-and-file resentment against "red company unionism," open red-baiting, and repression by the corporations and the government, and the sectarian policies of the Communists themselves sealed the isolation of the left from the mass of industrial workers. In the steel industry, many older workers became openly hostile to "communism" after the Soviet takeover of the countries of their birth or ancestry. The Steelworkers leadership was particularly close to the Catholic Church, which conducted active propaganda against the repression of organized religion in Hungary, Poland, and elsewhere. Many Steelworkers local leaders were among those who most frequented Communion breakfasts that often served as thinly veiled occasions for anti-communist discourses. In those years the Catholic Church, particularly its Jesuit wing, became extremely influential in such sections of the labor movement as steelworkers, electrical workers, New England textile workers, and the building trades. These industries were centered in the Northeastern region of the country, and in several large cities of the Midwest where the bulk of American Catholic workers lived. Of course, the church was concerned that communist influence, built up in the labor movement during the Depression years, would constitute a serious challenge to its constituency. There was a close connection between the fierce anti-communism of the steelworkers, CIO electrical workers, textile workers unions with the importance of Eastern and Southern European Catholics among their membership, and in the ranks of the officialdom.

Some radicals in the unions survived the Cold War. They were trade unionists who functioned as open socialists, who vigorously fought with workers against the deterioration of working conditions, and who refused to become part of the trade union bureaucracy. They included members of all radical tendencies. Their distinguishing feature was not their political affiliation. It was their radical sensibility.

In the auto industry workers distinguished for shop floor militancy, who had been members of Trotskyist groups or even of the CP, remained in the plants throughout the darkest days of the Cold War. Elsewhere, known radicals remained active shop leaders among metal miners, fur workers, electrical workers, and in the railroad and trucking industries. These workers were by no means immune from company or union discrimination because of their political views. Many were fired from their jobs with the implicit approval of the union. But in many cases their fellow workers rose to the defense of the left-wingers because of their honest political views as much as their ability to fight effectively over day-to-day grievances.

Yet there is no doubt about the effectiveness of the Cold War campaign against the political left among the working class. By the mid-1950s left-wing influence was all but erased from the plants, the mining industry, and transportation sectors. The fragments of radical influence that remained were never of sufficient weight to influence the outcome of major trade union policies or struggles. In the cases where left-wingers threw their limited resources into factional fights against the conservative trade union leaders, their influence was almost always separate from their political position. In the steelworkers' fight against the McDonald leadership in the late 1950s, a few radicals participated both on the insurgents' staff and among rank-and-file workers, but, just as in the 1930s, they played no independent role as *radicals*. Instead, in the farmworkers, hospital workers, and public employees unionization efforts, they were merely good labor organizers. Most of them felt, with some justice, that their ideas had no currency among workers, therefore the best they could do was to aid the most progressive sections of the labor movement as technicians rather than political influences.

In 1950, following a period of rhetorical militancy, the articulate former Socialist, Walter Reuther, engineered a five-year contract with the auto industry. The contract signaled the end of an era in industrial unionism. Saddled with a no-strike provision which permitted the company to speed up the assembly line without effective counteraction within the framework of collective bargaining, the rank and file was forced to act outside the union structure. The wildcat movement in the auto industry during 1953–5 embraced all major companies and sections of the country. Thousands of workers participated in flash walkouts as the companies tried to increase production from forty-eight to fifty cars per hour to more than sixty. Often the walkouts were initiated by the body-shop workers, who do the heaviest and dirtiest jobs in the plant, or by the workers in wet-sanding departments, most of whom were black.

The extent and frequency of the walkouts forced the union to restore the right to strike in the next contract and to cut down the contract duration. But strikes were permitted only when management changed the pace of work or for safety reasons. Even then, workers were not permitted to walk out at the point of the change. They could elect to strike only after enduring a long period of aggrievement through the procedure established by the contract. In one stroke, Reuther bowed to the realities of the situation and tried to cool workers' militancy by placing conditions on the strike weapon.

In 1955 the UAW and other industrial unions became concerned with automation and other forms of major technological change that would create joblessness among the workers. During the year, a large conference on the shorter work week was sponsored by the UAW to coincide with the opening of negotiations of a new contract. However, the new contract, when it was finalized, merely contained an agreement that companies would provide supplementary unemployment benefits to laid-off workers. Shortly thereafter, steel followed suit with a similar agreement and the shorter work week was dead.

Although the wildcat strikes of the early 1950s were smashed, the challenge to the unions did not abate. The next phase of the rank-and-file attempt to capture control over their own conditions was the mushrooming of movements to replace the old leadership. Beginning in the late '50s and early '60s, there was a parade of electoral challenges to the leaders of many key industrial unions. Although most of the pretenders to the thrones were middle-rank, full-time paid leaders, they rode to power on the strength of membership discontent. Such contests took place in the Steelworkers Union, in the Rubber Workers, Textile Workers, Oil and Chemical Workers, Teachers, State, County and Municipal Employees, the Electrical Workers, and in many locals of the Auto Workers where each collective bargaining defeat was followed by the defeat of a raft of local union incumbents.

The outcome of the movement for internal reform was surely disappointing to union members who hoped for the reawakening of the aggressive brand of trade unionism that was characteristic of the CIO prior to World War II. At best, the new leaders who emerged from the factional struggles in the 1960s offered more collective bargaining militancy and a determination to conduct active organizing drives among open-shop employers. The promise of internal democracy was almost never fulfilled. I. W. Abel, who had defeated McDonald, carried on the tradition of centralization of union command. And more ironically, he began a concerted campaign in 1970 to persuade union members to cooperate with employers to raise productivity and prevent foreign competition from eating away at their jobs. This plea corresponded to a period of high capital investment within the industry that resulted in substantial layoffs because of the introduction of labor-saving equipment. As tonnage increased, steel employment was dropping steadily. The Steelworkers Union was becoming an instrument of modernization, speedup, and labor discipline for the steel industry.

Another manifestation of the emergence of rank-and-file discontent in the '60s was the rise of the Teamsters Union as a major challenger to traditional union jurisdictions. The apparent militancy of this "outlawed" union meshed neatly with rank-and file disgust with the softness of the now middle-aged CIO labor statesmen. The merger of the AFL and the CIO had prevented workers from seeking alternative representation when their unions revealed company union practices. The expulsion of the Teamsters from the House of Labor in 1957 provided disgruntled workers with a powerful alternative to the old labor unions.

But by the late '60s the initial enthusiasm of the workers for competitive unionism and internal union reform had ebbed. Real wages had declined each year since 1967 and, after a period of economic growth as a result of the Vietnam War, the economy began to slow down. The first effects of the slowdown were reflected in rising layoffs and the elimination of overtime, which took the gloss from pay envelopes. But the slowdown in production and employment did not have a counterpart in the movement of prices, which kept rising.

The last two years of the 1960s and the opening of the '70s were marked by the reawakening of rank-and-file militancy. This militancy took different forms in different sectors of the work force. Among public workers and workers in voluntary institutions such as hospitals, a wave of union organizing and strike movements took place. This wave was led by teachers and hospital workers. The impact of public employee organizing was peculiar because every strike of this group of workers is, perforce, a strike against the state. In many places, the pent-up frustration of these workers, who had borne the worst effects of the inflation and the fiscal crisis of the public sector, caused widespread disrespect for laws prohibiting strikes of public employees and court injunctions aimed at enforcing the law. In many cities, particularly on the Eastern seaboard, the leaders riding the crest of the wave of militancy became important political figures and were ultimately absorbed by the municipal governments as warm allies and important sources of political power. But the chronic shortage of funds available to local governments prevents a secure alliance of the workers with government authority.

Another manifestation of militancy has been the reappearance of the wildcat strike. The vaunted authority of the Teamsters over the membership, its reputation for militancy and toughness at the bargaining table, its myth of invincibility, collapsed beneath the insurgent rank and file, which acted independent of the bureaucracy for the first time. The wildcat strike of postal workers in 1970 took place over the heads of the union leadership and became a national strike without central coordination or direction. The strike was preceded by the twenty-year efforts of the national postal union leadership to operate within approved legislative channels through lobbying methods and political pressure on the administrative directorate. Even more dramatic than the postal rebellion was the extraordinary 1969–70 wildcat strike by 100,000 Teamsters in the Middle West and the West Coast in rejection of the contract negotiated by their national leaders.

Unionism in the public sector is still somewhat raucous and unpredictable from management's standpoint. Even when labor leaders fervently desire close relations with public officials and are prepared to cooperate in confining membership action to approved channels, the workers in hospitals, schools, post offices, and city agencies often succeed in changing the script.

Among the most important reasons for the rise of public employee unionism is the entrance of large numbers of young workers and blacks into this branch of employment. The privileged status accorded veterans in civil service examinations, the sharp rise of public sector jobs during the '50s and '60s compared to manufacturing, and the relatively high pay of these jobs made public service an attractive option for black people and women. The changing attitudes of young people toward their labor, particularly their relative indifference to the old values that motivated civil servants (job security and a moderate commitment to useful work) made them less subordinate to supervisors and more impatient with the infinitesimal steps of the job leaders in civil services. They were not content to wait a full year for a $200 raise, or study for the civil service examination providing an opportunity for promotion. Many came to public employment with the understanding that they were workers like anybody else and were there for the money. The old appeals that suggested white-collar work as a privilege reserved for the best of the working class had clearly lost their force. Postal workers, for example, could not mistake their jobs for anything but industrial labor.

III

The bureaucratization of the trade unions, their integrative role within production, their conservative political ideology, and their dependence on the Democratic Party are not primarily the result of the consciousness of the leading actors in the rise of industrial unionism. To the extent that the left participated in redefining the trade unions as part of the corporate system, it must now undertake a merciless critique of its own role before a new working-class strategy can be developed.

It is not enough to admit bureaucratic tendencies in the unions or in their left leadership, however. The strategy flowing from this focus is to reform the unions from within in order to perfect their fighting ability and rank-and-file class consciousness. This line of thinking categorically denies that the unions can remain a dependent variable within the political economy dominated by corporate capitalism.

One of the important concepts of Marxist orthodoxy is that economic crisis is an inevitable feature of capitalist development, and that the tendency of employers will be to attack and reduce the power of trade unions during periods of declining production. Accordingly, it is believed that the government-employer attempts to circumscribe workers' power by restricting trade union functions will produce rank-and-file pressure confronting the leadership with the choice of struggle against capital or their own displacement. Thus the unions become objectively radical in their view despite their conservative consciousness.

However, strategies for rank-and-file reform ignore the bureaucracy and conservatism inherent in the present union structure and function, as well as the role of the unions in the division of labor. The growth of bureaucracy and the decline of rank-and file initiative is built into the theory and practice of collective bargaining.

During periods of crisis or stagnation, the union bureaucracy seeks an accommodation with management on the basis of the parochial interests of its immediate constituency. This practice can be observed in the settlement of the 1969 GE strike, where the unions agreed to a long-term contract which partially protected workers from inflationary pressures, but made no substantive advances. The forty-month contract provision of the agreement was a sign that the leadership was prepared to settle for consolidating its gains in the wake of the recession in the economy. Long-term agreements have been viewed traditionally as a management tool to stabilize production and labor costs. Militant unionism has always fought for one-year contracts based on its view of contracts as per se a limitation on workers' power to deal effectively with problems on the job.

GE workers were forced to strike against inflation and the attempt by the company to make gains against wages and working conditions. The company's attack was repulsed. But the struggle to prevent GE from making up for wage increases by other devices was not won. In this area, top leadership of the unions permitted the company to raise prices and increase productivity without protest and resistance. Local struggles to deal with the problems of women workers, production norms, and new machinery were fragmented. All unions, except the independent United Electrical Workers (UE) agreed to drop their demands for an end to discriminatory wages for women and for workers in the South. Since the International Union of Electrical Workers AFL-CIO (IUE), the largest union in the coalition, provides for contract ratification by its top committees, this meant the rank and file had no genuine voice in accepting or rejecting the settlement except through elected representatives.

But there is a more structural difficulty confronting trade unions in dealing effectively with the day-to-day issues on the shop floor. An increasing tendency can be observed in many unions toward the elimination, or the severe modification, of the shop steward system. One of the most progressive features of the CIO at its inception was the insistence of many of the new unions such as the Auto Workers and Electrical Workers that the members' basic grievances should be resolved at the workplace, since it was at the point of production that workers came face to face with problems of working conditions. Shop stewards were elected in each department, or even in each section of a department, on the basis of one steward for every twenty-five to thirty workers. The steward was not paid for union business either by the company or by the union and only left her/his work station when there was a grievance. In the early days of industrial management, foremen were still accorded more than marginal authority over the workforces. Foremen often performed the hiring and firing functions as well as distributing work and overtime to employees. Even as late as the early 1950s line supervisors and stewards fought out "beefs" right on the shop floor; failing a settlement, workers sometimes took "job actions," that is, refused to work or slowed down until the grievance was settled.

The centralization of management in the 1950s relieved the foremen of a great deal of their decision-making power. Nearly all decisions affecting production, including discipline, were now defined as policy issues reserved for professional personnel, directors, or middle supervisors. Now nothing could be settled on the shop floor without direct independent action by the workers. Such action was opposed by union hierarchies.

In some instances, this opposition was not the result of venality or class betrayal by the union officials. For one thing, the Taft Hartley Labor Relations Act imposed severe penalties for walkouts in violation of the terms of the labor agreement. Even when the walkout is not authorized by the union officials, the union is held responsible for penalties that may be ordered by a court. Some unions that have refused to order members to return to their jobs during wildcat strikes have been subjected to heavy fines and imprisonment of union officials by courts. Most union leaders have rejected the job action or the "quickie" as a self-defeating measure that can solve nothing and, on the contrary, make more problems.

Labor leaders attempted to adjust the grievance machinery to the realities of corporate power that removed decision-making from the work station. The rank-and-file steward was replaced by the "committeeman" in the United Auto Workers agreement with the "Big Three" manufacturers of the industry in 1946. The committeeman is employed virtually full time on union business and is paid by the company to deal with grievances. Instead of representing a small group of workers who do the same or similar labor in a relatively small area, the typical committeeman represents several hundred workers scattered over many different jobs and even geographic locations in the shop. He becomes the organizing force in the shop instead of the workers themselves. The argument for this system relies on the perception that the company will not deal with a steward because it has robbed its own line supervisor of real power.

The early version of the committeeman or business agent, the "walking delegate," was a post originally invented by craft unions whose membership was scattered over a large number of small shops. The commonly held belief among these workers in the latter half of the last century was that they must have a representative who was not paid by the company and was not required to work all day at the bench. But the introduction of the committee system into industrial plants can only have bureaucratic justifications. In large workplaces, this system has produced a union structure that is as alien to the line worker as to the company. The committeeman is perceived as a "man in the middle," having interests that are neither those of the rank and file nor those of management. His structural position is untenable from any point of view other than the performance of his main task: to police the union contract as well as possible and prevent both the rank and file and the management from going outside of it to solve problems. Many committeemen are sincerely interested in the welfare of union members and are frequently able to thwart the most arbitrary of management's actions against individuals. But they are powerless to deal with the issues that have produced the unauthorized job actions and wildcat strikes: the speedup of production, introduction of labor-saving machinery, plant removal, and disciplinary layoffs that do not result in immediate discharge.

The last thirty-five years of industrial unionism have failed to effect any substantive change in the distribution of income. Trade unionism under conditions of partial unionization of the labor force can do no more than redistribute income *within* the working class. Workers in heavily organized industries such as auto, rubber, and steel have relatively high wages compared to workers in consumer goods industries such as garments and shoes (which have migrated to the South), retail and wholesale workers, and most categories of government and agricultural workers.

The high wages of certain categories of industrial workers depend as much on the high proportion of capital to living labor and the monopoly character of basic industries as they do on trade union struggle. The tendency for employers in heavy industry to give in to union wage demands presupposes their ability to raise prices and productivity. In competitive industries such as light manufacturing, the unions have been transformed into stabilizers of industrial conflict in order to permit high rates of profits where no technological changes can be introduced. The result has been low wages for large numbers of blacks, Puerto Ricans, and poor whites locked into these jobs.

Since advanced capitalism requires consumerism both as ideology and as practice to preserve commodity production, its payment of high wages to large segments of the working class—and minimum income to those excluded from the labor markets—is not objectively in the workers' interest. It is a means to take care of the market or demand side of production.

The ability of workers to purchase a relatively large quantity of consumer goods is dependent on the forces of production, which include the productivity and skill of the labor force and the scale and complexity of technology. Technological development, in turn, is dependent on the availability of raw materials and the degree of scientific and technical knowledge in society.

The most important issue to be addressed in defining the tasks ahead is not the question of inflation, wages, or general economic conditions. No matter how inequitable the distribution of income, no matter how deep the crisis, these conditions will never, by themselves, be the soil for revolutionary consciousness.

Revolutionary consciousness arises out of the conditions of alienated labor, which include economic conditions but are not limited to them. Its starting point is in the production process. It is at the point of mental and manual production, where the world of commodities is produced, that the worker experiences his exploitation. Consumption of waste production, trade union objectives in the direction of enlarging wages and social benefits, and the division of labor into industries and sections are all mediations which stand between the workers' existential exploitation at the workplace and their ability to comprehend alienated labor as class exploitation.

Radicals of most persuasions have tended to address the problem of consciousness from the wrong end. Some believe that racism, trade unionism, conservatism, will be dissolved by discussion and exhortation alone, while other believe that "objective" conditions will force new understandings among workers. The notion that ideologies can be changed through ideological means or that capitalist contradictions will change consciousness with an assist from ideologically correct lines or propaganda is a nonrevolutionary position: in both cases, the role of practice is ignored. Nor will workers' struggles against economic hardship necessarily raise political consciousness.

In this connection one must reevaluate the rise of industrial unionism in the 1930s. Many radicals and labor historians have interpreted the failure of the CIO to emerge as an important force for social change as a function of the misleadership of its officials and the opportunism of the Communist Party and other radical parties that participated in its formation.[15] According to a recent work on the development of the CIO by Art Preis, a contemporary labor reporter writing from a Trotskyist position, the 1930s were a prerevolutionary period. Preis writes: "The first stage of awakening class consciousness was achieved, in fact, with the rise and consolidation of the CIO. The second stage will be marked by a further giant step, the formation of a new class party based on the unions.[16]

No important left-wing critique exists of unionism itself. Left-wing evaluations of the 1930s find the economic crisis a necessary condition for the development of class consciousness, but blame the Communist and Socialist policies for the fact that no significant radical force developed among the mass of workers.

I would dispute this theory since there is no genuine evidence that the CIO could ever have become an organized expression of a new class politics in America, or that trade unionism in the era of state capitalism and imperialism can be other than a force for integrating workers. After the disappearance of the IWW from the labor scene, there was no radical alternative offered within the working class. The trade union activists who belonged to Marxist parties functioned, in the main, as instruments for liberal union leaders. Their political thrust was dissipated by two factors. First, they were unwilling to become pariahs by opposing the rise of industrial unionism within the liberal consensus. Instead, they hoped to gain an operational foothold in the mass industrial unions from which to develop radical politics later on. Second, radical politics gradually became more rhetorical than practical for the left-wingers who entered the CIO. And it did not matter whether the left-winger was in the CP or anti-CP; the central thread was the same. Most radicals were all too willing to follow John L. Lewis. To them, he was performing the necessary preparatory work for socialism, later—despite his procapitalist bias, now.

Most non-Communist radicals within the labor movement refused to follow the CIO leadership into the New Deal coalition. It was the one distinguishing feature separating their politics from those of the CP. But insofar as they supported the CIO itself and subordinated themselves to its program, they could not but aid the despised Democratic Party.

In sum, radical ideologies and organizations played virtually no independent role in the trade unions after 1935. The few dissenters were swiftly cast aside in the triumphant march of industrial unionism.

One hundred years ago workers fought desperately for their right to form unions and to strike for economic and social demands. Unions arose out of the needs of workers. In the period of the expansion of American capitalism they were important means for restraining the bestiality of capital. Even into the twentieth century, long after the labor movement as a whole stopped reflecting their interests, workers fought for unions. But their hope was not to become new agents of social transformation. Industrial workers joined unions in the twentieth century seeking a share in the expansion of American capitalism, not its downfall.

Since the 1920s, the ideology of expansion has permeated working-class consciousness. On the one hand, many workers have no faith that the corporations will provide for their needs unless forced to do so by powerful organizations. On the other, American expansion abroad and the intervention of the government into the operation of the economy have convinced workers that the frontier of economic opportunity is not closed to them. The persistence of the idea of individual mobility amidst recognition of the necessity for collective action is partially attributable to the immigrant base of a large portion of the industrial working class in the first half of the twentieth century. As previously noted, the comparative advantages of American capitalism over the semifeudal agrarian societies of Europe in the early part of this century remained vital influences on workers' consciousness despite the Great Depression. For the minority of radical immigrant workers who didn't accept the expansionist ideology, corporations and the government reacted with constant deportation, and jail terms.

Thus the violence of American labor struggles has had a contradictory influence upon the development of working-class consciousness. Although it indicates the militancy with which workers have been prepared to conduct their struggles, the readiness of employers and the government to use methods of severe repression to break strikes and purge the working class of its most militant elements has become a powerful object lesson. Working-class consciousness is suffused with a sense of the awesome power of the corporations over American life. Workers have sought and helped create unions which mirror the hierarchical structure of corporations and can compete with them in marshaling resources to bargain effectively with them. To many, James Hoffa was a hero not because he represented a challenge to the robber baron but because he was the labor equivalent of him; as the quintessential business union, the Teamsters was seen as a formidable opponent of the corporations.

Strikes in the United States are of longer duration than in any other advanced capitalist country. Workers know that large corporations cannot be immediately crippled by walkouts and that corporate resources are usually ample to withstand months of labor struggle. Moreover, in some industries employers have created strike insurance plans to protect themselves. Similarly, unions have developed institutional forms of strike insurance. The largest unions boast of huge strike funds. Although the threat of starvation is no longer an immediate deterrent to militancy, the legitimacy of labor unions among workers is reinforced by their ability to raise money and to render concrete assistance to strikers' families. During the 1970 auto strike, however, the multimillions in the United Auto Workers strike chest were exhausted within a few months, even though benefits never exceeded $25 a week for the several hundred thousand GM workers. At the same time, thousands of workers lost their savings. The companies had driven home another lesson to the workers; despite unions, strikes are expensive.

In 1946, the workers in most large American industries conducted a mass strike for substantial wage increases. The strike was largely successful since workers had been forced to endure a wage freeze for the entire period of World War II. Neither union leaders nor corporate opposition could thwart the resolve of industrial workers to walk out, and neither union leaders nor the corporations were anxious for the strike. Its resolution, however, did have an important influence on the course of the postwar economy. The companies finally acceded to the workers' demands, but exacted a major concession from the unions. The immediate consequence of the wage settlement was the announcement by the steel companies of a significant price increase. Union leaders remained mute, thus giving tacit support to the companies. Together, unions and corporations imposed the pattern of the wage-price spiral on the whole society. Organized workers learned that their power was sufficient to make gains in real wages, provided they did not make social demands; that is, challenge the profits of the companies or the commodities they produced. Further, they were convinced that the growing international role of the United States, particularly in rebuilding Europe, was necessary for their economic well-being. The 1946 mass strikes ended in reinforcing the ideology of expansion among workers. Consciousness was fragmented, since the workers could separate their role as producers from their role as citizens and consumers.

When the Communists, following the lead of the Soviet Union and the world Communist movement, opposed the extension of US hegemony abroad, they were not supported by the workers. Of course, it was true that the CP had lost much prestige by its wartime support of repressive labor policies. But, more important, it was also true that workers perceived the opposition to US foreign policy as a threat to their own welfare; they watched in silence while the government, aided by liberal union leaders, put Communists in jail for violating the non-Communist affidavit required by the Taft-Hartley Act.

It cannot be denied that working-class militancy has generally been ambivalent in the United States. Workers are no less antiemployer than any other working class in the world. Strikes are bloodier, conducted for longer periods, and often manifest a degree of solidarity unmatched by any other group of workers. But working-class consciousness is industry-oriented, if not always job-oriented. Workers will fight their unions and the companies through wildcat strikes and other means outside the established framework of collective bargaining. But they are ideologically and culturally tied to the prevailing system of power, because until now it has shown the capacity to share its expansion with a large segment of the working class.

These ideological ties, however, are much weaker among those segments of the working class that have historically been excluded from these shares—black workers, women, and youth. But since 1919 it has not been accurate to claim that black workers are not integrated at all into the industrial work force. Although they are excluded from unions representing skilled construction workers and underrepresented within the top echelons of union leadership, blacks constitute between one and two thirds of the workforce in the auto and steel industries, and smaller but significant proportions of other mass production industries. Most union response to the large number of black workers has been characterized at best by tokenism.

Union discrimination against blacks and, to a lesser extent, young white workers, has led to the formation of caucus movements, particularly inside the auto and steel unions, based on the specific sectoral demands of these groups. Some black caucuses seek more union power and, at the same time, demand upgrading to better-paying skilled jobs. Youth caucuses have been organized within the UAW making similar demands, but have gone further to suggest that the rigidity of industrial labor be relaxed. Some caucuses have asked that the uniform starting time of most workplaces be rescinded, that supervision be less severe, and that ways be found to enlarge job responsibility so that the monotony and meaninglessness of most assembly line tasks be mitigated. Young workers are groping for ways to control their own work, even though they are making piecemeal demands. Black workers are demanding liberation from the least satisfying of industrial tasks and more control over union decision-making processes.

But these are only tentative movements toward a different kind of working-class consciousness. Workers are still oriented toward making demands on companies and unions, and do not aim at taking autonomous control over their own lives. Within the American working class, no significant movement or section of workers defines itself as a class and sees its mission to be the same as the liberation of society from corporate capitalist social relations.

Such consciousness will never arise in America from abject material deprivation. The position of the United States in the world has become more precarious since the end of World War II, but workers know that American capitalism has not reached a dead end. However, the consciousness that most work in our society is deadening and much of it unnecessary has permeated the minds of young people, including the new entrants into the factories and offices. The growing awareness of the need for new forms of labor manifests itself in spontaneous ways. Corporations are becoming more concerned that young workers are not sufficiently disciplined to come to work on time or even every day. The new ideas for fewer workdays, even if the 40-hour work week is retained, are not likely to catch fire in the near future. But they indicate that corporations are searching for new methods of coping with the manifest breakdown of industrial discipline among the millions of workers who have entered the labor force in the past decade and have not experienced the conservatizing influence of the Depression. After all, if poverty is really not a threat for large numbers within our society, how can they be expected to endure the specialization of work functions and their repetitive character? The specter that haunts American industry is not yet the specter of communism, as Marx claimed. It is the specter of social breakdown leading to a new conscious synthesis among workers.

It is the practice of trade unions and their position within production that determines their role in the social process. The transformation of the working class from one among many competing interests groups to capitalism's revolutionary gravedigger depends on whether working-class practice can be freed from the institutions which direct its power into bargaining and participation within the corporate structure and can move instead toward workers' control.

The trade unions are likely to remain both a deterrent to the workers' initiative and a "third-party" force at the workplace, objectively serving corporate interests both ideologically and in the daily life of the shop, and remaining a diminishing instrument of workers' struggles to be employed selectively by them. But the impulse to dual forms of struggle—shop committees, wildcat strikes, steward movements—may become important in the labor movements of the future.

The rise of new instruments of workers' struggle would have to reject the institutionalization represented by the legally sanctioned labor agreement administered by trade union bureaucracies. Workers would have to make conscious their rejection of limitations on their freedom to take direct action to meet their elementary needs at the workplace. Although many wildcat strikes are implicitly caused by issues which go beyond wage demands, these remain hidden beneath the more gross economic issues. Labor unions are not likely to become formally committed to the ideas of workers' control over working conditions, investment decisions, and the objects of labor. On the contrary, they will remain "benefits"-oriented, fighting incessantly to improve the economic position of their own membership in relation to other sections of the workforce rather than in relation to the employers. They will oppose workers' efforts to take direct action beyond the scope of the union agreement and to make agreements with the boss on the informal basis of power relations on the shop floor.

The forms of consciousness that transcend trade unionism within the working class are still undeveloped and have not caught up with practice. Moreover, the perception that unions have become less useful institutions in the defensive as well as offensive struggles of workers, is confined to long-organized sections of the working class that have experienced the deterioration of the labor bureaucracies into instruments for the suppression of independent workers action. But barely twenty-five per cent of the workforce are members of trade unions. Workers in service industries and government employment who have been without union representation often regard trade unionism as a social mission.

For example, trade unionism still appears as a progressive force among the mass of working poor, such as farm and hospital workers, who labor under conditions of severe degradation. At first, unionization seems to be a kind of deliverance from bondage. But after the initial upsurge has been spent, most unions fall back into patterns of class collaboration and repression. At the point when grinding poverty has been overcome and unions have settled into their conservative groove, their bureaucratic character becomes manifest to workers.

We are now in the midst of a massive reevaluation by organized industrial workers of the viability of the unions. However, it is an action critique, rather than an ideological criticism of the union's role and the legal implications of it. It is still too early to predict its precise configuration in the United States. In the end, the spontaneous revolt will have to develop its own alternative forms of collective struggle and demands.

NOTES

1. Collective Agreement between Oil, Chemical, and Atomic Workers International Union and Gulf Oil Co., Port Arthur, Texas, 1966–9.

2. Matthew Josephson, *Sidney Hillman: Statesman of American Labor* (New York: Doubleday & Company, 1952), 124–5.

3. Walter Galenson, *The CIO Challenge to the AFL* (Cambridge, Mass.: Harvard University Press, 1960), 112.

4. Ibid. 112.

5. Robert R. R. Brooks, *As Steel Goes* (New Haven: 1940), 147, as quoted in Galenson, ibid.

6. Steelworkers Organizing Committee Proceedings of the Second International Wage and Policy Convention (1940), 132.

7. Earl Browder, Speech at Extraordinary Conference, July 1933, Communist Party of the United States in *The Communist*, Summer 1933.

8. Saul Alinsky, *John L. Lewis: An Unauthorized Biography* (New York: G.P. Putnam & Sons, 1949), 72.

9. Earl Browder, *The People's Front* (New York: International Publishers, 1938), 40.

10. Alexander Bittleman's Review of the Month in, *The Communist*, July 1937, 583.

11. Ibid., 584.

12. William Z. Foster, "Twenty Years of Communist Trade Union Policy," *The Communist*, November 1939.

13. Ibid.

14. Steelworker's Organizing Committee, Proceedings of the Second International Wage and Policy Convention (1940), 137, quoted in Galenson, op. cit. 114.

15. For a recent example see Staughton Lynd, "The Possibility of Radicalism in the

early 1930s: The Case of Steel," *Radical America*, 6/6 (Nov.–Dec. 1972). In this article, Lynd ascribed the failure of union democracy in the Steelworkers Union to the ambivalent position of the Communist Party in pursuing its trade union policy.

16. Art Preis, *Labor's Giant Step* (New York: Pioneer Publishers, 1964), xvi.

.

CHAPTER FIVE

The Decline and Rise
of Working-Class Identity

"The passing of Marxism-Leninism first from China and then from the Soviet Union will mean its death as a living ideology of world historical significance." So ends Francis Fukuyama's lament for the end of history, "a very sad time."[1] In his version of the end of ideology thesis, there are no Hegelian-Marxist contradictions that can be solved only by a relentless struggle for a "communist utopia." To be sure, according to Fukuyama, the Third World will remain "mired in history," but the triumph of liberalism, at least at the ideological level, means that change is bound to be incremental or, to be exact, simply characterized by perfections of a system already in place, at least consensually.

Whatever the political merits of this thesis, first enunciated, in various ways, more than thirty years ago by, among others, Daniel Bell and Seymour Martin Lipset, the implications of its key tenets—that our era is marked by conflict but not struggle, problems but not contradictions, unions but not classes, and, most important, that no concrete utopias can animate broad social movements—have barely been explored.[2] In the heady days of the 1960s, which appeared to be submerged in ideology and animated by the not-too-distant dreams of a "new morning" (later to be appropriated by Ronald Reagan), the American and European New Lefts had no doubt what agents of historical change there were. Although some abandoned the "old" working class for revolutionary youth, women, and, especially, the Third World, the framework of theoretical and political dispute remained "class analysis." For example, Shulamith Firestone's pathbreaking *Dialectic of Sex* and Nancy Hartsock's attempt to assert a "feminist" historical materialism, no less than the Mao-inspired works of Samir Amin privileging the agency of the Third World, adopted the class standpoint, only changing the actors.[3] In addition, the numerous "new" communist parties in the early seventies were persuaded that their versions of Marxism-Leninism would ultimately prevail over the pack of rival revisionists.

By the early 1980s, Marxism-Leninism appeared to have definitively passed into history, even before its standard-bearers, the State Socialist societies of Eastern Europe, Asia, and Cuba, entered their period of crisis. In retrospect, the last great working-class upheavals might have been those of the French May 1968 and the Italian "Hot Autumn" of the following year.[4] For the 1970s were, in consequence of these unprecedented events, in part marked by a long economic crisis and consequent world capitalist restructuring, the effect of which has been to shift the scenes of industrial production to the global South and East, leaving in its wake high levels of permanent unemployment, drastically reduced trade union strength and, perhaps most telling, except in Sweden and Southern Europe, the relegation of labor and socialist parties to perennial and embattled minorities.

The question has been boldly, if narrowly, raised by Fukuyama: if the industrial working class of the West no longer carries the social weight of world historical transformation is the concept of agency, itself, dead? For without agency, there can be no history except an automatic kind. Or are agents destined to play within the rules of the liberal-democratic game within a capitalist framework? If this is the case, what is the status of class in contemporary western societies, in the Third World, in Eastern Europe? And, are there new social and political agents—women, people of color, gays and lesbians, the radicalized ecological and consumer-minded middle classes? Finally, what is the relation between social movements and class? Do social movements replace or displace class as a new "motor force" of history? Surely, the proponents of the new social movements reject the old dialectical theoretical framework but, insofar as they still work within historical discourse, that is, remain in the problematic of the "new," they cannot fully escape historical materialism.

In what follows, my focus will be, in the main, on the United States, but I will address these issues in comparative perspective. While, at least on the surface, the US case may be considered "exceptional" to the European pattern of capitalist development the differences, I think, are not fundamental but are, instead, variations on the same economic, political and cultural themes. For European socialism abandoned revolutionary perspectives during the interwar period and adopted, instead, a long-term reform strategy that has entailed collaboration with its own rulers, much as the American labor movement and popular left which, in retrospect, were in the vanguard of this drift. The differences between the US and Europe relate to the differences of their history, respective political systems, and effectiveness. But welfare state progressivism based upon the struggle for economic justice, although not invented in the US, was developed most fully in the US of the 1930s, which was the crucial example of "regulated" capitalism.[5] The 1980s did not merely sound the death knell to the remains of revolutionary doctrine, but it has witnessed the NADIR of the strategy of class-based reform. Austerity has become a permanent slogan of the capitalist state in proportion as capital accumulation has slowed and taken different forms, making enlarging the social wage a zero-sum game. The working class and its main political vehicles have been forced to retreat on a broad front of increasing privatization, of production and social benefits in the US and in Europe. Although the US stands at one extreme of the end of capitalist regulation and Sweden at the other, various labor and socialist movements have arranged themselves along a spectrum of progressively deregulated national economies and weakened welfare state programs. The degree of resistance and solidarity determines the pace but not the direction of the retreat. Today, European labor and socialist movements rest on a higher level of the social wage, but have, with the exception of the German metalworkers' strike for a shorter work week, made no new dramatic gains.

I

In the face of the apparent passing of the era of workers' power, albeit in the reformist mode, the past decade is marked by the appearance of a new politics of "identity," the terms of which are defined by the ruins of the old universal values of modernity. These values—industrialism within a market capitalist system, a liberal state that guarantees parliamentary democracy and individual rights—and identities that are defined, at least for political purposes, by economic position and interest, live an uncomfortable existence in late capitalist societies of Western Europe and North America. As a political program, modernity enjoyed an initial ascendancy against the authoritarian state socialist regimes of Eastern Europe in the 1980s and became hegemonic, briefly, with the fall of Eastern European communism. However, when the Berlin Wall toppled, and it became evident that the revolution was reasonably secure from a possible counterattack by the old leaderships, nearly every brand of long-suppressed identities surfaced: nationalism, Catholicism, monarchism, agrarianism, all of which owed their animus to premodern culture. And, especially in the West, there has developed a new politics based on race and gender identities.

The politics of identity takes no universal form. In Eastern Europe and what is, mistakenly, termed the "Middle East," nationalism is conditioned by historical subordination of former client states to the Soviet Union or, in the case of the Arab and Muslim world, to Great Britain, France, and the United States. Lifting the Soviet yoke revealed the plain truth that under the rock of suppression seethed yearnings that cloaked strong authoritarian currents, despite the liberal-democratic program by which the anti-communist movement rode to power.

Of course, Arab nationalism requires no democratic veneer. The modernist tendencies, identified as specifically Western values, were soundly defeated by the Iranian revolution and subsequently submerged, if not eradicated, in normally secular Iraq and Egypt. As the Shah was ousted so were equal rights for women, closely linked in the Iranian context to anti-clericalism and, as it turned out, so were the possibilities for trade unionism and other forms of open class politics. Anti-imperialism, directed especially against the United States and Britain, has combined with a resurgent Islamic fundamentalism to produce a powerful pan-Arab movement that has subsumed class movements. Recently weakened by the Vietnam trauma, recession, and waves of new, apparently unmeltable immigrants from Asia, Latin America, and the Caribbean whose faith in the "American Dream" is tempered by virulent nativism, American nationalism is on the rise again in the wake of the Gulf War. This nationalism was preceded by a resurgent ethnicity in the 1970s, when large sections of the white working class—especially those with Eastern and Southern European roots—began to reevaluate the merits of assimilation and discovered one aspect of their oppression. In the Reagan era, the United States recovered its rampant militarism, which has been a crucial component of that peculiarly American idea of progress. For US reliance on force to achieve state objectives is a feature both of a foreign policy that has bathed its expansionist aims in the blood of others and of the various internal wars that have been the moral equivalent of the welfare state: the "wars" on crime, sex, drugs, terrorism, dissent, the labor movement, radicals.

Certainly, American nationality has lost its utopic dimension. Militarism is no longer mediated by vital democratic and libertarian traditions, no longer masked by America's image as the "golden door" to economic opportunity and social and political freedom, no longer opposed by progressivism that tried to link US imperial aims with the provision of domestic social justice. Like the British at the turn of the twentieth century, but also in the late 1940s, and the French just after the War, when their efforts to preserve empire in Southeast Asia and Algeria ended in bitter defeat and national humiliation, American nationalism rises in inverse proportion to declining US global hegemony. While it is premature to announce the invasions of Grenada, Panama, and the Persian Gulf as a "last gasp" of the US imperium which, for most of the past half century, was the leading economic and military power in the world, the government's almost ritual reversion to the use of force to reestablish its dominance is surely a sign of weakness.

At the same time, as the coalition that pursued the Gulf War shows, the global metastate is alive and well. In this context, descriptions of US imperialism are simply inadequate. Rather, US-based transnational corporations, together with an international political directorate closely linked to them, pursue their own version of imperial intervention with, of course, the nation-state performing an important, if subordinate function.

Recall that American troops have been deployed for the past century as instruments of US foreign policy in five major wars and an equal number of "delightful" skirmishes on foreign soil. Between 1898 and the Gulf War, US military has been involved in the following interventions to protect American interests:

- 1898: Spanish-American War. US occupies Puerto Rico, Philippines, Cuba
- 1911: Nicaragua
- 1917–8: World War I
- 1920: US joins twenty-one foreign armies, invades Soviet Union
- 1934: Nicaragua against the guerrilla forces of Sandino
- 1941–5: World War II
- 1950–4: Korea
- 1962: Cuba
- 1961–74: Southeast Asia
- 1964: Dominican Republic
- 1984: Grenada
- 1989: Panama
- 1990: Gulf War

Needless to say, the list here of small wars is incomplete but it is sufficient to belie the well-publicized isolationist impulse of the American people. Nor was the century devoid of discontinuous but powerful patriotic fervor linked, in the main, to the reality of US and transnational interests. I would venture the hypothesis that these interests were and are an extension of that intrinsic internal will to expansionism that has marked the entire compass of US history, the signals of which are the French and Indian War of 1763, the Lewis and Clark expedition (1804), the wholesale theft of African tribes to enlarge the slave labor force, the Civil War, and the Indian wars of the latter half of the nineteenth century. The recent and very naive idea, that one may join the armed forces for purely educational and training reasons or for the vague aim of "defense," may be ascribed to the post-Vietnam syndrome, the illusion of the end of the Cold War, or anything else you like. What is abundantly clear is this: if young Americans believed that they would be spared the toils, but not the spoils, of war, they were deeply mistaken. After the Gulf War, the symbol of American identity remains the centaur, electronically mediated, of course. The American as policeman is supplemented by what has become a national scandal: the emergence of a permanent covert intelligence force that not only plays a vital role in foreign policy—keeping tabs on other governments, toppling or undermining them when they show signs of independence, and so forth—but also in domestic. The CIA is only the most visible of a complex network whose internal surveillance of US citizens, labor unions, and social movements has never relaxed since the 1920s. The other side to identity politics is no less disruptive of the older assumptions that social divisions were defined by national boundaries and class affiliations. Although national identity retains its mesmerizing power among large sections of the underlying population, the last two decades have been marked, in nearly all major countries of the late capitalist West, by a discernable decline in politics in which class, rather than race, gender, or ethnicity, was a crucial element. Of course, this is especially true of the United States, where class-defined movements have been weak throughout its history, but also Britain, France, Germany, and Italy, where socialist and labor movements constituted the heart of the social and political opposition for most of the twentieth century. With the exception of the United States, socialist and labor parties still occupy the space of the alternative to capitalist hegemonies, but no longer represent what might be termed the *determinate negation of the prevailing order*. Rather, they have settled for the position of "loyal opposition." Socialist parties and the former Italian Communist Party (now the Democratic Party of the Left) are national parties of order. Similarly, the class struggle is relentlessly waged, but, with few exceptions, the initiative has passed, perhaps decisively to capital and its political retainers. With few exceptions, the labor movements, still the mass organizations of workers, have become almost reflexively shy of militant strike action; their most fervent wish is that the status quo will remain in force.

231

II

Inevitably, the concept of class entails abstraction and a severe reduction. The multiplicities of concrete relations and, in contemporary parlance, of identities of individuals and collectivities are understood in one reading of historical materialism that, until recently, was dominant within Marxism, as mediations of what is conveniently described as a *fundamental* structuring relation of capital to exploited labor. Or, in the structuralist mode of analysis, the polarity of Marx's two-class model is, within this, ascribed the highest level of abstraction, termed "mode of production." Below this, the "social formation," the so-called intermediate classes, may play a larger or smaller political role depending on the specificity of a country's history.[6] However, in all versions of Marxism, class retains its dominance as a *structuring* relation. Within the paradigm, identities that may motivate political mobilization, such as gender, race and ethnicity, and even nationality, are named *displacements* of class relations and are ascribed to the unevenness of capitalist development or the specific conjuncture of the social formation which, typically, produces caste and stratification within those classes that structure the system.

Marx defined capital as a social relation the hidden term of which was that it is constituted by *labor*.[7] Capital appears in the forms not only of money, but also machinery, buildings, and raw materials, which are merely materializations of quantities of living labor. In Hegel's master-slave dialectic, the slave is the object of domination by the master but, in turn, is the vehicle through which humans dominate nature.[8] Living labor, as the embodiment of the multiplicity of nature's endowments is, for Marx, the condition for the reproduction of the entire social order, most particularly the relations of production and the social relations, the multiplicity of which is what we mean by the term "society." For Marx, the mode of appropriation of the surplus—in capitalist production relations the extraction of surplus value—is, at the end of the day, the fundamental structuring relation that determines all other social forms, including the state and politics.

Although Marx never denies the importance of considering that multiplicity of relations and, especially in his historical writings, insists on their pertinence for explaining concrete events at the political and social levels, he is chiefly concerned to reveal the underlying logic that governs the long wave of historical transformation. The subject term in the celebrated phrase "All history is the history of class struggles"[9] is "history" which, for Marx, connotes, in the first instance, the act in which "the production of the means to satisfy...needs, the production of material life itself."[10] Since this production depends on the means that nature provides, the degree to which production becomes a historical act seems to be inversely linked to the natural endowments any group of people confronts. The more nature provides, the less history is made. (This, of course, is an over-coded inference but would explain many wars and other acts of conquest.)

Conversely, human communities that are obliged to use relatively scarce natural resources to produce their means of subsistence tend to become the first sites of history—making in proportion as labor develops its various skills and cultivates its talents. Among these societies obliged by deficits in natural endowments to engage in the appropriation of nature for human ends, science (even in its mythic form) and technology, the names we give to the codification and further development of crafts, on the one hand, and magic, on the other, come to occupy a privileged place within the capitalist epoch. For science, like commodity exchange, entails processes of abstraction, such as quantification, from particular differences to achieve homogeneity among apparently diverse objects.

Thus, the concept of the common denominator, a basic mathematical procedure, is crucial for understanding the meaning of class. The Marxist notion of class can only be fully grasped as a concept that conforms to the requirement of any scientific object that it be stripped of its overdeterminations, that is, the effects of conjunction and contingency and the multiplicity of relations on its constitution. In turn, the problem for a scientific theory of class is to specify those characteristics that link one type of social object with another, even at the risk of ignoring those characteristics that differentiate them.

For historical materialism, the significance of religion in earlier modes of production is that its agents—shamans, medicine men, priests—are not only the first intellectuals but also the nascent ruling class. And priests, philosophers, the early scientists, medicine men, and rainmakers are the first repositors, in the form of ritual, of intellectual knowledge as a distinct social category. In the division of labor, the bearers of intellectual knowledge gradually become the first ruling class, while the bearers of "know-how"—possessors of practical knowledge—women who are the first farmers, and men, the hunters, gatherers, and craftpersons, constitute the subaltern classes, but not, of course, on an equal footing. Although women are assigned, within the division of labor, to cultivation of animals and the land which, accordingly, is perhaps the first "history-making" occupation, their agency is erased by male force. For hunters and gatherers possess lethal weapons with which to assure domestic tranquility on the basis of their own dominance.

Ironically, women's identity remains—despite the anthropological dispute about the existence of matrilineal, even the possibility of matriarchal, societies at the dawn of civilization—that of domestic servants to men, the history-makers. Although it would not be difficult to show that women engage in production as well as reproduction of the species, not only physically but socially, and women's work is the absolutely necessary precondition of social production—especially in agrarian societies where a significant portion of the means of existence is produced in the household by women and children—women's identity remains intractably gendered.[11] The class reduction does not seem to work here, except economically. With the advent of ancient society—Greece, Rome, and Mesopotamia among other states, women remain doubly subordinate—to the lord or the capitalist, and to their husbands—in various social formations within what might be termed "modern" history, that is, the epoch beginning with the transition from feudalism to capitalism.

From what is euphemistically described as "pre-history" to the present times, bearers of intellectual and technical knowledge have themselves entered into ruling groups as professional servants, but also as members of the "council of elders" that sometimes governs and, as often, constitutes a sort of secret or at least discrete government, deposes governments from kings to democratically elected officials.

I shall discuss other irreducible identities, such as ethnicity and race, in this essay. For now, I simply want to signal some of the problems entailed by the claim for class as the central problematic of history. It is simply not the case that women have, except in "pre"-civilized societies, been able to enter history when they engage in social production. Nor does class formation overcome racial and ethnic formations, except under very particular circumstances. When Marx claims in the *Eighteenth Brumaire* "Men make their own history," we should misread this statement to refer to gendered actors.

As is well known, historical materialism claims that modes of production are constituted by class divisions that, until the rise of capitalism, were most relevant, in political terms, among various sections of ruling classes. The subordinate classes of slave and feudal societies were simply incapable of presenting themselves to themselves much less to their masters as alternative forces of social rule. There were, of course, examples of slave and peasant revolts—some of which, notably the English peasant uprising in 1381, were virtual harbingers of things to come.[12] More to the point, subaltern resistances, expressed in slowdowns and sabotage, when not in direct strike action, have always constrained the economic and political power of ruling groups. Yet it is the antagonism between the producers and masters that remains, in every epoch, the fundamental one, while intra-class conflicts among sections of the ruling class depend, in the last analysis, on the surplus generated by labor.

In Marxist terms, the working class in the capitalist epoch is the first exploited class in human history capable of both making a revolution and of universalizing its own interests. Marx's logic, that "the specific form in which unpaid surplus labor is pumped out of the direct producers determines the relationship between those who dominate and those who are in subjection," is cited in a multiplicity of forms to assert that domination "grows directly out of production itself and reacts upon it as a determining element in its turn."[13] The centrality of class to social conflict derives from this theoretical argument; and the historical evidence that the working class in the most technologically and industrially developed societies has made a series of long-term compromises with capital and the political directorate has not, in the main, dissuaded Marxist intellectuals and revolutionary socialist activists. All efforts to amend socialist theory in the light of historical analysis and political experience are rudely condemned as "revisionism"; and the consequence of this virtual epithet has been that debates within Marxism and other elements of revolutionary socialism are circumscribed by the simple truths uttered by Marx more than a century ago, that:

> It is always the direct relationship of the owners of the conditions of production to the immediate producers—a relation *always* [emphasis mine] naturally corresponding to a definite stage in the development of the nature and method of labour and consequently of its social productivity— which reveals the innermost secret, the hidden foundation of the entire social structure and therefore of the political form of the relations of sovereignty dependency, in short the corresponding specific form of the state.[14]

G. E. M. de Ste. Croix has, I think correctly, singled this passage out as one of the crucial statements of what might be described as "classical" historical materialism. For Marx, the literal sense of the relations of production is the "hidden foundation of the entire social structure," a formulation that would refute attempts by revisionists, especially cultural Marxists, to claim Marx for their own by citing different passages from the early manuscripts, and especially the *Grundrisse*, where this archetonic prose is surely modified and otherwise qualified. When combined with some similarly decisive passages from *Capital*, Ste. Croix is able to claim that history is, indeed, the history of class struggles. In this interpretation, the fundamental class question is the mode by which surplus is extracted at the point of production; the "direct relationship" between owners of the conditions of production and the producers can be periodized and the forms will vary, but the structure remains constant. History becomes an account of the different forms of domination determined by the mode of surplus extraction. When confronted by this elegant formulation of class and class struggle the New Left had little or no use for the social-democratic alternative (or, in the United States, progressive liberalism) because these forces and their reformist doctrines were considered hopelessly compromised by the welfare capitalism and, equally important, stand condemned of theoretical and ideological emptiness, a charge that was, to say the least, harsh. The new revolutionary left arose as a rejection of progressivist premises, if not entirely their program.

The way the story of class compromises is told by some strands of neo-Marxist historiography and sociological analysis, workers have been frequently betrayed by trusted leaders—party and trade union bureaucrats or rank-and-file heroes who, even when not for personal gain, have misdirected the class struggle into reformist blind alleys.[15] This version of the past assumes that the workers have the will but not the capacity for self-organization, owing to their educational deficits; their ideological backwardness generated by such elements of false consciousness as racism, nationalism, and sexism; or their de-skilled position. Within this explanatory paradigm, the possibility that workers, themselves, made what they considered to be rational choices is inadmissible. At the same time, considering the power of the trade union and party bureaucracies in Northwestern Europe after World War I and throughout Europe after the 1940s, the considerable conservative influence of organization acted as a constraint upon the workers' movement. Recall the French, Italian, and US wildcat strikes of the early 1970s which were fiercely opposed by the leadership before, in some cases, being coopted.[16] Yet, their existence attests to the growing ability of more highly qualified industrial workers to form their own leadership because the "objective" conditions of highly concentrated capitalist production, combined with the freeing of laborer from feudal dependency, generated social movements capable of articulating their own demands on the political as well as the economic level. In contrast, those who suffered domination and were rendered powerless by social marginalization—peasants, women, sub-proletarians, that is, workers not linked to the decisive sectors in the social division of labor within mature capitalism—were certainly worse off, at least in many respects, than most industrial workers. Yet, their ability to enter history, that is, to become agents of social transformation, remained limited by their chronic incapacity for self-organization, especially at the political level.

In contrast to nineteenth-century England and turn-of-the-century Europe, when the class problematic dominated economic and political struggles, the tendency of contemporary politics has been to privilege the struggle against domination over exploitation. This has occurred, in part, as a consequence of the decline of working-class social and political hegemony over the systemic opposition, but also the rise of new problems: the significance of consumption as a social and political problematic, especially for the growing legions of intellectual labor within late capitalism; the re-emergence of what might be called caste struggles; and, most especially, the declining significance of work. Surplus value is still extracted from workers, especially, in recent times, from tens of millions of workers in the southern portion of the globe—which has stimulated the rise of workers' movements in countries such as constitute themselves as an independent, extra-parliamentary, and extra-trade union force. In turn, the partial breakdown of this historic postwar compromise between organized labor and capital played a crucial role in stimulating the world capitalist restructuring that, among other things, was directed against the workers' power to resist.

We must distinguish exploitation from domination, although this distinction is ambiguous in Marx's writings. Recall, Marx never claimed the working class was the most *oppressed* or *dominated* class in the capitalist mode of production, only the most exploited. His concept of exploitation, linked to the labor process, the crucial site of the intersection of humans and nature, endowed labor with its history making power. As we have already seen, for Marx, the mode of surplus extraction is the structuring relation of the entire mode of production, including the forms of the state.

Marx argued that the character of the specifically capitalist mode of production enabled labor to become a class in the historical sense, because capital freed labor, however brutally, from the "idyllic relations" of feudal dependency. While this evaluation proved somewhat optimistic in the wake of working-class history since the mid-1850s, its crucial point— that serfs and other peasants were freed from bondage to become wage laborers—possessed considerable force. Like all previous laboring classes, the proletariat remained exploited, but was no longer dominated by capital, if by that term we signify relations of dependency. Workers possessed the capacity for self-organization, in Brazil, South Africa, and Korea, to name the most prominent. In these regions the class problematic is alive and well, even if, in both South Africa and Brazil, mediated by racial domination. Yet, the long-term movement, especially in the "West" and in Eastern Europe, is away from an exclusive or even predominant focus on traditional class identities and towards their (partial) replacement by considerations of gender and color which raise caste questions.

The two-class model that Marx proposed to grasp the structure of mature capitalism, its probable political struggles and historic outcomes—where intermediate classes, such as independent, commercial proprietors, professions, and peasants, are proletarianized (if this term is confined to loss of property)—has been largely fulfilled. On the one hand, we have witnessed the appearance of new categories of salaried scientific/technical intellectuals whose class position, at once powerful and ambiguous, has become the object of considerable debate. On the other hand, the end of regulated capitalism in the late 1960s has been accompanied by vast shifts in the sites of production from north to south; the domination of intellectual over manual labor; and the shift in the psychological and political scene of conflicts from the realm of production to the sphere of consumption owing, among other things, to a growing popular perception of ecological crisis. Clearly, the emergence of what has become known as "consumer society" does not signify that Marx's argument—that consumption is the flip side of production—is thereby refuted.[17] But, struggles over the conditions of work, which occupied such a prominent place in the late 1960s and early 1970s, became somewhat muted in the face of what must be described as a historically significant defeat for the working class, which suffered extensive decomposition and recomposition during the following decade.

The potential power of the industrial working class emanated from its social location—chiefly from the concentration of production in large cities; from the relatively homogeneous experience of migration from the country to the city shared by millions of people within, but not across national boundaries; and from its juridical independence from the employer, if not from the state. In contrast to the widely scattered small peasants, for example, the new industrial workers possessed means of communication facilitated by the proximity of work-sites and home-sites. Their capacity for self-organization was overdetermined by these features which, however, were each a part of a structured totality. While neither Marx nor his more discerning followers claimed that revolution inevitably flows from features such as large-scale enterprises situated in large cities, there remained a high probability that, under certain conditions, they would conjoin to produce the revolutionary conditions. Here is Marx on communications:

> A relatively thinly populated country, with well developed means of communication, has a denser population than the more numerously populated country, with badly developed means of communication; and in this sense the Northern States of the American Union, for instance, are more thickly populated than India.[18]

Thus, one can derive a theory of class struggle and class consciousness from the crucial part played by communication for insuring the conditions for solidarity. When Marx argues that the French peasants could not form a class because of the isolated conditions of their existence, the presence of social communications would, presumably, facilitate class formation among a group having a common position with respect to production relations. "Communication" is the condition for the constitution of a common cultural community without which political self-representation is not possible. What is explicitly lacking here, but implied by the category of communication, is a concrete theory that links these "objective" preconditions to the process of self-consciousness of a group as a group. How do groups take themselves as their own objects, placing their particular situation in a historical rather than local context? In this respect, the great American Hegelian pragmatist George Herbert Mead may provide a clue in his explicit invocation of communication in which self and other are fused.[19] For Mead, the "I" becomes the "me" when, through communication, the ego moves from action based on personal needs to group action, a development that presupposes its recognition as a social self. What remains indeterminate in this narrative is the nature of the group that becomes the basis of the social self. As we shall see, communication may not lead to class consciousness but may, instead, produce a social self in other terms, especially race, nationality, and gender. The revolution might not inevitably succeed, but the *possibility* that the proletariat could make society in its image was produced by the conditions for capitalism's expansion, and concomitant development, of means of communication that provide the necessary population *density* without which class consciousness cannot congeal. This indeterminacy is the space of the relative autonomy of politics and organization that became the core of Leninist doctrine.

For mature capitalist states of the nineteenth century and the first half of the twentieth century, social and cultural identities were forged by the categories of class and strata: everyday life, aesthetic expressions, and cognitive mappings articulated with production relations. People who lived in cities and towns settled in subcommunities or neighborhoods composed mainly of factory and white-collar workers or, on the other side of town, professionals and entrepreneurs. Until suburbanization in the late twentieth century tended to blur these lines, friendships, extended families, and consumption patterns rarely violated class boundaries—even in the United States. The major exception, and one which has had a powerful impact on American ideology, was the relative fluidity of the boundary between working class and small business— exemplified by those industries such as farming, needle trades, small machine shops, and stores such as grocery shops or bars, where a small, but significant, fraction of skilled workers went in and out of business throughout their working lives.

III

Before embarking on a more detailed exploration of the fate of class discourse in the United States, I am compelled to enter a small digression. Deleuze has called attention to Bergson's discussion on the importance of the correct posing ofproblems.[20] Within this context Bergson has identified three wrong moves.

The assumption of questioners is that disorder precedes order, that non-being precedes being, and that one must ask questions about the "real" rather than the "possible." With respect to class, the problem has been posed in the following form: Do classes "exist" in the United States? Specifically, is there a "working class" in US society? The assumption is that we can know whether classes actually exist by invoking a determinate series of scientific criteria for class formation to which the supposed reality would conform. For example, some have defined classes by economic identification that is, posit axiomatically, that a working class exists when those engaged in production neither own nor control the decisive means of production.[21] Or, in a somewhat more sophisticated argument, do wage workers in a particular national context act collectively and independently to further their interests at the workplace, in the political arenas, and constitute independent cultural communities?

Obviously, we have here versions of the correspondence theory of truth where scientific statements are made about a reality that is said to preexist outside of them. But, if we pose the problem differently, asking, historically, what has been the fate of the *possibility* of workers forming a class or, more broadly, of class discourse to structure political and cultural life?, then the solution is far more tentative. One cannot answer the existential question by scientific statements, but must trace the fairly complex disrupted history of class through *discursive* analysis within any given social formation. In this inquiry, class is taken as a prospect whose "being" is never permanent or fixed in national life. Like nationalism, it is a contingent identity whose power is not fixed, but must be evaluated within a determined set of circumstances.

The official ideology insists that, unlike industrial Europe, there are no classes in the United States, if by this term we connote that political and cultural identities are typically forged by a definite relationship of individuals and groups to the ownership and control of the means of production, but more specifically to communities in which labor shares similar conditions of life, a common culture, and means of communication. These characteristics facilitate cohesive organization and, penultimately, political self-representation. Stated more broadly, the American popular, as well as sociological, imagination remains solidly infused with the idea that America is set off from all other societies, virtually, by the opportunities it affords for vertical mobility. In its more sophisticated "progressive" variants, the "rags-to-riches" doctrine is easily dismissed, especially after the Great Depression. But, liberal/progressive thought celebrates the chance, principally through universal access to higher education, for the son or daughter of a laborer to advance to professional and technical occupations. Thus, professionalization has largely replaced entrepreneurship as the basis for the widespread view, even among the popular left, that America isa middle-class society. Within this context

discrimination—against people of color, women, and sexual minorities—
is deplored as a historical anomaly within a generally democratic culture.
Surely, full civil rights requires, according to this view, a resolute struggle against ingrained prejudices, as well as short-term interests of employers who might benefit from the lowered wages that result from racial
or gender exclusions. But, progressivism stands on the optimistic judgment that economic expansion successfully combined with democratic
vision and strong trade unions can overcome the remaining inequalities.

As Abercrombie and Urry have pointed out,[22] American sociology
virtually equates class and status: skilled versus unskilled, intellectual
versus manual labor, professionals opposed to "lay" people, seem the
more urgent basis of distinction than relations of ownership. In turn,
especially after the 1920s, when a new "Fordist" credit system was introduced,[23] status is achieved not exclusively through occupational or
production relations but, as well, through *consumption*. The new status
symbols are home ownership; possessing other consumer durable goods,
such as late model automobiles and appliances; higher education that
now can be purchased, just like houses and cars, on the installment plan;
and the increasingly important status signifier—travel opportunities.
The replacement of class by a new status order antedates World War II,
but it was more closely articulated, at first, with traditional class boundaries. Professions such as law, medicine, and the clergy were typically
part of the old middle class of small entrepreneurs who, in towns and
small cities, constituted a significant part of the civic leadership.

However, the vast expansion of consumer credit after the War meant
that wages and salaries no longer expressed rigid boundary conditions
to consumption; they differentiated the *quality* of houses and cars, not
whether workers could buy them. With the growing importance of scientifically based technologies in the production sectors, the expansion
of financial services, and the emergence of the scientific management
of society as a crucial element of the American social imagination, not
only in factories but also in the welfare sector and the military, postsecondary education became increasingly important. Perhaps the most significant new development in what Marx termed the *forces* of production
was the growing centrality of knowledge and the dramatic expansion of

universities as its crucial site. The shift from an emphasis on manual to intellectual labor in production has had far-reaching effects. It has altered the terms of politics in all late-capitalist societies, and more globally has transformed the culture. One change in the twentieth century was the formation of the *salaried employee* as a prototype of the new worker. This shift applied not only to engineering and other technically based professions which were created in the era of the large corporation, but also the traditional occupations of law and medicine. By the 1970s, most medical and law school graduates could expect to work for health or legal organizations: lawyers may never become partners, physicians never open their own practice.

In sum, the advent of postwar mass higher education and the perfection of consumer society through the development of new communications arenas, such as television, combined with dramatic US economic expansion to vitiate the social weight of the classes linked to the older industrial order. That order has been described as "regulated" or "organized" capitalism, the heart of which was the close articulation of production and consumption, of work and leisure, and of the state with the production system.[24] Workers in the mass production industries which, after the 1930s, tended to be unionized, and technical and other stable white-collar occupations (which were not typically in unions), enjoyed a level of material well-being that was, until the 1960s when Europe largely recovered from war-devastation, unprecedented in world history.

These achievements eliminated neither distinction nor conflict. People were differentiated on new bases that bore, at most, an indirect relation to class. And, consumerism introduced new types of social conflict. Yet, what counts here is that, notwithstanding the increasing *objective* proletarianization of more than eighty per cent of the US population,[25] identities based on relations of production were significantly loosened.

In the postwar era, we have witnessed the emergence of social movements organized around a new conception of rights that marks the shifts of identity. From the burning passions of the first decades of this century to secure social justice, the new social movements have focused on the quality of life-values that articulate with the emergence of the scientific and technical intelligentsia as significant social and cultural actors. These movements have focused attention in some of the leading late-capitalist countries on the nutritional and chemical content of food, the purity of air and water, the need to protect forests and other "wilderness" areas from industrial exploitation, but also the right to pleasure, to be free of social domination. In contrast to what might be termed the politics of environmental purity that were propelled, at the turn of the twentieth century, by a fairly narrow layer of the intelligentsia, these movements have grown to such proportions that qualitative issues have replaced the old struggles for social justice at the cutting edge of political and social practices. This shift has occurred even as, ironically, living standards for most Americans, evaluated in quantitative measures, have steadily declined.

For example, from a relatively insignificant band of what were called "conservationists"—zealot birdwatchers and hikers who objected to the exploitation by industrial corporations and land developers of "wilderness" preserves for oil exploration, lumber, and suburban housing—the ecology movement has grown into a worldview as much as a series of institutions and popular protests which have challenged, intellectually, many of the sacred assumptions about progress through industrial expansion and, equally importantly, have forced reluctant national and local governments, which, whatever their ideological hue in the old terms, are relentless modernizers, to reform both practices and laws affecting the environment. Ecological thought questions whether *growth* is acceptable in the light of the greenhouse effect and other long-term threats to human survival.[26] Some argue that centralized, mass production regimes are deleterious to the environment, and that most human needs should be provided on a regional, even local basis;[27] and, social ecology powerfully challenges the premise that consumerism is a viable life-style in the face of ecological crisis, even in the face of evidence that its ideological influence may be attributed to the growth of consumerism as a social concern.[28]

In the past twenty years, the environmental movement has constituted a powerful force for eliminating chemicals in food processing, purifying water, controlling industrial and auto pollution, as well as fought the nuclear industry to a virtual standstill in the late 1970s and early 1980s.[29] In a major struggle of 1989–90, environmentalists have, for example, stopped the lumber industry in Oregon from felling old trees.

Earlier, spurred by intellectuals grouped around what became known as Public Interest Groups, the New York Public Interest Research Group halted New York's Westway project that would have replaced Manhattan's decayed highway system with a larger superfreeway. Environmentalists have come close to making oil spills, such as Exxon's Valdez spill off Alaska's coast, a crime punishable by imprisonment for corporate officials. In the 1990s, the scourge of overflowing garbage in major metropolitan areas, the alarming rise of big-city pollution attributed to automobile fuel emissions, and similar issues that strike to the core of what constitutes decent urban life are good candidates to dominate local politics rather than struggles to house the growing number of homeless in large cities, the massive increase in permanent joblessness, or deteriorating school and health facilities and services.[30]

But, as opposed to the solid achievements of specific environmental struggles, ecology has scored its most important success by entering the social imaginary. Ecology proposes not only repairing environmental damage through greater state regulation, but a new mode of life in which nature is taken not as an antagonist to culture, but as a partner. There are, of course, conservative versions of this imaginary, particularly the movement known as *Earth First* or deep ecology, in which human priorities are subordinate to those of the supposed natural order. Moreover, nature-loving is inherent in some versions of fascist ideology. And, it has been shown that a powerful ecological strain emanates from Malthusian assumptions, especially the relationship between earth's natural endowments and human appetites.[31] But, these conservative theories only serve to emphasize that ecology is a social movement, if by that term we designate movements that propose new ways of ordering our lives, in this case, new possibilities of social being. As social movements mature, their unity is often sundered by their growing popular character. People are attracted to them from different sides of the ideological spectrum. In the most powerful cases—laborism, socialism and anarchism, race and sex gender, for example—we can observe ideological realignment. What counted as "left" and "right" changes according to whether individuals or groups support the worldview (rather than the concrete demands) of the movement. In this respect, ecology is no exception. For example, the old wisdom, according to which achieving social justice crucially depends on the effectiveness of policies of economic growth in the global South as well as the North, is in crisis because of the claims of ecological theory. Moreover, consumerism as a way of life is in serious trouble, not only because of the world economic restructuring, but also because of the permeation of the ecological challenge into the collective belief systems of significant elements of the population.

Similarly, feminism has made an enormous impact. Its demands— from the fairly consensual call for gender equality in employment, income, and education, to the more controversial abortion rights struggle, to the radical argument for sharing child-rearing-have shaken the foundations of patriarchal culture. For when child-rearing is no longer, in the last instance, the mother's responsibility, working hours and, more profoundly, production expectations would be transformed. For example, the common practice of compulsory overtime for both industrial workers and managers would be, in the main, abolished in a regime of equal responsibility between males and females for child-rearing. Even if this proposal has not reached the stage of social practice or even of concrete political demands, it is a logical consequence of a thoroughgoing regime of social and economic equality.[32]

Moreover, some strands of feminism have developed a sweeping critique of contemporary culture as ineluctably gendered—production relations, social and personal relations, and knowledge, especially science—that, taken together, approaches the status of a social and political theory that may be considered an alternative to both liberalism and Marxism. Some writers, such as Ursula K. Le Guin and Joanna Russ, have constructed concrete utopias the effect of which would be to abolish reproductive difference, which, in their conceptions, grounds gender domination.[33] Others, such as Donna J. Haraway, Evelyn Fox Keller, and Sandra Harding[34] have shown that the universalist claims of science can be successfully challenged on the grounds that science is gendered. (For Haraway, for instance, science is constitutive and is constituted by the imperium, the will to expansion, the male imaginary of power.) And cultural radicals have, despite the counterattack by cultural conservatives of the left as well as the right, maintained their insistence on a woman's right to pleasure and, most recently, have joined with civil libertarians in opposing the efforts of some feminists to ban pornography on the argument that it is a form of violence against women.

Like other social movements, feminists divide ideologically the more the social imaginary becomes a burning issue. Yet, these differences can hardly obscure the fact that the debate concerns the conditions of possibility of alternative ways of life and that the persistent struggles for concrete reforms are not merely ameliorative of contemporary conditions, but are comprehended by a substantial fraction of the movement as part of a larger strategy of blurring the line between being-subordinate and the non-being of liberation whose boundaries are continually shifting.

These last two decades have witnessed contradictory developments for black Americans. On the one hand, the general decline of the labor movement that has resulted in the political marginalization of the discourse of social justice constitutes nothing less than a catastrophe for blacks. By every economic indicator—employment and income, housing, healthcare and mortality, education—material conditions of life have drastically deteriorated for blacks. The black poor are growing much faster than any other section of the population, and black communities suffered extreme hardship during the 1980s, when many other groups were prospering. On the other hand, these have been years of unprecedented expansion of the black middle class. Large corporations, federal, state, and local governments, universities, and leading social welfare institutions have actively promoted hiring programs for black managers and professionals.

Among the consequences of these developments is a distinctly new ideology that seeks to shift the Black Freedom Movement from its focus on racial discrimination and exclusion to constituting black identity within an ethnic context. The term "African-American" is now widely employed in universities. This strategy attempts to reproduce the hyphen between earlier immigrants' country of origin and their adaptation to American nationality. The designation "African" becomes an equivalent of, say, "Polish" or "Irish," and is designed to obliterate the significance of racial designation which has been both a class and a caste displacement throughout US history. Although racial identification has been the bane of their social and political existence and has been condemned by liberal social science as a crass instance of social Darwinism,[35] its ironic adoption by the most militant sections of the Black Freedom Movement since the nineteenth century was a strategic maneuver designed to forge greater solidarity among people of color. The declaration "I'm a race man" signified that the speaker recognized black people in the United States as a *class* sharing a common economic, political, and cultural fate that was not only different from that of whites, even the most disadvantaged ethnic minorities such as Latinos or Italian-Americans, but was ultimately antagonistic.

"African-American" stands on the boundary of ethnicity and nationality. It proclaims difference and the right to cultural autonomy, but identifies with the dominant nation. In effect, the term can be read as a reconciliation with the dominant economic and political arrangements after the age of the civil rights upsurge in which blacks won partial citizenship. But it is also profoundly shaped by the ebbing of hope among the black working class in the wake of the triumph of economic liberalism over regulated capitalism, and especially of doctrines that the market, rather than the state, should regulate economic gains. As the race/class matrix becomes increasingly sharp, sections of the black intelligentsia have come down for ethnicity. The implication of the shift toward a more subcultural identification is that legal remedies—if not legislation then juridical decisions—can partially erase the profound exclusions that have remained, historically, relatively intractable for the majority of blacks.

Of course, there can be no doubt that, since the mid-1960s, federal courts have been an extremely effective force for making room for a significant layer of black professionals and managers within corporations, universities, and state and local governments, even as conditions for the black working class have badly deteriorated—especially in the 1980s, when federal policy reversed the two decades during which, through national welfare policy, some sub-proletarian strata of the black working class made economic advances. However, deindustrialization, combined with the Reagan administration's program to slowly strangle the welfare state, has resulted in impoverishment for millions of blacks and other people of color.[36]

Class identities, which received their underpinning from ideology as well as culture, are severely undercut by these competing identities, especially because ecology and feminism have articulated new global ideologies that transgress the compromise that workers have conventionally made with the prevailing order and are linked to movements that are publicly visible. Just as the Black Freedom Movement of the 1950s and 1960s challenged the conventional class identity of many African-Americans with a racial or ethnic alternative that held out the possibility of a separate politics, economics, and culture that revived the memory of social movements cannot be divorced from the relative weakness of the old interest-based class in the political and cultural debates. Later, I shall explore some of the reasons for this state of affairs. In contrast, Europeans are far more resistant to global displacements, preferring to "make space" for racial, ecological, and feminist issues within the framework of the (hegemonic) socialist movement whose fealty to class ideology, even if eroded (especially in France and Britain), is still powerful. There are parallel developments in the US Democratic Party and, to a lesser degree, in the US labor movement as well. The difference is this: European socialisms, including the communists, may have abandoned their revolutionary doctrines, but remain ideologically wedded to the class compromise under which the welfare state was established after World War II, a series of reforms that recognized the working class as a crucial component of national solidarity, and the provision of universal social welfare as a human right.

Nevertheless, as the fifteen-year history of the German and Belgian Green Parties demonstrates, the integrative capacities of social democracy remain strained by the introduction of the new social paradigms of ecology, feminism, and racial justice—strained because these are precisely the issues that were historically sacrificed by the compromise with capital. Thus, although social democratic parties and communists have belatedly "gone along" with the issues deriving from the new paradigm, the gap between their traditional philosophy and program and the new philosophical premises of the Greens remains wide. The question for traditional socialism is whether it will be able to *theorize* its relationships to the new social movements or whether it will continue to "adapt" to their democratic demands. Since social democracy has renounced theory as political discourse, this is not a likely eventuality. For both social democracy and US progressivism are wedded to the "pragmatic" dictum according to which the movement is committed to being the "left wing of the possible," a field that continually shifts rightward.

American progressive liberalism has all but renounced its New Deal redistributive ideology, but has not replaced it with an alternative universal vision. Consequently, feminists, environmentalists, and the black and Latino civil rights advocates constitute, by default, the soul, if not the power of the Democratic Party, and have occupied the center of a new liberal/progressive vision that, despite considerable economistic tendencies, is struggling to find a meeting ground between the new paradigm and the older social justice ideology. In turn, the leadership of the increasingly weakened labor movement is, perhaps, the remaining relatively powerful guardian of the social justice worldview, but has witnessed the disappearance of large chunks of its active constituency and, therefore, despite its still considerable membership, appears increasingly less relevant to American political life towards the dawn of the twenty-first century.

The decline of the labor movement has put in jeopardy even the medium-term vitality of such programs as the long-awaited national healthcare program, educational reform, and urban revitalization, much less the more mainstream issues of employment, training, and income equity. As for healthcare, the AFL-CIO executive council, which consists of the top officers of the leading unions, has been split for a decade between those favoring universal government-sponsored insurance similar to Canada's program that would provide strong controls over doctors, hospitals, and insurance companies, and a "moderate" group that favors a compromise with the insurance carriers to give them the most important role in administering the program.

Since the Depression, workers in mass production industries, at least in the Northeast and the Midwest, typically organized into relatively powerful unions that, from time to time, conducted militant and, frequently, prolonged strikes. Moreover, in addition to their Fordist role in providing substantial income from which expanded private consumption was made possible, the union contract became, in the wake of the political weakness of the progressives, the repository of social welfare for union members and their families.[37] And when they voted in national elections, until 1968, workers mainly supported the Cold War welfare liberalism of the Democratic Party which, in the era of union and industrial expansion, accounted for the fact that Democrats occupied the presidency and controlled Congress for all but eight of the thirty-five years after Roosevelt's inauguration in March 1933. These conditions obtained as long as large industrial plants, each employing thousands of workers, were concentrated in urban metropoles and dominated an ever-expanding national economy whose world position was effectively unchallenged. The troubles began to mount when capitalism was obliged to restructure its global relations.

IV

From the turn of the twentieth century, industrial workers were the most cohesive and the largest category of the urban populations, and most Americans lived in cities or working-class suburbs surrounding them. The genius of the Democratic (and sometimes Republican) urban political machine was to incorporate many (but not all) of the basic demands of the new immigrant and migrant groups that constituted the majority of the working class in major industries. In turn, the discourse of social justice was integrated into what became known as "progressive" ideology, which reformulated social justice in statist terms but carefully marginalized demands for power-sharing with the working class. As in the famous passage from Marx's *Eighteenth Brumaire*, gains, within the progressives' plan, must appear as good things rained from above—a gift from on high. In this reprise, Franklin D. Roosevelt took on the aspect of a savior; in many union households his picture was placed next to that of Jesus Christ until the 1960s, when Christ remained but the Kennedys replaced that almost forgotten charmer.

The power of these machines was among the crucial "external" influences upon would-be politicized trade unions. Internally, independent working-class political action was contested early in the century by an insurgent anarchist tendency on the "left" and African pasts, whether they participated in the civil rights struggle or not, so the discourses of gender and ecology have, at least for a generation, overshadowed that of social class for large segments of their constituents.

Some commentators have argued that, in contrast to the old social movements whose links to classes were a cardinal feature, the "new" social movements are drawn from various strands of the population, and that class considerations play little or no part in their composition. Although there is no doubt that activists in the new social movements are attracted not by traditional conceptions of interest but by the power of the new paradigm, it is also the case that their leaderships are typically drawn from the ranks of various strata of technical, scientific, and cultural intellectuals. These are often people who have been reared in what Alvin Gouldner has termed a "culture of critical discourse."[38] Even if many of the movements are situated, not at the workplace, but in the sphere of social and cultural life, of which consumption occupies considerable space, the emergence of these movements can hardly be separated from their social composition. The wide diffusion of their values may signify the appearance of intellectuals as a class of a new type—one situated not only in a unique relationship to the process of production, but in a specific way to the dominant ideology. For if knowledge has become a crucial site of power, then it cannot be located at any one particular place in the social structure, but encompasses the entire range of relations.

Of course, the success of emergent discourses of these new "pure and simple" trade unionists on the "right" who feared that (class) politics, like religion, could sunder the solidarity of workers on the job. Both sides were anti-state, although the AFL, once the bastion of anti-political thought within the labor movement, gradually shifted at the turn of the century to a kind of corporatist perspective under the aegis of the business-dominated National Civil Federation and, later, President Woodrow Wilson.[39]

In retrospect, Wilson's concerted effort to bring labor into full partnership with the Democratic Party and, later, into the war effort, was a turning point. Recall, the first decade of the twentieth century were years of dramatic growth for the workers' movements, both unions and the socialists. And, left gains were made among non-immigrant as well as immigrant groups—as the significant growth of the party and the IWW in the West attests. But, adroitly, the big-city Democratic bosses and the party's progressive wing had already forged an alliance with a large populist fraction exemplified by the three-time presidential candidacy of William Jennings Bryan. When in 1912 the Socialist presidential candidate Eugene V. Debs garnered nearly a million votes in his highly engaging campaign, the die was cast. Wilson understood that he owed victory to the split between progressives and conservative Republicans, but needed to mend fences with an insurgent working class that was beginning to engage seriously in a politics of class.[40]

Roosevelt transformed the Democratic Party into a vehicle for a liberal/progressive version of social justice that entailed enlarging the scope of state intervention to include the provision of social welfare. More important than the New Deal's relatively modest program, at least compared to Europe, especially after the War, was the explicit alliance it forged with even greater force than had Wilson with the new labor movement. The task of the socialists who, throughout the first half of the century, were the main proponents of labor's political independence, became nearly impossible, especially when, in 1936, most trade unions socialists—left and right—were incorporated in various ways within the New Deal coalition as they had not been during World War I.[41] The transformation of the labor movement into an arm of the coalition was always contested by the AFL, whose antagonism to Roosevelt was based on its traditional opposition, revived by Gompers's successor, William Green, to state intervention into labor relations, as much as the conservative Republican affiliations of a considerable segment of its leadership.

Pure and simple unionism, which retained substantial ideological force among important sections of the labor movement, was not really possible as the state increasingly intervened in industrial and labor relations—a measure that was much more important, in terms of the new capitalist regulation, than the few elements of social security enacted by the New Deal. While Wilson, as a wartime emergency, had established a board to mediate industrial disputes, the New Deal made permanent a variety of apparatuses, designed to regulate labor and industrial relations, and thereby make wage levels a known factor in production costs, that retain considerable force to this day.

Until World War I, the leading forces for the development of a class-identified workers' movement were the Industrial Workers of the

World, whose key figures adopted a version of anarchist ideology, and, especially, the Socialist Party (SP). The SP engaged tirelessly in both political education, urging workers to break from the two major capitalist parties, and ran its own candidates at all levels of elective office. Its efforts, although minoritarian, were, nevertheless, crowned with some success. The party sent two members to Congress characteristically from districts in which large numbers of immigrants, concentrated in a few large urban-based industries, lived. At the same time, it made considerable inroads into some key rural districts, notably in Oklahoma and the Dakotas.[42] I want to reserve further discussion of the factors that contributed to the decline of the mass influence of the socialist movement after the War for the final section of this essay. For now, it is important to note that the periodic upsurge of union activity among workers, especially in the 1930s and the 1960s, when millions streamed into industrial and then public employees' organizations, did not advance the political and social practices that comprise the congealing of a specifically class identification. As I shall argue, until the 1960s, when feminism and consumerism, and their various manifestations, became popular movements, race and ethnic identities were carefully cultivated by urban political machines to the detriment of class—even though "objective" indicators point to economic class as a powerful barrier to vertical mobility, particularly for Southern and Eastern European immigrants and even their children, and were a boundary condition for social and cultural life. However, Roosevelt amplified the weight of these municipal political machines, not only by channelling considerable patronage to them, but also by permitting them to identify with the apparently pro-labor program of the second New Deal, the ideologically redistributive face of the Roosevelt coalition after 1935.

Any undergraduate sociology student can easily demonstrate that certain occupations—mostly factory and low-level clerical labor—structure workers' children's "life chances," and may even be a rough predictor of political behavior and social and cultural relationships such as marriage, friendships, and organizational affiliation. While intermarriage of partners belonging to different white subcultural groups is fairly common in this century, class intermarriage is far less frequent. And educational research shows that, despite a veritable explosion of postsecondary education after World War II, in which as many as fifty per cent of high school graduates, by the 1970s, entered college, those which Marxism would classify as workers either never graduate from secondary schools, are school leavers after high school graduation, or drop out from colleges and universities within two years of admission.

But, the power of ideology consists not principally in its capacity to reproduce "false" consciousness in the face of the stubborn facts, but in the degree to which, in Althusser's terms, it becomes (as opposed to *corresponds to*) lived experience.[43] For there is more than a grain of truth to the thesis of American "classlessness." There is no doubt that, under ordinary circumstances, subjectivities are structured by identities other than class, especially among workers. When working people are asked about their class affiliation they often respond "middle class" and rarely as members of a working class or even "lower" class. But, the web of group affiliations outside the workplace provides a more enduring set of identities on the basis of ethnicity (better described in this context as *subcultures*), in some cases as among Italians and Puerto Ricans, for example, regionally mediated within the same national origin.

I want to argue that America has never produced the conditions that would foster class identification as a category with effects on everyday existence. Social clubs, civic associations, and political organizations were frequently organized along subcultural rather than overtly class lines, even if their composition was delineated by class membership. For example, in the Eastern Europe neighborhoods of many large industrial cities—Pittsburgh, Chicago, Detroit—and Pennsylvania mining towns, such as Scranton and Pottsville, the unions—even when beloved—did not provide the main social and cultural center for Poles, Hungarians, Ukrainians, and other East European workers. The local branch of the Polish-, Ukrainian-, or Russian-based national "home," equipped with a bar, dance hall, and meeting rooms, provided the gathering place within which politics as well as friendships were forged. In the twentieth century, both political parties cultivated the leadership of these institutions, which was composed of workers, but also small businesspeople, such as funeral directors, lawyers, and merchants. Consequently, organizers cultivated subcultural ties, and local unions sought to meet in ethnic social halls and churches, the second crucial site of class displacement, rather than their offices which, increasingly, became administrative rather than social and cultural centers.

In contrast, the European workers' movement, particularly in Germany and Scandinavian countries, embraced a kind of trinitarian formula: trade unions, which by the late nineteenth century were imbued with class ideologies; geographically situated political parties dominated by professional politicians and intellectuals, although some local organizations had worker-members as well; and social and cultural institutions directed specifically to workers such as socialist singing societies, sports organizations, schools that were alternative indoctrination sites to Church-sponsored Sunday schools, and summer camps for children and adults. As Carl E. Schorske has demonstrated, the socialist movement created a "state within a state" which provided for a wide range of interests and needs of its constituents, even as it inured workers from entering the mainstream of their society.[44] In the United Kingdom perhaps the crucial social site has been the working-class pub. But even here, the pub was never a distinctly class institution; it is more appropriately designated a national institution differentiated by class patronage.

Working-class identities were reproduced by more than ideology and program. They were forged in the sinews of everyday life—at play as well as at work. At the turn of the century in Germany and, later, in Sweden and Norway, it was possible to live one's entire life in the socialist and labor movements. Thus, the workers' movement was not merely a "worldview" combined with organizations that "represented" the immediate and long-term interests of the working class, but a "lifeworld" defining the horizons of existence.[45] In the advanced capitalist social formations of North America and Western Europe, this lifeworld often encouraged intense class loyalties and consciousness. But its unintended consequence was, in given periods, to isolate workers from other strata and social categories, a situation that frequently contributed to political defeat.

Such may have been the case with the 1984–5 miners strike in Britain. Recall the miners, faced with wholesale mine closings by the Thatcher government, staged the most militant strike in Britain's postwar history.

The Labour Party quickly split over the degree to which it should support the miners' action. The more left-wing national executive pressed for wholehearted backing. But the parliamentary party was reluctant: "The leadership and the PLP right wingers, however, believed the dispute, or more specifically its conduct, would damage support for Labour among the social democratic middle ground" (read new middle classes). "Opposition leader Neil Kinnock struggled to maintain unity while distancing the LP from the miners' strike."[46]

One can easily cite parallel examples in the relationship between militant union struggles against concessions during the 1980s and the Democratic Party and US trade union leadership. In the first example of sustained resistance, members of local P-9 of the Food and Commercial Workers at the Hormel plant in Austin, Minnesota struck in summer 1985 to restore wage levels that had been previously reduced by a concessions agreement. The International union at first supported the strike, but withdrew when the workers refused to heed the leadership's order to return to work without an agreement. The state Democratic Party not only distanced itself from the struggle, but many condemned the "irresponsibility" of the local leadership. Moreover, union labor was split both locally and nationally. For the most part, the strikers successfully mobilized a segment of the unions in their support, but remained fairly isolated from both the major segments of the union movement and potential supporters among middle classes.[47]

Indeed, the socialist movement in the United States adopted the German model, in part because a large segment of it was comprised of descendants of the generation of 1848, German political refugees of the failed revolution, and partly because of the incredible success of the turn-of-the-century German Social-Democrats. The tripartite principle of organization was carried to the letter after 1900 by the newly formed Socialist Party which, with strategic acumen, competed with some success for the hearts and minds of newly arrived Eastern European immigrants. "Nationality federations," among some of the most important Eastern European immigrants, emerged as dual organizations to the more mainstream National Homes. In most cases, particularly among those immigrants whose Christian and agrarian roots were still deep—Poles, Italians, Hungarians,

Ukrainians, and Russians—the Socialists had limited success. But they were more influential among immigrants from urban environments or countries such as Finland, where early immigrants had been "landless peasant laborers"[48] rather than peasants, such as Italians or Russians, who were subordinated within semi-feudal systems of land tenure.

Jewish immigration until the 1880s was largely of businesspeople and professionals from Germany and Austria. But the Eastern European Jewish immigration was largely a working-class phenomenon, and, in this respect, bore strong resemblances to the second wave of Finns who arrived after 1898. They were urban workers and intellectuals whose decision to emigrate was motivated as much by political as by economic considerations. These were, frequently, refugees from various anti-radical repressions that paralleled the earlier German experience. In both cases, these immigrants carried their socialist and labor culture with them to US shores and managed to build powerful institutions that endured through the first half of the twentieth century.

Unlike the Germans, who had been skilled workers in the industrializing cities of the 1850s, 1860s, and 1870s, the Finns were mainly unskilled, from the perspective of industrial society. Germans organized the skilled trades—cigar makers, brewery workers, bakers, metal workers. Finnish miners and skilled Jewish needle trades workers, particularly the women condemned for the most part to semi-skilled "section work," were, however, at the forefront of the industrial union movements at the turn of the century. There were similar tendencies within both migrations of people who had been influenced by socialist and trade union ideas and, equally importantly, they brought a strong store of organizational experience in the labor and socialist movements of their countries.

Among the Finns of Wisconsin and Minnesota and among New York and Chicago Jews, working-class and socialist discourse was highly visible and enjoyed a considerable measure of popular support during the first half of the twentieth century. After the Bolshevik Revolution, two Yiddish language daily newspapers—one ostensibly social-democratic and the other communist—were widely read among garment workers, fur and leather workers, and the older generation of intellectuals. Like the Jews, many Finns affiliated with the Socialist Party or, as in the case of Minnesota, were the organizational heart of the Farmer-Labor Party that ruled that state for forty years. The socialist and communist movements in the United States were, in addition to their specific political interventions, constituted by a series of subcultures organized along nationality lines that were united by the thread of a common ideology. Concentrated in large industrial cities, the left-wing ethnic subcultures resembled, in microcosm, their European forebears. Their members were largely, if not exclusively, working-class. They sustained a wide array of institutions that, until the immediate post-World War II period provided health and burial benefits, as well as cultural and political activities. Given the weakness of the state system of social welfare, even after the New Deal, trade unions and the socialist movement with which they were loosely affiliated assumed many of these functions: unemployment benefits, a system of health clinics, paid holidays, pensions, and vacations paid in lieu of wages by employers and secured by collective bargaining agreements. Their welfare institutions were fatally weakened when, in the 1930s and in the 1940s, many unions negotiated these benefits through the collective bargaining agreement, and the Roosevelt administration enacted a series of measures, especially pensions, relief payments, and unemployment insurance.

But, labor and the left did not generate this infrastructure for reasons of economic necessity alone. Neither the socialist vision nor the redistributive vision implicit in collective bargaining could sustain the movement without the ties that only culture can provide. Where the left formed successful and enduring mass parties, especially in New York, Minnesota, and Wisconsin, the political club was more than an electoral vehicle and a counseling service for people having trouble with landlords or government. The socialist or labor party political club was mainly a male social center, providing library facilities, rehearsal rooms for music and drama groups, Sunday schools, and, especially, space for card games and games of chess. Saturday nights were times for youth or adult dances, concerts, sings, and other social activities involving the whole family. Electoral activity arose "organically" from these social and cultural activities.

When the Communists expanded their membership in the 1930s, so did their youth movement and cultural sections. Much of the Socialist-

Communist split after 1919 occurred on the battleground of the national minority social and cultural organizations. The Communists emerged from these battles with strong sections among Hungarians, Finns, and Yugoslavs, as well as weaker, but still substantial sections among Italians, Germans, Poles, and Jews who, in the majority, remained close to the social-democrats. However, pro-Soviet sentiment among Jews and CP influence in the needle trades insured the party and same unions that had a large Jewish membership of a significant minority. The Fur and Leather Workers, an exception in the otherwise socialist-dominated needle trades (although until World War II there were strong CP caucuses in the ILGWU), New York department store workers, wholesale and retail workers, public employees, teachers, social workers, and other "sub"-professionals were close to the Communist Party.

The CP organized its work among these "national minorities" along classic social-democratic lines, not only in style but, given the reform perspectives of the popular front, ideologically as well. The International Workers Order, the communist alternative to the socialist Workmen's Circle, a much larger organization, provided life insurance, medical and dental services, and burial benefits. The party's cultural sections sponsored Sunday schools, summer camps, women's organizations, and so forth. The CP-affiliated youth movement was strongest in working-class neighborhoods where, like the Lower East Side of New York, the Fairfax District of Los Angeles, or Chicago's Near North Side, strong subcultural fraternal organizations had been established.

The Communist affiliation with the New Deal was motivated, in part, by the popular front strategy of alliances between the various tendencies among the working class and the "progressive," that is, anti-fascist, wing of capital. Inevitably, the terms of this alliance entailed substantial ideological concessions by the left, not the least of which was the doctrine according to which workers and capitalists had diametrically opposed interests. Despite tactical left turns in 1939–40 and 1945–8, the popular front period from 1935 to the early 1950s—the span of an entire generation—was marked by noticeable softening of class struggle discourse, even in the midst of militant industrial struggles for unionization that were frequently organized and led by Communists and Socialists.

The most important intervention of the CP and its organizations among the native born was in several large urban black communities (although the party made significant efforts in rural districts as well). The party was an influential force in Harlem, Chicago's South Side, Detroit, and in black areas of Philadelphia and Baltimore, among others. The basis of this influence was first, its ability to stretch its hand towards the nationalist and religious culture of American black people; second, its determined and often militant struggles around the immediate issues affecting these communities, particularly housing and employment, and against police brutality; and third its willingness to elevate many of its black cadre to district and national leadership. Thus, despite the many shifts in the party line regarding black Americans and its declining influence within the labor movement and other sectors where it was once influential, the Communists retained considerable respect within black activist circles well into the 1960s.[49]

One can plausibly claim that the relative absence of class politics in the industrial workers' upsurge of this period was abetted by circumstances, namely, the threat of fascism. Yet, when put in context of the largely, if not exclusively, subcultural base of radical movements from the turn of the century, which also formed the context for unionization in mining, steel, and many other industries, the reason for the relatively weak class identity in the labor movement in the period of its most dramatic growth becomes clearer. Even the class-oriented left felt obliged to work through other identities—including race identities—because they believed these were, for various reasons, primary among those they sought to reach. This was true, not only of those who spoke foreign tongues, but also of English speakers. I want to consider two cases, the Irish-Americans who played an enormously important role throughout this century in the leadership of mass industrial unions and the "native-born" whites in the Southwest who, emerging from the populist explosion of the 1880s and 1890s, briefly affiliated with the Socialist Party.

Irish socialism and laborism were, like many colonial movements, closely tied to nationalism. James Connolly, the leading figure of Irish socialism until his death in the Easter rising of 1916 for Irish independence, posed the problem of socialism in terms that were strikingly similar to Lenin's conception of national liberation. Connolly argued that the working class had a double task: to lead the movement for national independence and to struggle for socialism. In the context of the heated debates within the Socialist International, this was by no means a majority position.[50]

But, Connolly symbolized the problem of generations of Irish radicals who felt obliged to work within the nationalist movement or risk isolation. Consequently, nationalism became, for the not inconsiderable radical wing of Irish immigration of the early twentieth century, an important dimension of their ideological arsenal. This was the imperative faced by Connolly's collaborator, James Larkin, who migrated to the United States and helped organize the largely Irish-American Transport Workers Union, as well as the Transport and General Workers Union of Ireland.[51] Larkin's legatee and long-time communist leader of the Transport Workers Union, Michael Quill, who was also an elected New York City Council member, was identified as closely by his Irish heritage and cultural ties as he was by his trade union and radical credentials. Like many other radicals, it was simply not possible, despite his considerable support in the Jewish working-class community of the Bronx, to build a political base outside the framework of close subcultural identification.

In the case of the "grassroots" agrarian socialism that, briefly, inherited the populist movements following among poor Southern and Western US farmers (who Lawrence Goodwyn has called agricultural laborers because they really didn't own the land), the category of the "people," even "poor people," always dominated class identity.[52] (This, despite Goodwyn's and James Green's convincing argument that the populist and the socialist movements of the South and Southwest were largely working-class and not middle-class movements.) The two parties successively organized around anti-capitalist issues, specifically against the big banks, the railroads, and the food-processing corporations that had reduced them to little more than workers, even though they ostensibly held title to the land.

But, what remains unanswered by these class analyses is why the aspirations of the farmers were for land ownership, why the images of cooperative ownership of the land did not accompany proposals for cooperative graineries and processing plants. As Craig Calhoun has shown in his detailed critique of E. P. Thompson's *Making of the English Working Class*, "class" struggle is often fought in the name of the "people," itself an ambiguous category that signifies a broader stratum within society.[53] When we speak of "class," the practices to which this signifier refers may be termed a "bloc" that is comprised of a multitude of social groups. Our designation of class refers as much to the negative object of struggle, the fractions of capital that are arrayed against the people, as it is to a group of concrete actors, the composition of which frequently belies class identity.

In these two examples, the Irish-dominated Transport Workers Union of the 1920s and 1930s and the turn-of-the-century agrarian radicals, we see that class is, at most, an empirical description made from the outside with the assistance of Marxist categories. Class is often part of the political vocabulary of actors who, nevertheless, are impelled to use a different language—either nationalism, cultural or otherwise, or populism—to achieve their organizational goals. Of course, this is not merely another example of American exceptionalism. For, not only did Connolly face the problem of reconciling socialism with Irish independence, but socialist movements everywhere in Europe have been forced to mediate class ideologies with the heterogeneity of their constituents and the complex traditions they find already in place. A good example of this are the strong laborist traditions of Scotland and Wales which, nevertheless, are laced with heavy doses of nationalism. Similarly, the older US socialist movement entered its long-term decline much earlier but still retained remnants of the old cultural organizations, particularly the largely Jewish Workmen's Circle (renamed the Workers Circle in the 1970s, in deference to feminism), that, together with the Jewish Bund, upheld *Yiddishkeit* against the twin threats of assimilation and Zionism (which favored Hebrew as the language of Jewish ethnic identity and dissolved class politics into nationalism). Even in the labor-Zionist movement that eventually became the first government after Israeli independence, the relation of labor to nation was characteristically resolved in favor of the latter.

In the wake of the restructuring of world capitalism, in which the most technologically advanced societies exhibit features of post-

industrialism, as much as postmodern culture; and the splintering of Soviet power—especially the precipitous decline of its persistent ideological
influence over significant fractions of workers' movements and intellectuals during the past seventy years—working-class identity has increasingly
become local, when not entirely incoherent. For even when workers and
intellectuals linked to workers' and socialist movements did not adhere
to the proposition that really existing socialism was a kind of global vanguard, in every country the left, old and new, responded to the Soviet
example. Nor could left anti-communism escape from the entanglement.

The Russian Revolution was understood in terms that extended beyond its real or imagined economic and political achievements. More to
the point was the fact that the Soviets systematically disseminated revolutionary Marxist culture and proved, through sometimes-orchestrated
example, that capitalism's invincibility was a mirage. Even when its own
version of socialism or Marxism was held in contempt, the survival of the
Soviet Union provided a target for debate—and hope for socialist prospects in a single lifetime. Dissenters from the Soviet model could claim
that if only a different strategy had been pursued by Lenin—or Stalin—,
if only they...were more democratic;[54] let the NEP (New Economic Policy)
work for a prolonged period of market relations;[55] had not beaten the
peasantry into submission;[56] established workers' control over production;[57] supported a vital civil society and a public sphere within which
important issues and ideas could freely be debated; and so on. If one or
more of these goals had been pursued by the revolution's leaders and
legatees, today the world would look different. Prospects for revolution
were, according to this position, indefinitely postponed, if not smashed,
by the repugnant Soviet experience.

During the past seventy years, when the parties of social-democracy,
and the labor parties, especially the Germans and the British, seemed to
yield both revolutionary and working-class ground to welfarism, colonialism, and nationalism, the communist world, notwithstanding its strategic and tactical twists and turns, maintained rhetorical fealty to the
revolutionary doctrines of Marx and Lenin, to internationalism and anti-imperialism. Even most Trotskyists, long implacable opponents of Stalinism, readily acknowledged that the socialist project, itself ineluctably

tied to the fate of the workers' movements, depended, among other things, on the solution to the "deformation" of the Bolshevik revolution and its international consequences.

But, the issue goes beyond various assessments of Soviet leadership offered by leaders and intellectuals connected to workers' and socialist movements, or of the character of Soviet society as a workers' state, or its brand of Marxism. As important as these are for comprehending the world-historical significance of the collapse, the whole question of the historical agency of the working class became wrapped up after 1917 with the fate of the Russian Revolution and its global influence, tentacles which reached into nearly all countries. The greatest international victory of the Russian Revolution was to impose upon at least two generations of radicals a new class imaginary in advanced capitalist societies, countries of the so-called semi-periphery and, especially, the colonial and postcolonial world where the Leninist linkage of anti-imperialism with global class struggle took on the status of a political religion. It hardly matters that the idea of the Soviet Union as a workers' state could be easily refuted by various measures, including the determination of whether workers were genuine participants in running the factories, the neighborhood, or the state. More important was that disputes among people who should have known better turned on whether it was a *degenerate* or healthy workers' state.

With the exception of one (tiny) faction of Trotskyists, and an even tinier enclave of anti-Leninist libertarian communists—Marxist as well as anarchists—there was a consensus during the interwar years among revolutionaries that the Soviet Union was the living embodiment of workers' power. Further, the question of the international class struggle gradually evolved toward the idea of the absolute necessity to defend the Soviet Union against capitalist economic and military aggression, a position that widened with the postwar establishment of the Eastern European "people's democracies," China, and Cuba.

Of course, it is important to remember that working-class identity and its most ubiquitous political expressions, socialism and anarchism, predated the advent of the Bolsheviks and their Stalinist legatees. But, the example of the Bolsheviks captured the hearts and minds of the

overwhelming majority of the world's radicals. Neither anarchist purity nor social-democratic realism were able to halt the flood of new adherents among most left-wing intellectuals and militants, especially in
the popular front period of the 1930s and, again, after the War. Even
where social-democracy retained its firm electoral and trade union base
it was unable or unwilling to go beyond the politics of the "real" and,
perhaps more damaging, remained incapable of attracting the bearers of
avant-garde political and cultural thought or the activist youth.

Which meant that social democracy became moribund in the period
of the rise of the generational movement called the New Left, the 1960s.
Although this was the period during which the German social democrats
gained government power for the first time since the immediate years
after World War I, and British Labour was able to grasp the reins of
government after more than a decade of conservative rule, these were not
parties of *movement* and ideology, but parties of order. For this reason,
the main dialogue of the young, independent left was with the various
tendencies of communists: in France and Italy with the communist parties and their intellectuals, in Britain and Germany with Marxist theory
and the question of Soviet power. This was a measure of the degree to
which, notwithstanding its reformist *practice*, the theoretical and ideological communist commitment to revolutionary doctrine enabled the
various parties of revolutionary socialism to retain their appeal to the
new radical generation of 1968.[58] Surely, the idea of the working class as
liberator of all humanity because of its status as the most exploited of all
oppressed groups—the term signifying a definite relation to the capitalist labor process rather than poverty or discrimination—has died hard,
despite the mounting evidence of working-class fragmentation and defeat
by restructured global capital.

There can be no doubt that the past two decades have been marked,
in most countries of the West and the most industrially developed postcolonial and Eastern European states, by the decline of working-class
economic and political power. In Western Europe and the United States,
conservative political ascendancy is accompanied by world economic
restructuration. As is well known, one of the key elements of the new
world economic order has been the massive shutdowns of plants in heavy

industrial sectors, such as steel, engineering, and mining. In the course of this development, centers of working-class power—such as the English midlands, northern England and Wales, the French steelmaking Lorraine region, and the US "heartland," from Pittsburgh's Mon Valley to Chicago—were decimated. For much of the 1980s, these areas experienced depression-level unemployment rates; trade unions were reduced to a fraction of their former strength; significant portions of the population migrated in search of work. Equally significant, these regions lost their traditional left-workerist character. Communists and left socialist electoral strength in France was reduced, the Labour Party lost considerable strength in Britain, and the social justice wing of the Democrats became almost marginal within the party. From signs of "advanced industrial societies" these once-proud areas became economic backwaters of what became known as "post-industrial" capitalism.[59]

In Eastern Europe and the Soviet Union, sites of the celebrated sudden collapse of what may be called oligarchic collectivist regimes, one of the distinguishing features of the dramatic transformations already underway was the attempt by the more "liberal," reform-minded sections of the oligarchy to break much of the social compact with the workers that had prevailed for nearly forty years. Beginning with the Solidarity Labor Union and its nationwide strike against the government's attempt to rescind the substantial food subsidies that had sustained working-class support for decades, the 1980s were marked by increasing tension between these governments and the workers.

Although the victory of Solidarity in Poland was not typical of the pattern in the rest of the region which, in the main, turned to intellectuals to lead the new regimes, working-class ascent was a necessary condition for the victory of the liberal-democratic forces. However, the workers were not necessarily motivated by the same republican impulses as intellectuals. For them, the birth of a new civil society where free public debate about public issues could be carried on, a multiparty parliamentary political system, and a market system for determining the rules for production and distribution were necessary, but not sufficient, conditions for change. In the last analysis, the almost forgotten promises of egalitarian socialism remain powerful forces among industrial workers, particularly the chance to gain genuine power in the workplace—whether in concert with markets or not. Moreover, many workers—in the mining and metallurgical industries of Russia and Poland—are hostile to the creation of any economic system that would widen the privileges of the emerging economic elites. For many, there is no special virtue in replacing the party bureaucrats, with their special stores, country homes, and state-financed cars, with entrepreneurs who would enjoy even greater wealth.

Those who came to political power in Eastern Europe (including the leader of the Solidarity Labor Union, Lech Wałęsa) have been little inclined to reestablish the old social contract with the workers, one which guaranteed a measure of job and income security, an extensive welfare program, and fairly good working conditions. Instead, they demonstrated the truism that only revolutionaries are able to impose austerity. The first post-Communist Polish government took decisions that made the gestures towards economic rationality of the last Communist government of General Jaruszelski appear extremely modest, even inadequate. For when the World Bank and other Western lenders finally called a halt to lending to East Europe and the postcolonial world in the mid-1980s, the Communists were literally forced against their will to take draconian measures, such as reducing subsidies for food and housing, thereby driving prices up, but were unwilling to share the decision-making so that the victims of austerity could consent in their own pain. For a time, the new democratic regimes have benefited from their legitimacy gained at the expense of the discredited oligarchs. They took even more harsh decisions to cut subsidies, shut archaic factories, and introduced the market as the arbiter of many, but not yet most, economic decisions. Needless to say, after a year of popular jubilation in the face of liberalization, despite the economic hardships, Eastern Europe is already hearing cries for justice from working classes which have suffered not only disastrous wage cuts, but also serious erosion of one of the basic tenets of socialist religion—the welfare state. And, of course, in Yugoslavia, the Soviet Union, and Czechoslovakia, nationalism, sometimes under the patronage of former communist parties and leaders, has reared its sometimes ugly head to displace, but also exacerbate resentments. East European nationalism has expressed in its political choices its preference for the long-suppressed nationalities struggle to assert its autonomy from central power to the forced march toward modernity prescribed by communist rule—even if the price of independence might be a long slide into the "Third World." In addition to economic motives, the appeal of a reunited Germany proved too powerful for the skeptics and doubters to prevail, even if unification will prove extremely painful for the former East Germans, at least in the near term. Eventually, they may dramatically raise their levels of private consumption, but they have already lost important public goods, such as abortion on demand and unlimited healthcare. And, in the long run, one should not be surprised if the draconian measures of the conservative Christian Democratic regime ignites memories of socialism among the East Germans.

We are also witnessing the resurgence of pan-Africanism, modulated by the demand for racial equality and radical democracy that replaced the revolutionary communist turn of the late 1960s, which, although not extinct, no longer enjoys ideological hegemony in postcolonial politics after the breakup of the communist world. Today, at least in Africa and the Caribbean, the term and even the content of "national liberation" has been replaced, at best, by the ideas of freedom, equality, and democracy—a kind of black social democracy, as interpreted by concrete movements, whose meanings vary with specific circumstances. At worst, many countries of Africa and the Caribbean have turned to more authoritarian forms of rule.

The two visible, and, indeed, most important instances of growing workers' organization and political influence are in Brazil—where the newly formed Workers Party (PT) has emerged as the likely alternative to the center-right coalition that governs the country—and South Africa— where a black trade union federation closely aligned with the African National Congress has recruited more than a million adherents over the past five years. Some highly publicized successful strikes conducted by the trade union federation during the 1980s became a significant factor in the emergence of the ANC and its apparently successful efforts to crack the color bar, if not the political white monopoly. While these movements are, in many ways, incommensurable, either with traditional workers' movements in the history of Western capitalism or with each other, they are, nonetheless, signs that reports of the death of the working class are, to say the least, premature.

The common link between Solidarity, the upsurge of Korean workers and those of Brazil and South Africa is that they have emerged in the context of industrializing societies, as opposed to the societies of late capitalism suffering, to various degrees, from the prevailing deindustrialization of Western Europe and, especially, the US and the UK. In the majority of instances where workers' movements are on the rise, their fate is ineluctably tied to investment decisions by international capital and, therefore, directly to the losses suffered by workers in the so-called "First World." In a situation of worldwide stagnation in industrial production, the industrialization of postcolonial and otherwise dependent regions of the world constitutes losses for the older developed areas. This situation has exacerbated what is already present in late capitalist societies that have experienced new waves of immigration, a phenomenon that is perceived by many workers, correctly, as a depressing influence on wages. For beyond nativism, nationalism is exhibited within the United States in the form of protectionism. The sentiment to prohibit or otherwise restrict imports from Japan, Korea, and Western Europe has accompanied a marked decline in domestic production of automobiles, steel, machine tools, and other basic commodities, and the virtual demise of the once buoyant domestic electronic industry.

European and US workers are aware of this relationship. Now, foreign investment is labeled "capital flight," in contrast to the immediate postwar era when overseas investment represented "expansion." This pattern is well illustrated by the growth of the petrochemical industry on Puerto Rico's southern coast in the 1960s and the establishment of a parallel pharmaceutical sector. As a recent suit by the US-based Oil, Chemical, and Atomic Workers union alleges, the recent transfer of production by American Home Products Corporation to Puerto Rico was at direct expense of its Indiana plant, where hundreds of workers are scheduled to lose their jobs. In some cases, notably Germany and France, postwar labor shortages were addressed by opening up their respective borders to Middle Eastern and North African migrants, just as the United States admitted, legally and illegally, millions of Caribbean and Latin American immigrants to work in industrialized agriculture, as well as in low-wage factories which produced light consumer goods.

For this reason, protectionist ideology among American workers and their unions was not uncommon in the 1950s and '60s. But as consumer goods imports from Japan and Korea rose in the 1970s, the first signs of US plants closings within the same industries were immediately linked up to growing trade imbalances. Of course, the United States has, since the nineteenth century, exported a third of its agricultural production, a proportion that rose to forty per cent during the 1970s, when imports of finished manufactured products dramatically increased. Lacking prospects for industrial revitalization, these facts could hardly be expected to ease the demands for restrictive import quotas by workers in these sectors of production industries that were shrinking in the 1980s. That protectionist demands were combined with expressions of xenophobia and outright racism should come as no surprise in a situation in which no strong left ideological constraints were present. Unfortunately, the situation has been no better in Labour Britain in the wake of new waves of Indian, Caribbean, and African immigrations. To its credit, the French Socialists *have* made some efforts to combat racism, sponsoring in 1987–8 a fairly vigorous antiracist campaign in connection with the presidential and legislative elections.

The world economic crisis of the 1970s and '80s was experienced differently in various countries of advanced industrial capitalism. Hidden from most Americans by the paucity of news, was the extremely high jobless rates of the United Kingdom and most Western European countries. Beginning in the early 1970s, unemployment attained a level of about ten per cent in France and Germany, and slightly higher in Italy. During these years, the UK was hit hardest; its official rate was nearly fifteen per cent in the late '70s and early '80s, close to the rates of the Great Depression.

The official US rate was never that high until the "Reagan" recession of 1981–3, when the US joined its European counterparts in double-digit joblessness, although it never dipped below six per cent throughout the 1970s. When added to the large number of discouraged workers (about one per cent) who stopped looking for jobs, and part-time workers unable to find full-time jobs (another two per cent), the US rate was close to Europe's. But in 1982, the official rate had climbed to eleven per cent, the worst since the Depression.

However, statistics tell only part of the story. For by the end of the recession, the face of industrial America had profoundly changed. America had been transformed from the leading industrial power into what many economists and journalists called a "service" economy which is, to say the least, an overstatement. There are still twenty-five million industrial workers in the United States, but their number has stagnated for most of the past twenty years and, in the past five years, has embarked on a steady decline. The key factor is both the declining proportion of Americans producing, transporting, and handling capital and consumer goods and, perhaps more importantly, the dispersal of production sites from cities and large towns dominated by factories to small communities and rural areas where industrial workers are isolated. By the middle of the 1980s, the major US service products were financial services, computer software, wholesale and retail trades, including the highly visible fast food industry that absorbed more than half the US beef output and employed millions of (mostly young) workers, many on a part-time basis.

However, popular images tend to obliterate the fact that the manufacturing sector which, although considerably reduced by labor-saving technologies and the recessions of 1981–3 and the late '80s and early '90s, remains strong in autos, trucks, machine tools, agricultural equipment (which is an export industry), oil refining and chemicals, massive military production, and even the declining but substantial textile and garment industries. Yet, with the shift of *perception*[60] from industrial to post-industrial society and the incredible denaturing of the cities—even Detroit, Pittsburgh, and Chicago—the heart of the industrial heartland—we have witnessed a fracturing of traditional working-class identities which depended crucially on the proliferate local cultures that sustained them. For, it is clearly not enough to infer from either labor statistics or even political participation data that a working class "exists" as a sociological object. The one element of class identity that had been powerful until the 1960s, a strong sense of union solidarity, especially among workers in the so-called "basic" industries, has been considerably weakened in the past twenty years. What must be shown is that the several instances of the persistence of a labor ethic—notably in the late 1980s and early '90s Eastern Airline and *Daily News* strikes—are more than evidences of rearguard actions.

V

In the United States and the United Kingdom, where there are large populations of people of African, Asian, and Caribbean descent that have been enlarged by recent and massive waves of immigration, assertions of race or national identities are punctuated by demands for inclusion into the dominant society and culture. People of color from postcolonial societies simply cannot afford to turn their backs on the opportunities afforded by economic and political inclusion, despite the increasingly insistent attacks by intellectuals on Eurocentrism. This postmodern paradox is entirely understandable once we give up the expectation that strategic intervention can obey the rule of linear consistency. What is involved here is a series of contradictions: between the permeation by US culture—commercial and popular—of postcolonial societies, such that the blunt statement that contemporary popular culture is American seems as obvious as it is horrific to those who would preserve the older identities, not only embodied in "folk" art and cultures but also in national musical and other artistic forms; between the relative openness of US society compared to those of Western Europe, where immigration is strictly regulated and the growing degree of draconian police surveillance of "guest" workers by the Immigration and Naturalization service. Moreover, we are witnessing a powerful counterattack against efforts, especially in school curricula, to recognize the integrity of immigrant cultures. There is a new campaign by many erstwhile liberals, as well as conservatives, to assert the cultural imperiousness of the discourse of assimilation with respect to those who wish to preserve their own language and culture. We note the deepening conflict between the fact of growing immigration among subaltern peoples, despite restrictive laws and blatant nativist sentiments that are designed to limit their entrance.

We have not yet experienced the full scope of the consequences of the new immigrant millions who have arrived in the United States in the past fifteen years. In California, Spanish-surnamed people will constitute a majority of the state's population before the end of the century. This tendency has already changed the political climate of the state's most populous area—Los Angeles. In New York, New Jersey, and Connecticut, Latino and Caribbean populations soared in the 1990 census, and the average increase of Asians in these states was thirty-three per cent. Even in the Midwest, where Asian, Latino, and Caribbean populations are smaller than on both coasts, there are significant gains.

In this regard, the difference between race and ethnic identities comes to the surface. The searing reality of race discrimination in the US, the effect of which has been to sharpen the exclusion of African-Americans from many sectors of economic, political, and cultural life—despite the concerted effort by the Black Freedom Movement and its (periodic) white allies over the past half century—has strengthened race consciousness among blacks who experience the multiple pains of exclusion from the dominant society and culture. At the same time, ethnicity signifies assimilation, and many people of color continue to act *as if* this objective has been achieved, and the remaining task for subalterns is to acquire the credentials of inclusion, principally through education, training, and legal protection against discrimination.

The cacophonic themes of race and ethnicity reveal the discursive power of American ideology. For while race invariably signifies exclusion, ethnicity signifies subculture. Ethnicity is a term that contains within it the presumption of structured class inequality, but not a problematic nationality. The prevailing perception of Southern and Eastern European communities within the United States is that of *deficit* born of the exigencies of origin. For example, Italian-American youth may suffer the third-highest dropout rates in New York City, just above Latinos and blacks, and their inability to rise into business, professional, and managerial strata has been amply documented.[61] But there is little imputation of institutionalized discrimination to this situation. Educators may recognize that Italian-American students have formidable obstacles to overcome, but these are considered to be primarily cultural in nature. Since the overwhelming majority of Italian-Americans migrated from Sicily and other regions of southern Italy marked by a low level of industrial and urban development, their lack of school success is correlated to the absence of cosmopolitan, i.e. intellectual culture in these areas. Peasant areas are traditionally preliterate.

Like all Southern and Eastern European immigrant groups, Italians brought significant aspects of their peasant culture with them to the United States. Among them, placing high priority on maintaining close-knit families whose solidarity at work and at play was and remains valued above any other form of social adherence is only the most visible. Another legacy of their agricultural background was their relative lack of industrial skills, a deficit that obliged Italians to seek to establish labor monopolies over unskilled and semi-skilled occupations within industries available to them. Consequently, according to this account, the relatively low level of Italian-American class mobility is intimately linked to the close-knit communities that Italians have established in the United States which are, in turn, linked to their claim to ownership over manual occupations in specific industries, notably transportation—particularly the waterfront—mining, steelmaking, and, above all, the trowel trades in the construction industry (such as bricklaying; street, road, and building labor; and roofing, none of which is highly technical in nature and requires little education or formal training).

But, acknowledging that Italians fought for job property rights in these sectors and that the partial monopolies they enjoyed in some of them exist(ed)—the past tense signifying erosion and even losses due to massive technological and urban shifts in the past two decades—what remains to be explained is their relative disadvantage compared to Northern European migrations. What led them to seek perquisites in trades that, until the postwar era, were at or near the bottom of the job hierarchy? A close examination of the economic position of Italian-Americans, together with the representations of Italians in the popular imagination, abetted by media depictions, might reveal the degree to which they became the object of racial stereotypes, such as are perpetuated, for example, by the seemingly endless series of films, television series, and novels about underworld life or the more recent *Rocky* series.

Italians were recruited for some of the heaviest and most dangerous occupations in the US industrial structure. For example, they were, together with Slavs, the heart of the coal mining and steelmaking industries, but were also heavily represented in the construction, textile, garment, and shoe production when these were among the most important, but lower-paid, industries of the Northeast. In the pre-mechanized era, they were the dockers in Brooklyn, once the largest port on the East

Coast, and constituted a significant portion of the waterfront labor force in New Jersey as well. All of these industries had skilled workers, but the Italians were not represented, to any significant degree, among them. Rather, Northern Europeans, largely migrants from the older industrial areas of Wales, England, Scotland, and Germany dominated the mechanical trades in both light and heavy industry; they brought their skills with them, skills which entailed a relatively high level of reading and writing and formal training. In many cases, it was the Northern Europeans who later became both managers and foremen and, equally importantly, dominated the unions.

It was not until late in the development of industrial unions—the 1960s—that some Italians—and Eastern Europeans—were elevated to the skilled trades in some of these industries, and were elected to important local and national union posts. Peter Bommarito became president of the United Rubber Workers; William DuChessi was secretary-treasurer of the Textile Workers; Tony Mazzocchi became a national leader of the Oil, Chemical, and Atomic Workers; and Anthony Scotto, the president of the Brooklyn dockers union was, until his indictment and conviction, a major figure in the International Longshoremen's Association (ILA). But, despite some gains in Italian-American representation, the top offices in the ILA stayed with Irish-Americans, whose representation among the rank and file dropped sharply after the 1950s. A similar experience can be recorded about Eastern Europeans, both in the labor movement and the skilled trades in US industry. It is significant that these men achieved leadership during the period of declining memberships in their respective organizations.

As Robert Viscusi has demonstrated, the common thread in nearly all representations of Italian-American men, especially since the War, has been their penchant for violence (to which I would add sexist relations with women).[62] These images have become a routine feature of American popular culture and have contributed to the reproduction of their subordination. Even in relatively dignified portrayals such as *Moonstruck*, the male lead is depicted as an angry, often irrational person who frequently flies into rages, particularly against his brother but, more generally, against his fate.

Needless to say, the dominant mass-mediated image of Italian-Americans since the 1930s has been that of the Mafia and other crime syndicates. From Edward G. Robinson's fictional representation of Al Capone in *Little Caesar* (1932) to the sophisticated figure of the postmodern Godfather by Al Pacino in 1990, the underlying themes persist: the heroic figures of the Italian immigration are those who beat up people or kill them. Martin Scorsese's three commentaries on this hegemonic narrative, *Mean Streets, Raging Bull,* and *Goodfellas,* are obliged to work within the genre while simultaneously attempting to deconstruct it. This is achieved by disrupting the relationship between private and "public" practices, between character and action. Certainly, there is no effort, in Scorsese's films, from his early work in *Mean Streets* (1973) and on, to disguise the utter futility of the choices his characters are obliged to make, whether those choices center on Jake La Motta's boxing career and his subsequent work as an entertainer, or the conflict between family loyalty and a life of crime in the *Goodfellas.* He does not romanticize or attempt to hide the violence that accompanies underworld life or the parallel world of professional boxing. What is different is that the inhabitants of these worlds for whom crime is a skilled trade, even a passion, view certain practices, such as beating opponents in the boxing ring or killing them in the course of underworld activity, as routine, often distasteful necessities.

Compared to one of the canonical works in this genre of an earlier generation, *Kiss of Death* (1947)—which became famous for Richard Widmark's ghoulish characterization of a sadistic hitman who, in one scene, pushes a crippled, wheelchaired mother of an intended victim down several flights of stairs—Scorsese's people enjoy their families, friends, and lovers, which, in the context of mob life, serve to blur the distinction between private and public. They perform the distasteful tasks of murder only with some embarrassment, but really live for the intimate relationships that they struggle to maintain in the wake of the chaotic life they publicly lead.

Six decades of Hollywood stereotypes articulated with more than a century of discrimination within working-class hierarchies, especially the fairly limited Italian-American mobility compared to Northern Europeans. This record invites comparison with others who have suffered the stigma of stereotypical cultural representations that correspond to their marginal position within the economic and social hierarchies, notably African-Americans. I do not want to claim that the resemblance is exactly parallel or that Italian-Americans suffer the same degree of economic and social exclusion. Needless to say, the brutal dichotomy of white and black that constitutes one of the characteristic divisions in the US has provided Italians with a (marginal) comparative advantage to that of blacks. Nevertheless, the comparison is apt. Italian-Americans are the most numerous white subcultural minority within the American population and are chronically underrepresented in the professions, among managerial strata, in the political directorate. Their signal achievement has been to win a secure place in the industrial working class as semi-skilled and, especially in the construction and needle trades, as skilled workers.

However, as we have seen, most of these places are rapidly disappearing, and many younger Italian-Americans, lacking education or union seniority, are being driven into the ranks of the unemployed and the working poor. The public representations of their rise within the corporate world, the Giannini group that controlled Bank of America and the Pope family that developed a successful food business as well as owned the largest Italian language daily newspaper, are notable as exceptions. And, of course, the singular figure of Chrysler president Lee Iacocca distorts the fact that he is (merely) an extremely high-paid manager whose relation to the ruling corporate class has always been controversial. Or, to be more precise, he has been excluded from the commanding heights of economic and political power, one suspects, because of his ethnicity.

True to the experience of other newly arrived turn-of-the-century immigrants, Italian-Americans found that sports and entertainment and, of course, organized crime, provided the best routes to riches and to social status. In the past century, this has scarcely changed, as the careers of singers Frank Sinatra, Perry Como, and the recent meteoric rise of actors Al Pacino and Sylvester Stallone, Cher, and Madonna attest. Earlier, Joe DiMaggio, Rocky Graziano, Rocky Marciano, and the later stardom of 49ers quarterback Joe Montana demonstrated the significance of Italian-Americans in sports. Needless to say, a similar account can be rendered for blacks, especially from the 1920s to the present.

Now, the idea that Italian-Americans occupy structurally subordinate subject-positions despite their categorization as Caucasian, challenges the prevailing view that they, like immigrants from Northern Europe were, more or less successfully, assimilated into mainstream American economic, political, and cultural life. Accordingly, to argue, provisionally, for Italian "racial" identity as at least one among their several collective subject-positions is also to interrogate the corollary idea that Italians themselves *chose* a series of positions, the result of which was to limit their options. If "Italian-American" has been constructed within the terms of exclusion as well as a troubled inclusion, the recent and past incidents of their acts of violence against blacks may be understood as a form in which they themselves live the contradiction between the multiple realities of racial and subcultural identities. But, it also provides an illustration of one of the central ambiguities inherent in US working-class history since the Civil War.

Italian and Eastern Europeans are commonly identified with the broad social and racial category of "white," which is the result of the conflation of race with color and other biologically derived physical characteristics. Accordingly, since nearly all Europeans are socially constructed as "white," differences among various European migrations are ideologically and culturally, rather than physically, constructed. Accordingly, given the general recognition that sons and daughters of black slave lineage are, at least historically, objects of systematic institutional racism, white is a signifier of class privilege, just as "black" signifies economic oppression, political marginality, and cultural deprivation. Since Italians have achieved some purchase on sectors of the economy, albeit in manual labor occupations and small businesses linked to working-class communities, and Eastern Europeans, although often blond and fair-skinned have traveled a strikingly parallel course, to suggest that they occupy, in part, "racial" subject-positions seems incongruous with our common understanding.

With the de-industrialization, these major national minorities have suffered profound deterioration in their living standards and in their social position. But as the two largest "white" minorities in the United States, Eastern Europeans and Italians have suffered at the level of political representation as well. To state that blacks are politically excluded is hardly disputed; to claim the same for Southern and Eastern Europeans raises a series of doubts about the claims for the democratic character of the liberal American state.

When Spiro Agnew, a Greek-American, was nominated and elected Vice President of the United States in 1968, it was the first time in the history of the Republic that anyone of Southern European background had achieved national elective office. The feat was almost duplicated by the Democrats twenty years later, when Massachusetts governor Michael Dukakis was nominated to be their presidential candidate. It is arguable that he lost to Vice President George Bush, in part, because of the racial issue which focused on his pardon of a rapist, a black man named Willie Horton, who repeated his offense after release from prison. But, like Agnew who was tarred with the brush of corruption, Dukakis, who had spent his entire political career cultivating the image of technocratic efficiency, was finally nailed by his Northern European opponent for incompetence—the politician's deadliest sin in our technoculture. Dukakis left office in 1990, disgraced for having failed to stem a rather small state deficit that paled in comparison to the gargantuan debt piled up by the national administration of which his opponent was a player. America can ignore or otherwise forgive its Northern European leaders, but send those of Jewish or Southern European backgrounds to jail or political oblivion.

Which, I believe, goes far to explain the fiscal conservatism of New York's governor Mario Cuomo and New York City's black mayor David Dinkins. The unwritten code to which they must conform—especially as racially and ethnically targeted politicians—is hard-nosed administration that means, in times of recession and de-industrialization, layoffs of public employees and draconian public economies that further erode working-class living standards. The name of the political game, one that Governor Jim Florio of New Jersey entirely underestimated in his first year of office, is that Italian-American, black, and Latino elected officials may not make their jurisdictions the vehicles for a determined effort to achieve social, i.e. class justice, lest they be accused of reverse discrimination against the rich and upper middle class. Of course, neither Cuomo nor Dinkins has been seduced by the redistributive class rhetoric of their own campaign platforms, or the needs of their working-class constituents; but Florio attempted exactly such a legislative and political program and was instantly attacked by both conservatives and a substantial segment of his own working-class constituency and was forced to beat a rapid retreat to save his political future.

Thus, the absence of class discourse in American politics does not relieve white or black national minorities from the exigencies of class struggle. When Florio attempted to realign the state's tax system to benefit workers and poor blacks and other urban people of color by redistributing state education funds to the most disadvantaged districts, he was confronted by a carefully orchestrated outcry—masked as a citizens' lobby against taxes—from all segments of business. During his first year in office, he was forced to retreat until, by early 1991, his program was nearly dead. Of course, Florio was defeated as much by the weakness of the movements that he had to mobilize as by those that would be expected to oppose him. Since the discourse of justice is intimately tied to class, ethnicity, race, and gender, the absence of one of its most salient components—class—foredoomed his efforts.

It could be plausibly argued that Florio was equally victimized by the recession and the conservative ideological climate that accompanied his rise to power. But how to explain the caution of Mario Cuomo who, despite the fact that he presided over the most prosperous period in his state's economic history, fashioned an economic agenda that could have been pursued by any liberal Republican? On the one hand, the ideological climate of the '80s was distinctly unfavorable to programs that recalled the modest New Deal efforts to redistribute income through equitable taxation or, indeed, a substantial expansion of the critically enfeebled welfare state. This climate was produced, in part, by the doctrine of "trickle down" according to which what is good for business is good for the country—hence deregulation to encourage competition, wage restraint to discourage capital migration, and union-free work environments. It was made possible by the decline of the leading forces of redistributive justice, the labor movement and the Black Freedom Movements, both of which retained, despite many disclaimers, a keen sense of class interest.

The fractured identities that have disrupted the feminist movement in recent years serve as a useful reminder that external portrayals tend to simplify and reduce what are always complex multilayered realities. The discovery of *difference* among women—between lesbian and straight, married and unmarried, radical and liberal, cultural separatist and cultural radical and, what has become increasingly controversial, white and black—often overshadows the fragile unities that can be mustered around issues of rights, especially abortion and employment. What developed within the feminist movement is, to some extent, genuinely tragic. There is a tendency—admittedly underground—to *counterpose* social and cultural issues to those of economic justice. For example, even though there are liberal and leftist reformulations of abortion rights, the former emphasizing a woman's right to "choose" whether to have an abortion and the latter shifting the discourse to "reproductive rights," the statement that women have an unconditional right to control their own destinies, especially their bodies, has always been a controversial formulation among those who would soften the impact of abortion on religious sensibilities. For what is implied by self-control over one's body is sexual freedom, more specifically, the right to pleasure without suffering dire moral consequences. This formulation has been criticized from a number of different directions. Of course, the most powerful has been the traditional position of the Catholic Church's hierarchy, that a woman's sexual activity be limited to the aim of reproduction. Indeed, other objections offer what might be described as a secular version of the same argument. Among them, Christopher Lasch's indictment of cultural radicalism, whose cornerstone is the right to pleasure, has grafted the clinical concept of narcissism as an emotional disease to the social phenomenon of pleasure-seeking. As the argument goes, the demand for sexual freedom masks a deeply narcissistic social personality that tends to be irresponsible to family and community (read men). Although the call for the return of women's subordination is rarely blatant, the attack on abortion rights as selfish and sexual freedom as irresponsible is really an attack on women as moral agents, on their capacity to take responsibility for their own choices, for the determination of how they will permit their bodies to be deployed.

The film *Kramer vs. Kramer* (1979) was, in retrospect, the harbinger of a decade when the concept of woman as moral agent was under severe attack. A woman leaves her up-and-coming advertising executive husband and their five-year-old-male child. Having stopped paid labor after marriage, she wants to find something of her own to do; she wants a career outside the home. Eighteen months after her departure, she sues for custody of their child. She *has* found a vocation that pays a salary that approximates that of her former husband who, meanwhile, has struggled with the vicissitudes of single parenting. For him, the result has been a closer relationship to their son and a downwardly mobile professional career. He is fired from his job because of lateness in deadlines and other negligences, all of which are caused by the fact that he places his child's needs above the firm's. In the end, the wife wins the suit, but finds that she cannot bring herself to reclaim their son because she has come to realize that the boy is "at home" with the father. She has gained a job and sexual freedom but has forsaken the joys of family life, especially the responsibilities of motherhood, and has thereby threatened a major part of her identity. This film is properly interpreted in the context of the attack on feminism that began to gain momentum in the late 1970s, but it also accurately connotes the decisive and perhaps irreversible move of women out of the home.

The prevailing imagery shifted as millions of women entered the labor force in the 1980s under the conflicting influences of feminism and the decline and fall of the family wage (which obliged virtually half of America's households to seek two incomes to maintain living standards). At the same time, the family reeled. By the middle of the decade, half of all marriages could expect to end in divorce for reasons that were inexorably linked to women's growing independence. For men, whose intellectual voice was articulated well by Lasch, American culture was in crisis in proportion that their position in private life deteriorated.

What needs to be noticed here is that women have gradually become one of the mainstays of the labor movement, whose popular representation has been obliquely celebrated in the film *9 to 5* (1980), obliquely because there is no question of a union in the film, only the collective revolt by women against sexual harassment and other office horrors. In some ways, Sally Field's portrayal of a reluctant shop union leader in a textile mill, in the 1979 *Norma Rae*, is more to the point.

Although the majority of union members are still men, almost all of the organizing gains of the past fifteen years have been among women workers in clerical, service, and professional occupations, particularly teaching and nursing. At the same time, many of these women have become increasingly ambivalent about feminism, not only because of the religiously influenced moral conflicts generated by the controversies over abortion rights, but because of the weakness of the US welfare system that has failed to provide adequate medical care, child care, and a decent income for women heads of households. The loss of the nuclear family may or may not be mourned by working-class women in the wake of increasing male violence against women and their own perception of the limitations of married life. But the material and social costs of the breakdown of the family to themselves and their children have been substantial. The steep rise in single mothering has been accompanied by the feminization of poverty, because women's wages are still only two thirds of those of men. Moreover, many women experience a loss of status in the wake of the absence of a significant alternative community that can provide spiritual support for the decision to go it alone despite social disapproval.

Yet, rarely, if ever, are the questions of economic justice and cultural freedom articulated within feminist discourse. Part of the reason has to do with the genuine cultural differences between women intellectuals and working-class women. Class really becomes an operative difference in relation to culture because the economic and ideological environment of working-class life tends to frame cultural discourse. Working-class women are often *privately* bitter about their marriages, but are constrained to maintain public silence. One of the constraints is, plainly, the homophobia of ethnic working-class communities, where even the most indirect hint that women and, to a lesser extent, men are prepared to exercise sexual preferences that do not conform to the heterosexual norm becomes an occasion for verbal and physical abuse and, frequently, exile from the community.

A recent representation of this situation appears in the 1989 European-made film of the Hubert Selby Jr. novel, *Last Exit to Brooklyn*. Here we can see the binaries of 1950s ethnic working-class life: women are constructed as desexualized, unpaid domestic servants or sluts; the strict homophobic code of male culture completely closes off the opportunity of a shop steward to exercise gay desire freely. Blocked by the repressive code of his own community, the shop steward ends his life—but not before engaging in a lurid attempt to seduce a young boy that earns him the scorn and ultimate exclusion from his comrades. (This theme of homophobia within male working-class environments is repeated, with considerable variation, in Melvin Dixon's *Vanishing Rooms* (1991). The novel, set in the 1970s, devolves around a gang rape and murder of a gay white man by a group of young Italian Americans. One of the group, Lonnie Russo, is the son of a small painting contractor who, in a series of episodically arranged first-person narratives, reveals his own latent homosexuality during and after his encounter with the victim and his attempts to distance himself from the violence in which he played a reluctant role. Lonnie's widowed mother's refrain "Christ Jesus, he never had a chance" is a constant comment on his own double oppression: as an Italian-American and as a teenage boy seeking to come to terms with his own sexuality. The strict homophobic male working-class culture becomes the thisness of his own otherness. In contrast, the gay victim's black lover, Jesse, struggles over his own sexuality, but not his gay identity. The third main character, Rusella, an aspiring black woman dancer, comforts Lonnie after his loss and tries to find a way to reconcile her attraction for Jesse with his own search for the soul of his dead friend.)

At the same time as feminism and economic necessity have tugged women of different classes in sometimes different directions, or in the same direction for sometimes different reasons, so sexual practices have had their own class differences as well—at least until recently. Premarital sexual intercourse among young women of high school age is common within working-class communities, white and black, but is exceptional, if not rare, within the middle classes. It is here that the question of abortion takes on its most exquisite class dimension. Since the white working class is typically either Catholic or fundamentalist Protestant, especially in the South and Southwest, social sanctions against women as moral agents are the greatest amongst the working classes. For these young women moral strictures are radically dissociated from everyday life, but retain their coercive authority to produce profound emotional turmoil.

These examples illustrate some of the ways in which class culture remains powerful in everyday life. Even today, in cities such as Chicago, Hamtramck, Michigan, a Detroit industrial suburb, New York's Italian-American neighborhoods, such as Bensonhurst, Howard Beach, south Greenwich Village, and northern New Jersey and the Long Island suburbs, some blue-collar communities survive. And they are places of political mobilization, but not necessarily on behalf of the progressive agenda of the traditional labor movement or, indeed, the old Democratic political machine. To the extent that they are politicized, they have become hotbeds of patriotism, racism, and antifeminist control over the right of "their" women (and their young men) to make sexual choices, especially for men who are identified as people of color.

During the recent Gulf War, as with the earlier US invasions of Panama and Grenada, the deep-going patriotic fervor of working-class and lower middle-class Americans was amply demonstrated in the proliferation of American flags, yellow ribbons, and signs announcing "We Support our Troops in Operation Desert Storm" in windows, cars, and neighborhood shops. Absent a political left-wing counter weight that could address the economic and social insecurity of many people within these communities, anger and frustration—especially in the light of the growing youth joblessness and the fact that the army has become, for many, the employer of last resort—is directed against those whose destiny seems most reminiscent of their own condition. Working-class nationalism is an outgrowth of powerlessness, of the absence of viable alternatives, of a sense that war and violence against people of color is a way to ward off defeat.

Militarism cannot be understood exclusively as the product of a conspiracy of governing elites seeking solutions to their own economic and political weakness in a changing world. As Wilhelm Reich argued,[64] working-class authoritarianism arises because of the multiple dimensions of powerlessness, of which sexual deprivations are among the most crucial. Recall that Reich insisted that in the struggle against fascism, the left should take up the problem of the crisis of the family, and most especially the "sexual misery" of the masses. For him, the moral conservatism of the left was complicit in the ability of the right to build a base among the workers. Of course, Reich's analysis ran counter to the official communist position, that Nazism could be understood as the "open dictatorship of the most reactionary sections of finance capital"[65] whose mass base was virtually confined to the proletarianized petty bourgeoisie. Reich adduced statistical evidence to support his claim that a significant portion of workers voted for the National Socialists after 1930.

There is another problem not anticipated by Reich's cultural critique. The concept of citizenship is ingrained in the formation of the nineteenth-century nation-state, and there is no *practical*, as opposed to theoretical, notion of citizenship that corresponds to internationalism—except the fairly ambiguous idea of class, race, or gender solidarity. Of course, solidarity expresses itself even among trade unionists who, in other respects, are profoundly nationalistic on occasions such as major strikes. In Winter 1991, I saw a window of a south Brooklyn two-family home that had an American flag and yellow ribbons, the symbols of support for US troops in the Gulf War, next to a sign that read "Teamsters support *Daily News* Strikers." These were codes of solidarity that might appear incongruous to the radical intellectual. But, for this working-class, white household they made perfect sense.

And there is a small, but definite antiwar movement based on the ideological precepts of anti-capitalism (only the rich benefit from most wars) and anti-imperialism that spans the traditional left and progressive traditions. But, it must be admitted, these are exceptions to the rule that the rights of citizenship imply the contractual obligation to military and other types of service and to support that service when at war.

In the recent Gulf War, polls reported that while eighty per cent of all Americans approved of US aims, fifty per cent of blacks were opposed to military intervention. This sentiment must be comprehended within the framework of the perception shared by many within the black community that they are excluded from the substantive, if not the procedural aspects of citizenship. They may freely exercise their right to vote, at least in the North and West, but this ritual act does not necessarily obviate their profound feeling of powerlessness in economic, political, or social terms.

The structural exclusion of blacks has produced a strong strain of radicalism in ghetto communities, one that expresses itself as separatism,
revolutionary nationalism, strong antiwar positions and, to a lesser extent, internationalism of the Marxist or racial variants. In contrast, white
Americans, especially first- and second-generation Eastern and Southern
European immigrants, accepted, with varying degrees of enthusiasm, the
ideology of assimilation, but only unevenly its cultural practices. Assimilation means surrendering their language and their culture as the price
they paid for being granted citizenship rights and the extremely hazy idea
of "equality of opportunity" to achieve mobility. While, as I have argued,
the historical record is complex and not entirely convincing regarding
the extent to which they made it in America, elements of the American
Dream were achieved without, however, being attended by genuine power. As we have seen, Eastern and Southern European immigrants often
felt obliged to form economically powerful subcultures that sometimes
took the form of labor unions, to protect their gains against the incursion
by employers and competitive subcultural groups. These labor monopolies and the persistence of relatively closed family and neighborhood relationships—even in today's postmodern culture—are signs that the Deal
has not yet been entirely consummated. Nevertheless, during the Gulf
crisis, white subcultural working-class communities, responding, in part,
to the fact that their kids constitute a large part of the military forces,
rallied powerfully to the administration, even as they had united behind
policies of racial exclusion in the construction and other key industries in
which they had gained some degree of power.

Since the breakup of the old socialist and communist organizations,
and the decline of the New Left, the American left has been confined, in
the main, to cheerleading progressive ideology and programs and organizing for issues of economic justice and against US military intervention
abroad. The brief decade of the New Left was characterized, in part, by a
significant turn by many activists and intellectuals towards what became
known as "social issues"—sexuality, child-rearing, the problem of the youth
generation, their popular culture, the family, and other sites of everyday
life. Several strains of the New Left comprehended that these issues are inextricably linked to problems faced by working people, particularly youth.

However, since the middle 1970s, leftist intervention in working-class issues are confined, almost exclusively, to the predominantly defensive struggles of embattled trade unions against the employer offensive of the Reagan era. In effect, the left, conceived in its broadest connotation to include the still-formidable popular forces for economic and social justice, including significant elements of the feminist and civil rights movements, has reverted to vulgar economism and the politics of the lowest common denominator—features that also characterized the 1930s popular front against fascism, when social, cultural, and educational radicalism was viewed as an impediment to the aim of achieving maximum unity in the struggle.

Despite the recent upsurge of cultural and political authoritarianism at the commanding heights of economic and political power and among working people, an upsurge which has successfully masked the deepening of social inequality at every level, we are not in a prefascist era. Yet, bereft of intellectual seriousness, the American non-university left finds itself without either analytic resources or the political will to address the profound cultural crisis manifested in the decay and disorder that marks urban life, the surface tendencies towards violence against women and people of color, or even the massive attack from corporations and the political directorate against the remaining provisions of the welfare state.

VI

Class has always been powerful in the United States, but not mainly in the way classical Marxism or even socialist ideology assumes. To be sure, America has had its share of militant labor struggles and dramatic surges of union organizing that invoked the most repressive responses of police and the army and, for a time, changed the landscape of national politics. In every decade of the twentieth century, visible signs of class combat have been present; from the miners strike of 1902 and the uprising of the 20,000 needle trades women in 1909 to the recent Eastern Airlines and *Daily News* strikes, US workers, embattled by employers' offensives against their living conditions and elementary trade union rights, have engaged in monumental resistance. But, as Werner Sombart argued in 1907, the socialist movement has been weak and, one might add, the broader ideological left has been only a sporadic presence in American life. In the final accounting, the inability of the left to place the egalitarian ideas in the forefront of public debate, much less political solutions, accounts, in the main, for the absence of a clearly articulated discourse about class.

Needless to say, subcultures, new social movements concerned the quality of life, and the civil rights and feminist struggles are not *merely* class displacements. I have argued in this essay that the historically ex-clusive focus of class-based movements on a narrow definition of the is-sues of economic justice has frequently excluded gender, race, and qual-itative issues, questions of workers' control over production, and similar problems. The almost exclusive emphasis on narrow quantitative issues has narrowed the political base of labor and socialist movements and made all but inevitable the emergence of social movements which, as often as not, perceived class politics as inimical to their aims.

Nevertheless, class shapes the collective fate of most Americans, not only economically, but ideologically and spiritually as well. For example, the social issues, such as racial justice and sexual freedom, are medi-ated within working-class communities by class considerations. As we have seen, working-class women and girls are subject to considerably more stringent controls than women in middle-class neighborhoods. And while young people interacting more extensively with popular mu-sic and other social influences may view questions of race and sexuality differently from their elders, they are also constrained by both the psy-chological and social limits of class affiliation in their ability to act on sentiments other than those approved by the subculture. Class fatally shapes the relation of children to schooling which, in turn, has a great deal to do, not only with the economic dimensions of their lives, but their relation to politics and what is taken as legitimate knowledge and art.

Absent a vital discourse of class, many Americans have displaced their resentments resulting from what Sennett and Cobb called the "hid-den injuries" of class to patriotism and other varieties of nationalism.[66] Moreover, working-class racism and sexism mask the considerable in-security suffered by many white male workers in the face of capital mi-gration, depression and recession, and the deterioration of their living standards, particularly their ability to earn a "family wage"—a situation that has forced many women into the wage labor force and has had devastating consequences for the working-class family. These economic strains have combined with social and cultural strains, especially the influence on women of an otherwise maligned cultural radicalism, to produce the largest divorce rate in the history of the West. The further proletarianization of large chunks of the contemporary working class is particularly acute among young workers, whose best hope for job training and job security has become the armed forces.

Further, the more desperate situation confronting many white workers has strengthened what was once, in the halcyon era of assimilation, considered moribund: ethnically based subcultures. As economic independence becomes a distant shore for many white working-class youth, they are obliged to remain at home, and this compulsory extension of their childhood has thereby reinforced their subcultural identity, despite contrary pressures from the media and education systems. With the increasing identification of class fate with subculture, working-class life appears increasingly distinct, but "class consciousness," encased in largely segregated and culturally homogeneous neighborhoods, tends to become ideologically conservative and politically authoritarian. This is not the result of "inherent" tendencies in the constitution of the working class, but may be considered as part of a specific conjuncture of the strengthening of corporate capitalist hegemony and the profound weakness of the labor movement.

Despite job discrimination, segregation, and social exclusion, blacks have been, since the industrial union campaigns of the 1930s, when, for a brief period, they were invited, albeit ambivalently, into the House of Labor, among the most loyal and militant trade unionists. Similarly, women have streamed into the new public employees and service unions in large numbers since the 1960s and have become a counterweight to the relative decline of unionism engendered, in part, by recent disaffections among white men. From this follows the conclusion that class no longer has an autonomous ideological existence among US workers, but lives as a hybrid with the discourse of social movements, particularly of gender and race, not only in this country. For while class is no longer dominant over these emergent discourses, neither has it disappeared; it remains true that, at a concrete level, many workers still rely on the collective power of labor organizations to sustain, much less improve, their standard of living even when unions are no longer perceived as resolute champions of workers' interests on the shop floor.

The changing composition of the US labor movement corresponds to its increasing marginality within American life. Unions are strongest among public employees in the cities whose populations have in the past three decades become increasingly black and Latino. In turn, from its proudest monuments, the cities have become the backwater of what may be described as American civilization. In a nation without viable centers, the working class, whose power has always been crucially tied to these centers, becomes invisible or, alternatively, appears only when it disrupts the ordinary rhythms of public life. At such times, the "public," a term that is always a euphemism for the white middle class, looks on not only with puzzlement, but with ire, because it has become convinced that the "once mighty unions" are no longer a threat to their tranquility and resent the temerity of these people of color to believe they have the right to disrupt essential services in the interest of their salaries.

Of course, in the case of strikes by physicians, journalists, pilots, teachers, and social workers that have dotted the landscape in recent years, a fraction of the public itself becomes the object of public scorn and discovers the ambiguity of its own class affiliations. These events have become more frequent the more that employers, having successfully "taken out" many industrial unions, now concentrate on the organized part of the service sector. In these cases, the "public" seems more confused because it can easily identify with the respectable people walking the picket lines. Even television and press reports seem softer, less bellicosely anti-union. Perhaps, as confrontations between professionals, who have become the core of the public sphere, and large institutions and corporations become more frequent, the situation of class will take on a new and different coloration.

The working poor remain invisible in debates about class. Situated in casual, part-time, and extremely insecure labor in small, competitive workplaces, they typically earn incomes at, or below, the minimum wage.

Many of these workers are employed in the service sector or light manufacturing by employers whose positions in their respective industries
is shaky. Thus, they are frequently laid off, and are constantly seeking
work. Since, US and state labor laws favor the largest, most stable employers, the working poor find themselves deprived of jobless benefits,
decent health and child care, and chances for education and training.

Part-time work has become the fastest growing category of employment. There are nearly four-and-a-half million officially part-time workers, or about three and three-quarters per cent of the labor force and
tens of thousands in the underground economy. In the legal sector these
are the most vulnerable of all workers. Contrary to earlier periods when
many women with children sought part-time work during school hours
because of the absence of affordable all-day or after-school child care facilities, part-time work, some of it done in the home, has become the arrangement of choice for many employers who, beleaguered by increasing
competition, are anxious to reduce labor costs, such as health benefits,
paid holidays and vacations, and others that might accrue to unionized
workers. Part-time arrangements put many workers in a precarious position with respect to job security, especially where the work is casual.

The major unions have spent little effort trying to organize among the
millions who find themselves in these situations—most of whom are people
of color, women, often single mothers and youth. In the instances where
organizing has been relatively successful—hospital workers, agricultural
workers, needle trades workers—the unions have almost invariably been
part of what might be described as "social," as opposed to "business,"
unions—the distinction is one of ideology, if not always trade union practices. Yet, the fact that more than a half a million hospital workers have
joined unions in the past thirty years, especially in the large cities, and the
farm workers conducted heroic and often successful strikes throughout
the 1960s and '70s attests to the possibility that the most oppressed of the
working class are, indeed, likely candidates for membership, if the unions
fuse struggles for social justice with those of racial and gender dignity.

The considerable fraction of workers in the underground economy
who are not engaged in drug dealing, sexwork (commonly referred to
as prostitution), or other ostensibly illegal activities, has mostly escaped

scholarly, much less trade union, attention. Today, there are considerable sections of the garment, toy, and novelty, plastics, and other light manufacturing industries that operate outside various labor and health laws. The work force is composed, typically, of recent immigrants who are part of the wave of Latin, Caribbean, and Central American migrations, and Asians. Where unions, such as the Ladies Garment Workers, have made a concentrated drive to unionize these workers, they have met with some success and, even in failure, have elicited a gratifying response among undocumented workers who face deportation if their employer reports them to the INS.

Of course, the plight of immigrant workers, when discussed, is depicted in terms of issues of immigration because of the informal enforced silence about class discourse. The struggle of these workers entails, indeed, constant efforts to overcome the effects of the restrictive immigration laws and policies of the US government which are directed, not at immigration itself (indeed, tens of thousands continue to enter the US each month), but at the capacity of workers for self-organization, for class or other identity. Immigrant workers live an underground existence and are often terrorized by the knowledge that any overt resistance on their part is an invitation for deportation. However, as the second economy occupies a more important position, these restrictions appear increasingly irrational and have produced several misguided efforts at immigration reform which, despite the fact that they benefit some, have merely tightened the repressive controls of the federal government, making economic and political organization increasingly difficult.

The excruciating consequence of these compulsions is to further close off the most important resource to those who need it most: time. For the condition of achieving collective self-consciousness is the ability of individuals and groups to take the self as an object, to distance ourselves from our situation in order to recognize it and, potentially, to overcome it. This is not done primarily through introspection, although this is a necessary concomitant of self-evaluation. The formation of groups that study relationships—sexual and otherwise—that become able to understand broad economic and social developments and connect these to their own situation, is an absolutely crucial method for developing and sustaining the critical self.

However, large numbers of people are working at two or three jobs or are caught in the vise of consumption and overtime, as in the case of autoworkers. They are unable to read anything beyond the daily newspaper or receive news apart from that offered by the car radio or the television channels. For women, the "double shift" is devastating to their capacity to transcend conditions of their own oppression. Even when they walk out on their husbands or lovers, the pressures of earning a living and child care keep them chained to the home. Under these circumstances, it is all the more remarkable that so many women and men have succeeded in adopting one or another critical position with respect to everyday life, politics, and culture.

The American evasion of class is not universal. We have no trouble speaking of ourselves as a "middle-class" society or, indeed, endowing the economically and politically powerful with the rights and privileges of rule. American ideology identifies the middle class with power and, in its global reach, has attempted to incorporate manual workers into this family. The anomaly of the large and growing working poor, some of whom are hungry, others homeless and, indeed, the increasing insecurity suffered not only by industrial workers but also by professionals and clerical employees in the service sector, make some uneasy but have, until recently, failed to faze the ongoing celebration. Or, to be more accurate, class issues are given other names: crime, especially drugs; teenage pregnancy and suicide; homelessness and hunger; chronic "regional" unemployment that is grasped as an exception to an otherwise healthy national economy.

These will remain "disturbances" in a calm sea of progress so long as opposition is confined to resistance and alternatives remain murky. Needless to say, this essay has not been directed toward a revival of some antiquated idea of class. Instead, what I have tried to show is that class never appears in its pure form. It is always alloyed, short of what might be called the rare instances of "epochal" transformations, with other identities, discourses, movements. In the United States, where socialism, anarchism, and laborism have suffered marginal existences for most of this century, we are afflicted with a serious case of social amnesia, the only treatment for which is the emergence of a new radicalism at once sophisticated and militant.

NOTES

1. Francis Fukuyama, "The End of History?", *The National Interest*, 16 (Summer 1989).

2. Daniel Bell, *The End of Ideology* (Glencoe: Free Press, 1960); Daniel Bell, *The Coming of Post-Industrial Society* (New York: Basic Books, 1973); S. M. Lipset, *Political Man* (New York: Doubleday, 1960).

3. Nancy Hartsock, *Money, Sex and Power* (London: Longmans, 1984).

4. For a contemporary account see Henri Lefebvre, *The Explosion* (New York: Monthly Review Press, 1969); also Daniel Singer, *Prelude to Revolution: The French May 1968*. A more recent treatment is Laurent Joffrin, *Mai 1968: Histoire des événements* (Paris: Editions du Seuil, 1988). For the Italian situation, the best account in English is Joanne Barkan, *Visions of Emancipation* (New York: Praeger Publishers, 1985).

5. The most comprehensive and theoretically elaborated treatment of capitalist regulation in the US context is Michel Aglietta, *A Theory of Capitalist Regulation: The US Experience* (London: New Left Books, 1979).

6. Louis Althusser and Étienne Balibar, *Reading Capital* (London: New Left Books, 1970).

7. Karl Marx, *Capital*, vol. i (New York: Vintage Books, 1976).

8. G. W. F. Hegel, *Phenomenology of Spirit*, trans. A. V. Miller (London and New York: Oxford University Press, 1976).

9. Karl Marx, *Communist Manifesto*, in Marx, Selected Writings, vol. i (New York: International Publishers, n.d.).

10. Karl Marx, *German Ideology* (Moscow: Foreign Languages Publishing House), 39.

11. Even Engels acknowledges this. See Frederick Engels, *The Origins of the Family, Private Property and the State* (New York: International Publishers, 1935).

12. R. H. Hilton and H. Fagan, *The English Rising of 1381*; R. H. Hilton, *Bond Men Made Free* (New York: Viking Press, 1973), especially part 2.

13. Marx, *Capital*, vol. iii, quoted in G. E. M. de Ste. Croix, *The Class Struggle in the Ancient World* (London: Duckworth, 1981), 51–2.

14. Ste. Croix, *Class Struggle*.

15. For a representative example, see Art Preis, *Labor's Giant Step* (New York: Pioneer Press, 1964).

16. Stanley Aronowitz, *Working Class Hero: A New Strategy for Labor* (New York: Pilgrim Press, 1983).

17. See Karl Marx, "Introduction," *Grundrisse*, trans. Martin Nicholaus (London: Penguin Books, 1973).

18. Karl Marx, *Capital*, vol. i (Moscow: Foreign Languages Publishing House, 1964), 352.

19. George Herbert Mead, *Mind, Self and Society* (Chicago: University of Chicago Press, 1934).

20. Gilles Deleuze, *Bergsonism* (New York: Zone Books, 1989).

21. Erik Olin Wright, *Classes* (London: Verso Books, 1985).

22. Nicholas Abercrombie and John Urry, *Capital, Labour and the Middle Classes* (London: Allen and Unwin, 1983).

23. Michel Algietta, *A Theory of Capitalist Regulation*.

24. Scott Lash and John Urry, *The End of Organized Capitalism* (Madison: University of Wisconsin Press, 1987), chs. 1 and 2.

25. By "objective" I mean the striking increase in the number of wage and salaried workers in proportion to the absolute decline of the family farm and the relative decline of small business with respect, particularly, to its share of total production of goods and services.

26. For the best theoretical statement of the position of social ecology, see Murray Bookchin, *The Ecology of Freedom* (Palo Alto, Calif.: Cheshire Books, 1982). Also Bookchin's earlier book, *Our Synthetic Environment* (New York: Alfred A. Knopf, 1962). This book appeared in the same year as Rachel Carson's immensely influential *Silent Spring*, but was more far-reaching and, therefore, less easily accepted. See also Barry Commoner, *Closing Circle* (New York: Alfred A. Knopf, 1972) and Stephen H. Schneider, *Global Warming* (New York: Vintage Books, 1989).

27. Kirkpatrick Sale, *Human Scale* (New York: 1985).

28. Bookchin, *Ecology of Freedom*.

29. However, the danger now presented by the sluggish economy, especially rising unemployment and reduced consumer spending, is that employers can effectively threaten plant shutdowns if state-imposed sanctions become more stringent. A case in point is the argument made by the US automobile industry that safety measures, such as air bags, more efficient pollution control devices, and legislation that would restrict the use of internal combustion engines, would drive up costs and reduce their ability to compete with Japanese, Korean, and European imports.

30. Of course, the advancing decay of our major cities is more than just one more "social problem." Our cities have been sites of cultural avant-gardes, social movements, and political left-liberalism. While rapid suburbanization has spawned new ecologically linked consumer movements, the widespread support enjoyed by movements for social justice has been eroded by the acceleration of *de facto* racial segregation since the 1960s.

31. Anne Bramwell, *Ecology in the Twentieth Century: A History* (New Haven: Yale University Press, 1989).

32. Ellen Willis, "Is Motherhood Moonlighting?", *Newsday*, 12 March, 1991.

33. Ursula K. Le Guin, *The Left Hand of Darkness*; Joanne Russ, *The Female Man*.

34. Donna J. Haraway, *Primate Visions* (New York: Routledge, 1990); Evelyn Fox Kelle *Reflections on Gender and Science* (New Haven: Yale University Press, 1985); Sandra Harding, *The Science Question in Feminism* (Ithaca: Cornell University Press, 1986).

35. Ashley Montagu, *Man's Most Dangerous Myth: The Fallacy of Race*.

36. William Julius Wilson, *The Truly Disadvantaged* (Chicago: 1985).

37. Alvin Gouldner, *The Future of Intellectuals and the Rise of the New Class* (New York: Continuum Books, 1979).

38. For a discussion of these issues, see Stanley Aronowitz, *False Promises: The Shaping of American Working Class Consciousness* (2nd edn., Durham: Duke University Press, 1992).

39. James Weinstein, *The Corporate Ideal and the Liberal State* (Boston: Beacon Press, 1966).

40. Weinstein, *Corporate Ideal*.

41. William Leuchtenburg, *Franklin Delano Roosevelt and the New Deal* (New York: Harper and Row, 1963), 188–9; also Stanley Aronowitz, *Working Class Hero*, 75ff.

42. James Green, *Grass Roots Socialism* (Baton Rouge: Louisiana University Press, 1978).

43. Louis Althusser, "Ideology and Ideological State Apparatuses," in *Lenin and Philosophy and Other Essays* (New York: Monthly Review Press, 1971).

44. Carl Schorske, *German Social Democracy 1905–1917* (Cambridge: Harvard University Press, 1955).

45. Alfred Schutz and Thomas Luckmann, *Structures of the Life World*, trans. Richard Zaner and H. Tristram Engelhardt Jr. (Evanston: Northwestern University Press, 1973), 3: "The everyday life-world is the region of reality in which man can engage himself and which he can change while he operates in it by means of his animate organism. At the same time, the objectivities and events which are already found in this realm (including the acts and the results of the actions of other men) limit his possibility of action... Furthermore only within this realm can one be understood by his fellow men and only in it can he work together with them. Only in the world of everyday life can a common communicative surrounding world be constituted." Schutz relies here on Husserl. See particularly, Edmund Husserl, *Ideas: General Introduction to Pure Phenomenology*, trans. W. R. Boyce

Gibson (New York: Humanities Press,1931); and Edmund Husserl, *Crisis in European Sciences and Transcendental Phenomenology*, trans. David Carr (Evanston, Northwestern University Press, 1970).

46. John and Ruth Winterton, *Coal, Crisis and Conflict: The 1984 Miners Strike in Yorkshire* (Manchester: Manchester University Press, 1989), 109–10.

47. Hardy Green, *On Strike at Hormel* (Philadelphia: Temple University Press, 1990).

48. Carl Ross, *The Finn Factor in American Labor, Culture and Society* (New York: Mills MN Parta Press, 1977), 12.

49. This can be seen in the fact that Angela Davis's stature far outlasted that of the Communist Party of which she is a leader, so too the enduring popularity of W. E. B. DuBois and Paul Robeson, both of whom had long associations with the communist movement.

50. James Connolly, *Nationalism and Socialism.*

51. Emmet Larkin, *James Larkin.*

52. Lawrence Goodwyn, *Democratic Promise* (New York: Oxford University Press, 1976).

53. Craig Calhoun, *The Question of Class Struggle* (Chicago: University of Chicago Press, 1981).

54. Samuel Farber, *Before Stalin* (London: Verso Books, 1990).

55. Stephen F. Cohen, *Bukharin and the Bolshevik Revolution* (New York: Alfred A. Knopf, 1974).

56. Moshe Lewin, *Russian Peasant and Soviet Power.*

57. Carmen Siriani, *Workers Control and Workers Democracy* (London: Verso Books, 1982).

58. Daniel Singer, *Prelude to Revolution: The French May 1968*; Alain Touraine, *The May Movement* (New York: Random House, 1970).

59. Bell, *The Coming of Post-Industrial Society*; Alain Touraine, *Post-Industrial Society.*

60. The idea of the material significance of economic and social perception still unfortunately requires argument. Here are two examples: despite the enormous decline of US working-class living standards during the past twenty years, many workers perceive themselves and are perceived by others as members of the "middle class." By all statistical measures, blacks have suffered an even greater economic disaster in the same period. Still, many whites perceive that blacks are privileged by the welfare system; that they do not work because they don't choose to. Liberals may deplore such widespread misperceptions of the contemporary black economic conditions, but they have serious political consequences.

61. Joseph Cescelca and Vincenzo Milione, "Statistical Profile of Educational Attendance of Italian Americans," John D. Calandra Institute.

62. Robert Viscusi.

63. Christopher Lasch, *Haven in a Heartless World* (New York: Norton, 1977).

64. Wilhelm Reich, *Mass Psychology of Fascism*, trans.Theodore Wolfe (Orgone Press, 1946).

65. George Dimitroff, *United Front Against Fascism and War* (New York: International Publishers, 1935).

66. Richard Sennett and Jonathan Cobb, *The Hidden Injuries of Class* (New York: Random House, 1972).

CHAPTER SIX

The Last Good Job in America

Prologue

There's a wonderful museum of eighteenth- and nineteenth-century material culture in Shelburne, Vermont. Last summer our family joined thousands who marveled at exhibits of toys, miniature soldiers and battle scenes, and the many transported authentic artifacts or replicas of living rooms, kitchens, pantries, and other objects of everyday life. My favorites were the working blacksmith's and print shops. The print shop reminded me of old movies about courageous small-town editors crowded into a single room with their presses. The Shelburne presses were more industrial but the technology was the same. Amid the fire and the heat and the clanging hammers hitting the forge, one had a vivid picture of what skilled manual work might have been like before the automobile displaced the horse and buggy and cold type all but destroyed the old printer's craft.

These were good jobs. They paid well and, perhaps equally important, engaged the worker's mind and body. Apart from the laborious task of typesetting, which was done by hand, the printer had to carefully set the controls on the machine just right. It was a time-consuming but supremely intellectual activity. Through reenactments of popular material culture—for example, the blacksmith let our daughter participate by forging a metal hook—as well as through artistic representations, the

Shelburne museum reminds us how rural and small-town people once lived and worked.

Walking through the museum's sprawling acres I could not help drawing an analogy with the disappearing professoriat. One day some academic entrepreneur—a *Lingua Franca* publisher Jeffrey Kittay of the future—will hit on the idea of exhibiting mid-twentieth-century academic material culture. There will be a replica of a professor's study: On her desk sits the old Olympia typewriter, an ashtray, and some yellow pads filled with notes for an article or book or the next day's lecture. The study is book-lined, many volumes surfeited with dust. A leather jacket and denim work shirt hang on the door's hook.

The magazine rack is filled to the brim with scholarly journals, along with the *New York Review of Books* and *Lingua Franca*, those quintessentially academic feuilletons which went out of business about 2010 because there were too few professors around to read them. By then most of us had been retread as part-time discussion leaders—freeway or turnpike flyers—and could manage only to scan the day's video of the famous scholar's lecture on whatever before meeting the fifty students at the local American Legion hall where the group meets. The actual postsecondary faculty member of the future may still own a desk, but the shelves may contain as many video cassettes as books and there might or might not be a magazine rack.

Diary

It's Wednesday, one of my writing days. Today I'm writing this piece, for which George Yudice and Andrew Ross have been nudging me for a couple of days. Nona will return home about three o'clock and it's my turn to get her to her after-school music class and prepare dinner. As it turns out she brings a friend home so I have a little extension on my writing time. I couldn't begin working on the piece yesterday because on Tuesdays I go to the City University of New York (CUNY) Graduate Center. Even so, after making Nona's breakfast and sending her off to school (as I do every other day), reading the *Times* and selected articles from the *Wall Street Journal* and the *Financial Times*, and checking my e-mail, I usually spend the morning editing my Monday writing. But yesterday

Nona was home with a stomach bug and, because Ellen, her mother, had umpteen student advisements at New York University (NYU), it fell to me to make her tea, minister to the puking, get some videotapes, and commiserate. Anyway, Monday morning after my usual reading routine I had finished an op-ed for *The Nation* on the future of the left. Otherwise I would have started this article a day earlier.

I was somewhat out of the writing mode on Monday because I had a second (oral) exam to attend. I'm chair for a candidate who was examined in cultural studies, psychoanalysis, and feminist theory. She knew her stuff but took some time to get rolling, after which the exam was quite good. After the exam I answered my calls, wrote two recommendations for job applicants, attended a colloqium in the early evening given by Elizabeth Grosz and Manuel DeLanda, and arrived home about nine o'clock, after which Ellen and I prepared our dinner (Nona eats earlier).

On Tuesday afternoons I meet with students. At this time of year (mid-December) many sessions are devoted to discussing their papers, which are due at the end of January. This semester I preside at a seminar on Marx. We are reading only four texts but a lot of pages: the early manuscripts, *Critique of Hegel's Philosophy of the State*, *Capital*, and the *Grundrisse*. There are about twenty-five students in the group, who form three study groups that meet weekly to address the critiques and commentaries as well as to study the texts more extensively than the two-hour session with me could possibly accomplish. Sometimes after class I meet with one of the study groups to help with the reading. Yesterday I did some career counseling in the early evening for a friend who is thinking about quitting his job and trying to work for the labor movement.

Tonight I'll read in the *Economic and Philosophical Manuscripts* because tomorrow one of the groups is making a presentation. Yesterday, a few of my students met with me individually to discuss, among other things, the merits of Althusser's argument for an epistemological break between the early and late Marx, the state/civil society distinction, and whether Marx's *Capital* retains the category of alienation in the fetishism section of volume one. Tomorrow after checking my e-mail I will edit some of this stuff I am writing and arrive at school around noon to meet with a student about last semester's paper for a course called "Literature as Social Knowledge." Then I'll try to work on this piece until my office hour, which is simply a continuation of what I do on Tuesday, except some of my dissertation students may drop in to give me chapters or to talk. At 4:15 I'll meet my seminar, after which a small group of students has asked to meet about publication chances for a collective paper they wrote on what the novels of Woolf, Lessing, and Winterson tell us about the gendering of social life. I'll probably get home by nine o'clock.

Friday is committee and colloquium day in the sociology Ph.D. program in which I work. While I serve on no departmental committees, I am involved in seventeen other committees this year, either as dissertation advisor or as chair of a CUNY-wide committee that raised some money to help faculty do interdisciplinary curriculum planning. But I will try to attend the colloquium. I often invite my advisees to meet me at home because life is too hectic in my office. My office is a place where students hang out, where there are myriad telephone interruptions, and where I am called on to handle a lot of administrative business, such as change-of-grade forms, recommendation letters, and so on.

Over the weekend I'll have time for my family, having hopefully finished a draft of this piece. I also have to finish a longer collectively written article for a book called *Postwork*, which came out of a conference sponsored by the Center for Cultural Studies, of which I am director. The group will meet on Monday evening to go over my collation. I may get it done on Sunday or Monday. And next week Jonathan Cutler, the coeditor of the volume, will work with me on writing an introduction.

I am one of a shrinking minority of the professoriat who have what may be the last good job in America. Except for the requirement that I teach or preside at one or two classes and seminars a week and direct at least five dissertations at a time, I pretty much control my paid worktime. I work hard but it's mostly self-directed. I don't experience "leisure" as time out of work because the lines are blurred. What is included in this form of academic labor anyway? For example, I read a fair amount of detective and science fiction, but sometimes I write and teach what begins as entertainment. The same goes for reading philosophy and social and cultural theory. I really enjoy a lot of it and experience it as recreation but often integrate what I have learned into my teaching and writing repertoire. In any case, much reading is intellectual refreshment. And even though I must appear for some four hours a week at a seminar or two, I don't experience this as institutional robbery of my own time. It's not only that I like to "teach" or whatever you call my appearance in the classroom. I'm not convinced that even the best of my lectures "teaches" anybody more than providing some background on the topic. (I hardly ever give a "talk" in class that lasts more than ten minutes without student interruptions, either questions or interventions.) Most of the time I work from texts; I do close readings of particular passages, inviting critique and commentary and offering some of my own.

When I meet with study groups I do so voluntarily. Needless to say, the job description really doesn't require it, since few of my colleagues encourage such groups to form. And my assent to serve on more than twenty dissertation committees, about a quarter of those outside the sociology program, and to direct a number of tutorials and independent studies is by no means "required" by some mandated workload. Whatever I take on is for the personal and intellectual gratification or obligation which I have adopted.

As a professor in a research school and a teacher of Ph.D. students, I feel I should also raise money to help support students in addition to doing whatever I can to help them find jobs and get their dissertations published. And as director of a center, I need to find money for its public life: talks, conferences, and postdoctoral fellowships. Now, in my situation I don't have to do any of this work, but I feel that I should go back to undergraduate teaching if I won't or can't contribute to meeting these urgent student needs. So I raise between $15,000 and $50,000 a year for student support and for conferences and research projects.

Finally, for all practical purposes my career is over, so none of this work is motivated by the ambition or necessity of academic advancement. I am a full professor with tenure and have reached the top of a very modest salary scale, at least for New York. I earn more by some $5,000 a year than an auto worker who puts in a sixty-hour week but less than a beginning associate in a large New York corporate law firm or a physician/specialist in a New York health maintenance organization (HMO). But most of them work under the gun of a manager and, in the case of the law firm, only five of every hundred attorneys will ever make partner. With a two-paycheck household we can afford to eat dinner out regularly, send Nona to camp, give her the benefit of piano lessons, fix the car, and own and maintain a couple of early- and late-model computers and a decent audio system. And we pay a mortgage on an old ill-heated farm house in Upstate New York where we spend summers and some autumn and spring weekends. But because in my academic situation I have nothing career-wise to strive for, I'm reasonably free of most external impositions. Before every semester my chair asks me what I want to teach. What's left is the work, and with the warts—administrative garbage, too many students (a result of my own hubris), and taking on too many assignments, writing and otherwise—I enjoy it.

What I enjoy most is the ability to procrastinate and control my own worktime, especially its pace: taking a walk in the middle of the day, reading between the writing, listening to a CD or tape anytime I want, calling up a friend for a chat. And I like the intellectual and political independence the job affords. I can speak out on any public issue without risk of reprisal from the administration or from my program. Organizations such as the AAUP originally fought for tenure because, contrary to popular, even academic, belief, there was no tradition of academic freedom in the American university until the twentieth century, and then only for the most conventional and apolitical scholars. On the whole, postsecondary administrations were not sympathetic to intellectual, let alone political, dissenters, the Scopeses of the day. Through the 1950s most faculty were hired on year-to-year contracts by presidents and other institutional officers who simply failed to renew the contracts of teachers they found politically, intellectually, or personally objectionable.

For example, until well into the 1960s the number of public Marxists, open gays, blacks, and women with secure mainstream academic jobs could be counted on ten fingers. And contrary to myth it wasn't all due to McCarthyism, although the handful of Marxists in American academia were drummed out of academia by congressional investigations and administrative inquisitions. The liberal Lionel Trilling was a year-to-year lecturer at Columbia for a decade, not only because he had been a radical but because he was a Jew. The not-so-hidden secret of English departments in the first half of the twentieth century was their genteel anti-Semitism. For example, Irving Howe didn't land a college teaching job until the early 1950s, and then it was at Brandeis. Women fared even worse. There's the notorious case of Margaret Mead, one of America's outstanding anthropologists and its most distinguished permanent adjunct at Columbia University. Her regular job was at the Museum of Natural History. She was a best-selling author, celebrated in some intellectual circles, but there was no question of a permanent academic appointment. Her colleagues Gene Weltfish and Ruth Benedict, no small figures in anthropology, were accorded similar treatment.

It's not surprising that the University of Minnesota administration recently decided to try to turn back the clock forty years and rescind tenure. Only the threat of an AAUP-conducted union representation election caused the board of trustees and the president to (temporarily) withdraw the proposal. In the absence of a powerful enough left there is little, other than market considerations, to prevent university administrations from abrogating the cardinal feature of academic work: the promise that, after five or six years of servitude, mainly to the discipline and to the profession, a teacher may be relatively free of fear that fashion will render his or her work obsolete and, for this reason, not worthy of continued employment. The irony of the current situation is that many who win tenure nonetheless risk not being promoted, harassment, and, probably most painful of all, utter marginalization for dissenting intellectual work. For those who have been incompletely socialized into their professions, tenure turns out to be a chimerical reward. With some notable exceptions, by the time the teacher has achieved tenure, at least in the major schools, internalized conformity is often the condition of long-term survival.

In this respect, in addition to protecting genuine political dissent in conventionally political terms, tenure can protect academic dissidents—scholars and intellectuals who depart, sometimes critically, from the presuppositions of conventional science, literature, or philosophy. But tenure is job security only in the last instance. Typically the successful candidate must demonstrate her/his lack of independence, originality, and hubris. Peer review is often used as a way to weed out nonconformity. It works at all levels: getting tenure and, in many systems for which pay raises depend almost entirely on "merit," climbing the pay scale often entail publishing in the "right" journals (in the double-entendre sense) and prestigious academic presses. For example, I know a wonderful younger scholar coming up for tenure in a quasi-Ivy League college who decided to accept an offer from Stuffy University Press rather than one from an aggressive hotter house. He admitted his book might end up in annual sales, but it would do the tenure trick. It's hard to say whether the other choice would have been as efficacious. But he felt in no position to take a chance. The second question is, How much did this decision take out of his chance to become an intellectual rather than a professional clerk of the institution?

Now, it must be admitted that most faculty have long since capitulated to the strictures of the conservative disciplines and to the civility and professionalization demanded by academic culture. Many define their intellectual work in terms of these strictures and, in the bargain, measure their contribution not by the degree to which they might be organic intellectuals of a social movement but, at best, how they might make piecemeal, incremental changes in the subfield to which they are affiliated. The overwhelming majority do not aspire to genuine influence. Moreover, they disdain any discourse or activity that cannot be coded as civil: the idea of confrontation as a means of clarification is beyond the bounds of acceptability. Insofar as institutional power continues to reward conformity, tenure is quite beside the point for the overwhelming majority of the professoriat.

I have a "central line" appointment, which means that I teach exclusively in the graduate school and nearly all of my students are working toward the Ph.D. With the exception of approximately a hundred others, most of the teaching and advising at the school is performed by college-based faculty who rarely teach more than one graduate course a year. My situation is enviable by CUNY and most other colleges' standards.

For the time being I write what I please without the sword of unemployment or ostracism hanging over my head. If I were on the job market today most sociology departments would not hire me because I don't follow either the discursive or the methodological rules of the discipline and first and foremost I'm a *political* intellectual whose views occasionally are in public view. I doubt I would have gotten a tenured professorship at the University of California at Irvine in 1977 if the program into which I was hired, although sympathetic with my political views, grasped that my work on labor was informed by cultural studies and what it has come to mean. But I did, and they were stuck with me until I left in 1982 to teach at CUNY. CUNY Graduate School hired me because they believed I was a labor sociologist, even though I had published several articles in social and cultural theory during the late 1970s. They had good reason to focus on my work on labor. I had helped organize the Center for Worker Education at City College while teaching at Columbia during 1980-1. It is a thriving BA program for working adults, many of whom are union members or their family members. Then I became a visiting professor in the Center. Shortly after I was hired in the sociology program at CUNY I organized a cultural studies center and, in addition to what I had been hired to teach—political economy and labor—I began teaching courses in cultural studies, social studies of science and technology, and social theory. Some of my colleagues were astonished and some were chagrined. I am glad to report most got used to my eclecticism, but not immediately or easily.

Now there are some who view my teaching and writing as a luxury which should be ended at the earliest possible convenience and, indeed, are waiting for me to retire or leave by any other possible circumstance. Sometimes it's about me, but mostly it's about the structural position of the full professor in research institutions. According to some, they/I have too many privileges. I offer another perspective on this position. I am a radical because I believe that people work too hard for too little and that their work is more like labor, not under their control. The situation of the few holding the last good job should be universalized, not suppressed. I do not hold to the view that there should be an equality of misery; on the contrary, we need a movement for less externally imposed labor and more self-directed activity. People should be able to write their stuff independent of whether it is necessary for promotion, tenure, or anything except to share their knowledge and/or their art. People would be better served by cutting working hours for more pay rather than by working without end. I believe that the work ethic is, literally, a cornerstone of the prevailing ideology of capital. That some are swimming against the stream should be defended, not attacked on phony populist grounds.

In fact, the salaries and working conditions that some enjoy in universities should be held up as a standard for everybody. Work without end is the scourge of every radical idea because it colonizes our most precious possession: time. Participatory governance at the workplace, in the community, and in the home; free time for personal development and pleasure; and social and cultural equality are next to impossible when work-time is so long that the worker (intellectual as well as manual) can barely keep her/his eyes open at the end of the day. Back-breaking manual labor and work that separates body and mind should be eliminated by technology and democratic work organization. And rather than excoriate those who are able to avoid the most degrading jobs, the left should excoriate those jobs and not romanticize them. In a word, most paid labor is shit, and those who are lucky enough to avoid it, make it more pleasant and self-managed, or reduce it to the barest minimum should be emulated.

A Little Political Economy of Teacher Work

Most of us who work for wages and salaries are subject to external compulsion throughout the workday. Signifying one of the most dramatic shifts in work culture, the ten- and twelve-hour workday has become almost mandatory for many factory, clerical, and professional employees. Forty years ago looming automation was accompanied by the threat of unemployment and the promise of shorter hours. It was also a time when the so-called mass culture debate exploded in universities and in the media: Would the increased leisure made possible by technological change be subordinated to the same compulsions as paid labor? Would television, for example, crowd free time? Or would the late twentieth century become an epoch of such innovations as life-long education, the recreation of civil society (imagine all the cafes filled with people who have the working lives of full professors), a flowering of the participatory arts, a golden age of amateur sports?

One of the predictions of that period has been richly fulfilled. World unemployment and underemployment reached a billion in 1996, thirty per cent of the working population. And this is the moment when part-time, temporary, and contingent work is threatening to displace the full-time job as the characteristic mode of employment in the new millenium. But the part-timers have little space for individual development or community participation. You may have heard the joke: the politician announces that the Clinton administration has created ten million jobs in its first four-year term. "Yeah," says the voter, "and I have three of them."

This is a time of work without end for many Americans and a work shortage for many others: youths, blacks, other "minorities," and women (whose jobless rate is higher by a third than men's). Behind the statistics lies a political and cultural transformation that has already wiped out the gains of three generations. A hundred years ago the dream of the eight hour day animated the labor movement to a new level of organization and militancy.

In the main, unions embraced technology because, if its benefits were distributed to producers, it could provide the material condition for freedom from the scourge of compulsory labor and the basis for a new culture where, for the first time in history, people could enter into free associations dedicated to the full development of individuality. In the aftermath of the defeat of the Paris Commune, where for a brief moment workers ran the city, Marx's son-in-law railed against the dogma of work and insisted on the right to be lazy. Some workers, imbued with the protestant ethic, vehemently disagreed with this utopic vision—many of the best labor activists were temperance advocates—but did not dispute the goal of shortening the workday so they could fix the roof or repair the car. Whether your goal was to spend more time fishing or drinking or at "productive" but self-generated pursuits, nearly everyone in the labor movement agreed, mediated for some by the scurrilous doctrine of a "fair day's pay for a fair day's work," to do as little as possible to line the bosses' pockets.

As everyone knows, we are having our technological revolution and the cornucopia of plenty is no longer grist for the social imagination; it is a material possibility. As, among others, Robert Spiegelman, Herbert Marcuse, and Murray Bookchin have argued, scarcity is the scourge of freedom and, from the perspective of the rulers, must be artificially reproduced to maintain the system of domination. Hence, working hours are longer, supervision—call it surveillance—more intense, accidents and injuries more frequent, and wages and salaries lower. Marx's belief that the more the worker produces the more he or she is diminished, enriching only the owners, seems more relevant today than it did in 1844 when he first wrote this idea.

Technology is deployed as management's weapon against its historic implication of freedom. It permits radically shorter working hours but, instead, has been organized to produce a three- or four-tier social system. At the bottom, millions are bereft of the good life because computer-mediated work destroys jobs faster than the economy creates them. Many are fully unemployed, some still receive government support. Others are casual laborers who "shape up" everyday at the docks of companies such as United Parcel Service and FedEx for a day's work or are migrant farm workers. You can see the shape-up any morning in the South Bronx or on Chicago's West Side where mostly Latino workers await a furniture or vegetable truck for a day's hard labor.

At the pinnacle of the working class a shrinking elite—industrial workers in the large enterprises, craftspersons, and technical employees—still have relatively well-paid, full-time jobs and enjoy a battery of eroding benefits: paid vacations, healthcare (with the appropriate deductibles), and pensions. In between are the at-risk categories of labor: laid-off workers rehired as "contractors" or "consultants," both euphemisms for contingent workers; workers in smaller enterprises with lower-paying, full-time jobs and fewer benefits; and, of course, the bulk of college teaching adjuncts.

As capital reorganizes and recomposes labor, the idea of a job in contrast to paid labor is increasingly called into question. Here I won't dwell on the political economy of capital's offensive. Many of its salient features are well known: sharpened international competition, declining profit rates, global mergers and acquisitions. But it is important to underline the crucial fact of the decline, even disappearance, of the opposition and alternative to capital. It's not only the disarray into which the socialist project has fallen but also the inability of powerful national labor movements to confront global capital with more than sporadic resistance.

Corporate capitalism and its fictions, especially the "free market," have become the new ideological buzzwords of world politics and culture. They penetrate every itch and scratch of everyday life. Under the sign of privatization public goods are being disassembled: healthcare, environmental protection, and, of course, state-sponsored culture, signified by, among other things, the legislative evisceration of the National and State Endowments and Councils on the Arts and Humanities and their replacement by corporate-sponsored arts programs, notably those aired by PBS (the Petroleum Broadcasting System), countless corporate-funded museum exhibits, and the reemergence of corporate sponsorship of all kinds of music, especially middle-brow classical music. Sixty million Americans obtain their healthcare from HMOs, private consortia of hospitals, managers, and owners. The mission of these groups is to get rid of patients, not disease. And they operate under the sign of cost containment, with ultimate success measured by the number of subscribers turned away from service.

No more startling change has occurred than the growing tendency by local school boards to use their funds to outsource instruction, curricula, and other educational services to private contractors. Meanwhile, the drumbeat of vouchers gets louder as public perception that elementary and secondary schools are "failing" prompts an orgy of straw grasping. As a recent report using standard measures indicated, these arrangements do not seem to have a noticeable effect on improving school performance, but it is not clear that panic will not overcome reason. Teacher's unions have resisted privatization, but the propaganda campaign on behalf of "free choice," the euphemism for privatization, appears, at times, overwhelming.

It was perhaps inevitable that the steamroller should have arrived at the doorstep of America's universities and colleges. By 1990, in contrast to the general decline of the labor movement's density in the workforce, faculty and staff were joining unions in record numbers. By the 1990s some 130,000 faculty and staff (exclusive of clerical workers) were represented by the three major unions in higher education, the American Federation of Teachers (AFT), the American Association of University Professors (AAUP), and the National Education Association (NEA). Thousands of college and university clerical workers organized into a wide diversity of organizations, including AFT, but mostly others such as the United Auto Workers (UAW) and, in public universities, the American Federation of State, County, and Municipal Employees (AFSCME). To pay for rising salaries for clerical workers and faculty and to compensate for falling revenues for research, many administrations imposed tuition increases that exceeded the inflation rate and beefed up their endowments from— you guessed it—large donations from corporations and the individuals who headed them.

The growing influence of corporate giving on private and public research universities has been supplemented by a cultural corporatization of higher education. Once limited to community and technical colleges, vocationalization has become a virus infecting the liberal arts undergraduate curriculum. In many institutions social science and humanities departments have been reduced to service departments for business and technical programs. Many colleges have agreed to offer degrees, majors, and specially tailored courses to corporate employees in return for company reimbursements of tuition and other revenues and have accepted money from corporations to endow chairs in vocationally oriented fields. In some cases, notably the Olin Foundation, not only chairs are offered to universities but also the right-wing professors to sit on them.

This configuration is not confined to technical and managerial areas: it has become one of the solutions for the sciences, which have progressively lost public funding for research in fundamental areas. Now, many scientific departments must justify their faculty lines by raising outside money to perform (mostly) product-oriented research. Most famously, Massachusetts Institute of Technology molecular biologists entered a hotly contested Faustian bargain with drug companies, which have subsidized research in return for patent ownership. This model has been reproduced in many other institutions and has, to some extent, become the norm. Of course, American scientists are accustomed to subordination to higher authorities; their involvement with the defense establishment is a sixty-year marriage.

Faculty unions are not entirely a solution to the conditions that generate them: an acute power switch from the faculty to administration and to government and corporations over some hiring, curricular, and academic priorities; sagging salaries except for the high-profile stars and top administrators; and, at least in the public universities, legislatively mandated budget cuts which, in most instances, buttressed the power switch and resulted in some layoffs, a much tighter market for real jobs, increased workloads for those who have them, restrictions on promotions, and pay raises calibrated to the inflation rate. In sum, faculty members see their unions as a means to restore their lost autonomy and shrinking power as well as to redress salary and benefits inequities.

Academic labor, like most labor, is rapidly being decomposed and recomposed. The full professor, like the spotted owl, is becoming an endangered species in private as well as public universities. When professors retire or die their lines frequently follow them. Instead, many universities, even, as we have recently learned, in the Ivy League, convert a portion of the full line to adjunct-driven teaching, whether occupied by part-timers or by graduate teaching assistants. At the top, the last good job in America is reserved for a relatively small elite. Fewer assistant and associate lines are being made available for newly minted Ph.D.s. As the recently organized Yale University graduate teaching assistants discovered, they are no longer, if they ever were, teachers-in-training. Much of the undergraduate curriculum in public and private research universities is taught by graduate students who, in effect, have joined the swelling ranks of part-timers, most of whom are Ph.D.s. Together they form an emerging academic proletariat. They make from $12,000 to $20,000 a year, depending on how many courses they teach and where, whether they teach summers, and whether they are hired as adjunct instructors or assistant professors. Except for those termed *graduate teaching assistants*, most do not get benefits or have offices or, indeed, any of the amenities enjoyed by full-time faculty.

It reminds me of my semester teaching at the University of Paris at Saint-Denis. Only the chair of the department had an office. Faculty from part-timers to full professors crowded into a single large room where they deposited their outer clothing and some papers while they taught. After class, they picked up their belongings and headed home. In most French universities the university as a public sphere is simply unthinkable, a situation which once described the American community or technical colleges. The postsecondary scene of the future may, unless reversed by indignant and well-organized students and faculty, resemble more the second-tier European and Third World universities than the "groves" celebrated in the popular press.

Administrators offer contradictory accounts of this emerging configuration of academic teacher work. They claim teaching is merely part of the academic apprenticeship of graduate students and a means to support them through school. On the other hand they are wont to claim that the proliferation of adjuncts is a sad but necessary aspect of the imperative of cost cutting. According to this line, if they could they would create many new full-time lines. But they can't. At CUNY, where the number of new full-time lines has slowed to a slow faucet leak, approximately half of all courses in the undergraduate curricula are taught by adjuncts; in community colleges the figure is sixty per cent. Even in schools such as New York University, which has made substantial efforts to rebuild its full-time faculty, some key programs such as the School of Continuing Education and many traditional departments' undergraduate lower-division offerings are largely taught by adjuncts.

In the largest middle-level state systems such as California State University and CUNY, research is not genuinely encouraged except in the natural sciences. Nonetheless, it remains a sorting device to get rid of faculty by denying tenure to those who fail to meet the criterion of producing the requisite quantity of publications. In these schools, many full-timers teach four and five courses a semester and have dozens of student advisees. In some instances, the professor who defies gravity's law by remaining intellectually active is labeled a rate-buster by the exhausted or burned out majority of her or his colleagues. When combined with committee work, many faculty are transformed into human teaching machines, while others, in despair, desperately seek alternatives to classroom teaching, even stooping to accept administrative positions, and not just for the money or power. The old joke that the relationship between a tenured professor and a dean is the same as that between a dog and a fire hydrant has become one of the anomalies of the waning century. Now the adminstrators are the cat and the faculty the catbox.

318

A Margin of Hope?

In *The Jobless Future* William DiFazio and I have argued that academic teacher work is heteronomous. Salaries, working conditions, and expectations are crucially shaped by where the teacher is employed and in what capacity. I have already alluded to the heavier teaching loads in middle- and lower-tier colleges. In community colleges and state non-research four-year institutions, teaching loads and student advisement have been rising in the 1990s. And many more professors are teaching introductory courses where texts are prescribed by the department, especially but not exclusively in community colleges, which enroll half of the fifteen million students in postsecondary education. As teacher/student ratios skyrocket class size increases; at one CUNY campus an introductory course enrolled eighty students. The graduate assistant told me that she had no teaching assistant or grader. And this narrative is fairly typical of many public four-year colleges. When the course load was three for full-time faculty and classes enrolled no more than thirty students, the professor had time to read and write and pay close attention to students' work. It was at least one of the better jobs. Now many institutions of postsecondary education have an industrial atmosphere, especially with the increasingly vocational curricula in the liberal arts.

Research universities have smaller classroom teaching loads in order to facilitate faculty research, at least in the social and natural sciences. Apart from composition and other required introductory courses which have increasingly become the meat and potatoes of English departments in community colleges and middle-level universities, philosophy, criticism, and history are activities treated as ornaments. The leading figures in these disciplines enhance the institution's prestige, which has implications for fundraising and, in some instances, provides administrative leaders for elite schools. Deans, provosts, and presidents are frequently recruited from the humanities in high-prestige liberal arts colleges and private research universities, although the public universities lean toward natural scientists.

Many faculty maintain their intellectual and social distance from students, even graduate students. It's not only that they are busy with their grant-funded research, their writing, and their narrowly circumscribed celebrity. The distance is produced by the growing gap between the professoriat, who in the elite universities almost completely identify with the institution, and graduate students' growing recognition that collective action rather than individual merit holds the key to their futures. For example, when I was invited to address a meeting of hundreds of members of the recently organized Yale Graduate Assistants union in spring 1995, I was dismayed but not surprised to find only three senior faculty in attendance, one of whom promptly resigned his job in the sociology department to return to the labor movement. The other two, David Montgomery and Michael Denning, and a few others who could not make this particular event, are union stalwarts in this otherwise snow-blinded community of scholar-managers. "Left" critics and scholars along with more conservative faculty were prominent by their absence. A year later I was informed that a distinguished historian turned in a graduate assistant who had participated in an action to withhold grades as a protest against the administration's refusal to recognize the union.

The formation of an academic proletariat, even in the elite universities, must be denied by the professoriat, who have gained richly from the labor of their "students." The professors must continue to believe that those who teach the bulk of the undergraduate classes are privileged crybabies destined to become the new privileged caste. Strikes, demonstrations, and other militant activity are expressions of graduate students' flirtation with outworn ideologies of class and class struggle and not to be taken seriously. These professors are not only indifferent to the new graduate assistants' unions, they are hostile to them. In effect, they take the position of the administration and its corporate trustees because they identify themselves as its supplicants.

Some who are acutely aware that they hold the last good job in America believe that their best chance to preserve it lies in becoming what the infamous Yeshiva decision alleges: that faculty in private schools are managers and therefore ineligible for union protections under the law. It is not merely that they are highly paid and enjoy the prestige of institutions standing at the pinnacle of the academic system. Their identities are bound up with their ornamental role. To break with the institution on behalf of graduate students would acknowledge that higher education at all levels is being restructured and that they may be the last generation of privileged scholars. This admission would prevent them from playing their part in closing the gates.

The Yale struggle is only the most publicized of a growing movement whose main sites are in state research universities. The University of Iowa, the University of Michigan, the University of California at Berkeley, Los Angeles, and San Diego, the State University of New York at Binghamton, and the University of Wisconsin are among the dozen major universities with graduate assistant unions, many of them affiliated with conventional blue-collar organizations such as UAW, as well as AFT. In many cases the AFT or AAUP contract covers adjunct faculty, but graduate assistants must organize separately.

But academic unionism has, in general, not yet addressed the very core of the crisis: the restructuring of universities and colleges along the lines of global capitalism. Most of us are situated in less privileged precincts of the academic system. We have witnessed relatively declining salaries and the erosion of our benefits. And like many industrial workers we have been driven into an impossibly defensive posture and are huddled in the cold, awaiting the next blow. We know that full-time lines are being retired with their bearers, that more courses are taught by part-timers at incredibly low pay and few if any benefits. We are aware of the tendency of elite as well as middle-tier universities toward privatization and toward aligning the curriculum with the job market, and we are experiencing the transformation of nearly all the humanities and many social sciences into services for business, computer technology, and other vocational programs.

In short, although more highly unionized than at any time in history, academic labor has not yet devised a collective strategy to address its own future. We know that the charges against us—that university teaching is a scam, that much research is not "useful," that scholarship is hopelessly privileged—emanate from a right that wants us to put our noses to the grindstone just like everybody else. So far we have not asserted that the erosion of the working conditions for the bulk of the professoriat is an assault on one of the nation's more precious resources, its intellectuals. Guilt-tripped by mindless populism, whose roots are not so far from the religious morality of hard work as redemption, we have not celebrated the idea of thinking as a full-time activity and the importance of producing what the system terms "useless" knowledge. Most of all, we have not conducted a struggle for universalizing the self-managed time some of us still enjoy.

CHAPTER SEVEN

The Jobless Future?

Is Work a Need?

"Men like to work. It's a funny thing, but they do. They may moan about it every Monday morning and they may agitate for shorter hours and longer holidays, but they need to work for their self-respect."

"That's just conditioning. People can get used to life without work."

"Could you? I thought you enjoyed your work."

"That's different."

"Why?"

"Well, it's nice work. It's meaningful. It's rewarding. I don't mean in money terms. It would be worth doing even if one wasn't paid anything at all. And the conditions are decent-not like this."[1]

This conversation between Vic Wilcox and Robyn Penrose, a lecturer in English at a thinly disguised University of Birmingham, is from David Lodge's novel *Nice Work*. Penrose has been assigned to "shadow" Wilcox, the managing director of Pringle, a medium-sized, diversified, metal-working company in the increasingly deindustrialized Midlands region of England. In this dialogue, Vic summarizes one of the crucial elements of what has commonly been designated as the "work ethic." It is not merely the comparative economic advantage of paid labor over an increasingly inferior "dole" that motivates "men" to take jobs. Nor does the meaning of work derive from its intrinsic interest; in principle, technology eliminates the workers' skills and, finally, the workers themselves. Instead, we are driven by the fact that the "self" is constituted, at least for most of us, by membership in the labor force, as a member of either the job bourgeoisie—the "professions"—or the working class.

Thus paid work is, in Penrose's amendment, a socially and psychologically constructed "need" shared by those who have been successfully habituated to think that the link between holding a job and having "dignity" is a given. Put bluntly, in this view the self is identical to its place in the paid labor force. No job, no (secure) self. Individuals under retirement age (an increasingly indeterminate threshold) are motivated, indeed urged, to seek and hold paid labor when, for whatever reason, they experience a need that does not depend entirely on rational considerations such as how much a job pays or fear of sinking into penury—better to take pride in the fact that, as workers, they are able to provide for self and family without state aid or charity.

Even when one-third of the US labor force was officially unemployed throughout the 1930s, and many workers were on short-time schedules, they still blamed themselves for their joblessness. There was no dignity for those who could not find jobs; the conventional wisdom, shaken for more than a decade but not displaced, was that there was "always" plenty of work for those who wanted it. This homily derives from the larger American ideology according to which there cannot, by *definition*, be a disjunction between broad economic growth and jobs. Individuals, not the economic and social system, are ultimately responsible for their fate; the market adjusts itself at a level approximating full employment, and any joblessness is "frictional"—that is, temporary—for responsible and able-bodied individuals. This key precept of the dominant ideology resumed its virtually uncontested hegemony after World War II, when official statistics recorded jobless rates of less than six per cent until the early 1980s.

There are, of course, exceptions to the universal principle of paid labor as the sole path to male (and, increasingly, female) dignity, but these turn out to be only variations on the theme that work is a "need." One may retain "dignity" if income has been "earned" through past usury or ownership of business. Unwork becomes dignified only if income is derived from retirement or disability. The implicit assumption is that the retired and the disabled would have remained in the paid labor force if they were able-bodied or younger. Retirement is still considered a reward for a lifetime of faithful paid work, although some research has contended that relatively few retirees in the United States prosper unless they have income acquired through labor or property in addition to their Social Security benefits. From the standpoint of the conventional ethic, paid labor is considered optional for women.

Inherited income is ambiguous. Even when heirs do not need to take paid work in order to live, it is always implied that they should be subject to the work ethic. Even in higher circles the "playboy" and "playgirl" are morally condemned; heirs who live on income that derives from trust funds and other repositories of the past labor of others but are unwilling to engage in socially useful activities face censure from peers. The socially responsible heir seeks redemption through performing good "works" in charities or other civic activities or may become a patron of the arts, science, or other types of knowledge.

Although Robyn Penrose objects to the notion of paid work and its surrogates as a "need," she invokes another criterion for working: it is "meaningful" in nonmonetary terms. Intellectual work yields its own rewards when it fulfills two principal criteria: it is done under decent conditions and it produces new knowledge that, by implication, transcends its intrinsic pleasures for the producer. The work is produced not only for subjective gratification or survival, but has a larger meaning.

Much of David Lodge's novel concerns Robyn's struggle to reconcile her desire to hold a permanent teaching job at a time of contraction for academic institutions with her belief that intellectual work is intrinsically meaningful. She is oppressively aware that her chances to land a job are enhanced if she writes and publishes a second book. That she is interested in what she wants to write about is plainly secondary to the requirement that it be written and published.

Robyn must secure paid labor in order to live, but she cannot envision life other than teaching and writing. Her "self" is clearly intertwined with being an intellectual, which generally entails holding an academic post. As the narrative unfolds, we are made aware that her pursuit of a job is indistinguishable from the production of a suitable text, the contents of which, although putatively significant, are subordinate to its role in enhancing the commodity value of her labor.

Vic, alternately her antagonist and her lover (he is an archetypal anti-intellectual), also lives to work. Despite the apparent gulf that separates their interests, he derives as much pleasure from playing the power game, as much "meaning" from building the company, as Robyn does from writing a book or delivering a successful lecture. He suffers from the inevitable petty intrigues in his situation, as does Robyn in hers: she must curry favor and lobby intellectual "inferiors" in the quest for a job. What unites them is the satisfaction they get from the *nature* of their work rather than merely its monetary rewards. Yet their identities are impelled in different ways by the requirement that they occupy a definite position within their respective job hierarchies and can thereby manage a determined, if unequal, living standard. The product the workers at Lodge's fictional company, Pringle, make is far less important than how much of it they make and how cheaply. Craftspeople and common laborers work for the sake of making a living, not to fulfill themselves. Vic, like Hegel's master, is driven by the hope that, via mastery, he can achieve recognition and, perhaps more to the point, a dwelling place through the labor of "his" workers. He deplores the present orientation of managers and employers in much of British industry; he takes considerable care to make sure that "his" firm recovers from years of unprofitability and is prepared by what he calls "rationalization"— new-product development, technological innovation, and organizational efficiency—a program that implies that the firm would be willing to abandon its diversified character and become more specialized. Despite his success in achieving these goals, which he was hired to pursue, Vic loses his job when the firm is sold to its archcompetitor by the holding company that owns it; his interest in Robyn and the intellectual life has made him suspect among his peers. In the end, he is a victim of the creed by which he lives: rationalization. A manager is a manager and an intellectual is just that. Robyn fares better, but she learns that the university is subject to the same bottom-line rationality.

A Distinction between Labor and Work?

Hannah Arendt has insisted on the distinction between labor and work; she calls work a reified activity—that is, it has an objective existence independent of the immediate needs of the producer or, for that matter, of its role in consumption.[2] In fact, Arendt argues, proceeding from Marx but not from the same standpoint, labor and consumption are part of the same system. Both function to reproduce human labor power and, while they are necessary human activities, they have a profoundly different significance from that of work.

Arendt sees the products of labor as transitory; all that counts is their reproductive function. In contrast, work ensures the "durability of the world":

> It is this durability which gives the things of the world their relative independence from men who produce and use them, their "objectivity" which makes them withstand, "stand against" and endure, at least for a time, the voracious needs and wants of their living makers and users. From this viewpoint, the things of the world have the function of stabilizing human life, and their objectivity lies in the fact that—in contradiction to the Heraclitean saying that the same man cannot enter the same stream— men, their ever-changing nature notwithstanding—can retrieve their sameness, that is, their identity, by being related to the same chair and the same table. In other words, against the subjectivity of men stands the objectivity of the man-made world rather than the sublime indifference of an untouched nature.[3]

Arendt does not accept the Platonic claim for the ontological status of pure "form"; she recognizes the relativity of durability. Tables and chairs disintegrate, if they are neglected or worn out, to their state as wood (but not as trees; their artificial character is irreversible). They require "care in preservation" just as the "tilled soil, if it is to remain cultivated, needs to be labored upon time and again." There is no permanence, no objectivity that can resist the sands of time. But just as the artwork, whatever its satisfactions from the point of view of consumption, remains independent of the labor/consumption system, so the "works" of science and technology and of craft can be separated from their incorporation into the commodity-form.

Far from constituting a manifestation of the alienation of labor, the independence of fabricated things from the conditions of their production and consumption is that they remain objects that retrieve the self, which is ineluctably lost in the never-ending life process. When, in Arendt's terms, Marx "joyfully" announced the primacy of labor as the historical and ethical equivalent of the production and reproduction of "life," he also proclaimed the subordination of the individual to the social character of life's flow.

But Arendt discovers a contradiction in Marx's thought. On the one hand, he shows that labor is the means by which humans and nature constitute and reproduce the metabolism by which nature is humanized and humans are naturalized. In this perspective humans are part of nature: *Homo sapiens* are the latest evolutionary stage of natural history. Accordingly, the reproduction of labor power is equivalent to the reproduction not only of human life, but of life itself. On the other hand, Marx never tires of restating his claim that communism consists not merely of the emancipation of the laborer from exploitation, but of the emancipation of labor itself. Communism develops the productive forces that are brought into existence by capitalism but remain "fettered" by the class system. With the full development, through scientifically based technology of human powers over nature, it becomes possible to liberate the worker from labor and to reinstate work, which, however, is neither subsumed under the commodity form nor free to become a form of play.

Arendt argues that with the advent of these productive forces the link between humans and nature is severed. In the age of automation (and, one might add, cybernetics), nature becomes a playground to indulge the new leisure needs produced by massive labor displacement. For Marx and Engels, the passage from the realm of necessity to that of freedom signifies the abolition not only of the specific form of wage labor, but also of the close identification of the head with the hand, of the constitution of the self with its role in making the object world. Perhaps only the designers of machines that make things—the architects of automatic production— retain anything like the sense of a self that is identified with fabrication, with self-objectification. Against Marx, Arendt wants to separate means from ends. In her view, historical materialism does not get us very far from being laboring animals for whom reproduction is the sole end. Relegating art and other works to the realm of play only compounds the problem, for we have no reliable means of achieving a specifically *human* identity without our ability to attain a "free disposition of tools"—free from the division of labor and the rhythmically repetitive labor process in which the individual is subordinated to the requirements of organizational precision. Arendt writes that "what dominates the labor process and all work processes which are performed in the mode of laboring is neither man's purposeful effort nor the product he may desire, but the motion of the process itself and the rhythm it imposes on the laborers."[4]

The incorporation of machines into the labor process in order to make the activity of laboring easier has failed to restore laborers to their humanity. Instead it has further subordinated workers to the machine and to the forces of nature by imposing a regime in which the process of re(production) mimics the physical processes of animal existence and dominates life. As Marx himself remarked, under capitalism we engage in production for the sake of production. The age of automation, according to Arendt, has been so organized that humans do not produce in order to provide themselves with a "dwelling place" but to further the efficiency and operational capacity of the machines:

> For the society of laborers, the world of machines has become a substitute for the real world, even though this pseudo world cannot fulfill the most important task of the human artifice, which is to offer mortals a dwelling place more permanent and more stable than themselves.[5]

Rather, machines are seen, as Marshall McLuhan noted, as "extensions" of our biological selves. In turn, we are attached to machines as to ourselves.

Arendt rejects the collapse of work into labor, and also what she considers Marx's error of relegating work to "play," his protestations to the contrary notwithstanding.[6] In the final accounting, for Arendt and for many intellectual critics of technology, the artwork remains the best repository of that dwelling place where thought and action are fused, ends are not subordinated to means, and, perhaps most important, *Homo faber* and *vita activa* (fabricating "man" and active life),[7] may create a durable world. Arendt deplores the degree to which virtually all human purposes and relations that once found their apogee in the political realm have been transformed into a process of production of goods that may be exchanged in the marketplace. Since for Arendt social production becomes an extension of biological reproduction aimed at the reproduction of labor power, people are not really "doing something" that can be distinguished from the labor of animals, *work* as opposed to labor consists in the fusion of thought and making in activity that contributes to that which really constitutes freedom—politics, the one sphere in which specifically *human* interaction is possible. Yet when politics is not possible because all activity has been subsumed under labor or, more precisely, science, which may be the most powerful force of modernity, she tragically but triumphantly concludes that it is better to do nothing, to be alone.

Of course, Arendt's privileging of politics over labor is by no means unique in the history of social and political thought. This view, most powerfully expressed in Plato's *Dialogues* and Aristotle's *Ethics*, and whose most recent manifestation is Habermas's theory of communicative action, accepts the instrumental character of the relation of humans to nature.[8] According to this school of thought, work, however necessary, is ultimately no measure of man. The repository of truly human action is language. In Habermas's version of "discursive" ethics, speech is directed toward rational decision making outside the consensual sphere of production.[9]

This perspective explicitly denies that humans negotiate their relationship to nature through labor and thus form themselves. For this reason, there is little consideration in Arendt's and Habermas's theoretical discourse of the ethical dimensions and implications of ecological questions; labor and nature having been relegated to a nether world, the "social" is removed from its natural referent. In making this separation, Arendt and Habermas follow a tendency that embraces a wide spectrum of contemporary thought. The question we wish to explore here is its *defensibility*.

330

The Decline of "Work"

Both Arendt's discourse on the significance of work as opposed to labor and David Lodge's skeptical response to this view raise the fundamental question of whether there is work worth doing in a regime in which production is merely a means to make profits and, for the rest, to reproduce life; in which apart from the important qualification that under current conditions labor displacement results in economic pain, workers, engineers, and managers have no reason to defend labor itself and are right to be indifferent to both the process and the product of labor. In fact, when they are given the opportunity, workers—skilled and unskilled alike—are pleased to be relieved of participation in the labor process provided they are guaranteed an income adequate to the current "decent" standard of living.

With the decisive passing of craft, except in the crevices of the modern labor system, the main value of having a job (besides its economic function for individuals and households) is that it once provided a "community," which for many men replaced the traditional agricultural family. With the partial breakdown of the urban family, many women found the workplace a source of social solidarity as well. Moreover, contrary to popular depiction of craft labor as intrinsically satisfying in comparison to stupefying mass production, historical and ethnographic evidence demonstrates that skilled workers were no less eager to be liberated from the workshop than assemblers and laborers. Much of Arendt's invocation of the "reified" object as the permanent testament to humanized work turns out to be as mythological as the supposed beneficent effects of the slave system on its subjects, for it was not the object that provided satisfaction for the craftspersons, but the opportunity for a richer human interaction. This benefit of collective labor was not generally available to assembly-line and other less-qualified laborers. Production workers found after-hours conviviality in bars and social clubs.

But the culture of the factory and the large office is dying; for most workers, even those classified as "skilled," the old bonds are considerably loosened, even when they have not completely disappeared, for a very good reason: most craftspersons—in construction, in factories, car and instrument mechanics—know that the division of labor and the computer rationalize craft nearly as much as they do manual labor. Most auto and instrument mechanics, for example, rely on computer-mediated electronic tests for diagnostic purposes and work with parts that are engineered as modules. When Vic tells Robyn that the men like to work, what he forgets to mention is the reason for this affection. It certainly does not lie in work "satisfaction," that ambiguous sociological and psychological category that might issue from the substantial aspects of the tasks, but in the reality of the shop as a "dwelling place," a home that has little to do with the end product of their collective labors.

Achieving a home in the traditional industrial culture did not entail crafting a reified object that represented suprabiological dignity, as Arendt and so many romantic accounts of the artisanal era have claimed. The "bonds" of labor derive from the immanence of laborers' collective power and shared recognition of their collective subordination. The markers of these bonds are less "tools," instruments of fabrication, than a shared discursive universe replete with rituals, linguistic codes, jokes, and world-views—in a word, a culture. The shop or office may be regarded as a universe that visits exhaustion and frustration upon its inhabitants but provides, at least for some workers, an irreplaceable network of relationships and, taken in its multiple significations, a discourse, which together constitute the class culture of the factory.

Contrary to the ideologically conditioned theory shared by sociologists, psychologists, and policy analysts that "nonwork" produces, and is produced by, social disorganization and is symbolic of irresponsibility and personal dysfunctionality, recipients of guaranteed annual income who are relieved of most obligations to engage in labor do not fall apart. The incidence of alcoholism, divorce, and other social ills associated with conditions of dysfunctionality does not increase among men who are not working. Nor do they tend to experience higher rates of mortality than those of comparable age who are engaged in full-time work. Given the opportunity to engage in active nonwork, they choose this option virtually every time.[10]

For example, East Coast longshoremen who are not working but receive adequate income find many things to occupy their time. Many spend more time with their families, some engage in side businesses, and

332

others take up hobbies or fix up the house. They retain their industrial community and much of its culture. Most important, they are happier because they do not have to labor every day at a hard, often life-threatening job where the dangers associated with loading and unloading cargo are compounded by the need to handle materials that are frequently hazardous to their health. Because of the pleasures of nonwork—work in the specific sense used here, paid labor under a hierarchical management system—the men are not pleased to be called to put in a day's labor.

Most of all, they have regained "free" time. This freedom, perhaps more than the activities in which they become absorbed as an alternative to paid labor, fulfills the premier promise of technological displacement that in its earlier ideological expressions was heralded by the labor movement and intellectuals as the main historical benefit of industrialization. An alarming number of workers, both intellectual and manual, surrender nearly all of their waking and even dreaming time to labor. The by now ancient slogan of the movement for shorter hours—"eight hours work, eight hours sleep, and eight hours to do with what we will"— has been abandoned. The notion of free time is as distant from most people's everyday experience as open space. Labor has been dispersed into all corners of the social world, eating space and time, crowding out any remnants of civil society that remained after the advent of consumer society, and colonizing the life world. We are able neither to work nor to play; unlike the older industrial model where labor was experienced as an imposition from above, the dispersal of work makes the enemy invisible because labor is now experienced as a compulsion dictated by economic anxiety more than by the "need" to work.

Under current economic and social conditions, the major casualties of technological changes on the waterfront and, increasingly, in the auto, electronics, and communications industries, are the children and grandchildren who will never have the chance to work on the docks or in the factories and accumulate enough time to achieve dignified nonwork. The time of the new generations of never-to-be industrial workers is not free even though they are relieved of paid labor. Instead, it is suffused with anxiety that they may never again enter the cycle of labor and consumption that defined working lives in the Fordist era, or they displace the anxiety of nonwork without income in lives of petty crime (in which case they need not apply for public assistance). Whereas before containerization, as late as 1960, sons of longshoremen certainly would have followed their fathers onto the waterfront, in the postwork society, life for the children of dockers is in most respects harder than it was for their parents. Many among the next generation who have been unable to accumulate the requisite cultural capital to qualify for employment in one of the knowledge industries or have not had the luck to find a job in one of them are, lacking guaranteed income, reduced to undignified nonwork—or worse, are driven to seek low-wage, dead-end jobs because they are suited neither for unemployment nor for lives as drug dealers or petty thieves.

The remaining repositories of "work" within the wage-labor system are, despite the ruthless transformations of virtually all of its products and producers into commodities, the diminishing instances of petty craft production (occupations that are frequently suffused with the uncertainties connected with self-employment), art, and the products of the relatively small proportion of those who produce knowledge of all kinds, even those, like teachers and writers, who through transmission (or translation) re-produce knowledge. This work retains its objectivity, depending on neither a knowing subject nor the immediacy of the labor process.

It may be objected that this argument seems Eurocentric; it applies at best to the fate of work in so-called "advanced" industrial countries. As industrial production moves away from the United States and Europe, especially to Latin America and Asia, some have envisioned the rebirth of the industrial proletariat. And presumably, because of this shift, few of these issues such as joblessness and class decomposition apply. According to this view, the old slogans of labor solidarity have not disappeared; they have merely been deterritorialized. This thesis, however, ignores the fact that industrialization in formerly agricultural regions is occurring at an accelerating rate under the new scientific-technological regimes, which are by no means local. Computer-mediated labor processes are the standard against which global labor is measured, not merely labor in the traditionally industrialized countries. For example, some of the *maquiladoras* on the Mexico-US border are often

334

more technologically developed than older US plants that produce the same products. They make auto parts, computers, and other high-tech commodities as well as furniture and textiles, which, as we have seen, are increasingly produced with computer-mediated and laser technologies. Thus, whereas earlier capital migrations relied on low and intermediate technologies because the advantages of employing low-wage labor outweighed the costs of introducing advanced machine processes, we may now observe new forms of capital migration that tend to make the labor process—if not (yet) wages and working conditions—uniform.

Workers on the Mexican side of the border may earn at most about eighty dollars a week, but they are often paid much less. And even though Mexico has some protective factory and environmental legislation, it is observed more in the breach than by enforcement. Moreover, as workers organize in Mexican factories, employers have not hesitated to steal away in the night to other areas in the country where wages are even lower and workers are less prepared to form independent unions.[11]

The North American Free Trade Agreement (NAFTA) may be viewed as merely the conclusion of the first chapter in a long process of overcoming some aspects of the traditional unequal division of labor between north and south. In the next decade, US wages and living standards are likely to continue to deteriorate. If labor organization emerges in Mexico and other parts of Latin America, wages there will rise, but not by enough to deter migration of US plants, at least during the 1990s. In the near future, Texans and Californians will cross the border in greater numbers every day to work in Mexico and Mexican workers will continue to migrate to certain jobs in the United States, approximating the situation at the already blurred US-Canadian border. At the same time, as in Canada, Mexican industry is increasingly subject to US investment; this will set a pattern for transnational investment in other countries of Latin America, particularly Brazil, which, along with Mexico, had before the current economic crisis succeeded to some extent in developing its own industrial base.

Deterritorialized production applies also to knowledge. By the early 1990s, for example, China and India were offering US, Japanese, and European capital access to highly qualified scientific and technical labor.

US computer corporations began to let contracts to software corporations in India. Du Pont and other chemical corporations were building petrochemical complexes in Shanghai, employing Chinese engineers and chemists at eighty dollars a month. The fairly well developed Mexican bioengineering sector is actively negotiating with US corporations to "share" discoveries and technical achievements.

Even in science and technology, whose products are situated in their own historical and institutional contexts and as often as not are appropriated for socially dubious purposes, the product never entirely "disappears" into consumption but is incorporated into the common built environment. Yet although the work of some of those engaged in the production of arts and science retains excitement, challenge, and end products that possess genuine durability, few have the good fortune to be custom cabinetmakers, theoretical physicists, literary critics, social scientists, molecular biologists, or computer engineers.

Just as the scientific-technological revolution has utterly transformed the workplace in all categories of labor, we are obliged to examine its consequences for the conception of work that undergirds cultural identity, the self, and our collective understanding of the norms by which the moral order imposes a mode of conduct upon us. In his notebooks, Marx wrote in 1857–8:

The free development of individualities, and hence not the reduction of necessary labour time so as to posit surplus labor, but rather the general reduction of the necessary labor of society to a minimum, which then corresponds to the artistic, scientific etc. development of the individuals in the time set free, and with the means created, for all of them. Capital itself is the moving contradiction [in] that it presses to reduce labour time to a minimum, while it posits labor time, on the other side, as the sole measure and source of wealth.[12]

It may be argued that the history of capitalism during the last hundred years may be recounted in terms of this contradiction. This transformation in industrial production has stunningly fulfilled the tendencies that were prefigured in Marx's description: once based chiefly on the practical knowledge handed down to succeeding generations by craft traditions, production is now based on abstractions of organization and on science.

The promise of this movement, however, has been subsumed almost entirely under the sign of capital reproduction. Capital fears its own moving spirit. Vast quantities of labor are set free from the labor process, but rather than fostering full individual development, production and reproduction penetrate all corners of the life world, transforming it into a commodity world not merely as consumption but also in the most intimate processes of human interaction. Intellectual labor, its ideology of professional autonomy in tatters as a result of its subordination to technoscience and organization, becomes a form of human capital the components of which are specialized knowledge and differentially accumulated cultural capital determined mainly by hierarchically-arranged credentials. Most professionals, let alone "liberated" manual workers, enjoy little free time for artistic and scientific development, either of their individuality or indeed of the productive forces. To the contrary, we live in a time when not only are individuals thwarted, but the political economy of late capitalism appears—at least in one crucial area, research and development—to fetter the new productive force: knowledge.

On June 30, 1993, the *New York Times* reported that US companies are cutting funds for scientific and technological research:

> Scientific research by private industry, the traditional powerhouse of innovation and technological leadership in the United States, is suffering deeper financial woes than previously disclosed, suggesting that America is slipping in the international race for discoveries that form the basis of new goods and services. The National Science Foundation reported in February that industrial research on research and development had begun to shrink after decades of growth.[13]

Of course, much of the previous growth was military, and was therefore driven by and dependent on public funds. But with recession, the tapering off of the Cold War, and the enormous deficits accumulated by government and by corporations caught up in the swirl of the leveraged buyout mania of the 1980s, funds have dried up. For example, as we noted earlier, the National Institutes of Health, which formerly funded a third of the research proposals submitted to the agency, supported only ten per cent in 1991. More to the point, the priorities of the federal scientific and technical bureaucracies, which are increasingly tied to the requirements of corporations, have restricted the *kind* of research they are willing to support. Consequently, there is almost no hope that biomedical projects that fall outside the purview of molecular biology and biophysics will be funded. And, as we have seen, research scientists are feeling pressure to make arrangements with private corporations in order to obtain desperately needed research funds. In short, the commodification of basic science, combined with its increasingly technical character and declining funds, may in the future all but seal the fate of the United States as a major economic power.

For the plain truth is that overfunding and "useless" knowledge is the key to discovery. From the discoveries of Galileo to the "idle" ruminations of Frege, Gödel, Einstein, and Bohr, patronage, whether public or private, permitted unbounded dreaming that led to new ways of seeing and ultimately—but only ultimately—new modes of producing. When government and corporate policymakers insist on "dedicated" research as a condition of support, they announce that they have opted for failure rather than long-range innovation. This blatant act of research shooting itself in the foot is by no means intentional. Rather, it is the result of the logic of technoscience and the human capital paradigm according to which unsubordinated knowledge is perceived to threaten the social order either by draining economic resources or by proposing unpalatable jolts to the imagination. Moreover, it signals a profound failure of nerve, a refusal to take the risk that some knowledge can never be translated into technology and will remain outside the framework of accepted science and that some knowledge might even subvert cherished beliefs within the prevailing social order. For the social sciences and the humanities, cost reductions exacted a steep toll on research, but during the Reagan-Bush era many projects were rejected by conservative leaders of the National Endowment for the Arts and the National Endowment for the Humanities on political grounds, a manifestation of the conservative ideological attack on postmodern cultural expression.

The crisis in research of course has serious consequences for the US national economy, but it augurs equally badly for hope that intellectual work will be possible for more than a tiny fraction of scientists and artists in the future. Its effects are even more far-reaching. For, in a higher education system already incurring severe criticism for the low number of US-born scientific and technical majors and graduates at the undergraduate and graduate levels, the decline in basic research constitutes a disincentive for young people to enter the sciences. At leading universities, many if not most advanced-level physics, mathematics, and chemistry students are foreign born.

The irony of this situation is that the completion of the process by which science is almost entirely subsumed under capital and which, concomitantly, transformed intellectual work into human capital, is by no means in the system's interest. For just as the emergence of knowledge as a productive force "solves" the problem of productivity while at the same time intensifying the problem of how capital valorizes itself, so the subordination of knowledge to the imperative of technical innovation undermines one of the central presuppositions of innovation: *unfettered* free time for knowledge producers.

In recent years this contradiction has been at play in universities, even in first-tier institutions, which place increasing administrative burdens on faculty; the second and third tiers impose, in addition, heavier teaching loads. Under the impact of economic constraints we have entered a new era of academic cost cutting and of surveillance whose intended as well as unintended effects are to discourage independent intellectual work. For a society that trumpets the growth imperative as the key to its survival, and for which knowledge is the acknowledged economic spur, such measures are, of course, self-defeating.

Clearly, the promise that the scientific and technological revolution will usher in an epoch in which the full development of the individual is finally fulfilled is thwarted as long as Bentham's Panopticon dominates the political unconscious of established authorities. The current tendency is to "resolve" the contradictions prompted by the emergence of knowledge as both the salvation of capitalism and its nemesis by transforming the intellect, as it did craft, into human capital.

339

Toward a New Labor Policy

Ours is a time when questions are much more easily posed than answered, when the fragmentation of economic and political perception among both experts and what may be termed the "public" prevents solutions that have a chance to garner wide support. Further, the question What is to be done? has become tainted because it points to calumnies committed in the name of traditional ideologies of emancipation. Indeed, to speak of liberation, of the emancipation of labor, appears utopian, in the bad sense; in a period of the transformation of global politics by the breakup of the Soviet Union, the intellectual discrediting of Marxism, even by some of its erstwhile practitioners, and, on a larger canvas the steep decline of socialism recalling these words conjures images of betrayal.

Nevertheless, without bold alternatives, we condemn ourselves to the present state of affairs. This is the fundamental conundrum of the Frankfurt School, of some French philosophers and social theorists, and of others who have, with some reason, concluded that ours is the epoch of the death of the subject. If this means the subject as God's surrogate, solitary consciousness, or human dominion over nature, we have little to quarrel about. What is often meant by this phrase, however, is the possibility of agency, of opposition, or even of resistance. To posit the end of this kind of agency is a kind of reconciliation with the established order.

This book situates itself in the discourses of human emancipation, freedom, and hope because we align ourselves with the agents of opposition and alternative: the "new" social movements—feminism, ecology, sexual self-determination—and elements of the "old" social movements, particularly in black, Latino, and Asian freedom movements and the labor movement. Needless to say, in arguing for a perspective on the future of work that takes into account the scientific-technological revolution of our time, we make no claim to be doing more than suggesting some pathways. As intellectuals we speak to, not for, other intellectuals and those in the social movements who might find our viewpoint useful.

Our proposals are based on the presuppositions of this study: that economic growth grounded in technological innovation does not necessarily increase employment unless there is a sharp reduction in working hours, and even then may not be sufficient to sustain a level approaching full employment; and that since a considerable number of recently created jobs are part-time, poorly paid dead ends, there is a powerful argument that we have reached the moment when less work is entirely justified. In addition, our proposals assume the goal of assuring the *possibility* of the full development of individual and social capacities.

These statements further imply that—if our assertions that the world economy will not sustain full employment in the coming decades and the social safety net will remain full of holes are correct—we need to reconsider the pace of technological change and the effects of corporate reorganizations that have shed tens of thousands of employees in the past several years. Until measures such as a substantial reduction of working hours, a guaranteed income plan, a genuine national health scheme, and the revitalization of the progressive tax system have been introduced into law and union contracts, job-destroying technologies and mergers and acquisitions should be rigorously *evaluated* in terms of their implications for the well-being of communities and workers. In an era of uncontrolled growth amid economic stagnation, corporate efforts to make workers and communities pay the costs of falling profits are exacting heavy tolls and should be stopped.

We have used the general concept "evaluation" to connote the urgent need for social controls, perhaps in the form of re-regulation of business, over untrammeled labor-saving technological change and mergers that result in permanent reductions of labor forces. Needless to say, this proposal directly opposes the dominant strategy of US, European, and Japanese corporations and would assume a political situation in which national states were independent of these corporate interests. Unfortunately, for the most part this is the case among neither conservative nor social-democratic and social-liberal regimes. Free enterprise and free market ideology enjoy global hegemony in the current political and economic environment. Thus, even the suggestion that technological change and mergers may not be in the public interest flies in the face of the prevailing common sense.

Needless to say, we do not support technophobic perspectives on technological transformation. As our critique of Arendt and the earlier discussion of work and skill show, we do not mourn the passing of craft. Given guaranteed income, shorter hours, and work sharing, we welcome the coming of a postwork society and have tried to refute the sociological and psychological "wisdom" that labor is an intrinsic need beyond survival. In fact, we have claimed that, as a mode of life, its historicity has been demonstrated by the nature and the spread of cybernetic technologies.

We wish to point out, however, that deregulation has been most consistently applied to corporate prerogatives: to reduce labor in production; to relocate, at will, factories and professional services; to eliminate workers through consolidation; to put labor in competition with itself by breaking and otherwise reducing the traditional protections provided by union contracts for decent wages and against working conditions that threaten health and safety; and to weaken employer- or government-financed health and pension benefits.

When it comes to regulating the poor, there is no absence of programs: workfare; more prisons for convicted drug dealers and users; armed guards in urban high schools. The largest corporations have never insisted upon competition for government contracts, nor have they hesitated to support tariff and trade restrictions when their particular interests are at stake. Nor have conservatives failed to temper their opposition to open borders to Latin American, Caribbean, and Asian immigrants, demanding draconian measures to regulate their flow.

Recall the words of economic historian Karl Polanyi: "It should need no elaboration that a process of undirected change, the pace of which is deemed too fast, should be slowed down, if possible, so as to safeguard the welfare of the community. Such household truths of traditional statesmanship...were in the nineteenth century erased from the thoughts of the educated by the corrosive of a crude utilitarianism combined with an uncritical reliance on the alleged self-healing virtues of unconscious growth."[14]

Finally, social ecology, which has emerged as a major paradigm of social and economic theory as much as it is a significant social movement, has taught us that untrammeled growth is by no means an unmixed blessing. At the most fundamental level, ecological thought is a powerful counterweight to the Western idea of progress. We have learned that technologically driven growth has had disastrous consequences that can no longer be ignored. Hazardous waste, industrial pollution and its consequent global warming, life-threatening power sources (alternating-current electricity, nuclear energy), and increased radiation resulting from high-powered computer technologies are some of the most visible results of the rapid expansion of industrial and consumer societies.

To be sure, a theoretical model according to which human survival depends on maintaining a sustainable biosphere and stable ecosystems suggests that there may be enormous costs to uncontrolled economic growth, but no consensus has emerged, even among the most insistent critics of uncontrolled growth, concerning possible solutions. At one end of the spectrum are those who warn that unless growth is arrested, even reversed, the ecosystems that sustain life are in imminent jeopardy. This view proceeds from the indisputable fact that "development," one of the cherished names for capital accumulation and urbanization, has exacerbated what are called "natural" disasters—soil erosion, floods, global warming, the cancer epidemic that afflicts nearly a third of all people in industrial societies (by the year 2000, the figure may rise to forty per cent). Cancer, which many biologists argue is directly linked to living and working conditions, is rapidly becoming the major disease of industrial societies. Beyond industrial and commercial pollution, it is linked to the spreading contamination of food and water. This position argues for elimination of entire sectors of industry—especially nuclear energy, many branches of chemical production, the use of most fossil fuels—and conversion of the highly centralized electric power industry to locally based water, wind, and solar energy. Decentralizing power production suggests bioregional economies in which communities produce and distribute their own basic foods and many other everyday products. In this economic arrangement, the scale of production is reduced. This regime would not entirely eliminate the division of labor and commodity exchanges, but would limit these activities in order to minimize disturbances to the ecosystem.

At the other end are the proponents of environmental protection through state and voluntary regulation by industrial corporations and developers. This group includes many social liberal governments and their professional retainers, who insist that the political and economic

343

climate is permanently unfavorable to draconian ecological regulations. Growth can be selectively moderated by conservation measures such as creating national parks and wilderness areas, limiting the use of fossil fuels, encouraging industrial and consumer recycling, and requiring business to clean up after itself. In the United States, a federal law imposes heavier taxes on polluters but relies on market mechanisms for remedial action. Large employers, most public policy professionals, and some trade unionists are largely hostile to proposals to restrict automobile travel and expand mass transit; to declare a moratorium on many types of industrial and residential development, especially in rain forests and rural areas; and to restructure industrial production to eliminate or sharply curtail carcinogenic processes and products. Faced with declining profits, corporate capital resists innovations that add to the cost of doing business. Lacking an alternative to jobs, many trade unions and their members have opposed ecological protections. For example, most union labor sided with timber companies in Oregon against environmentalists' demands for substantial restrictions on timber production and in the fights over nuclear power during the 1970s and '80s almost invariably ignored warnings by ecologists and public interest groups that reactors endangered the safety and health of workers and of neighboring communities. Nor have some unions been willing to insist on strict health protections lest plants be shut down and jobs lost. There are exceptions, notably the Oil, Chemical and Atomic Workers, which played a crucial role in the passage of the Occupational Safety and Health Act in 1971.

In light of the mounting evidence of ecological crisis, the idea that economic policy can no longer fail to incorporate fairly sweeping ecological perspectives seems to us to be incontrovertible. However, if this argument is accepted, we can no longer rely on growth to address problems such as technologically induced unemployment and to improve living standards. Yet, in a remarkable example of failure of political imagination and will, uncontrolled growth remains the basis of world and national efforts to resolve long-term economic woes in nearly every major country. The ideological hegemony of growth economics, combined with the powerful threat of globalization, has virtually eliminated from public debate the characteristic industrial-era imperatives of social justice and equality. Since the social justice left and the labor movement have largely dropped their traditional demands for redistributive justice in favor of growth, the political environment seems more unfavorable than at any time in recent memory for addressing ecological issues. In addition, what might be called the spread of *virulent nationalism* in nearly all industrialized countries as well as in Eastern Europe militates against international efforts to deal with ecological disaster. The breakup of communism, which from a democratic perspective may prove to be an important milestone in human history, has done nothing to improve the chance to revitalize the world's ecosystems. On the contrary, having embraced the doctrine of the free market, many governments and political forces in Eastern Europe seem resigned to accepting the trade-off of economic vitality for ecological disaster, an approach that was consistent with the policies of the former communist regimes.

Given ecological and economic crisis and world economic and political restructuring, there is an urgent need for thinking that refuses to remain mired in the impossibilities of the present. For to insist in advance that possibilities are limited to the givens of the social and political world leads to the conclusion that no genuine transformation is possible, which in turn gives rise to the dark conservatism that holds that change is not desirable, and even is evil. Since it can be easily demonstrated that international "competition" is only one and perhaps a minor feature of the current economic situation but that we have entered an unprecedented period of central power over most economic decisions on a global scale, we have no compunctions in offering a practical and necessary discussion of how and why the new era of postwork may be addressed.

The Need to Reduce Working Hours

There has been no significant reduction in working hours since the implementation of the eight-hour day through collective bargaining and the 1938 enactment of the federal wage and hour law. Since then, we have witnessed a slow increase of working time despite the most profoundly labor-displacing era of technological change since the industrial revolution. People are laboring their lives away, which, perhaps as much as unemployment and poverty, has resulted in many serious family and health problems. In turn, the lengthening of working hours has contributed to unemployment and poverty among those excluded from the labor system.

Therefore, there is an urgent need for a sharp reduction in the workweek from its current forty hours—a reduction of, *initially*, at least ten hours. The thirty-hour week at *no reduction in pay* would create new jobs only if overtime was eliminated for most categories of labor. And, although some people may prefer flexible working arrangements that are more compatible with child-rearing needs or personal preference, the basic workday should, to begin with, be reduced to six hours, both as a health and safety measure and in order to provide more freedom from labor in everyday life. Finally, we envision a progressive reduction of working hours as technological transformation and the elimination of what might be termed makework in both private and public employment reduces the amount of labor necessary for the production of goods and services. That is, productivity gains would not necessarily, as in the past, be shared between employers and employees in the form of increased income, but would result first in fewer laboring hours.

Obviously, restricting laboring hours raises some important questions: How do families maintain their living standards if income is substantially reduced by restricting overtime and other work-sharing arrangements? Will people use free time to develop their capacities or will time be absorbed destructively? Who will pay for work-sharing? Is it feasible in a global economy where capital moves freely in search of cheap labor? We will address the last question first because, although it is politically agonizing, it poses fewer conceptual problems.

The experience of the German labor movement is instructive in this regard. In 1985, the Metalworkers Union (IG Metall), which represents auto, steel, and metal fabricating workers, struck for reduced hours. After a relatively short walkout involving millions of workers in the most technologically advanced sectors of the economy, employers yielded to the demand for a thirty-five-hour workweek, to be implemented in stages over five years. Gradually, other sectors have adopted the shorter workweek, but there is no federal law because the labor-supported Social Democrats are out of power. The competitive position of German industries is not suffering because of this innovation, in part because of the tremendous productivity of German workers made possible by cutting-edge technologies that have been widely introduced in production. Moreover, in countries such as Germany where the social wage includes substantial government-administered health benefits and guaranteed income and pensions, labor costs to employers may be lower than in the United States, which does not have these state-sponsored provisions, even when wages are higher. In the United States, employers have shouldered much of the burden of the welfare state, spending as much as forty per cent of wages on fringe benefits.

While notions of solidarity have suffered in Europe in the past several decades, particularly in the wake of a major influx of immigrants from the Middle East and Africa, Italian and German labor movements nevertheless retain considerable ideological loyalty to concepts such as class unity. The victory of the German metalworkers—and a parallel struggle by public employees—attests to the power of discursive and ideological influences in determining the shape of the politics of work. Although the German economy has suffered during the recession of the past decade and there is considerable xenophobia throughout German society against immigrants during a period of high joblessness, the discourse of social justice has not disappeared because the labor movement insists that employers share the pain of economic woes. Moreover, the unions have insisted that the promise of pay equity between East and West Germany be fulfilled.

This is not the case in the United States, where public discourse is dominated by demands that business be protected at all costs. The privatization of welfare and antediluvian social policies, especially the lack of national healthcare and a strong pension system, places onerous burdens on enterprise labor costs to provide these social wages. Of course, to require industries to be "competitive" presumably entails a sharp curtailment of these company-paid benefits. But if workers agree that they have a "responsibility" to help their own companies, current conditions demand that they accept wage and benefit reductions and suspension of hard-won work rules that protect their health and their jobs. Clearly, US workers and their unions gave back many of their previously won gains in the 1980s, but these concessions failed to reverse capital flight. Although movements of capital, especially from north to south, are often meant to reduce labor costs, there are other factors that motivate such shifts. One of them is historical. After World War II, strong US unions were able to increase wages and benefits in the private sector even as social wages remained static. But technological innovations developed within this country were on the whole translated into reinvestment in a wide range of intermediate (that is, mechanical), technology industries such as steel, machine tools, and metal fabrication. As a result, US industries remained stuck in earlier technological regimes while other countries, through computerization, were transforming their labor processes. In the United States, advanced technologies were introduced mainly in military-related industries.

Regulating Capital

In some countries, capital may not freely export jobs without consultation with unions and the government. Clearly, reducing working hours without simultaneously addressing the issue of capital flight is unthinkable. In 1988 the US Congress passed modest plant-closing legislation requiring employers only to notify employees and the community of their plans to close a facility. This law could be strengthened to compel collective bargaining with unions and local governments over the conditions of capital flight, including the extent of compensation and effects on the community. To discourage plant closings, employers could be required to pay substantial compensation to displaced workers and to communities, and they could be required to offer transfer rights to their employees. Unions have sought to protect jobs by persuading Congress to pass the so-called domestic content bill according to which a percentage of the components of commodities (autos and garments, for example) sold in the United States would have to be produced by US workers. This provision has been incorporated into the North American Free Trade Agreement (NAFTA) for some items; it could be extended to become a basis of plant-closing legislation.

The most important issue raised by our proposals is international coordination of labor demands. It is evident that the purely national framework within which labor movements operate is for many purposes archaic. But although there are some instances of genuine coordination of strikes, bargaining, and even legislation, labor movements are often at loggerheads over their own position in the international division of labor. In the face of global competition, it is nothing short of suicidal for labor to remain in competition with itself. Unless these issues are addressed, discussions of the need for shorter hours can never advance beyond the proposal stage.

The question of living standards strikes at the heart of the cultural dimension of this issue. For millions of Americans, working almost all the time is the only way they can maintain their homes and provide for the care and education of their children. Here we offer three suggestions. First, single-family, privately owned homes should not be the most important source of new housing. Publicly financed, affordable, multiple-dwelling rental housing would lift an enormous burden from the shoulders of working people. The value of their homes—whether they were cooperatively owned or rented—would no longer depend on market fluctuations that have in recent years severely reduced equity in millions of homes and, perhaps more egregiously, spurred lender-provoked evictions. Second, we need free, publicly provided child care services like those in many European countries. Since mortgage payments or rent plus child care absorb as much as fifty per cent of the income of many households, they bear on laboring practices. Third, the United States could adopt the European system of treating postsecondary education as a public resource therefore a public expense.

At the same time, we would propose that higher education be a right rather than a privilege reserved for a minority of the population, as it is in most of Europe and the countries of the Americas. Here we can observe considerable differences between the United States, Western Europe, and developing countries. In most of the world, all education is paid for by the state, but access to education is severely regulated. In Europe, a relatively small percentage of students enter postsecondary programs, including technical institutes. In most of the less developed regions of the world, most people are denied a decent elementary and secondary education, much less opportunities for university degrees.

Since the 1960s, US colleges and universities have been more accessible to students than they used to be. Some fifty per cent of high school students enter some kind of postsecondary education program; about half of them go to community colleges and technical schools. Dropout rates, however, are enormous, and sometimes as high as seventy per cent. Plainly, if the revolution in scientific and technical knowledge has occurred, fairly high levels of educational achievement are now a necessity for larger numbers of young people. Just as secondary education became a right at the beginning of the twentieth century, so higher education must become a right at the turn of the twenty-first.

Paradoxically, just at the historical juncture when knowledge work becomes more important, US colleges and universities have entered into a period of downsizing due to budget constraints. Public universities have been especially affected by massive cutbacks. In 1992 and '93 the University of California suffered a budget cut of nearly ten per cent; plans to build new campuses were shelved; graduate admissions were restricted; and professors were obliged to accept a five per cent salary reduction. New York's City University, the country's largest urban university whose student body is mostly black and Latino, sustained four consecutive years of cutbacks totaling twenty per cent. The huge California State University system was similarly beleaguered by reductions, and parallel developments occurred in New Jersey and Massachusetts, among many other states. In the midst of these cuts, enrollments were still rising, placing a huge burden on an already depleted faculty. William Honan, writing in the *New York Times*, cited Robert Zemsky of the University of Pennsylvania's Institute for Research in Higher Education, who argues that if faculty members do not adjust to the new "realities" by accepting the new austerity, changes will be imposed from without: "The 'without' are the brute economic realities for private institutions and further cutbacks by city, state and federal legislatures for the public institutions."[15]

Zemsky, echoing the views of university administrators, cannot envision an alternative to the reality of austerity, a regime that has already forced administrators to consider measures such as eliminating programs and departments, laying off faculty, and eliminating a wide range of services such as private telephones, faculty access to duplicating facilities, and paid sabbaticals. Many universities have encouraged senior faculty to take early retirement, but have not offered to replace them on anything near a one-to one basis, even with assistant professors.

All over the United States, faculty have said no to cutbacks, but have failed to propose alternative schemes to preserve democratic access to higher education. Rather, they have been cast, in Honan's article and elsewhere, as staunch defenders of the status quo. To be sure, some faculty unions have lobbied legislatures against budget reductions, and faculty senates have refused to accept the elimination of departments, especially in the traditional disciplines. But the trend toward restoring the concept of higher education as a *privilege* rather than a *right* is pervasive.

At a basic level, our proposals involve much more than an effective legislative struggle. They also require a significant effort to pose alternatives to the values that have propelled American cultural ideals since the end of World War I. The persistence of the old values, many of them crucially tied to the period of American economic expansion and world dominance, has constituted one of the most significant tools in the arsenal of insurgent conservatism. The conservatives have been able to mobilize working-class and professional constituencies with a populism that is based on resisting the implications of change.

We do not want to be interpreted as falling in line with the belt-tightening, anti-pleasure ideologies of the communitarians. To the contrary, we are arguing that the only chance to maintain and advance our living standards is by means of a bold, intelligent reassertion of the values of more equality and more high-quality public services as the basis of social policy. The fifteen-year bipartisan experiment in deregulation has failed, miserably, to reach any of its major goals, except that of lining the pockets of a small cabal of business interests. In the wake of deregulation many small businesses have failed, workers have lost their jobs, and services have deteriorated. Moreover, the private sector has failed to provide moderate-cost housing, day care, and education while the public sector has been ruthlessly gutted in an orgy of cost-cutting measures.

There Is Still Work to Do
Despite labor-saving technologies, there is still much work to do. Our roads, bridges, water systems, schools, and cities need rebuilding and

repair. We need a mass-transit system to counteract traffic jams and the deleterious effects of auto and truck emissions. With a growing population, we require more garbage collection, cleaner streets, and refurbished parks, forests, and other public spaces. And, as always, there is an urgent need to reclaim "wilderness" areas that have been subjected to industrial and real-estate development. Surely we require a new, balanced development policy, since the long-awaited era of the post-paper, steel, and fossil fuels society seems still far in the future. We could spend vastly more funds to research, develop, and produce solar, windmill, and water power.

This work is frequently labor-intensive and physically hard, but, because it improves the quality of life, it is worth doing. And because much of it is onerous but necessary, pay should be higher than for many other occupations. Workers should be paid on a principle of what might be called *reverse renumeration*, that is, paying more for jobs that are more unpleasant but enhance "public goods": manual, routine, or dirty tasks such as cleaning the streets and parks and collecting garbage; heavy work and routine mass production tasks; caring for children, older people, and the sick. If we are serious about the arrival of the so-called post-Cold War era, paying for these services should pose few additional burdens on ordinary incomes because the military budget still hovers around $300 billion. Even a fifty per cent reduction in the military budget and transfer of funds would result in a net increase in jobs, since much current military spending is extremely capital intensive. At the same time, a long-range commitment to expanding public services such as mass transit is expensive.

We should replace the current tax system, which favors the rich, and reintroduce the progressive tax, dropping the fiction that tax incentives are a major impetus to new investment within the US economy. As the experience of the 1980s—when the Reagan administration presided over not only a tax giveaway but also one of the sharpest redistributive tax measures in history—amply demonstrates, putting more money in the pockets of the rich does not guarantee new investment within the borders of the United States or, indeed, better-paying jobs.

If we were committed to abolishing the hierarchical division of intellectual and manual labor, such tasks could be shared through a program of universal public service. A new commitment to universal public education to prepare the multivalenced worker would replace the current focus on specialization. Many if not all tasks in what is conventionally regarded as "mental" work could be shared among a wider portion of the labor force. In this regime of task equalization, every person would be obliged to perform some of the least desirable tasks, regardless of accumulated credentials; these jobs would not be permanently assigned to any class of people.

This is a long-term perspective, but in the wake of the objective possibilities inherent in new technologies for eliminating vast quantities of manual and clerical labor in both "advanced" and developing areas of the world, the question before us is whether the polity is prepared to tolerate *permanent mass unwork* or whether share-work values and programs will begin to bridge the gulf between knowledge-based labor and manual and clerical work.

A Guaranteed Income

Accordingly, if unwork is fated to be no longer the exception to the rule of nearly full employment, we need an entirely new approach to the social wage and, more generally, "welfare" policy. If there is work to be done, everyone should do some of it; additional remuneration would depend on the kind of work an individual performs. But shorter work days, longer vacations, and earlier retirement imply that most of us should never work anything like "full time" as measured by the standards of the industrial-izing era. We need a political and social commitment to a national guaranteed income that is equal to the historical level of material culture. That is, everyone would be guaranteed a standard of living that meets basic nutritional, housing, and recreational requirements. Everyone would assume the responsibilities of producing and maintaining public goods, so no able citizen would be freed of the obligation to work. This would place a large burden on the private production sectors to induce people to engage in routine labor, presumably at wage rates higher than the guaranteed income and equal to tasks in the public sector. These rates would constitute a further incentive to invest in labor-saving technologies, which would free people from routine tasks without plunging them into a state of penury.

There would be no welfare system because the distinction between workers and "idlers" would disappear. Services such as healthcare (including counseling and therapy), education, and social work would expand and be paid for through general tax levies, but, assuming a new perspective on "jobs" and the division of labor, would shift their emphasis from work toward solving problems, exploring possibilities, and finding new ethical and social meaning.

School curricula, for example, could concentrate on broadening students' cultural purview: music, athletics, art, and science would assume a more central place in the curriculum and there would be a renewed emphasis on the aesthetic as well as the vocational aspects of traditional crafts. We suppose this would lead to a revival of what has become known as "leisure studies": psychologists and sociologists would study, prescriptively as well as analytically, what people do with their time, no longer described in precisely the same terms as it was thirty years ago. Concomitantly, space and time themselves become objects both of knowledge and, in the more conventional science fiction sense, of personal and social exploration. Consequently, lifelong learning, travel, avocations, small business, and artisanship take on new significance as they become possible for all people, not just the middle and upper classes. Some may choose to participate in the technoculture as a crucial component of the exercise of the right to *pleasure* as well as work. Others may avoid the technological construction of social and personal meaning.

Only when social policy has been transformed can the conditions that have produced the ecological crisis—consumerism, for example—be redirected. In a society in which the preferred route to pleasure is buying commodities, to propose a new asceticism in the name of ethical renewal, as Lasch and others have done, merely perpetuates the repressive cultural regime of our era. Concomitantly, those who will not address issues of social justice and economic equality should keep silent about ecological disaster, for to expect that the vast majority of people will sacrifice their living standards to preserve the spotted owl without provision for the means of life is either naive or blatantly class biased.

Clearly, there is an urgent need for a new ethic that addresses the proliferation of waste in our communities. No observer of urban politics can fail to notice the struggles in black, Asian, and Latino communities against government plans to build incinerators to deal with the mountains of garbage that have accumulated in overcrowded cities and suburbs. Yet it is not enough to resist the most polluting methods of garbage disposal, nor will alternatives that do not ask the hard questions about how we have constructed our lives around consumption be adequate.

A New Research Agenda

In the immediate as well as the medium-range future, we need a renewed public commitment to scientific and technological research. Research would not be confined to developing new products or motivated exclusively by considerations such as enhancing the national economy in an era of global competition. Fighting disease, protecting the environment, and finding new ways to construe time and space in both "wilderness" and urban settings would absorb considerable resources.

Expert opinion, echoing similar conclusions after World War II, reached a virtual consensus that the Reagan and Bush administrations lacked science, energy, and technology policies beyond those required by the military. In fact, the Bush administration had an active science policy: using the pared-down federal research budget to encourage collaboration between government agencies, universities, and private corporations in the pursuit of growth-directed research. Federal courts, for example, ruled that private corporations could "own" patents on new life forms; the federal government reduced its direct participation in scientific research and instead encouraged collaborative arrangements between universities and biotechnology companies. As we have noted, funding for basic research was reduced by almost two-thirds, even as European countries were increasing their public funds for these purposes. Production and exploration of domestic oil, gas, solar power, synthetic fuels, and wind power were actively discouraged in favor of increasing oil imports. Research on alternative fuel sources was reduced to the vanishing point as the United States became increasingly dependent on imported fossil fuels.

Clearly, ecological considerations impel seeking alternatives to reliance on oil as our primary energy resource and on plastics as the major packaging material and as a substitute for natural fibers, among other nefarious uses. We should reexamine the almost universal use of alternating current for electricity in the wake of strong suspicion that large, centralized generators may contribute to cancer. Direct current and solar and wind energy might not be as dangerous. In any case, this is a vital part of the research agenda. In addition, a concerted effort to curtail and in some instances ban automobile use, especially in cities, is long overdue. Mass transit and new patterns of settlement in multifamily dwellings would create jobs and at the same time address ecological concerns.

It is by now evident that among the costs of a relentless pursuit of industrialization was pollution of our water and air. Congress has established a national cleanup fund and imposed some regulation on industrial polluters, but so far has not been willing to reexamine the historical costs of industrial enterprise. More than forty years ago, R. William Kapp took the first steps when he argued that we have failed to calculate the "social costs of private enterprise":[16] when a coal mine or a metal plant is abandoned, even if the employer is required to "clean up" the surrounding area, people from miles around have already suffered the deleterious effects of air and water pollution. To be sure, public agencies have made our drinking water safer; the Clean Air Act imposed regulations on employers but provided extremely small inspection and enforcement teams.

Even if they were vigorously enforced, these measures are all after the fact. They take for granted the historical regime of industrial production that requires huge quantities of fossil fuels, employs large-scale power plants and disposes of waste in large dumps that pollute the water bed. We erect regimes of treatment to counter the cancer- and heart disease-causing effects of industrialization and spend billions of dollars to construct hospitals and other medical facilities; we produce pharmaceuticals as our primary life-preserving weapon against the identification of industrialization with civilization itself. We take for granted that capital provides jobs, and the job culture becomes the new religion of advanced industrial societies.

We do not yet fully possess the knowledge required to fundamentally and radically shift the basis of our production regimes: wind, solar, and hydro energy are still in their infancy; we have only scant experience with radically decentralized small-scale production methods, except in agriculture;

and alternatives to the life-threatening (as well as life-enhancing) effects of medical treatment require more work (some alternative methods, based on traditional cultures and organicist worldviews, have proven effective against certain diseases, while others remain hypothetical).

There is little doubt that the two main killers—cancer and heart disease—and another key cause of premature death—automobile accidents —can be reduced only if we decide to reverse the blind, compulsive march of industrial culture. In the interest of averting the health crisis as well as the ecological crisis—not for saving labor costs—we need to deploy cybernetic and other labor-saving technologies in conjunction with the development of small-scale, ecologically sound production regimes. Undoubtedly we will find that some of these technologies, especially those that use large quantities of energy, are ecologically problematic; others will certainly prove to be ecologically beneficial.

One of the major issues in our emerging ecological crisis is how to reduce the amount of nonbiodegradable synthetic materials that have replaced cotton, wool, and wood products in packaging, furniture, clothing, cars, houses, and appliances. Despite claims that many plastics are biodegradable, some have argued that they seep into and pollute the water supply. Obviously, for "convenience" and cost savings, we have agreed to the trade-off, just as Americans have become addicted to their cars and single family homes.

Clearly, the inevitability of both the jobless future and the ecological crisis demands a conclusive cultural shift, for we cannot simply legislate a change of this scope. But this shift cannot be achieved without a national and international effort to reduce the degree to which people would be required to give up some components of the "good life" associated with consumer goods. For just as we do not advocate nonwork without adequate income, we see the need to mobilize the scientific and technological revolution to meet ecological and health needs. In the last instance, this becomes the basic goal of science and technology policy.

Ending Endless Work

Since the democratic revolutions of the eighteenth and nineteenth centuries, images of the Athenian city-state have suffused the work of

357

political philosophers. Hannah Arendt's polemic against Marx, for example, is directed not chiefly to the glorification of work over labor (although this remains a significant aspect of her picture of an ideal civilization), but to the notion of the primacy of politics. For Arendt as well as other political theorists, among the more egregious consequences of the Enlightenment was the displacement of politics by social relations and, indirectly, our relations with nature. Accordingly, Marx's critique of the relation of power to domination erased the very idea of the polity since it could be shown that "citizenship" was an ideology that masked what should have been evident: that the individual as the subject of politics had not yet emerged—indeed, could not emerge until the relations of production were decisively transformed. For the people as a self-governing body presupposed, as in ancient Athens, rough economic equality, at least for a fraction of the nonslave population.

Like many who have come before us, we believe that among the crucial tools of domination is the practice of "work without end," which chains workers to machines and especially to the authority of those who own and control them—capital and its managerial retainers. To be sure, labor did not enter these relations of domination without thereby gaining some benefit. In the Fordist era, as Hunnicutt has brilliantly shown, organized labor exchanged work for consumption and abandoned its historical claim of the right to be lazy, as Paul Lafargue put it.[17] Here, within limits, we affirm that right but confess another: the freedom of people emancipated from labor to become social agents.

Needless to say, we reject the idea that liberal democratic states have already conferred citizenship and that apathy is the crucial barrier preventing many from participating in decision making. Such optimism, unfortunately promulgated by many intellectuals of the left as well as the right, blithely ignores the social conditions that produce "apathy," especially the structural determinants of disempowerment, among them endless work. Nor are we prepared to designate the economic sphere, including the shop floor "rational-purposive" activity that on the whole has been effectively depoliticized and functions only in terms of the perimeters of instrumental, technical rationality.[18] Management's control over the workplace is an activity of politics. There are winners and losers in the labor process. To render the workplace rational entails a transformation of what we mean by rationality in production, including our conception of skill and its implied "other," unskill; a transformation of what we mean by mental as opposed to physical labor and our judgment of who has the capacity to make decisions under regimes of advanced technologies.

Politics as rational discourse—as opposed to a naked struggle for power—awaits social and economic emancipation. Among the constitutive elements of freedom is *self-managed time*. Our argument is that there are, for the first time in human history, the material preconditions for the emergence of the individual and, potentially, for a popular politics. The core material precondition is that labor need no longer occupy a central place in our collective lives, nor in our imagination. We do not advocate the emancipation from labor as a purely negative freedom. Its positive content is that, unlike the regime of work without end, it stages the objective possibility of citizenship.

Under these circumstances, we envision civil society as the privileged site for the development of individuals who really are free to participate in a public sphere of their own making. In such a civil society, politics consists not so much in the ritual act of selection, through voting, of one elite over another, but in popular assemblies that could, given sufficient space and time, be both the legislative and the administrative organs. The scope of popular governance would extend from the workplace to the neighborhood. For as Ernest Mandel has argued, there is no possibility of worker self-management, much less the self-management of society, without ample time for decision making.[19] Thus, in order to realize a program of democratization, we must create a new civil society in which freedom consists in the first place (but only in the first place) in the liberation of time from the external constraints imposed by nature and other persons on the individual.

The development of the individual—not economic growth, cost cutting, or profits—must be the fundamental goal of scientific and technological innovation. The crucial obstacle to the achievement of this democratic objective is the persistence of the dogma of work, which increasingly appears, in its religious-ethical and instrumental-rational modalities, as an obvious instrument of domination.

NOTES

1. David Lodge, *Nice Work* (New York: Macmillan, 1986), 85–6.

2. Hannah Arendt, *Human Condition* (Chicago: University of Chicago Press, 1958).

3. Ibid. 137.

4. Ibid. 146.

5. Ibid. 152.

6. There is a long polemic in the *Grundrisse* against Fourier's utopian program to transform work into play. Apparently these passages escaped Arendt's notice.

7. Arendt, *Human Condition*, 207–19, 325.

8. Jürgen Habermas, *Theory of Communicative Action*, vol. i (Boston: Beacon, 1984).

9. Jürgen Habermas, *Moral Consciousness and Communicative Action* (Cambridge: MIT Press, 1991).

10. William DiFazio, *Longshoremen* (South Hadley, Mass.: Bergin and Garvey, 1985).

11. *Solidarity*, a publication of the United Auto Workers (AFL-CIO), May 1993.

12. Karl Marx, *Grundrisse* (New York: Vintage, 1973), 706.

13. "Companies Cutting Funds for Scientific Research," *New York Times*, 30 June 1993.

14. Karl Polanyi, *The Great Transformation* (Boston: Beacon, 1957), 33.

15. William Honan, "New Pressures on the University," *New York Times Education Life*, 8 January 1993, 18.

16. R. William Kapp, *The Social Costs of Private Enterprise* (New York: Schocken, 1951).

17. Paul Lafargue, *The Right to Be Lazy* (Chicago: Charles Kerr, 1907).

18. This is a major argument of Jürgen Habermas's theory of communicative action. See especially Habermas's "Toward a Reconstruction of Historical Materialism," in *Communication and the Evolution of Society* (Boston: Beacon, 1979), 131–8.

19. Ernest Mandel, *Late Capitalism* (London: New Left Books, 1979).

PART THREE

Culture

CHAPTER EIGHT

Literature as Social Knowledge: Mikhail Bakhtin and the Reemergence of the Human Sciences

Introduction

Scholarship is seldom more charming than when it exhumes and recycles dead souls. In the late sixties, a social theorist was resurrected on the mistaken premise that he was primarily a literary critic. Mikhail Bakhtin was introduced to English-speaking readers as a new voice in late medieval studies, perhaps the greatest commentator on Rabelais. We are only now realizing, twenty years after the first English-language translation of his work, that Bakhtin is one of the giants of twentieth century social and cultural theory.

Since Bakhtin's death in 1975, his writing has slowly made its way into literary circles, and a small cottage industry has grown up around him in the American academy. One curious feature of his reception is that no one is quite sure which "Bakhtin" works were actually written by Bakhtin, despite a recent full-scale biography by Katerina Clark and Michael Holquist.

Born in 1895 to an aristocratic family, Bakhtin was an early convert to the life of the mind. He entered Saint Petersburg University in 1914 and immediately became involved in both philosophical and religious study. According to Clark and Holquist, he appeared to be less interested in political activity. After the revolution, he found himself in Nevel, a small town near Petersburg, teaching school. There he discovered a scattering

363

of intellectuals similarly dealing with hard times by working in the provinces. A "circle" formed to study philosophy and debate ideas. The Bakhtin Circle was unique, even for Russia, because it combined study with collective literary production in sufficient volume to constitute a "school" of social theory and criticism. But it also presented future scholars with a problem. The work of "Bakhtin"—books about Freud, the philosophy of language, and literary formalism—was first published under the names of other members of the Bakhtin Circle.

It is even curious that Bakhtin has been received so warmly by the same generation that was so smitten by formalism it forced even Marxism to take the French way. Bakhtin and his friends were the precursors of *antiformalist* criticism: *Freudianism* is a pitiless critique of psychoanalysis from a sociohistorical perspective; *Marxism and the Philosophy of Language* takes the linguistics of Ferdinand de Saussure to task for its biophysiological view of language. Against Saussure's argument that the structure of language is given to all humans, Bakhtin counterposes the idea that language derives its meanings from dialogue, which in turn is grounded in asocial context. He insists that the study of language and literature provides a crucial clue to understanding such social questions as class conflict, the construction of communities, and history. While structuralism and Russian formalism emphasize the spatial dimension of social life and literary texts, Bakhtin adheres to the idea that social and aesthetic forms are produced under particular circumstances, and the task of language study is another kind of historiography: the analysis of everyday life.

All of us have submitted to a historical pedagogy that highlights "great men" and abstracts "key events" from the details of daily existence. The heroic has no place in Bakhtin's historiography. For him, traditional histories are the narratives from which the myth that the past belongs only to the victors is fashioned. To hear the voices of the "people," Bakhtin seeks out imaginative rather than scientific literature; the novel is constructed from the details of ordinary existence, just as discourses are the stuff of communication between people.

Bakhtin is neither modernist nor postmodernist. On the contrary, his work may be described as populism of a special type. As Bakhtin becomes the center of a history revival, his literary executors, like Benjamin's, are fighting over the treasure and its interpretation. Slavicists such as Michael Holquist have recruited Bakhtin in the struggle against Soviet repression, and have portrayed him as a "religious man" persecuted by the Russians for his faith. His writings about Rabelais and Dostoevsky, as well as his work about language, psychoanalysis, and literary forms, are said to be a coded antiauthoritarian response to the Stalin era.

In Dostoevsky, Bakhtin discovers his Moby Dick, his Dora, his Molly Bloom. The Dostoevsky in *Problems of Dostoevsky's Poetics* is not the existentialist precursor of Sartre and Camus, but a master of polyphony, creator of a multiplicity of voices and consciousnesses. According to Bakhtin, the interior voice is not a monologue, but is in constant dialogue with the outside world. It is through dialogue that the self is constituted in Dostoevsky's fiction; his psychology is always a signifier of the ways in which social life sets the boundaries of individual will. In Bakhtin's reading, there is no solitary hero. Rather, Dostoevsky dredges up the voices of those excluded from history, revealing the details of everyday life in order to decode the social world, not aestheticize it. Although Bakhtin acknowledges that Dostoevsky is a novelist of ideas, those ideas are transformed by the characters; they never appear as an aspect of the authorial voice. This point is no more strongly made than in Bakhtin's interpretation of *Notes From Underground*:

> There is literally nothing we can say about the hero of *Notes From Underground* that he does not already know himself: his typicality for his time and social group, the sober psychological or even psychopathological delineation of his internal profile, the category of character to which his consciousness belongs, his comic as well as his tragic side, all possible moral definitions of his personality, and so on...he stubbornly and agonizingly soaks up all these definitions from within. Any point of view from without is rendered powerless in advance and denied the finalizing word.

Instead of reflecting a powerful, alienated, inner self, the Underground Man is a mirror of what everybody else says about him: "he knows all possible refractions of his image in those mirrors...and he takes into account the point of view of a 'third person.'" Dostoevsky's Underground Man is engaged in furious dialogue with opposing consciousnesses; he is the condensation of the "other" of society. His self-consciousness is constructed, not primal.

Despite Bakhtin's critique of formalism, his magisterial study of Dostoevsky demonstrates the power of a formal method. This method presupposes a theory that places the relation of the individual to his social context at the center of the novel's formation of character, its ideas and ideology; even its narrative structure. Bakhtin is not a literary critic either of the school where the reader becomes the subject of discourse, or of the scientific formalism that focuses primarily on language and its vicissitudes. He is a *social* theorist. Bakhtin's main purpose in studying literature is to plumb the depths of social, not psychological, relations. He wants to discover how we negotiate our circumstances, how we constitute ourselves as eminently individual yet supremely typical characters of our time, our social class, our social relations. And his point is to discover history in and through works of art as privileged.

I

In recent years, literary methods have been widely used to reread some of the texts of social sciences, particularly ethnography. Clifford's and Marcus's collection, *Writing Culture*,[1] showed us that "evidence" can be taken as discourse, specifically, that the ethnographer engages in rhetoric and other weapons of persuasion—metaphor and metonymy, tropes and so on—which render power to discourse. Moreover, as the recent debate over ethnography has shown, the researcher is bound, ethically, to take responsibility for her or his choice of subjects as well as the method of inquiry. The notion that anthropology, for example, is assigned by a neutral division of intellectual labor to study the subaltern in "Third World" settings is today completely shattered. The investigator is obliged to set out her or his social and political presuppositions, including what may be described as the "intention" of the investigation. In sum, knowledge for knowledge's sake is under severe attack.

The problem of taking literary and other artistic works as reliable sources of social knowledge presents somewhat greater difficulties. In

366

the first place, artists, critics, and philosophers have, since the eight-eenth-century, insisted upon the "autonomy" of art—especially from the economic and political matrix we call "society."[2] Others have modified this judgment by admitting that art is intertwined with moral and ethical precepts of a given culture, in which case the relation of art to philosophy and other forms of systematic knowledge is a reasonable inference. At the same time, the art world—artists, critics, theorists, patrons—tends to acknowledge an internal relation of art to everyday life or, in anoth-er register, to what Bakhtin often refers to as "culture."[3] Literature may be self-referential insofar as its formal attributes, such as narrative and linguistic traditions, play a significant part in artistic production, and aesthetics insists that the creative act is autobiographical, that is, objec-tivates what Bataille has called "inner experience."[4] Yet, as we know, the common root of both self and other precludes a purely subjective origin.[5] We are ineluctably bound to our social relations; culture may be taken as *both* the civilizing process—where the assimilation of art and its tradi-tions is understood as one of the crucial elements of self-creation—and in the anthropological sense, as the practices (and as Bakhtin argues, utterances) that constitute everyday life.[6]

The second difficulty is the conventional separation of science, in-cluding the sciences of society, from art. According to the so-called "two cultures" thesis,[7] the methods and the apprehended knowledge derived from these spheres of human existence are both logically and existen-tially separate. While literature provides insight into the subjective or psychological aspects of being, its ability to provide reliable systematic, conceptual, and generalizable knowledge as compared to, for example, history or sociology is, considered within this reprise, quite limited.

Until the discovery of the work of Mikhail Bakhtin by European and US theorists and critics, the debate concerning the possibility that liter-ature may be a source of social knowledge was determined by the tenets of realist epistemology, according to which the literary text corresponds to an objective reality and, in fact, is determined by it, albeit not in a one-to-one copy. Even in the more sophisticated versions of this position, such as that of Georg Lukács, the problem of the epistemological status of representation is never avoided. Within this framework one needs no theory of language, only a theory of narrative. Recall that in Lukács's second excursions into literary criticism and theory (chiefly in the 1930s) he argues that narratives are constituted formally by social types derived as an abstraction from social life and are, consequently, independent of the text or literary traditions. The "great" novelists in his canon—among them Balzac, Scott, Thomas Mann—draw their sources from these typifications of bourgeois society; the contradictions of everyday existence refer to real, historical contradictions and, in the best novels, narratives lose their self-referential character. Lukács draws his canon of European literature from those works that conform to the requirement that the economic and social character of a period are expressed in and through concrete characters and situations.

Of course, in this paradigm of literature as social knowledge literary forms themselves are taken as mediations of an external reality that is quite independent of them. In our time of keen interest in formal methods of criticism, Lukács's work has become a monument to an important but apparently surpassed discourse, precisely because of its realist historical epistemology. Consequently, for much of the interwar period, when literature and art were not understood in their formal-aesthetic dimensions to the exclusion of any possible social referent (a move conditioned by Marxism's intellectual hegemony over much of the literary intelligentsia during the 1930s), the social investigation of literature was subordinated by conceptions according to which literature may be taken as a kind of language game that obeys certain rules, some of which owe their effectivity to literary conventions. In semiotic criticism the text is a signifying practice whose meaning can only be derived from how it functions with a specific context. In turn, "context" connotes not chiefly a sociohistorical "reality" but a system of codes. For example, Roland Barthes's *S/Z*—which may be taken as anti-Lukács—purports to show that the literary text of Balzac is actually fractured by a gaggle of codes, the interplay of which constitutes the narrative. Barthes transforms the social code from a master discourse into only one of six relatively autonomous systems the juxtapositions and combinations of which constitute the text. As with other works of structuralist criticism, diachronicity is subordinate to synchronicity, but equally important, the social loses its privileged place in reflection upon literary production. Barthes's methodological move consisted not in obliterating the social referent, a position easily dismissed by the perspective of critical realism. Rather, the social code is relativized; its effectivity becomes indeterminate in advance and must be evaluated anew in every concrete situation.

At first glance, the recent interest in Bakhtin may be considered paradoxical, since he appears to privilege *parole* over *langue*, time (history) over space, and, perhaps more puzzling, his work may be interpreted as profoundly ensconced in a subtle but unmistakable realist epistemology which, despite its differences from Lukácsian Marxist criticism, shares a sociohistorical referent.[8] Indeed, the similarities in these respects between the two are by no means frivolous. Yet, as I argue, by exploring Bakhtin's category of chronotope, and perhaps more urgently his use of the musical figure of polyphony, we have here neither a conventional materialist discourse abetted by dialectical logic, nor a precursor to poststructuralism. For the chronotope, along with Bakhtin's other key categories—heteroglossia, dialogic narrative, and polyphony—may be seen as a critique of historicism from the perspectives of a new conception of historicity.

Bakhtin offers a theory of language which privileges agency over structure but works with, but not within, linguistic boundaries.[9] Most important of all from the perspective of social and cultural theory, his perspective addresses, within a critique of literary texts, the complex relationships between humans and nature and social relations, without, however succumbing to correspondence theory. In fact, as I shall argue below, Bakhtin offers an incipient theory of the relation of nature to human relations which falls into neither biological nor social reductionism. It remains virtually singular in the past century of literary scholarship, during which the culturalist position of the *Geisteswissenschaften* (spiritual or human sciences) have dominated cultural studies.

Perhaps his stature as a social historian is unknown to literary scholarship. But Bakhtin's wide influence on European social history is largely due to the pertinence of his "method," not uncontested, to historical sociology of the medieval and early-Renaissance period. For what Bakhtin achieved, long before the richly detailed historical and sociological studies by George Rude, Eric Hobsbawm, and E. P. Thompson, to name

369

only some of the best known, of what is variously termed the Crowd, the "people" or simply popular culture, was to provide a series of rigorously constituted categories of description. Yet some admiring historians have persisted in privileging social scientific methods that purport to achieve direct knowledge of the past. Here is Carlo Ginzburg:

> The stereotyped and saccharine image of popular culture that results from this research is very different from what is outlined by Mikhail Bakhtin in a lively and fundamental book on the relations between Rabelais and the popular culture of his day. Here it is suggested that Gargantua or Pantagruel books, that perhaps no peasant ever read, teach us more about peasant culture than the *Almanach des Bergers*, which must have circulated widely in the French countryside. The center of the culture portrayed by Bakhtin is the carnival, myth and ritual in which converge the celebration of fertility and abundance, the jesting inversion of all values and established orders, the cosmic sense of the destructive and regenerative passage of time.[10]

According to Bakhtin, this vision of the world, which had evolved through popular culture over the course of centuries, was in marked contrast to the dogmatism and conservatism of the culture of the dominant classes, especially in the Middle Ages. By keeping this disparity in mind, the work of Rabelais becomes comprehensible, its comic quality linked directly to the carnival themes of popular culture: cultural dichotomy, then—but also a circular, reciprocal influence between the cultures of subordination and the ruling classes that was especially intense in the first half of the sixteenth century.

> These are hypotheses to a certain extent and not all of them equally well documented. But the principal failing in Bakhtin's fine book is probably something else. The protagonists of popular culture whom he has tried to describe, the peasants and the artisans speak almost exclusively through the words of Rabelais.

But what is the epistemological status of Ginzburg's own text? Can the "reports" of his own protagonist the miller Menocchio's captors be called more "reliable" than Bakhtin's protagonists of popular culture read from Rabelais's *Gargantua*? Says Ginzburg:

> the very wealth of research possibilities indicated by Bakhtin makes us wish for a direct study of lower class society free of intermediaries. But for reasons already mentioned, it is extremely difficult in this area of scholarship to find a direct rather than an indirect method of approach.[11]

Ginzburg believes that we can avoid the "indirect approach," yet is properly concerned that this claim exposes him to the charge of positivism:

> But the fear of falling into a notorious, naive positivism combined with the exasperated awareness of the ideological distortion that may lurk behind the most normal and seemingly innocent process of perception prompts many historians today to disregard popular culture together with the sources that provide a more or less distorted picture of it.[12]

Ginzburg implies that something other than "distortion" can be derived from a direct method of research, that historical research can reliably get back to the "things themselves," that history can be recovered in some extratextual manner. So, like other social historians such as the Annales school (Bloch, Braudel, Febvre, Le Roi Ladurie), he scans official records in an effort to capture the moral economy of the period, the rhythms of everyday life, and the elusive, but discernable agency of the people. Yet his method is inevitably indirect; the people rarely if ever "speak for themselves." They cannot represent themselves, either because they cannot read or write, or because they are denied access to preserved documents. They must be represented through the reports of official bodies which, until fairly recently, monopolized the means of communication, and whose texts are always edited. Social history is, regrettably, an indirect history, subject to the exclusions and inclusions of interested informants. The texts of social history, however valuable, are warranted inferences whose epistemological status may be compared in their documentary status to that of the novel. Events are inevitably and doubly fictionalized: by the institutional authority of the Church and its courts, and by the professional authority of the historian. While it is admirable that some, notably the various schools of social history, choose to construct the agency of the people, the methodological ensnarements are frequently severe.

Bakhtin seems to anticipate these criticisms. In his essay on the "text" he claims that:

> The text (written and oral) is the primary given of all these distinct disciplines and of all thought in the human sciences and philosophy in general (including theological and philosophical thought at its sources). The text is the unmediated reality...the only one from which these disciplines and this thought can emerge. Where there is no text there is no object of study and no object of thought either.[13]

Even the social historian (of which genre Carlo Ginzburg is an unsurpassed practitioner) relies on texts—letters and diaries, and in order to get at everyday life (especially of the nonliterate classes) the historian or ethnographer is obliged to construct a narrative out of the raw materials provided by public records—court transcripts, tax rolls, among which Fernand Braudel and other members of the Annales school found lists of agricultural products and their money or barter values, property deeds, and so forth. And others such as Ladurie and de Goff worked in the genre of historical scholarship that relied, in part, on civil and ecclesiastical courts. If Bakhtin is right that, whatever its form, "the implied text (if the word is understood in its broadest sense as any coherent complex of signs),"[14] then even the study of art deals with texts. For Bakhtin "our discipline" is not literary criticism or social history, but the "human sciences," which, for him, are distinguished by the centrality of interpretation in them, in contrast to the natural sciences' penchant for direct modes of authentication.

However, if it can be shown that natural sciences are themselves theory-laden and, therefore, evidence is heavily mediated by interpretation, we may refer to the positivist doctrine of authentication through experiment, rational calculation, or whatever, but the actual as opposed to the imputed difference between the two broad disciplines begin to break down. Bakhtin:

We will give the name chronotope (literally 'time space') to the intrinsic connectedness of temporal and spatial relationships that are artistically expressed in literature. This term (space-time) is employed in mathematics, and was introduced as part of Einstein's Theory of Relativity. The special meaning it has in relativity theory is not important for our purposes; we are borrowing it for literary criticism almost as a metaphor (almost but not entirely). What counts for us is that it expresses the inseparability of space and time (time as the fourth dimension of space). We understand the chronotope as a formally constitutive category of literature; we will not deal with the chronotope in other areas of culture.[15]

For Bakhtin, in literature the primary category of the chronotope is *time*. And, as this essay shows, time constructs narratives by its intersection with social and symbolic space. Moreover, in the sections on Rabelais in the Chronotope essay, Bakhtin shows that the history of the novel itself may be configured in relation to chronotopic categories, as multitudes of spatiality whose cores are forms of temporality. Bakhtin abstracts from the texts of Rabelais, for example, no less than seven forms of what he calls "productive and generative time"[16] in the preclass agricultural stage of human societies (the folkloric time), all of which are marked in various ways as "unified and unmediated" totalities in which means of production, ritual, and everyday life are not yet differentiated into private and public spheres. Rabelais's *Gargantua* comes at the end of this epoch: its series are primarily spatial since, as Bakhtin says, "the folkloric basis of (even) the entire grotesque images is patently obvious."[17]

Laughter and grotesquerie mark these series of eating, copulation, death, and so forth, that are, despite their phantasmagoric imagery, still ensconced in the worldview according to which we are part of natural history. Thus, in contrast to the sublimated form of sexuality—love—that transmogrifies the romantic novel in the eighteenth century, Rabelais invokes the popular conception according to which sex is a natural practice unmediated by extrinsic influences such as religious morality, all of which are concentrated in the spatio-temporal specificity of the carnival.

In contrast, modernity is marked by the separation of public from private, that is, the separation of means of production, ritual, and everyday life, each of which becomes the site of the well-known fragmentation of the social world in which the commodity form, in all of its permutations, gradually displaces (but does not destroy) popular culture.[18] With the rise of the individual, the social chronotope is replaced by the individual chronotope. We must now speak of the multitude, not so much of series, but of voices, the combinatory effects of which are polyphonic, a term that signifies the dissonant harmonies of individual voices.

Bakhtin:

> When the immanent unity of time disintegrated, when individual life-sequences were separated out, lives in which the gross realities of communal life had become merely petty private matters; when collective labor and the struggle with nature had ceased to be the only arena for man's encounter with nature and the world—then nature itself ceased to be a living participant in the events of life. Then nature became, by and large, "a setting for action" its backdrop; it was turned into landscape it was fragmented into metaphors and comparisons serving to sublimate individual and private affairs and adventures not connected in any real and intrinsic way with nature itself.
>
> But the treasure-house of language and in certain kinds of folklore this immanent unity of time is preserved insofar as language and folklore continue to insist on a relation to the world and its phenomena based on collective labor. It is in these that the real basis of the ancient matrix is preserved, the authentic logic of a primitive enchaining of images and motives.[19]

In these lines we can hear echoes of the neo-Marxist critique of modernity associated with Lukács and the Frankfurt School, but with a significant and perhaps a decisive difference: Bakhtin insists on the primacy of the popular which, itself, is associated with the unity of humans and nature mediated through labor. His vision—against all privileging of high culture—is the idea that what appears as trivial to culture as what Norbert Elias calls the "civilizing process,"[20] may be taken as the authentic when seen from the perspective of its historicity. For a unique conception of historicity underlies Bakhtin's chronotope, within which all categories of

374

social space-time are employed. Since in the final accounting language is subject to temporally induced transformations but also stands outside, one may infer its relative transhistoricity as well. Otherwise how could language "preserve" the "immanent" unity of time? But folklore enjoys the same status. Contrary to the myths of modernity, Bakhtin shows that, although fundamentally marked by the totality (in which subject-object are unified by the body), folkloric time is anything but static. Unlike the later incarnation, history is not coded as a series of external events to which private life is consigned to "petty affairs," but consists in the chronotope of the carnival which, however, is part of everyday existence. Although Bakhtin's object of knowledge are the texts of literature, from the sources literature derives its narratives are plainly "extraliterary": folklore (popular culture) which are part of the oral tradition.

Surely the idea that literary texts may be, among other sources, taken as reliable objects of social knowledge is precisely what Bakhtin has in mind in his *Rabelais* or *Dostoevsky*. The distinction between the social sciences, including history and the so-called humanities, is refuted in Bakhtin's invocation of the *Geisteswissenschaften* (human sciences), a term he employs to signify what he calls "the unity of culture" to describe his own discourse.[21] Of course, the appropriation of his categories by the disciplines and subdisciplines in the United States, without showing the implications of the large claim represented by the chronotope for constituting categories of experience, literary or otherwise, is entirely conventional, just as Bakhtin's own disclaimer for the universality of the chronotope in relation to the natural sciences may be comprehended within the framework of Marxist-Leninist scientism to which he was subject, at least bureaucratically. However, if we recall the ambiguity of his own statement, he proposes to employ space-time as a fourth dimension in literature but not really metaphorically. For his meticulous typology of the various series that constitute the temporal-spatial contexts for the medieval and Renaissance novel and the modern novel illustrates the claims of contemporary philosophy of science that all empirical science is theory-laden. The "chronotope" as a physical category mediates observation, measurement, and their results. Bakhtin uses space-time in a fairly rigorous way, from which he derives his own categories of narrative.

Moreover, in the work of Vernadsky, Oparin, and other biologist contemporaries, from whom Bakhtin drew as much as from Einstein's relativity theory, the chronotope, one of the main ideas that appears in the Rabelais has become a crucial element in the study of the evolution of the biosphere and problems such as the origin of life.[22] In the mid-1920s Soviet biologists and biochemists, together with some German and British colleagues, developed a theory of biochemical evolution that abandoned the older view that posited the appearance of life in images of linear temporality. They held that green plants fed by radiation made the earliest appearance, followed by other organisms. These scientists, led by Vernadsky and Oparin, advanced the hypothesis of heterotrophic sources for life, the simultaneous appearance of life forms and the close relation and ultimate interdependence of organisms and their organic and inorganic environments, which interact interdependently. That is, once having emerged, life-forms enrich or impoverish the environment. And Vernadsky employs the category of chronotope to describe and explain the series of events that constitute evolution. It is a Darwinian hypothesis, but also one in which synchronic relations of a horizontal kind remain pertinent.

So, although Bakhtin identifies with the view according to which literary studies are part of the human sciences, he departs from one of its major tenets: the logical and existential divide between natural and human sciences corresponding to a parallel gulf between nature and history. The concept of the "unity" of culture refers to art, everyday life, and postmodern scientific culture. But unity does not assume identity. Into time-space he inserts polyphony; that is, the multiplicity of voices which are definitively not dialectical, if by this term we connote internal contradictions that are resolved through the subordination of one of the terms by the other and its incorporation into a "higher" unity.

Thus, Bakhtin's philosophical position resembles more that of Nietzsche than of Hegel. While the rhetoric of the eternal return is absent from his discourse, there is also an emphatic, albeit implied, argument for the continuity of formal categories in the wake of historically determined transformations of speech genres. Yet the chronotope is constituted as a heterogeneity of voices. Utterance is a dynamic category through which time may be apprehended. The importance of utterance

376

in Bakhtin's later thought can be understood in several dimensions: its role in literary production, its centrality to what we mean when we speak of "style." But Bakhtin's ambition is, finally, to read history through discourse, especially through a close reading of the transformations of utterances. In his essay on speech genres, Bakhtin comments on Goethe's description of geographical terrain in his *Italian Journey*:

> The living, dynamic marker provided by flowing rivers and streams also gives a graphic idea of the country's water basins, its topography, its natural boundaries and natural connections, its land and water routes and transshipment points, its fertile and arid areas and so on. This is not an abstract geological and geographical landscape. For Goethe, it reveals potential for historical life. This is an arena of historical events, a firmly delineated boundary of that spatial riverbed along which the current of historical time flows. Historically active man is placed in this living, graphic, visual system of mountains waterways, boundaries and routes.... One sees the *essential* and *necessary* character of man's historical activity.[23]

Bakhtin draws on travel genre as he draws on novels, to demonstrate that embedded in the writer's craft of invoking nature is human activity, that writing is a kind of speech whose status is fundamentally historical even when its ostensible referent is the natural world.

II

Bakhtin commends his work to our attention now because, underneath the current fashion of European-inspired formalisms, other currents are struggling for a place in the critical sun: the new literary history, much of which is not new; a strong claim inspired by the later works of Roland Barthes for relieving criticism of its obligation to produce science in favor of a return to the text of fiction, to discover its pleasures. In some ways, interest in Bakhtin is unlikely in either literary criticism or linguistics because, until now, his social perspective on literature was out of fashion. Since the '60s American critics have been smitten by formalisms of various sorts: structuralism, semiotics, and deconstruction; and a considerable coterie hangs onto the New Criticism. Even Marxism, which is historical, whatever else it might be, was forced to adapt to the French turn or face marginality in current debates. Bakhtin and his friends were the collective precursor of antiformalist criticism; *Freudianism* is a pitiless critique of the fundamental psychoanalytic ideas from the point of view of a social linguistics. Their theory of language, which forms the basis of all of work of what became known as the Bakhtin Circle, is fully developed in *Marxism and the Philosophy of Language*—like the Freud book, ostensibly written by V. N. Vološinov. In the language work, Vološinov's fire is directed against Saussure's *Course in General Linguistics*, which took Soviet linguistics of the 1920s by storm and provided a broad basis for a new literary formalism against which the Bakhtin Circle argued throughout the decade. *Marxism* is perhaps the most persuasive statement in our century of an alternative conception of language to that of Saussurian structuralism, for which the structure of language really inheres in the biophysiological makeup of humans and, like the gene, is relatively independent of its social and historical environment. Long before Saussure's French legatees discovered the pragmatic rule that signification was situated not chiefly in its structure but in the uses of language, Bakhtin insisted that, even if the capacity for language is given, its structure as well as its meaning derive from its uses (and its consequences) within a definite social context. Words and sentences do not refer principally to their structure but to the dialogues in which they are employed.

Speech, or as Bakhtin calls it, utterance, is intimately linked to the space-time (chronotope) which constitutes the speech act as well as narrative. In fact, the analysis of utterances in literature as much as in daily communication is the crucial source of knowledge about modernist daily life. We learn about what people are saying, but even more important, inner and outer dialogues (conversations between people and between the self and its own other) tell us by the mode of expression who these people are.[24] And, as we have seen, descriptions of the external world are signifiers of conditions of historically situated time—signs of the self-production of humans.

So, although taken up in the United States mostly by literary critics because most of the translated work under his own name concerns methods of literary theory or studies of such novelists as Dostoevsky and Rabelais, Bakhtin may be considered better as a close student of culture, both in the anthropological and in the art sense; his wide use of historical, sociological, and aesthetic categories defies the neat cubbies of academic disciplines, although this has not prevented them from recoding his work in terms of their specialized debates.

Like Walter Benjamin, whose writings animated the literary critical scene in the late 1960s and '70s,[26] Bakhtin is rapidly becoming the subject of literary studies. Among others of course, the Slavicists have appropriated him. In the context of the anti-Stalinist revival of the post Brezhnev era, he is portrayed as a "religious man" persecuted by the Soviets for his faith. Consequently, his writing, ostensibly about Rabelais and Dostoevsky, as well as works about language, psychoanalysis, and literary forms, is sometimes taken as code for an antiauthoritarian political intervention precisely during the Stalin era.[27] On the other side, the Marxists have gravitated to Bakhtin after long years in the modernist wilderness, where their insistence on socially rooted interpretations of literature were considered by the critical avant-garde to be quaint, when not dangerous in the light of Zhdanovian repression of artistic dissent until the partial thaw of the late 1950s.[28]

More than Benjamin who, despite his communist fellow-traveling, was among the first of the truly modernist critics, Bakhtin rails against modernism in art and criticism on both technical and ideological grounds. His attack against formalism, the revolution's most daring and internationally appreciated aesthetic experiment, not only puts him, at least in the immediate postrevolutionary decade, outside the cultural mainstream in his own country, but also places him out of step with modern art of the first half of the twentieth-century. If he remained relatively obscure after the 1920s until his belated and conjunctural discovery in the highly charged political context of the waning years of the Khrushchev era, modernists could argue "with good reason," that his obscurity was well deserved for even when Bakhtin reads Dostoevsky, he looks for different things. What he wants to discover in the novels are the voices of those excluded from written history; he wants to dredge up the details of everyday life, not until very recently a legitimate object of the historian's eye.

But Bakhtin is not just another critic for whom the popular voice constitutes the basis of the aesthetic and social value of a literary work. Although there is a good case to be made that he is not a literary critic, historian, aesthetician, but is really a social theorist and a social linguist for whom literature functions as social knowledge, his great attraction for us, despite his denunciation of formalisms of all sorts, is his penchant for category-making which corresponds, ironically, to our (if not Bakhtin's own) will to scientificity. Bakhtin's "will to scientificity" is revealed most saliently in his penchant for category-making, an elective affinity that places him, loosely, in the Kantian mode of cultural criticism that was extremely powerful in the years just prior to and immediately after the Russian Revolution. At the same time, his great admiration for Goethe belies any facile attempt to place him in either the religious or the Kantian camp:

> All we have said reveals the exceedingly chronotopic nature of Goethe's mode of visualization and thought in all areas and spheres of his multifaceted activity. He saw everything not *sub specie aeternitatis* (from the point of view of eternity) as his teacher Spinoza did, but in time, and in the power of time. Everything—from an abstract idea to a piece of rock on the bank of a stream—bears the stamp of time, and is saturated with time and assumes its form and meaning in time.

To Goethe's world of "emergence" Bakhtin counterposes the "mechanical materialism of Holbach and others.... These same two aspects clearly separate Goethe from subsequent romantic historicity as well."[29] Unlike the old literary essayists whose discursive meditations grabbed the reader by their sheer force of style, and who performed criticism by making the assumption that the work of art violated or was sympathetic to our collective sensibilities, Bakhtin's power is to get us to think in his categories. If you already know that Dostoevsky is the modernist whose major achievement was to capture interior dialogue, really our first great modern psychological writer, Bakhtin shows that this is merely an instance of a far greater contribution—his polyphony, the multitude of voices that inhabit his texts, the master narrator of the vicissitudes of modernity where the petty affairs of private life become identical to the excluded history of the space-time that his characters inhabit.[30]

Bakhtin contrasts the monologue in which the authorial voice dominates the text, and dialogue where characters speak for themselves, voices that Dostoevsky articulates against his own political will, speaking of values and ways of life that are in profound disagreement with his own precepts. For Bakhtin, Dostoevsky's greatness consists in his loyalty to truth, even if this truth of diversity, of plurality, opposes his own exquisitely hierarchical religious worldview. Like his critics and biographers, Dostoevsky may have believed he was a chronicler of the existential choices to which humans were ineluctably wedded, but Bakhtin persuades us that his work provides, first of all, a window to the Russian middle class which forms the context of nearly all his most important novels and stories. Not that Bakhtin's Dostoevsky is a sociological naturalist who, like Émile Zola, contents himself with recording the world as a botanist classifies the forest flora. The novels and stories do not describe a social environment "objectively." Bakhtin:

> Not a single element of the work is structured from the point of view of a nonparticipating "third person." In the novel itself, nonparticipating "third persons" are not represented in any way.... [Dostoevsky has created a] plurality of equally authoritative ideological positions and an extreme heterogeneity of material...[31]

This achievement Bakhtin calls polyphony. The musical metaphor could be transposed to a political metaphor, since Bakhtin's study was published when Stalin's dominance in Soviet life was just taking hold. And 1929 was the year of Bakhtin's arrest for his religious activities, an event which led to his exile from the Soviet metropolis to the provinces, where he was to spend most of the rest of his life, except for the last decade, after being "discovered" by a post-Stalinist student generation. He returned to Moscow in the late 1960s when the Soviet Union was still in the first period of post-Stalin-era reform. In fact, this obscure provincial teacher of linguistics and literature who was rediscovered in the context of the debate, initiated by Nikita Khrushchev, about the political and cultural monologism of the previous era, may have made the important contribution.

For a new intellectual generation Bakhtin became a democratic prophet, but also a great Marxist critic. Certainly it is this "Marxism" that many current claimants to the Bakhtinian legacy would deny, substituting instead an aestheticist interpretation of this work which may be perhaps the least literary of all twentieth-century schools of thought for which textual criticism is the crucial method.

The first chapter of *Problems of Dostoevsky's Poetics* lays out his standpoint: Dostoevsky has invented the polyphonic novel out of his own ambiguous and ultimately contradictory personality and ideological position. Although the work is rooted in its own time, the validity of the achievement does not die when the conditions under which it was produced have been surpassed. Like only Dante, and perhaps Dickens, Dostoevsky has the gift of presenting many voices simultaneously and with equal amplitude. The dialogic imagination reaches its highest point here, precisely because Dostoevsky cannot resolve the conflicts that constitute his life and art. Nor can Bakhtin. For he was a religious individual, profoundly at odds with postrevolutionary Russia. At the same time that he is influenced by Marxism's *intention* to deliver literature from its formal bonds, especially in his attempt to develop a truly social theory of literature in which not only whole discourses and even sentences embody the dialogic principle, but even the word itself become an instance of discursive activity, a sign of the "subject." A member of the so-called Bakhtin Circle (Medvedev) writes a harsh critique of Russian formalism, and another, Vološinov, produces a theory of language as a system of signs, the meaning of which depend upon their use within the context of communication. The social semiotics suggested in this work is sufficiently compelling to members of French poststructuralist circles, particularly Julia Kristeva, who finds in Bakhtin a precursor to her own work, which, however formalistic, nevertheless adopts the idea that language means as language acts.[32]

We resonate to Bakhtin, particularly his conception of the plurality of voices, and the intimate link of language to action, in part because his position bears some affinities to pragmatism, which I understand here as democratic philosophy, according to which a discourse may be evaluated chiefly not in relation to a transcendent "truth," but in terms of its practical consequences. He offers criticism a way to explore the relationship between text and context that is resolutely antireductionist, but instead insists that social life is imbedded in the narrative in a way not available to more abstracted disciplines such as sociology, economics, and even historiography.

For what is found here is the experience of the ordinary—retold and recast in the novelistic text which, since the seventeenth century, has taken the quotidian as the discursive object. For Bakhtin there are no resolutions of the contradictory, "heteroglossic" nature of human interactions in terms of categories of class, history, or other categories that inevitably transcode experience into information. Which is not to deny that Bakhtin is acutely aware of the class dimension to the novels of the bourgeois epoch. What he refuses, precisely, is the tendency towards class reductionism, to encode all experience and its aspects in terms of a version of social relations that derives from a priori, eternal essences such as those he perceives in Spinoza.

This is Bakhtin's strong program for a criticism that seeks to recover experience, wiped out by the processes of abstraction—both social and scientific—among other monologisms. Bakhtin demands that we reconstruct history through explorations of literature because, in his view, "life below the waist" is erased from our collective memory by official historians, those employed by the victors to tell the past in images of the present. This perspective is perhaps made clearest in his dissertation, *Rabelais and His World*, published belatedly after Bakhtin's rehabilitation in 1963. Judged by leading historians and critics to be "merely" a comic masterpiece, Bakhtin argues that the two major Rabelais novels, *Gargantua* and *Pantagruel*, are profound constructions of the popular critique of aristocratic society and culture, monuments to the power of laughter as political and social criticism. Moreover, the novels are veritable snapshots of the social worlds of the transition between peasant and bourgeois societies, portraits hidden in the preponderant histories for which peasant culture remains otherwise invisible.

Bakhtin's *Rabelais* has become a major influence on recent social history of the sixteenth century, as we have seen in the work of Carlo Ginzburg, discussed earlier. Rabelais's peasants work hard all year, too hard, under the stern authority of the Church and the aristocracy, and their retainers, the local officials. The carnival is that time when the peasants are free to break the rules, rules imposed from on high, and to appropriate by inversion the sacred practices of high culture by means of parody and ridicule. The carnival is a *ritualized transgression*, the place to display gross violations of conventional sexual morality, to engage in a temporary raucous public celebration of the body, a sphere strictly interdicted by established authorities. Bakhtin shows that the wild peasant dances, the laughter, and other outrages creep into high culture just as popular culture absorbs, albeit in comic form, the art of the masters. Even the Church is infected with popular art, so that, although possibly not a single peasant could or did read *Gargantua*, Rabelais's novels represent the intervention of the popular into literature, an art of the ruling classes by definition.

Ginzburg, still tied to the positivist premises of historiography, does not grasp the full power of Bakhtin's approach. It is not that Bakhtin has somehow avoided dredging up direct evidence to demonstrate resistance through popular culture and other means; he is making two different points. The first is that high culture does not stand as the polar opposite of the popular. The split between intellectual and manual labor is a wall created by ideology, but does not, in fact, describe the real relationship between the two. And he is tacitly making a crucial historiographic point: he challenges the positivist assumptions of social historians who, since Thompson's magisterial *Making of the English Working Class* and Trempé's *Les Mineurs de Carmaux*, have revolutionized the writing of working-class history through their archaeological investigations of everyday life. Bakhtin invokes the social world through literature because, among other things, he holds that the novel is the premier form through which the popular is defined by an oral tradition not available to historiography except through *indirect* accounts. Moreover, he shows that much of high culture is constituted, in part, by its appropriation of the popular, and that since the popular is an oral tradition, it can speak only indirectly through its incorporation by high-cultural works. The people of Rabelais's time cannot speak for themselves directly, but in order to enter "history" require intermediaries.

Our knowledge of their hidden history, even information culled from records, of ecclesiastic courts in Ginzburg's justly famous studies, or of manorial rolls where clerks record commodity exchanges between lord, serf, and merchants, and accumulated debits and credits, is always filtered information, since our informants are servants of the mighty. Of course, Rabelais's account differs only in degree; his eyes and ears are unique only because the novel is a form that depicts everyday life and is not restricted by the function within which peasants appear—as defendants, debtors, or whatever additional subordinate position they occupy. The historian is not likely to discover the grotesque—as representations of aristocratic culture or the orgies of pleasure—in the trial of a heretic, or a highwayman apprehended by the county police (the trial records are sources from which many social histories of the last centuries of the old regimes are gleaned). Nor can members of the lower classes emerge as real subjects, no matter how much we learn about them through dredging official records, without the historian's narrative constructions. The formal context of a tribunal tells one thing, a novel another.

Consistent with his work on the early modern novel, Bakhtin investigates later novels to reveal the underside of the space-time of the characters they represent. Unlike criticism derived from structural linguistics, which recognizes that signification derives from its use, but disdains its historicity, Bakhtin holds language as a historical category; utterance is the clue to the "socioideological" situation of characters:

> the novel is an expression of a Galilean perception of language, one that denies the absolutism of a single and unitary language—that is, that refuses to acknowledge its own language as the sole verbal and semantic center of the ideological world. It is a perception that has been made conscious of the vast plentitude of national and more to the point social languages...all of which are equally relative, reified and limited, as they are merely the languages of social groups, professions and other cross-sections of everyday life.[33]

According to Bakhtin, the modern novel is marked by "linguistic homelessness of literary consciousness," by which he means that authorial individuality, prized by some critics as the mark of great writing, is "decentered" by what might be described as the experience of modernity itself. The fragmentation of the social world, the relativity, and relationality of the worldviews of any of its actors, is the real subject of the novel. Against poetry, which preserves the myth of language—that the singular voice may be contained in the form itself—the "truth" of the novel is its "vast plentitude" of voices. The best works of fiction dissolve the singular voice of the author—the characters take over, as in Pirandello's play, *Six Characters in Search of an Author* where the authorial voice is sought but has, regrettably, disappeared.

This theory of literature, and its companion theory of language, are analogous to the propositions of relativity and quantum physics, both of which put the observer in the observational field, and therefore can make no statements about nature that are independent of the framework of investigation. Poetry may be described as the Newtonian period in art; its ideological assumption is the separation of the inner and outer life, its language is characteristically the monologue. This was precisely the reason that the New Criticism privileged poetry over fiction. Stories and novels have a quality of anonymity, especially if they fulfill Bakhtin's critical criteria, while poetry is still the work of the ego, whose sole possession, a mythic yet individual language, aspires to transcend the muck of everyday existence to achieve higher truth. Of course, much of twentieth-century poetry has violated these rules by its aspiration to descend "below the waist." One hears the otherwise muffled voices of the populace in the epic of William Carlos Williams, or in the declamations of Mayakovsky. These are not the world-weary consciousness of a Pound or Eliot, who speak the unified voice of their generation, however distinctively. What many critics find wanting in Williams is precisely the degree to which his utterance approaches the vernacular; they complain that there are too many separate voices in his long poem, *Paterson*, that the transcendental monologic subject, the unique personal voice that has become the subject of modern poetry, disappears. Besides the cardinal sin of merging aesthetics and politics, Mayakovsky feels too "prosy": he has taken everyday speech as the vehicle of his poetry.

Still, despite the blurring of the lines between prose and poetry in a growing genre of poetic works that explicitly renounce the evaluative criteria enunciated by high-cultural critics for this form, Bakhtin prefers prose, because:

> In the poetic image narrowly conceived (in the image-as-trope) all activity—the dynamics of the image-as-word—is completely exhausted by the play between the word [with all its aspects] and the object [in all its aspects]. The word forgets that its object has its own history of contradictory acts of verbal recognition, as well as that heteroglossia that is always present in such acts of recognition.[34]

The word cannot stand alone apart from its object, but the object does not exist solely for the wordsmith; Bakhtin insists that language refers to something outside the speaker's sensibility. Or, to be more precise, the poetic trope cannot be the product of pure consciousness or stylistic convention, but points to an inexhaustible variety of expressions whose reference is the space-time of the world. For Bakhtin, rather than stretching the multiplicity of its uses and its references, poetry closes down the word.

My point in this chapter is emphatically distanced from an attempt to appropriate Bakhtin for the social sciences but to show instead how Bakhtin, through his paradigm shift from the standpoint of the disciplines to that of the human sciences—makes an antidisciplinary intervention into the construction of knowledge, to transform the disciplinary basis of historical, literary, and social knowledge, all of which are separated in contemporary culture by parameters which are institutionally and ideologically derived. Bakhtin's is the way of the transgressor, for the disciplines have fiercely defended their respective domains and, with few exceptions, have clung to that portion of their canons and methodological presuppositions that justify their separate existences.

Needless to say, this work points to the emergence of the intervention that has appeared under the rubric of "cultural studies." This intellectual movement has been marked by three distinct features, all of which have been elaborated by Bakhtin. We have already seen the interplay of the "low" culture of Rabelais's peasants with high-church culture, that there is *mutual* appropriation of each by the other, although the forms of utterance are dissimilar: peasant appropriation is accompanied by mockery and laughter; the Church incorporates peasant culture within its own rituals, but without calling attention to it. The second feature is cultural studies' alternative to the monologism of the dominant culture's canonical works of literature and art, proposing instead that the human sciences recognize the diversity of voices, not only with respect to the emerging discourses of women, people of color, lesbians and gays, and workers, but also the criteria for privileging utterance. This request articulates with Bakhtin's emphasis on *genre*, which provide space for "emotion, evaluation and expression" which are foreign to the mainstream.[35] Finally, as I have argued, Bakhtin introduces the concept that literature may be an authentic site, perhaps *the* privileged site, of social knowledge, precisely because of its polyphonic character, as opposed to the monologisms of the philosophy of language and historical writing that remain unaware of their passive character.

I suspect that it is Bakhtin's challenge to the claims of science with its positivist methodologies of discovery, particularly its artificial separation of fact and fiction, of theory and observation on one hand, and "expressive" forms on the other, that is the most enduring contribution of this amazingly prescient thinker. If we are on the verge of a paradigm shift in the constitution of social knowledge, in which the categories developed by literary theory, especially of discourse, utterance, and polyphony, are no longer conceived as an internal, aesthetically saturated discourse, and where the distinction between nature and culture is once more blurred, then it is in Bakhtin's work that we will find a beacon for the new.

III

Bakhtin proposes to abolish literary history and criticism in favor of a poetics that aims to uncover the social relations other critics reify or submerge. Despite its formal elegance, this is a kind of populism, and therefore likely to cause anxiety in American academic critics. For just as Benjamin is often approached from his kabbalistic side, his Marxism regarded as an aberration better left unexamined, so Bakhtin is dubbed a pluralist, a freedom fighter, a soldier in the new Cold War. His Marxism is dismissed as the necessary compromise any intellectual had to make in the Stalin era. Clark and Holquist find themselves in a cul-de-sac when they claim that almost all of the work, including the Marxist critiques of structural linguistics, formalism, and Freud, was written by Bakhtin himself, or that he was the primary author and that he wrote the work in which such overt ideological positions are not emphasized, such as the Dostoevsky and Rabelais books. To Clark and Holquist, the Marxist discourse was Aesopian; it could not be Marxist and formally complex, since Marxism is a crude economic determinist doctrine explicitly excoriated by Bakhtin.

"*Marxism and the Philosophy of Language* is the most comprehensive account of Bakhtin's translinguistics. It sets out the major presuppositions on which all his other works are based," write Katerina Clark and Michael Holquist of a work that they attribute to Bakhtin, though it bears Vološinov's name.[36] Not that they don't have reason to be confused. The controversy still rages over the issue of authorial voice. Some recent research purports to show that the writing in the language book differs from Bakhtin's unique style. But this is a relatively trivial consideration, of interest only to the cognoscenti.

The real issue is whether the claim that Bakhtin's Marxism is really a cover for another orientation can be supported. Clark and Holquist insist on Bakhtin's conception of language as a primarily social field, yet they ignore the Marxism of *Marxism and the Philosophy of Language* along with the contribution of Vološinov. This omission is not, of course, innocent, since the biographers try to show that both the Circle and Bakhtin himself were quite separated from Marxism in the postrevolutionary twenties.

We can understand this mode of appropriation only if we remember that literary resurrections intervene in the conflicts of the present, in Bakhtin's case, recent developments in Eastern Europe. That Bakhtin could have been a practicing religionist and a political and literary radical is a proposition never entertained by his anti-Marxist interlocutors. Clark and Holquist show the link in the circle's theory of language between ideology and systems of signs, but they offer no independent discussion of the concept of ideology either in Bakhtin or in Marxism. Yet here's Vološinov-Bakhtin:

> Any ideological product is not only itself a part of a reality (natural or social)…it also, in contradistinction to these other phenomena [physical bodies, instruments of production, products for consumption] reflects and refracts another reality outside itself. Everything ideological possesses *meaning*; it represents, depicts or stands for something lying outside itself. In other words, it is a sign. Without signs there is no ideology.[37]

For the Bakhtin Circle, ideology is not located in consciousness as a subjective reflection on reality. It consists of practices, not disembodied thoughts. Ideology is inscribed in the way we deal with the practical problems of daily life, in the things we buy and eat, the ways we "spend" time, which movies and TV shows we watch, the kinds of friends we choose to keep. The idea of ideology as objective, linked to systems of signs, is fully consistent with several tendencies in modern neo-Marxist thought. The work of Fredric Jameson, Raymond Williams, Terry Eagleton, and others echoes the Bakhtin Circle's interpretation of language as a social semiotic whose meaning theory and criticism try to decode by integrating text and context. But you would never know this from Clark and Holquist's Bakhtin.

Bakhtin's biographers could relax if they realized that it matters little whether he wrote all, most, or none of the books and articles upon which his name does not appear. If the Circle was really an intellectual collective, then Bakhtin is a movement, not a new academic icon. Bakhtin hoped that his social semiotics would change our view of social life and shed new light on history. His work prefigures some recent critical accounts of historiography that suggest this activity is little more than mythmaking, where reverence replaces archaeology. Bakhtin recommends Dostoevsky's portrayal of contradictions that never get resolved. In this tableau, the passage of time does not equal progress, and history is not a dialectical spiral from lower to higher levels. Everything exists on the same plane, an insight that foreshadows Levi-Strauss's "ahistorical" polemic against Sartre's progressivism. Bakhtin's explorations of excess in rural culture were meant to remind the middle class of the price it had paid for the mind-body split, for its self-sacrifice on the altar of modernity. Sadly, the Bakhtin "revival"—its discussions of the significance of utterance, of social context, its passionately baroque metaphors—seems to invoke a time out of joint with ours.

It may be that the age of epic appetites is over. We have experienced a massive assault on our own excessive moment, complete with regrets, self-renunciations, communitarian journeys cloaked in the garb of religious fundamentalism, or of humanism, the "left wing" of neo conservative discourse. Humanism is just another kind of religion: the idea of progress is more or less unimpeachable; rationalism enjoys the status of holy writ. Yet, just as art often prefigures politics and everyday culture, we can speculate that the rediscovery of Bakhtin, which antedated *glasnost* by fifteen years, will mesh with a postmodern social theory that challenges the assumptions of the scientific-technological age. Bakhtin is the social theorist of difference, who, unlike Derrida and Foucault, gives top billing to historical agents and agency. For Bakhtin, there are no privileged protagonists, no final solutions, only a panoply of divergent voices which somehow make their own music.

NOTES

1. James Clifford and George Marcus (eds.), *Writing Culture: The Poetics and Politics of Ethnography* (Berkeley and Los Angeles: University of California Press, 1988).

2. Herbert Marcuse, *The Aesthetic Dimension* (Boston: Beacon Press, 1978).

3. M. M. Bakhtin, *Speech Genres and Other Late Essays* (Austin: University of Texas Press, 1986), 3–6. In this interview with the cultural journal *Novy Mir*, which appeared in November 1970, Bakhtin reveals clearly his argument that one may not consider the literary text apart from "the history of culture." He explicitly resumes his earlier critique of the formalist tendency to abstract text from context.

4. George Bataille, *Inner Experience*, trans. Leslie Anne Boldt (Albany: State University of New York Press, 1988).

5. George Herbert Mead, *Mind, Self and Society* (Chicago: University of Chicago Press, 1934).

6. "Insofar as stratification of the communal whole into social classes occurs, the complex undergoes fundamental changes; the motifs and narratives that correspond to those strata are subject to a reinterpretation. A gradual differentiation of ideological spheres sets in. Cultic activity separates itself from undifferentiated production; the sphere of

consumption is made more distinct and, to a certain extent, compartmentalized. Members of the complex experience in internal decline and transformation. Such elements of the matrix as food, drink, the sexual act, death abandon the matrix and enter *everyday life* which is already in the process of being compartmentalized." M. M. Bakhtin, *The Dialogic Imagination* (Austin: University of Texas Press, 1981), 211. In this description, Bakhtin accounts for the appearance of everyday life in terms of the critical idea of differentiation.

7. C. P. Snow, *The Two Cultures*.

8. However, Bakhtin's referent is the "rich treasury of folk humor" in his study of Rabelais or, as in the studies of Dostoevsky's poetics, the multiplicity of voices or "consciousnesses" that do not reduce to a series of "types" as in Lukács's Weberian formulation.

9. V. N. Vološinov, *Marxism and the Philosophy of Language* (New York Academic Press, 1973).

10. Carlo Ginzburg, *The Cheese and the Worms*.

11. Ginzburg, ibid. vii-viii.

12. Ginzburg, ibid.

13. Bakhtin, "The Problem of the Text in Linguistics, Philology and the Human Sciences," in *Speech Genres*, 103.

14. Bakhtin, "The Problem of the Text," ibid.

15. Bakhtin, *The Dialogic Imagination*, 84.

16. Ibid. 206.

17. Ibid. 209.

18. Georg Lukács, "Reification and the Consciousness of the Proletariat," in *History and Class Consciousness* (London: Merlin Press, 1971). Of course, Lukács would not agree with the judgment that popular culture is "displaced, but not destroyed" by the penetration of the commodity form to all corners of the social world, the division of labor and its consequent alienation effects.

19. Bakhtin, "Forms of Time and the Chronotope in the Novel," in *The Dialogic Imagination*, 217.

20. Norbert Elias, *The Civilizing Process* (New York: Urizen Books, 1980).

21. Bakhtin, "Discourse and the Novel," in *The Dialogic Imagination*, 270.

22. M. M. Kamshilov, *Evolution of the Biosphere*, trans. Minna Brodskaya (Moscow: MIR Publishers, 1978), 40–1.

23. Bakhtin, "The Bildungsroman," in *Speech Genres*, 37.

24. Bakhtin, "The Problem of Speech Genres," in *Speech Genres*.

25. Bakhtin, *Speech Genres*, 72–3.

26. The boom was initiated by Hannah Arendt who, in 1967, edited the first collection in English of a selection of Benjamin's essays. Walter Benjamin, *Illuminations*, ed. with an introduction by Hannah Arendt (New York: Schocken Books, 1967). But it was not until Fredric Jameson's discussion of Benjamin in *Marxism and Form* (Princeton: Princeton University Press, 1972) and articles in *The New York Review of Books* and other periodicals in the 1970s that he was recognized by scholars and critics beyond the Germanists and Frankfurt School mavens.

27. These themes are repeated in the various works of Michael Holquist, Caryl Emerson, Saul Morson, and Tzvetan Todorov. Todorov's pithy remarks on the subject of Bakhtin's relation to Marxism are extremely instructive in this regard. While, as he points out, Bakhtin never published a "single polemical text under his own name," there is, according to Todorov, little doubt that the Marxist works of members of the circle to which he was affiliated had his approbation, and their debates with various orthodoxies were conducted from inside Marxism. See Tzvetan Todorov, *Mikhail Bakhtin: The Dialogic Principle* (Minneapolis: University of Minnesota Press), 9–10.

28. Andrei Zhdanov, "Tire Richest in Ideas, the Most Advanced Literature," in Maxim Gorky, et al., *Soviet Writers Congress 1934* (London: Lawrence and Wishart, 1977).

29. Bakhtin, *Speech Genres*, 42.

30. Bakhtin, *Problems of Dostoevsky's Poetics*, ed. and trans. Caryl Emerson, with an introduction by Wayne C. Booth (Minneapolis: University of Minnesota Press, 1984).

31. Bakhtin, *Problems*, 18.

32. Julia Kristeva, "Word, Dialogue and the Novel," in *Desire in Language* (New York: Columbia University Press, 1980). In this essay Kristeva underlines dialogism as "transgression giving itself a law" (71).

33. Bakhtin, "Discourse and the Novel," in *The Dialogic Imagination*, 366–7.

34. Ibid. 278.

35. This point is elaborated in "The Problem of Speech Genres," in *Speech Genres*.

36. Katerina Clark and Michael Holquist, *Mikhail Bakhtin* (Cambridge: Harvard University Press, 1984).

37. V. N. Vološinov, *Marxism and The Philosophy of Language*, trans. Ladislav Matejka and I. R. Titunik (New York Seminar Press, 1973), 9.

CHAPTER NINE

Film: The Art Form of Late Capitalism

History is not and can never become a seamless narrative. Historical narrative becomes myth when it performs the function of representing society to itself as forgetting and makes present only the surfaces of the material practices that constitute history, recuperating the past for the present. If we view film as ontology rather than representation we can understand how filmic images have shaped our beliefs about the history of the Bolshevik revolution more than the writings of John Reed, Lenin, and Trotsky. The task of the filmmaker, according to Sergei Eisenstein, is to involve the spectator in the process of creating the film. For Eisenstein montage (the creation of a new image from two *partial representations*) solves the problem of making the physical reality palpable without reproducing it. The filmmaker makes the viewer "experience the emergence and assemblage of the image."

By revealing the process as much as the result of the creation of film image, the filmmaker literally produces a new reality rather than merely representing it. Eisenstein and the various schools of Soviet filmmakers strove to achieve a "synchronization of the senses" through the film such that all the elements of perception are woven into whole cloth. For Eisenstein, Vertov, and other filmmakers of the Bolshevik revolution, the task was not to make a report about social reality, but to produce it: "consequently, in the actual method of creating images, a work of art must reproduce the process whereby, *in life itself,* new images are built up in the human consciousness and feelings."[1]

Thus, the international cultural function of the "glorious years" of Soviet art has been to structure our remembrance of the past. For us Eisenstein's *October* is the Russian Revolution, not a representation of it, not a report. Its power to evoke a nostalgia for that which was never present to us yet is part of our political repertoire just as Griffith's *Birth of a Nation* constitutes itself not only in films like *Gone with the Wind* but in the whole political repertoire of the right wing. It is only by deconstructing these films that the structure of desire can be revealed and the desiring machine, to borrow a phrase from Deleuze and Guattari, that "records" and actually creates a mediated reality be surpassed. The real question raised by the political films of the revolution and counterrevolution is the question about the status of film as an object-form of which the entire repertoire of human emotions is the subject-form.

I

In his essay "Americanitis," the pioneering Soviet filmmaker Lev Kuleshov tells how montage was born. Even before the revolution, the Russian film industry was concerned that American films were more popular,

> among audiences than their own. The public *feels* American films. When there is a clever maneuver by the hero, a desperate pursuit, a bold struggle, there is such excited whistling, howling, whooping, and intensity that interested figures leap from their seats, so as to see the gripping action better.[2]

According to Kuleshov, "The success of American motion pictures lies in the greatest common measure of film-ness, in the presence of maximum movement and in primitive heroism, in an organic relationship to contemporaneity." On the other side, Russian films were marked by their "literariness, i.e. the externally actionless (sic) of a given plot." This early theorist of the Soviet film, teacher of Pudovkin and Eisenstein, placed the development of montage, the relentless use of the shears to assemble images from disparate shots (Eisenstein even claimed these shots ought to be "in collision"), within a set of social and commercial problems. The Russian, and subsequently, the Soviet film, was not reaching audiences, while the Americans (particularly Chaplin and Griffith) had captured them.

What is filmness? It differs from photography in that it moves and introduces the temporal dimension. The pre-montage filmmakers had failed to understand these defining characteristics. Individual scenes were too long. They had a static quality. The Americans, it seemed, had solved the problem of film-ness by "shortening the length of each component part of the film, by shooting only the element of movement without which at any given moment a necessary vital action could not occur."[3]

For Soviet filmmakers (most of the leading film theorists were also film workers), the key concepts behind "film-ness" were frequent alternation, editing, and predetermined assemblage of shots, so as to form a scene that produced signification not reflection—and without reflection. The technique, of course, was informed by the manipulation of conventional symbolization. Montage depended on the use of internalized cultural codes and conventions so that images could be comprehended instantly, since the movement of the scene was too fast to allow the critical distance necessary to solve puzzles.

Herein lay the difference between film and other artforms. According to Eisenstein, film stands "at the intersection of nature and industry."[4] The purposive intervention of the film effects a series of collisions between the representation of the physicality of nature and the production/reproduction of life, transforming their separateness into a single ontic fact. The film, posing as mediation, becomes an independent entity. The facticity of the film transcends the integrity of both nature and social life since it consisted in the concatenation of the two into a distinct third. This third, the "physical palpability" of the film, could no more be reduced to its cinematic raw materials, than the machine could be disassembled into the nuts and bolts, the casting and the instruments from which it becomes something else.

I do not believe the analogy of film and the machine to be merely metaphorical. For photography and film are the first art forms in which mechanical reproduction is internal to the form itself. But while photography must be content to reproduce the object as a static image, even as it attempts to simulate movement, the film succeeds "in penetrating deeply into the web" of reality. Benjamin aptly compares the relation of the painter to the camera operator to that between magician and surgeon. While the painter and the magician maintain a respectful distance from reality and thus can gain a "total" picture, the picture obtained by the camera operators "consists of multiple fragments which are assembled under a new law."

Benjamin, however, is still caught in the notion of the film's "representation of reality." What the Soviet filmmakers clearly understood is that filmness is an intervention into reality such that the "real" is utterly transformed by "the permeation of mechanical equipment." We get a new object "free of mechanical equipment" precisely because film tries to abolish the category of mediation.[5]

In different ways, both Benjamin and Brecht rejected the traditional high-cultural distaste for the mechanical reproducibility of the work of art. For the advocate of "authentic" art, the photograph and the film signaled the end of the identification of art with the concrete individual. In fact, as early as the printing press the hand of the writer was absent from the text. When we arrive at photography there is no longer the visible semblance of authorship—the film negative has obliterated the artist's signature.

Benjamin celebrates mechanical reproducibility precisely because it abolishes aura in this sense. Only when we can no longer find the artist appearing as an individual subject in the work of art will the democratization of art be possible. Adorno reflected on this judgment and found that aura is not destroyed by mechanical reproducibility; it has been displaced to the star, who appropriates the original halo.[6] I agree with Adorno that aura remains despite the repetition of images, but the maintenance of aura is not produced by the star's ability to recuperate its traces. Rather, aura lives in the film's power to produce a reality that never was and to represent the never-was as history. Aura lives in montage, as the absence of the deconstructed producer.

The technological apparatus of film does not stand between the observer and the observed in the manner of the photograph, reinterpreting that which is seen. The synchronization of the senses is also the suspension of time, its collapse into spatial relationships. When Eisenstein tells us that he will involve the spectator in the processes of film production, he is achieving more than that. He is transforming our memory into forgetting. *October* is not the representation of the Bolshevik revolution. It is history made present to us as a new reality. The collisions that are worked up in these revolutionary films connect us to a past we have never experienced, but may now produce. Eisenstein will grab our senses; images are all that is left of the revolution. We remember only the action abstracted from its concrete determinations as historical events. What remains in the mind's eye are fragments of faces conjured by the camera's closeups, running masses storming the Winter Palace. Yet this is our Bolshevik revolution. Of course, we know that there were complex economic, political, and social issues fought out in rooms not subject to the camera's eye. But Eisenstein has given us the streets, the conflict—a compression into minutes of the whole historical process. We have relived that which we never lived outside the movie house *as if* that is the way it really was.

Kracauer argues that film differs from the photograph in establishing physical existence by "representing reality as it evolves in time."[7] Of course, it is only a *representation* of time reworked as a sequence of spatial relationships. Film pares history, social structure, social life down to size. Its compression of distances, historical epochs, personal relationships into the span of the two-hour narrative punctuated by fragments, particles of existence metonymically arranged according to conventional symbolisms, simulates the continuous while effectively destroying it. Montage constructs order out of the chaos of history and social life, dragging the spectator under the wheels of a train, cutting to the cab, panning to an entirely different scene and back to the underside of the train in thirty seconds. The totality becomes the filmmaker's "organization of the visible world."[8]

The ability of the Soviet film to problematize history was itself unproblematic for Eisenstein and Vertov. For them montage was a way of expressing ideology as an artform. For Eisenstein montage was "a means before all else of revealing the ideological conception of the film."[9] For he knew that the question was not one of accurately depicting a social and natural reality that was pregiven; the task was to transform consciousness by making the masses remember selectively even that which they may have experienced and by constructing reality rather than reporting it.

Although Eisenstein was prone to evoke painting and literature to support his perspective on film, even going so far as to quote a highly filmic description by Leonardo for a projected painting, there was a sharp break between film and literature implied in montage. Gone were the narrative styles, common in literature, in which the seamless story concealed the contradictions of the social world. For the important filmmakers of the revolutionary period in Soviet history, the film could, through politically informed shooting and editing, reveal the degradation of human existence, showing its stitches and depicting historical upheavals as orderly yet discontinuous events—orderly insofar as the sequences were purposively motivated by the political filmmakers, discontinuous in that conflict could only be "represented" by metaphoric, metonymic, and synecdochic means. Film was the Joseph's coat of art and the filmmaker was a rag picker and then a textile remnant recycler. The object was to render the cloth whole even as the processing machine remains visible. The spectator knows that s/he is experiencing a fiction; however, the camera's lies are like truth, certainly more real than reality, because it evokes a physicality that is palpable.

Although much Soviet filmmaking in this period was modeled after a documentary characterization, a visual newspaper so to speak, it was actually a highly stylized presentation of the ideology of the collective subject, a more or less deliberate abstraction from the details of everyday life—a view of history in which the hero is masses and classes rather than the distraught bourgeois. Or to be more exact, history was the subject, so that the individual or, indeed, the masses were a function of movement, whose exemplification was no more than a moment in the historical process. The documentary was a fiction depicted as historical fact. It was the absence of the individual, as much as the juxtaposition of images, that gave authority to the revolutionary claims of the presentation. The filmmaker, acting for history, pieces together that which is itself unknowable and abstracts from all concrete temporal contexts only those elements that can be made to point in a specific ideological direction.

Those who forget the political aspirations of Soviet filmmakers in the revolutionary period while praising their aesthetic or technical achievements have missed the essential element of these films: they attempt, in theme and form, to reorganize consciousness in accordance with the ideological precepts of revolutionary communism by abolishing the still existing forms of consciousness. The later, degraded films mark the end of the revolutionary phase of Soviet culture and are constructed as paeans to the primacy of administration, now elevated above its dirty bureaucratic manifestation to mythic proportion. Indeed, Eisenstein, in his writings, is constrained to point out that "governments disappear, art remains." Yet, to the last, the main directors of the early period, now significantly eclipsed during the early 1930s in the Soviet film industry by more pedestrian filmmakers, remained wedded to their project. In both periods, Eisenstein, Vertov, and Kuleshov held firm to the objectives of montage and its ideological precepts.

Surely Eisenstein and Vertov have to be distinguished in several respects, especially in their different perceptions of the task of the filmmaker and their actual work. However, the efforts of both to generate a truly revolutionary film are undermined not only by the circumstances under which they labored (the shortage of film stock in the early years of the revolution; the tensions both shared with the party and the administration of the Soviet film industry whose tolerance for experimentation was rather short) but also by the limits intrinsic to film form. For film is the synchronous art form of late capitalism. The film machine is the enemy of time no less than mass production; it reproduces desire as its product, removes the referent, the signified, and leaves only the act of signifying. It removes the critical distance which Brecht correctly understood as the basis for a transformed consciousness that distinguishes the emotions from reason—not only by reorganizing perception but by taking the emotions as raw materials for artistic production. Brecht himself remains as ambivalent as his friend Walter Benjamin about the film as form. While acknowledging that film's "splendid inductive method" provides a level of detail about human existence not available to the "bourgeois novel," he says that the film is the quintessential capitalist art form:

What the film really demands is external action and not introspective psychology. Capitalism operates in this way by taking given needs on a massive scale, exorcizing them, organizing them and mechanizing them so as to revolutionize everything. Great areas of ideology are destroyed when capitalism concentrates on external action, dissolves everything into processes, abandons the hero as the vehicle for everything and mankind as the measure, and thereby smashes the introspective psychology of the bourgeois novel.[10]

It is not only because America had the technological means and massive capital to generate film that may account for its development as a mass form early in the century. The rise of advertising in the US was a consequence of the entrance of the US into its late-capitalist phase; "late" in the sense that the intimate connection between production and consumption had now become the condition for the reproduction of capitalism as such. For the production of the consumer became as important as the production of things. And, in Brecht's terms, taking "needs on a massive scale" and organizing them, "dissolving everything into processes" is the key to creating the new consumer, a task that the ruling classes recognized in the first decades of the century.[11] Brecht's analogy between film and capitalism is not accidental. Late capitalism marks the "mechanization of everything" in order to make itself infinitely reproducible, and film is that art form which requires no ideological justification other than its own production and no legitimation other than its reception. Notwithstanding Brecht's own desire to employ the film for his non-Aristotelian drama, film's "splendid inductive method" reduces everything to particles that are reorganized into sheer process, perpetual motion, and thus problematizes any project tied to critical reason. If Brecht could celebrate film's abolition of the bourgeois subject by its dissolve into pure external motion/action, he could not sustain his own critique because he was among those who regarded capitalism's forces of production as an autonomous and progressive unintended consequence of capital accumulation. Just as Soviet engineers and managers in the 1920s and '30s became devoted followers of Henry Ford and F. W. Taylor, so the critical dramatist could not transcend his own period. For him, Marxism builds on the achievement of the bourgeois epoch, seizing those elements of progress which even the bourgeoisie in its twilight years must repress. If Benjamin was to argue for the democratization of culture in the wake of its degradation in the era of mechanical reproducibility, so Brecht could happily imagine surrendering the tools of the novelist and playwright in order to engage mass needs for socialist ends by becoming a filmmaker.

The logic of capital has generated mass production in which labor is degraded at the work place by rationalized methods, replaced and maimed by machines, and de-skilled by the particlization of tasks. Capital becomes the historical subject of production, appears as the creator of all things and persons. And film, penetrating the web of human needs and emotions, smashes mankind as the measure of all things. Capital/ film tends to rule everything. What the machine achieves at the point of production, the film achieves in the sphere of consumption. The infinite mechanical reproducibility of all objects not only demolishes the bourgeois hero, the introspective subjective consciousness, but separates form from content, lets processes dominate things and makes administration the ruler of art as much as any form of labor.

In the first ten years of the revolution, the official Soviet line called for the expunging of individualism if not individuality. Montage was intended to be more than a technique; it was conceived as nothing less than a way to transcode a world view into the language of film, to piece together the disparate elements of reality into a coherent whole establishing new conventions of visual perception by tying emotions to certain visual and aural effects. Although Eisenstein's well-known debt to Griffith is important to mention, his use of these conventions was intended to oppose the ideological presuppositions of the master since his use of the filmic linguistic codes would be grounded in different social and political a prioris. The question is whether immediate context could transform a series of techniques born within the larger context of the logic of capital.

Film arose from the same sources as nineteenth-century science, the concern with the microscopic particles of matter. If science and industry could harness nature to meet human ends, so could humans be harnessed. Eisenstein and Vertov, each in his own manner, wished to produce revolutionary consciousness on a mass scale. They became the vanguard of the production of a new human, one whose senses are sychronized to the visual. Since the communication processes of film had to at once evoke cultural conventions by montage and reorganize needs by effectively destroying the ideology of the individual and transforming it into a system of external action, the intentions of the filmmaker are systematically subverted by the form. Brecht's wish to escape the static forms of the Aristotelian theater by using this dynamic new vehicle for didactic ends, had to contend with the essentially *American* characteristic of the form. "History is bunk" said Henry Ford, because the past weighs heavily on the shoulders of the capitalist. Mass production wipes out the memory and in its place *produces* the past, just as it produces the future as a version of the present. The assembly line appears to the worker as a series of discrete actions and other workers are similarly serialized. Only "scientific management" can comprehend the whole, now seen as a purposive arrangement of the parts according to criteria that defy the notion of the "organic" unity; the mechanical unity produced by capital is always a pastiche masked as natural object. Nature is subsumed by the production process just as the worker is subsumed by capital in the course of production. From the center of production, capital reduces the worker to a factor of production whose subject is capital. What is remembered becomes the same as what is present since the production process aims only at infinite reproduction.[12]

October presents us with a series of images in which revolution is experienced erotically, that is, as a constant high since excitement is the main emotion. Duration is obliterated even though there is swift movement and the sequence evokes temporality, because there is nothing but action. Yet, true to the program that required the abolition of psychology, of introspection, activities which require spaces for reflection (therefore time that is free of space-filling action), all time is filled by light and dark, music and loud silences, and, later, speech.

Let it be said that Eisenstein is an unwilling conspirator in the mockery that mechanical reproducibility visits upon memory as it transforms it into forgetting. The early Eisenstein is filled with the romance of the masses as makers of history. His revulsion against the bourgeois novel of personal heroism is carried through as the sheer evocation of mass action. Here the difference with Griffith's view that the rise of the masses was tantamount to the end of civilization is most poignant since he cannot avoid participating in the generation of "massification," the hypostatizing of the people as a series of interchangeable parts. Even though Eisenstein's political codes were antagonistic to those of his American teacher, their cultural codes are remarkably similar. Later Eisenstein, as though recognizing this unintended convergence, writes of the primacy of inner speech in the formation of images. Inner speech, the "flow and sequence of thinking unformulated into logical construction" as uttered speech is, lies at the basis of film form. Film attempts to invade the prelogical; its form is the utterance of the prelogical now organized and mechanized by ideological criteria. Eisenstein goes on to make explicit the use of part/whole substitutions in montage and for the first time acknowledges art as a narcotic: "Art is nothing else but an artificial retrogression in the field of psychology towards the forms of earlier thought processes, i.e. a phenomenon identical with any given form of drug, alcohol, shamanism, religion, etc." Art for Eisenstein has a dual unity. On the one side, explicit steps towards the raising of consciousness; simultaneously, the penetration to the prelogical, that is, the unconscious. Then he enters a remarkable defense of the relation between art and the unconscious and the renunciation of the reliance on ideological and didactic criteria for the performance and creation of the work of art, i.e. the film. Eisenstein ascribes film form to the expressive mode, its affective side gains ascendancy over the logical. Thus, Eisenstein's concept of the common basis of all film, which emerges with his refusal to privilege the didactic, corresponds to Brecht's and Benjamin's argument for the power of film, its imperious quality.[13]

The question of whether the means used to produce meaning had become dominant over artistic intention clearly concerned Eisenstein. But his reversion to depth psychology to explain the inversion can only be explained by the permutations of Soviet reality after 1929.

These were years of the passing of the revolutionary phase. The regime was obliged in its period of stability to acknowledge the persistence of the old, prerevolutionary cultural and political forms. This was the period of the Stalinist reversal of the revolutionary experimentation in economics, politics, and art. The task of the Soviet state and Communist Party was to legitimate its link to the Revolution by tying it to prerevolutionary traditions. Literary, architectural, musical, and cinematic modernism were eschewed in the same measure as political and cultural oppositional movements. Mayakovsky, the crown prince of Soviet futurism, committed suicide in 1931, three years before Stalin's literary arbiter Andrei Zhdanov declared "socialist realism" the official party cultural doctrine. For the next twenty-five years, Soviet composers, novelists, and filmmakers were admonished to mine their raw materials from folk culture. The folk idioms became standard form, and tales, legends, and myths the accepted content. "Partyness in art" meant the subordination of the discontinuous to the continuous, the ruptured narrative and the anti-narrative to an epic tale in which the future was depicted as the present, at the same time as the utopian element in art was strictly excluded.[14]

In Eisenstein's 1935 speech, cited above, it was plain that he understood culture as the invariant underpinning of art, just as his earlier position ascribed the production of film to the interaction between the audience and filmmaker. But whereas in the earlier period Eisenstein was speaking exclusively in terms of the formation of social consciousness through film, now the form became subordinate to culture.

Yet depth psychology or, more precisely, the philosophical anthropology of the collective unconscious, is not as important as the processes implicit in the logic of capital and their relation to film as capital's own psychological weapon. It is not a question of ideology, if we mean by that the imposition of a world view upon consciousness. Instead, film generates its own ideology; its way of seeing constitutes technically its ideological parameters. That is, the subsumption of perception, emotion, desire under film's reproductive powers circumscribes experience.

Michael Herr describes the Vietnam War in cinematic terms, a war in which American soldiers try to understand what they are going through in terms of the only references they have for comparison, World War II movies, Westerns, and cartoons. The NAM paradigm is no war movie, for Herr, yet the comparative structures of thought cannot escape the filmness of all contemporary experience. Herr's *Dispatches* is a fragment consisting of fragments that can only evoke the war as a montage whose order can only be inferred from the accumulation of scenes; because Herr only reports, shows the world, he refuses to organize, mechanize, or consciously penetrate its web as does the camera. The war is a series of film cameos in which the reality appears as a film script—always being compared to a John Wayne movie or the film versions of the Battle of Bataan.[15]

Montage opposes duration with a film form of optical effects that are linked to needs that have been produced technologically by the effects themselves. After seventy-five years of the mass produced film, has the audience become the product rather than a participant in the production? Is Eisenstein's overture to depth psychology, written after the golden year, an admission that the experiment gave rise to a Frankenstein? And is his effort to subordinate the film to culture merely an inversion of the actual process by which the culture became an effect of the film?

These are the questions that strike to the roots of the debate about mass culture in general. Marx's description of the reified form in which the logic of production makes labor appear to be the product of capital presupposed an understanding that labor alone could produce value, that its relation to nature was privileged but obscured by the fetish. Yet lived experience does not attain sovereignty; the fetish is the real, and the social relations must be apprehended theoretically, if at all. The transformation of consciousness produced by the rise of film as a dominant cultural form is the other side of the restricted consciousness resulting from the degradation and segmentation of labor. The world is experienced as design and execution, a series not a unity, because craft has disappeared except as a marginal phenomenon in late capitalism. The film-ness of the private sphere is not only produced by "going to the movies" or watching television in the home. The division of private from public itself makes lived experience fragmentary such that the attempt to recapture the whole appears naive.

II

But what of that vilified, marginalized figure of Soviet cinema, Dziga Vertov? Can the claim be made that his differences with Eisenstein are merely tactical? Did he not depart from the montage of Kuleshov and Eisenstein, as Annette Michelson claims, by creating a new epistemology of film, one that may compare with the findings of twentieth-century science in providing a "grasp upon the nature of causality"?[16]

For Michelson, Vertov is incomparable because of his inversion of action, his reversal of time, his "subversion of the cinematic illusion" by means of distortion and abstraction. Michelson finds Vertov stretching the potential of the medium, more, rediscovering reality. But in what does this rediscovery consist? "It is above all...that Vertov has seized upon the trope as a master strategy elevating it to the function of a radical innovation." This point, illustrated but never elaborated, suggests that Vertov's use of figures (the figure of the elegant ladies promenading from a peasant market followed by the freezing of the image and then a portrait of a peasant woman in the market) amounts to a stylistic device, collision/distortion, which removes Vertov from the didactic and into the maieutic.

It is clear that what Michelson and other Vertov commentators like about him is his literariness, his adoption of the figural as a central focus of his film. There is in Vertov, the metacommentator, a kind of reflexivity which is absent in most of his contemporaries. The camera mediates while it constructs reality—the subject-object dichotomy remains because the project of deconstruction does not give way to the vicissitudes of ideological imperatives. Yet we cannot avoid noticing that the brilliant editing of *Man with a Movie Camera*, however dialogic, retains that element of cinema for instruction that animated montage. For while Vertov insists that the screen is a surface, and that the filmmaker must destroy illusions, especially those of linear time and harmonious action, it may not be said that synchrony is, in itself, a virtue. There is, in Vertov's *Man with a Movie Camera*, the trope of the machine, of processes, of the dominance of the rhythmic over things. His juxtapositions are those of the machine age, both in his selection of the machine as the crucial metaphor of the movie which links the cycle of life and the reflexive commentary on the camera as the producer of life itself.

It may be, then, that Vertov was the master of the revolutionary decade of Soviet cinema precisely because he internalized into his art the politics of industrialization, the massification of images, not presented as a fiction, but represented as fact. It is the conscious subsumption of social life under the ethic and imperative of production that marks this film and that made Vertov the supreme documentary filmmaker of the early years of the revolution.

Consider Vertov's treatment of the separation of the private from the public. We see workers at their machines, cut to a group doing gymnastics in the same rhythms as the machine, back to the machine. A few moments later the image of birth—the rhythms of the machine are again evoked. Street scenes: there are no walkers in the city; everyone is swept up in purposive and rapid locomotion. The camera grinds away, reproducing itself and its images in a mechanical hymn.

So, the trope of reproduction comprises the essence of the Soviet spirit, a revolution that must devour its people so as to prevent being devoured by its enemies. This is the age of Gladkov's *Cement*, of music and novels that glorified the factory, of architecture that was proposed in purely functional modes, especially buildings that were designed to represent economy, a break with the lurid past of gargoyles and purely decorative frills. Vertov deconstructs time to show its synchrony; in avoiding the illusion that duration is produced by sequential action, Vertov actually suppresses duration itself—with montage. His disruptions collide with the trope of the machine, which achieves hegemony over the Socratic, the epistemological project. Production, movement, reproduction, these are the causal figures that overcome the distinctions of private and public, rich and poor, birth and death. Vertov is only the most consistent modernist of this era, only the most relentless in erasing the bourgeois subject, the romantic heart of the individual. But there is a substitution of the romance of action, of the surfaces of the naturalness of humans, their lack of distinction with nature and the apparatus. Vertov's depiction of desire is the desiring machine. There are no "needs" that can be specified as uniquely human. We are of one piece with nature.

Vertov does not mess with history. The surface now is all we can speak about. If time can be reversed, if the camera can intervene in social processes, if things can be dissolved by distortion so that materiality becomes pure energy, how does this differ from the fundamental assumptions of contemporary science and technology? Vertov's epistemology is that of the transformation of nature and humans by the machine, the forms of appearance of an essence having now become the totality; even the word "surface," which implies depth, must be abolished.

The revolutionary cinema is, in the last instance, as much a part of its time as it is a shaper of its times. Wishing to "lay the foundations of human kindness," Soviet filmmakers could not themselves escape the profound influence of Soviet economic and political life, "which could not be kind."[17] Art could subvert that reality as long as the artist worked alone, in private rooms. But film has always been, in the first place, an industry. Its "art" is named by theoreticians and by those who make films, but only if one adopts the rather dubious claims of the authorial school of film theory can film's status as art remain unambiguous. Vertov began his career as a documentary filmmaker, perhaps the Soviet Union's most famous journalist. His "reports" were inevitably reconstructions of the news. One of his newsreels, *Kino-Pravda No. 22*, contains these words:

> WE find the soul of machinery, we love the worker sitting at his table, we love the farmer on his his tractor, the engineer in his train.
> WE cause the joy of creation in all mechanical activities
> WE make peace between man and the machine
> WE train the new man.[16]

Vertov was aware that his work bore a close relation to the objectives of the revolution as Lenin characterized them. "Electrification plus planning equals socialism"—that slogan expressed the priority of industrialization for Soviet policy. In a period when the allocation of scarce material resources became a basic issue in the arts, particularly theater and film, Vertov occupied a position of privilege because he had "organized the visible world" as the "organization of motion" through the camera which he said would stop copying reality and start organizing, mechanizing, and otherwise penetrating the real.

This was a period of danger for the new Soviet state. Its existence depended on whether it could "achieve state capitalism" in the poignant reply of Lenin to a critic of the new economic policy that, after 1922, invited the formation of private capital under the watchful eyes of the state. The key to development was the acculturation of the people to industrialization. It was no easy task. Here was a largely peasant population accustomed to hand labor, to a relation with the external world not marked by the ethic of domination. The "new man" had to be put into motion, reorganized, awakened to the task of transforming the world. The image of Soviet man was "a giant shaking the earth," a metaphor of the instrumentalization of nature. It was a scientific attitude that Vertov brought to his task. His was the doctrine of the reduction of things to particles of energy and their quantification, so that the camera, the machine, can rework them to "train the new man" in the Soviet style of the "joy of creation" through mechanical activity.

I am objecting to those who, by aestheticizing Vertov and celebrating his modernism, tear his work out of its historical context. Futurism, a major modernist form in the early Soviet period, anticipated the economic and political project of the revolution—the domination of nature and the transformation of the human being. The preoccupation with surfaces, the exploration of the possibilities of synchrony, and experimentation in technique are all consonant with the demands of Soviet life. The implicit Taylorism of Vertov, his administration of the visible world through the transformation of the camera from observer to producer, may be understood as an important "element," of which conditioned reflex psychology is another, in the effort by the Soviets to move into the twentieth century, skipping the stages of social, political, and economic development experienced by Western European countries. Art served industry in the quest for the domination of nature.

For this was a race against time. "Organic" processes could not be respected because these redounded to the benefit of the enemies of the new Soviet system. Time had to be dominated if survival was to be insured. The ability to control time, of course, is the central task of capital for duration always violates the business of accumulation since, unless harnessed, it shrinks surplus value. Michelson is right, Vertov's grasp of causality proposes a new epistemology—one in which the world is produced; that which *appears* external is merely the object-form of our creative action. What remains problematic is whether technology has become hegemonic in Vertov's conception of knowledge and action, or whether "man" is the subject.

"WE" are the organizers, the trainers, the administrators of the new man. But "WE" are the soul of machinery, capital. Michelson says that

Vertov's camera was engaged in "rendering uncertainty more certain"—
that is, the camera as technology does mediate between the subject (human beings) and the object (nature) but reconstitutes and controls both.

How else could it have been? Can the film be anything but the art
form of late capitalism? Can the distortions of compressed and reversed
time be themselves reversed so that politics may be expressed in and
through film as the determining moment, rather than remaining subsumed under its technological reduction?

III

The films of Ozu and Tanner may be seen as attempts to solve various
problems raised by the employment of montage as a political weapon.
These directors are interested in the social world as both object of investigation and as the context within which humans act. Each of them sees
the task of the film as fostering distance between the audience and the
screen. But the process is not deconstructed as Vertov does in *Man with
a Movie Camera*. Where Vertov insists that the camera operator makes
reality and shows the possibilities of reordering the visible world through
film, Ozu violates this accepted code of external action and tries to make
the camera the servant of the human drama unfolding. The camera moves
slowly as we watch family life in modern Japan dissolve under the weight
of urbanization and migration. As we view such films as *Tokyo Story, Late
Spring*, and others, we are conscious of duration, of the details of daily
life that are suppressed in the apparent flood of details in an Eisenstein or
Vertov film. While Soviet film was written on a large canvas but divided
the world into particles, in a manner not unlike the physicist who tries to
find the ultimate unit of matter so as to manipulate it for human ends,
Ozu tries to capture a totality, even if necessarily partial and unfulfilled.
His narrative attempts to open up the spaces of perception, by granting
the spectator the chance for reflection. It is as if his camera is struggling
with film-ness, to negate its inevitable march. The portrayal of the intimate details of private life, such as the folding of sheets and towels on a
bed, the repressed argument between husband and wife, the brooding
rebellion of a daughter against her parents, the painful distance created
by the city between family members, the awkwardness of death, this is

the stuff of which social time is made. And it is slow, deliberate, reluctant time as against natural time that dissolves everything, including life.

It cannot be claimed that Ozu wins the struggle against the film of optical effects. Duration is simulated by montage, for example, the activity of toenail cutting, of train riding, the training of the camera on family photographs which achieves a consonance between the photo stills and the stillness of the camera. In the end, we are surprised by Ozu's films because he tries, more or less aggressively, to deny the intrinsic characteristic of film imputed to it by nearly all worker and theoretician movements. Ozu is the filmmaker of the nostalgia for spaces that are not taken up in the frantic motion of life. For him life is to be fondled, dock-time fought. When he employs the seasons as a metaphor for the cycle of life, there is a savoring of the turning of the leaves, the changes in weather, but there is a sadness too.

At first glance, Ozu appears the arch-conservative. His shooting style, as Donald Richie shows in his excellent account of Ozu's work, is free of optical effects. "The camera rarely pans..., fades in and fades out are seldom found..., and dissolves are very rare."[19] Moreover, Ozu believed that the dissolve "is a form of cheating." He tried to reproduce the natureness of life by denying film-ness, at least in the terms that most Soviet filmmakers would comprehend the meaning of the word. His is not a film of surfaces: he tries to depict the depths of emotion rather than organizing these emotions into processes. Thus Ozu considers editing the least important phase of film production, for his is an art of words and images in which the camera is silent, or at least relegated to the role of observer.

The sharpest issue raised by Ozu's work is whether the film can avoid Americanitis. His scenes are long, the action is progressive not regressive. There is an effort to construct a story, sequentially linear yet fraught with significance that is expressed within the terms of the narrative rather than through technical gyrations. That is, meaning is produced by the interaction of the characters, by their relation to the social context, their work, and their family life and their collision with the seasons, with living and dying, growth and decay.

Ozu, unlike the Soviet filmmakers, is preoccupied by modernity, intensely worried about it. Since his is the collective subject, the family, its disintegration marks the foregrounding of the machine as the new subject. It is as if the technique is made to express the loathing of technique itself by minimizing the filmness of the film. Nevertheless, Ozu is inhibited by the form. One senses the tension between his film-paintings and photographs and the wish of the medium to move; the stillness of the images cannot avoid suggesting what is absent in the films' movement. The weapons of the filmmaker are there amid his contemplations, but they are expressed photographically as a series of frames rather than as particles in motion, yet it is the movement of the everyday that, in the end, penetrates the spectator's desire for action. Ozu's meticulous attention to details forces him to come to terms with industrial society; the collision is between the stillness of the family, its rootedness in traditions, and the waves of the machine in motion. Motion is produced by the man looking out a train window so that even if motion is backgrounded, it is present. There is a kind of tension impossible on the stage because the stage cannot reveal the subtleties of facial expression. It is here that the storms rage—in the pain of the parents whose child has renounced their way of life, in the tense face of the professional whose work is ever in conflict with the sedate style of the traditional Japanese family, or the tranquility of two older persons sitting on a stone fence overlooking the water, their hands not touching, but plainly in communion with each other.

Despite the renunciation of montage, Ozu succeeds, perhaps against his wishes, in producing a kind of ideology, the imaginary relation of the older generation to the reality of urbanism and industrialism. He affirms that which can no longer be, privileging the past as the dream forever deferred by the mechanical present. The everyday has the force of the concrete, while the city is portrayed as the abstract, a smoky alien world whose landscape stands as an ugly reminder of what humans have brought upon themselves. We see an exterior of a railstation in *Tokyo Story* with hundreds of persons on the platform passively waiting to board the train. The very city glorified in its mechanical motion for Vertov becomes a grim reminder to us all of what we have lost in our quest for salvation through material rewards. Thus, there is *general* montage in Ozu's films, produced not by cutting, panning, and dissolves but by contrast between fully realized scenes, in which the judgment of the director is made perfectly clear. Ozu privileges the personal, the private, the routines of ordinary existence. His is the desire for the peace that was said to be the legacy of the "old man," a looking backward that remains synchronous and repetitive but now disguised as narrative. Ozu is still caught in the problem of film as such. As metonymic as his Soviet adversaries, he has selected images of family history, produced a silent tirade against the present and offered a future in which the present is eternal except in the vivid remembrance of those things he offers us as the legacy of the past. It is a pastoral image of the past, heightened in its palpable physical existence by means of the contrasts we are offered to a present plainly inferior and degraded. Just forty years after the golden age of Soviet cinema, which gloried the present as the future, Ozu has provided a commentary that reverses time and, like the painter, recalls the wholeness that the machine has disrupted. As in the later Eisenstein, culture is privileged over the camera and humans over the machine.

IV

Tanner's solution to the problem of creating a political film may be the most successful, if our criterion hinges upon reflexivity and thus critical distance. Certainly, as Robert Stam points out, *Jonah* is not free of flaws from the perspective of political content. But Tanner is aware of the contradictions within his project: he is trying to make a political statement to a wide audience at a time when social movements have foundered and when capitalism has entered a stabilized phase. There is an effort to link the private with the public sphere in both *La Salamandre* and *Jonah* by infusing the routines of daily life with political conversation, with the grievances of inflation and degraded labor. Tanner tries to combine respect for the routines of daily life (the art of purchasing cigarettes) and montage (the combination of songs with conversation, scenes of differing lengths juxtaposed to produce discontinuous action), a sense of rupture in the organization of the film so that narrative linearity is broken. It is plain that *Jonah* tries to slow down the action while remaining playful and evoking the unexpected. There are long political conversations among the eight people who live in the country together, but are forced, in various ways, to live in the regular world, so that the imaginary and the real have materializations in the binary of country and city without the former assuming a privileged place.

Above all; Tanner plays in the interstices of fragment and imposes temporal juxtapositions and spatial decentering—thus working between the antinomies of the opposing tradition from which he draws. Stam has remarked that Tanner follows Godard in producing a deconstructed film, one in which the camera, the technique, is brought to the surface and the narrative disruptions, the jagged edges of the flow, call attention to the "art" so as to demystify it.[20] Tanner is careful not to foreground past or future, but to locate each of their fates in the present—a present tormented by the contradiction between advanced sensibilities and the objective possibilities of action where the future has an edge only because children are part of the community. Yet, he is scrupulous to force the spectator out of chains of romantic illusions. The images are those of dynamic stasis, at least on the surface. Thus the real subject of the film is desire, not the desiring machine that reproduces its own emotions as the objects of self-exploitation, but as hope. In Tanner, the utopian side of art is revealed in the refusal of the characters to submit to their degraded jobs, their lost chances, or the barriers that threaten their existence. Of course, the overcoming is not, properly speaking, revolutionary because there is no collective action that goes beyond particular grievances. But the possibility for action, however molecular, is shown in the form of a local struggle against land speculators who threaten to displace the communards who are the protagonists of the film.

Tanner relentlessly refuses nostalgia and retains a realism in the midst of his exploration of modernism: the frequent quotations from other films are an acknowledgment of his debt to tradition; the refusal to pose solutions makes this a film of disrupted action in which, as if to remind us that external action mystifies, Tanner insists that the narrative pause so that the spectators may ponder what has occurred; the juxtaposition of the splice with the still makes a statement about the contradictions in creating a political film that also sells.

Jonah feels like a gentle likeable film because there are no personified villains and all of the people are really like us: slightly absurd, troubled, wondering how we can insert ourselves in history, or alternatively, become free of it. However, I would like to assert that its profoundly troubled tone is not only a reflection of questions without answers about our political time, or the impossibility of elevating the everyday as Ozu has done to a new totality, but a sign that the political film remains problematic because the form is problematic. Or, the form is not inherently compatible with a socialist or radical art, yet socialist artists cannot avoid working with it.

Tanner has denounced history as narrative, has tried to make us remember that art is constructed and that life is disrupted, that linearity is an ideological production, and even the coherent is myth. But he is constrained to link the unlinkable, just as Godard, Eisenstein, and Vertov must in order to capture an audience for whom duration is a threat to the contemporary human project of forgetting. Perhaps unintentionally, Tanner has offered us what amounts to a protagonist. He is a socialist and a teacher who works to integrate his politics into his pedagogy. In a brilliant scene the teacher is trying to explain both the history and mechanism of capitalist development, so that his young students may not forget that the present is not immutable. Tanner wants us to remember history, but his teacher can only *tell* us that history is forgetting and to remember the way in which Western lives are built on the misery of others, to remember that plunder forms the bases of capitalist wealth. Once again we are reminded how the past may be constructed coherently imagistically, but it is the filmmaker who has produced the past. This paradox, that history needs images to make itself present is played as a counterpoint to the rest of the film. As a critical interruption it contains both subversive and integrative elements. For to produce history as ideology an imagined past which instructs rather than generating myths, undermines the imagined naturalness of the present by insisting on its temporality and origins. In the lesson Tanner introduces a length of sausage links to symbolize the continuities and disruption of history. Yet, the lesson has no context; it is sprung upon the class as a disruption, a surprise intended to draw us back, in the end a theatrical device. The motion of the film, the inevitability that it must move on, promotes the forgetting of even the content of the history lesson. All that remains is the long sausage, Tanner's symbolic leitmotif for the continuities of social existence. The sausage embodies the teacher's father, a butcher, the object form in which history presents itself to us metonymic, decontextualized, ephemeral, yet above all continuous. The insistence on the continuity as well as the discontinuity of history marks off Tanner from other filmmakers. For cinematic modernism consists in its inversion of reification—it posits the fragment, the surface, the facticity of things as a partial totalization. That is, the film as form occludes essences. Its law is the sum of appearances, rich in their detail, yet curiously hollow.

What Tanner has done is to live inside the contradiction of film as form because he cannot refuse it. Together with Ozu he has refused to abandon the search for depth and therein lies his strength. Unlike Ozu he recognizes that modernism is the characteristic modality of contemporary cinema, indeed of all twentieth-century art. Just as, after Schoenberg, our music cannot return to the classic style, except, as in Stravinsky, as irony, the film cannot be truly novelistic.

V

Let us now turn to Bertolucci's *1900*, where we find that the attempt to create a political film as a nineteenth-century saga lapses into the soap opera—a left-wing *Gone with the Wind*. Bertolucci's solution to the problem of generating a political film in times of revolutionary defeat is a return to the romantic mode. When events cannot circumscribe history, when the times are not ripe for the ruptures that mark great historical leaps, the past once more becomes a model for future activity, albeit a decoded past. For *1900* is history, a narrative in which disruptions are suppressed and time appears to recover duration. This is a family chronicle set in industrializing northern Italy where the idyllic relations of semi-feudal agriculture give way to capitalism and mechanization. On the one side, Bertolucci has restored the organic civilization, the cliche of all romantic anti-capitalism. On the other side, he condenses all the contradictions of modernization, that felicitous word that describes the sundering of the private and the public, the replacing of human labor by the machine, the struggle of the peasantry to maintain solidarity against the absentee landlord-capitalist and against its own proletarian existence. But Bertolucci's story is the failure of a new public creed, socialism, to weld the proletariat into a coherent political force for restoring solidarity. Berto-lucci brilliantly quotes the great film commentator on Italian fascism, Pasolini, to show the link between capitalism and sadism, but transforms this powerful montage (the third here is fascism) into evidence that, un-der capitalism, the only option available for those who wish to transcend the barbaric present is a retreat to private life.

Lacking the ruptured unity that may produce (and be produced by) a revolutionary subject, *1900* degenerates into the abstract myth of the lordship/bondage relation. It nullifies history by reducing it to the struc-tural relation of domination/dependence between the two families whose symbiotic relation it has traced. The failure of the revolution, its defeat by fascism, masked as modernism, leaves nothing but the eternal strug-gle for mutual recognition. Bertolucci's regression to a "genre" of film is an admission that the heroic epoch is over, at least for the time being, and that the political film as epic is not possible.

Thus we have arrived at a point when the political filmmaker tries to transcode politics into the discourse of the bestseller—attesting to the end of a political art that can generate its own forms in a world in which both politics and art have become problematic as subversive activities. *1900* is a testament to the depoliticization of the audience insofar as mass culture reveals, however unintentionally, as much about its recep-tion as about its production. If politics can be tolerated only within dia-chronic and sometimes sentimental modality whose underpinnings are "realistic" in the nineteenth-century meaning of the term, it may signify the surrender of a politics of form to the extent that revolutionary art has always insisted that forms are themselves a content that requires over-turning. Bertolucci refuses Eisenstein who may be the canonical figure of the political film, not for the authoritarianism of his formal innova-tions (an objection that might have occurred to another artist who wish-es to make a metacommentary on the "organization of the visible world" that excludes critique), but for reasons having to do with the necessity of having to come to terms with new conditions of reception as well as the political economy of production. For, in regard to its distribution, this is a film which must address the ennui of the post-1968 middle strata in all advanced capitalist societies.

For this is not a period in which revolution appears to be a serious alternative to the crisis. On the contrary, the left in Europe presents itself as a better manager of the crisis. Its argument, that the old liberal coalitions that have ruled the major Western European countries since the War, have failed to provide a framework for meeting the needs of the working classes and the middle strata, does not imply the disruption of history. It is not so much that Bertolucci has produced a bad film for reasons having to do with the deficiencies of his art; the social and historical framework has changed. The student generation of the 1960s has now taken its place in various bureaucracies in the social liberal governments, the trade unions of white collar and professional employees and the institutions of mass communications. Those who occupied the barricades of a decade ago and found in the films of Eisenstein and French and Italian neo-realism a spiritual equivalent to political activism, are now seeking a new language of spiritual confirmation. It remains to be seen whether the language of Bertolucci succeeds in providing this confirmation. But the comparisons between *1900* and the 1950s are inevitable. This export film can no longer foreground the revolution or even the process of the class struggle's emergence from the idyllic relations of the feudal system of mutual obligations. Instead, this epochal transformation at the beginning of the twentieth century is counterpointed with the drama of personal ties between a family of owners and a single peasant family. Historical transformation becomes the context in which the codes of personal interactions are worked through.

The conventional narrative structure of the Hollywood film is preserved, presumably the *sine qua non* of mass audience reception since the 1920s. The public and private realms do not connect with one another, despite the illusion of their connection; the narrative is produced by simply establishing a metaphorical relation between public and private. Unlike the modernist expressionism of the early postwar French avant-garde, *1900* eschews all codes of ambiguity, save the irreconcilability between the code of friendship and the code of class conflict. The focus on "content"—the storyline which may easily be described—precludes a metalevel of discourse such as are provided by making time an arbitrary category and representing or foregrounding the social structure of the society or even the farm by any device besides the rather obvious symbolic imagery employed. Bertolucci has chosen to suspend the vertical density of both social relations and social structure. The popular, novelistic character of the film excludes such considerations.

It may be argued that the narrative has been permitted to unfold in accordance with its own inner logic. The bold interventions of both the political filmmakers of the revolutionary period after World War I and those of the 1960s were attempts to generate ideology rather than permitting the actors to work out the logic of their situation. But Bertolucci is no Tanner or Ozu. These are not efforts to elevate everyday life, its slow routines in that dense, thick texture in which events are folded into the minute practices of social reproduction. In *1900* narration has remained episodic. The camera and editing shears no less active in the occlusion of the everyday. What we have here is the simulation of ordinary existence mediated by American stars, melodramatics, and asymbolic closure that itself produces ideology in the guise of rapportage. The camera, to be sure, shoots as if the flatness of labor is to become the subject of the action. But the representation of work is, as in all commercial films, truncated, prettified by the voiceover of the film-director, that is, denied its own rhythms and backgrounded in the service of the narrative. Its representation is always focused upon scenes where the plot is the principal center of interest.

It is the subordination of all action to the plot that marks this film as ultimately within the genre of Hollywood bestseller. Gone are the efforts of a Godard or the neo-realists to make degradation present to us, or of Vertov's proposed emergence of a new historical subject. Bertolucci's film is about films about families that were important in the American culture industry of the 1950s and have returned on US television in the 1970s. He has, through the device of the historical narrative, linked politics with the nostalgia for family dynasty, or at least the collective desire to order the world in terms of private existence that can have meaning as geneology corresponding to Alex Haley's *Roots*. Insofar as *1900* suggests the possibility of a simple origin from which we may recover the self, it falls within the emergent genre which dignifies the slave as slave.

The reversal of the political that occurs in this film is the privileging of the private existence, the subordination of the macro- to the micro-social level rather than following the line of the neo-realists who represented the details of daily existence as the concrete universals of a ravaged postwar Italy.

VI

Can the film be an oppositional artform? This is not merely the question of whether the political film is possible, and under what circumstances. Rather if a central problem of social life in the twentieth century is the forgetting that is produced by an art that has renounced essences, continuous time in favor of the rupture, then film itself must be interrogated.

But it will not do to merely condemn film as the quintessential mass cultural form and reduce it to an industry. Such a course privileges an anterior art, one that corresponds to handicraft production. Just as it is not possible, even on ecological grounds to argue for the return to the handloom, the horse and buggy, or the guild system, so painting, poetry, and the novel cannot replace the photograph and the film. These late forms have inserted themselves in our world so indelibly that even the earlier arts are subsumed under them. We can only notice the relative autonomy of the artisan mode of artistic production in the context of late capitalism. The novel that wishes to escape from the cinematic becomes a mere inversion, an antinomy so to speak, of the film. A novel like John Hawkes's *Second Skin* has the mark of stasis, abstract because it fails to come to terms with the hegemony of its antagonists.

Yet it cannot be claimed that all inversions are futile. Ozu's inversion works within the film form and his violation of the code of movement of disrupted time, of montage as defining element of cinematography, is all the more oppositional precisely because these characteristics of film are the absent presence. His reversal of classic film form is startling and calls attention to the juxtaposition of film and industrialism. Just as the black person on a poster labelled "black is beautiful" is caught in the contradiction between the master's standards of beauty and the servant's desire to assert otherness boldly, Ozu's painterly films cannot avoid the discourse of the machine. This play of contradictions may define the limits of oppositional art in our epoch. In a period in which disruptions, juxtapositions, that is, modernism, has become the cliched art, the assertion of the continuous becomes oppositional, however much we cannot return to Dickens or Tolstoy.

But Ozu and Tanner succeed in going beyond the assertion of unreflexive otherness which only shows the cracks in the smooth surfaces of cliches. Although making the protagonist of a film or novel gay (a recent example, *Outrageous*, succeeds in calling the codes of heterosexual love into question) or black marks an advance towards the politicization of film while remaining within the form's constraints, these filmmakers achieve something more. Their presentation of the everyday violates the routine film practice of abstraction from the details of ordinary existence in order to generate the heroic, to make film characters larger than life. The film that shows the ordinary points to the surreal that is endemic in all film, its "asphalt-paving" character in which the cobblestones of history are enshrouded.[21] Thus the didactic element is restored in *Jonah* and *Tokyo Story* by reminding us that life is boring, reminding us of our own times, where revolution appears suspended, where the ruptures are concealed in the everyday.

Since administered capitalism tends to suppress the ordinary, making it an aspect of the general forgetting, and allows us to remember only the highlights of life, the film becomes oppositional not only when it attempts to go beyond the technicism of cinematic modernism without returning to the romantic narrative, but also becomes a political statement when it points to the ruptures by slowing the camera down.

But, can the film create an anti-cinematic language, one in which the form itself is not merely subverted, but is appropriated, in Enzensberger's terms, by a counterhegemonic politics? In raising this issue, we are forced to return to the debates in the early years of the Russian Revolution concerning the possibilities of a proletarian art. Recall Trotsky's argument: In the prolonged transition from capitalism to socialism, there can be no proletarian art, if by such a term we mean an art that creates its own language/culture embodying the determinate negation of bourgeois art. Trotsky may have gone too far in asserting only the possibility of appropriating existing bourgeois forms for revolutionary education. His point that the proletariat cannot create its own culture because the negation of the bourgeois epoch entails the destruction of the proletariat as well as the elimination of its class enemy proved too optimistic in the wake of historical events. Yet his central point remains persuasive: the ruling ideas of any epoch are the ideas of the ruling class. Its culture will subsume opposition as long as the conditions of capital's reproduction remain.[22]

What is objectionable about Trotsky's argument is that it remains, at the core, one-sided. The subsumption of art by capital, even the creation of art forms by capital is always a two-sided process. On the one side, the logic of subsumption prevents the formation of oppositional artistic languages, just as this logic prevents the working class, gays, blacks, and all others locked in capital's orbit from establishing their own hegemony *before* the revolution. But, capital can never completely pave the cobblestones nor can the unconscious remain repressed by the superego. An oppositional art emerges from the cracks in the hegemony of dominant culture, from the insertion of the other into public sphere dominated by capital. For while this insertion lays the groundwork for administration and integration of the other into the dominant language and culture, it also makes the invisible visible in a way that allows for new forces to emerge. Such is the history of the formation of trade unions: workers' struggles were legalized and made subject to capital's requirement that the price of labor power become merely a "factor" of production; at the same time, they signal the self-organization of the class, the first step to its political self-representation. Similarly, the dialectic of discontinuity/continuity places severe restrictions on the conditions for artistic hegemony. The politicization of filmmakers, like the radicalization of a fragment of the technocracy, subverts the rule of capital from within the apparatus. This is by no means a proletarian art, any more than Eisenstein or Vertov were aspects of the working class itself. Even if a working-class culture is impossible to realize in the same way that bourgeois culture has been victorious, the struggle for that counter-hegemonic culture within and without the dominant forms of political and cultural discourse, remains necessary if emancipatory politics is to become possible.

NOTES

1. Sergei Eisenstein, *Film Sense* (New York: Harcourt, Brace and Jovanovich, 1942), 18.

2. Lev Kuleshov, "Americanitis," in *Kuleshov on Film* (Berkeley: University of California Press, 1974), 127.

3. Ibid., 128.

4. Sergei Eisenstein, *Film Form* (New York: Harcourt, Brace and Jovanovich, 1949), 46.

5. Walter Benjamin, "The Work of Art in the Age of Mechanical Reproduction," in *Illuminations* (New York: Schocken, 1969).

6. Ibid.

7. Siegfried Kracauer, *Theory of Film* (New York: Oxford University Press, 1960).

8. Dziga Vertov, quoted in Judith Mayne, "Man with a Movie Camera," *The Minnesota Review* (Spring 1976).

9. Eisenstein, *Film Form.*

10. *Brecht on Theatre*, ed. and trans. John Willett (New York: Hill and Wang, 1966), 50.

11. Stewart Ewen, *Captains of Consciousness* (New York: McGraw-Hill, 1976).

12. Harry Braverman, *Labor and Monopoly Capital* (New York: Monthly Review Press, 1974), and Roman Rosdolsky, *The Making of Marx's Capital* (London: Pluto Press, 1977).

13. Eisenstein, *Film Form*, especially "Film Form: New Problems," 122–49.

14. Ibid.

15. Michael Herr, *Dispatches* (New York: Alfred Knopf, 1978).

16. Annette Michelson, "The Man with a Movie Camera: From Magician to Epistemologist," *Art Form*, 7 (March 1972), 60–72.

17. The quotation is from Bertolt Brecht's poem "To Posterity."

18. Quoted in Seth Feldman, *Evolution of Style in the Early Work of Dziga Vertov* (New York: Arno Press, 1975), 85.

19. Donald Richie, *Ozu* (Berkeley: University of California Press, 1974), 105. Space does not allow extensive commentary on Marc Holthof's evaluation of Ozu's work as "reactionary" (see *JumpCut*, 18). Suffice it to say that Holthof's Marxism reads films as exemplars of "hidden ideology," consisting principally in their content. Ozu is depicted as a sentimentalist whose efforts to preserve the feudal traditions, particularly the family, from their rout by capitalism and, at the same time, to keep the customers attending the film. Such a perspective justifies the charges of those who criticize Marxist views of culture as reductionist. While appearing to be concerned with form, Holthof merely regurgitates the same old ideological critique of Marxist orthodoxy whereby ideology is viewed as "false consciousness" in the service of profit.

20. Robert Stam, "Tanner's *Jonah*," *JumpCut*, 17.

21. The reference here is to the paving of the cobblestone streets of Paris's fifth arrondissement by the authorities after the May 1968 student/worker uprisings.

22. Leon Trotsky, *Literature and Revolution* (New York: International Publishers, 1924).

CHAPTER TEN

Against Schooling: Education and Social Class

The crisis in American education, on the one hand, announces the bankruptcy of progressive education, and, on the other hand, presents a problem of immense difficulty because it has arisen under the conditions and in response to the demands of a mass society.

—Hannah Arendt, 1961

Americans have great expectations of their schools. We tend to invest them with the primary responsibility for providing our children with the means by which they may succeed in an increasingly uncertain work world. Moreover, if the child fails to be inducted, through academic discipline, into the rituals of labor, we blame teachers and school administrators. Indirectly, schools have been burdened with addressing many of the world's ills. Along with two world wars and various revolutions, the twentieth century witnessed great hopes for democracy but experienced its demise in the wake of the rise of many dictatorships. We knew that education was the key to technological transformation, which became the main engine of economic growth. Schooling was a bulwark of secularism, but that function has buckled under the onslaught produced by the revival of religious fundamentalism. And in almost every economically "developed" country, we count on schools to smooth the transition of huge populations from rural to urban habitats, from "foreign" languages and cultures to English and Americanism.

At the dawn of the new century, no American institution is vested with a greater role in bringing the young and their parents into the modernist regime than are public schools. The common school is charged with the task of preparing children and youth for their dual responsibilities to the social order: citizenship and—perhaps its primary task–labor. On the one hand, in the older curriculum on the road to citizenship in a democratic, secular society, schools are supposed to transmit the jewels of the Enlightenment, especially literature and science. On the other, students are to be prepared for the work world by means of a loose but definite stress on the redemptive value of work; the importance of family; and, of course, the imperative of love and loyalty to one's country. Under the Enlightenment's concept of citizenship, students are, at least putatively, encouraged to engage in independent, critical thinking.

But the socializing functions of schooling play to the opposite idea: Children of the working and professional and middle classes are to be molded to the industrial and technological imperatives of contemporary society. Students learn science and mathematics not as a discourse of liberation from myth and religious superstition but as a series of algorithms, the mastery of which is presumed to improve the student's logical capacities, with no aim other than fulfilling academic requirements. In most places the social studies do not emphasize the choices between authoritarian and democratic forms of social organization, or democratic values, particularly criticism and renewal, but instead are disseminated as bits of information that have little significance for the conduct of life. Perhaps the teaching and learning of world literature in which some students are inspired by the power of the story to, in John Dewey's terms, "reconstruct" experience are a partial exception to the rule that for most students high school is endured rather than experienced as a series of exciting explorations of self and society.[1]

Fiscal exigency and a changing mission have combined to leave public education in the United States in a chronic state of crisis. For some the main issue is whether schools are failing to transmit the general intellectual culture, even to the most able students. What is at stake in this critique is the fate of America as a civilization—particularly the condition of its democratic institutions and the citizens who are, in the final analysis, responsible for maintaining them. Hannah Arendt goes so far as to ask whether we "love the world" and our children enough to devise an educational system capable of transmitting the salient cultural traditions. Other critics complain that schools are failing to fulfill the promise to working-class students, black, Latino, and white, of equality of opportunity for good jobs. Although such critics are concerned with addressing the class bias of schooling, they unwittingly reinforce it by ignoring its content. The two positions, both with respect to their goals and to their implied educational philosophies, may not necessarily be contradictory, but their simultaneous enunciation produces considerable tension, for, with exceptions to be discussed later in this chapter, the American workplace has virtually no room for dissent and individual or collective initiative not sanctioned by management. The corporate factory, which includes sites of goods and symbolic production alike, is perhaps the nation's most authoritarian institution. But any reasonable concept of democratic citizenship requires an individual who is able to discern knowledge from propaganda, is competent to choose among conflicting claims and programs, and is capable of actively participating in the affairs of the polity. Yet the political system offers few opportunities, beyond the ritual of voting, for active citizen participation.[2]

Even identifying the problem of why and how schools fail has proven to be controversial. For those who would define mass education as a form of training for the contemporary workplace, the problem can be traced to the crisis of authority—particularly school authority. That some of the same educational analysts favor a curriculum that stresses critical thinking for a small number of students in a restricted number of sites is consistent with the dominant trends of schooling since the turn of the twenty-first century. In its quest to restore authority, conservative educational policy has forcefully caused schools to abandon, both rhetorically and practically, the so-called child-centered curriculum and pedagogy. Instead, it favors a series of measures that not only hold students accountable for passing standardized tests and for a definite quantity of school knowledge (on penalty of being left back from promotion or expelled) but also impose performance-based criteria on administrators and teachers. For example, in New York City the schools chancellor has issued "report cards" to principals and has threatened to fire those whose schools do not meet standards established by high-stakes tests. These tests are the antithesis of critical thought. Their precise object is to evaluate the student's ability to imbibe and regurgitate information and to solve problems according to prescribed algorithms. A recent agreement between the New

York City Department of Education and the teachers' union offers economic incentives to teachers whose students perform to preestablished testing standards, a sharp departure for a union that has traditionally contended that "merit"-pay schemes destroy solidarity.

On the other side, the progressives, who misread John Dewey's educational philosophy as meaning that the past need not be studied too seriously, have offered little resistance to the gradual vocationalizing and dumbing down of the mass education curriculum. In fact, historically they were advocates of making the curriculum less formal; reducing requirements; and, on the basis of a degraded argument that children learn best by "doing," promoting practical, work-oriented programs for high school students. Curricular deformalization was often justified on interdisciplinary criteria, which resulted in watering down course content and deemphasizing writing. Most American high school students, in the affluent as well as the "inner-city" districts, may write short papers, which amount to book reviews and autobiographical essays, but most graduate without ever having to perform research and write a paper of considerable length. Moreover, in an attempt to make the study of history more "relevant" to students' lives, since the late 1960s the student is no longer required to memorize dates; he may have learned the narratives but is often unable to place them in a specific chronological context. Similarly, economics has been eliminated in many schools or taught as a "unit" of a general social studies course. And if philosophy is taught at all, it is construed in terms of "values clarification," a kind of ethics in which the student is assisted in discovering and examining her own values.

That after more than a century of universal schooling the relationship between education and class has once more been thrust to the forefront is just one more signal of the crisis in American education. The educational left, never strong on promoting intellectual knowledge as a substantive demand, clings to one of the crucial precepts of progressive educational philosophy: under the sign of egalitarianism, the idea that class deficits can be overcome by equalizing access to school opportunities without questioning what those opportunities have to do with genuine education. The access question has been in the forefront of higher education debates since the early 1970s; even conservatives who favor vouchers and other forms of public funding for private and parochial schools have justified privatizing instruction on the grounds of access.

The structure of schooling already embodies the class system of society, and for this reason the access debate is mired in a web of misplaced concreteness. To gain entrance into schools always entails placement into that system. "Equality of opportunity" for class mobility is the system's tacit recognition that inequality is normative. In the system of mass education, schools are no longer constituted to transmit the Enlightenment intellectual traditions or the fundamental prerequisites of participatory citizenship, even for a substantial minority. Although acquiring credentials that are conferred by schools remains an important prerequisite for many occupations, the conflation of schooling with education is mistaken. Schooling is surely a source of training, both by its disciplinary regimen and its credentialing system. But schools do not transmit a "love for the world" or "for our children," as Arendt suggests; instead, contrary to their democratic pretensions, they teach conformity to the social, cultural, and occupational hierarchy. In our contemporary world, they are not constituted to foster independent thought, let alone encourage independence of thought and action. School knowledge is not the only source of education for students—perhaps not even the most important source.

On the contrary, in black and Latino working-class districts, schools are, for many students, way stations more to the military or to prison than to the civilian paid labor force. As Michelle Fine observes, "Visit a South Bronx high school these days and you'll find yourself surrounded by propaganda from the army/navy and marines.... Look at the 'stats' and you'll see that seventy percent of the men and women in prison have neither a GED nor a diploma; go to Ocean Hill-Brownsville 40ish years later, and you'll see a juvenile justice facility on the very site that they wanted to a build their own schools" (personal communication). In the current fiscal crisis afflicting education and other social services, there is an outstanding exception: Prisons continue to be well funded, and despite the decline of violent crimes in the cities, drug busts keep prisons full and rural communities working.

Young people learn, for ill as well as good, from popular culture, especially music; from parents and family structure; and, perhaps most important, from their peers. Schools are the stand in for "society," the aggregation of individuals who, by contract or by coercion, are subject to governing authorities, in return for which they may be admitted into the world, albeit on the basis of different degrees of reward. To the extent that they signify solidarity and embody common dreams, popular culture, parents, and peers are the worlds of quasi-communities that are more powerful influences on their members.

Access to What?

In the main, the critique of education has been directed to the question of access, particularly in terms of the credentials that presumably open up the gates to higher learning or better jobs. Generally speaking, critical education analysis focuses on the degree to which schools are willing and able to open their doors to working-class students because, through their mechanisms of differential access, schools are viewed as, perhaps, the principal reproductive institutions of economically and technologically advanced capitalist societies. With some exceptions, most critics of schooling have paid scant attention to school authority; to the conditions for the accumulation of social capital—the intricate network of personal relations that articulate occupational access; or to cultural capital—the accumulation of the signs, if not the substance, of kinds of knowledge that are markers of distinction.

The progressives assume that the heart of the class question is whether schooling provides working-class kids with equality of opportunity to acquire legitimate knowledge and marketable academic credentials. They have adduced overwhelming evidence that contradicts schooling's reigning doctrine: that despite class, race, or gender hierarchies in the economic and political system, public education provides every individual with the tools to overcome conditions of birth. In reality, only about a quarter of people of working-class origin attain professional, technical, and managerial careers through the credentialing system. They find occupational niches, but not at the top of their respective domains. They typically graduate from third-tier, nonresearch colleges and universities, and their training does not entail acquiring the type of knowledge connected with substantial intellectual work: theory, extensive writing, and independent research. Students leaving these institutions find jobs as line supervisors, computer technicians, teachers, nurses, or social workers and in other niches in the social service professions.

A small number may join their better-educated colleagues in getting no-collar jobs, where "no-collar"—Andrew Ross's term—designates occupations that afford considerable work autonomy, such as computer design, which, although salaried, cannot be comfortably folded into the conventional division of manual and intellectual labor. The fact that so-called social mobility was a product of the specific conditions of American economic development at a particular time—the first quarter of the twentieth century—and was due principally to the absence of an indigenous peasantry during the US industrial revolution and the forced confinement of millions of blacks to Southern agricultural lands—is conveniently forgotten or ignored by consensus opinion. Nor do the celebrants of mobility take into account the labor shortages provoked by World War II and the subsequent US dominance of world capitalism until 1973. Economic stagnation has afflicted the US economy for more than three decades, and despite the well-known high-tech bubble of the 1990s, the US economic position has deteriorated in the world market. Yet the mythology of mobility retains a powerful grip over the popular mind. The notion that schooling makes credentials available to anyone, regardless of rank or status, forms one of the sturdy pillars of American ideology.[3]

In recent years, the constitutional and legal assignment to the states and local communities of responsibility for public education has been undermined by what has been termed the "standards" movement, which is today the prevailing national educational policy, enforced not so much by federal law as by political and ideological coercion. At the state and district levels, the invocation to "tough love" has attained widespread support. We are witnessing the abrogation, both in practice and in rhetoric, of the tradition of social promotion whereby students moved through the system without acquiring academic skills. Having proven unable to provide to most working-class kids the necessary educational experiences that qualify them for academic promotion, more than a decade after its installation, the standards movement has revealed its underlying content: It is the latest means of exclusion, whose success depends on placing the onus for failure to achieve academic credentials on the individual rather than on the system. Although state departments of education frequently mandate that certain subjects be taught in every school and have established standards based on high-stakes tests applicable to all districts, everyone knows that districts with working-class majorities provide neither a curriculum and pedagogy nor facilities that meet these standards because, among other problems, they are chronically underfunded. But there is no shortage of money for the private corporations that are making huge profits on school systems.

High-stakes testing, a form of privatization, transfers huge amounts of public money to publishers, testing organizations, and large consulting companies. The state aid formulas, which, since the advent of conservative policy hegemony, have rewarded those districts whose students perform well on high-stakes standardized tests, tend to be unequal. Performance-based aid policies mean that school districts where the affluent live get more than their share and make up for state budget deficits by raising local property taxes and soliciting annual subventions from parents, measures not affordable by even the top layer of wage workers and low-level salaried employees. The result is overcrowded classrooms; poor facilities, especially laboratories and libraries; and underpaid, often poorly prepared teachers, an outcome of financially starved education schools in public universities.

Standards presuppose students' prior possession of cultural capital—an acquisition that almost invariably entails having been reared in a professional or otherwise upper-class family. In the main, even the most privileged elementary and secondary schools are ill equipped to compensate for home backgrounds in which reading and writing are virtually absent, a fact that has become a matter of indifference for school authorities. In this era of social Darwinism, poor school performance is likely to be coded as genetic deficit rather than being ascribed to social policy. Of course the idea that working-class kids, whatever their gender, race, or ethnic backgrounds, were selected by evolution or by God to perform material rather than immaterial labor is not new; this view is as old as class-divided societies. But in an epoch in which the chances of obtaining a good working-class job have sharply diminished, most kids face dire consequences if they don't acquire the skills needed in the world of immaterial labor. Not only are seventy-five percent assigned to working-class jobs but, in the absence of a shrinking pool of unionized industrial jobs, which often pay more than some professions such as teaching and social work, they must accept low-paying service sector employment, enter the informal economy, or join the ranks of the chronically unemployed.

From 1890 to 1920, the greatest period of social protest in American history before the industrial union upsurge of the 1930s, John Dewey, the leading educational philosopher of the progressive era, decisively transformed class discourse about education into a discourse of class leveling. Dewey's philosophy of education is a brilliant piece of bricolage: It combines an acute sensitivity to the prevailing inequalities in society with a pluralist theory, which by definition excludes class struggles as a strategy for achieving democracy. It was a feat that could have been achieved only by tapping into the prevailing radical critique of the limits of American democracy. But Dewey's aim was far from founding a new educational or political radicalism. True to the pragmatist tradition of "tinkering" rather than transforming institutions, Dewey sought to heal the breach between labor and capital through schooling. To the extent that schools afforded workers' children access to genuine education, American democracy—and the Americanization of waves of new immigrants—would be secure.

Dewey was not only America's preeminent philosopher, he was also a major intellectual spokesperson for the progressive movement at a time when social reform had achieved high visibility and had enormous influence over both legislation and public opinion, principally among wide sections of the middle class and in the higher circles of power. His writings helped bring education into the center of intellectual and political discourse by arguing that a society that wished to overcome the stigma of class distinction associated with industrial capitalism had to fervently embrace universal schooling. In addition, he was able to elaborate the doctrine that schooling was the heart of education, the core institution for the reproduction of liberal democratic society, and the basis for the objective of class leveling. In the end, "democracy in education" signifies that by means of universal schooling, all children, regardless of class origins, could have access to social mobility. Which is not egalitarian at all.

Democracy and Education (1916), Dewey's main philosophical statement on education, may be viewed in the context of the turn of-the-
twentieth-century emergence of mass public education, which, among
other goals, was designed to address a multitude of problems that accompanied the advent of industrial society and the emergence of the
United States as a world power. Among these problems were the enormous task of "Americanizing"—ideological education—millions of immigrants' children, most of whom were of the working class; the rise of
scientifically based industrial and commercial technologies that, in the
service of capital, required a certain level of verbal, scientific, and mathematical literacy among a substantial portion of the wage-labor force;
the hard-won recognition by economic and political authorities as well
as the labor movement that child labor had deleterious consequences for
the future of the capitalist system; and, in an era of rapid technological
change, the fact that industrial labor had become relatively expendable.
In this context the high school became an important aging vat or ware-
house, whether adolescents learned anything or not. As Michael B. Katz
has shown, this concern was the basis of the public education movement
in the nineteenth century because the question for educators, law enforcement officials, and political and economic leaders was what to do
with unemployed youth during the day. The day prison was one solution, but Horace Mann prevailed upon his colleagues to establish public
schools as a more "productive" way of containing unruly youngsters.
Later the institution was expanded from six to twelve grades, and the
minimum age for leaving rose from twelve to sixteen. After a century of
compulsory secondary schooling, the educational value of high schools
is still in doubt.[4]

At the outset, Dewey specifies the purposes of education: through
adult transmission and communication, assisting the young to direct
their own lives. Dewey cautions that because the young hold society's
future in their hands, the nature of adults' transmissions inevitably has
serious consequences. Yet, having recognized, briefly, the role of "informal" education in the self-formation of the young, Dewey establishes
the rule for virtually all subsequent educational philosophy. Consistent
with a liberal democratic society, he exhorts educators to devise a formal

method for directing the future: by organization of a common school that provides the necessary discipline, array of learning, and methods by which learning that reproduces the social order may occur. Although transmitting and communicating knowledge are intended to provide "meaning to experience," and Dewey invokes "democratic criteria" as the basis for his concept of the "reconstruction of experience," the objective of "control and growth" in order to achieve "social continuity" occupies an equally important place in any enterprise that seeks to explore the creative possibilities of education.[5]

Dewey walks a tightrope between the creative side of education as a playful and imaginative reflection on experience and the necessary task of reproducing the social order, in which work, albeit as much as possible creative, remains the key educational goal. But he also endorses the role of the school in training the labor force. Dewey advocates for the ability of children to obtain the knowledge that could aid in their quest for an autonomous future even as he approaches the problem of moral education (character building, values) from the perspective of society's need to reproduce itself on the basis of the criteria inherited from the past. He deplores the separation of labor and leisure, the cleavage of liberal arts and vocational education in which the former is regarded as activity to be tolerated but not enjoyed. Labor should be viewed not as a "job" but rather, as much as possible, as a "calling." Without addressing the nature of the rationalized labor to which wage workers, including most professional and technical workers, are subjected, Dewey's educational philosophy is directed mostly to the ideal of educational humanism. Class distinctions are not denied but are assumed to be blurred, if not eliminated, by democratic education.

In both their critical and celebratory variants of his philosophy, Dewey's intellectual children, with few exceptions, have not addressed the issue of whether, given their conflictual purposes and hierarchical organization, schools can fulfill their liberal democratic, let alone egalitarian, promise. Having narrowly confined itself to school practices, post-Deweyan progressive educational thought has recoded Dewey's philosophy by invoking phrases such as "self-realization" and "child-centered" to describe education's goals. Or, worse, Dewey has been used to justify a relentless instrumentalism in curriculum design: In the name of antitraditionalism and nationalism, high schools do not teach philosophy or social history—principally the role of social movements in making history—or treat world literature as a legitimate object of academic study. Needless to say, few if any critics have challenged the curricular exclusions of working-class history, let alone the histories of women and of blacks. Nor have curricular critics addressed the exclusion of philosophy and social theory.

In recent years the philosophy of education has waned and been replaced by a series of policy-oriented empirical research projects that conflate democracy with access and openly subordinate school knowledge to the priorities of the state and the corporations. Educational thought has lost, even renounced, Dewey's program directed to the reconstruction of experience. In fact, after the early grades, student experience is viewed by many educators and administrators with suspicion, even hostility. Recent educational policy has veered toward delineating preschool and kindergarten as sites for academic and vocational preparation. If the child is to grow to become a productive member of society—where productive is equated with work-ready—play must be directed, free time severely constrained. The message emanating from school authorities is to "forget" all other forms and sites of learning. Academic and technical knowledge become the only legitimate forms, and the school is, the only reliable site. Whatever their defects, in contrast with the penchant of modern educational researchers for focusing on "policy" to the detriment of historical and theoretical analysis, Dewey's ideas demonstrate a passion for citizenship and ambivalence about the subordination of education to the imperatives of the system. He deplored the subordination of knowledge to the priorities of the state while, at the same time, extolling the virtues of the liberal state, and he subjected vocational education to the scrutiny of the Enlightenment prescription that education be critical of the existing state of affairs while at the same time approving the reproductive function of schools.

The rise of higher education since World War II has been seen by many as a repudiation of academic elitism. Do not the booming higher-education enrollments validate the propositions of social mobility and democratic education? Not at all. Rather than constituting a sign of rising qualifications and widening opportunity, burgeoning college and university enrollments signify changing economic and political trends. The scientific and technical nature of our production and service sectors increasingly requires qualified and credentialed workers (it would be a mistake to regard those two things as identical). Students who would have sought good factory jobs in the past now believe, with reason, that they need credentials to qualify for a well-paying job. On the other hand, even as politicians and educators decry social promotion and most high schools with working-class constituencies remain aging vats, mass higher education is, to a great extent, a holding pen because it effectively masks unemployment and underemployment. This function may account for its rapid expansion over the past thirty-five years of chronic economic stagnation, deindustrialization, and proliferation of part-time and temporary jobs, largely in the low-paid service sectors. Consequently, working-class students are able, even encouraged, to enter universities and colleges at the bottom of the academic hierarchy—community colleges but also public four-year colleges—thus fulfilling the formal pledge of equal opportunity for class mobility even as most of these institutions suppress the pledge's content. But grade-point averages, which in the standards era depend as much as the Scholastic Aptitude Test on high-stakes testing, measure the student's acquired knowledge and restrict her/his access to elite institutions of higher learning, the obligatory training grounds for professional and managerial occupations. Because all credentials are not equal, graduating from third- and fourth-tier institutions does not confer on the successful candidate the prerequisites for entering a leading graduate school—the preparatory institution for professional or managerial occupations—or for the most desirable entry-level service jobs that require only a bachelor's degree.[6]

Pierre Bourdieu argues that schools reproduce class relations by reinforcing rather than reducing class-based differential access to social and cultural capital, key markers of class affiliation and mobility. These forms of capital, he argues, are always already possessed by children of the wealthy, professionals, and the intelligentsia. Far from making possible a rich intellectual education or providing the chance to affiliate with networks of students and faculty who have handles on better jobs, schooling uses mechanisms of discipline and punishment to habituate working-class students to the bottom rungs of the work world, or the academic world, by subordinating or expelling them.[7] Poorly prepared for academic work by their primary and secondary schools, and having few alternatives to acquiring some kind of credential, many who stay the course and graduate high school and third- and fourth-tier colleges inevitably confront a series of severely limited occupational choices—or none at all. Their life chances are just a cut above those of the students who do not complete high school or college. Their school performances seem to validate what common sense has always suspected: Given equal opportunity to attain school knowledge, the cream always rises to the top, and those stuck at the bottom must be biologically impaired or victimized by the infamous "culture of poverty." The fact that most working-class high school and college students are obliged to hold full- or part-time jobs in order to stay in school fails to temper this judgment, for, as is well known, preconceptions usually trump facts.[8] Nor does the fact that children of the recent twenty million immigrants from Latin America and Asia speak their native languages at home, in the neighborhood, and to each other in school evoke more than hand-wringing from educational leaders; in this era of tight school budgets, funds for teaching English as a second language have been cut or eliminated at every level of schooling.

But Paul Willis insists that working-class kids get working-class jobs by means of their refusal to accept the discipline entailed in curricular mastery and by their rebellion against school authority. Challenging the familiar "socialization" thesis, of which Bourdieu's is perhaps the most sophisticated version, according to which working-class kids "fail" because they are culturally deprived—or, in the American critical version, are assaulted by the hidden curriculum and school pedagogy, which subsumes kids under the prevailing order—Willis recodes kids' failure as refusal of (school) work.[9] This refusal lands them in the factory or low-level service jobs. Willis offers no alternative educational model to schooling: His discovery functions as critique. Indeed, as Willis himself acknowledges, the school remains, in Louis Althusser's famous phrase, the main "ideological state apparatus," but working-class kids are not victims.

Implicitly rejecting Sennett and Cobb's notion that school failure is a "hidden injury" of class insofar as working class kids internalize poor school performance as a sign of personal deficit, he argues that most early school leavers are active agents in the production of their own class position.[10] Although students' antipathy to school authority is enacted at the site of the school, its origin is the working-class culture from which it springs. Workers do not like bosses, and kids do not like school bosses, the deans and principals, but often the teachers as well, whose main job in the urban centers is to keep order. The source of working-class kids' education is not the school but the shop floor where their parents work, the home, and the neighborhood. I'll discuss this concept in more detail later in this chapter.

In the past half century the class question has been inflected by race and gender discrimination, and, in the American way, the "race, gender, class" phrase implies that these domains are ontologically distinct, if not entirely separate. Many educational theorists have conceived of the race and gender question not as a class issue but as an attribute of biological identities. In fact, in the era of identity politics, class itself stands alongside race and gender as just another identity. Having made the easy, inaccurate judgment that white students, regardless of their class or gender, stand in a qualitatively different relation to school-related opportunities than blacks, these theorists often suppress the notion of class as a sign of exclusion. In privileging issues of access, not only is the curriculum presupposed, in which case Bourdieu's insistence on the concept of cultural capital is ignored, but also the entire question of whether schooling may be conflated with education is elided. Only rarely do writers examine other forms of education. In both the Marxist and the liberal tradition, schooling is presumed to remain, over a vast spectrum of spatial and temporal situations, the theater within which life chances are determined.

Education and Immaterial Labor

Education may be defined as the collective and individual reflection on the totality of life experiences: what we learn from peers, parents and the socially situated cultures of which they are a part, media, and schools. By "reflection" I mean the transformation of experience into a multitude of concepts that constitute the abstractions we call "knowledge." Which of the forms of learning predominate is always configured historically. The exclusive focus by theorists and researchers on school knowledge-indeed, the implication that school is the principal site of what we mean by education-reflects the degree to which they have internalized the equation of education with school knowledge and its preconditions. The key learning is to habituate students to a specific regimen of intellectual labor that entails a high level. of self-discipline, the acquisition of the skills of reading and writing, and the career expectations associated with professionalization.

To say this constitutes the self-reflection by intellectuals—in the broadest sense of the term—of their own relation to schooling. In the age of the decline of critical intelligence and the proliferation of technical intelligence, "intellectual" in its current connotation designates immaterial labor rather than those engaged in traditional intellectual pursuits such as literature, philosophy, and art. Immaterial labor describes those who work not with objects or administration of things and people but with ideas, symbols, and signs. Some of the occupations grouped under immaterial labor have an affective dimension, particularly people who, in one way or another, care for each other. Such work demands the complete subordination of brain, emotion, and body to the task while requiring the worker to exercise considerable judgment and imagination in its performance.[11] At sites such as "new economy" private-sector software workplaces; some law firms that deal with questions of intellectual property, public interest, constitutional, and international law; research universities and independent research institutes; and small, innovative design, architectural, and engineering firms, the informality of the labor process, close collaborative relationships among members of task-oriented teams, and the overflow of the space of the shop floor into the spaces of home and play can evoke a high level of exhilaration, even giddiness, among workers.[12] But such relationships are also present in such work as teaching; child care; care for seniors; and the whole array of therapeutic services, including psychotherapy.

Immaterial workers, in the interest of having self-generated work, surrender much of their unfettered time. They are obliged to sunder the conventional separation of work and leisure, to adopt the view that time

442

devoted to creative, albeit commodified, labor is actually "free." To be more exact, even play must be engaged in as serious business. For many, the golf course, the bar, the weekend at the beach are workplaces in which dreams are shared, plans formulated, and deals made. Just as time becomes unified around work, so work loses its geographic specificity. As Andrew Ross shows in his pathbreaking ethnography of a New York new economy workplace during and after the dot-com boom, the headiness for the pioneers of this new work world was, tacitly, a function of the halcyon period of the computer software industry when everyone felt the sky was no longer the limit. When the economic crunch descended on thousands of workplaces, people were laid off, and those who remained experienced a heavy dose of market reality.

It may be argued that among elite students and institutions. not only does schooling prepare students for immaterial labor by transmitting a bundle of legitimate knowledge, but the diligent, academically successful student internalizes the blur between the classroom, play, and the home by spending a great deal of time in the library or ostensibly playing at the computer. Thus, the price of the promise of autonomy, a situation that is intrinsic to professional ideology, if not always its practice in the context of bureaucratic and hierarchical corporate systems, is to accept work as a mode of life: One lives to work, rather than the reverse. The hopes and expectations of people in these strata are formed in the process of schooling; indeed, they are the ones who most completely assimilate the ideologies linked to school knowledge and to the credentials conferred by the system. Thus, even if they are not professional school people or educational researchers. they tend to evaluate people by the criteria to which they themselves were subjected. If the child has not fully embraced work as life. he is consigned to the educational netherworld. Even the egalitarians (better read as populists) accept this regime: Their object is to indoctrinate those for whom work is a necessary evil into the social world where work is the mission.

Media and Popular Culture

Most educators and critics acknowledge the enormous role of media in contemporary life. The ubiquity and penetration of visual media such as

TV, VCR and DVD players, videogames, and electronic sound equipment such as CD and tape players into the home has called into question the separation of the public and private spheres and challenged the notion that autonomous private life any longer exists. Writers such as Hannah Arendt insist on the importance of maintaining the separation of the two spheres.[13] When taken together with the advent, in the technical as well as metaphoric sense, of "Big Brother"—with the government now openly announcing its intention to subject every telephone and computer to surveillance—it is difficult to avoid the conclusion that media are a crucial source of education and may, in comparison to schools, exercise a greater influence on children and youth. Many claim that television, for example, is the prime source of political education, certainly the major source of news, for perhaps a majority of the population. And there is a growing academic discourse on the importance of popular culture, especially music and film, in shaping the values, but more to the point the cultural imagination, of children and adolescents. Many writers have noted the influence of media images on children's dream work; on their aspirations; on their measurement of self-worth, both physical and emotional. Of course debate rages as to what is learned—for example, the implied frameworks that are masked by the face of objectivity presented by television news and by fiction, which, as everybody knows, is suffused with ethical perspective on everyday relations.[14]

Nor does every critic accept the conventional wisdom that, in the wake of the dominance of visual media in everyday life, we are, in the phrase of a leading commentator, "amusing ourselves to death," or that the ideological messages of popular music, sitcoms, and other TV fare are simply conformist.[15] But it must be admitted that since the 1920s and '30s, when critics argued that the possibility of a radical democracy in which ordinary people participated in the great and small decisions affecting their lives was undermined by the advent of the culture industry, popular culture has to a large degree become a weapon against, as well as for, the people. As a general rule, in periods of upsurge—when social movements succeed in transforming aspects of everyday life as well as the political landscape—art, in its "high" as well as popular genres, expresses a popular yearning for a better world. In this vein, a vast literature, written

444

largely by participants in the popular culture since the 1960s, rejects the sharp divide between high and low art. Many contemporary cultural critics such as Greil Marcus and Robert Christgau acknowledge their debt to the work of the critical theory of the Frankfurt School, particularly that of Herbert Marcuse and Theodor Adorno, owing both to their independent judgment and to the influence of Walter Benjamin—who, despite his elective affinity to critical theory, welcomed, with some trepidation, the eclipse of high art. However, these same critics find a subversive dimension in rock-and-roll music.[16] It maybe that the 1960s phrase "sex, drugs, and rock-and-roll" no longer resonates as a universal sign of rebellion. Yet, when evaluated from the perspective of a society that remains obsessed with drug use and premarital sex among youth and "blames" the music for kids' nonconformity, the competition between school and popular culture still rages. From anthems of rebellion to musical expressions of youth rejection of conventional sexual and political morality, critics have detected signs of resistance to official mores.

Of course even as punk signaled the conclusion of a sort of "golden age" of rock-and-roll and the succeeding genres—heavy metal, alternative, and techno, among others—were confined to market niches, hip-hop took on some of the trappings of a universal oppositional cultural form and by the 1990s had captured the imagination of white as well as black kids. Out of the "bonfires" of the Bronx came a new generation of artists whose music and poetry enflamed the embers of discontent. Figures such as Ice-T, Tupac Shakur, Biggie Smalls, and many others articulated the still vibrant rebellion against what George Bernard Shaw once called "middle-class morality" and the smug, suburban confidence that the cities could be safely consigned to the margins. Like Dylan, some of the hip-hop artists were superb poets: Tupac had many imitators, and eventually the genre became fully absorbed by the culture industry, a development that, like the advent of the Velvets, the Who, and other avant-garde rock groups of the early 1970s, gave rise to an underground. And, just as rock-and-roll musicians were accused of leading young people astray into the dungeons of drugs and illicit sex, the proponents of hip-hop suffered a similar fate. Some record producers succumbed to demands that they censor artistic material; radio stations

445

refused to air some hip-hop songs; and record stores, especially in suburban malls, were advised to restrict sales of certain artists and records.

What white kids have learned from successive waves of rock-and-roll and hip-hop music is chiefly their right to defy ordinary conventions. After the mid-1950s, the varied genres of rock, rhythm and blues, and hip-hop steadily challenged the class, racial, and sexual constructs of this ostensibly egalitarian but puritanical culture. Bored and dissatisfied with middle-class morality and its cultural values, teenagers flooded the concerts of rock and hip-hop stars, smoked dope, and violated the precepts of conventional sexual morality to the best of their abilities. Many adopt black rhetoric, language, and disdain for mainstream values. Of course middle-class kids are obliged to lead a double life because their preferred artistic and cultural forms are accorded absolutely no recognition in the world of legitimate school knowledge. Also, for reasons I have already stated, they are in a double bind: Since the 1960s their shared music and the messages of rebellion against a racist, conventional, suburban, middle-class culture have constituted a quasi-countercommunity. Yet, on penalty of proscription, they must absorb school knowledge without invoking the counterknowledge of popular culture.

The products of visual culture, particularly film and television, are no less powerful sources of knowledge. Since movies became a leading form of recreation early in the twentieth century, critics have distinguished schlock from "films" produced both by the Hollywood system and by a beleaguered corps of independent filmmakers. In the 1920s, elaborating the dynamic film technique pioneered by D. W. Griffith, the Soviet filmmakers, notably Sergei Eisenstein and Zhiga Vertov, and the great cultural critic Siegfried Kracauer fully comprehended the power of visual culture in its ornamental, aesthetic sense, and gave pride of place to film as a source of mass education. Vertov's *Man with a Movie Camera* and Eisenstein's *October* were not only great works of art, they also possessed enormous didactic power.[17] Vertov evoked the romance of industrial reconstruction in the new Soviet regime and the imperative of popular participation in building a new technologically directed social reality. And in most of his films, Eisenstein was the master of revolutionary memory: The people should not forget how brutal was the ancient regime and that the future was in their hands, and he would produce the images that created a new "memory" even among those who had never experienced the heady days of the revolution. Of course, Griffith conveyed a different kind of memory: In his classic *The Birth of a Nation*, he deconstructed the nobility and romance of the US Civil War and the Reconstruction period by depicting those events as a corrupt alliance of blacks and Northern carpetbaggers, the epithet applied to the staff of the Freedmen's Bureau and the military who were dispatched to guarantee the newly won civil rights of millions of African-Americans.

In 1950, the anthropologist Hortense Powdermaker termed Hollywood "the dream factory." Although we were entertained by the movies, she argued, a whole world of hopes and dreams was being manufactured that had profound effects on our collective unconscious. Rather than coding these experiences as "illusion," she accorded them genuine social influence. With the later writings of critics André Bazin, François Truffaut, Christian Metz, Stephen Heath, Laura Mulvey, and Pauline Kael, movies came into their own as an art form but also as a massive influence on what we know and how we learn. Film, which for critical theory was just another product of the culture industry, is now taken seriously by several generations of critics and enthusiasts as a many-sided cultural force. At the same time, film criticism has evolved from reviews in the daily and weekly press and television (whose main function is to advise the public whether to choose a particular film or to hire a babysitter to attend a movie) into a historical and critical discipline worthy of academic departments and programs, and whose practitioners are eligible for academic rank.[18]

Despite their ubiquity and vast influence, the kinds of knowledge derived from mass media and popular music remain largely unexamined by the secondary school curriculum. In this respect, public education may be regarded as one of the last bastions of high-cultural convention and of the book. Perhaps more to the point, by consistently refusing to treat popular culture—television, film, music, and video games—as objects of legitimate intellectual knowledge, schools deny the validity of student experiences, even if the objective were to deconstruct them. Thus, a century after mass-mediated music and visual arts captured our collective imagination, popular culture remains subversive, notwithstanding its undeniable commodification and regardless of its content, because it continues to be outlawed in official precincts. By failing to address this epochal phenomenon, even as its forms are overwhelmingly influential in everyday life, school knowledge loses its capacity to capture the hearts and minds of its main constituents. And if schools cannot enter the students' collective imagination, other forms of knowledge are destined to fill the vacuum.

Of course the power of television in shaping the political culture is far less well understood. If the overwhelming majority of the population receives its news and viewpoints from television sources, then, without such counterweights as those that may be provided by social movements, counterhegemonic intellectuals, and independent media, the people are inevitably subjected to the ruling common sense. Alternatives to the official stories lack legitimacy, even when they are reported in the back pages or in a thirty-second spot on the eleven o'clock news. Even journalists have discovered that the integration of major news organizations with the ruling circles inhibits their ability to accurately report the news. For example, on October 26, 2002, more than 100,000 people descended on Washington, D.C. to protest the Bush administration's plan to wage war against Iraq. The *New York Times* reporter on the scene estimated the crowd in the "thousands" and stated that the turnout had disappointed organizers, who had expected more than 100,000 demonstrators to show up. Since the *Times* functions as a guide to the rest of the American news media, including television and radio news, the coverage of the demonstration throughout the nation was scanty, in part because other media relied on the *Times*'s understated numbers. For the majority of Americans, the original report and its numerous recapitulations left the impression that the demonstration was a bust. But the *Washington Post*, perhaps the *Times*'s only competitor in daily print journalism, estimated the number of demonstrators more or less accurately, and by the evening of the event a wealth of information and furious condemnation of the *Times*'s biased coverage had swarmed over the internet. Days later, in an obscure little piece, the paper's editors issued a correction without referring the readers to the previous report.

But more importantly, the relation of education and class is indicated by the way in which issues are framed by experts, opinion surveys, and the media, which faithfully feature them. That Iraq's president, Saddam Hussein, and his government constituted an imminent threat to US security—a judgment for which neither the media nor the Bush administration seemed to require proof—was the starting point of virtually all of the media's coverage of US foreign policy during the first years of the US war on Iraq. On the nightly news or the Public Broadcasting System's (PBS's) many programs of talking expert heads, no less than on Sunday-morning talk shows on commercial networks in which experts mingle with the political directorate to discuss world and national events, the question of whether there is warrant for this evaluation was almost never posed. Instead, discussion revolved around the issue not of *whether* the United States should go to war to disarm the Iraqi regime but of *when* the invasion would inevitably occur. The taken-for-granted assumption was that Saddam had viable "weapons of mass destruction" in his possession, whether or not the United Nations inspectors dispatched by the Security Council to investigate this allegation could affirm this US government-manufactured "fact." Since the Bush administration knew that there was nothing as efficient as a war to unify the underlying population behind its policies, and the media were complicit, citizens were deprived of countervailing assessments unless they emanated from within the establishment. And even then, there was only a small chance that these views would play prominently.

Thus, when Brent Scowcroft, the national security adviser in the first Bush administration, and retiring Republican conservative US Representative Dick Armey expressed reservations about the current administration's war plans, neither received the notice that such an ideological breach might deserve. Only the tiny fraction of the population that reads a handful of liberal-newspapers and opinion magazines were likely to know about their objections. From the perspective of the leading media, Americans (except for African-Americans) were, in the months leading up to the US invasion, in virtual unanimous agreement that we should and would go to war against Iraq. Yet, according to the results of some polls that were poorly reported in most media, we know that support for the war was not only soft but was qualified; whereas few were opposed to a war on any terms, many Americans objected to a unilateral attack by US forces, a belief that was partially responsible for the administration's formation of a "coalition" to undertake the tasks of invasion and occupation. But there were ample indications that the administration proceeded *as if* public opinion were unified around its policy. In this mode of governance, absent massive protest that might manifest directly or electorally, silence is tantamount to consent. Without visible dissent—a visibility routinely denied by the media to protestors—the administration interpreted the Republican victory in the 2002 midterm elections as a retrospective mandate for its war policies.

The pattern of government vetting and censorship of war news was established during World War II, but the first Bush administration elevated it to an art form. During the 1991 Gulf War, the administration took pains to shield reporters from the battlefield and insisted that they be quartered in Saudi hotels, miles away from the action. Journalists received all of the war news from government sources, including video footage and photographs shown to them in special briefings. According to the contemporary and subsequent testimony of some journalists who were assigned to cover the events, the Bush administration was intent on not repeating the mistakes of the Vietnam War, when the Johnson administration permitted the press full access to American and enemy troops and to the battle scenes. Historians and political observers agree that this policy may have had a major impact on building the antiwar movement—especially the images of body bags being loaded onto airplanes and the human gore associated with any close combat supplied by staff photographers. In 1991 Americans never got the chance to view the physical and human destruction visited by US bombs and missiles on Baghdad or the extent of US casualties. The war was short-lived, so the political damage at home was relatively light. Needless to say, the fact that some 150.000 of the 700,000 troops who entered the combat area have since reported psychological or physical injuries barely makes it to the back pages of most newspapers, let alone the visual media.

Note well that at its inception, some educators and producers touted the educational value of television. Indeed, perhaps the major impact of the dominance of visual culture on our everyday knowledge is that to be is to be seen. "Celebrity" is a word reserved for people whose names become "household" words. Celebrity is produced by the repetition of appearances of an individual on the multitude of television talk shows—*The Oprah Winfrey Show*, the *Today Show*, Jay Leno's *Tonight Show*, and the *Late Show with David Letterman*, among others—in which personalities constitute the substance of the event. The point of the typical interview between the anchor and her or his subject is not what is said, or even that the guest is currently appearing in a film or television show, the ostensible purpose of the segment. The interview is a statement of who exists and, by implication, who doesn't. The event has little to do with economic or high-level political power, for these people are largely invisible, or on occasion may appear on *The Charlie Rose Show* on PBS or, formerly, on ABC's *Nightline*. The making of sports, entertainment, political, or literary celebrities defines the boundary of popular hope or aspiration. The leading television celebrity talk shows are instances of the American credo that, however high the barrier, anyone can become a star. This is not an instance of having charisma or exuding aura: The celebs are not larger than life but are shown to be ordinary in an almost banal sense. Fix your nose, cap your teeth, lose weight, take acting lessons, and, with a little luck, the person on the screen could be you.

The Labor and Radical Movements as Educational Sites

The working-class intellectual as a social type precedes and parallels the emergence of universal public education. At the dawn of the public school movement in the 1830s, the antebellum labor movement, which consisted largely of literate skilled workers, favored six years of schooling in order to transmit to children the basics of reading and writing but opposed compulsory attendance in secondary schools. The reasons were bound up with the movement's congenital suspicion of the state, which it believed never exhibited sympathy for the workers' cause. Although opposed to child labor, the early workers' movement was convinced that the substance of education—literature, history, philosophy—should be supplied by the movement itself. Consequently, in both the oral and the written tradition, workers' organizations often constituted an alternative university to that of public schools. The active program of many workers' and radical movements until World War II consisted largely in education through newspapers, literacy classes for immigrants in which the reading materials were drawn from labor and socialist classics, and world literature. These were supplemented by lectures offered by independent scholars who toured the country in the employ of lecture organizations commissioned by the unions and radical organizations.[19]

The shop floor was also a site of education. Skilled workers were usually literate in their own language and in English, and many were voracious readers and writers. Union and radical newspapers often printed poetry and stories written by workers. Socialist-led unions such as those in the needle, machinist, brewery, and bakery trades sponsored educational programs; in the era when the union contract was still a rarity, the union was not so much an agency of contract negotiation and enforcement as an educational, political, and social association. In his autobiography, Samuel Gompers, the founding president of the American Federation of Labor, remembers his fellow cigar makers in the 1870s hiring a "reader" who sat at the center of the work floor and read from literary and historical classics as well as more contemporary works of political and economic analysis such as the writings of Marx and Engels. Reading groups met in the backs of bars, in union halls, or in the offices of local affiliates of socialist wings of nationality federations. Often these groups were ostensibly devoted to preparing immigrants to pass the obligatory language test for citizenship status. But reading, in addition to labor and socialist newspapers and magazines, was often supplemented by works by Shakespeare, the great nineteenth-century novelists and poets, and Marx and Karl Kautsky. In the anarchist incarnation of these readings, Pyotr Kropotkin, Moses Hess, and Mikhail Bakunin were the required texts.[20]

In New York, Chicago, San Francisco, and other large cities where the socialist and communist movements had considerable membership and a fairly substantial periphery of sympathizers, the parties established adult schools that not only offered courses pertaining to political and ideological knowledge but were also vehicles for many working-and middle-class students to gain a general education. Among them, in New York the socialist-oriented Rand School and the communist-sponsored

Jefferson School (formerly the Workers School) lasted until the early 1950s, when, owing to the decline of a leftist intellectual culture among workers as much as the repressive political environment, they closed. But in their respective heydays, from the 1920s to the late 1940s, for tens of thousands of working-class people—many of them high school students and industrial workers—these schools were alternative universities. They didn't offer only courses that promoted the party's ideology and program; many courses concerned history, literature, and philosophy, and—at least at the Jefferson School—students could also study art, drama, and music, and so could their children. The tradition was revived briefly by the 1960s New Left, which sponsored free universities for which the term "free" designated not an absence of tuition but the fact that the schools were ideologically and intellectually unbound to either the traditional left parties or the conventional school system. I participated in organizing New York's Free University and two of its successors. Although not affiliated to the labor movement or socialist parties, it succeeded in attracting more than a thousand students—mostly young—in each of its semesters and offered a broad range of courses that were taught by people of divergent intellectual and political orientations, including some free-market libertarians who were attracted to the school's nonsectarianism.

When I worked in a steel mill in the late 1950s, some of us formed a group that read current literature, labor history, and economics. I discussed books and magazine articles with some of my fellow workers in bars as well as on breaks. Tony Mazzocchi, who was at the same time a worker and an officer of a Long Island local of the Oil, Chemical and Atomic Workers Union, organized a similar group, and I knew of several other cases of young workers doing the same. Some of these groups evolved into rank-and-file caucuses that eventually contested the leadership of their local unions; others were mainly for the self-edification of the participants and had no particular political goals.

Beyond formal programs, ever since the industrializing era the working-class intellectual, although by no means visible in the United States, has been part of shop-floor culture. In almost every workplace there is a person or persons to whom other workers turn for information about the law, the union contract, or contemporary politics—or, equally important, as a source of general education. These individuals may or may not be schooled but, until the late 1950s, rarely had any college. Schools were not the primary source of their knowledge. They were, and are, largely self-educated. In my own case, having left Brooklyn College after less than a year, I worked in a variety of industrial production jobs. When I worked the midnight shift, I got off at 8:00 in the morning, ate breakfast, and spent four hours in the library before going home. Mostly I read American and European history and political economy, particularly the physiocrats, Adam Smith, David Ricardo, John Maynard Keynes, and Joseph Schumpeter. Marx's *Das Kapital* I read in high school and owned the three volumes.

My friend Russell Rommele, who worked in a nearby mill, was also an autodidact. His father was a first-generation German-American brewery worker with no particular literary interests. But Russell had been exposed to a wide range of historical and philosophical works as a high school student at Saint Benedict's Prep, a Jesuit institution. The priests singled out Russell for the priesthood and mentored him in theology and social theory. The experience radicalized him, and he decided not to answer the call but to enter the industrial working class instead. Like me, he was active in the union and Newark Democratic Party politics. Working as an educator with a local union in the auto industry recently, I met several active unionists who are intellectuals. The major difference between them and those of my generation is that they are college graduates, although none claim to have acquired their love of learning or their analytic perspective from schools. One is a former member of a radical organization; another learned his politics from participation in a shop-based study group and union caucus organized by a member of a socialist group that dissolved in the mid-1990s when the group lost a crucial union election. In both instances, even after the demise of their organizational affiliations, they remain habituated to reading, writing, and union activity.

Parents, Neighborhood, and Class Culture

John Locke observes that, consistent with his rejection of innate ideas, even if conceptions of good and evil are present in divine or civil law, morality is constituted by reference to our parents, our relatives, and especially the "club" of peers to which we belong:

454

He who imagines commendation and disgrace not to be strong motives to men to accommodate themselves to the opinions and rules of those with whom they converse seems little skilled in the nature or the history of mankind: the greatest part whereof we shall find govern themselves, chiefly, if not solely by this law of *fashion*; and so they do what keeps them in reputation with their company, little regard for the laws of God or the magistrate.[21]

William James put the matter equally succinctly:

A man's social self is the recognition which he gets from his mates. We are not only gregarious animals, liking to be in the sight of our fellows, but we have an innate propensity to get ourselves noticed, and noticed favorably, by our kind. No more fiendish punishment could be devised, were such a thing physically possible, than that we should be turned loose in society and remain absolutely unnoticed by all the members thereof.[22]

That the social worlds of peers and family are the chief referents for the formation of the social self, neither, philosopher had a doubt. Each in his own fashion situates the individual in social context, which provides a "common measure of virtue and vice"[23] even as they acknowledge that the ultimate choice resides with the individual self. These and not the institutions, even those that have the force of law, are the primary sources of authority.

Hannah Arendt argues that education "by its very nature cannot forgo either authority or tradition." Nor can it base itself on the presumption that children share an autonomous existence from adults.[24] Yet schooling ignores the reality of the society of kids at the cost of undermining its own authority. The society of kids is in virtually all classes an alternative and opposition site of knowledge and of moral valuation. We have already seen how working-class kids get working-class jobs by means of their rebellion against school authority. Since refusal and resistance are hallmarks of the moral order, the few who will not obey the invocation to fail or to perform indifferently in school often find themselves marginalized or expelled from the community of kids. Although they adopt a rationality that can be justified on eminently practical grounds, the long tradition of rejection of academic culture has proven hard to break, even in the wake of evidence that those working-class jobs to which such students were oriented no longer exist. What is at stake in adolescent resistance is the kids' perception that the blandishments of the adult world are vastly inferior to the pleasures of their own. In the first place, the new service economy offers few inducements: Wages are low, the jobs are boring, and the future is bleak. And since the schools now openly present themselves as a link in the general system of control, it may appear to some students that cooperation is a form of self-deception.

If not invariably then in many households, parents provide to the young a wealth of knowledge: the family mythologies that feature an uncle or aunt, a grandparent, or an absent parent. These stories are loosely based on actual events in which the family member has distinguished her- or himself in various ways that (usually) illustrate a moral virtue or defect so that the telling constitutes a kind of didactic message. Even when the lessons are not attached to an overt narrative, parable, or myth, we learn from our parents by their actions in relation to us and others. How do they deal with adversity? How do they address ordinary, everyday problems? What do they learn from their own trials and tribulations, and what do they say to us? What are our parents' attitudes toward money, joblessness, everyday life disruptions such as sudden acute illness or accidents? What do they learn from the endless conflicts with their parents over issues of sex, money, and household responsibilities?

The relative weight of parental as opposed to peer authority is an empirical question that cannot be decided in advance; what both have in common is their location within everyday life. The parents are likely to be more susceptible to the authority of law and its magistrates and, in a world of increasing uncertainty, will worry that if their children choose badly, they may be left behind. But the associations we make with our peers in everyday life provide the recognition that we crave, define what is worthy of praise or blame, and confer approbation or disapproval on our decisions. If an individual makes a choice that runs counter to that of his or her "company" or club, he or she must form or join a new "company" to confer the judgment of virtue on her or his action. This company must, of necessity, consist of "peers," the definition of which has proven fungible.

Religion, the law, and, among kids, school authorities face the obstacles erected by the powerful rewards and punishments meted out by the clubs with which people are affiliated. At a historical conjunction when the relentless pressure imposed by capital works to transform all labor into wage labor, thereby forcing every adult into the paid labor force, the society of kids increasingly occupies the space of civil society. The neighborhood, once dominated by women and small shopkeepers, has all but disappeared save for the presence of children and youth. As parents toil for endless hours to pay the ever-mounting debts incurred by home ownership, perpetual car and appliance payments, and the costs of health care, kids are increasingly on their own, and their relationships with each other have consequences for their conceptions of education and life.

Some recent studies and teacher observations have discovered a not inconsiderable reluctance among black students in elite universities to perform well in school, even those of professional and managerial family backgrounds. Many seem indifferent to arguments that show that school performance is a central prerequisite to better jobs and higher status in the larger work world. Among the more acute speculations is the conclusion that black students' resistance reflects an anti-intellectual bias and a hesitation, if not refusal, to enter the mainstream corporate world. Perhaps the charge of anti-intellectualism is better understood as healthy skepticism about the chance that a corporate career will provide the well-publicized satisfactions. There are similar indications among some relatively affluent white students. Although by no means a majority, some students are less enamored by the work world to which they, presumably, have been habituated by school, and especially by the prospect of perpetual work. In the third-tier universities, state and private alike, many students, apparently forced by their parents to enroll, wonder out loud why they are there. Skepticism about schooling still abounds even as they graduate high school and enroll in postsecondary schools in record numbers. According to one colleague of mine who teaches in a third-tier private university in the New York metropolitan area, many of these mostly suburban students "sleepwalk" through their classes, do not participate in class discussions, and are lucky to get C grades.

In the working-class neighborhoods—white, black, and Latino—the word is out: Given the absence of viable alternatives, you must try to obtain that degree, but this defines the limit of loyalty to the enterprise. Based on testimonies of high school and community college teachers, for every student who takes school knowledge seriously, there are twenty or more who are timeservers. Most are ill prepared to perform academic work, and since the community colleges and state four-year colleges and "teaching" universities simply lack the resources to provide the means by which such students' school performance can improve, there is little motivation for them beyond the credential to try to get an education.

In some instances, those who break from their club and enter the regime of school knowledge risk being drummed out of a lifetime of relationships with their peers. What has euphemistically been described as "peer pressure" bears, among other moral structures, on the degree to which kids are permitted to cross over the line into the precincts of adult authority. Although being a success in school is not equivalent to squealing on a friend or to the cops or transgressing some sacred moral code of the society of kids, it can come close to committing an act of betrayal. This is comprehensible only if the reader is willing to suspend the prejudice that schooling is tantamount to education and is an unqualified "good," as compared to the presumed evil of school failure or the decision of the slacker to rebel by refusing to succeed.

The concept of class, when invoked in either educational debates or any other politically charged discourse, generally refers to the white working class. Educational theory and practice treat blacks and Latinos, regardless of their economic positions, as unified, biological identities. That black kids from professional, managerial, and business backgrounds share more with their white counterparts than with working-class blacks is a fact generally ignored by most educational writers. Just as, in race discourse, "whites" are undifferentiated, since World War II, "race"—which refers in slightly different registers to people of African origin and those who migrated from Latin countries of Central and South America and the Caribbean—is treated as a unified category. The narrowing of the concept limits our ability to discern class at all. Although we must stipulate ethnic, gender, race, and occupational distinctions among differentiated strata of wage labor, with the exception of children of salaried professional and technical groups where the culture of schooling plays a decisive role, I want to suggest that class education transcends these distinctions. No doubt there are gradations among the strata that comprise this social formation. But the most privileged professional strata (physicians, attorneys, scientists, professors) and high-level managers are self-reproducing, not principally through schooling but through social networks. These include private schools, some of which are residential; clubs and associations; and, in suburban public schools, the self-selection of students on the basis of distinctions. Show me a school friendship between the son or daughter of a corporate manager and the child of a janitor or factory worker and I will show you a community service project to get the poorer student into one of the "select" colleges or universities such as Brown, Oberlin, or Wesleyan.

Schooling selects a fairly small number of children of the class of wage labor for genuine class mobility. In the first half of the twentieth century, having lost its appeal along middle-class youth, the Catholic Church turned to working-class students as a source of cadre recruitment. In my neighborhood of the East Bronx, two of my close childhood friends, both of Italian background, entered the priesthood. They were sons of construction workers, so the Church provided their best chance to escape the hardships and economic uncertainties of manual labor. Another kid became a pharmacist because the local Catholic college, Fordham University, offered scholarships. A fourth was among the tiny coterie of students who passed the test for Bronx Science, one of the city's special schools, and became a science teacher. Almost everybody else remained a worker or, like my best friend, Kenny, went to prison.

Despite the well-publicized claim that anyone can escape their condition of social and economic birth—a claim reproduced by schools and by the media with numbing regularity-most working-class students, many of whom have some college credits but often do not graduate—end up in low-and middle-level service jobs that often do not pay a decent working-class wage. Owing to the steep decline of unionized industrial production jobs, those who enter factories increasingly draw wages that are substantially below union standards. Those who do graduate find work in computer jobs, although rarely at the professional levels. The relatively low paid become K-12 teachers and healthcare professionals, mostly nurses and technicians, or enter the social services field as case workers, medical social workers, or line social welfare workers. The question I want to pose is whether these "professional" occupations represent genuine mobility.

During the postwar economic boom, which made possible a significant expansion of spending for schools, the social services, and administration of public goods, the public sector workplace became a favored site of black and Latino recruitment, mainly for clerical, maintenance, and entry-level patient care jobs in hospitals and other health care facilities. Within several decades, a good number advanced to middle-level jobs such as registered nursing, but not in all sections of the country. As unionization spread to the nonprofit private sector as well as to public employment in the 1960s and 1970s, these jobs paid enough to enable many to enjoy what became known as a "middle-class" living standard as well as a measure of job security offered by union security and civil service status. Although it is true that such "security" has often been observed in its breach, the traditional deal made by teachers, nurses, and social workers was to trade higher incomes for job security. But after about 1960, spurred by the resurgent civil rights movement, these "second-level" professionals—white and black—began to see themselves as workers more than professionals: They formed unions, struck for higher pay and shorter hours, and assumed a very unprofessional adversarial stance toward institutional authority. Contracts stipulated higher salaries; definite hours—a sharp departure from professional ideology—seniority as a basis for layoffs, just like any industrial contract; and substantial vacation and sick leave.

Their assertion of working-class values and social position may have been strategic; indeed, it inspired the largest wave of union organizing since the 1930s. But, together with the entrance of huge numbers of women and blacks into the public and quasi-public sector workforces, it was also a symptom of the proletarianization of the second-tier professions.

Several decades later, salaried physicians made a similar discovery; they formed unions and struck against high malpractice insurance costs as much as the onerous conditions imposed on their autonomy by health maintenance organizations and government authorities bent on cost containment, often at the physicians' expense. More to the point, the steep rise of public employees' salaries and benefits posed the question of how to maintain services in times of fiscal austerity, which might be due to an economic downturn or to probusiness tax policies. The answer has been that the political and public officials told employees that the temporary respite from the classical trade union trade-off was over. All public employees have suffered relative deterioration in their salaries and benefits. Since the mid-1970s fiscal crises, beginning in New York City, they have experienced layoffs for the first time since the Depression. And their unions have been in a continuous concessionary bargaining mode for decades. In the politically and ideologically repressive environment of the past twenty-five years, the class divide has sharpened. Ironically, in the wake of the attacks by legislatures and business against their hard-won gains, in the early 1980s the teachers' unions abandoned their militant class posture and reverted to professionalism and to a center-right political strategy.

In truth, schools are learning sites, even if only for a handful of intellectual knowledge. In the main, they transmit the instrumental logic of credentialism, together with their transformation from institutions of discipline to those of control, especially in working-class districts. Even talented, dedicated teachers have more difficulty reaching kids and convincing them that the life of the mind may hold unexpected rewards, even if the career implications of critical thought are not apparent. The breakdown of the mission of public schools has produced varied forms of disaffection; if school violence has abated in some places, it does not signify the decline of gangs and other clubs that signify the autonomous world of youth. The society of kids is more autonomous because, in contrast to the 1960s, today's authorities no longer offer hope. Instead, under the doctrine of control they threaten punishment, which includes, although it is not necessarily associated with, incarceration. However, the large number of drug busts of young black and Latino men should not be minimized. With over a million blacks, more than three per cent of the African-American population—most of them young—is within the purview of the criminal justice system; thus, the law may be viewed as a more or less concerted effort to counter by force of the power of peers. This may be regarded in the context of the failure of schools. Of course, more than 300 years ago, John Locke knew the limits of the ability of the magistrates—indeed, of any adult authority—to overcome the power of the society of kids.[25]

Conclusion

What are the requisite changes that would transform schools from credential mills and institutions of control to a site of education that prepares young people to see themselves as active participants in the world? As my analysis implies, the fundamental condition is to abolish the high-stakes standardized tests that dominate the curriculum, subordinate teachers to the role of drill masters, and subject students to stringent controls. I do not mean to eliminate the need for evaluative tools. The essay is a fine measure of both writing ability and the student's grasp of literature, social science, and history. Although I must admit that math and science as much as language proficiency require considerable rote learning, the current curriculum and pedagogy in these fields include neither a historical account of the changes in scientific and mathematical theory nor a metaconceptual explanation of what the disciplines are about. Nor are courses in language at the secondary level ever concerned with etymological issues, comparative cultural study of semantic differences, or other topics that might relieve the boredom of rote learning by providing depth of understanding. The broader understanding of science in the modern world—its relation to technology, war, and medicine, for example—should surely be integrated into the curriculum; some of these issues appear in the textbooks, but teachers rarely discuss them because they are busy preparing students for the high-stakes tests in which knowledge of the social contexts for science, language, and math are not included.

I agree with Arendt that education "cannot forgo either authority or tradition." But authority must be earned rather than assumed, and the transmission of tradition needs to be critical rather than worshipful. If teachers were allowed to acknowledge student skepticism and incorporate kids' knowledge into the curriculum by making what they know—especially popular music and television—the object of rigorous study, they might be treated with greater respect. But there is no point denying the canon; one of the more egregious conditions of subordination is the failure of schools to expose students to their best exemplars, for people who have no cultural capital are condemned to social and political marginality, let alone deprived of some of the pleasures to be derived from encounters with genuine works of art. The New York City Board of Education (now the Department of Education) mandates that during every semester high school English classes read a Shakespeare play and one or two works of nineteenth-century English literature. However, it affords little or no access to the best Russian novels of the nineteenth century; no opportunities to examine some of the most influential works of Western philosophy, beginning and carrying on from the Milesians through Plato, Aristotle, and the major figures of "modern philosophy"; and no social and historical context for what is learned—thus, tradition is observed more in the breach than in its practice. And when, under budgetary pressures, elementary and secondary schools cut music and art from the curriculum, they deprive students of the best sources for cultivating the creative imagination. Schools fulfill their responsibility to students and their communities when, at every level, they offer a program of systematic, critical learning that simultaneously provides students with access to the rich traditions of so-called Western thought, history, and the arts, including literature, and opens parallel vistas of Africa, Asia, and Latin America.[26]

Finally, the schools should relieve themselves of their ties to corporate interests and reconstruct the curriculum along lines of genuine intellectual endeavor. Nor should the schools be seen as career conduits, although this function will be difficult to displace—among other reasons because in an era of high economic anxiety, many kids and their parents worry about the future and seek some practical purchase on it. It will take some doing to convince them that their best leg up is an education. It is unlikely in the present environment but possible in some places.

I could elaborate these options; this chapter is only an outline. In order to come close to their fulfillment, at least three things are needed. First, we require a conversation concerning the nature and scope of education and the limits of schooling as an educational site. Along with this, theorists and researchers need to link their knowledge of popular culture, and culture in the anthropological sense—that is, everyday life—with the politics of education. Specifically, we need to examine why in late capitalist societies, the public sphere withers while the corporatization process penetrates every sphere of life.

Second, we need teachers who, by their own education, are intellectuals who respect children and want to help them obtain a genuine education, regardless of their social class. For this we need a new regime of teacher education founded on the idea that the educator must be well educated. It would surely entail abolishing the current curricula of most education schools, if not the schools themselves. The endless courses on "teaching methods" would be replaced with courses in the natural and social sciences, mathematics, philosophy, history, and literature. Some of these courses would address the relation of education, in all its forms, to these subjects' social and historical context. In effect, the teacher would become an intellectual, capable of the critical appropriation of world histories and cultures.

Third, we need a movement of parents, students, teachers, and the labor movement armed with a political program directed toward forcing legislatures to adequately fund schooling at the federal, state, and local levels and boards of education to deauthorize the high-stakes standardized tests that currently drive the curriculum and pedagogy.[27]

Having proposed these changes, we need to remain mindful of the limitations of schooling and the likelihood that youth will acquire knowledge outside schools that prepares them for life, such as sex, the arts, where to find jobs, how to bind with other people, how to fight, how to love and hate. The deinstitutionalization of education does not require abandoning schools. But they should be rendered benign, removed as much as possible from the tightening grip of the corporate warfare state. In turn, teachers must resist becoming agents of the prison system, of the drug companies, of corporate capital. In the last instance, the best chance for education resides in the communities, in social movements, and in the kids themselves.

NOTES

1. John Dewey, *Democracy and Education* (Carbondale: Southern Illinois University Press, 1980).

2. Hannah Arendt, "The Crisis in Education," in *Between Past and Future* (New York: Penguin Books, 1961).

3. Andrew Ross, *No-Collar: The Humane Workplace and Its Hidden Costs* (Philadelphia: Temple University Press, 2003).

4. Michael B. Katz, *The Irony of Early School Reform: Educational Innovation in Mid-Nineteenth-Century Massachusetts* (Boston: Beacon Press: 1970).

5. Dewey, op. cit. 331.

6. Stanley Aronowitz, *The Knowledge Factory: Dismantling the Corporate University and Creating True Higher Education* (Boston: Beacon Press, 2000).

7. Pierre Bourdieu and Jean-Claude Passeron, *Reproduction in Education, Culture and Society* (London: Sage Publications, 1977).

8. Aaron Cicourel and John Kitrae, *The Education Decision-Makers* (New York: Bobbs-Merrill, 1963).

9. Paul Willis, *Learning to Labor: How Working Class Kids Get Working Class Jobs* (New York: Columbia University Press, 1981).

10. Louis Althusser, "Ideology and Ideological Apparatuses," in *Lenin and Philosophy* (New York: Monthly Review Press, 1971); Richard Sennett and Jonathan Cobb, *The Hidden Injuries of Class* (New York: Vintage, 1973).

11. Michael Hardt and Antonio Negri, *Labor of Dionysus* (Minneapolis: University of Minnesota Press, 1994).

12. Ross, op. cit.

13. Hannah Arendt, *The Human Condition* (Chicago: University of Chicago Press, 1958).

14. Max Horkheimer and Theodor Adorno, *Dialectic of the Enlightenment*, trans. Edmund Jephcott, (Palo Alto, Calif., Stanford University Press, 2002); Dwight Macdonald, *Against the American Grain* (New York: DaCapo Press, 1983); Marshall McLuhan, *Understanding Media* (New York: McGrawHill, 1964).

15. Neil Postman, *Amusing Ourselves to Death* (New York: Viking, 1986).

16. Robert Christgau, *Any Old Way You Choose It* (Cambridge: Harvard University Press, 1973); Greil Marcus, *Mystery Train* (New York: Random House, 1975).

17. Siegfried Kracauer, *The Mass Ornament* (Cambridge: Harvard University Press, 1995).

18. André Bazin, *What Is Cinema?* (Berkeley: University of California Press, 1989); Christian Metz, *Film Language: A Semiotics of the Cinema* (Chicago: University of Chicago Press, 1991); Pauline Kael, *I Lost It at the Movies* (New York: Marion Boyers, 1994); Hortense Powdermaker, *Hollywood: The Dream Factory* (Boston: Little, Brown, 1950).

19. Kenneth Teitelbaum, *Schooling for "Good Rebels": Socialism, American Education, and the Search for Radical Curriculum* (New York: Teachers College Press, 1995).

20. Samuel Gompers, *Seventy Years of Life and Labor: An Autobiography* (New York: E. P. Dutton, 1924).

21. John Locke, *An Essay Concerning the Human Understanding* (New York: Dover., 1954), bk. 1, ch. 28, no. 12, 478; emphasis in the original.

22. William James, *Principles of Psychology* (New York: H. Holt, 1890).

23. Locke, op. cit.

24. Arendt, "The Crisis in Education," 180–1.

25. Henry Giroux, *Stealing Innocence: Youth, Corporate Power, and the Politics of Culture* (New York: St. Martin's Press, 2000).

26. Aronowitz, *The Knowledge Factory*, ch. 7.

27. Stanley Aronowitz and Henry Giroux, *Education Under Siege* (South Hadley, Mass.: Bergin and Garvey, 1985).

PART FOUR

Politics

CHAPTER ELEVEN

Marxism and Democracy

Introduction

Some of the more significant contributions to social theory in the '60s and '70s were made by Marxists who endeavored to "bring the state back in" to considerations of both the nature of the structure of social relations and to prospects for historical transformation. Following the large divisions of this period between structuralism, critical theory and "plain" Marxism (the approach according to which the economic infrastructure determined, in rough correspondence, the crucial institutions of the superstructure), the precise location of the state in social relations, its effectivity and its vulnerability to protest and reform were the crucial issues in dispute. Notwithstanding these differences, Marxist theory remained largely immune to some of the major debates that had animated the socialist and working-class movements of the nineteenth century, especially the question of democracy. No doubt this glaring omission can be ascribed in a significant measure to the certainties of the post-Bolshevik left which lingered throughout the postwar period, at least until the collapse of "Eurocommunism" in the late '70s. For social democrats the body of liberal democracy was to be incorporated into the new socialist societies. In fact, the predominant social-democratic critique of capitalist politics was not substantive but, rather its failure to extend to the economic sphere. The political limitation of democracy under capitalism was not imbedded in its institutions. Effectively, therefore, democracy was identical with the definition of socialism, but made more global.

On the other side, those who followed Marx's and Engel's critique of "bourgeois" democracy (of which more below), agreed that the working-class movement needed the liberal state for the sole purpose of organizing to overturn and replace it—without civil liberties, not only the right to strike but also to "use" the state to ameliorate working conditions such as health and safety regulations, abolition of child and sweated labor, and a measure of social security. But, in the main, the left followed the Leninist critique of the capitalist state as a stacked deck. Therefore, liberal democracy could never be conceived as a goal of working-class political struggle, but only as a means to another end, the abolition of the state and politics as such.

The breakup of communist ideology in the '70s has led to the revival of discourses of left republicanism, citizenship, and liberal versions of parliamentary democracy according to which representatives, accountable to their constituencies, are to supplement, but not replace, party politics. In effect, the left, including many Marxists and those influenced by Marxism have made a startling rediscovery of liberal political theory. Norberto Bobbio,[1] Adam Przeworski,[2] Ernesto Laclau and Chantal Mouffe[3] have, in somewhat different ways, gone so far as to displace the social in favor of a conception of human relations in the model of politics, a return to both Greek and early bourgeois conceptions of society.

The present essay is an examination of this turn in the light of the history of the Marxist discourse on democracy. As will become evident, I defend a conception of democracy which, deriving from Hegel and Marx as well as some tendencies in anarchism, argues that democratic society can be constituted only by understanding citizenship as self-management in economic, social, and cultural aspects. In this framework, the idea of participation by producers and consumers of goods (whether of the means of subsistence, services or formal knowledge) in the decisions that affect their lives, can constitute democracy. In this conception, socialist democracy consists in a "free association" of individuals each of whom is expected to participate fully in the decisions affecting the collective. Obviously, the republican virtue is to insist upon rules which ensure equality, and the observance of which sanctions participation. Among these none stands higher on the ethical scale than the creation of a public sphere of dialogue and debate among members, a substantive intervention that, hopefully, limits the degree to which crucial decisions are made by elites and undermines the side of the meaning of "consent" that signifies passive approbation by means of formal procedures.

Clearly, this program would entail considerable transformations—in institutions of representation, the availability of knowledge, channels of communication, length of the working day, patterns of childcare which prohibit women from participation in the public sphere, the scale of production and distribution of goods and services, and governance. Broadly speaking, it would require a radically different conception of what we mean by and expect from "state" power because it would reverse the substantive elements of sovereignty by making all crucial public decisions subject to review and amendment by the people.

Some of the discussion around these issues, especially by Bobbio, focuses on the question concerning representation or, more precisely, on ways of expressing popular will. As I will describe it below, one of the core arguments against radical democracy turns out to rely on the notion of "complexity" in modern societies. Critics of radical democracy presuppose this complexity in their proposal to support strengthening liberal democracy as a socialist end. In this essay I offer the argument that among the errors of nearly all previous Marxist and social thought has been its failure to entertain, seriously (except polemically) the anarchist objection to both the nation-state and large-scale, centralized economic and political subdivisions. Just as the idea of self-managed socialism was developed most fully in the anarchist tradition, particularly by Pierre-Joseph Proudhon, Gustav Landauer and, in a more Marxist vein by council communism, so the critique of the authoritarian features of even the most liberal state fell to the anarchists because Marxism had failed to recognize the relative autonomy of the state, politics and bureaucracies from their economic infrastructure, even in the wake of Engels's warnings against economic determinism. Marxism excoriated the capitalist state for its role as defenders of bourgeois relations of production. But it was not until Louis Althusser and Nicos Poulantzas[4] derived the relative autonomy of the state from their anti-Hegelian critique of the base-superstructure model that a major Marxist tendency made an opening for state theory, and more particularly for a theory of politics. For even if the critical theory of the Frankfurt School had adopted Weber's understanding of the growing sovereignty of the state bureaucracy, the crucial link between the state and monopoly capital formed the foundation of their modern conception of the state. (Here Franz Neumann and Otto Kirchheimer may be considered partial exceptions especially in their work on fascism.) Ironically, the import of Althusser's work has been to provide a new Marxist appreciation of the possibilities of working-class intervention into the capitalist state, an insight brought home most forcefully in Poulantzas's last book, *State, Power, Socialism*, where both the ideal of proletarian dictatorship in the transition to socialism is renounced as well as the classical Marxist instrumental state theory. Henceforth, the state is to become an arena, perhaps the arena for proletarian class struggle.

My essay appears at the precise moment when the full implications of Althusserian theory for a post-Marxist discourse on democracy are becoming more evident. I share much of the structuralist critique of automatic Marxism, but not the political conclusions derived from this critique. Rather, I hold that the relative autonomy of the state signifies that the struggle against exploitation in production relations and domination in the political sphere are inseparable elements in a discourse of emancipation.

I

With respect to the proletariat the republic differs from the monarchy only in that it is a ready-for-use political form for the future rule of the proletariat. You are at an advantage compared with us in already having it; we for our part shall have to spend twenty-four hours to make it. But a republic, like every other form of government, is determined by its content. So long as it is a form of bourgeois democracy it is hostile to us as any monarchy (except for the forms of hostility). It is therefore a wholly baseless illusion to regard it as essentially socialist in form or to entrust socialist tasks to it while it is dominated by the bourgeoisie. We shall be able to wrest concessions from it but never to put it in charge of the execution of what is our own concern, even if we should be able to control it by a minority strong enough to change into a majority overnight.

(Engels to Lafargue, 6 March 1894)

The proletariat too needs democratic forms for the seizure of political power but to it they are, like all political forms, mere means. But if today democracy is wanted as an end one must seek support in the peasantry and petty bourgeoisie, i.e. in classes that are in process of dissolution and reactionary in relation to the proletariat as soon as they try to maintain themselves artificially. Furthermore, it must not be forgotten that precisely the democratic republic is the logical form of bourgeois rule... And yet the democratic republic always remains the last form of bourgeois rule, that in which it goes to pieces.[5]

(Engels to Bernstein)

For Marx and Engels the republic is a specifically bourgeois democratic form capable of yielding to organized working-class demands for reforms, but incapable of making room for a proletarian takeover within the framework of parliamentary representation. In any case, democracy cannot be an end, only a means of working-class action: it is hard to envision the development of powerful trade unions and workers' parties under repressive conditions. The working class and its organs of struggle must enjoy rights: so to speak, to publish their press, to assemble freely. Yet, for Marx and Engels, the movements cannot nourish the illusion that emancipation (socialism and beyond) may be brought about by controlling the bourgeois state, even if workers' representatives enjoy majorities in legislative bodies.

Despite these warnings, social-democratic parties persisted in holding the view that bourgeois democratic forms were adequate, given a high level of working-class mobilization, to the achievement of substantial, i.e. structural reforms. These views were held particularly by Bernstein and his followers through the period leading up to World War I and beyond. Even the intellectual defeats suffered by the revisionists at turn-of-the-century German Social-Democratic congresses at the hands of revolutionary Marxist critics such as Karl Kautsky and Rosa Luxemburg, did not prevent the spread of the argument, more vital in the late twentieth century than when it was first articulated, that the achievement of democratic rights and universal suffrage encompassing the working class and other hitherto deprived strata, constituted a permanent gain which would not be replaced by new forms of rule. The working class and its organizations, particularly its political parties which represented it in parliaments, could under the new circumstances of suffrage, which eventually included women, reform the bourgeois state to near death. Nor could these be regarded as mere "concessions" as Engels was prone to do. The structure of rule could be affected as well by such major reforms as are embodied in the broad rubric of the welfare state, the provisions of which amounted to a significantly different social order. In substance, the quality of life could be permanently altered for the working class, provided it remained class-conscious and politically vigilant.

Of course, these gains and the ideology that accompanied them depended, at their root, upon the given nation having attained a relatively high level of development of productive forces. Equally important, capitalism itself had to have become organized so that the allocation of surplus value between capital and labor was now regulated by the state, corresponding to the growing power of the working-class parties. In turn, this power reflected the spread of trade-unionism and cooperatives, the flowering of socialist culture and therefore the necessity, from capital's standpoint, to forge new terms of political compromise in which consent replaced coercion as the key basis of social rule.

In effect, Bernstein, the recipient of Engels's "lecture" on bourgeois democracy, separated the concept of democracy from the pejorative prefix under conditions where the working class had successfully taken the offensive against capital. He insisted that political action (as opposed to industrial action) did not merely wring concessions but changed the nature of the state and these reflected, not merely a growing alliance with the petty bourgeoisie or even the peasantry, but, more importantly, a new level of proletarian power—the power to control, or at least participate in, determining the destiny of society as a whole. For it was not only the direction of state expenditures that were transformed by agitation and legislation but the configuration of the capitalist system itself, an outcome entirely unexpected by the founders of scientific socialism.[6]

Underlying Bernstein's evolutionary perspective was his judgement that capitalism had stabilized economically, that cartel and monopoly development signified increased rationalization (taken as a neutral, universal category). In effect, having solved the problem of the anarchy of production, advanced capitalism was prepared, in the new situation, to accommodate to working-class demands, even to democratically alter the state form in its own interest. For among the vital presuppositions of organized capitalism, none stood higher than stable industrial and labor relations. Therefore, a new industrial order, marked by workers' participation, through enlightened representatives, in some key decisions of the enterprise as well as the system as a whole, was thoroughly consistent with the idea that uncertainty had to be removed from the economic and hence the political equation. It is important to separate this program from the charge that it signified a surrender of class struggle or socialist ideology. Despite his departure from the orthodox Marxist doctrine that only proletarian revolution could bring social emancipation, Bernstein attributed the new state of affairs to class action. The slogan that the "movement is everything, the goal is nothing" reinforces this idea; for Bernstein there is no question of a permanent arrangement whereby the social-democrats would lay down their "arms," only the need to jettison the dogmatic doctrine according to which only the seizure of power by force could bring into being a new social order.

In practice, even Bernstein's opponents were obliged to work for reforms, especially those which extended democratic rights and the amelioration through legislation of working and living conditions. The chief difference became one of interpretation. For Rosa Luxemburg, these gains were at best temporary; the inevitable economic collapse resulting from chronic underconsumption at home and the closing of the frontiers for capital investment abroad would force the bourgeoisie to seek attenuation of the falling profit rate by cancelling or reducing major welfare-state provisions and cutting wages. These measures would exacerbate workers' resistance, which would likely be met by the now-covert, now-overt state coercion against the movement and its representatives.

This resistance, combined with the inherent limits to world capital accumulation would lead to complete collapse of the system.[7]

The debate within German social democracy was reproduced, with appropriate national variations, in all major capitalist countries. Everywhere socialists were perplexed by the distance between classical Marxist crisis theory and the apparent development of an organized capitalism on a world scale. Under these circumstances, victories by the workers' movement in extending social benefits, the level of trade-union organization and the parliamentary strength of the socialist and labor parties produced a definite tendency within the left toward reformism, a tendency that seemed to merge with left support for national as well as class politics.

Germany's entrance into World War I found the socialist movement divided: a majority of the SPD representatives supported the government's request for war credits and even some revolutionaries such as Kautsky refused to wage "war against war" on behalf of the working class. This experience was reproduced in other democratic countries, where thousands of socialists who actively opposed the war were jailed by their own governments, regardless of the existence of constitutional or legislatively-induced bourgeois freedoms won in the previous decades. Luxemburg herself languished in jail for much of the war, the liberal Democrat Woodrow Wilson sanctioned the imprisonment of Eugene Debs, the leading American socialist, and hundreds of others were either jailed or deported. These experiences, combined with the deteriorating economic conditions after the war in Germany, the Austro-Hungarian Empire and Russia led to revolutionary upsurge in several major European countries in 1917–9, uprisings that renounced, for the most part, the Bernsteinian arguments of the prior two decades. As Lenin disbanded the Constituent Assembly in Russia, a signpost of the democratic revolution of February 1917, the characterizations of Marx and Engels, that republican democracy was, after all, inextricably linked to bourgeois rule, was revived and became the basis of the political ideology of Leninism. To the main features of democratic freedoms, including parliamentary rule, Lenin posed the alternative of proletarian democracy, a concept drawn from his reading of Marx's *Critique of the Gotha Program*, the practical examples of the Paris Commune and of the creation of workers' councils during the 1905

Russian Revolution, which Lenin as well as Luxemburg understood as forms of dual power to that of the monarchy and its Duma. Recall the Duma was a representative body that lacked even the power of a proper bourgeois parliament. In contrast, the soviets were meant to exercise sovereign power over state decisions; they were to be both legislative and administrative bodies which, according to Lenin, amounted to a parallel state to that of the monarchy. During the height of the 1905 revolution Lenin theorized that a state of dual power existed because the monarchy was unable to assert its hegemony, which, for Lenin meant a monopoly over the means of violence. The soviets were powerful to the extent that they had obtained the arms necessary to make their "state" organs effective.

The fundamental difference between bourgeois and proletarian democracy has often been portrayed in the phrase "dictatorship of the proletariat." For Marx, this concept signified a transformation in the content as well as the state form in the transition between capitalism and socialism. Since democracy under capitalism was always a form of bourgeois rule, the cards were inevitably stacked against the workers, especially if they managed to achieve a level of representation in legislative bodies approaching a majority or, in the alternative, were able to project their own minority government with the support of parties of other subordinate strata. Engels's judgement that such a republic was already "too dangerous" suggests that we could expect the bourgeoisie to mount a counter-offensive as soon as the left parties attempted to intervene in the process of capital accumulation and alter patterns of distribution of the social surplus through legislation, or the trade unions engage in mass strikes to lower working-hours or achieve more far-reaching political reforms. Engels's rather linear scenario was only indirectly fulfilled in the wake of the collapse of the Weimar Republic, but there is enough prescience in the evaluation of the limits of representative democracy to explain the persistence of revolutionary scepticism regarding the strategic value of this form for the working class well into the later decade of this century.

However, the experience of the early years of the Bolshevik revolution appeared to validate Engels's judgement that the bourgeoisie, both internal and international, would not stand by and permit the new Soviet state to survive without making counter-revolutionary moves to over-throw the new regime. Recall that the new regime immediately faced armed opposition from representatives of the old order, recalcitrant peasants who were organized by both the right and the anarchists into militia that opposed the Red Army (although the Makhnovist movement of anarchist peasants attempted to come to agreements with Trotsky and Lenin and were treated cynically by the Bolsheviks).[8] In 1920, twenty-one foreign armies invaded Russia, hoping to topple the regime. These expe-riences, as much as the Leninist reading of Marx's late writings on the transition from capitalism to socialism convinced the Bolsheviks that the remnants of the liberal state should not be revived in the wake of capitalist encirclement. In any case, according to this argument, rep-resentative democracy was inherently a middle-class demand and had never really enjoyed a mass base in Russia. Beneath the Menshevik (social-democratic) judgement that a prolonged period of parliamentary democracy was necessary in a regime of capitalist social relations, were two elements of second international Marxism: from Marx (the famous preface to the *Contribution to the Critique of Political Economy*) came the proposition that no social order ever disappears before all the forces of production within it have been fully developed. Russia, a relatively industrially-backward society, was simply unprepared to accommodate socialist production relations. And there was the by now canonical view, adapted from Bernstein's, that socialism inherits the main elements of bourgeois freedoms and does not abolish them, particularly representa-tive democracy and civil liberties. These articles of prewar socialist faith were rudely dismissed by Lenin in the wake of the civil war that broke out soon after the Bolshevik seizure of power.

It is important to note that the left criticism of bourgeois democracy paralleled the right-wing criticism of such theorists as Carl Schmitt, who argued that the bourgeoisie was incapable of preserving social order, be-cause of its essentially apolitical stand. Among Schmitt's most power-ful arguments is the disappearance of genuine debate concerning public issues in parliamentary regimes. Schmitt derides the liberal claim that these regimes make vital political decisions "through representative in-stitutions, through public discussion, that is, reason."

The reality of parliamentary and party political life and public convictions are today far removed from such beliefs. Great political and economic decisions on which the fate of mankind rests no longer result today (if they ever did) from balancing opinions in public debate and counterdebate. Such decisions are no longer the outcome of parliamentary debate...the whole system of freedom of speech, assembly, and the press, of public meetings, parliamentary immunities and privileges, is losing its rationale. Small and exclusive committees of parties or of party coalitions make their decisions behind closed doors and what representatives of big capitalist interest groups agree to in the smallest committees is more important for the fate of millions of people, perhaps, than any political decision.[9]

This from one of the most articulate theorists of the coming antidemocratic German state. As Ellen Kennedy has argued, Schmitt's crucial distinction between "true" democracy, where there is an identity of the rulers and the ruled, and representative democracy, where this principle is compromised, was initially influential on such left-wing political theorists as Franz Neumann and particularly Otto Kirchheimer.[10] Both were students of Schmitt around 1930 when left and right critiques of democracy dominated the intellectual space of Weimar politics. For both tendencies the legitimation of representative democracy was undermined by the growing tendency toward secret government so long as there was no substantive agreement on a set of values from which policies could be fashioned. Owing to the absence of consensus, secret government was bound to replace open, public debate because these societies, in which representative democracy existed, were fatally heterogeneous with respect to social interests, a situation which prevented the emergence of a public sphere of political discourse in which reason rather than violence could prevail. For Schmitt, violence was the inevitable consequence of social fissures, themselves exacerbated by neutrality of the liberal state while the social order is torn apart under it.

Underlying these judgements is a critique of the dominance, in political theory, of formal rationality (constitutionalism) and instrumental rationality (pluralism). What united left and right in this respect was the search for a new foundation for substantive reason, a category abandoned with the ascendancy of the scientific world-view that has won ideological hegemony in the bourgeois social and political order. What Norbert Bobbio is, approvingly, to call the "rules of the game," is an explicit abandonment of the search for consensual values upon which to base social decisions except the acceptance by all parties of a procedural definition of democracy.[11] According to this conception, unilateral methods for resolving political differences are renounced, especially the use of violence. What marks the idea of proletarian democracy as an alternative to both the liberal state and parliamentary forms of decision-making is its claim to have grounded political theory in a consensus in which the universal interest has replaced the unprincipled compromises that recognize the ineluctability of difference as the basis for politics which is really the cornerstone of liberal theory. There are, of course, several varieties of liberalism, the leading versions of which are individualism, really an adaptation of Lockean and Smithian conceptions and the interest-group theories of American political science. In neither case does the concept of universality occupy a significant theoretical space. Therefore, the logical necessity of proceduralist views of social rule.

The new form of post-revolutionary workers' democracy, the soviet or workers' council, was understood as nearly identical to the concept of the transitional state, replacing the bourgeois state by representatives of workers' parties which, however, supported the revolution and the necessity of its defense by force against internal and external enemies but might disagree on such questions as economic strategy, social policy, and so on. Since the soviet was not merely a legislative body but an organ of administration as well, it would thwart, at least in concept, the emergence of a new bureaucratic class whose existence could undermine workers' power in the name of efficiency and expertise. Additionally, Lenin and Leon Trotsky feared that this new "socialist" bureaucratic class would administer in its own interest.[12] Similarly, the role of the manager in enterprises was placed in contention by the revolutionary left, which argued that workers' councils should legislate and administer the labor process, distribution, and other ordinary industrial functions. As is well known, Lenin rejected these arguments on practical grounds: the urgent necessity to rapidly develop the productive forces needed to solve the twin military and economic crises made the demand for workers' control a luxury in enterprises as much as in the state. For others the soviets would not, necessarily, replace the representative character of legislative assemblies. The left proponents of retaining elements of representative democracy remained persuaded that developed industrial society was simply too complex for direct democracy–that is, fulfilling legislative and administrative functions in the manner of the Athenian *polis*. Lenin's own optimism on the eve of the October Revolution that a system of direct democracy was possible during the transition, expressed in his pamphlet *State and Revolution*, was rapidly dissipated in the wake of the civil war and the foreign invasion of 1921, events that were to permanently alter the content of the revolutionary dictatorship in the lexicon of Soviet Marxism. Henceforth, demands for direct proletarian democracy were labelled "ultra-left" or ultra-democratic, which endangered the revolution. A minority has always disagreed, insisting that, even if representatives are needed for "higher" functions, the base of the entire system should consist of popular assemblies that would really run shop-level and neighborhood affairs and can send delegates to higher bodies recallable at any time if they failed to reflect the will of shopfloor and neighborhood groups (not merely represent them in the larger sense). This system would suggest a radical redefinition of socialist democracy which sharply diverges both in composition as well as intention from its bourgeois form. The minority view was articulated best by the group of council communists which in the early years after the war had considerable influence in both the Dutch and German communist movements. The names of the key figures—Karl Korsch, Anton Pannekoek, Herman Gorter and Henriette Roland Holst— suffered eclipse until the 1960s, largely because their views, paralleling those of Rosa Luxemburg and the "workers' opposition" in the Soviet Union, were discredited by the apparent success of the Bolshevik Revolution and particularly the prestige of Lenin.[13] Lenin's pamphlet, *Left-Wing Communism: An Infantile Disorder* (1920), was directed to both attacking their petition on workers' democracy and establishing a new line for the world communist movement which, recognizing that world capitalism had achieved "temporary" stabilization (again) after the initial revolutionary upsurge of the immediate postwar years, counselled moderation, especially toward bourgeois democratic governments and those socialist parties that adhered to parliamentary struggle as the substance of working-class and socialist action. Lenin's critique of left-wing communism may be seen as a repudiation of his own utopian *State and Revolution; Left-Wing Communism*'s wide dissemination made communist short-term strategy virtually identical with that of its arch-rival, social democracy. (Of course, the new policy of the United Front with social democratic workers and parties was understood as a temporary expedient dictated by contemporary conditions. However, with the exception of the short-lived "third-period" sectarianism (1928–34) it turned out to be the dominant communist perspective of the twentieth century, in part, because although stabilized capitalism proved a temporary phenomenon, the development of fascism reaffirmed the United Front policy, but on different grounds.)

For virtually half a century, the communists and other elements of the revolutionary Marxist left (Trotskyists, left social democrats, Maoists and "democratic" Leninists of various stripes) held fast to the dual perspectives of Leninism: the need for a non-sectarian united front against the right whose common basis is the defense of bourgeois democracy, especially civil liberties and representative government; at the same time, this tendency, which has encompassed the overwhelming majority of Marxist parties and intellectuals influenced by Leninism and the Bolshevik Revolution, retained the idea of the proletarian dictatorship as the model of postrevolutionary transition. For the communists, the degree of democracy consistent with the transition was determined by the reality of capitalist encirclement. Accordingly, ultra-democratic demands could only weaken the revolution, especially workers' control at the factory level and multi-party political democracy in councils and parliaments. Therefore, the Soviet model, although increasingly criticized, after Stalin's death, for its harsh repression of dissent, was viewed by the CP and its periphery as a more or less adequate representation of the degree to which democracy could be implemented by a socialist state in a world dominated by aggressive capitalist powers on the hand, and the relative underdevelopment of productive forces in socialist societies. Although critical of the failure of the Soviet Communists to address the problems of inner party democracy in a Leninist spirit, namely, to guarantee the right to (socialist) dissent, especially the right of workers to strike and the right of political dissenters to form factions and publish independently of official party organs, mainstream Trotskyism and other independent Leninist lefts have defended the achievement of the Soviet Union, Cuba, and China, especially the abolition of private property in the decisive means of production. Thus did the bulk of revolutionary Marxism until about 1970 maintain the classic duality between reform and revolution. One judges the postrevolutionary regime differently from those enclosed within the capitalist orbit and ascribes the shortcomings of socialism with respect to its democratic institutions to the hegemony of global imperialism. Gone, for all intents and purposes, was the earlier quest for substantive democracy, since the possibility of ideological and material homogeneity had been, for the time being at least, foreclosed. Nor were the Leninists prepared to accept the main propositions of procedural democracy proposed by social democrats.

Under this regime, most Marxists evaluate bourgeois democracy by separate criteria from those that might be applied to countries such as the Soviet Union. Bourgeois countries were evaluated by this section of the left by the degree to which the working class and other popular movements enjoy the ability to organize on the shopfloor and in the legislatures for the amelioration of their working and living conditions. For example, American communists and Trotskyists placed considerable emphasis upon civil liberties and civil rights and were, until very recently, leading defenders of these freedoms. But, since Marxists expected little, if any, popular control over the workplace and the state so long as capitalist social relations prevail, demands such as workers' self-management of the labor process without altering ownership of the means of production by capital were regarded as contemporary examples of ultra-leftism or utopianism, judgements that reflected the ideological dualism of Marxist perspectives on democracy. In sum for the revolutionary left, except for the New Left of the 1960s, socialism was the absolute condition for true democratic initiatives at the point of production as well as in other sectors of social relations; under capitalism the job of the workers' movements is to battle for concessions, even far-reaching reforms that institutionalize these concessions as "rights" which accompany the formation of a sector of the state bureaucracy to enforce them. Simultaneously, the ever-present danger of right-wing attacks upon basic bourgeois liberties forces the left to devote considerable energies to protecting them. As for the rights of minorities, particularly blacks and immigrants, some Marxists have theorized that the struggle against discrimination in employment, housing, and civil liberties, represents a crucial blow against capital's effort to maintain a large industrial reserve army by the method of exclusion of large sections of the labor force from any but the most menial employment. To fight against discrimination in employment, housing, and education is to fight for working-class unity, because its success tends to remove the differences in the technical division of labor between blacks and whites which, in the orthodox view, is the material basis of ideological racism.

The separation of present and future by the revolutionary left is undoubtedly influenced by the realities of the social and political environments of leading Western democracies. With crucial caveats, to be discussed below, workers' movements have succeeded beyond the expectations of revolutionary Marxists in winning substantial gains through the capitalist state, an achievement that seems to validate Bernstein's judgement that an apocalyptic future is decisively foreclosed by the capacity of capital to learn how to attenuate its own contradictions, to which Keynes has added a crucial verification in his widely-accepted political economy of state intervention into investment and consumption.[14] It is important at this point to note that many socialist theorists nourished in post-World War II European environment, particularly Jürgen Habermas, Wolfgang Abendroth and Claus Offe, among others, interpreted the rise of the welfare state as a substantive historical achievement in the direction of "redeeming the promise of representative democracy" by establishing a new consensus regarding social equality. As this view has evolved, socialism has been redefined as "more equality" which may or may not entail the social ownership of the means of production, a demand now relegated to a conjunctural outcome of the resistance of big capital to structural reforms that aim at substantial redistributive justice. The

welfare state is understood by Habermas and Offe as a two-headed phenomenon: on one side, it would not have come about without the powerful
workers' movement that imposed such measures as income guarantees
during unemployment on an unwilling capitalist class; on the other, the
welfare state legitimates the liberal state and blunts the chance that a
new form of social rule will replace it. In any case, the great compromise struck between labor and capital after the War in nearly all Western countries restructured both accumulation and the terms upon which
the underlying population were prepared to grant consent to the state.
Capital was now obliged to take into account the relatively fixed transfer
payments bill when considering options for investment unless it could
persuade voters, particularly workers, of a different form of legitimation.

After World War II, capital demanded of trade unions and socialist
and labor parties that they consent to the Atlantic Alliance's international aims. The majority of movements under social-democratic leadership
responded by demanding substantial concessions in the provision of
transfer payments whether they succeeded as in Britain in winning parliamentary majorities or not. The welfare state became the price exacted
by the labor movement for the new postwar corporativism.

Communist opposition was confined, almost entirely, to questions of
international relations since their own conception of socialist organization and mobilization tended to support a commitment to enlarged state
intervention, especially in Europe, where substantial arms expenditures
were not assumed by the leading governments during most of the postwar period. Given the weakness of the insurgent right during the first
two decades after World War II, democracy as such remained off the political agenda, giving way to debates concerning the pace and direction
of state intervention. Most of the left remained unconcerned about the
problems of the formation of a sovereign state bureaucracy that accompanied the growth of the economic and legitimation functions of the
state. After all, with the exception of Trotsky's writings, particularly his
neglected critique of early signs of bureaucratism in the Soviet Union,
The New Course, neither communists nor social democrats had confronted this question at a theoretical level, reproducing the relative neglect of
explicit treatments in the works of Marx and Lenin and the key theorists

of the Socialist International, Kautsky, Bernstein and Luxemburg, although the Austro-Marxists seemed keenly aware of the problem in the first decades of the twentieth century.

Nor did the profound threats to democracy in metropolitan countries posed by imperialist intervention in the Third World produce a serious postwar debate. Even the rise of national liberation movements in the colonial world did not initially disturb left complacency. The Western left became, at the same time, a national left, one almost wants to say "nationalist," a position which rendered both major wings, communist and socialist, relatively indifferent when not outright supportive of their own governments' foreign policy. With the exception of a non-Communist extreme left and small pacifist movements, both communists and social democrats remained aloof until the US intervention in Vietnam, principally because (with the notable exception of the East/West divide) the left ignored or gave little more than lip service to the North/South cleavage. For example, French socialists actually supported the French colonial policy in Southeast Asia and may be held partially culpable in the notorious war-aims of the French government against liberation movements in the region. Similarly it was not until the Algerian War in 1960 that the Communists finally actively opposed the position of their own government. While ritualistically critical of French colonial policies, the Communists had to be forced from the extreme left to take direct action. As for the powerful British Labour Party which formed three postwar governments, the Irish question was treated as all former, and subsequent governments had: Catholic demands for Irish unity were rejected and the virtual occupation of the country by British troops has been a continuous feature of the Irish policy, whether under Labour or Conservative rule.

II

It was the rise of the New Left in Europe and the United States that revived political and theoretical interest on the left concerning questions of democracy. The core of the New Left critique of bourgeois democracy consisted in the claim that representative government was a shell; far from being delegates of groups of people, whether geographically or institutionally based, representatives increasingly responded to the discipline of their own parties which, like the trade union and corporate bureaucracies which constitute their fundamental organizational base, have come to represent a constellation of autonomous interests. The party leaders are obliged to factor in the concrete grievances of the underlying population, but subsume them under the historical compromise between the labor bureaucracy and capital which forms the core of the capitalist state. Far from being an unambiguous benefit to ordinary people, interventionist economic and social-state policies have centralized power in fewer hands. Trotsky and Weber had, in different ways, called attention to the dangers for popular democracy represented by the emergence of a relatively powerful bureaucracy in societies in which the state and industrial development were intimately linked, but socialists and communists were fairly supportive of this development. The New Left claimed that the reason for the lack of concern with bureaucracy was inherent in the transformation of the official left into a self-interested organizational colossus itself which is bound by innumerable ties to the established order.

Although in both the United States and Western Europe the New Left emerges around opposition to the efforts of capitalist states to retain colonial empires, its roots are as much in the struggle to redefine categories such as democracy and freedom and to reconstruct them. In the United States, the generation born just before the War which reached adulthood between the late '50s and the mid-'60s rejected both the middle-class suburban culture into which they were inducted and the "ideological state apparatuses," particularly schools, which purported to prepare them for citizenship but merely delivered them to the economic order as workers and professionals. This generation also perceived representative democracy as a shell, a series of institutions marked more by its exclusions than inclusions. In the United States this perception was buttressed by the emerging civil rights movement of the mid-'50s which called the disenfranchisement of blacks to the attention of white America, most particularly the Montgomery Bus boycott of 1955 and the school integration struggles of the late '50s.

Under the mostly indirect influence of the mass society critics Herbert Marcuse and especially C. Wright Mills, the student movement begins to challenge the equivalence of representation with democracy by arguing

that the military/industrial complex, Big Labor, and the welfare bureaucracies really run the country, subordinating Congress to the rank of
junior partner of an economic and social monolith. To this oligarchy, the
American New Left counterposed the concept of participatory democracy which invokes images of the New England town meeting and other
forms of direct decision-making.[15] Of course, few advocates of participatory democracy would surrender the struggle for full voting rights for
minorities in representation elections or would derogate the importance
of electing genuine peoples' representatives to legislatures and congress.
It was never a question of either/or, but clearly the movement's emphasis
was always on the creation of new ways to enlarge direct popular control
over key social institutions—schools, health facilities, workplaces and the
Black Panthers raised, in the late '60s, the "impossible" demand for community control over the police.

These initiatives went beyond ideological debate or slogans at demonstrations at the height of the civil rights movement's strength, the late
'60s. In many local communities, legislatures and executive authorities
felt compelled to support, with varying degrees of seriousness, new arrangements that took direct account of popular voices and positions; in
1968, the New York City Board of Education surrendered some of its powers to newly-constituted local school boards; hospitals established community advisory boards which had influence, but not real power over
administration decisions regarding community access to healthcare.
Civilian boards were established to monitor police behavior and community planning boards, which had been fairly weak previously, gained
a genuine voice over urban renewal decisions. Under federal antipoverty
guidelines, the poor had to be represented on boards charged with determining how funds were to be spent at the local level.

Of course, none of these innovations was unambiguously a form of
popular power; all of them operated under severe constraints, reflecting the still-dominant position of bureaucracies and legislatures which
had agreed to share authority only under severe duress. Few of the new
avenues of participation were substantively routinized; on the contrary, when the demonstrations died down and the riots were finally contained in the 1970s, these incipient inroads either disappeared or were

reduced to ritualized performances of citizens' participation. Since the major political parties never genuinely supported either in principle or practice the formation of participatory democratic institutions which did not resemble direct democracy, but broadened the base of representation to quasi-legislative bodies, only the militancy of the movements sustained them. And these movements were not themselves secure enough to withstand the inevitable counter-attack which came almost with the direct-action phase.

It was not difficult for New Left critics of American democracy to invoke the past as a guide to the future. The '50s were seen as eminently undemocratic, even in representative terms. Millions of Southern blacks were literally deprived, by state repression and unofficial terrorism, of citizenship despite constitutional guarantees of voting rights to all qualified citizens; youth under twenty-one could not vote while, at the same time, subjected to an almost continuous postwar draft, political dissent was ruthlessly suppressed and higher education, far from conforming to the ideal of free, self-directed inquiry, was increasingly regimented by academic administration that had drawn closer to the goals of the corporations and their state allies. Perhaps more important, the concept of the Atlantic Alliance, the cornerstone of the international policy of Western capitalist countries, was removed from the agenda of political debate by bipartisanship, an agreement between the Democrats and Republicans to leave such matters to the executive branch of government. In this connection the one important instance of debate about international issues prior to the '60s occurred in 1956 when the Democratic presidential candidate challenged the Eisenhower administration's opposition to welfare state expansion. The Republicans regarded the relationship between defense spending and social benefits a zero-sum game. According to this doctrine, even the vigorous economy could not provide both. Adlai Stevenson argued that we could have "guns and butter" and the Republican opposition to expanded welfare masked as a problem of budgets, was really ideologically motivated. On the other hand, allusions to Jeffersonian democracy (absent its regrettable dependence on slavery) provided an ideological basis for asserting an alternative. American New Left theorists such as Tom Hayden[16] grasped the issue as a struggle for power to control the conditions of social life conceived in personal terms. The American New Left did not renounce the individualism characteristic of American ideology; it asserted boldly that the aim of democratic renovation was to empower individuals to take control over the decisions that affected their lives. For the New Left, the field of battle was to be found, in the main, at the local level, where public bodies regulated electrical rates, decided how many units of public housing might be constructed, who should teach the children of people of color and the poor, how often garbage would be collected, or whether a street light was to be installed. Some of these decisions bear on which party is elected to public office but New Left activists and theorists argued that empowerment was best achieved by direct action since the candidates presented by the leading political parties may be elected by, but rarely took direction from, their constituency.[17] The relationship between the electors and their representatives was mediated by the directing force of national and international capitalist economic power, the domination by bureaucracies inured from public responsibility, which often neutralized the political weight of elected representatives. This state of affairs rendered the claim to genuine democracy under the current setup suspect. The critique of bureaucracy was no less powerful in New Left theory. The doctrine of corporate liberalism asserted among other things that the individual could be reconciled with a corporate-dominated polity, provided a series of institutional arrangements were developed which cushioned the effects of rapid, large-scale changes in the economy, in social and political life. These arrangements always entail, for this doctrine, a compromise among leaders and administrators of large-scale organizations to insure that private associations control public life, but succeed in winning the approbation of the masses. The private control over public authority consequently excludes anything resembling Lockean and Jeffersonian conceptions of democracy. On the contrary, Cold War liberal doctrine asserts the priority of the national security state over everyday life while preserving the doctrine of particularism that is generally confused with individuality. Group interests may be served by state policy to the extent that they become powerful through direct or legislative pressure, but there is no question of sharing power broadly.

The new lefts of Western Europe were products of the powerful communist and social democratic movements of the previous century, but especially of the postwar era even as they broke in certain respects from them. Socialist rather than populist orientation meant that the language of the movements of students and intellectuals was imbedded in Marxist theory, working-class concerns, North/South struggles, and later in problems of immigration and sexuality which they joined with the questions associated with class formation.[18] It did not take much to persuade this generation in Italy that the state and its representative institutions were little more than a caricature of genuine democracy. Political parties offered various and often conflicting programs for society, but the real levers of power seemed to many Italians to be pulled elsewhere, by the Agnellis, the owners of Fiat, for example. Similarly, after an extended period after the War during which political power was barely exercised by the government, but seemed to be lodged in the American State Department, international investors and NATO, the French in a nationalist outburst elected de Gaulle to rule the country in a kind of democratic despotism that lasted from the mid-'50s until the May events of 1968 sent his government reeling.

As is well known, the French May and the Italian "hot autumn" the following year marked the high point of the influence and power of the New Left, just as the pinnacle of antiwar protest occurred during these years in the United States. These explosive movements were directed against the perceived charade of parliamentary and republican democracy as much as against the increasing centralization of all political decisions in autonomous bureaucracies of the political parties as well as state and corporate institutions. On questions that were settled during the immediate postwar period by large-scale institutional compromises, such as those bearing on foreign affairs, parliaments and mainstream political parties remained intransigent to popular pressure. Equally obdurate were the bureaucracies which controlled public services such as housing, healthcare, and education. The New Left's demand for a radical restructuring of these services to allow a large measure of popular participation in administration were usually brusquely rejected as a violation of the principle of delegation of powers to professional experts when bureaucrats did not claim that such arrangements would be grossly inefficient. The Italian workers' movement raised sharply the issue of worker's control over production, an issue far removed from parliamentary action. When employers in the North, especially Fiat, flatly refused to subject the conditions of labor to workers' self-management but insisted that the responsibility of the unions ceased at the cusp of managerial prerogatives to direct the workforce according to criteria of efficiency, a series of wildcat strikes broke out, demanding radically different industrial relations. These struggles found both Communist and Socialist leaders unprepared. When they were not denouncing the wildcat strikes as irresponsible, provoked by the far left, or potentially destructive to the survival of the labor movement itself, they were running furiously to head the movement in order, according to extra-parliamentary critics, to head it off.[19]

In sum, the New Left attack was directed equally to parliamentary and administrative institutions of the bourgeois state and the giant monopolistic corporations. As in an earlier sectarian period in the history of the Third Communist International, social-democracy (or, in the United States, the Democratic Party) shared considerable blame for the late-twentieth-century phenomenon of mass alienation in the wake of unprecedented mass political rights. The neo-Marxist critique of bourgeois democracy was directed as much to the so-called welfare state as it was to parliament, as much against trade unions which, because of their corporativism, refused to lead the battle for shopfloor workers' control, for new measures to ensure the workers power over investment, as it was against the owners of large enterprises.

And, of course, the explosive student opposition to the Vietnam War capped a worldwide break with the *de facto* detente between the mass electoral left and its own capitalist states on global issues. The term "explosive" expresses my conviction that the antiwar and anti-colonialist movement in the most industrially developed societies challenged one of the crucial pillars of class compromise, the linchpin of the drift to parliamentary democratic ends among left parties after the War. Of course, antiwar struggles can be linked to specific features of government policy, notably the draft which, in the United States, has been employed selectively throughout its history. But youth objections to the draft are, in turn, related to the larger issue of disaffection, the loosening of patriotic, nationalistic fervor which was effective in recruiting millions of soldiers in the two world wars and during the Korean War. Although the draft was instituted in order to meet troop requirements, no mass opposition appeared in these instances. In contrast, the Vietnam War proved immensely unpopular after 1965 when President Johnson dramatically increased US troop commitments to support the South Vietnam government forces. Clearly, among the generation of 1940–50 at least, something had changed in the conditions of consent. American society was experiencing considerable difficulty reproducing consent even as the economy was ostensibly in a boom phase. The national administration responded to what became a consent crisis by alternate tactics of repression and concessions. Draft-evaders were prosecuted and jailed, deserters condemned, battlefield indiscipline was severely punished. But Congress also reduced the voting age to eighteen and similar state laws were enacted to reduce the minimum drinking age. Funds for education were made available to Vietnam-era veterans as an incentive to youth to give approbation to US war aims and, of primary importance the American welfare state was dramatically expanded beyond its New Deal borders, particularly in elementary and secondary education for the poor, income payments, and special compensatory programs for racial and ethnic minorities.

After insisting on universal draft, the administration finally capitulated to student demonstrations by granting mass exemptions to active students, permitting exemptions for those who agreed to teach in elementary and secondary schools, and other concessions for workers engaged in work strategically linked to military production. In retrospect, the movement committed a grievous error by separating its own middle-class base from the sons and daughters of workers and farmers who had no means to claim exemptions and who were, on the whole, not inclined to take the route of dissent even as later developments revealed the degree to which the war was unpopular among American combat troops.

Clearly, the global New Left attributed its relative successes to having adopted an extra-parliamentary strategy, to its liberation from reliance on legal methods of attaining its objectives. Moreover, the mass strikes in France and Italy, the university occupations in Britain, Germany, and the United States over issues of both university complicity in war-related research, of academic freedom and institutional governance, and the huge antiwar demonstrations in all countries, even those of the South such as Mexico and Argentina, contested the liberal and social democratic claim that the extra-parliamentary opposition represented a small fragment of the broad population. The New Left theorized the sometimes heady events in two ways. The more orthodox Marxists of the extreme left detected a huge breakaway among the industrial working class which established its partial hegemony over factions of the (new) petty bourgeoisie of students and technical intelligentsia. Another (minority) theoretical tendency argued that new social movements were in the process of coming into existence, composed largely of members of a new stratum of increasingly educated and qualified workers who, owing to the fact that modern industry was now largely knowledge-based, faced the contradiction between their proletarianization and their capacity for self-management of the labor process. Mass estrangement from the prevailing social and political compromises was situated in new, emerging strata which constituted a kind of vanguard of a different kind of class struggle. This theoretical tendency, unlike its orthodox counterpart, placed the cultural revolution on a plane with the proletarian revolution, insisting that questions of race and sex, intimately linked to class, occupied a crucial space in late capitalist society. For the "new working class" theorists, the problem of domination was a central issue, even if it did not displace the question of exploitation. The issue of workers' control, made difficult by the progressive dequalification of manual workers in the first industrializing era, was now thrust to center stage in the period during which knowledge had become the chief productive force. According to neo-Marxist theory, the new workforce remains in the thrall of capital. Despite its relative wage privileges, its position of subordination amounts to a degradation of the quality of working life.

André Gorz and others in Italy and Germany argued that, in a period of capitalist rationalization of quantitative crisis-tendencies in the system, the qualitative issues occupied central importance in the struggle for emancipation. Legislatures and bureaucracies of various sorts have demonstrated their capacity to accommodate to quantitative grievances, but cannot yield in any permanent way to the new demands, precisely because these challenge capitalist ideological hegemony and, equally important, power relations in the key institutions of the state and in the enterprises. Gorz's theory, borrowed heavily from the work of Italian and German neo-Marxism, particularly that of Mario Tronti, Rudi Dutschke, and older work of the council communists, provided a theoretical as well as historical basis for the extra-parliamentary departure from the half-century of parliamentary strategy of the mainstream left. No sooner had these positions been staked out than the New Left began to unravel in all advanced capitalist societies through a series of developments that provided the basis for a new state offensive against the extreme left.[20]

Another tendency, identified with later Tronti, Antonio Negri and the Italian '70s movement Proletarian Democracy took the argument another step: late capitalism had decisively destroyed even the vestiges of meaningful work. The program of self-management assumed that work could still be invested with significance.[21] Contemporary technological developments had foreclosed these possibilities. The latent tendency of the workers' movement was the refusal to work. The refusal to work had become not merely a demand to be presented to executive or legislative authorities, but was inherent in the workers' practices on the shopfloor—taking informal rest periods, blue Mondays and absent Fridays, sabotage on the line, job actions of short duration that disrupted production, and so forth. While the working class might appeal through their unions and parliamentary representatives for shorter work weeks or more rest periods, their self-organization in small groups, their extra-parliamentary radicalism, often devoid of explicit ideological premises, was the heart of the new class struggle. As usual a close student of latest Italian theoretical and political developments on the far left, Gorz followed suit by positing the identity of industrial labor with a prison, a metaphoric turn of phrase which legitimated the refusal to work as a key element of the workers' struggle.

These developments were influenced, beyond doubt, by the defeat of the revolutionary goals of the May events, particularly abetted by the ability of communist parties in France and Italy to head off the movement by alternate tactics of denunciation, cooptation and, in the case of France, open collaboration with government forces to break the general strike. In the course of advocating new elections, a substantial wage increase and an end to the strikes, the Communists experienced a sudden conversion to workers' control, a demand they previously condemned as utopian. Similarly, the PCI, motivated by dissident currents within the party as well as a breakdown in its trade union base, temporarily turned to the left, even as its early response to an insurgent feminist movement that was attaining mass proportions was initially hostile owing to its efforts to cement a neutrality pact with the Catholic Church hierarchy which was directly under attack for its abortion and divorce stands by the feminists. During this period, the PCI lost considerable ground among intellectuals and militants in all sectors of Italian society, but regained as the '70s proved inhospitable to New Left ideology.

As the new movements ebbed, a recalcitrant tendency emerged on the extreme left, stemming from profound frustration at the unwillingness of the official left to depart from its denunciations of the militants and its simultaneous efforts to coopt the movements and their own left. The extra-parliamentary movements were treated by established agencies, especially the media, as outlaws, which prompted many who had participated in direct action of a peaceful variety to become actual outlaws, to engage in activities that called attention to the kabuki dance between the official left and the capitalist state that effectively thwarted the attempts of the people to break the rules of the game without facing dire consequences. For it had become clear to some in the New Left that parliamentary regimes were more than merely inadequate for the project of socialist transformation; when the "base" chose to sidestep the usual channels of protest and petition, they were met by the full force of the combined powers of capital and their own judases, the official left. Parliamentary institutions were no longer democratic; they formed a barrier to genuine change, just as Engels had forecast.

Of course the emergence of the Red Brigades in Italy, the Red Army faction in Germany, and the Weather Underground in the United States did not signify a unified political tendency; programatically and politically these groups harbored major differences. But they shared a single vision: the revolution was a break with the past, a new cultural and social equality in which privilege was abandoned in favor of arrangements that had to recognize the priority of Third World needs in the allocation of world resources, the uncompromising end of old cultural forms of sexual and family relationships. Influenced by the spate of peasant revolutions in China, Cuba, and especially Vietnam, these groups demanded that the left resurrect violence as an instrument of political and social change. Thousands of those reared in the New Left were, for a brief historical moment, attracted by what was described as a kind of nihilistic, anarchist tendency in Marxism which, at once, was driven by the anarchist critique of the established left and the doctrine of Third Worldism, or, alternatively proletarian internationalism.

Now, there is no doubt that this "movement" was animated by contradictory ideas and sentiments as well as an unrealistic evaluation of the contemporary political situation both within their own countries and in the capitalist world. For one thing, the economic and cultural crises of the early '70s signified radicalization but not a specifically political break with the liberal state. Although millions of workers, students, and professionals had come to question the degree to which representative institutions remained a vehicle through which their grievances could be resolved, there was no consensus on alternative forms of social and political rule nor were the radicalized prepared to create new political vehicles. Under these circumstances, it was relatively easy for the state and the parties to recoup their losses of the 1968 period. By the mid-'70s, voters, in Europe at least, were turning up at the polls in undiminished numbers compared to the historical data. The considerable fractions of the adult population which were opting out of public life in the United States and Western Europe had failed to manifest a strong tendency toward an alternate politics. Instead, as Jean Baudrillard has commented, the '70s are marked by the rise of anti-politics, a mood of pure refusal that has no articulated form except in a widespread cynicism, especially among the young, concerning electorism as such.[22] The issue babble of established forces, entreaties from official sources to stimulate voter turnout have fallen on increasingly deaf ears. Of course, of all advanced countries, this tendency is most apparent in the United States which has a long history of electoral nonparticipation. But, it is also a growing trend in France which experienced a thirty-four per cent abstention rate in the 1988 leg-islative elections, compared to slightly less than fifty per cent in the US presidential election during the same year. Since the left parties typically capture the votes of poorer and younger sections of the population (and this is where abstention is heaviest), it may be inferred that staying away from the polls is one way potential dissident voters show their distrust of those parties to which they would ordinarily gravitate and, more globally, of the parliamentary democratic system as such.

The growing crisis of citizenship is clearly one of the major politi-cal tendencies in advanced capitalist countries, which is not properly de-scribed as apathy. Except for a brief period in the early '70s when some established institutions in the major countries of the West were moved to accommodate the new militancy, the last fifteen years are marked by a definite hardening of battle lines between official agents and the underly-ing population which, of course, did not support the "terrorists" who had misread their mood. If the crisis of citizenship is predominantly a cultural crisis, then what marks this period most is the narrowing of the electorate which, implicitly includes only those whose political perception is that voting as an activity is in their interest. To be sure, the constituency for parliamentary democracy includes diverse social movements as well as the older business, professional, agricultural, and trade union interests. The Green parties in Germany, Belgium, Sweden, and Italy contest par-liamentary and local elections. The Greens have won small but signif-icant victories and, equally importantly, have constituted a permanent electoral and extra electoral constituency. After considerable debate in the late '70s, their electoral participation signifies a strategic decision to wring concessions on ecological and feminist concerns precisely because extra-parliamentary struggle, although necessary, remains insufficient in the wake of the urgency of issues. That a Swedish social-democratic government announced in 1988 its decision to implement the popular ref-erendum that supported closing the nuclear energy plants of that country attests to the possibility of winning substantial victories at the ballot box, even if not strictly by parliamentary means. Similarly, Italian feminists secured abortion rights and the right to divorce by referendum. In the 1988 US elections California voters supported a twenty per cent reduction in auto insurance rates by similar means, a victory against the private insurance companies which was quickly subjected to judicial review as to the constitutionality of the measure.

Although employing the electoral system, these popular victories were not secured through representative institutions, chiefly because the movements perceived these institutions no longer amenable to structural reforms, especially those that propose to intervene from the base in determining accumulation priorities and on social rights. In this respect, it is noteworthy that abortion rights in the United States were won by a decision of the United States Supreme Court rather than by Congress, which had blocked action on proposed legislation and undoubtedly would have continued to stonewall these freedoms indefinitely. In this connection, it is valuable to remember that the first major civil rights victory for blacks was obtained as a result of another Supreme Court decision, *Brown v Board of Education* (1954), fully a decade prior to congressional approval of a comprehensive civil rights law, a measure enacted in the midst of massive civil disobedience by a rejuvenated civil rights movement, ghetto riots and a stepped-up US military intervention in Southeast Asia. At the time of writing, gay rights await both court and legislative sanctions which, in the increasingly conservative social environment of the country are not likely to be forthcoming in the near future.

At the same time, the United States Congress, despite a Democratic majority, passed, in the waning days of its 1988 session, two pieces of legislation that augur badly for the premise that representative democracy has popular roots in the country. The most egregious, a new drug law, will impose heavy penalties for drug abuse by individuals; the second, euphemistically labelled welfare "reform," removes income rights for physically able-bodied individuals receiving transfer payments if they refuse work. Of course, there is considerable sentiment for such measures among voters who are, after all, largely recruited from the upper reaches of the society and the most stable sections of the working class; those most saliently affected by these measures are largely unrepresented, even tendentially, in Congress and state legislatures. Nevertheless, the character of the legislation signifies a major shift in the direction of this crucial institution of representative government in the United States.

The welfare reform is particularly onerous for single mothers, blacks and youth. It opens the possibility for flagrant violations in labor standards, further weakening trade unions. The drug bill is a historical reversal of the traditional right to privacy, by making use of regulated substances subject to civil penalties (previously it was relegated to the status of misdemeanor which carries much lighter penalties but were honored more for the fact that they were ignored by law enforcement agencies).

Apart from constitutional guarantees for both individual freedoms and local governmental forms, Britain, under conservative rule, has exhibited the dark side of parliamentary representative government and evidence that majority rule is not necessarily democratic: the government's shameful treatment of the Catholic minority in Northern Ireland; its flagrant violation of the spirit, if not the letter, of democratic process by dissolving the left-led Greater London Council and recent measures to restrict civil liberties on national security grounds have revealed the limitation of popular reliance on representative institutions to guarantee liberty. The Greater London Council was premised on the notion of democracy as participatory; its aim was to involve large numbers of people in directing local government through decision-making in the governance of a wide variety of neighborhood and city-wide planning and welfare institutions. The Conservative national government understood well the implications of this experiment: its hegemony was threatened by a radicalized local government which claimed considerable autonomy. The only recourse, to dissolve the entire arrangement, was entirely within its powers, but was profoundly authoritarian.

For those experiencing the relative impotence of parliamentary institutions to resist the initiatives of executive authorities against fundamental "bourgeois" freedoms masked in the language of retributive justice and legal legitimacy, the current revival of the defense of representative democratic institutions within socialist and Marxist debates may, at first, appear puzzling. After all, we who live in these societies in which bourgeois democracy has reached its zenith, at least in comparison not only to Third World societies, but to most of the countries of continental Europe and the Eastern bloc as well, have become acutely aware of the limits of legislative institutions, especially in the glare focused by heavy corporate intervention in political campaigns to the point where even liberal observers have raised questions about whether the procedural processes such as elections provide voters with meaningful choices. In the 1988 elections, ninety-eight per cent of members of the United States House of Representatives were reelected, in part, because substantial contributions to both political parties were made by corporate-funded political action committees. The differences between the presidential candidates were limited to social issues, at once a tribute to the permanent influence of cultural radicalism and the virtual consensus between competing elites on economic and foreign policy issues. I will reserve a discussion of the reasons for this appalling state of affairs for the last section of this essay.

Since the demise of the New Left in the early '70s and the relative decline of the social movements such as feminism and ecology in the '80s (relative to the strong position each occupied in some major countries through the '70s), especially in the US, Britain, and southern Europe, social-democratic political theory has breathed new life. In the last fifteen years the concept of representative, parliamentary democracy is argued by Norberto Bobbio, recently a socialist senator in the Italian Parliament, and academic political theorists such as Adam Przeworski, whose Marxist perspectives are influenced by the historical experience of social democracy. To these must be added the recently-articulated idea of the ineluctable link between democracy and markets asserted by Alec Nove and Charles Lindbloom, among others. In short, we are in the midst of a new theoretical defense of Bernsteinism. And the audience for this position is by no means confined to the advanced capitalist countries where extra-parliamentary radicalism seems to have passed into history, except among small groups of Green activists. It has achieved popularity in some Third World societies, especially Chile and Brazil where many Marxists and socialists regard parliamentary democracy as an achievement devoutly to be wished and remains to be won.

Since Bobbio's influence in the current debate is fairly widespread, I will examine his claims with special care. For, not only in the clarity of his arguments, but also in his political trajectory, it is easy to see why many once in the revolutionary extra-parliamentary left now look to his work. His works are widely read in parts of Latin America as well as the

United States and Western Europe because they present, in an uncompromising way, not only an argument for the priority of democracy over socialism, but for the liberal state not as a convenience, from the point of view of the left, but a permanent legacy. He makes absolutely no apology for advocating representative democracy as an end of socialist political struggle rather than a means, and defends the actual historical choices of social democratic movements to take the parliamentary road as the best chance of the workers and other popular movements to attain their needs.

Bobbio writes in the shadow of European history where left-wing critiques of parliamentary democracy preceded the rise of fascism which came to power in the name of national unity and, counterposed a racist and nationalist spirit for liberal pluralism. In contrast to those who defend parliamentary, representative democracy from the point of view of social liberalism or conservative anti-left doctrines, his is a socialist defense of representative institutions and a vigorous attack on the practical viability of their left-wing alternatives. What renders his arguments particularly persuasive is that he recognizes both the historical and structural weaknesses of the democratic claims of parliamentary government. This strategy can disarm opponents whose assault easily demolishes liberal arguments on the contemporary evidence of increasing authoritarian practices in Western democracies, if not historical failures. We know that even the most secure democracies are prone to suspend civil liberties on national emergency grounds, that their commitment to freedom ends at the water's edge and that they ascribe many of the blatantly undemocratic practices of parliamentary states to conjunctural deformities rather than being inherent in some features of the system.

Bobbio begins by defining democracy as a "set of rules (primary or basic) which establish who is authorized to take collective decisions and which procedures are to be applied." Of course, these collectivities are more democratic the more inclusive the "who" is, and the closer their procedures correspond to the idea of majority rule. And Bobbio is a strong proponent of constitutional norms that "are not rules of the game as such: they are preliminary rules which allow the game to take place."[23] His distinction between the liberal and democratic state consists in this: "liberalism provides those liberties necessary for the proper exercize of democratic power, democracy guarantees the existence and persistence of fundamental liberties." For Bobbio, "the real society underlying democratic government is pluralist."[24] This pluralism is inevitably a pluralism of elites who are in "competition with each other for votes of the public." This idea, borrowed freely from Max Weber and Joseph Schumpeter,[25] is offered in the spirit of a realistic assessment of the chances for anything approaching grassroots control over political decisions. With many others, Bobbio's pessimism is rooted in a history that leads to the judgement that we must settle for the possible: better to have a plurality of elites competing for the popular mandate than a single elite whose intrusion into every aspect of the social world chokes individual and collective autonomy. in any case, as we shall see, for this school of thought, the liberal state becomes the best chance for avoiding authoritarian rule.

Bobbio advances several basic arguments for taking representative democracy as a foundation for democracy as such: it is the only form of democracy which actually exists, its obverse, direct democracy, is impractical in increasingly complex societies which render the revival of the Athenian *polis* a pipedream; democracy in the workplace and other social institutions outside the state is merely the extension of political to social democracy; the demand for participation is satisfied by voting, an activity which implies that the subject is exercizing decision-making powers through the delegation of authority. For compared to those societies in which such delegation, whether parliamentary or presidential, is not regularly granted, the vote is vastly superior.

Beneath these assertions is Bobbio's fundamental political philosophy. Society consists of groups rather than individuals, each of which has interests. These groups, organized as constellations, form political parties which, however constituted as elites, can win political power by drawing on the interests of the groups to which they are ultimately responsible. That government governs best which governs openly, a statement not of fact, but of value. Decisions openly arrived at are the only assurance that the representative procedures are valid as democratic indicators. In the context of most advanced capitalist democracies, open government appears as normative rather than corresponding to actual practice. While the minimal definition described above of democracy surely exists in many states, two crucial components of its maximum definition are missing: citizens join political parties and other voluntary associations in smaller numbers in proportion as the separation between public and private widens. While the intervention of the state in the economy, social life, and personal affairs has been enlarged in the past half-century, popular perception is that the state is increasingly dominated by powerful elites over which they have little control. We now confront a pervasive phenomenon in Western countries of anti-politics; the power of corporate and bureaucratic elites has resulted in a studied, deliberate retreat of large sections of the population into private life, even when they vote. In contrast, for radical democrats the act of voting is a process of aggregation rather than participation. While an element of decision-making is entailed by this activity, there is a much more important element of ritual, something like singing "The Star-Spangled Banner" or "God Save the Queen" which, for many, are songs without words, sung in public to avoid embarrassment. Ritual behavior is not an insignificant aspect of voting, especially in those democracies where voting takes place on Sunday, a day when large numbers of people view the polling place as a social site. US voting shows a similar dynamic, but only in small towns and the shrinking number of tightly-knit neighborhoods of large and middle-sized cities where identity is still forged by ethnicity, occupation, or club membership. But, for the anonymous working and underclasses living in areas where the architecture, urban sprawl, and the consequent absence of a sense of place is reinforced by frequent job-changes and changes in living arrangements, voting is, increasingly, a purely individual and not a group activity; lacking real differences between the parties, people in these situations turn their backs on voting (it does not matter that logical argument can demonstrate, if not "prove" that electing Democrats would benefit the poor and the workers at least in comparison to electing the Republicans: for many, the price of granting legitimacy to the elites is simply too high).

I realize these observations may be taken as deliberate provocations, for many voters do take their franchise seriously. However, if we allow that the practical unfolding of late capitalist democracies are identified with consensual rather than conflictual relations among leading political parties, for example, that the traditional opposition in Italy, the Communists, were capable during the '70s of announcing a policy of historic compromise with the bourgeois parties in order to achieve a stable government (a measure that we understood to be in the working-class interest), then reported cynicism concerning the real choices involved in the act of voting should be taken as an index of the legitimation crisis of contemporary capitalist democracies. For even as Bobbio enters his fervent defense of representative institutions, he is obliged to acknowledge the existence of invisible government, of powerful and increasingly intractable elites which are not responsive to the sovereign claims of the electorate and, in the Italian context, of the prevalence of corruption in public life. At the same time, he has ontologized representativeness as democracy itself, which obliges him to systematically deny the viability of direct democracy. Moreover, he fails to address the large areas of state policy that have effectively been removed from parliamentary debate: the important decisions made by central governments regarding science and technological investments; the most general direction of foreign relations; the question of immigration (where differences between Socialists/Democrats and their conservative opponents vary with only the severity of restriction and punishment); and broad areas of tax policy which are debates conducted among elites but rarely shared with the broad electorate. The questions are indeed complex. Do the parties really discuss these issues in an informed and detailed manner? Are the parliamentary committees charged with considering relevant legislation fully apprised of the issues, much less have access to relevant information? Or are these matters assigned to the scientific, foreign affairs, defense, or whatever establishments whose apposite relations are to large corporations not to the voting public? Moreover, as the fate of the dollar in international markets attests, the task of government policy is to achieve closer and more symbiotic links with financial interests; the executives communicate to each other concerning such issues as budget deficits, loans to debtor nations, but also the fundamental direction of foreign policy beyond economic issues.

The point is that the last two decades are marked, in both Anglo-American and continental instances, by the more or less open acknowledgement by executive authorities of the existence of a massive invisible government on an international plane. In the United States this has produced much tension between the President and Congress who disagree on the extent to which the executive branch may take autonomous action. While Congress passes many laws and resolutions restricting the authority of the executive to legislate by means of the "executive order," not only in matters of ethics but also foreign military intervention, the administration shows few signs of honoring such restrictions as representative bodies may impose. This executive "lawlessness" is rationalized by the emerging doctrine of the National Security State according to which the President reserves the right to restrict domestic freedoms, especially press access and expression, and the constitutional requirement for seeking the advice and consent of Congress for its actions, when a state of emergency or other extraordinary situations arise. In short, in all countries representative parliamentary institutions have powers limited to those matters deemed beyond the purview of the security state, a purview whose tentacles have expanded enormously since the War.

In his critique of alternative proposals to representative democracy, Bobbio enters what is perhaps his most telling set of arguments. Two of the most powerful analytic arguments advanced for alternatives are that these societies in which democratic governments prevail are marked by powerful bureaucratic domination and alongside this phenomenon we can observe the development of a cultural industry, one of whose sectors is a political industry that manipulates votes through propaganda and through images which massify the electorate rather than providing the space in which interests can be adequately represented. Bobbio agrees that these are dangerous tendencies in late capitalist societies but insists that the enlargement of state intervention is driven by the emergence of new demands by an enfranchised electorate that demands such functions be assumed. Therefore, bureaucracy is a welcome feature of democratization. Second, the politics industry is an eluctable feature of a society which requires the "organization of a consensus" as a precondition of political rule:

> Let us be quite clear on this, no full scale democracy without some sort of
> political industry. It would be nonsensical and, what is more, unrealistic,

at least at the present stage of social and intellectual development in our culture to postulate that a society could exist in which all adults have the right to influence directly or indirectly the way political decisions are made, and who must be taken into account by those in power to a greater or lesser extent (but in any case to a greater extent than in oligarchic societies, where the vast majority of subjects remain politically irrelevant). All societies require the use of techniques for the organization of consensus, though in varying degrees of intensity and intrusiveness.[26]

While acknowledging that mass demonstrations are necessary for the purposes of influencing public opinion and are, under certain circumstances, "civic duty" Bobbio argues that "their effectiveness is short-lived, because once the crowd has dispersed, the excitement that has been whipped up rapidly melts away, and with it also the will to act (without which there is no politics for politics is not only feeling or opinion, but action)." These lines are quite revealing. Rather than understanding demonstrations, disruptions, civil disobedience as historic commentaries on the inadequacy of representative institutions from the point of view of those, increasing in both numbers and categories, who are marginalized, he sees them as parallel to representation, an aspect of participation of which voting is the other side. Since demonstrations may or may not be expressions of elite efforts to intervene in the political process, it is convenient for Bobbio to insist that they are merely "opinion" molders rather than incipient expressions of alternative politics. Further, Bobbio engages in a sleight-of-hand statement: demonstrations are not forms of political action as if the mass-marches of the civil rights and antiwar movements, the student occupations of French and German universities, the massive Paris march of the left against the Algerian War in 1960, or the uprisings in Paris in 1968 were not forms of action. Bobbio's discourse shows a prejudicial side when in one paragraph he nullifies the history of the sixties, even in his own country, by the demeaning phrases that link direct action with the expression of "heady emotions," " whipped-up excitement," and so on.

However, his defense of bureaucracy is far more serious. Here Bobbio stands in a long line of socialist and progressive thought for which the state intervention is the means by which the struggle for equality becomes institutionally legitimate. Legislatures pass welfare state measures, enact occupational and health legislation, are forced to provide some minimum protections against further ecological deterioration and must, as a consequence, provide the mechanisms of enforcement and administration. These always entail the expansion of the bureaucracy which tends to promote, in its own interest, a technocratic ideology to replace the class victories to which it owes its very existence. Bobbio notes the paradox, but stubbornly insists that in advanced democratic states expertise does not replace the citizen as the sovereign power, but he cannot offer more concrete analytic arguments for the belief that technocratic domination is subject to representative institutions. His claim ultimately rests on an ethical rather than historical foundation.

Now Bobbio's dilemma reflects an admirable trait in his coherent defense of "bourgeois" democracy, his honest acknowledgement of its constraints and limits. He will not surrender popular sovereignty while admitting that it is threatened by the very successes of social-democratic struggles. Part of his problem lies in a certain realism that permeates Bobbio's discourse. For example, the increasing complexity of advanced industrial society is taken as a given framework for democratic discourse.

Surely, for Bobbio to posit direct democracy on the basis of decentralized political jurisdictions is utopian. We cannot revive the Athenian *polis* because we cannot cope with an increasingly technological culture without representative institutions, expertise, and most egregiously a technical/managerial class that is profoundly anti-democratic insofar as it disdains popular sovereignty. But the hope that parliament or executive authorities which derive their legitimacy from voters who freely choose them, will be genuinely accountable to their constituents is, for Bobbio a "realistic" expectation. I submit that Bobbio's appeal to realism (for example, his flat statement that representative democracy is the only kind which exists), is a rhetorical gesture that unwittingly sidesteps the implication of his own critique of the historical development of democracy, the degree to which it departs, empirically, from the model he proposes. For Bobbio's invocation to socialists to observe the rules of the game is founded on another paradox: "where the rules of the democratic game have been observed socialism so far has not come about and does not even seem imminent" in part, according to Bobbio, because socialism has made the critique of bourgeois democracy one of the corner stones of its program. Democracy is "subversive," "wherever it spreads, it subverts the most traditional sense of power, one so traditional it has come to be considered natural, based on the assumption that power flows downward. By conceiving power as flowing upwards, democracy is in some ways more subversive than socialism..." if we take the definition of socialism to mean "the transfer of ownership of the means of production from the hands of private individuals to the state,"[27] in other words, the model proposed by actually existing socialist states. While this may be true, and I think it is, there are two problems here: Bobbio bases his conception of power flowing upward on the ideal type of democracy that has, by his own admission, only restricted application in even the most advanced democratic countries; and his conception of socialism is quite statist, precisely the objection of radical democratic-socialists for whom social rather than state ownership constitutes a starting point (but not the limit) of democracy. Since Bobbio cannot conceive of a practical way to achieve genuine social ownership or control, he cannot define socialism other than the ways it has been conceived by state bureaucracies, East and West. His own statism is in logical contradiction to the only reliable way that democracy can flow upward—if power is genuinely lodged at the base and representative institutions are subordinated to those that afford to popular forces the opportunities for administration typically reserved to executive and bureaucratic bodies. Under this regime a "state" does not disappear but it is radically altered both with respect to its sovereignty and to its relationship to other forms of autonomous power. We are not speaking here of some ultimate arrangement whereby all human relations are self-regulated; however desirable, this state of affairs requires a fairly long period during which we learn to live in collectivities not grounded in particular interests but have freely chosen to become individuals in the sense this term has been philosophically conceived, people able to solve problems, not by means of compromises grounded in power relations, but by reason. This situation presupposes a profound change in the nature of property, of course, but also a radical restructuring of our collective selves. And this restructuring takes both time and the transformative effects of social praxis.

In sum, there is a yawning gap between the normative assertion of the necessity of popular sovereignty and its practical definition as representative democracy. When Bobbio confronts his own use of utopian ideas, he recoils from drawing the implications of these norms for practice. For in his *Realpolitik* defense of bureaucracy, technical bases for decision-making, the cultural and political industries, as well as his devaluation of direct action as, in the main, quasi-religious catharsis, Bobbio reveals that he is engaged in little more than a polemic against the '60s, that his apologia is directed against the left, which, despite the validity of its critique of the course of bourgeois democracies has failed, in his view, to understand the necessity of the liberal state.

It is not surprising that these views have impressed many peripheral and Third World intellectuals and militants. For the '60s in Latin America were marked by efforts by the extreme left to mechanically emulate the strategy and tactics of the Cuban and Chinese revolutions, especially among far-left factions in Columbia, Uruguay, Venezuela, and Bolivia and, on the other hand, a powerful effort in Chile and among some leftists in Brazil to place the question of socialism on the political agenda, and bring it about by parliamentary-democratic means. The repressive and long military dictatorships in both countries that followed leftist electoral victories did not encourage socialist revolutionary ideas. On the contrary, Marxists and socialists have been chastened by the revelation that the political culture of these countries was, at its base, dominated by authoritarian forces. Therefore, what has emerged in the '80s is nothing less than a spate of theoretical and political declarations on the left that declare the priority of representative democracy to socialism, that argue for the restoration of the liberal state as a strategic objective of the left as the best chance to secure liberties and a parliament that will ensure the right of various parties to represent their respective constituents. But, we must note that the left-wing conversions to representative democracy after two decades of revolutionary activity are dictated as much by the effects of militarism, the worldwide economic crisis and the recognition that US imperialism remains a forceful presence in the Americas capable of thwarting radical democratic movements, directly or indirectly, as it is by ideological shifts. Moreover, Latin Americans have been affected by the examples of the civil war in El Salvador, the US assault on Nicaraguan sovereignty, and by the Mexican constitutional crisis of 1988 where the United States remains perhaps the determining power in deciding the fate of these societies. Like those in Eastern Europe who seek freedom from Soviet economic and military domination, Latin Americans believe their first step to fundamental social transformation is to secure representative democracy, which has emerged as the most immediate alternative to authoritarian rule.

After the experience of really existing socialism and militarism in the periphery and semiperiphery, few would argue against the proposition that one of the pillars of the liberal state, the guarantee of speech, assembly and, more widely, dissent and opposition must be considered a permanent legacy of the past. No social order which purports to be considered democratic can argue, even under conditions of hostile encirclement such as exists in Nicaragua, or as existed in the Soviet Union prior to World War II, that repression of these liberties is justified. While condemning the pressure brought to bear on the revolution by the United States government and its agents, radicals must be critical of the victim's refusal to depart from the historical script. The tragedy is, of course, that its periodic suspension of press freedom and other forms of political expression is often a reaction to what the state perceives to be imminent US invasion and constant subversion of its institutions; the Nicaraguan government has lost a crucial opportunity to take the ideological and political initiative by defending all liberties, even for its most virulent internal enemies. What gives the socialist defense of the liberal state more weight is the unwillingness of the revolutionary left to acknowledge that freedom of political expression is a non-reversible legacy of the political philosophy of left-liberalism, since other varieties, especially the Burkean and Hobbesian traditions, are prepared to forgo these in the service of social discipline, an ideology shared by authoritarian communist states.

Since the Nicaraguan revolution succeeded in 1979 in deposing the hated Somoza regime, it has been US policy, following the sacred precepts of the Monroe doctrine, to aid, by diplomatic, economic, and military means, the overthrow of the Sandinista regime. The US government has done everything possible to reduce the Nicaraguan economy to a shambles by denying normal trade and diplomatic relations to the new government and by financing a group of exiles and ex-Somoza guards to conduct a long war of attrition designed, finally, to drain the new government's economic and moral resources.

The policy has been brilliantly successful in all but its ultimate aim of counter-revolutionary overthrow. The Nicaraguan economy is on its knees and the Sandinista government has lost its once tremendous prestige among an exhausted and increasingly impoverished population. Many of the regime's left supporters have quietly retreated to the background as Nicaragua has become a garrison state. Within the United States, official policy is to label the regime a "Marxist" government (which it is not) to charge it with molesting its neighbors (it has engaged in only defensive incursions into Honduras, the base of the rebel forces) and, on this "evidence," to continue to give financial and military aid to the counter-revolution. In the face of this US-sponsored terrorism, it is understandable that many on the left hesitate to criticize the Sandinistas in any way, fearing that criticism will give aid and comfort to its rightist enemies. Similarly, many on the left bracket the emergence of Solidarity in Poland from their general support for insurgent workers' movements precisely because the Reagan administration and its successor have made Solidarity an element of their Cold War policy. The problem with this stance is that it reproduces the reception to Stalinism when, in the wake of the terror of the 1930s Soviet regime against the internal left opposition, the pro-Soviet left and left-liberals were silent or preferred to accept the explanations for events such as the Moscow trials from Stalin's minions. I would not want to attribute anti-communism as a political ideology entirely or even principally to this history, but those who will not acknowledge its contribution to the postwar phenomenon of a growing conservative defense of capitalist democracy among ex-leftists, have reduced the Cold War to "objectivist" explanations.

Of course, I do not mean to equate the Sandinistas with the Stalinist state; the comparison made by neo-conservative discourse is scurrilous. I am, however, calling attention to the analogy, at the level of reception, of the position of many in the global left for whom the enemy of my enemy is my friend. These groups and individuals seem unable to distinguish between an unremitting defense of the right of the revolution to exist, and support for its behavior. Clearly, to defend the right to self-government has been conflated by the American right with support for regimes whose democratic record is subject to criticism. When the democratic left refuses to bare its criticism of revolutionary and socialist regimes it merely compounds the error of these regimes and condemns itself.

The burden of the history of Western capitalism as well as really existing socialism is that democracy, in any meaningful sense, remains an elusive goal. Riding the Paris subway in May 1988, I was impressed by the frequent searches by police of people who looked like African immigrants to discern whether they had the proper papers; ordinary police practice in black and other minority communities in the United States consists in search and seizure practices; motorists are often stopped, their cars searched without warrants, presumably for drug possession. The American prisons are bulging with victims of an increasingly retributive criminal justice system which seems to have jettisoned, except where politically inadvisable, the rehabilitation ideology it temporarily adopted in the late '60s. But the US remains a paragon of liberty in comparison to most other countries even if, in comparison to Western Europe, its representative institutions are fairly narrow sites for public debate on crucial issues. In Western Europe, the loyalty of the representative to the party exceeds her/his sensitivity to constituents who were responsible for her/his election. This discrepancy is underlined by the fact that parliament is obliged to deal with national and international issues which are rarely contested in locally-based elections. There are, of course, exceptions to this rule, notably the 1988 national elections in Israel and Canada, where major national issues were really at the heart of parliamentary elections, and smaller northern European countries, particularly Sweden, where social-democratic parties are much more open to popular will than their comrades in countries such as France and Italy.

The presidential systems of France and the United States, for example, do not lend themselves to such referenda. Although there are broad ideological orientations behind media images of candidates that seem to dominate the selection process, the convergence at the ideological as well as practical plane is surely a stunning verification of the radical claim that the parties offer less and less for the voters to choose. This state of affairs demonstrates another claim of Marxist analysis: although nationalism has become a more important legitimating ideology in recent years (not only of colonial peoples, but also those that are hegemonic), the dominant tendency of economic and political relations is towards integration on a global scale, or at least for the surrender of national autonomy to regional blocs. American cultural hegemony is even more stunning in both Third World societies and Europe, East and West. These centrifugal forces may not eliminate the reality of competing elites, the dream/analysis of "organized capitalism" has never materialized; but there is little question of the closing of autonomous spaces within which politics may become truly democratic. Which makes Bobbio's discourse on democracy peculiar. He has described the reality of Western democracy in utopian terms while attacking those who argue for direct participatory democracy as "unrealistic." The fact is, neither form of democracy has resulted in permanently broadening the base of participation because, despite considerable deterritorialization of industrial production, popular culture, and political hegemony, abetted by the widening of the technological sensorium (the development of means of communication as a social and personal wraparound, for example), power has been increasingly linked to knowledge which is rarely, if ever subject to popular sovereignty. Knowledge is the new locus of sovereignty which forms a kind of dual power to that of the national state, which has depended upon the accumulation of physical capital for its economic and cultural viability. With the exception of Green politics, which insists that scientific knowledge and technology be subject to a public sphere of debate, traditional political parties or parliaments are not sites for such appraisal. Science and technology policy are treated as technical, not political, issues. Or when they were subject to political determination, as in France during the 1981 presidential elections, the Socialist demand was for increasing the state budget for research but did not specify, beyond industrial policy, how it should be spent. One of the reasons for this is the historic socialist and communist support for science and technology as the best hope for economic growth and their consequent refusal to enter a critical discourse on these questions. The political dynamic for democratic revitalization has come from the new social movements which have insisted not only on an upward flow of democratic power, but the creation of new arrangements that would facilitate a horizontal flow as well as widening the purview of issues subject to public debate and decision-making

Bobbio represents a tendency of political theory stuck in the vertical models of power. Horizontal power can only flourish by reconstituting local communities as powerful. This proposal entails a transfer of many decisions reserved to executive authorities, over welfare, educational, technological, international, and repressive institutions to local control as well as the transfer of power in the workplace to the producers. However, if my description of the increasing centralization of power is right, achieving direct democracy entails new arrangements in the production and distribution of goods at the regional and local level so that decision-making regarding what is produced, how it is to be produced and distributed and how much, can really come within the purview of the base community. Further it would require disaggregation of many now-centralized economic activities to accommodate the productive capacity of individual enterprises as well as regionalization for the purposes of creating an ecologically sound physical environment.

The discerning reader will already have asked how this proposal is possible, given the nature of scientifically-based technologies, the possession of which is crucial for reproducing central ownership of the means of production, whether by the state or large privately-held corporations. Obviously, the will to direct democracy or representative forms that make delegates effectively recallable, requires at least two crucial pre-rules: knowledge must be widely shared, through education and free information-flows, so that scientific and technological decisions may be made by people who possess neither capital nor credentials; and the basis of productive activity must be radically dispersed, not only to facilitate control but also on ecological grounds. For it can be easily demonstrated that especially in large countries and regions, the concentration of industry, polluting motor vehicles and population, generates unhealthy living and working conditions and has· wreaked significant damage to the homeostatic relations of societies to their external physical environments. As I have argued, domination among humans is interlocked with domination of nature. For this reason, decentralization of crucial social functions is a necessary condition for the achievement of a grassroots-generated society and ecological relations that improve the quality of life.

Some of these arguments have been elaborated by others, but only a few theorists have made the link between democracy and ecology. There is, of course, a second argument that can be made for direct democracy, the normative goal of empowerment which implies recognizing that one of the crucial weaknesses of orthodox Marxism has been to privilege the struggle against exploitation over the fight to overcome alienation. For it can be argued that alienation, engendered by such developments as the concentration and centralization of capital, the emergence of the "new" urban spaces organized with a nightmarish vision of expressionist, if net modernist abstraction (skyscrapers dotting the landscape, monoliths as living spaces, empty deserted streets even in daytime and so on), is really the problematic of late capitalism just as exploitation was crucial for the intensive regime of industrialism. Some have conceptualized this as the cultural question and this surely comprehends an important feature of the question of empowerment; but the loss of control presupposes an entire historical compromise that we have made with the search for the good life or, to be more precise, the good life has been framed in the music of the machine and its consequences. The articulation of this regime of domination with patriarchy, with exploitation and technological progress, is precisely what is at issue in the rejection of the adequacy of representative democracy. For its procedures are necessarily aggregative and do not address the everyday consequences of large social questions. For example, lacking the votes in legislative bodies to win abortion rights, American feminists have been forced to declare control over a woman's body an individual matter free of public determination in order to qualify under constitutional guarantees. This strategic judgement, as I have indicated earlier, resulted from the overwhelming evidence that, despite opinion polls which show substantial public support for abortion rights, legislative bodies have effectively blocked them.

For even though the US Supreme Court has ruled that states may not deny these rights, Congress and many state legislatures have refused to appropriate funds to ensure access to abortions for poor women. This example demonstrates the structural unresponsiveness of legislatures to the popular will when party alliances prohibit them. Further it illustrates the degree to which party elites are separate interest-groups from those they purport to represent.

Which raises a final objection to exclusive or even predominant reliance for ensuring democracy by means of representative institutions. For just as it may be argued that bureaucracies tend to class formation with their own ideologies and political programs, so political elites often tend to class formation, the nature of which varies in relation to knowledge and bureaucratic hierarchies. They tend now to become fractions of the same class, even when they are plainly subordinate to capital, at least "in the last instance." In Third World countries where the various elites have combined as a class which controls, if not owns the decisive economic instruments, representative democracy which presupposes the existence of an opposition able to freely exercize civil liberties is far from realization. In Western democracies, what is in question is whether elites are "delegates" rather than merely seeking the legitimacy that constituencies may confer on their programs. The presumption of delegation of authority is compatible with one of the crucial mediations of direct democracy that recognizes the validity of certain situations of representation provided it is considered a mandate for certain actions fully discussed and determined by popular assemblies. In its most uncompromising form, the control over delegates is provided by recallability, to which Bobbio replies, "By whom?" The question cannot be answered without addressing the problem of the scale of governance, upon which the form of self-regulation depends. Clearly, his objection to a mode of direct democracy that assumes the large-scale centralized jurisdictions characteristic of many urban areas is valid. But, if decentralized power is actually implemented it might be possible to restore the delegated basis of representation rather than resigning ourselves to choices between competing elites, such as is the case in the selection of enterprise committees in France and Italy, where trade union "parties" compete for votes on the basis of agitation and propaganda but rarely, especially in large enterprises, genuine delegation from a participating base.

At the root of this debate are diverging conceptions of the meaning of citizenship. For those accepting the minimalist assumptions of the liberal state, that most decisions that have effects on everyday life take place beyond the powers of any possible or given public sphere of debate and dialogue, voting is an adequate measure of participation and therefore citizenship, at least in larger jurisdictions. If one takes a more comprehensive and therefore optimistic view, democratic citizenship is intertwined with a significant restructuring of social relations so that horizontal and vertical power flows from the base of society and representative institutions, to the extent that they are a necessary outgrowth of popular assemblies which are delegated and not constituted by elites who derive a mandate from electoral victories or alliances. Obviously, the crisis of Marxism in this regard consists largely in its historic ambivalence towards the support of either representative or direct democracy, that is, its failure to adopt a thoroughly democratic ethos and political commitment, especially when as a political practice, it captures state power. Further, its traditional split between reform and revolution resulted from its antipathy to a more evolutionary conception of the path to direct popular rule. Parties which adopted the Marxist perspective regarded proposals to reorganize the basis of bourgeois citizenship within the capitalist order as disruptive and "reformist." Clearly, times have changed so that Marxism finds itself caught between its strategic commitment to the liberal state (so long as capitalism prevails) and a transitional authoritarian state that is currently in the final stages of crisis. As a result, socialists and Marxists are, more often than not, counted in the ranks of those who defend one kind of hegemony or another and those whose position on existing state forms ranges from dissent to opposition, and who are obliged to distance themselves from both Marxism and really existing socialism.

For those, like myself, whose socialism is rooted in the belief that what Negt and Kluge called, in the late '60s, a "proletarian" public sphere (or more appropriately now a popular public sphere), questions of democracy remain at the center of the emancipatory project. This project differs from really existing social democracy and communist orthodoxies insofar as it holds to the revolutionary metaphor that social transformation entails a change, root and branch, in relation to the old order. This means, following the spirit of Ernst Bloch[28] that direct democracy is viewed as a practical utopia, the not-yet conscious of social life that is expressed, not only in the resistance to domination characteristic of shopfloor action and the refusal of students to learn the prescribed curriculum in schools but is revealed in the high divorce rates in Western countries when women really do have some rights, and the anti-politics of voter abstention. Of course, resistance is not enough. Periodically, throughout history people have tried to create popular public spheres in the form of alternative schools and cooperatives, rebellious unions, and voluntary associations that organize around impossible demands. Sometimes these alternative forms take a right-wing direction in part because the left is perceived by many people to be part of, and not in opposition to, the prevailing order. As the struggles in Poland and South Africa demonstrate, the will to direct democracy is not identical to liberal, social-democratic politics no matter how much these are a necessary ingredient in the struggle against authoritarianism. Perhaps only another explosion can put new democratic expression back on the political agenda. In any case, the vehemence of the arguments for representative democracy indicates that despite the nadir of this alternative movement, political theorists are still looking over their shoulders.

NOTES

1. Norberto Bobbio, *The Future of Democracy* (London and Minneapolis: Polity Press and University of Minnesota Press, 1987); *Which Socialism?*, (London: Polity Press, 1987).

2. Adam Przeworski, *Capitalism and Social Democracy* (London and New York: Cambridge University Press, 1985).

3. Ernesto Laclau and Chantal Mouffe, *Hegemony and Socialist Strategy* (London: Verso Books, 1986).

4. Louis Althusser, "Ideology and Ideological State Apparatuses," in *Lenin and Philosophy* (London: New Left Books, 1971); Nicos Poulantzas, *State, Power, Socialism* (London, New Left Books, 1978).

5. Karl Marx and Frederich Engels, *Selected Correspondence* (Moscow: Foreign Languages Publishing House, n.d.).

6. Eduard Bernstein, *Evolutionary Socialism* (New York: Schocken Books, 1961).

7. Rosa Luxemburg, "Social Reform and Revolution," in *Selected Political Writings*, ed. Dick Howard (New York: Monthly Review Press, 1971).

8. For a detailed account of the movement and its relations with the Bolsheviks see Voline, *The Unknown Revolution, 1917–1921* (London and Detroit: Black and Red/Solidarity).

9. Carl Schmitt, *Crisis of Parliamentary Democracy*, trans. Ellen Kennedy (Cambridge: MIT Press, 1988), 49–50.

10. Ellen Kennedy, "Introduction," in Schmitt, *Crisis*, op. cit.

11. Which, of course, is the heart of republican doctrine.

12. For a classic statement of the Leninist fear of bureaucracy in the transitional state see Leon Trotsky, *The New Course* (1923).

13. For an excellent introduction to the left-communist tendency see Serge Bricianer (ed.), *Pannekoek and the Workers' Councils* (St Louis: Telos Press, 1975).

14. John Maynard Keynes, *The General Theory of Employment, Interest and Money* (New York: Harcourt, Brace and World, 1969).

15. See especially C. Wright Mills, "The New Left," in *Power, Politics and People* (New York: Oxford University Press, 1963).

16. SDS, *The Port Huron Statement* (New York, 1962); James Miller, *Democracy Is in the Streets* (New York: Simon and Shuster, 1987). Hayden drafted the Statement, integrating sections written by others on the committee.

17. See James Miller, *Democracy Is in the Streets*, op. cit.

18. For a good summary of the politics of the European New Left, see George Kastiaficas, *The Imagination of the New Left: A Global Analysis of 1968* (Boston: South End Press, 1987).

19. For the best account of the left critique of the PCI position and of the program of the radical workers' movement in Italy, see Joann Barkan, *Visions of Emancipation* (New York: Praeger Publishers, 1984).

20. André Gorz, *Strategy for Labor* (Boston: Beacon Press, 1967); Serge Mallet, *The New Left* (London: Spearman Press, 1975).

21. Mario Tronti, *Ouvriers et capital*, translated into French by Y. Moulier and G. Bezzo (Paris: Christian Bourgeois Editeur, n.d.).

22. Jean Baudrillard, *In the Shadow of Silent Majorities* (New York: Foreign Agents Series, Semio-Text, 1986).

23. Bobbio, *Future of Democracy*, op. cit. 18.

24. Ibid. 28.

25. See David Held, *Models of Democracy* (Palo Alto, Calif.: Stanford University Press, 1987), ch. 5.

26. Bobbio, *Future of Democracy*, op. cit.

27. Ibid.

28. See Ernst Bloch, *Principle of Hope*, 3 vols. (Cambridge: MIT Press, 1986), vol. i.

CHAPTER TWELVE

Class in Political and Social Philosophy

"Seeing is believing?"

"I'm from Missouri, show me."

"The proof of the pudding is in the eating."

Classification: How We Make Sense of the World

These time-honored sayings encompass two of the ways humans figure out what's going on: by their and others' observations; and by reflecting on the multitude of everyday practices by which we constantly negotiate our relationships with our built and social environments—principally at work, in the home, on the street, and in our dreamwork. Making sense also entails making and forming concepts of two kinds: classification of objects, material and social, and creating concepts that select from the welter of experiences that would otherwise remain random and confusing. Apart from those who think and write about concepts and produce them intentionally, ordinary concept formation is mostly unacknowledged by producers. Concepts are extrapolated from elements of the cultural climate as well as more enduring world-views. Without them neither observation nor practice would take shape in our collective understanding of the social world and of material objects.

Just as concepts such as atoms and molecules—most recently quarks and strings—help us grasp and order our material world, the concept of class is a typical way of organizing and understanding the social world. Despite the humanist/liberal cry to treat persons equally, without prejudice, and ultimately as individuals rather than as a "class" or collective, ordering experience demands we classify people and thereby discern difference. Concepts are also used to evaluate our observations and social interactions. How we differentiate the elements of our social environment and organize them, in a system of classification both in public discourse and in our imagination, changes with historical situations. What is crucial in one social space/time, may be marginal, ancillary or absent in another. Although some modes of classification disappear, at least for a time, the most persistent concept used for ordering the social world is to divide people by how they earn their living, by their occupation and its place in the historically evolved imaginary social hierarchies. Here the term "imaginary" signifies a model, that is, a fiction that, nevertheless, we believe describes how social things are really ordered. "Fiction" does not imply that the model is false. It refers to the Real but does not necessarily correspond to it. Yet, since we tend to act on our concepts—which are also reworkings of social life—these fictions become social things and assume an independent existence. To be sure the system of classification often becomes a prison-house of thought and action. Few can shift their categories to accommodate the new. Our concepts are as habitual as any ordinary routine. They prevent us from making sense of new experiences; they are the dead past that tend to "weigh on the brains of the living."[1]

We may cite some of the worst examples of this process. As good industrial and craft jobs become hard to find a majority of high school graduates who once might have become electricians or relatively well-paid assemblers enter tertiary (or "higher" education) hoping to qualify for available jobs in administration, technology, or in the "helping" professions—education, social work, and healthcare. In the last twenty-five years of the twentieth century, those obliged to enter semi-skilled manual labor or low paid service jobs have been stigmatized; their low paid jobs are taken as signs of social character rather than a reflection of the labor market situation. If these workers had any talent or initiative they would not be working at McDonald's, unless they were attending school as well. The student who, under earlier circumstances, might have held in a blue

collar job "forgets" that he has been obliged to seek educational credentials out of necessity rather than choice. The perch from which to pejoratively evaluate manual and clerical labor is as wobbly as a termite-ridden
platform. A man observes a woman driver creeping along the highway at
forty miles per hour in the outside lane and, in irritation and contempt,
ascribes her inept behavior to gender difference. She is not seen as an
individual; she is a member of a class—women—who, among other characteristics, are not risk-takers and because of this inherent conservatism,
unintentionally drive in a thoughtless and dangerous manner. Similarly,
reading an account of a murder in the newspaper it is not surprising to
many whites that the perpetrator of the crime is a black man. The class
of poor black men is identified in the minds of many with murder, rape,
and robbery. Needless to say these judgments are not rooted in nature,
they are conditioned by a multiplicity of social influences, not the least
that, in many circles, color is a marker of anti-social behavior. Unfortunately given the prevailing conception of blacks as beings congenitally
incapable of self-control, an everyday encounter with a black male on a
deserted street, even in daylight, may provoke considerable anxiety in his
Caucasian interlocutor.

How social or economic class helps us interpret events may be illustrated by our evaluation of statistics showing that students attending
schools in working-class districts perform below the national average
when measured by standardized tests. We may ascribe this performance
"deficit" to the lack of educational attainment in their families which
might be reflected in the absence of books and other artifacts of cultural
capital in their homes; or, before the conflation of racial thinking with
color (say, the nineteenth century), attribute poor grades to inherent or
cultural characteristics of certain immigrant groups such as Irish, Poles,
and Italians. In nineteenth- and early twentieth-century parlance, these
groups had racial designations. They were the subjects of phrenological
investigations which purported to show that they had smaller brains than
members of the white race, an allegation that was also pinned on blacks
as a justification for slavery. In these times white working-class school
performances are largely ignored by the media and by education policymakers. Despite ample evidence that high school and college drop-out

rates among working-class white students are far higher than for middle class students and not much lower than that of blacks and Latinos, these statistics are ignored because white working-class kids rarely make it into public discourse except when they commit acts of mass suicide or mass murder. In public discourse, the fundamental class divide is between the undifferentiated class of whites and a parallel aggregation of "minorities." The reason is fairly plain: in the post-World War II period, nearly all whites have been recoded as "middle class," a designation that connotes not occupational position but levels of consumption that, for a considerable fraction of blue-collar industrial workers, compare with some professional and technical occupations. Since the middle class is presumed to have no significant educational deficits as measured by the norms set by school authorities, whites who fail to meet the standards are assumed to suffer individually but not as a class.

But, class is beginning to be recognized as a basis for affirmative social policy. For example, against conservative arguments for race neutral policies for access to higher education and other mainstream public goods, Glenn Loury insists that blacks be treated by institutions of higher education as a class with historical deficits that need remedy. He distinguishes between "race-blind" and "race-neutral" criteria for awarding access to scarce public goods such as elite higher education. In this view schools should not admit blacks who do not meet their academic standards. On the other hand, failing to adopt a policy of black admissions on race-neutral grounds will surely have deleterious consequences, particularly in relation to the goal of diversifying the intellectual and managerial elite. If society wishes to make sure that access to membership is broadly distributed given limitations such as the number of places, schools have little choice but to adopt special measures to assure black admissions. Otherwise, in a race-blind policy, blacks would be required to perform at a higher level than whites in order to secure their place(s).[2]

For the present, I want to evoke class loosely rather than subjecting it to rigorous definition. My main point here is not to engage in the scientific debate about what are the determinants of classes. Here I want to focus on its importance in organizing both individual and social perception. I make the further claim that the most salient concepts are those of difference, which constitutes the foundation of knowledge. Something or somebody is this and not that; we measure and know thisness with reference to thatness. In the course of making everyday judgments we tend to define them in relation to what they are not. The manual worker is not an intellectual worker; in turn the intellectual works with her/his brains rather than with her/his hands. These binaries are extreme reductions. They contradict what, with a little reflection, is obvious: that nearly all work has both physical and intellectual components. The labor of producing things and services is not literally divided by head and hand. Intellectuals use tools such as pens, word-processors, calculators, and other machines which are operated manually. And from the highly skilled toolmaker or plumber to the "unskilled" laborer, manual work involves knowledge of science and technology and the considerable use of judgment. Homeowners understand that the plumber is a prestigious possessor of rare and necessary knowledge whose manual tasks are accompanied by analysis and prognosis. Everybody who has cleaned her or his home knows the variety of skills needed to get the job done. In the contemporary household, the worker (whether the unpaid member or a professional cleaner) must know how to use a variety of tools and operate various machines such as vacuum cleaners (an instrument which requires more than a little maintenance), perhaps a waxing machine and dishwashers. In addition, the cleaner knows and uses a wide array of cleaning chemicals ranging from soaps to sprays and oils. That many experimental physicists spend considerable time and energy literally making their own tools of observation and experiment goes unnoticed as a descriptor of their job. Despite this indisputable fact they are still classified as intellectual rather than manual workers. Thus there is a measure physical toil in most work but all work involves knowledge and judgment, the hallmarks of intellectual labor. Still we know what we mean when we divide labor in this manner. We are designating educational credentials as a marker of social difference.

Concept-formation is not limited to the social world. They help us as well to understand what we have called "nature," that is, visible and the invisible heterogeneous material objects and processes. Whether these concepts are always already present in the sinews of comprehension itself, on our inherent capacity for making sense, or are produced in conjunction with our historically conditioned social existence belongs to the problem of explanation. For now it is enough to remark that we cannot do without organizing concepts, in science and in everyday life. The Ancient Greek scientists/philosophers debated what substances constituted the material world. Some reduced matter to four: earth, air, fire, and water. Thales, who has been called the first scientist in written history, proclaimed that water is the fundamental substance of nature. But Leucippus and Democritus theorized the world as consisting of an infinite number of closely packed atoms and provided a detailed account of their origin and development. As opposed to later physical theory they posited no empty space, although others thought that space was the void between material objects. In their view, atoms are invisible and indivisible. Despite different permutations, for 2,500 years atomic theory has been a leading concept of physics and has withstood frequent attempts to override its fundamental premise. While some have challenged its adequacy as a description of the physical world, declaring that the matter is also organized in waves or strings, even as atomic theory has been refined by adding several layers of microparticles under atoms and molecules, the world understood as particle remains at the leading edge of both description and explanation. While many believe its persistence, despite the invisibility of several classes of microparticles, is a testament to the veracity of (sub)atomic theory—that it corresponds to the actual organization of the physical world—for our purposes what counts is that it remains an organizing concept in science and in our collective understanding.[3]

Who is a Citizen?

There is a long tradition in Western political philosophy which understands human societies as, in part, constituted by social differences and some even recognize that there are not merely distinctions between individuals and groups but some of these are antagonistic. Marx was not the first to discover that the concept of interest was rooted in the position people occupied in society. In fact, it may be argued that class pervades the entire history of Western political philosophy and is among its organizing principles. From Plato to James Madison, political theorists believed social relations were inherently hierarchical and conflictual. Not suprisingly, perhaps the first written class discourse occurs in ancient Athens where, alongside its democratic polity, there flourished a system of slavery. Owned by landowners and proprietors of medium-sized and large businesses, slaves performed a considerable portion of the agricultural and urban labor. They were considered non-persons and appear in the great works of classical Greek philosophy as the "other" of the human community or a tool of the citizen's household. The condition of slavery is employed as a continuous sign of that which the citizenry—invariably composed of free, leisured men—must avoid.[4]

Plato informs us in his *Republic* that slavery is the condition a free man most abhors. But this does not mean that all others are to be accorded equal status. In *The Republic* and other dialogues, he names the classes of society: rich landowners, artisans, guardians—a very small "class" charged with the protection of the whole state—the urban poor who, he infers, are often the repository of evil, and the slaves who are invoked in a variety of contexts. *The Republic* accords a special significance to mastery and slavery. These terms are employed as metaphors for Socrates's ideal State as much as descriptions of the state of Athenian society:

> There is something ridiculous in the expression 'master of himself'; for the master is also the servant and the servant the master, and in all these modes of speaking the same person is denoted.
>
> Certainly the meaning is, I believe, that in the human soul there is a better and also a worse principle, and when the better has the worse under control, then a man is said to be master of himself; and this is a term of praise: but when, owing to evil education or association, the better principle, which is also the smaller, is overwhelmed by the greater mass of the worse—in this case he is blamed and called the slave of self and unprincipled.[5]

How are classes determined? To this day conservative philosophers following Plato's formula claim that classes are formed from nature's endowment of intrinsic qualities in each individual. While through education and association one learns a profession or craft, the capacity to learn and perform the duties appropriate to these occupations is always already given many now claim, by genetic predisposition. Accordingly the necessary qualifications for ruling the state are present only in a very few individuals whose nature it is to be more wise and enlightened than those of other classes. Book Seven, where one finds the famous allegory of the cave, poses the limits of mass education and Book Eight is a sustained argument for the view that social rule should be grounded neither in oligarchic nor democratic principles but in a natural aristocracy of the intellect. In Plato's view, most humans are shackled in the chains of illusion and are incapable of liberating themselves from ignorance without the guidance of the precious few who, in his allegory, are naturally endowed with the capacity to see the light.

Socrates contrasts the status quo with his own vision of the Ideal State. As he makes clear in Book Four: "any city, however small, is in fact divided into two: one the city of the poor, the other of the rich; these are at war with one another."[6] In the existing state of affairs, the powerful rich and political leaders have defined justice in terms of their own interest and have construed the law in this image. But the economically and politically strong are by no means necessarily endowed with qualities of wisdom or of genuine justice. For the just ruler acts in the interest of the weak rather than defining justice as the self-interest of the strong. Socrates's solution to the state of affairs that defines justice in terms of the interests of the strong is to install a small class of philosopher-kings at the helm—a frank aristocracy of intellect—and to educate a class of guardians to provide the means of force by which they may rule.

These guardians, too, must possess the natural talents to perform their task. But they require moral as much as physical education. Accordingly, Socrates outlines a curriculum that, in sum, may be the first open enunciation of education as ideology, if by that term we mean knowledge presenting itself as truth but actually disseminated in the interest of a particular class in society The guardians will be spared knowledge of Homer's statement that the gods are the source of evil as well as good and will be taught the values appropriate to the new form of rule. In these passages it may be said that Plato invents the concept, but not the name, ideology. The education of those assigned the security of the state is plainly partial and, perhaps more to the point, in sync with the prevailing values.

While the guardians and the philosophers would share goods in common and eschew material riches, Socrates has no intention of disturbing the economic class system of the Greek city-states. Instead he wants to found the state on natural intellectual superiority and to construct civil society on the basis of a "natural" division of labor. Each is to remain in her or his place, as the gods have decreed.

For those who regard this perspective as profoundly inegalitarian and properly consigned to historical memory, they might find it useful to consult the early influential writings of the American journalist and political philosopher, Walter Lippmann. In his widely read book *Public Opinion*, published in the aftermath of World War I, Lippmann argues that mass democracy is, regrettably, not possible in a society rent by large and petty rivalries, mass media which, even at the turn of the century, had gripped the popular imagination and irreparably twisted it, and particular interests that distort the public interest. Like Plato's slaves, the masses could only see one side of the truth—their own. But public life cannot be held hostage to perennially warring factions. Its management requires a modern version of the philosopher-king, the expert. Lippmann favors a democracy of consent rather than broad participation, if only to control the few experts who, by virtue of their broad educational preparation and technical skill, are charged with the responsivity of managing large-scale governmental institutions and managing the multifarious functions of public life. If the professional managers must run society, the political class acts as the mediator between these largely shadowy figures and the electorate. The electorate remains the final judge of expert actions but must be excluded from day-to-day decisions. Needless to say, what Lippmann so bluntly describes is our own representative democracies today.

In many respects Aristotle's *Politics*[7] is a reply to his teacher, Plato. Aristotle focuses on the question: who is entitled to citizenship? Consistent with his abiding passion for the "mean" he rejects the "extremes" of oligarchy—an option to Statecraft equally abjured by Plato— and a State of "extreme" democracy, the definition of which is that the "working class" (the term is Aristotle's) has citizenship and, in accordance with the norm of Greek society, entitled to participate in making state decisions. Like his mentor, he warns against the rule of the mob. But Aristotle takes the argument against mass democracy a step further. He argues that the tasks of labor and the tasks of citizenship are in fundamental contradiction: "Certainly the good man and the statesman and the good citizen ought not to learn the crafts of inferiors except for their own occasional use; if they habitually practice them, there will cease to be a distinction between master and slave"[8] and again, "That in a well ordered state the citizens should have leisure and not have to provide for their daily wants is generally acknowledged..."[9] Like Plato, the necessary work of keeping the polity going must be performed by "inferiors"; more, labor is *de facto* equated with slavery for reasons that will become clear.

Aristotle's "mean" is a democracy in which citizens are able to participate in rule: "He who has the power to take part in the deliberative judicial administration of any state is said by us to be a citizen of that state; and speaking generally a state is a body of citizens sufficing for the purposes of life."[10] What enables a citizen to acquire the power to participate? That he is the head of a household and performs only the limited work of management and has the time needed to enter the public arena. Women, although vital for the State because they perform the work of raising children and other household duties are disqualified, as are artisans, because they are too busy performing the labor of the physical reproduction of the household to concern themselves with affairs of state. As for the slaves or servants, they are excluded from citizenship by definition: since they are property, they cannot freely participate in any activity; they serve at the pleasure of their master.

Aristotle reserves a special discussion for a class of freeholders, the merchants. Summoned into existence by need—one household cannot provide all of its needs so it must trade with others—the merchant becomes the mediator of these exchange relationships. At a certain stage direct barter no longer suffices to satisfy trade requirements so the instrument of money is invented as a universal medium of multiple, complex exchanges. As long as money is exchanged for goods used to satisfy naturally endowed and the merchant remains a necessary intermediary, he serves the good. The problem arises when merchants and some other property owners accumulate money for its own sake, engage in chrematistics, the "freeing of the (monetary) sign of any relation to its natural referent."[11] Thus, the city becomes "emptied" and is no longer a presence to itself:

> the most hated sort of trade and with the greatest reason, usury, which makes a gain out of money itself, and not for the purposes it was meant to serve. For money was intended to be used in exchange, but not to increase at interest. And this term interest, which means the birth of money from money...is applied to the breeding of money because the offspring resembles the parent. That is why all modes of getting wealth this is the most unnatural.[12]

Unnatural because it is not earned but instead is the consequence of the self-birth of money. That is, "interest" accrues only because one possesses it and lends it for a specified period of time to another and not as the "natural" product of the exchange of commodities needed for "life." Accordingly the merchants must be excluded because they are too busy making money.[13]

Aristotle's discourse on class calls attention to the question of the good and bad uses of time. The "leisure class" is always a relative term: those who have power over their own time are ill-advised to squander it on frivolous pleasures or on the pursuit of money for its own sake: their leisure makes possible their participation in the juridical functions of the State and this is an ethical obligation. As in Plato, the inference here is that nature should rule human conduct. But the deformation of time and money in the service of avarice, their abstraction from concrete material and juridical need, is a violation of nature. As Aristotle makes plain, the chief difference between his conceptions of democracy and of citizenship and that of the "extremists" rests on class doctrine. The fundamental distinction is between those who are masters of their time and those who are not. Seen in the context of political economy "slavery" consists not only in the fact that some humans have become the property of other humans but also that propertylessness condemns those who are ostensibly free to labor and therefore cannot engage in statecraft. Throughout most of the subsequent millennia political theory has adopted the core of Aristotle's position, which integrates some, but not all, of Plato's arguments. In sum, only those who are freed from the concerns of labor and of commerce can rule.[14] Since Plato and Aristotle, political and social philosophy has, tacitly or explicitly, recognized that class is for society what atoms are for nature, a building block upon which the whole edifice of being rests. Some, like Aristotle, have viewed the distinction between those who hold productive property and those who are obliged to labor to provide the necessities of physical existence, as a benign division of labor: slaves, women, and artisans work in the Household or to supply goods. The work of the master and, by extension, a fraction of the nobility and capitalists in subsequent feudal and bourgeois eras is to rule. In the ancient sense their role in the social order is to practice the art of government.

But in the modern epoch many political theorists argued that the division between the ruler and the ruled has become an antagonistic relationship. While the underlying population has been formally freed of bondage to a master or to the land, until the nineteenth and twentieth centuries they remained deprived of citizenship. At the dusk of the feudal order Machiavelli was among the first to recognize that a new situation had arisen in the Italian city-state. However powerful the monarch, a new social group, the people, had come into being which called into question his claim to divine right. Although subordinate to the Prince, the people would no longer automatically view him as God's representative on earth and award him their undying loyalty. While riches can facilitate the Prince's ascendancy to power, Machiavelli argued wealth could no longer secure its maintenance. Security of rule can be achieved only if the Prince wins the loyalty of the people. Anticipating the emergence of a democratic populace rather than taking their fealty for granted Machiavelli urges the Prince—an abstraction from the class of rulers in the multitude of Italian city-states—to win the consent of the masses by, among other innovations, to live among them. Tacitly recognizing their citizenship, Machiavelli argues that in order to "hold" the cities the Prince should not rely on coercion as the prime instrument of direct rule and, instead, recognize the right of the people to self-government. Although favoring the maintenance of a strong militia as a guarantee of independence from foreign armies, Machiavelli advises the Prince to forge friendly relations with those accustomed to liberty, on condition that they "pay tribute" and recognize his ultimate sovereignty.[15]

A century later, having been expropriated from the land, millions of individuals presented themselves in the market as possessors of a single commodity, their own labor, Thomas Hobbes argued that, left to itself, civil "society" had devolved into a morass of incessant competition between individuals which always threatened to break out into war, the war of all against all. In the situation of sixteenth- and seventeenth-century English capitalism, the concept of the social order was more hope than reality. As Karl Polanyi has shown, the Enclosures, whose effects were to drive hundreds of thousands of peasants into the city and amounted to a "revolution of the rich against the poor," may have increased the domestic food supply but constituted a "catastrophic dislocation in the lives of the common people."[16] The peasants were "freed" from feudal obligations but were also deprived of their collective livelihoods. Possessing formal freedom but lacking Rights—to vote, to organize into trade unions and other voluntary associations, to form political factions, and to stay out of jail or workhouses—the most dangerous class was the "bondsmen made free," the newly formed multitude of wage workers.[17] But at the dawn of the industrial revolution they were offered few jobs. In the absence of opportunities to earn a living many crowded the narrow streets of the major English cities begging for change, engaging in petty crimes and periodically staging bread riots. In a chaotic economic situation, far from remaining a nightwatchman whose job was to protect owners' property but to stand aside of the marketplace, the State was charged with the task of keeping order and typically came down on the poor and destitute with an iron fist. Moreover, the liberal dogma of free market capitalism became untenable: in the seventeenth and eighteenth century the disruptive effects of geographical and industrial dislocation drove some of the most enthusiastic proponents of market liberalism to propose state intervention to provide subsistence income to the long-term poor.

In the wake of the English revolutions of 1640 and 1688 it was impossible for political philosophers to ignore class in their consideration of the proper form of government. Led by an emergent middle class of proprietors and their intellectual and political allies these revolts were directed against the monarchy's oligarchic power. Writing in the heat of

535

the civil war of 1640 that challenged the traditional monarchy, Hobbes's treatise *The Leviathan* was received at the time as a spirited defense of the need for a state in which sovereignty would be concentrated in the royalty. Like Plato and Aristotle, Hobbes argued from the perspective in which politics derived from human nature. Reflecting the prevailing social philosophy of his day, he viewed society as an agglomeration of individuals who, he added, were possessed of appetites and desires that were, for some, uncontrollable. In contrast to Adam Smith who later postulated that the market was regulated by the "invisible hand of God," Hobbes viewed the market of individuals seeking to satisfy their appetites with alarm. Although most members of society are peace-loving because they can be induced to exercise self-control over their natural appetites, a small number of individuals will inevitably disrupt the peace and act aggressively towards others. Civil war was the outcome of the anarchy of civil society, that is, of the chaos that attends untrammeled liberty. Left to itself the marketplace results in the "war of all against all." Hence, in the interest of peace there is need for members of society to surrender their sovereignty to a higher secular power.[18] As C. B. Macpherson points out, Hobbes was sharply critical of "bourgeois morality." Hobbes observes that "'the generality of citizens and inhabitants of market-towns' being at ease with 'the lucrative vices of men of trade or handicraft; such as are feigning, lying, cozening, hypocrisy, or other uncharitableness' and about merchants 'whose only glory [is] to grow excessively rich by the wisdom of buying and selling' and 'by making poor people sell their labor to them at their own prices.'"[19] Hobbes's model of man is derived from the very social relations he criticizes. His scientific hypothesis is that avarice is constitutive of human nature and that market society provides the occasion for the manifestation of its most detestable features. On the other hand, he shares Aristotle's loathing for making of money for the sake of money and views the self-aggrandizing merchant as the exemplary figure from which to argue for a system of constraint. For it was the merchant class as much as the small manufacturers who strained against the remnants of the old feudal system, especially the monarchic oligarchy which, they believed, were standing in the way of progress.

The historian William Appleman Williams argued, referring to the relation of the rising industrial and commercial classes in eighteenth- and nineteenth-century America, that "laissez faire" never meant a genuine free market to which, as John Locke theorized, individuals brought the products of their own labor and should be paid to the extent of their own labor rather than trading on the labor of others. From a Hobbesian point of view the slogan "laissez-faire" meant laissez nous faire (let us do what we please) and this was the main obstacle standing in the way of the quest for perpetual peace.[20] No less that the gluttonous industrialists of the late nineteenth century, the new middle class of the early capitalist era, whose greatest prophet was John Locke, wished to transfer sovereignty over the state to themselves in order to insure their unfettered ability to produce commodities and trade them. If Locke's *Two Treatises of Government* were written to justify, in advance, the 'glorious revolution' of 1688 whose objective it was to lay the monarchy to rest since it had survived the earlier civil war, his justification was based on a conception of human nature that marked a breakthrough in political theory. For Locke as much as Rousseau, nearly a century later, God has created us all equal and, as individuals we are free in a state of nature. Government is constituted, according to Locke, to preserve the natural rights of individuals. Its main job is punish those who would inhibit the individual's freedom. As Peter Laslett points out, the exception to this rule is that parents must impose their authority on children because, while they are born to reason, they have not yet attained a state of reason.[21]

Locke believed that in primitive societies—his chief contemporary example was the American Indian civilization, at least before the European conquest—humans shared the fruits of the earth in common.[22] So how does he justify the cornerstone of middle-class society, bourgeois, that is, individual property?

> Though the earth, and all inferior creatures be common to all men, yet every man has a Property in his own Person. This no Body has any right to but himself. The Labour of his Body, and the work of his Hands, we may say are properly his.[23]

So the products of our individual direct labor are inalienable, "no man but he can have a right to what is once joyned to, at least where there is enough, as any good left in common for others."[24] In these sentences we can see the model of a society of individual producers, each of whom has property rights only to the extent of their own labor. This is the model that impelled many American revolutionaries for whom Locke's political philosophy was inspiration. As we shall see, however much the doctrine of natural law and individual freedom infused revolutionary slogans, Hobbes's pessimism informed the ideas by which conservatives who dominated the Constitutional convention developed the model of American government.

But Locke himself could not reconcile his labor theory of property with his acknowledgement that the emergence of money as the intermediary of exchange renders the theory more than problematic. While in the end he maintains that labor is the measure of exchange value—a discovery which precedes Smith's nearly a century later and Marx's further development of the labor theory more than one hundred fifty years after the publication of the *Second Treatise*, the concept that a person should limit their accumulation of capital to the extent of their own labor, and its relation to natural law, yields to a theory of contract:

> it is plain, that Men have agreed to disproportionate and unequal possession of the Earth, they have by a tacit and voluntary consent found out a way, how a man may fairly possess more land than he, himself, can use the product of, by receiving in exchange for the overplus, Gold and Silver, which may be hoarded up without injury to any one, these metals not spoiling or decaying in the hands of the possessor. This portage of things, in an inequality of private possessions, men have made practicable out of the bounds of Societies, and without compact, only by putting a value on gold and silver and tacitly agreeing in the use of money. For in Governments the Laws regulate the rights of property and the possession of land is determined by positive constitutions.[25]

Once again, here is Aristotle's position on the corrosive role of money in altering human relations but without the condemnation of accumulation

538

for its own sake. Locke's conception of history's stages corresponds to some modern anthropological periodizations: we start with primitive communism which gives way to property, but only as the result the labor of its possessor, to a money economy where accumulation for its own sake produces inequality, but which is instituted by the tacit consent of free men. While he sees no reason why, in the vast expanse of America's riches in natural resources, property should exceed products that individuals can themselves use, in Europe the scarcity of land gives rise to "controversies" over Title and the appearance of certain individuals who will exchange their "overplus" for silver and gold. That Locke retreats from the implications of his own philosophical anthropology is not surprising in the light of the stark inequalities that surrounded him, both in England and in France. Then, as many political theorists do now, he ends up on the confident note that a society of laws can remedy the inevitable contradiction between natural equality and social inequality. And, at the same time, Locke introduces the by now commonplace fiction that those whose labor is bought and sold by Hobbes's hypocritical merchants and manufacturers have done so voluntarily and blithely ignores the tyranny of economic necessity motivating people to sell their labor.

To Rousseau fell the task of reversing many of the precepts of his philosophical ancestors. That human action is ruled by the passions he readily admits. But instead of insisting that the passions are rooted in the evil side of human nature and the exercise of reason is the solution to most social problems, he argues that the passions are grounded in needs which are clearly good and that the civilization's attempt to suppress bodily needs is at the heart of social ills. For the fundamental criterion of the good society is that which conforms most nearly to how man lived in a state of nature, born free and equal. But his most vociferous criticism is reserved for capitalism: "the extreme inequalities in the manner of living of the several classes of mankind, the excess of idleness in some, and of labor in others, the facility of irritating and satisfying our sensuality, and our appetites, the too exquisite and out of the way foods of the rich, which fill them with fiery juices, and bring on indigestions, and the unwholesome food of the poor, of which even, bad as it is, they very often fall short, and the want of which tempts them, every opportunity that offers, to eat greedily and overload their stomachs;" and, he adds many other batterings we administer to our own bodies; "these are the fatal proofs that most of our ills are of our own making," especially the drive to accumulate property.[26]

In contrast to his friends, the Philosophers who, like Diderot, proclaimed the interests of the bourgeoisie to be identical with those of mankind, Rousseau breaks ranks and declares the revolution had already failed to bridge the gap between rich and poor, master and slave in England, and is further seriously flawed because, no less than the monarchy against which it was arrayed, it represents particular interests, those of property owners. If Rousseau's own version of ethics depends on a reading of human nature as inherently good, his critique of contemporary social relationships and the consequences of a civil society governed by the accumulation of wealth is, together with the writings of Vico, the first modern discourse of social science. For unlike his forbearers, he ascribes the origin of inequality not to innate natural gifts or to evil passions but to the exact machinery that makes the capitalist world go round: private property in the means by which survival of each and of all depends. In consequence an inquiry into the origin and causes of inequality must seek purely social causes.

Moreover, rather than viewing government as the mediator of social conflicts that flare up in civil society, he sees the state as a mirror of these conflicts: "The various forms of government owe their origin to the various degrees of inequality which existed between individuals at the time of their execution." Therefore "where a man happened to be preeminent in power, virtue, riches or credit, he became the sole magistrate, and the State assumed a monarchical form." Concomitantly the aristocratic form reflects the dominance of "several of pretty equal eminence" and democracy is the expression of a society which has deviated "less from a state of nature" and is of greater, but not necessarily perfect, equality.[27] But sadly, according to Rousseau, the revolutions do not occur to produce greater democracy but, rather, to "authorize" existing inequalities. Whatever the governmental form, as long as it is based on the class divisions of rich and poor, powerful and weak, and master and slave they will not result in greater human freedom.[28] Thus unlike Hobbes and Locke, Rousseau places little weight on reform of the state and its laws.

Class is as American as Cherry Pie

Contrary to the loud proclamations among American critics and social theorists that class is an imported idea, class is as American as cherry pie. When, in the wake of what is sometimes termed the "age of democratic revolutions," political expediency, if not always conviction, requires that farmers, merchants and artisans (but not the economically and socially disinherited), be included in the polity their rights must be specified, but also limited by constitution and by statute. Thus, the concept of passive participation enters political discourse, as in the definition of democracy as government which rules by "the consent of the governed." In addition, even the minimalist idea of citizenship remains defined by property pos-session, a stricture which insures that only those who have a genuine interest in state affairs—taxation, foreign and internal trade, and wheth-er the government can appropriate private property for public purpos-es, such as roads—can constitute the electorate. Since the propertyless are governed by their passions, are hostile to government and especially to taxation, have no interest in the preservation of private property and have shown throughout history to be indifferent to the national interest in times of war, they must be disqualified from voting.[29]

In the debate that preceded the adoption of the constitution of the new American nation, Alexander Hamilton, John Jay and James Madi-son published a series of essays directed to their fellow citizens intended to argue for a new form of government and a conception of citizenship which, remarkably, set the contours of the American state for more than two hundred years. Among other objectives, *The Federalist Papers* were addressed to the problem of how to achieve national unity in the wake of the pervasive factionalism—the contemporary term for class—within the post-revolutionary America. For the American victory over the British did not erase the internal factionalism that, even in times of war flickered now, raged then. Even as the three political leaders wrote their epistles to the fledgling nation, the danger to the fragile unity forged in 1776 was ever present: farmers, the overwhelming majority of whom were small-holders, were arrayed against merchants for whom money was the end rather than the means of economic activity; slave-holders were opposed by artisans and laborers for whom free labor was identical to the idea of liberty; groups that had sympathized with the British and even collaborated against patriots of all social classes. Perhaps no more eloquent statement of the problem was written than Madison's in *Federalist 10*:

> By a faction, I understand a number of citizens whether amounting to a majority or a minority of the whole, who are united and actuated by some common impulse of passion, or of interests, adverse to the rights of other citizens, or to the permanent and aggregate interests of the community. So strong is this propensity of mankind to fall into mutual animosities that where no substantial occasion presents itself, the most frivolous and fanciful distinctions have been sufficient to kindle their unfriendly passions and excite their most violent conflicts. But the most common and durable source of factions has been the various and unequal distribution of property. Those who hold and those who are without property have forever formed distinct interests in society. Those who are creditors, and those who are debtors fall under a like discrimination. A landed interest, a manufacturing interest, a mercantile interest, a moneyed interest, and with many lesser interests, grow up of necessity in civilized nations, and divide them into different classes, actuated by different sentiments and views. The regulation of these various and interfering interests forms the principal task of modern legislation, and involves the spirit of party and faction in the necessary and ordinary operations of the government... No man is allowed to be a judge of his own cause, because his interest would certainly bias his judgment, and, not improbably, corrupt his integrity...[30]

Since "the latent causes of faction are thus sown in the nature of man" the question of how to form a nation that is unified in purpose and particularly able to resist incursions into its territory from foreign powers, becomes the decisive issue facing the leading framers of the constitution. Hamilton put the matter even more bluntly: "A firm Union will be of the utmost moment to the peace and liberty of the States, as a barrier against domestic faction and insurrection."[31] In Hamilton's view, a strong central government which commands a near monopoly over the means of violence and has the legal power to issue money and to intervene to deal with the excesses of faction (as represented, for example in Shays's Rebellion, a veteran's movement demanding public support for its largely indigent constituents).[32] Madison finds little hope for "adjusting these clashing interests" through reliance on the prevailing political party, even if its leaders are composed of enlightened statesmen.[33]

Since social difference is natural, one way to cure the causes of factionalism would be to suppress the liberties of one or more of the contending parties. In Madison's view, this course of action is unacceptable. "The inference to which we are brought is, that the causes of faction cannot be removed [because they are rooted in human nature] and that relief is only to be sought in the means of controlling its effects."[34] One solution that was quite popular among small farmers and some intellectuals in the early of post-revolutionary years was "pure democracy" which, as in the Greek *polis*, inevitably consists of a small number of citizens who make, in person, all decisions for the community, inevitably because, in its Aristotelian mode, citizenship is restricted to the minority of property holders who can make the time to deal with affairs of state. Of course the anti-federalists who advocated this form of governance also favored a highly decentralized state, where the small community would retain a high degree of sovereignty, especially on questions of taxation and what later became known as "eminent domain"—the power of government to seize property for public purposes such as the construction of roads and dams.[35] According to Madison the *de facto* exclusions entailed by direct democracy will only exacerbate factionalism and interest politics. To cure the problem, Madison proposes a Republican form of government, in which representatives may claim the public good and thereby can legitimately suppress the insurrectionary impulses of the minority—small holders on the farm or in the workshops, and the city laborers—which is chronically discontented with the state of things.[36]

Hamilton and Jay were the leading advocates of establishing a third branch of government to mediate the excesses of the elected executive and legislative branches. They urged the formation of an independent judicial system to adjudicate conflicting property claims, contract disputes and other civil matters. More to the point of their proposals for the constitution, the three authors sought other mechanisms to settle disputes between the factions and to correct the excesses of Congress which, from their perspective was much too subject to the popular will—a Supreme Court. The highest court would have the power to override congress when it exceeded its powers under the constitution. It would present itself as the chief arbiter of disputes between the states and the federal government and between a recalcitrant, underlying population driven by its particular interests and wanton passions, and the state. In order to safeguard its impartiality, at least between various disputants among the propertied classes, members of various levels of the federal courts would not be elected but would be appointed by the president subject to the advice and consent of the Congress. In other words, the more distant from the popular will, the better the courts would be able to perform their mediating and overriding functions.

Among their many objections to the proposals advanced in *The Federalist*, the anti-federalists were vehemently opposed to the establishment of a separate judicial department of government. They understood this proposal to be directed against popular sovereignty, specifically against legislative powers, at a time when many at the local level were close to being popular assemblies. In fact, the insurrections that Hamilton feared often flared up against efforts by state governments to form independent judiciaries even before the passage of the Constitution in 1789. A crowd burned down a Massachusetts courthouse in 1783. Moreover they read the courts as voices of the most oligarchic among the federalists, that is, those who would centralize power against the farming and working classes.[37]

In general, the anti-federalists were proponents of what Madison had termed "pure" or "direct" democracy, holding that "representatives" tended to be recruited from the upper reaches of society. Needless to say, they were defeated at the convention but, contrary to the consensual accounts of historians, the convention was by no means a love-fest of national unity. It was, at times, raucous because it mirrored the class divisions that were the real subject of many of the *Federalist Papers*. The main features of the Constitution, excluding the first ten amendments which were added after the initial draft under pressure from the Jeffersonians and the anti-federalists, ratified republican, representative government, the tri-department structure of government rather than the English parliamentary system but, like England, provided a bi-cameral legislature—a popular chamber and an aristocratic chamber, aristocratic because it was not directly chosen by the electorate and, since it equalized representation between the states regardless of the size of their populations, discriminated against those which had large urban populations. Since no legislative proposal could become law without approval of both houses and of the President who, like the senate was not elected directly, it enlarged the power of the executive and undercut the sovereignty of the popularly elected House, many of whose members were of distinctly modest means and were often seen by the statists and large landholders as tribunes for the rabble. It further reinforced the class system by refusing to challenge slavery (in order to win the support of the slave states for the constitution they permitted slaves to be counted as three fifths of a person, thereby increasing the South's congressional delegations), the exclusion of women from suffrage, and maintained the English system of property qualifications for voting. As Hamilton averred it was patterned, in part, on Montesquieu's notion of the confederated republic and on the Hobbesian idea that at its pinnacle the national state should constitute a "supreme authority"—a formulation echoed by Montesquieu.[38]

The English proved unable to abolish the monarchy even as they established a House of Commons that gradually assumed the supreme state authority. A hundred years later, the French Revolution crushed the royal Court and proclaimed the "Rights of Man," England remained in the partial thrall of the Crown. It was the French Revolution rather than the English that inspired the young George Wilhelm Frederich Hegel to believe that humankind was on the threshold of Freedom. For Hegel, Freedom was more than the establishment of individual right; it signified the unity of humans with nature and the unification of humankind in an indissoluble bond. Eleven years before the birth of Karl Marx, in 1807 Hegel published his monumental *Phenomenology of the Spirit*, perhaps the most influential work of philosophy in the nineteenth century. Its most compelling concept is, perhaps, the development of the dialectic as the leading thread of Being, natural and social. The dialectic is the immanence of nature, including human affairs, according to which things are constantly in flux and in the process of becoming and passing away, a proposition that underlies the work of the ancient "presocratic" Ionian philosophers, Thales, Anaximander, and especially Heraclites.[39]

Hegel's development of the dialectic was inspired by his strong attraction to the ancient Greeks and to Spinoza but also to the example of the French Revolution which, at first, seemed to have sounded the death knell to the two thousand years of the economic subordination of the overwhelming majority of people and their political disenfranchisement by aristocratic rulers. The slogans of the revolution used to overthrow the monarchy posed freedom as the defining political as well as philosophical question of his as well as our century. The thirty-seven-year-old Hegel lived in a Germany that had not yet come to terms with the political ideas of the Enlightenment let alone modernity with their powerful invocation of the individual and of freedom. After all, echoing Hobbes, the great Immanuel Kant, still promulgated a political philosophy which, in the interest of perpetual peace demanded obedience to the oligarchic German state.[40]

The dialectic attempts to answer the question of how, in the wake of centuries of human oppression change and the movement toward freedom is possible. Hegel's answer has a strong element of teleology: the end is present as a kernel at the very beginning of the process. Even if One, as opposed to antagonistic interests is the goal, Hegel refuses to posit the unity and self-identity of Being in advance of History. History is the process of the unfolding of the Totality through contradiction and negation. "Men" are obliged to fight it out without guarantees of victory either on the side of the status quo or of the revolutionaries. As with the Greeks, strife is ineluctably constitutive of being. The dialectic presents itself as the "unfolding" through a spiral of contradictions—resolution of "warring opposites" through their mutual destruction, preservation, and transformation at a higher level—only to give rise to new contradictions until the final unity of opposites is reached. If, for Hegel, the end is always already present at the beginning the passage from being to essence and back to Being is, nevertheless, a process of overcoming a series of contradictions within being, not the result of external force. To make concrete these highly abstract concepts, Hegel is compelled to offer an allegory. We may represent human relationships and their fate in the image of the fissure of lordship and bondage.

For Hegel as for Locke, Labor is the mediation between humans and nature, the mode of appropriation of the external world by man, an appropriation necessary for the preservation of humanity. But if, as Locke argued, there once was a primitive communist society marked by collective, egalitarian sharing of the fruits of labor, by the turn of the nineteenth century it was clear that society was rent by two great classes opposed over the division of the products of labor. The Lord commands the results of the bondsman's labor and dominates him in the social sphere. But the bondsman enjoys one element of superiority over the Lord, his direct interaction with nature. Thus, although subordinated to the Lord in social relations, the bondsman is the master of nature upon which human life depends. The Lord gains material satisfaction from appropriation of another's labor and retains the power over the laborer. But the lack of equality between the two deprives the Lord of that which he craves: Recognition by the Other. For even if the bondsman grants his superior his desire, it is the recognition of a slave for the master, and not of peers. Inevitably after stages of self-consciousness in which he, successively is proud of his station in life and hostile to the Lord, but still subservient, the bondsman finally understands the disparity between the sovereignty he enjoys in his relation to the natural world which his labor commands and his alienation from ownership and control over the products of his labor. He begins to see the Lord as a parasite on his labor and, finally, an antagonist. But in Hegel's dialectical allegory the contradiction cannot be resolved because the bondsman's consciousness of exploitation and oppression is not followed by the means by which bondage can be overcome. Like Aristotle and Plato, Hegel cannot imagine the bondsman transcending his alienation; he can achieve only an Unhappy Consciousness of his own oppression, unhappy because he has no power to overcome his subordination. The laborer cannot achieve freedom by his own efforts and become the master of his own destiny. As Kojève has argued, in the fight the "slave" fails because he refuses to risk life while the "master" is dominant precisely because he is willing to risk death.[41]

Following the publication of the *Phenomenology*, Hegel continued to grapple with the problem of how freedom was possible if the class divide could not be overcome. In *The Philosophy of Right* (1821) he returns to the unfinished problem posed in the Lordship/Bondage dialectic, unfinished because, contrary to Hegel's logical principle of overcoming, the contradiction between the two antagonists is never resolved. The *Philosophy of Right* begins with a discussion of two central social forms, the family and civil society. Hegel finds the protagonists of family life, husband and wife, parent and child, in perpetual conflict. In civil society he finds commodity owners confront each other as competitors in the marketplace, including labor and capital. The eighteenth century ideal of a civil society of individuals who, as peers discuss the affairs of state and of everyday life and may reproduce the condition of Greek Democracy without the encumbrance of slavery, has been irreversibly submerged in the triumph of commerce as a new cultural as much as an economic norm. Even at the level of the relatively privileged, the war of all against all arising from commodity exchange in the market dominates the public sphere. At the level of the family and of economic relations which, he argues, increasingly occupies the space of civil society there is no possibility for the resolution of social cleavages. The classes of modern society—the peasantry, the commercial class (which includes wage workers, in a subsumed form) the businessmen—are engaged in constant mutual strife. These contradictions can only be resolved only at a higher level, the State, particularly the German State which negates the opposition while preserving the classes within civil society.[42]

The class which constitutes the institutional apparatuses of the state, the bureaucracy, is charged with the task of transcending the limitations of family which remains in the private sphere, and of civil society which, albeit a public sphere, is reduced by exchange to an agglomeration of self-interested individuals and groups. Although suffused with his characteristic dialectical language, in this last great work Hegel succeeds in returning to themes first developed by Hobbes: only by surrendering their sovereignty, gained in the private sphere, to the State and the Laws can citizens achieve human freedom. As Marx notes, every particular class in Germany lacks not only the consistency, the penetration, the courage, or the ruthlessness that could stamp it as a negative representative of society. No more has any estate [class] the breadth of soul that identifies itself, even for a moment, with the soul of the nation, the geniality that inspires material might to political violence or that revolutionary daring which flings at the adversary the defiant words: *I am nothing, I must be Everything* [emphasis in the original].[43]

As one of the so-called Young Hegelians which, in addition to Marx included Arnold Ruge, Moses Hess, and Max Stirner, whose obsession with Hegel's allegory of alienation and domination defined German philosophy in the 1840s, who later inspired a flowering of anarchist thought, Marx was alone to draw the ineluctable conclusion from Hegel's failure to resolve the political contradiction among classes, except by reproducing in the State the subordination of the proletariat to the dominant class, especially the bourgeoisie. The consequence of Hegel's logic of negation and contradiction was, for Marx, that human emancipation is only possible through the:

formation of a class in radical chains, a class in civil society which is not a class of civil society, an estate which is the dissolution of all estates, a sphere which has a universal character by its universal suffering and claims no particular right because no particular wrong but wrong generally is perpetrated against it; which can invoke no historical but only its human title;…a sphere finally which cannot emancipate itself without emancipating itself from all other spheres of society, and thereby emancipating all other spheres of society, which, in a word, is the complete loss of man, and hence can win itself only through the complete rewinning of man. The dissolution of society as a particular estate is the proletariat.[44]

Marx argues that the proletariat is a universal class because unlike all other previous classes, the outcome of its struggle is to abolish classes as such rather than to reproduce domination by achieving its own particular interest against those of others. Or, put another way, as the propertyless class whose labor which, as Hegel discovered, is the absolute condition for the production and reproduction of human life and of society,

549

its "interest" is the abolition of private property in the ownership and control of the means of production. According to Marx, what Hegel and the German "ideologists" who followed him could not envision is that the self-emancipation of the proletariat is only possible if everyone is liberated from the bondage of the wage relation and of the private mode of capital accumulation which, for Marx, is the abstract, that is, money form, of surplus labor. Although "production for the sake of production" has increased economic wealth many-fold, Marx is not so far from Aristotle's condemnation of merchants whose goal is to accumulate money. The main contradiction of capitalism is the cleavage between production as an activity of creating "use" values and its production of exchange values whose aim is not to increase the personal consumption of employers and workers but accumulation for its own sake.[45]

Four years after the critique of Hegel's philosophy of politics when, in *The Communist Manifesto*, Marx and his collaborator Friedrich Engels declare that "All History is the History of Class Struggles," they are linking two distinct concepts in all previous social theory: history and class. For philosophers from Plato through Hegel the slaves, serfs, and the workers were, however subordinated by property relations, hardly capable of becoming history-makers; the two concepts were considered virtually incommensurable by those who came before them. By "history" Marx and Engels signify not only events but underlying changes in the relations of humans to nature and to each other that propel societies forward. According to the theoretical framework developed in their materialist conception of history, humans organize themselves into social groups, in the first place, to effectively conduct the struggle with their external environment in order to extract their fundamental means of existence. Facing the wrath of the physical world as well as other animals, they are obliged to band together and, at least in the process of production of use values, to cooperate. Human groups gain greater mastery over nature by the development of the means of production—tools, practical and theoretical knowledge of the cosmos, including the weather, how the earth yields or does not yield crops and, of course through observation of how their fellow animals and other living things negotiate their own relation to nature.[46]

These ideas were developed in *The German Ideology*, written by Marx and Engels only a year after the critique of Hegel's doctrine of the state and law and *The Economic and Philosophical Manuscripts*, which developed the concept of alienation, but no longer in allegorical form, but as a philosophical anthropology of the condition of the working class and a further argument for its emancipatory task. Marx and Engels do not construct a model of historically evolved class divisions in the analogy of a biological need or of any other natural necessity. Consistent with their evolutionary perspective, they draw on Rousseau and Hegel's social theories of inequality and exploitation and on contemporary anthropological studies which show that early human societies, the hunters and gatherers, organized themselves in an egalitarian manner. Citing the American, Lewis Henry Morgan, whose work among the Iroquois in New York State demonstrated a "primitive" communist community but also one based upon Mother Right rather than patriarchy, they develop a theory of historical periodization that purports to verify Locke's postulate of primitive communism at the dawn of humanity.[47] The materialist conception views humans in the context of natural history. As if to underscore this point the first material act is the physical reproduction of humans. As humans produce their livelihood by transforming nature, so they produce themselves. Only after thousands of years of hunting and gathering do human groups discover the value of engaging in cultivation. From the development of agriculture we first acquire the knowledges that produce technologies of production, communications, and the means of violence. As these technologies enable groups to produce a surplus beyond their immediate needs, they begin to engage in trade with others at first by barter, and, at the same time, as they recognize other groups, they develop "collective" private property. In time, through war and other means, the expansion of clans to tribes to "nations" in the ancient sense, gives rise to private property within the society. To these correspond the forms of social power and the ideas by which humans live.

The concept of class, according to Marx, signifies the development of collective or individual private property which, at a certain moment of social time, replaces a system of collective labor based on more or less equal sharing. Consequently, whereas earlier groups collectively wrested from nature their means of subsistence, now the process and product of labor is "owned" by relatively exclusive groups or by individuals, and sometimes they own labor itself as slaves, the main means of production. Classes are formed in the course of struggle over the division of social production. The outcome is determined by the power of those who own "productive" property, that is, property in means of production and the means of distribution which, in turn, determines the level and the differentiation of consumption. This is the class that ordinarily rules and reinforces its rule by its monopoly over the means of violence.

Although class struggles have existed throughout history, the outcome is never, or almost never, in doubt: the dispossessed lose because, even if united in opposition to those in power over the means of production, in the first place they lack force. Or, put another way, they lack the means of violence to effectively oppose and displace those who own the means of production and their retainers. But, since among the characteristic forms of their subordination none is more powerful than illiteracy, they also lack the means of generating knowledge of their social situation and the tools of communications by which to disseminate their ideas. Since humans do not live by bread alone—they have so-called spiritual as well as material needs, Marx argues that the ideas about how we should live are crucial aspects of social power. The ruling ideas are the ideas of the ruling class. It is the class which owns productive property and extracts the "surplus" from the laborer that imposes its cosmology, the moral code, the idea of Right, the values of everyday life.[48] If articulated and circulated, the ideas of the dispossessed are usually ignored or marginalized by those whose possession of productive property—including the means of communication—enables them to define the common sense of society.[49]

Since the emergence of Aegean city-states based on slave labor about six thousand years ago, societies have been structured along the model of social hierarchy based on the labor of subordinate classes. But in each stage of human history, the forms of class struggle differ according to the level of development of the productive forces—tools, skills, and scientific knowledge of nature—and the specific relations between those who own the means of production and those who don't. According to Marx's historical perspective, only with the development of capitalism is the laboring class capable, by virtue of its organization by capital as collective labor, of organizing itself on a continuous basis as a major social force: At first spontaneous resistance to its expulsion from the land, its degradation by the factory system from skilled to semi-skilled labor and through protests against its immiseration and finally, through its self-organization in trade and industrial unions and the formation of its own political parties, is the working class able to contest the power of capital.

Contest for what? Not for power over the existing state in order to substitute itself for capital on the same terms as it has been subordinated. In various writings Marx is unmistakably clear that he means to bring into being communist society. But unlike early or primitive communist societies, Marx views the coming communism as emergent from capitalism itself. The argument goes something like this: With the development of large-scale industry and the concentration and centralization of capital, capitalism has already "socialized" the productive forces; in comparison to the early capitalist regimes—the society of Adam Smith and the classical economists—production and distribution are no longer dispersed in many small firms. Moreover, labor is not only socialized labor in the technical sense that its products are exchanged for the products of other laborers or, indeed, that it sells its labor power as a commodity in order to reproduce itself and its family. Owing to the concentration and centralization of capital which brings labor into huge workplaces for the first time in human history labor can recognize its own exploitation, its own position in society and draw the necessary conclusions from this knowledge. In time it goes beyond contesting shares of its own labor and begins to pose the question of emancipation from the wage relation as such. At the same time capital advances towards the consolidation of its own economic and political power.[50]

In the late nineteenth century, Marx could only observe the beginnings of a high degree of capital concentration. In effect, his forecast of the erosion of competition awaited the emergence of what one of his followers, Rudolf Hilferding, termed "finance" capital—the merger of banking and industrial capital into huge, international combines that dominate the extent and rate of technological change, the markets for capital, labor and goods. Since the turn of the twentieth century the tendency towards oligopoly—the control by a few large firms of markets and patents within a given industrial sector has accelerated tremendously. For example, today the world's oil supply is essentially held by a few oil-producing nations and transnational corporations with whom they are allied. There are only two commercial aircraft-producing companies in the world and car corporations are merging across national borders so that a handful of transnational companies produce the lion's share of the world's vehicles. And, with each passing year, the global concentration of ownership and control of the latest computer mediated communications technologies in a few hands is becoming evident. For example, a recent United States government anti-trust suit against Microsoft revealed that it controls eighty-five per cent of the computer software industry.

What remains an obstacle to the further progress in humankind's quest for social and economic equality and for the development of the productive forces was the private appropriation of achievements of labor, intellectual as well as manual. Marx viewed the struggle between labor and capital as inevitable. With the exception of the *Manifesto* which, after all, was a call to arms as much as an analysis of the contemporary state of affairs, his later writing was concerned with the question of whether communism, in which the means of production would be held in common by the producers was the inevitable result of the tendency of capitalism to produce ever deepening economic crises which lead to the material immiseration of a large fraction of the working class through unemployment and reduced wages. Surely, in his later writings Marx reiterated and expanded Rousseau's critique of the state form as the means by which the contradictions in civil society could be resolved; but he did envision a "transitional" state to secure the victory of the revolution which he termed a "dictatorship of the proletariat."[51]

For Marx, as for his contemporary and adversary, the anarchist intellectual and agitator, Mikhail Bakunin, there was no question of positing a permanent state, proletarian or otherwise. Marx envisioned communism as a "free association" of producers, not congealed into a conventional political party that would seize the capitalist state. The *Communist Manifesto* was written more than one hundred fifty years ago. If Marx refused to engage in utopian speculation there are indications in his works that he fully expected the first stage of communism to be forged in the near term, if not in his lifetime. In fact, during his lifetime (he died in 1883) a vital labor and socialist movement emerged in nearly all of the leading capitalist countries, including the United States, and he witnessed the Paris Commune (1871), perhaps the first instance of a (short-lived) workers democracy, he had reason for optimism that sooner than later vast epochal changes would be made.

That his concept of the transitional state of proletarian dictatorship—largely drawn from the Commune's example—became the justification for many tyrannical regimes of social inequality and oligarchical power may be traced to the concrete circumstances of economic and cultural "backwardness" that attended their creation, as much as to the characteristic exercise of arbitrary power and brutality of their rulers. The question that arises from the miscarriage of Marx's vision of the good society in the plethora of twentieth-century revolutions carried out in the name of his theory of human development has always been whether the crimes of Stalin and of lesser despots who invoked Marx as the inspiration for their perfidy can be traced to a fatal flaw in the elements of historical materialism. Some have answered by carefully separating its methodological and descriptive components from the prescriptive side, particularly the doctrines of socialism and communism. But for Marx, the resolution of the class struggles under capitalism is bringing the relations of production into line with social character of the productive forces. This resolution entails a society of rough economic and social equality based on the abolition of private property in the ownership of the decisive means of production even if, according to Marx, the accumulation of surplus labor for the purposes of the further development of the productive forces remains necessary in order to shorten working hours, a condition of the full development of individuality, and provide the resources for raising living standards and universal education and health.

It is not a question of whether the new society Marx envisioned was inevitable; he almost always posed the question of the consequences that might attend the failure of the proletariat to carry out its historical "mission" of abolishing private ownership of productive property and hence the growing inequality arising out of it. He and many of his followers

saw that "barbarism" would return if capitalism was not overturned—
where the term came to mean that capital on an international scale would
ignore or otherwise abrogate even the feeble constraints placed upon it
by the working class and her social movements and by state regulation.
In the dark corners of his later writing, Marx theorized that, in the words
of the philosopher Georg Lukács, "the commodity-form penetrates every
corner of the social world."[52] If left unabated, capital could sweep before
it every manifestation of economic, political, and cultural autonomy, by
transforming all social relations into little more than goods to be bought
and sold. That we are not too far from this hideous eventuality is a leading theme of social criticism since the middle of the twentieth century,
but has picked up considerable steam in the last decade of state deregulation, the defeats suffered by the labor movement and the completing
of the globalization process. Needless to say, as if to justify these developments the formal elements of representative democracy have spread
around the globe, simultaneously, the only real freedom has become the
freedom of capital to transgress national borders in order to exploit new
sources of wage labor, as much as seeking raw material by scavenging
hitherto pristine spaces of the earth.

Born in 1864, three years in advance of the publication of the first volume of Marx's monumental critique of political economy, *Capital*, Max
Weber was educated in the shadow of the explosion of social-democratic
movements which, in Germany, were based on Marx's ideas. Although an
economist by training, as was often the case among the intellectual elite
of his time, his was not a "specialist" in the late modern sense. For example, he wrote pioneering works in history, notably his early "Marxist"
agrarian history of the ancient world, investigated world religions and
made important contributions to the study of the origins and development of capitalism. And perhaps most significant he is honored as one of
the three founders of sociology as an intellectual pursuit and an academic
discipline. But however much he strayed from the pursuit of professional
economics his education in the prevailing neo-classical economic doctrines, the precursor to contemporary neo-liberalism at the turn of the
twentieth century, infused his social theory throughout the length of his
intellectual life. At the same time, he was fervently attached of the ideas

of Kant, particularly the concept that scientific knowledge could not be obtained through the senses alone but required a synthetic "method" of combining observations of the social world with theoretical hypotheses to construct ideal types against which to measure accumulated data.[53]

Weber's political liberalism was matched by his adherence to the idea that market relations are both the context for the development of social classes and as the best guarantor of freedom. In contrast to the tradition that asserted that the culture and politics as well as the economic relations of society were structured by class antagonisms, Weber argued that classes were formed on a contingent basis when groups sought access to goods and employment. Trade union and professional associations might demand employers respond affirmatively to their grievances and, lacking agreement, withhold their labor. In turn laborers might combine through political parties or legislative pressure to enlist the state to intervene in their behalf. Professional Associations too seek to limit the supply of intellectual labor in order to drive up its price but also to enhance their status. In the last century their main weapon to create a degree of labor scarcity was the credentialing systems of higher education and state certification through examinations. Since neo-classical theories are confident that the market, itself sensitive to the movement of supply and demand, will ultimately adapt to these demands, Weber argues that classes are not the key social category. As soon as a group attains its objectives, it tends to break apart, only to be reconstituted by other groups who seek the same advantages. So class and class conflict in industrial societies is temporally specific; moreover the effects of these specific struggles were empirically variable. No epochal changes could be inferred from them.[54]

Weber did not hold that social justice would result from resolute class struggle. Its achievement was, instead, made possible by the rationalization of social life, especially the formation of bureaucratic procedures for the revindication of grievances. Like many others before and after him as a liberal he placed considerable reliance on the rule of Law to mediate and resolve social conflicts. Bureaucracy in its state form had the deficit of flattening the romance of social conflict, including workers struggles. It was a form of what might be called the "disenchantment" of history. Thus the revolutions of the eighteenth and nineteenth centuries had the

unintended consequence of creating the liberal state where faceless functionaries such as judges and administrative officials administered laws
that often settled disputes between contending parties through negotiation and mediation. But for Weber who witnessed the great strikes of the
turn of the twentieth century and particularly the violence and devasta-
tion of World War I, opposed his own conception of the democratic constitution to the socialist revolutions in Germany, Russia, and Hungary
which he regarded as continuous with the irrationality that many of his
generation had attributed to both the dying monarchies and their leftist
opponents. For him the revolutions were made by aggressive politicians
who, loudly proclaiming emancipation would, if successful, result in another repressive regime. In this regard it might be argued that Weber's
liberalism—which saw no alternative to a society of individuals who face
each other in a complex series of market relations—infused both his social theory and his political judgment.

Perhaps the most influential of the twentieth-century ideas for explaining social relations is the concept of the unconscious. According to
its most important theorist, Sigmund Freud, the unconscious is the basis
of our psyche and is rooted in the instinctual structure. In this respect,
Freud follows the main drift of political and social thought from Plato
through Hobbes to locate the "passions" in nature which, in turn are
situated, in social terms, within the underlying classes. The seat of the
pleasure principle, the sex drive, may be likened to the cunning of nature,
a common theme in political philosophy. Political philosophers locate
reason in the state and the upper reaches of society. The task of the state
was to prevent the passions/drives of the lower classes from overflowing
social order. As we have seen, early philosophers were more explicit than
later scientific thinkers like Freud about the class location of these drives.
Hence the basis of the mind/body split. But it is no long stretch to note
the homology between political philosophy's class discourse and Freud's
theory of the psychic structure. We may understand the body as the site
of turmoil, the mind as the hope for the rule of reason.

The foundation of human action, Freud held, is propelled "behind
our backs" by forces over which we have only a small measure of control. Psychoanalysis may be understood as the science of the "irrational"

which, according to Freud, governs human actions far more than any of the products of conscious activity like law. In truth, for psychoanalysis human institutions such as religion, concepts like civilization, political ideologies and other human productions are due to the cunning, not of reason as Hegel thought, but of the unconscious whose driving force is sex. The pleasure principle or, in another locution, the id may be viewed as the suppressed proletariat of the psychic structure. In the last instance, Freud believed that history could best be understood as the monumental struggle between the unconscious drive for pleasure and society's demand upon individuals and groups to address the vicissitudes of nature and social life through the repression or sublimation of sexuality which, if indulged, may disrupt or destroy the building and maintenance of civilized society. As he correctly understood it, if alienated labor is the condition for the reproduction of civilization, the ineluctable rebellion against it, in the first place the instinctual drives for pleasure, must be suppressed by the imposition of a repressive morality and then by coercion. Of course the best mechanism is sublimation. According to Freud only those engaged in art and science can expect to find fulfillment in the actual work they perform. The rest require religion to provide spiritual solace from society's demand for the subordination of pleasure. The activity that fulfills this demand is labor which, in the best circumstance, becomes the moral imperative of human activity even if only a few of us can truly achieve satisfaction in the content of our work.[55]

Freud was not the first to discover the unconscious but, even among his colleagues and followers, most of whom remained tied to the clinical side of the new science, he was perhaps the pioneer in elaborating the ways in which the unconscious has broad social power. At the beginning of the development of psychoanalysis through often-successful clinical work, he thought possible an accommodation between the demand for happiness and the inevitable demands of civilization that pleasure be subordinated in a large measure, to the rigors of labor. But, prompted by the huge sacrifice of human life during World War I, Freud conceded that, lacking the means to find satisfaction in the routines of everyday life, including work, family, and sexuality, humanity increasingly succumbed to its own collective destructiveness. He speculated that life itself was a struggle to harness the destructive effects of what he came to believe was the necessary work of repression of the most basic instincts. In the course of his investigations he discovered that, at best, we could achieve only a modicum of control over them. Thwarted by civilized institutions the id or libido, the core of the pleasure principle, tends to seek expression either in war and civil disorder, or death, the final triumph of pleasure.[56]

For others who followed Freud's theoretical precepts, but not his political and social prognostications, the discovery of the unconscious provided hope that humans could eventually achieve rational social arrangements. Wilhelm Reich, Erich Fromm (until his final work), Norman O. Brown, and Herbert Marcuse, among others, refused Freud's "discovery" of the death instinct, nor were they resigned to the triumph of the destructive and repressive tendencies of society. Instead, while fully embracing the power of the pleasure principle and acknowledging the role of labor in building and sustaining social life, their writing may be seen as an attempt to realize the unfinished task of finding ways to achieve universal happiness, not primarily through individual therapy or social resignation but through social transformation. In agreement with Freud, most of the so-called radical or left Freudians viewed labor as a problem rather than a solution, as religious and liberal thought would have it. And like Freud they focused on the distorted relationship between sex and the authoritarianism of the family. While Marcuse and other writers in the critical theory tradition were already familiar with the importance of economic relationships in shaping individual and social destinies, particularly social class, those trained in medicine and clinical psychoanalytic practice were obliged to turn their attention to the study of class in order to "complete" their grasp of the factors that influence mental pathologies. For example, they found that the place of individuals, their families and their associations in the social structure had profound influence on how they experienced the world.[57]

While Freud drew many of his conclusions from a close reflection on his clinical practice, largely among middle-class patients, some analysts who worked in the environment of postwar Germany of the 1920s were exposed to people suffering emotional dislocations from an assortment of social backgrounds. In order to deepen their knowledge of how different individuals and groups responded to the poverty and social chaos of the postwar world they turned to Marxism, or more precisely to historical materialism which understood history, the nature of social conflicts and such apparent "personal" problems such as health and family troubles in the perspective of the fate and struggle between social classes. If Freud joined the preponderant tendency of evolutionary theory to argue that "biology" was individual and group destiny, many of his followers came to understand that "class" was also destiny for most people. In the late 1920s and early '30s, Reich and later members of the Frankfurt School, especially Erich Fromm and Herbert Marcuse, conjoined the struggle for class emancipation with the emancipation of pleasure from the shackles imposed by patriarchal and class society. In this struggle the proletariat is at once the object of repressive sublimation in the form of what Reich called the "imposition" of a repressive sexual morality which, in Fromm's terms manifests itself in the "fear of freedom."[58]

To be sure, there are differences among these thinkers. After his migration to the United States, Fromm largely abandoned the language of collective action and focused, conventionally, on the individual who suffers. Reich maintained that the central contradiction was the biological-energetic need for orgasmic fulfillment and society's damming up of the pathways to happiness. He argues that patriarchical capitalism, which tends towards fascism, constitutes the barrier to the essence of human happiness and identifies the working class as the subject and the object of the struggle to achieve it. Twenty years after Reich analyzed the Nazi cultural dimension and showed that the hierarchical structure of the family prepared the repressive fascist state, Marcuse adapted many of Reich's ideas to advanced industrial society Marcuse advanced the notion of repressive desublimation, where "pseudo" pleasures are permitted within modern democratic societies, but genuine sexual fulfillment still inhabits the space of the underground. Still the bedroom remains a crucial scene of combat and, as Reich first argued, it bears close relationship to the authoritarian state, where democracy is reduced to the ritual of voting, to the militarized workplace and to consumer society which, for Marcuse is, in the wake of alienated labor and the fragmented family, the key mechanism of desublimation.[59]

In the 1960s these arguments found fertile reception among radical youth who became the energy and motivators of popular social movements. Now at the tail end of a counter-revolutionary period, critical psychological reflection has fallen into disrepute as questions of freedom are subordinated to elementary survival and preservation of already-punctured institutions of liberal democracy. What unites the Freudian left is its argument that freedom and pleasure are class issues, that is, are struggles intimately bound with the struggle against Capital.[60] That these ideas, forged more than seventy years ago, remain controversial is both a testament to their continuing challenge to all forms of authoritarianism and their relevance to the constitution of class relations in our time. For while the names may have dimmed in our collective memories, there is considerable reason to insist that the confident postmodern prognostications that we have transcended scarcity and for this reason have no need for class analysis, ideological flags, and utopias are premature, to say the least.

Class and Political Theory Today

In the wake of the rise of Stalinism as the leading form of "really existing" socialism and the perceived integration—"territorialization"—of the working classes of advanced capitalist societies, political philosophy since World War II has, in the main, drifted toward endless disquisitions on the limits and possibilities of representative, liberal democracy. At the level of perception the labor question has faded, if not disappeared in political and social theory in proportion, as the main sites of material production have shifted from the global North to the global South and the composition of the labor force in industrial production has gradually shifted from manual to intellectual and administrative labor. As capitalism has entered its epoch of global interdependence, any discerning observer must conclude that the working class has not disappeared; it has been recomposed and deterritorialized. Recomposed within advanced industrial societies from the predominance of manual labor to, on the one hand, a vastly expanded technical intelligentsia that leads industrial production as far as it concerns those aspects of the economy that engage in the functions of design, development, and distribution; and, on the other, to a plethora of low-wage factory and service jobs, most of which carry no benefits and no security. "Deterritorialization" refers chiefly to the exclusion of increasing numbers and sectors of workers from the legal framework within which production, distribution, and services occur. The emergence of an informal or underground economy, a symptom of what has been described as "Post-Fordism"—the disarticulation of mass production from mass consumption—places many workers at the margins of the prevailing system. Those who remain at the centers of industrial production are, in the main, desperately fighting to retain their niches, even as the largest industrial corporations cut the ground from under their feet. Material production has been partially displaced to what has come to be known as the developing or postcolonial world of former colonies and semicolonies; which, after World War II, gained formal political independence, even as they remained in the political and economic thrall of the metropolitan countries and transnational corporations. I say "partially" displaced for, contrary to the received wisdom about globalization, the United States and Western Europe, however diminished in their domination of the worldwide production of goods, retain control of the terms of distribution and investment in important sectors of production and of the general economy. For example, the Big Three auto companies have invested considerable capital in Mexico and Southeast Asia, even as capital flight has afflicted many US Northeast and Midwest cities; while Japanese and European car companies have established an impressive number of assembly plants in the Southern and border states of the US, almost always on a non-union basis. While the number of goods-producing workers in the car industry has shrunk, this reduction is due as much to the introduction of computer-mediated technologies as it is to offshore outsourcing. But flexible specialization (just in time production) dictates that parts be produced near assembly plants, a technology that limits offshoring. Much of parts production is increasingly non-union, but even when unionized these jobs offer wages and benefits below the standards established over many years. US steel output no longer leads, instead having given way to China, but the industry produces as much tonnage as it did twenty-five years ago when the migration of steel production began. Similarly one of the two leading global aircraft producing corporations, Boeing, has its main facilities in the United States,

although employment has plummeted because of technological innovation and increasing outsourcing off-shore. The highly automated oil and
chemical refining sectors are still here, although imports have increased,
but only because the big oil corporations refuse to build new refineries,
and technological transformation has reduced workforces by six or sev-
en hundred per cent. Appliances are still produced in the United States
and so is electrical machinery. And a myriad of small- and medium-sized
"niche" producers have survived the bleeding of industrial sectors and
provide many production jobs. What the United States has lost is the bulk
of its textile, apparel, and consumer electronics industries; the sum of
which were once the leading source of industrial jobs and accounted for
a substantial portion of the service industries as well.

Political and social theory has pronounced, in one account, these
transformations as the "coming of post-industrial society" (Daniel Bell),
a term which entails the definitive eclipse of one of the most striking
features of modernity, the emergence of a vast industrial working class
whose institutions—unions and political parties—once constituted the
heart of the era of social reform within a framework of representative
democratic governmentality. But Bell's retreat from class analysis is
only one of many: the oldest postwar version of American Exceptionalism, the doctrine of political pluralism, still dominates political theory. Even as its leading proponent, Robert Dahl, owing to observations
of growing social inequality, partially reversed his own 1950s exercise
in the American celebration, most of political philosophy and political
theory remained ensconced in the premises of consensus rather than
conflict in their descriptions of American social and political life. Perhaps the most celebrated alternative view is that of John Rawls who,
in his *Theory of Justice*, calls attention to the persistence of economic
inequality within the pluralist framework. While refusing any move to
challenge the institution of productive private property as an explanatory category of inequality, Rawls advocates a measure of distributive
justice that would allay the widening gap between rich and poor, an indication of an increasingly polarized society in which the "middle class"
(in income terms) is rapidly suffering economic erosion, even when it
has not entirely disappeared. Despite his gesture towards recognizing

class inequality, Rawls shrinks from drawing structural lessons from its ubiquity and, in the modern liberal tradition of "tinkering" rather than opting for radical transformation, he contents himself with offering a new series of palliatives.

Now, in the wake of the decline of interest in the labor question—and general disillusionment with not only prospects for fundamental change in the social and economic system, but also with its desirability—most have accepted the permanence of capitalism and agreed that, while representative democracy is imperfect, it remains preferable to authoritarianism, an evaluation that is little more than a version of the doctrine of the lesser evil. For, what political theory has learned from the collapse of the Soviet Union—indeed world communism—is that socialism was always identical to its regimes. Consequently, since class has been reduced and, for some, disappeared as a world-historical force, many Western political theorists have, openly or tacitly, embraced political pluralism as an adequate description of contemporary political power. Else, how to account for the pervasive preoccupation in mainstream political theory and philosophy with correcting some of the egregious features of representative democracy? We are speaking of the tendency to oligarchy in the executive branch manifested in a pervasive lack of transparency in government operations; in the name of the war on terror, widespread surveillance of citizens; corruption, even in parliamentary systems; and, for the self-proclaimed radical democrats, the decline of citizen participation in political decision-making in late capitalist societies, even where voting rates remain relatively high. (Of course, in the United States where, for national elections, voter participation has not reached sixty per cent in two generations and off-year congressional and local elections the rates are much lower, even the ritual is in jeopardy.) Hence the enthusiasm among a relatively wide swath of political commentators for the Obama phenomenon. In the United States, political philosophers sometimes bemoan our winner-take-all system and suggest that some version of proportional representation would broaden political representation, but have as yet failed to offer specific proposals to achieve this goal.

But the dominant tendency on the left, broadly conceived to include critical liberals, is made of various sorts of postmodern politics. It bears recalling that postmodernism renounces the totality as an intellectual framework; and it also renounces the subject-object dialectic, whose political expression is the revolutionary proletariat or in a more contemporary version a new overlapped historic bloc of workers, women, racialized minorities, and fractions of the professional/managerial class. In its political version, postmodern politics abjures the rhetoric and organizational forms of systemic change: if socialism, then it simply signifies an ethical ideal; if not, against its will, left postmodern political philosophy revives a version of Bernsteinism, that is, it has reverted to the belief that the movement is everything, the goal nothing. For left postmodern philosophers, like Sheldon Wolin, Ernesto Laclau, and Chantal Mouffe, "radical" democracy signifies a shift from the modern political parties and their class-based constituencies to "new" social movements based on identities—among them, race, sex, ethnicity.

And then there is the figure of Antonio Negri and his collaborator, Michael Hardt. Although they retain the fundamental proposition of historical materialism that society is divided into antagonistic classes, the subalterns are described, following a suggestion of Spinoza, as the "multitude," whose location, both spatially and historically, remains indefinite with respect to economic, political, and cultural relations. Moreover, after decades of advocating "workers power" in contrast to reformist socialist and communist movements, Negri remains vague on the basic issue of political organization, possibly because the experience of parties in the Italian context has been tragic, when not outright farcical. In fact, the practices of those who are inspired by his writing must be counted in the post-modern camp insofar as their politics remain, to put it in Sheldon Wolin's terms, "fugitive" and mainly local. Others, like Frances Fox Piven, walk a line between a perspective of protest and resistance characteristic of social movements and a close ideological affiliation with the progressive wing of the United States Democratic Party; and this being the case, they are hostile to proposals suggesting that the two-party duopoly and their respective ties to Big Capital is bankrupt and needs to be challenged by an independent electoral force. Finally, there are progressive and conservative versions of communitarianism, a political philosophy associated with Alasdair MacIntyre, Michael Sandel, and Amitai Etzioni.

This philosophy deplores the fragmentation of mass society and post-modern life and, in its stead, offers a program of the beloved community as the best guarantee of democratic participation, accompanied by a quasi-religious creed of mutual recognition and mutual aid. Of course, the political unconscious of the communitarians suppresses the class/race basis of the community. On the contrary, some argue that the community enjoys the right to set its own rules of inclusion and exclusion, an unintentional invitation to segregation, especially along racial lines.

It may be argued that much of contemporary political philosophy presupposes: *a*) a distinctly Western (Northern) orientation with respect to class. Ignored is the explosive expansion of the proletariat in the developing world, the mounting evidence of strikes, demonstrations, and riots in China and India, the growing political instability of many African countries many of whose economies have entered free-fall and where ethnic conflicts displace class relations, and the open class-based revolt against capital in the Global South, notably Latin America where once-stable political regimes have been toppled and new forces struggle to forge an alternative. *b*) a positivist view of politics and agencies—pluralist and "radical" democratic philosophies, excepting Negri and Wolin, have failed to analyze the enormous concentration of economic and political power in the global North and have absolutely no conception of the recomposition of class and other social forces. In sum they have not absorbed the contributions of social theory. *c*) Liberal political philosophy, in addition, has refused to undertake a reevaluation of state theory. In this connection, the work of Nicos Poulantzas, Bob Jessop, Giovanni Arrighi, and, more recently, Peter Bratsis, among others, is almost totally ignored. They have even failed to address the provocative critique of the liberal state offered by Carl Schmitt, whose work hoists liberalism on its own petard by calling into question the assumption of consensus as an empirical description of late capitalist states. As a result, the presupposition of most contemporary political philosophy is the liberal state, a hangover from seventeenth century political philosophy. It is no exaggeration to remark that we are witnessing the eclipse of the imagination in contemporary bourgeois political theory and philosophy. Always prone to substitute morality for sharp analysis, the most egregious tendency today is the absence of a fundamental theoretical framework for understanding the contemporary world. Instead, as in John Rawls's influential theory of distributive justice, we are treated to a series of prescriptions for making the division of the economic surplus slightly more equitable, but on the basis of the doctrine that private property, and therefore class privilege, is inviolate.

Needless to say, class theory is in need of significant rethinking and revision. Elsewhere, I have offered a new theory of class based on the concepts of power and the historicity of classes as a framework. If power is the referent, then in any historical moment formations that are deprived of power over the conditions of economic, political and social life constitute, in varying degrees, a "class." Conversely, holders of the main productive property (finance capital today) in alliance with fractions of the national and global political directorates constitute the ruling class. Since the composition of both main classes is entwined with their temporality, it does no good to remain faithful to the configuration of social forces as they existed, say, in 1848 or even 1948. One must perform a concrete analysis for our own time, taking into account the changes that have forced a realignment of class forces. It follows that the key agents of contestation of perhaps a half century ago may now still contest power, but at a different level and with differential effectivity. But mine is only one contribution to the project of theorizing and historicizing class in political philosophy. For those who adhere to the project of fundamental social transformation, there is no more urgent task than to enrich class theory.

Back to Aristotle

The main defect of mass representative democracy is its flawed conception of citizenship. Let us recall Walter Lippmann's less than rueful statement that the electorate should act exclusively as a veto over the sometimes irresponsible decisions of the bureaucratic elite. In Lippmann's scenario, ordinary citizens are better left to their banal lives and awakened only periodically. Needless to say, this formulation is not merely a prescription, it describes the state of political being. Politically, the individual citizen has been removed from history; and, to the degree that classes and movements accede to the prevailing political system, they too have, at best, the right to say "no" in the forms of protest and resistance. But, in their fragmented situation, they cannot reach for the "not yet" of an alternative, revolutionary future. The ritual of voting all but sets the boundary of political participation in contemporary societies; the process of governance is almost completely delegated to the vocation of politics and perhaps more saliently to the top experts: economists, professional bureaucrats, officials recruited from the top financial and industrial corporations and, occasionally, from the elite professoriate, who rotate from government service to the corporate board room, and the veritable army of capital's lobbyists. Various writers, especially the communitarians, have attempted to revive the fabled New England town meeting, where almost all decisions affecting the community were/are made in a face-to face-assembly, which John Dewey advocated in the 1920s. Many have said that the slogan "small is beautiful" remains a romantic projection of the frustration shared by many critics, but that it cannot serve as a practical program of reform. Yet, if the size remains so large that people cannot grasp, conceptually as well as in practice, the totality of decisions that constitute our polity, then any political philosophy that seeks to overcome the deeply disabled governance structures that dominate our corporate-dominated liberal capitalist reality must address the oligarchic character of its massive size or renounce the search for genuine democracy. Proposals such as those advanced by Kirkpatrick Sale, Murray Bookchin, and others would dismantle the huge national and global markets and create "human scale" regional economies that grow their own food, produce their own clothes and many other products on a subsistence basis, and also devise new forms of exchange that replace money and largely renounce planetary economic interdependence. In this context, they would, as well, create manageable structures of governance that depend on instituting direct democratic structures, such as town and regional meetings.

But most ideas that have been advanced to overcome the deficits of mass politics and global economics circumvent what Aristotle understood to be central to the problem of governmentality: genuine participation in every self-governance requires the individual to have time away from the burdens of necessary labor. As Marx argued, freedom presupposes that society distinguish industrial time from autonomous time for the self-development of the individual, a self-development that literally creates the individual who, in capitalist society, remains an ideological concept. If everyday life is liberated for most of the day from the labor needed to provide for basic material needs, questions of politics as well as education and art may be widely shared among the citizenry. And in terms of our present concern, the absolute precondition for the creation of a democratic polity is a drastic reduction of hours devoted to earning a living.

Many have called attention to the speeding up of everyday life. Intellectuals as well as other categories of labor are plagued with work without end. Intellectuals, proclaimed by Gramsci as key actors in the struggle for hegemony, have become *de facto* technicians of the existing setup. Their interventions are sporadic and, for the most part, they have been subsumed under the career imperatives of the system. Technical and scientific workers, professors, and those engaged in the tasks of running organizations find themselves taking their mostly-administrative work home, staying late most nights at the office or laboratory. When they return home, if their male partners do not share housework and childrearing, women are hit with the double shift; in the interest of advancing their careers or earning more money than their salaries allow, professionals take on extra jobs or administrative tasks or squander their creative activities on work which serves the organization, but has little lasting value.

We are reminded that self-organization and self-governance requires a considerable amount of unencumbered time. And, our encumbrances are not confined to workplace tasks, whether performed at a factory or office or at home. We are encumbered by the vicissitudes of a severely privatized everyday life. Raising children, performing housework, shopping, paying bills are activities that weigh upon an ever-shriveling family unit.

In the cities and suburbs, we have lost touch with collective living; even its concept evades the imagination. Child-care has become commodified and for most parents frightfully expensive. Even publicly-financed after-school programs are routinely reduced or eliminated; and wherever the state provides for child care, rigorous poverty-line income constraints prevent most working-class and professional people from qualifying.

Mass democracy and its concomitant creation of a self-valorized oligarchy is the result of the ability of capital and the state to impose a labor
regimen that, with the exception of a few hours a week, gobbles up all or
most of the time available to workers, professionals, and almost everybody else. The struggle for the shorter work day was linked to these considerations, but when the labor movement and its constituents literally
bought into consumerism, the prevailing wage was never enough and
gave rise to crippling personal and collective debt.

Aristotle argued that the sole consideration of those possessing time
unencumbered by necessary labor meant the exclusion of the bulk of the
Athenian population from citizenship. In this respect, the outcomes of
both the French and the Russian Revolution carried on the tradition of
exclusion. Amidst the praise for liberal democracy in most societies where
liberal democracy prevails, citizenship is, to a large extent, restricted to
the ritual of voting; civil society, in which ordinary people congregated in
cafes or in the town square to debate issues affecting the entire community, is increasingly "ideological"—by which I mean, it has been relegated
to nostalgia, to a past that never really existed, except in very specific
geographic and temporally narrow instances, notably some large cities of
Germany and France and small towns of New England. Unless we create
forms of organization that assert the primacy of the struggle for reducing
hours of paid labor, we can never resolve the 2,500-year-old problematic
that plagues all political philosophy. That is, must we capitulate to the notion that democracy is inevitably for the few, or will we create a situation
in which the individual emerges as the subject of history?

NOTES

1. Karl Marx, *The Eighteenth Brumaire of Louis Bonaparte*, trans. C. P. Dutt (New
York: International Publishers, 1969).

2. Glenn C. Loury, *The Anatomy of Racial Inequality* (Cambridge: Harvard University Press, 2003).

3. G. S. Kirk, J. E. Raven, and M. Schofield, *The Presocratic Philosophers* (2nd edition, Cambridge: Cambridge University Press, 1984).

4. Aristotle, *Politics*, trans. Ernest Barker (London: Oxford University Press, 1957).

5. Plato, *The Republic*, in *Collected Dialogues*, ed. Edith Hamilton and Hunnington Cairns (Princeton, Princeton University Press, 1961), 575–884.

6. Ibid.

7. Aristotle, *Politics*, trans. Ernest Barker (Oxford: Oxford University Press, 1957).

8. Ibid.

9. Ibid.

10. Ibid.

11. Ibid.

12. Ibid.

13. Ibid.

14. Walter Lippmann, *Public Opinion* (New York: The Free Press, 1962).

15. Niccolò Machiavelli, *The Prince*, trans. George Bull (New York: Penguin Classics, 2005).

16. Karl Polanyi, *The Great Transformation* (New York: Beacon Press, 2001).

17. Ibid.

18. Thomas Hobbes, *Leviathan*, with an introduction by C. B. MacPherson (New York: Penguin Classics, 1982).

19. Ibid.

20. Ibid.

21. John Locke, *Second Treatise on Government*, ed. C. B. MacPherson (New York: Hackett Publishing, 1980).

22. Ibid.

23. Ibid.

24. Ibid.

25. Ibid.

26. Jean-Jacques Rousseau, *The Discourses and Other Early Political Writings*, ed. and trans. Victor Gourevitch (Cambridge: Cambridge University Press, 1997).

27. Ibid.

28. Ibid.

29. Alexander Hamilton, John Jay, and James Madison, *The Federalist Papers: A Commentary on the Constitution of the United States*, ed. and with an introduction by Robert Scigliano (New York: Random House, 2000).

30. Ibid.

31. Ibid.

32. Ibid.

33. Ibid.

34. Ibid.

35. Ibid.

36. Ibid.

37. Ibid.

38. Montesquieu, *The Sprit of the Laws*, ed. by Anne Cohler, Basia Carolyn Miller, and Harold Samuel Stone (Cambridge: Cambridge University Press, 1989).

39. Kirk, Raven, and Schofield, *The Presocratic Philosophers*.

40. Kant's *Political Writings*, ed. H. S. Reiss and trans. H. B. Nisbet (Cambridge: Cambridge University Press, 1991).

41. G. W. F. Hegel, *The Phenomenology of Spirit*, trans. A. V. Miller. (Oxford: Clarendon Press, Oxford, 1977).

42. G. W. F. Hegel, *Philosophy of Right*, trans. T. Knox (Oxford: Oxford University Press, 1967).

43. Karl Marx, *Early Writings*, ed. Quentin Hoare, trans. Rodney Livingstone and Gregor Benton, and with an introduction by Lucio Colletti (New York: Vintage Press, 1975).

44. Ibid.

45. Ibid.

46. Ibid.

47. Ibid.

48. Friedrich Engels and Karl Marx, *Collected Works, 1845–1847*, v: *The German Ideology* (New York: International Publishers, 1976).

49. Ibid. This modern type of concentration of capital was anticipated by Marx in the 1840s.

50. Karl Marx, *Critique of the Gotha Programme*, ed. C. P. Dutt (3rd edn., New York: International Publishers, 1977).

51. Ibid.

52. Georg Lukács, *History and Class Consciousness*, trans. Rodney Livingstone (London: Merlin Press, 1971).

53. Max Weber, *Economy and Society*, vols. i and ii, ed. Guenther Roth and Claus Wittich (Berkeley: University of California Press, 1978).

54. Ibid.

55. Sigmund Freud, *The Future of an Illusion*, trans. James Strachey and with an introduction by Peter Gay (New York: Norton, 1989).

56. Ibid.

57. Max Horkheimer, "Authority and the Family," in *Critical Theory*, and with an introduction by Stanley Aronowitz (London: Continuum, 1972).

58. Wilhelm Reich, *Sex-Pol: Essays, 1929–1934*, ed. and with an introduction by Lee Baxandall (New York: Vintage, 1972).

51. Erich Fromm, *Escape from Freedom* (New York: Holt Paperback, 1994).

52. Herbert Marcuse, *Eros and Civilization: A Philosophical Inquiry into Freud* (Boston: Beacon Press, 1974).

CHAPTER THIRTEEN

When the New Left Was New

I

My '60s did not begin until 1962. I had been living in a different now, the worlds of the trade union movement, Newark peace and community organizing, and reform Democratic politics. These were the "nows" of the late '50s, a time which saw the rise of a new Southern-based civil rights movement, a northern struggle for black community empowerment, and a middle-class peace movement which was not unlike our current nuclear disarmament campaigns. The civil rights movement had just entered its civil disobedience stage (lunch-counter sit-ins and freedom rides) but was still five years away from "black power," despite the respected but largely ignored voice of Malcolm X.

The early years of the decade remained infused with the culture of the 1950s. Rock-and-roll, an urban adaptation of the music of the black migration from the South, had emerged, but Dylan was still playing acoustic guitar and the Beatles were barely visible in the Tin Pan Alley. The "high" culture of the era continued to smell of modernist sincerity and literary intensity. For the most part the Beats who gathered at the Cedar, White Horse, and other bars in Greenwich Village remained enraged suburbanites, their energy, too, flowing from the weariness often attributed to them. Columbia alumnus Allen Ginsberg fulminated against a society that could reduce the "best minds" of his generation to drugged impotence and the massively oedipalized Jack Kerouac, finding no home to replace Lowell, Mass., returned to his mother. John Clellon Holmes produced *Go!* and promptly vanished into college teaching. Like so many of the literary landmarks of the late 1950s, his work turned out to be a brief candle light rather than a sustained flame that could guide a movement. In fact, only Kerouac, Ginsberg, and San Francisco poet Lawrence Ferlinghetti survived the Beat movement. Most of their comrades literally sat out the 1960s; by the late 1950s their rebellion had degenerated into the cynical affectation characteristic of all failed romantic politics and art.

For most intellectuals, *Partisan Review* was still the measure of critical thought, even though its representative figures had long since abandoned the journal and been replaced by writers like Susan Sontag, for whom the tradition spawned by Philip Rahv and William Phillips was already a vague memory. For the succeeding generation preferred the aestheticism of Lionel Trilling, whose thesis of "authenticity" and "sincerity" had already been torn from the soil of revolutionary commitment, from the political radicalism of the founders of the magazine.

Before 1962, I used to hang out at the White Horse, where I gazed at Delmore Schwartz dying at his corner table, laughed at Brendan Behan's drunken tales (not realizing that he too was about to expire), and listened to the earnest conversations of the refugees of the political intelligentsia who had remained in the cities despite the suburban exodus of the 1950s. I was part of the group of young trade union organizers. Some of us worked for the Garment Workers Union, which was then trying to revive itself by importing intense young radicals into the movement. Gus Tyler, the former leader of the revolutionary faction of the Socialist Party and now the director of the union's Training Institute, knew then what labor leaders have still not learned: that rank-and-file mobilization is impossible when the members and the bureaucrats are too far apart. Tyler's experiment, in what might be called John L. Lewisism, failed under conditions of Cold War liberalism. The radical agitators, many recent college graduates such as Gus Sedares, Ted Bloom, and Bob Wolk, were simply unwilling to go along with the programs of top-down unionism unless the leadership permitted them to take the class struggle to the growing unorganized sector of the industry. What they failed to grasp was that collaboration had sunk deep roots into the psyche of the trade union bureaucracy, indeed that it had become a way of life, not just a set of practical measures to save a dying industry.

Sedares was frustrated in his efforts to push the sclerotic ILGWU towards a militant, aggressive organizing campaign, but he found an alternative outlet for his remarkable ability. He scandalized the old socialists who dominated the union not by mobilizing the rank and file, for the concept of an active membership had long since disappeared from the union's lexicon, but by organizing his fellow staffers into the first Federation of Union Representatives (FOUR). Sedares argued that if the union had lost its vision of class struggle, not to mention that of a new society, it could at least pay its cadres a decent wage and provide good benefits and tolerable working conditions. Today, the "union within a union" idea has gripped the masses of tired trade union functionaries. The staffs of many international unions have organized for collective bargaining. Of course, the Garment Workers remain an open shop. As far as their staff representatives are concerned, the house David Dubinsky built adheres to the principle of self-sacrifice.

The Training Institute is disbanded but an important truth survives it: that unions cannot hope to become a major force in American life once again until they attract the most dedicated among young radicals. On the other hand, it may be argued that the new social movements emerging in the 1960s were defined by their departure (in a double sense) from what C. Wright Mills called the labor metaphysic. The generation of the 1950s still saw the labor movement as the lightning rod of global social transformation; their hopes were framed within the heroic visions of the struggle against capital, by the romantic idea of the self-emancipation of the toilers.

The McCarthy era, the obvious deterioration of the labor movement's militancy, the advent of consumer society—nothing could daunt the small band of radicals who downed gallons of beer every Friday at the White Horse. How appropriate it was that they should jostle in that packed room with the Beats and the veterans of an already-eclipsed literary radicalism, a literary radicalism which had not been destroyed by the anti-Soviet denouement of the 1930s alone. Its final resting place, of course, turned out to be the graveyard known as the Congress for Cultural Freedom and its journal *Encounter*, if it wasn't *Commentary* or the *Partisan Review* of the 1950s. Max Eastman, perhaps the greatest of all radical journalists and editors, ended up writing for the ultra-conservative *Reader's Digest*.

There were exceptions to the rightward drift, some attempts to keep a distance from the Irving Kristols and the Sidney Hooks and other people for whom Stalin's betrayal had proved once and for all the superiority of liberal democracy over any possible revolutionary socialism. There was, for instance, the small group around *Dissent*, which had been founded by Irving Howe and Lewis Coser in 1952, and the even smaller group following *New Politics*, Julius Jacobson's attempt to preserve an independent Marxist presence in intellectual life. From one perspective, Howe's position resembled that of the emerging conservative/liberal majority among the formerly radical intellectuals. He concurred with Rahv's judgment that however egregiously awful capitalism remained, Stalinism and, by extension, Eastern Europe and China represented a worse alternative. Nonetheless, Howe retained his faith that democratic socialism could provide a realistic alternative to the antinomies of liberal exploitation and totalitarianism, while his peers lost faith altogether in the visions of an organized left.

The American Communist Party had broken apart following the post-Stalin crisis within the world communist movement, a crisis which had become acute with Khrushchev's famous report to the Twentieth Soviet Party Congress in 1956. Most young radicals, however, were relatively unaffected by this development since the American CP had virtually gone underground in the 1950s on the assumption that the political repression at the time was a dress rehearsal for fascism. Some, including myself, were sympathetic to the party but remained troubled by its conservatism and caution. We were moved by the internal party debates and the concomitant information about Stalin's crimes and taken aback by the clear errors of the party left. Our desire for some kind of radical affiliation was considerable, but it made no sense to join the decimated CP then, especially since the "right wing" of the party was already attracted to the pacifist A. J. Muste's call for regroupment among democratically minded leftists. Several evenings in 1957 and 1958, I journeyed across the Hudson River to hear leftists from various Trotskyist sects, so-called "right-wing" CP leaders and Muste himself debate prospects for a "new" left. They discussed the necessity of independence from the Soviet Union and the US, of unremitting commitment to democratic rights under socialist rule, of renewed efforts to revitalize the labor movement on the basis of rank-and-file militancy, of a strong intervention into the burgeoning peace movement, which had shown considerable strength since Adlai Stevenson's adoption of the nuclear test ban plank in his losing 1956 campaign.

Once the alliance between William Z. Foster's conservative faction and General Secretary Eugene Dennis's "centrist" group had foreclosed any hope of renovating the Communist Party along democratic lines, there began a debate among democratic socialists regarding possible affiliation with the reform-minded minority communists. At the same time, in 1959, the socialist-influenced League for Industrial Democracy decided that the moment had come to resuscitate its nearly moribund student group and invited the University of Michigan chapter to take charge of this task. It was symptomatic of the times that the concept of "industrial democracy" had lost entirely its meaning as a unifying slogan. The leading student figures Al Haber and Tom Hayden insisted, accordingly, that the name of the organization's student affiliate be changed to Students for a Democratic Society. Haber and Hayden shared the political perspective of LID's chairman, Michael Harrington, but abhorred the more conservative position of most of its board members. I first met Harrington at the White Horse during his literary neo-Trotskyist period, when he was better known for his literary criticism than the political writings. He was closer to Jacobson's *New Politics* than to the more staid *Dissent* in that he considered himself a revolutionary democratic socialist who believed in the formation of a labor party built around a strong labor-civil rights alliance. He supported the broad "third-camp" position of his organization, the Independent Socialist League, rather than the pro-Western line of *Dissent*.

As a trade unionist and Democratic Party activist influenced by the old Popular Front politics, I debated Harrington and other Trotskyists

in the early 1960s precisely on the issue that was to mark the break between SDS and the Harrington-Howe wing of the socialist movement a
few years later: I argued that working people and trade unionists had
no choice but to seek change within the Democratic Party, that the multiplicity of movements to reform party procedures and platforms which
had arisen out of the anticorruption, peace, and civil rights movements
of the late 1950s prefigured the chance for a new alliance that could at
least mount an effective challenge to the most conservative wing of the
party. Harrington at the time took the classic third-party position that
non-communist socialists have adopted since the turn of the century. Later in the decade Harrington changed his mind, but then found that there
were new radicals who had picked up where he and Howe had left off.

Because New York City was a Democratic stronghold, New York
Democrats were more concerned with the leadership question within the
party than with beating the Republicans. Ideology and power were contested in the primaries, not in the general elections. The Liberal Party,
composed of some trade unionists, mostly from the apparel trades, and
ambitious lawyers, had long since lost its role as the balance of power
and had become more or less harmless. The more "left-wing" American
Labor Party had disappeared after its disastrous performance in the 1954
election and some of its activists were now part of the Reform Democrats.
In this situation, the main issue for the Democratic Party was whether it
could become a mass liberal party, that is, whether it could mobilize the
new postwar professional constituencies in the shaping of party policy.

These were the last years of the political machine, a form of cultural
as well as more narrowly constructed political power. The machine was
founded on the institutions of patronage already weakened by the introduction of the civil service system of public employment and the professionalization of the service as a whole. Moreover, the immediate postwar
period had witnessed the suburbanization of the working-class and the
lowermiddle strata, the electoral base of the machine. When I had dinner in the early 1960s at Cannon's, an old-time Irish bar on Broadway
and 108th Street, I found Japanese food being served with the Guinness
stout, a sure sign of incipient gentrification on the Upper West Side.
Likewise, Greenwich Village, which was no longer a haven for artists,

housed the coming leaders of the Democratic reform movement: Stanley Geller, who owned a gorgeous townhouse on 12th Street; Ed Gold, a journalist for Fairchild Publications; Ed Koch, a lawyer with unbounded political ambition; and Sara Schoenkopf, a young professional politician whom I had first met during the Stevenson campaign when I was a leader of Young Democrats in New Jersey's Essex County.

Yorkville, once the neighborhood of German machinists, Hungarian laborers, and factories like American Cystoscope, where I had worked in the early 1950s, was fast becoming the fashionable East Side. The district had been represented in Congress by a succession of moderately liberal Rockefeller Republicans, but the area still contained a strong local Democratic machine with a working-class constituency. To these precincts there came a young left-wing lawyer who together with the Yorkville leader and erstwhile party regular John Harrington attached himself to the reform movement. Mark Lane had been a criminal lawyer specializing in hopeless criminal cases in behalf of blacks and Latinos. He possessed a talent singularly conducive to a successful political career, an unerring sense of publicity, a sixth sense for what would capture the public's political imagination.

He was not, however, endowed with a particularly vibrant or charismatic personality. Shy of personal encounters, his fiery social messages were delivered exclusively to larger audiences. He rented a small apartment in a slum building on Lexington Avenue in Yorkville, a sort of place that has all but disappeared now. He was also recently separated from his wife, the actress and folk singer Martha Schlamme. We were introduced by his brother-in-law Bill Nuchow, a Teamster official whose one moment of glory had been the presidency of an ill-fated taxi drivers' union in the late 1950s. He might in fact have become a major figure in New York labor, had the Teamsters not abandoned the unionization campaign, but now he was a business agent for a Teamster local. Nuchow asked me to join the effort to elect Lane to the state assembly, and even though I was living in Newark, NJ, I agreed. The position of the incumbent Democrat was less entrenched than usual, mainly because East Harlem's Puerto Rican voters, subordinate to the Irish and Italian machine politicians after the passing of Vito Marcantonio's left-wing machine, were beginning to strike out on their own, and Mark Lane had gained prominence by representing poor Puerto Rican clients.

Lane's subsequent stay in the legislature was luminous, controversial, and brief. His great achievement was the exposure of an illicit scheme between Republican Assembly Speaker Joseph Carlino and a coterie of businessmen to build fallout shelters, a scandal which led to Carlino's defeat in the next election and to instant stardom for Mark among the "clean government" types and the peace movement activists. By late 1961, he was calling small meetings of supporters, myself included, to determine if he should seek the nomination of the reform Democrats for the nineteenth congressional district, a horseshoe which came down the West Side and then curved around the Battery, ending up on the Lower East Side. Its representative was Leonard Farbstein, a product of the still-powerful Democratic machine led by the almost legendary Carmine DeSapio. Farbstein was no worse than most others among the New York congressional delegation. His political base outside the machine lay primarily in the substantial Orthodox Jewish community of the Lower East Side, but this once formidable sociopolitical force was now losing some of its weight because of the exodus to the suburbs and to Brooklyn, and because of the influx of Puerto Ricans. In 1960, the reformers had succeeded in beating DeSapio himself, winning control over most West Side clubs for the first time. Other strong challenges were mounted in Chelsea, where the new ILGWU-sponsored cooperative housing was replacing longshore slums. In order to take on Farbstein, Lane first had to get past the reform movement; although he was by far the best known reform legislator in Albany, he was not a resident of the district and other reformers wanted the nomination too.

Early in 1962, Mark asked me to become his campaign manager. We got together a rather high-powered inner circle that included Michael Harrington, who didn't see the campaign through; Susan Brownmiller, who had sparked his assembly campaign; and Ed Wallerstein, who was an old captain of the Vito Marcantonio organization and now active in the Yorkville Democratic Club. From the start, Lane was accused of being an outsider and of surrounding himself with carpetbaggers. But his campaign suffered from another and perhaps more crucial weakness:

WHEN THE NEW LEFT WAS NEW

he fought on substantive issues before a group for whom such questions were subordinate, if not entirely irrelevant. For the reform movement was a loose anti-machine coalition whose main concern was to eliminate corruption from the Democratic Party, by which was chiefly meant patronage. In short, "reform" entailed procedural renovation and a kind of civil service for professionals, making sure that elected officials were democratically chosen and that the most merited would get the jobs. Lane paid lip service to these issues but in fact could not have cared less who selected the candidates. He ran on public issues, although he was obliged to use the theme of anti-corruption extensively in his initial assembly campaign. In the spring of 1962, we tried to take the reformers by storm by raising such issues as the increasing US intervention in Vietnam, the growing concern over poverty, and the importance of better housing and jobs for residents of the district. Indeed, by the end of the designation campaign all the candidates were echoing Lane's platform down to the obscure and anomalous issue of Vietnam. Yet these were side issues as far as the movement was concerned. The reform Democrats of New York, Illinois, California, and elsewhere were plainly on the liberal wing of the party, but their chief interest lay in the question of control, for which purpose the issues of Vietnam, nuclear weapons, and civil rights had little relevance. Lane, on the other hand, considered Congress a place for national policy; procedural questions made him impatient.

The reform movement was an early expression of a new style in American politics. Large numbers of professional middle strata and small businessmen had participated in the Stevenson campaign, which raised the possibility that the Democratic Party for the first time could become a mass organization, something beyond a leadership coalition between labor, blacks, professional politicians, and a fraction of capital. The focus here lay on clean government and popular democracy rather than on peace, civil rights, and economic justice, though unquestionably the movement could become the vehicle for these traditional concerns. In fact, the greatest and last triumph of this new political "class" was the presidential nomination of its epitome, George McGovern, a history professor turned politician, from South Dakota.

Lane lost the designation fight and quit the assembly seat shortly thereafter. His politics, grounded in the primacy of questions of economic justice, was rapidly fading from the scene. Later, he was to reenter the discourse of the 60s in a rather peculiar way by his relentless conspiracy investigations of the John F. Kennedy assassination.

I entered the 1960s myself through my friendship with Evelyn Leopold, who, at the time of Lane's campaign, was running Ed Koch's losing primary fight for the assembly; Koch ran on behalf of the Village Independent Democrats. Evelyn was living on W 21st Street with several SDS leaders. She had met them in 1960 when editing the Douglass College paper. Hayden was then the editor of the *Michigan Daily* and was organizing college newspaper editors for civil rights. The first time I came to the 21st Street house, I was greeted by Al Haber, a resident and also the current head of SDS. Characteristically, he was drenched in mimeograph ink. Mike Harrington was still regarded by the SDS, in late spring 1962, as the closest thing to a mentor. Hayden, who lived in the apartment with his wife Casey, was, like Harrington, a middle-class Midwesterner of Irish Catholic background. Like Harrington, he exemplified the adage "you can take the boy out of the church but you can't take the church out of the boy."

Tom and Al were then preparing for the first national conference of this relatively new and very small organization. It was to be held in June at Port Huron, Michigan. Tom was responsible for writing the organization's political manifesto. He had returned recently from a trip to the South where he had gotten a fairly well-publicized beating during a civil rights demonstration. This had established his credentials as one who would put his body on the line. As the first SDS President, he was clearly its best known and probably most influential leader, but by no means the only one. He embodied the spiritual and intellectual energy of this small movement of no more than 200 members, most of whom could be found on major campuses like Michigan, Harvard, and Chicago. SDS held national meetings at Christmas and in the summer. The rest of the time people kept in touch by mail, telephone, and through campus visits by the two national leaders. The SDS became highly visible because some of its members were also key activists in the then powerful National

Students Association, and leading politicians and editors on some very important campuses. Despite its numerical insignificance, SDS thus organized an effective caucus for civil rights at the 1961 and 1962 NSA conventions. It became a veritable tribune for the growing movement for university reform, particularly the fight for a student voice in campus policymaking. It was also a catalyst in the student peace movement, helping to found the Student Peace Union.

I may have misunderstood the Democratic reform movement at the time, but I could not have mistaken the primacy of the moral in SDS. It was the most articulate expression of what became the leading theme of the ideology of the 1960s: the attempt to infuse life with a secular spiritual and moral content, to fill the quotidian with personal meaning and purpose. The reform Democrats and SDS shared the belief that they themselves were the new historical subjects. The spurious doctrines of the student as "nigger" or as a new class were merely clumsy ways for this generation to separate itself from the old labor metaphysic, to declare itself competent to name the system that oppressed humanity. The *Port Huron Statement*, written by Hayden but collected from many sources, retained the outline of a liberal argument: its pages resound with the rhetoric of economic and social justice. But the subtext concerned the generation after Ginsberg's, a generation which not only prided itself on having the best minds but also claimed its own subjectivity.

"Participatory democracy," fighting for "the people" to have "control over their own lives,"—this goal reflected self-interest as much as anything else. The students, who were too young and too far removed from direct power to be concerned with the electoral issues of reform Democrats, inveighed on the contrary against the institutions themselves. It was a matter of replacing the old institutions of control—control over their own lives—with other structures. In this sense reform was only useful to the extent it demobilized existing political power.

By June, I was practically living on 21st Street with Evelyn and the SDS staff. They came home from the office and I from my union, and we would immediately plunge into long discussions about the labor movement, civil rights, the Democratic Party, and the Kennedy Administration. As a relatively weak political movement, they recognized the need to find allies in all of these arenas. Hayden was trying to pry some money from Walter Reuther and the UAW and went to Detroit to meet with him. Yet, despite playing "student organization" for the adult counterparts, Hayden, Haber, Todd Gitlin from Harvard, Bob Ross and others, did not ingratiate themselves with trade union and liberal leaders because they believed that the labor-liberal coalition had no future in American politics. They were indeed deeply convinced that these were forces of the past which ought to be scrapped. While making compromises and seeking temporary alliances, they were actually looking for an alternative formula with which to transform the United States into a democratic utopia.

In this sense, the *Port Huron Statement* was remarkable for its continuity with traditional American ideas of popular self-government, egalitarian ethics, and social justice, and refused socialist discourse. It broke with the old left by ignoring entirely the question of the Soviet Union, Marxism, and communism. Not since Earl Browder's slogan "Communism is Twentieth Century Americanism" in the 1930s had there been such an attempt to invent an indigenous radical discourse. There was no "socialism," "revolution," or "workers' control" here, but "participatory democracy" instead, the tradition of Mills and Thorstein Veblen, the refusal of explicitly Marxist categories.

It was not the Cold War alone which had brought this about. It was the passion for a fundamental break with the radical past, with the sectarian debates, foreign subcultures, and sterile programs. The communist and socialist past was not repugnant, it was just irrelevant for contemporary purposes. A new language to forge group solidarity was therefore necessary—and Tom Hayden and his friends understood that.

Historians of this "new left" have frequently mocked the SDS for spending the first half of any meeting adopting the agenda and defining the rules of debate, and even sympathetic observers have sometimes ascribed this strange ritual to inexperience or to the absence of a viable political culture. This criticism misunderstands the nature of the New Left, summarized in a single word: process. It signaled an almost religious return to *experience* and a converse retreat from the abstractions of the red politics of yesterday. One worked out personal and procedural issues in great and often exhausting detail as a way of fusing the personal with the political, of creating a community not primarily of interest (political rationalism) but of *feeling*. So in some respects a national meeting of the SOS was an orgy of incantations. Rhetorical repetition, procedural debate, moral invocations to kindness and equality were all part of the process of community building, a psychopolitical experience in which duration played a purgative part in transforming traditional political interactions into what was described as "movement behavior." This style drove many left and liberal politicos to distraction.

From 1962–5, I attended these meetings, having been coopted along with several others as an advisor. This job actually began on 21st Street, but my interest then was not enough to bring me to SDS meetings. I was drawn in by the unfortunate aftermath of the *Port Huron Statement*. A CP-led youth group, the DuBois Club, had sent an observer to the conference. He was a rather timid fellow called Marvin Markman and was regarded by the SDS people as harmless. But when the word reached the League for Industrial Democracy that a bona fide communist had been permitted to observe the SDS convention, the roof fell in on the students. During a meeting (that has become part of the lore of the New Left), Harrington and other Board members excoriated the SDS leaders for political naivete: having had the bitter experience of witnessing communist hegemony on the American left during the 1930s and '40s, as staunch anti-Stalinists, the Board concluded that the CP was not merely wrong on a variety of political questions but that its presence was actually detrimental to the task of rebuilding the democratic left. It was not a question of political differences but of whether democracy and dictatorship, as they saw it, could coexist.

The incident would have blown over had the SDS leaders simply agreed to bar communists from future meetings, since there was never any proposal to admit them into the ranks, but SDS instead chose to treat the whole thing as a major issue between the old and new left. After this confrontation, SDS looked for other possible sources of contact with the mainstream of the labor and liberal communities. Ray Brown, a former union organizer and then an economist for the Federal Reserve Bank, myself, and others were asked to give talks at national meetings, hold workshops, and be available for consultation. I was twenty-nine years old at the time, Ray a little older. Most of the "students"—many were already in graduate school or working full time for some liberal or peace organization—were only between five or eight years younger, but had grown up under very different circumstances. We helped them because we shared their belief that a new movement was being born and that it would die if shackled to the past. I was convinced, like SDS, that the CP was little more than a nuisance, and I was also persuaded that anti-communism had been the scourge of the 1950s, that the labor and progressive movements had been seriously crippled by their preoccupation with issues like the Soviet Union. With C. Wright Mills, James Weinstein, William Appleman Williams and others of *Studies on the Left*, I shared, too, the belief that a genuinely American movement could arise only by adopting the stance of leftist isolationism.

SDS had no sympathy for the American Communist Party or the Soviet Union, but this was a generation which had just emerged from the dark days of political repression and intellectual censorship commonly known as the McCarthy era. It was believed that the American CP was being persecuted not so much for its ties with the Soviet Union as for its dissent from the main drift of American foreign policy. In this way, SDS became an important repository of "anti" anti-communism: it held that the Cold War was responsible for the destruction of participatory possibilities, that it was a mask for central control and management of everyday life, a metaphor for the reduction of the American Dream to rituals of conformity. In the pursuit of a new democratic ideal, of political redemption from the McCarthy terror, SDS was thus obliged to defend the rights of the CP. It also understood that the CP itself was no threat to democratic institutions, for the party was weak and in fact had to uphold these institutions in order to survive at all.

However, the new movement was determined to resist the examples of its elders. It chose neither the path of Marxist science as the historical equivalent of moral redemption after the capitulation by its political progenitors during the McCarthy era, nor the Cold War liberalism of the disillusioned radical intellectuals of the 1930s. Instead, SDS was the first organized expression of the postscarcity generation's new nationalism. Their idea was directed principally to the renewal of the atrophied institutions of American democracy, or more precisely, to the creation of new institutions of popular participation to replace existing bureaucratic structures. The problem was how to utilize the subversive possibilities that already existed in popular political culture. For the New Left, the question of the Soviet legacy was simply irrelevant except negatively; the obsession among the various groups of the old left with the character of actually existing socialisms was regarded as a central reason for the demise of the left in American life. At the same time, the New Left was deeply concerned with issues of race and Third World-revolutions, regarding the civil rights and independence movements as correlates to democratic renewal, the support of which could assist the moral regeneration of the middle classes.

Much of the New Left was guilty of a kind of collective amnesia, having rejected the idea that historical knowledge and living traditions could prevent repetition of past errors. Action/experience was to take precedence over history and memory. In this respect, one cannot but be impressed by the naivete of the widely disseminated notion "Don't trust anybody over thirty," the proposition that older people are somehow a priori plagued by memories and beliefs, habits of thought and action, that ought to be buried.

Furthermore, there was an almost paranoid fear of what Sartre called the *practico-inert*. To admit, in other words, the limits of action was to court defeat. Undoubtedly, this delusion produced a series of disasters. So it was with the ill-fated community organizing efforts of SDS's Economic Research and Action Program (ERAP), an intervention in the black ghettoes and white underclass slums which generated much publicity but little benefit for the residents. Hayden and Carl Whitman had written a strategy paper in 1963 called *Toward an Interracial Movement of the Poor*, in which they argued for a multiracial alliance combining the research and organizing skills of students and other middle-class types with the authentic anti-capitalist needs and demands of the poor, a "class" the authors believed to be distinct from the working class (big labor). These ideas were put into practice in the summer of 1964, which saw ERAP's entrance into Newark, Baltimore, Chicago, and other Northern cities. There were also the less radical but equally inspired efforts of the Northern

Student Movement, which conducted literacy programs for black kids and assisted the Harlem rent strikes in the winter of 1964–5. However, the unstated concept was that whites could redeem themselves only by helping blacks to become free. It was the adoption of the concept of responsibility which is as old in the American tradition as abolitionism.

Community organizing, voter registration (primarily by the black Student Non-Violent Coordinating Committee [SNCC] in the South), and education projects challenged the liberal state and the institutions that supported it, thus providing an opening for mass participation. For student radicals, the struggle for decent housing, for jobs and income, and against rats and roaches, pointed clearly towards the authoritarian side of liberal democracy.

Most of these projects folded within a few years but they produced some interesting lessons. Take the Newark project for instance. I had played a fairly active role in helping ERAP and the New York rent strikes get moving and was, until 1963, the vice-chair of the Clinton Hill Neighborhood Council in Newark. This was an organization dedicated both to preserving the interracial character of the community and improving living conditions. From its inception in 1955, the Council distinguished itself by waging successful struggles against federally sponsored urban renewal, a project heralded by corporations and liberals alike as the key to the development of the decrepit inner cities. Although the Council became a political power in this rapidly changing city and was able to slow down the process of what we called "people removal," we were resisting large demographic and economic forces that proved too strong to withstand. When SDS decided to make a commitment to off-campus organizing, they turned to me, among others, for information as to what to do. I arranged for SDS to be invited to assist the Council; this was a match not made in heaven.

The SDS group called itself the Newark Community Union Project (NCUP) and formed its base in the city's South Ward. Conflicts soon arose between the student organizers and the Council, who counted among its members many black and white homeowners interested in code enforcement and other ways of preserving neighborhood and property values. The SDS group regarded these objectives as both limited and hopelessly middle class and broke with the Council, moving its territorial claims to the lower part of the Hill, where the people were poorer and the homes more dilapidated. Thereby they had not only defined a turf but also an ideological difference, arguing that poor and working-class residents often had divergent needs and demands. The working-class homeowners wanted to make the neighborhood safe, the schools better and the streets cleaner and better lit. In the view of the NCUP, the poor welfare recipients of the dilapidated areas, with their ill-clothed and ill-fed children, wanted political power in order to improve their conditions. A "union" rather than a council was therefore the appropriate form for this desperate constituency. Analogously, while the Council was mired in electoral politics, NCUP favored direct action, especially since most of its underclass members were not registered to vote. It was not a question, then, of finding the least common denominator which could unite the greatest number of residents (the policy of the Council), but of sharpening the differences between the poor and the wealthy, the people and the state. Later, NCUP was nonetheless forced to defend its gains through electoral politics, and they entered conventional coalitions around specific issues, candidates, and programs. But the group had defined a new politics of community organizing that went beyond single-issue coalitions. A union was no longer conceived in terms of "trade" or "craft" but as "community," a site of popular fusion formed apart from, and in opposition to, the established interests.

This innovation was remarkable both for its sectarianism and its political originality. We need not linger, in this context, on Hayden's— by 1964 he had become the leader of NCUP—unfortunate tendency to factionalism and personal power politics. What made NCUP interesting, on the contrary, was its creative fusion of traditional symbols such as "community" and "union," and the recognition of the need for self-representation among the poor. Even more important, in retrospect, was the fact that SDS, SNCC, and other movements of this generation provided a model for others to challenge the prevailing modes of representation. It was not the organization they built that defined the New Left in American politics, but the deconstruction of the common conflations of aggregation and democracy, of interest and community, of voting and participation: a deconstruction which indeed created an ideological space for the multilayered movements of the late 1960s.

These were movements of a generation, not of a class, a race, or specific interests or issues. It was a generation shaped by its parental predecessor, by the postwar migration to the suburbs and professional communities adjacent to the big cities, where happiness had become synonymous with economic security and maximum consumption. As a reaction, the new generation tried to create more than a different sort of politics; it tried to create a utopian community and indeed one may argue that the new politics was a product of this communitarian impulse. Some sought this community in Southern rural slums and others in the ghettoes of Northern cities. A small but important segment created a counterculture within the core cities—art in the East Village, agriculture in Virginia, California, and Vermont, craft in Minnesota and Upstate New York. These avant-garde movements were not marked so much by their formal innovations as much as by their conviction that efforts to reform the system were doomed to be absorbed by the antagonists. Hence the critique of liberal society took the forms it did, from the attempt to sustain an alternate economy based upon subsistence farming and small-scale production to that of finding the link between art and life in the combination of working, living, and sexual space.

It might be objected that communitarian movements were naive, that their success depended on the longstanding affluence of the United States in general and the economic buoyancy generated by the Vietnam War in particular. And surely the notions of "participatory democracy," of the beloved community, of the counterculture, are overdetermined and historically specific. However, to reduce their character to class origin, or to dismiss their social and political significance as narcissism or something worse, is to see the whole thing from the perspective of social conservatism.

There were really two countercultures in the 1960s. My connection was mainly to the political counterculture, those who engaged in the politics of direct democracy, who organized traditional constituencies in new ways. The second were the cultural radicals, the artists, writers and, above all, the rock musicians and their audience, for whom the erotic revolution was a political movement. It is important to recognize the differences between these two tendencies. Even though there was some overlap, there was also considerable hostility between them. The cultural radicals believed the struggle within the state and its institutions hopeless and beside the point. For them the important question was freedom to be different, in political terms, freedom from the state. This doctrine did not foreclose political action, but its forms were different: smoke-ins and be-ins in Central Park and other places where ostensible law-breaking could visibly show defiance; building art and cultural communities on the Lower East Side, the Haight in San Francisco, and other cities; coffee houses where poetry and stories were recited; new dress codes, new sexual norms, concerts and so on where dope was passed around in an otherwise dark stadium or club.

It does not matter that such slogans as "sex, drugs and rock-and-roll" failed to encompass the many layers of social reality of the 1960s, or that economic countercultures, communes, and various other communities ultimately succumbed to interpersonal squabbles, external economic pressures, or the provocations of government agents and the like. What survives in memory is not the megalomania of this generation, which mistook its demographic proliferation for political power, nor the arrogance of those who invested themselves with magical powers; these excesses were merely symptoms of the affliction of historical amnesia. America's past is as mystified and weighs as heavily on the living as that of any other country. The difference is that widespread perception that only the glorious part constitutes our legacy and that to be American is to overcome all adversity. The New Left was thus American in a double sense: it tried to invent a new past that served the present rather than the "truth" of the past, and, in a sort of Nietzschean way, it proclaimed the triumph of the will, the limitless capacity to shape the future in its own images. This magical quality marked the cultural politics of the 1960s and distinguishes it from virtually every European counterpart except the French, where the slogan "All power to the imagination" replaced every traditional concern.

At the time, many older friends of the student and youth movements were amazed by the hubris of the new activists. We attributed their disregard for political and social boundaries to their inexperience, arrogance, and megalomania. Of course, much of this was accurate. Hayden was impervious to criticism; Carl Wittman, the person who really started the Newark project, was moralistic to the point of absurdity; and others were similarly afflicted with delusions about the omnipotence of their movement. These very qualities were the source of antagonism between SDS and other movements, like SNCC, the West Coast free-speech and antiwar activists, and the Northern Student Movement. On the other hand, the same confidence and sense of purpose brought about results, among them the magnificent SDS March on Washington in April 1965 against the Vietnam War. Nevertheless, it was symptomatic that the organization did not follow up on this event, which had been so skeptically regarded by an assortment of social democrats and radicals on the outside. Instead, others like A. J. Muste, Staughton Lynd, Jerry Rubin, and myself had to provide the links between the April demonstration and the growing antiwar movement. Astonishingly, the SDS leadership was still convinced that the future lay in local organizing among the poor and marginal groups. The chief promulgator of this view was Tom Hayden, later to become a very public antiwar activist.

II

Sometime in 1964, Jim Weinstein brought himself and the four-year-old *Studies on the Left* to New York from its birthplace in Madison, Wisconsin. The journal was started by students under the auspices of William Appleman Williams, a Wisconsin history professor who is now generally accredited with having spearheaded the school of American historical writing called "revisionism." Williams, together with C. Wright Mills, openly urged the generation of young intellectuals and political activists to break with all of the codes of traditional radicalism, especially the doctrines according to which the working class was anointed with sacred historical powers, and the Bolshevik Revolution was the transcendentally significant event for the fate of the American left.

In the late 1950s, Williams collected a large coterie of students, some of whom were refugees from the youth sections of the Communist Party. Among these were Jim Weinstein, Dave Eakins, Marty Sklar, Michael Leibowitz, and Ron Radosh. He added some of the more promising younger historians, many of them too young to have been part of the organized left in the 1950s but yet sympathetic to radical politics. Taken as a whole, this was probably the most resourceful and brilliant cohort that any American university possessed in that period. *Studies* was founded to provide the intellectual grist for the development of a new left. In its first issue, which appeared at the dawn of the new decade, it ran Mills's *Letter to the New Left*, a short document which served as the manifesto of this intellectual vanguard (but nonmovement) until the *Port Huron Statement*. It was Mills who first systematically laid out the doctrine of the American New Left: abandon the labor metaphysic, don't get bogged down politically and emotionally in the controversies regarding the Soviet Union, China, or any place besides the United States, rediscover American traditions, particularly the promise of a democratic society, equality, and community, oppose the domination of large corporations over all aspects of American life, support national liberation movements abroad, but avoid endorsing their particular form of government—these were the succinct imperatives, and they became the creed of *Studies*.

The project throughout its seven-year history thus became a concrete investigation of American history and contemporary politics from the outlined perspective. Weinstein assumed the leadership, partly because he raised almost all of the necessary money for the journal and partly because he among the many editors was the most dedicated to the major principles prescribed by Williams and Mills. In his own field, the history of American socialism, he applied these ideas to the issues that united and divided the historical left: electoral versus direct action, the question of the Soviet Union, class versus sectoral politics, socialist campaigns versus reform struggles within the Democratic Party, the mass party versus the vanguard party. Despite his communist past, or perhaps because of it, he came down squarely on the side of the old prewar socialists, finding that the betrayal of Debs's party by both left and right led to the demise of the American left. Indeed, from its inception, *Studies* aimed to reconstruct a multi-tendency socialist movement in the United States, one that could successfully contest electoral offices, provide room for education and cultural development, and play an important part in the peace, civil rights, and other social movements of the day. In the context of the 1960s, when the American left divided between those wanting simply to resurrect and humanize Leninism and those who thought socialism archaic and wished to replace it with "democracy" pure and simple, the Williams-Mills-Weinstein position seemed to be a serious and reasonable alternative.

In the early issues, Sklar wrote some wonderful papers on the Wilson era in which he traced the origins of what became known as "corporate liberalism." Sklar argued that such "reforms" as regulation of corporate economic activities were anything but expressions of popular power over capital, their being on the contrary signs of a new integration of state and big business. The Interstate Commerce Commission, railroad commissions, and other governmental agencies developed by all national administrations after the 1890s, were means to rationalize competition, to accelerate the process of monopolization of leading sectors, and resulted not in more popular power over government, but in less.

Writers like Williams himself, Gabriel Kolko, and Weinstein, whose book *The Corporate Ideal and the Liberal State* (1966) extended Sklar's argument to social welfare policy, shaped a new vision of the twentieth century in America; "corporate liberalism" became probably the most influential doctrine of American historiography in the 1960s. In the bargain, twentieth-century populist, trade union, social liberal, and other movements were dismissed as either objectively corporatist, regardless of intention, or as grievously misguided in their refusal to choose an explicitly socialist alternative to corporate power. By showing that the corporations themselves wanted reform—though this has since proved somewhat of an exaggeration—the New Left historians also hoped to demonstrate the futility of popular front politics according to which communists believed the Democratic Party to be a viable political arena for socialists. For if the New Deal, for instance, was little more than a brilliant and effective way of derailing radicalism, the success of the Communist Party in the 1930s was merely the left face of corporate liberalism. Sklar and Williams provided a powerful counterweight to the conventional left wisdom that the CP was a heroic and strong force for social progress until the Cold War destroyed it or, as in the anti-communist left version, until the CP was mortally wounded by Stalinism. They argued that even the communist contribution to the building of industrial unions could be discounted, if it were true that industrial unionism, whatever its benefits from the point of view of the workers, was irrelevant from a socialist perspective. *Studies* did not go as far as to denounce the labor metaphysic, since most of its editors still believed in the leading role of the working class. But it did hold that American trade unions were part of the corporate/liberal consensus and not its opponent, regardless of the frequent strikes and disputes with individual employers.

Since many of the editors remained in Wisconsin or scattered to various American and Canadian universities when Weinstein moved east, he, Lee Baxandall and Helen Kramer began to look for some new editors. Shortly after they arrived, *Studies* held a party to which I was invited. I had known Weinstein from my days as a high school organizer in New York in the late 1940s. I was an international representative for the Oil, Chemical and Atomic Workers based in the Northeast region. He asked me to join the *Studies* board and I agreed. For the next three years, till its demise, I was an active member of the board. Gene Genovese was also recruited, and within a year so was Norm Fruchter, an American writer who had been on the editorial committee of the *New Left Review* while living in England; Alan Cheuse, Fruchter's college friend and also a writer and a critic; Tom Hayden, now ensconced in Newark; and historian Staughton Lynd, who was ending his career at Yale.

The board divided along ideological lines from the start. It would be excessive to see the split as one between intellectuals and activists, but every meeting after 1965 reflected some aspect of this sort of dispute. Most salient was the issue of how important the new social movements of the decade were, and how they should be treated. Weinstein and Genovese could barely disguise their contempt for the mindlessness of the student, countercultural, and, to a lesser extent, civil rights movements. At best these were to be regarded with benevolent condescension. The main task was to provide consistent socialist analysis of the main political struggles of the time and an evaluation of the American past from the point of view of an undogmatic but incisive Marxism. I generally sided with the Weinstein faction concerning the politics of the journal, insisting that socialism was the determinate negation of corporate capitalism and that the journal had to place itself within a specifically socialist ideological tradition of American radicalism. At the same time, as a participant in many of the new movements, I was fearful that Genovese's old leftism would destroy the journal's receptivity to their originality. Unfortunately, as with many other debates on the American left, the controversies were too often framed as antinomies: either the new social movements or ideological politics (albeit one sharply critical of old leftist positions).

In the end, it was agreed to subject the movements to critical reportage and inquiry. My only signed articles for *Studies* were pieces on the labor movement and community organizing, written from the perspective of the corporate liberal theme: the idea was always to show the reformist nature of apparently radical organizations and movements which did not adopt an explicitly socialist or even anticorporate view. Lynd and Hayden, often supported by Fruchter, argued that the movements were everything. Though Lynd had been a Trotskyist in the 1950s and came from a distinguished left-wing academic family, he was deeply influenced by Muste's version of radical pacifism. It is worthwhile to review some of Muste's activities in the 1950s and early '60s since the importance of his ideas, and of the groups he guided, has been strangely underestimated by historians.

In his early career, Muste was a Methodist minister of the social-gospel variety, but in the 1930s he became a revolutionary Marxist, organizing the American Workers Party. This group played a key role in the famous Toledo auto strike of 1934, one of the three struggles that paved the way for the CIO. After a disastrous and sobering experience attempting to merge with the Trotskyists, Muste took a half-step back towards the religious left. From the late 1930s to his death in 1968, he organized and led a series of pacifist groups, most notably the Fellowship on Reconciliation, the War Resisters League, and the Congress of Racial Equality (CORE). During World War II he advised conscientious objection to some draftees, including Dave Dellinger, who was later to become his successor at the helm of the pacifist wing of the peace movement. In the 1950s and '60s he helped to articulate the aims of the nuclear disarmament campaigns and the resistance to the draft. Shortly before his death, he was fighting to establish the principle of nonexclusion within the antiwar coalitions so that communists, Trotskyists and other radicals could work with independent leftists, liberals and even some social democrats: no one was to be excluded in principle.

By the 1950s, Muste had become a kind of Christian socialist but he was also a radical organizer of unusual ability. His vision was fundamentally at variance with both communist and democratic socialist views. Although he respected and worked with progressive legislators on specific issues, he worked hardest on promoting direct, nonviolent resistance as the best and most morally defensible means to achieve social change. He was probably the preeminent exponent of Ghandism in the United States, but at the same time he adopted a unique version of Leninism, geared to the reality of radical American politics, exclusively as an organizational device. On the surface, Muste ran or advised a floating crap game of organizations that intervened on every major issue: peace, civil rights, African Freedom, religious and political liberty. He established informal relations with important figures of the developing movements on the strength of his personal stature: his quiet, firm way of speaking, his obvious political sophistication and enormous intelligence drew younger people to him, especially radicals seeking alternatives to social-liberal and sectarian left politics. He spoke a different tongue from the tired leftism of the 1950s. For him, direct action was not merely a dramatic tactic to achieve specific ends, it was a way of life. If you sat at a lunch counter, you were doing more than integrating a public facility and breaking Jim Crow practices, you were bearing witness to human inequality and to the possibility of creating the beloved community. Lynd was deeply influenced by Muste and so was I.

Muste had his own implicit theory of the student/middle-class professional as a historical agent. The working class had demonstrated its passion for both economic justice and social conformity, and Muste was therefore always looking for others who would be prepared to put themselves on the line to save humanity, to call attention to injustice, to initiate change. Hence the middle-class nature of his entourage, some of whom become public figures—notably Dellinger and Bayard Rustin. Most of his comrades, however, remained anonymous, creative apparatchiks willing to work long hours at low pay for idealistic reasons.

When Muste died, his co-workers scattered in different ideological directions. Bob Gilmore of Turn Toward Peace moved steadily to the right of the peace movement, became increasingly anti-communist and mainstream both in style and aspiration. Bayard Rustin, after brilliantly organizing the March on Washington together with Martin Luther King and a group of New York radicals, became President of the A. Phillip Randolph Institute, which, as time went by, came to oppose the militant wing of the Black Freedom Movement. Rustin was always torn between his radical pacifism and his fierce loyalty to a neo-Trotskyist version of the United Front which in the end led him to a strong alliance with the mainstream labor unions. Dellinger stayed on the left and modified his pacifist beliefs in the wake of the national liberation movements of the 1960s. He succeeded Muste as the leading pacifist activist but lacked the latter's authority and talent for compromise, both necessary qualities to keep an ideologically diverse group together.

I had first met Muste in 1963 when I was chair for the Committee for Miners. I was seeking "notables" for our effort to defend some Kentucky miners who were on trial for conspiracy, having staged a wildcat strike against both the companies and their own corrupt union. Muste, a respected figure in some religious circles, agreed to help reach others, including former minister and Socialist Party leader Norman Thomas, who was now a fairly crotchety old warrior. However, not until the early days of the antiwar movement did I get to know Muste well. We sat together on coordinating committees that began to gain momentum in the summer of 1965, following the boldly conducted SDS March on Washington. We lived in the same Upper West Side neighborhood, so I frequently drove him home to his West 90s apartment after meetings. I learned that the popular image of a saintly yet slightly irascible fighter was only part of the truth. Muste was a strategic thinker. By the last year of his life, he was absolutely convinced that the struggle against the American intervention was the key to mass radicalization and urged that view upon me.

Subsequently, I become part of the Labor for Peace network that Sid Lens, Tony Mazzocchi, and David Livingston of District 65 were organizing under the benign sponsorship of Pat Gorman of the Meatcutters, Frank Rosenblum of the Clothing Workers, and Emil Mazey of the UAW. Mazzocchi, a member of the Board of the Oil and Chemical Workers, was clearly the most talented rank-and-file activist in labor's wing of the antiwar movement. I was critical at the time of his cautious, even conservative approach to the war, but he had his ear to the ground. Given the deepseated anti-communism of American workers and their conviction that war work was needed for full employment, given George Meany's open hostility to any criticism of US foreign policy from within the AFL-CIO, Mazzocchi stepped just far enough out on the limb to keep his legs intact. I, of course, got mine cut off because by 1966 I had gone public in my antiwar activities inside and outside the trade unions.

Lynd, under Muste's influence, organized a conference in Washington in August 1965 for the purpose of providing a forum for the many new movements which were trying to mobilize poor people, students, and blacks. The *Congress of Unrepresented People*, as it was called, was intended as a protest against the hypocrisy of representative government, as a demonstration that direct action rather than traditional political participation was the only way to achieve justice. One of the by-results of the Congress was the first national coordinating committee for the new antiwar movement, a committee put together by Jerry Rubin, Frank Empspak and myself.

Lynd and Hayden disagreed with the old left less on the specific issues than on the reliance of the latter on state action, legislative methods, bureaucratic organization and the like. Furthermore, like many other new radicals, they were more interested in novel cultural and social relations than in reorganizing the principle of economic ownership as such. In this, they were early proponents of political and economic decentralization, the creation of nonbureaucratic forms which would "let the people decide" the questions affecting their lives, and the substitution of "community" for "society" (thus following Tonnies's famous distinction). The state was regarded not as an instrument of social justice and equality, but as an arena in which community, peace, and other issues of the "people" could be fought out. The ultimate object, however, was to dismantle as much of the state's power as possible.

The *Studies* board in 1965–6 was not split along personality lines— though Lynd's slow, pacific, and moral discourse was sometimes maddening to the New Yorkers—but on deep-rooted divergencies on the question of what the basis of a New Left was supposed to be. Weinstein and Genovese may have broken with the Communist Party on political grounds, but they were, root and branch, socialists of the Second and Third Internationals, respectively. Hayden and Lynd, on the other hand, had a deeply religious conception of the "movement." Their argument that *Studies* should report the activities of the emerging social movements was well received by other board members. The battle ensued over the problem as to whether the journal had the right and responsibility to provide a critique of these movements. Hayden was particularly insistent that intellectuals on the outside should confine themselves to publicity for them, at the very most asserting their centrality to contemporary political discourse and situating them in the general liberation movement.

This cut to the heart of the role of the journal. In these years, *Studies* was perhaps the most influential and widely read of the growing band of New Left periodicals. Despite its relatively modest circulation, its articles were widely discussed. Its editors were national figures in the movement, and its ideas were considered advanced. Weinstein, Genovese, and myself saw the journal as a theoretical organ of a putative new socialist party that would gradually gain hegemony among the key activists in the movements. Having abandoned the old left organizations did not for us signify the absence of any hope for a mass socialist party, which could run its own candidates for public office, constitute the leading cadre of the movements, and eventually find means of building influence within the trade unions and other working-class organizations. Hayden, Lynd, and Fruchter argued that these perspectives were far removed from reality. They, and the new radical generation, did not aspire to act within the confines of mainstream politics. They were searching, on the contrary, for a way to authenticate their own social and personal existence through action, for a way to construct a new moral order based on popular democracy as the antithesis of representation.

One can see in these debates the germ of what was to become the cause of the breakup of the movement in the later 1960s. Weinstein argued that movements without a political vehicle would inevitably collapse. But his often accurate criticisms failed to come to grips with the fundamental assumptions of Hayden and Lynd. For them, the issues had to be fought in order to build the movement, which was by no means intended to change the existing society but to presage an alternative one.

Weinstein had replaced the palpably erroneous economic determinism of the old left with the primacy of the political; Hayden and Lynd challenged politics itself as a form of domination infinitely more oppressive than economic exploitation.

We socialists on the board also missed a second principle of the new radicalism: the aspiration to absolute sovereignty for the individual, whose power had been systematically undercut by representative government, trade union bureaucracies and large, impersonal institutions. The New Left intended to restore power to the *person* (which is not to be confused, as it often was, with "power to the people," a formulation of the black civil rights movement where the individual was subordinated to group interest). Hayden and Lynd were, in this respect, early critics of what Gilles Deleuze and Felix Guattari were later to castigate as aggregate politics. Against the traditional macropolitics evinced by Weinstein, Genovese, and myself, Hayden and Lynd advocated a micropolitics of liberation.

Weinstein was finally also involved in the politics of *interest*, the underpinning of such notions as class struggle, corporate liberalism, and conventional conceptions of socialist revolution. Lynd, while not adopting Muste's reconciliatory stance, was less interested at this point in the political strategies deriving from rationalist assumptions, i.e. alliances, coalitions, and blocs, than he was in movements stemming from individuality, spiritual renewal, and love. The revolution would restore our humanity, bring us back to ourselves, and in Marx's words, recreate our "species-being." The movement had to be founded on the dignity of its subjects or it would inevitably degenerate into traditional interest group politics. The inspiration here was the early Marx and the left traditions of Protestant humanism, not revolutionary Marxism. Lynd's fundamental view was expressed in a book he wrote later with Alice Lynd, *Rank and File*, in which workers spoke for themselves about their work, their struggles, and their hopes for the future.

The differences within the board were too wide. Lynd, Hayden, and Fruchter finally resigned when they understood the intractability of Weinstein's position. Weinstein then disbanded the journal in 1967 and moved to the West where, three years later, he founded *Socialist Revolution* (now *Socialist Review*), a political journal seeking a new party. In

1972, Lynd and Weinstein came together again to form the New American Movement, a democratic-socialist organization which embodied the principles of both the communitarian and the traditional radical politics. From its inception, NAM was much closer to the ethos of the social movements of its time than to parliamentary politics. Its somewhat more conservative counterpart, the Democratic Socialist Organizing Committee, founded by Michael Harrington, Irving Howe, and others in the same year, was in fact more attuned to Weinstein's original stance than his own organization.

Lynd and Hayden, like Weinstein and Genovese, were serious intellectuals. Both groups were profoundly persuaded that the left had to be, in the first place, an *American* movement. This left isolationism did not affect their shared hatred of imperialism and global American corporate interests, or their admiration for national liberation movements abroad. The idea was to build the movement on American traditions. The trouble was that each of them discovered antagonistic traditions. Lynd admired Thoreau and Hayden wrote his master's thesis at Michigan on C. Wright Mills. Although Weinstein drew much from Mills's *Power Elite* and followed his political writings with interest, he was more of a Marxist. As for Genovese, he remained an unreconstructed Leninist of the Italian variety, which meant that he believed in a polycentric world communist movement, admired Gramsci, but he was also interested in building an American Marxist party that could one day contest state power. In 1964, he became a national figure by declaring, while still a junior history professor at Rutgers, that he favored victory for the National Liberation Front in Vietnam.

However, Lynd and Hayden became, as the 1960s wore on, more political activists than intellectuals. Like so many others, they were unable to break down the growing division between the two aspects of the radical movement, and ultimately came close to sharing the pervasive anti-intellectualism of the period. We, on the other side, increasingly defined the issue in terms of the need for *theory*. For Hayden, theory was a devaluation of concrete experience. On the other hand, what we meant by theory was not clear. Weinstein was hardly a theorist and Genovese's idea of theoretical discourse was mostly too traditional to be taken seriously by the other side. In fact, most of the writers of *Studies* were empirical historians. The journal did publish genuine contributions to theory. James O'Connor's two articles on community unions as a new form of social struggle advanced our collective understanding of the processes at hand very considerably; Harold Cruse produced a brilliant, if one-sided, historical critique of the role of the CP among blacks; and Martin Sklar, though no longer involved in the daily activities of the journal, succeeded in his few contributions to expand the historical perspective on corporate liberalism.

III

The antiwar struggle, in its first years an important but still sectoral movement, gradually came to consume almost the entire New Left, including Hayden, Lynd, and for a time myself. This transformation was due mainly to the escalation in the war and the attention it drew in American political life. As the 1968 election approached and the size of the movement increased, antiwar leaders like Hayden, Dellinger, Rubin, and Abbie Hoffman inevitably turned their attention to the Democratic Party convention in Chicago that summer. Many of them could not have cared less about the actual nomination, though others certainly were attracted to electoral politics after seeing how profoundly the protests had shaken the Democratic Party. Yet the coordinators of the movement, the majority of them either Muste's offspring, old SDS leaders, like Rennie Davis, or cultural radicals such as Hoffman, were still guided by communitarian ideas. Protest and confrontation would purge the sins of our culture: the antiwar movement was yet another occasion to exercise the popular will, to expose the sham of electoral representation, to mobilize the millions for control over their lives. Only a minority perceived the movement as a means to change power relations within the state or to create new alliances against imperialism.

The war, then, was seen largely as a symptom of the degeneration of our civilization, of the futility of bourgeois rationality, which had become the same as technological rationality. Antiwar protest, direct confrontation, was a politics of redemption. However, even as thousands of young people were battling with police in Chicago, the youth movement was beginning to fall apart. SDS, now a mass student organization with thousands of members all over the country, was beset by sectarian squabbles, squabbles which had begun in 1967 with the entry of a Maoist sect, Progressive Labor, into the movement. PL was formed in 1960 as a late spinoff from the Communist Party, partly as a product of the Sino-Soviet split, partly because the dissenters considered the CP hopelessly reformist. By the mid-1960s, PL had discovered that the student movement was more than an amusement for upper-middle-class kids and indeed worthy of political intervention.

PL forced the usually laconic SDS leadership into intense ideological struggle. For the first time, members were forced to declare their "politics" beyond the ordinary combination of vague democratic radicalism and strong antiwar position. PL pushed its own, fully worked-out Marxist-Leninist perspective from which it was never prepared to deviate upon an organization which was somewhat of an ideological vacuum at the time. For SDS had grown much faster than its political and administrative resources could handle. A good number of the first generation of student activists had already graduated into antiwar work, trade union and community organizing, academia or, occasionally, "mainstream" liberal politics and the professions. Many of the old New Leftists had gone to the media. It was a new leadership, then, that had to come up with a response to PL. For a time, they tried to rework the implicit ideology of their predecessors: "youth" became a class, a historical subject and the vanguard agent of change.

The early SDS leaders would never have seen their generation as "agent," "vanguard," or historical subject. For them it was always "the people," the poor, the blacks—in short, someone else. They had rejected the old left, but hesitated to go further than arguing for an anti-mass, antielite, anti-state position. Their successors had no choice but to engage in ideological combat, faced as they were with a competent and determined PL cadre. In addition, one could not deny the importance of Maoism and the Cuban Revolution in the context of mobilizing the political opposition. Maoism, as distinct from the actual achievements of the Chinese revolution, deeply influenced feminism and radicalized many youth, especially blacks. It also became a refuge for the multitude of radicals who abjured reformism but could not bear to support the Soviet Union.

The debate within SDS epitomized what was going on everywhere: it was just more visible because the discussion was open, had immediate organizational consequences, and took place in the most highly respected New Left outfit. The Trotskyist Socialist Workers Party, which had made a substantial contribution to the antiwar movement since 1965, was now challenging it to limit itself to minimalist slogans and leave broad ideological politics to the Leninist vanguard (like themselves)—a policy, incidentally, directly opposite that of the European Trotskyists. Other sects intervened too. By the end of the decade, the entire independent left was debating whether to transform its various organizations into preparty formations, and, if so, what one ought to do next. SDS split into four major factions, corresponding to the wider splits in the radical movement.

The first tendency, the Revolutionary Youth Movement, immediately became two. RYM 1, which was later to metamorphose into the Weather Underground, Prairie Fire, etc., argued that the United States was in a prerevolutionary situation, an old concept designating imminent armed struggle for political power. The perceived agents of this revolutionary upsurge were the oppressed black masses and the alienated, already countercultural youth. This alliance, forged through exemplary acts of violence against the symbols of white ruling-class power, would thus eventually topple the system. Now, critics have often labeled the Weather movement as nihilistic, juvenile, irresponsible, and paranoid; it has also been blamed in pulp magazines for sexual experimentation, elitism, and general zaniness. Yet one should be aware that the Weather people were an extension of the communitarian anarchic impulses of their entire generation. They misread American politics and the depth of the cultural rebellion. Like other isolated groups, they overestimated the repressive side of the state and of the large corporations, prophesying for a time the advent of fascism. As a result, they engaged in some dubious acts of symbolic violence to show the vulnerability of the system and their own power. Yet these sometimes grotesque actions were not out of sync with the ideal of a total reconstruction of the human community: these "action critiques" of an apparently closed universe of liberal discourse can be defended if one accepts the premise that pluralism is simply another authoritarian form.

A total critique of the existing society, one which finds nothing redeeming in it, requires a broad political consensus in the population at
large. Such was the case in Chiang's China, Batista's Cuba, Somoza's
Nicaragua. The tragedy of the Weather Underground did not consist so
much in the nature of its deeds as in the complete misunderstanding that
the United States was another one of these cases. The question, then, is
how they could fall into such an egregious error. Part of the answer lies
in the nature of community building. Like other sects, they created a
discourse for themselves which reinforced the self-imposed demand that
political work necessarily had to be a "family" expression. Just as the
family generates a series of behavioral rules, values, and assumptions,
so the Weather people insisted that its members endure rituals of initi-
ation, tight security as to their comings and goings, and a strict system
in which loyalty to the family was everything. The community in effect
created a new reality to fit the mode of intervention. The Weather Underground inherited the hubris of the New Left and added their own form
of solipsism. Their feelings, perceptions, and ideas were not represented
to others as their own. They had become tribunes of the masses of revolutionary youth waiting in the high schools and the streets for the deto-
nator to set them off in struggle—the new Weather vanguard. All others,
especially leftists, were hopelessly mired in the culture and politics of
liberal reform, inherently unable to make a real contribution to history
because they had been coopted. The violence of the Weather faction was
most acute in its language rather than the isolated acts of revolutionary
deeds such as bank bombings. These capers were informed by a deep
sense of righteousness. After a while, it was reinforced by blatant sub-
stitutionism. The masses had yielded to their masters and the Weather
family had to awaken their revolutionary temper by the deed.

The other RYM faction was a throwback to the 1930s. The notion
of youth as the vanguard was supplanted with an emphasis on working-class and black youth. Led by SDS vice-president Carl Davidson,
Michael Klonsky and Bob Avakian, this group renounced the American perspective of the New Left, replacing it with the figures of Mao
and/or Stalin and the policies of the Third Period of the Communist
International, that is to say, confrontation with social democrats and left

liberals. The party form of organization followed its course. It was the complete antithesis of the early New Left and the mirror image of PL. There was nothing libertarian or anarchist about it; it was deliberately mundane, glorifying the plodding and dogmatic style of the old left. For a time we witnessed a remake of an old film, but like all replays it suffered from having lost its original context.

The second tendency, the "mainstreamers," already in existence by the time of the split in 1969, gradually reverted to left-liberal politics though they retained its New Left ideology, at first. These were the community organizers: Mike Ansara, who was later to form MASS Fair Share; Paul and Heather Booth, who founded the Midwest Academy as a training institute for community and "citizens action" organizers; and policy-oriented activists like Lee Webb, a leader in the Vermont Citizens Action Network and later the founder of the Conference for Alternative State and Local Politics; and, of course, Hayden himself.

Seen historically, this group was old left in the sense of the popular front. Their task was to bring new constituents like environmentalists and working-class neighborhood movements into the faltering labor-liberal coalition and to put new issues on the national political agenda. One of the latter, the struggle for safe, clean and cheap energy, became a central focus for coalition politics in the 1970s under Heather Booth's direction. The Citizens Labor Energy Coalition is perhaps the quintessential formation of this mainstream tendency. It combines energy and utility organizations, trade unions and citizens' groups in anticorporate campaigns against big utilities that are responsible for advocating and producing nuclear energy, raising gas and electric rates to pay for it, and pressuring legislatures to give in. CLEC is a locally and nationally based model for this new citizens movement that pretty much denies any specific ideological politics except the anticorporate rubric. In recent years, citizens' action networks and coalitions have reentered local Democratic politics on behalf of liberal candidates and have reproduced the older orientation of progressive politics of the 1930s and '40s. Yet at the outset, electoral politics had been subordinate to extraparliamentary legislative and street activity. Although the mainstreamers came out of the 1960s, they have left it behind, taking their place in the left wing of the Democratic Party.

Third and perhaps most important was the formation of the new feminist movement about which much substantive has been said. Here I wish to emphasize that the socialist-feminist wing and a major segment of the radical feminists formed in opposition to the sexism of the male New Left. SDS, antiwar organizations and countercultural movements of various kinds shared one major characteristic: women were mimeo-operators, coffee and meal-makers, and convenient bedmates for male leaders. I cannot recall a single major woman figure in the early SDS, although women comprised a large proportion of the membership. When the movement entered community organizing or mass antiwar activity, women assumed responsible roles in the actual work, but were rarely, if ever, considered leaders. Upon reflection, I remember the exceptions: Casey Hayden in Chicago's North Side organizing white welfare mothers; Betty Garman on the West Coast and Jill Hamburg in Newark. I am sure there were more women leaders in the mid-1960s, but I am equally certain that they took a great deal of abuse and suffered humiliation. We were, simply, a male elite, on the *Studies* board, the leading antiwar coalitions, the counterculture affinity groups. The feminist movement became more than the property of a generation; it represented, mobilized, and embodied a large fraction of women as gender.

The fourth tendency was a small but not unimportant group which maintained the deep-seated beliefs of the New Left, i.e. its reverence for decentralization, communitarian goals, and democratic renovation of American society. Jeremy Brecher, Bruce and Kathy Brown, Paul Breines, Stu and Liz Ewen, and many others became writers and publicists of a new type of libertarian socialism, which was not exactly anarchist in ideological orientation but certainly antistatist and antibureaucratic. At the end of the 1960s, it was my tendency. For us the twin tragedy of the New Left was the Leninist intervention and the left-liberal cooptation. For the most part, we went back to the Marxism of Georg Lukács, Rosa Luxemburg, Karl Korsch, or the later Sartre, a Marxism without the sterile party politics and dogmatism of the new communist movement. At the same time, we tried to preserve the antiparliamentary or at least extraparliamentary perspective of the workers' councils. We celebrated the wildcat strikes of the late 1960s in Italy and derived much inspiration from the May '68 events in France.

This tendency was not a movement, but many of the new journals shared the general perspective (*Telos, Liberation, Root and Branch*, one part of *Socialist Revolution*, particularly Carl Boggs and James O'Connor). Some local organizing efforts were informed by it. Eventually, this neo-Marxism also spurred a major Marxist revival in the universities. The "tendency" faded but survives as a current of cultural Marxism among radicals within a wide spectrum of activities today.

IV

I left the trade unions in the 1960s determined to break with my own political and occupational past. My activities in formal New Left organizations terminated with enforced exile to Puerto Rico in 1966 when I was accused of being a leader of the "communist antiwar conspiracy in the labor movement." While sympathetic in the main, the President of the Oil, Chemical and Atomic Workers Union responded to right-wing pressure by sending me off on an organizing assignment in the Caribbean, thus avoiding having to dismiss me. Eventually, I took a leave of absence to write *False Promises*, and then, while I was on a trip back to the mainland, Russ Nixon, a Columbia professor, advised me to see some people in the New York City antipoverty program. I was hired subsequently by Bob Schrank, a former trade unionist and machinist, who had become assistant Commissioner of the Job Agency. I welcomed this. I was tired of traveling and living in motels, tired of trade union routine. Although the unions remained for me an important part of any possible movement for social transformation, the life of a labor functionary was not for me anymore.

After a year as program developer, I became director of a Lower East Side jobs program, spending the next two years as a community activist and administrator. My road was an alternate one to that of those radicals enamored of party or union building. The Lower East Side could not be organized along the same lines as citizens' action, most of which had been formed among white middle- and working-class constituencies. When we fought David Rockefeller's Lower Manhattan Expressway, when we tried to start coop housing movements in the slums and battled police in one of the several hot summers in the late 1960s, when we struggled to obtain more jobs for youth than the city or the federal government were willing to yield, then the movement was based on poor and working-class Puerto Ricans in alliance with the remaining Italians. The organizers were recruited from the many social agencies that dotted the community. For these were the golden years of community action, the time that prompted Daniel Patrick Moynihan to address the problem of disruption and underclass organizing by devising for Nixon a guaranteed-income program for the poor as an alternative to the sprawling activities that marked Johnson's antipoverty crusade.

Moynihan's *Maximum Feasible Misunderstanding* referred to a panel at the Socialist Scholars Conference in 1970 where Michael Harrington and I participated in a debate about the value of the antipoverty program. I had asserted somewhat casually that its best feature was the employment of some good organizers, and Moynihan took this as evidence that the program was hopelessly misdirected. In retrospect, I think the hodgepodge of programs directed to the needs of the poor was one of the most interesting features of the entire decade. These programs provided support for SDS community organizing (the first welfare rights movements since the Depression), helped stop urban "renewal" dead in its tracks, and, equally important, trained a generation of organizers who together with some in the civil rights, antiwar and student movements came close to revitalizing the labor movement through farm workers' struggles and the still unfinished organization of the public sector.

These community organizers avoided the Maoist and Trotskyist alternatives for two reasons. First, both positions struck them, and me, as authoritarian ideologies opposed to the ideas of a self-managed society. Second, to many of us, Marxism was the necessary but insufficient condition for understanding our situation, while Leninism, despite the major contributions of Lenin himself, was not at all appropriate to the building of our movement: we believed that an American socialism had to be internationalist, especially in regard to national liberation struggles in the Third World, but we were even more convinced that it had to build on specifically American traditions. While we were among the most active opponents of the war and fully grasped the danger of isolationist populism, we were more impressed by the perils of trying to relive the history of the American communists.

The "new communists" invaded the factories to constitute a workers' vanguard. Most of the time they fell on their faces, though locally they made intermittent gains. They produced weighty manifestos proclaiming the imminence of the socialist revolution and elaborated strategies for defeating the liberals and social democrats (for which read ourselves) who would, just as in 1919, betray the workers at the brink of revolution. They talked the language of violence as much to purge themselves of their deep rooted pacific feelings as to symbolically annihilate the enemy.

The various Trotskyist sects were considerably more sensible. For one thing, they refused violence and did not prophesy imminent fascism or revolutionary socialism. But they were no less workerist and vanguardist. Their trade union work was more successful because they supported the "most progressive" rank-and-file insurgencies in the Teamsters, Steelworkers and Communication workers' unions, and kept their leftism in the background. Yet, they found themselves in reform struggles against the most conservative bureaucrats along with other militants who were not socialist and for whom an honest contract and a democratic union was the limit; and that also tended to be the limit of this kind of entryism as such.

In the 1970s, an important fraction of the left "disappeared" into neighborhood activism, fights about nuclear power and opposition to the utilities which controlled it, feminist struggles for social autonomy and economic equality, and, of course, the academy where Marxism had secured some beachheads in various disciplines, notably economics and sociology. Often, we lost our distinct political identity as radicals, an identity that was not constituted by the sects, by the leftist journals, by the several socialist schools that survived the breakup of the New Left. Many independent radicals felt that the time had passed when national movements were possible or even desirable. Nor did the left constitute a definite ideological tendency; it had become a subculture, a strain of American life that still resonated among intellectuals and activists but had lost its specific constituency elsewhere.

I had become, in the late 1960s, a columnist for *The Guardian*, which was then the leading New Left weekly, the place where activists and intellectuals debated radical strategies. It was clear to me that the task was to broaden the left public sphere created by the mass movements and that the press was probably the best way to do it. I wrote two kinds of pieces: analyses of current politics and labor developments, and a series that tried to bring a sense of history and social theory to my readers. I wrote on Marcuse's philosophy, the debate about fascism, the fate of the trade unions, the state of the American left, and so on. I remained active, meanwhile, in the fight for urban space on the Lower East Side.

For me, the 1960s ended when a group of *Guardian* staffers seized the means of production in protest against the stance of the paper on one of the factions of the new communist movement, RYM 2. The insurgents were sympathizers of the Weather Underground or antiauthoritarian independents. I abandoned my column in March 1970 with a piece in the *Liberated Guardian*, the shortlived alternative paper set up by the "rank-and-file" movement; I condemned both factions for sectarianism and that was for me the end of the New Left.

By spring 1970, I was part of a project to start an alternative public high school in East Harlem, perhaps the first major institutionalization of the free school movement. We tried taking the long march through the bureaucracies, fighting for space inside the structure of prevailing power, waiting perhaps for the next conjuncture. Those dizzy years of building an institution would not erase the sense that this was a defensive struggle. We were now engaged in preserving our gains of the 1960s in bits and pieces. I knew it was going to get worse before it would get better.

The Depression of the 1930s would certainly not have produced a mass popular left if capital had not reneged on its promise of the good life to both immigrant and native youth. For the American Dream was synonymous with economic security. Capital had thus broken the social contract by closing the frontier of economic opportunity. Of course, young workers fared better than their older comrades who were consigned to the bread lines and Hoovervilles. But if one was lucky to have a job it did not mean dignity: wage labor in these times was self-evident humiliation. By 1933, mass organizing among the unskilled and semiskilled, most of them young, brought millions into both new industrial unions and old AFL craft unions.

The 1960s revolt was caused by another kind of broken contract, one generated by the very success of the system during the New Deal in reconstituting the American Dream. The generation born around 1940 and after never experienced the culture of deprivation and this opened the possibility of seeing the injustice of American foreign policy, racial discrimination, and poverty as signs of the moral decay of late capitalism. These concerns were in fact mirror images of the middle-class discomfort with the banality of everyday life in the suburbs. Consumer society obliged its white, middle-class beneficiaries to accept the end of history as the price of economic security. For the new historical subjects this was too steep a price to pay: a euphoria grounded in mediocrity.

The end of the war removed the one universal issue from the public eye. When activists were forced back into single, often locally based, issue movements, or into trying to recapture the initiative by forming national organizations that substituted somebody else's revolution for our own, the era had ended. Some years ago, Peter Clecak told me that the enduring achievement of the 1960s was the cultural changes it brought about, particularly the codification of a new morality in sex, gender, and race. The strategic failure of the left to create new institutions of conventional political power can be forgiven. There was a time when the movement could have created a viable independent electorate in many states, though not on the national level. These formations would surely have cut the losses we have sustained during the recent conservative onslaught. Yet, despite the right-wing victories in the 1980s, the betrayal by a whole generation of liberals of their most cherished beliefs, the disintegration of the progressive coalition within the Democratic Party, imagination had succeeded in creating both institutional and ideological practices resistant to reversal. Certainly, as Brecht wrote referring to the rise of fascism, we live in dark ages; our justice system is once more suffused with the doctrine of retribution and it is once more possible for a President to defend holding a billion tons of butter in government vats instead of feeding the hungry and thus presumably destabilizing farm prices. But, Grenada notwithstanding, the administration cannot successfully invoke the Monroe Doctrine in Central America. The "halls of Montezuma" are no longer welcome to the Marines and the shores of Tripoli are out of bounds and the majority of Americans know it. Nevertheless, we must recognize that the conservatives are entrenched in political power and dominate the discourses of public policy to an extent not seen since the 1920s. One important reason for this is that the upheavals of the 1960s showed how tenuous are the ideologies and institutions that reproduce consent. Conservatives learned that tolerance is reserved for a secure system and that, while repression may not be necessary as yet, the real test is whether workers will accept their part in the system by sacrificing hard-won gains, whether the middle strata will remain oriented to career aspirations, and whether the minorities and the women will agree that they have been permanently defeated. Perhaps the other worlds that remain the indisputable legacy of the 1960s will fade from memory like childhood itself. But if the new social movements are unlikely to play a central role in the near future, they persist in our own decade, reminding us that, contrary to the best efforts of reactionaries and to the most pessimistic prognoses of social theory, the future is not dead. It is just resting.

Biographical Note

Stanley Aronowitz (1933–2021), born and raised in New York City, grew up in the Bronx in a working-class family. His mother worked as a book-keeper for a textile wholesaler, and his father worked for the Work Projects Administration. Both of his parents were supportive of the American Labor Party.

Aronowitz often referred to himself, half-joking, as a "boy-Stalinist," highlighting his childhood participation in summer camps and educational programs that were sponsored by the Communist Party. Of particular importance was his time as a student at the Jefferson School, a school founded by the CPUSA that was dedicated to teaching working-class students. It was there, starting when he was fourteen years old, that Stanley started studying philosophy, political economy, and history. He emphasized the significance of his years there and of how fundamental the study of the classics—from the pre-Socratics and Aristotle onwards—was for his intellectual and political development. His experience at the Jefferson School played a significant role in shaping his views on education and schooling, as well as his insistence on the importance of popular education for left political movements. Concurrently, Stanley was a student at the High School of Music and Art, graduating in 1950. A violin player, Aronowitz maintained a strong interest in music throughout his life, often drawing inspiration from music and writing on the social and political significance of popular music. He was especially fond of jazz and classical music but was also very much a fan of folk and rock music, from the labor and folk songs that he learned in summer camp (and which he would occasionally perform at union events and parties) to Bob Dylan, Lou Reed, and Patti Smith. During his time as a high school student, Aronowitz was already politically engaged, outspoken on political matters, and active with the Young Progressives for America.

Aronowitz began as a student at Brooklyn College in 1950, but his tenure there was short lived. Continuing his proclivity for militancy and direct action, Aronowitz was suspended from school during his first semester for protesting the decision to discipline the student newspaper because it had broken a ban on publishing political articles. Aronowitz decided against returning to college after that, in part out of a desire to move away from his parents and live on his own, but largely because he found school to be boring and overly disciplinary. Whereas he had imagined that college would be liberating and dedicated to intellectual curiosity and exploration, he found it to be very much a continuation of high school.

Through the United Electrical Workers, Aronowitz found a job as a lens grinder (just like Spinoza he would note) in Midtown Manhattan, rising to be shop steward within the year. By 1952, Aronowitz had landed a job as a lathe operator for the Worthington Corporation in New Jersey. From 1955–60 he worked as a steelworker at the Driver-Harris plant. As a steelworker he helped organize readings groups with his fellow workers, and he also was very active in leading a takeover of the local. His future colleague at the City University of New York and a key figure within the Democratic Socialists of America, Bogdan Denitch, was also a worker at the plant and a participant in the shopfloor militancy. Marvin Miller, who would go on to lead the Baseball Players Association, was a key staff member for the United Steelworkers at that time and was very sympathetic to Aronowitz and his fellow militants (at one point inviting Aronowitz to join the staff at the Players Association). Despite some minor successes, the futility of the shopfloor struggles that he participated in shaped his views on the limits of bureaucratized labor unions and of contract unionism—views that he would later become well known for. Importantly, during this time as a steelworker he would spend many hours reading at the public library.

Aronowitz would be laid off during the recession of 1960. Now unemployed, he applied to the organizer training program of the International Ladies Garment Workers Union. He was accepted and, after a year-long training, was employed by the union as a field organizer before moving on to the Oil, Chemical and Atomic Workers—where he served as director of organizing for the Northeast region—from 1964–7. During these years, when he crisscrossed the country as an organizer, Aronowitz became much more politically active, often serving as a bridge between the labor movement and the political movements of the New Left. His experiences in the Bronx and in the factories of New Jersey, together with his political instincts and theoretical insights, led him to understand the importance of cultural factors, the necessity for multi-ethnic and anti-racist left organizations, the centrality of the labor question, and the fundamental importance of democratic organization.

From 1962 onwards—the true start of the 1960s according to Aronowitz—he would be an influential participant in left politics on a national level. In 1962, he collaborated with Tom Hayden and others in drafting the *Port Huron Statement*, a call to arms for the New Left and an indication of the significant role that the Students for a Democratic Society (SDS) would play in the political struggles of the 1960s (many years later, Aronowitz would go on to publish and write an introduction for Haden's intellectual biography of C. Wright Mills, *Radical Nomad*). Around the same time, Bayard Rustin enlisted Aronowitz to help mobilize support for the March on Washington that would take place in 1963. Aronowitz struggled to gain support from organized labor, with the United Auto Workers being the only major union to formally support the march. Rustin would go on to send Aronowitz to meet with Malcom X, hoping to get his support as well. Malcom X refused to publicly endorse the march, but nonetheless promised to send 5,000 of his supporters. A gifted and rousing speaker, Aronowitz was a frequent presence at radical political meetings and at demonstrations against the war in Vietnam. He became a regular columnist for the national left newspaper *The Guardian* and a contributor to and editorial board member of *Studies on the Left*, one of the main left journals of the '60s.

Aronowitz's antiwar activism and other political activities did not sit well with his employer. He was first banished to their offices in Puerto Rico, and was then pushed out altogether in 1967. Once again unemployed, Aronowitz was admitted to the New School in 1967 in a program that did not require him to take any classes but that gave him credits based on his previous writings, as well as requiring him to write one additional research paper. He graduated in 1968. In that same year he would start work as an associate director at the social work agency Mobilization for Youth in New York City. From there he would go on to found the experimental school Park East High School, which he ran from 1970–2.

Having landed a teaching position at Staten Island Community College in 1972, Aronowitz dedicated himself to completing a manuscript that combined his experiences in the labor movement with his intellectual background in Marxist theory and political economy. Strongly influenced by European Marxists such as Karl Korsch and Herbert Marcuse, as well as the American radical sociologist C. Wright Mills, *False Promises* was an attempt to give both a historical overview of the formation of the American working class and a critical assessment of the failures of the labor movement. It became widely discussed and debated. Free from jargon and scholastic formalities, it was a paradigm-breaking take on American labor that was accessible to activists as well as academics and that finally provided, from the left, an analytical foundation for understanding what had gone wrong with the labor movement. On the basis of the great success of *False Promises*, Aronowitz suddenly became much more employable. Having received a Ph.D. in 1975 from Union Graduate School (which, like Aronowitz's undergraduate experience at the New School, required no coursework), Aronowitz left for California, where he was a visiting professor at UC San Diego and then a tenured full professor at UC Irvine from 1977–82. In California, Aronowitz was close to Herbert Marcuse and participated in his study group. He also became good friends with Fredric Jameson, his colleague at UC San Diego. They would go on to co-found the influential cultural studies journal *Social Text* in 1979.

In the late 1960s, as SDS had become more fragmented and organizations like the Weather Underground emerged, Aronowitz had taken care
to distance himself from the vanguardism and adventurism of these new
groups. The New American Movement (NAM), which had formed in 1971,
represented the more democratic and non-sectarian elements of SDS and
the New Left. Aronowitz joined NAM in 1976. He was active in their Los
Angeles chapter at first, and taught classes for them. He would go on
to be one of their national leaders, and he was influential in their turn
to Antonio Gramsci as their key theoretical inspiration. Together with
Barbara Ehrenreich and others, Aronowitz taught summer workshops
that became important spaces for the theoretical and political development of the group. By 1982, Aronowitz was back in New York City and,
partly influenced by his old friend Denitch (who was very active in the
Democratic Socialist Organizing Committee led by Michael Harrington),
supported the merger of NAM with DSOC, which created the Democratic
Socialists of America (DSA). The merger took place in 1982, but in only
a few years it became obvious to Aronowitz and others that it had been a
mistake. The calculation had been that NAM was too small to have a national impact and that, by merging with a larger but more politically and
intellectually passive group, they would be likely to take the lead on the
important issues while gaining a much larger platform. It turned out that
the more conservative tendencies won out, and DSA was much more of a
social democratic force that aspired to work through the Democratic Party. Nonetheless, together with Denitch and others, Aronowitz cofounded
the Socialist Scholars Conference in 1983, which quickly became a fundamental space for yearly meetings of leftists from throughout the United States and beyond. It continued until 2004, when much of its board,
including Aronowitz, broke with the increasingly sectarian influence that
the DSA leadership was exerting over the conference. A new conference,
The Left Forum, was started and was independent of the DSA (it continues as the largest yearly left conference in the United States).

From 1983 until his retirement in 2017, Aronowitz taught sociology at
the Graduate Center of the City University of New York. In 1988, Aronowitz founded a new research center, the Center for Cultural Studies (later renamed the Center for the Study of Culture, Technology and Work), which

would become an important space for training radical organizers and for the coordination of critical research, publications, and conferences. Key works published by Aronowitz during this time include *The Crisis in Historical Materialism*, *The Jobless Future* (with Bill DiFazio), and *How Class Works*. In total he would author, co-author, or edit over thirty books that focused on questions of Marxist theory, the labor movement, education, and the study of culture. He is widely influential in all of these areas, and his many students have added to his impact on these topics.

Aronowitz never stopped being active in the labor movement and was a main figure in forming the New Caucus, a group of progressive academics at CUNY that took control of the leadership of the Professional Staff Congress—the over-30,000-member union of CUNY faculty and staff—in 2000. Aronowitz would go on to serve as an officer and contract negotiator for the PSC. In 2002, Aronowitz became the Green Party nominee for Governor of New York. Running on the platform of "tax and spend," Aronowitz toured the state and participated in debates and interviews in an attempt to shape popular opinion and to present radical ideas to the public. Aronowitz's dedication to radical education and to the need for imagination and thinking was a constant throughout his career, and toward that end he cofounded both the journal *Situations: Project of the Radical Imagination* (2005) and the Institute for the Radical Imagination (to organize programs for popular education and to sponsor critical research outside the control of universities). He remained faithful to the principles of democracy and the need to overcome capitalism, and he managed to be relevant to popular struggles and left movements from his days as a shopfloor militant in the 1950s until his death.

Publication Credits

The publishers gratefully acknowledge the permissions given by the original publishers to reproduce the following materials. Every effort has been made to trace copyright holders and obtain their permissions for the use of copyright material.

"The Necessity of Philosophy" and "Marxism and Democracy," in Stanley Aronowitz, *The Crisis in Historical Materialism: Class, Politics and Culture in Marxist Theory* (2nd edn., Houndmills: Macmillan, 1990), pp. 28–71 and 256–304 © 2024 by the Estate of Stanley Aronowitz.

"Marxism as a Positive Science," in Stanley Aronowitz, *Science as Power: Discourse and Ideology in Modern Society* (University of Minnesota Press, 1988), pp. 169–200 © 1988 by the University of Minnesota.

"Marx, Braverman, and the Logic of Capital" and "The Decline and Rise of Working-Class Identity," in Stanley Aronowitz, *The Politics of Identity: Class, Culture, Social Movements* (New York: Routledge, 1992), pp. 76–124 and 10–75 © 1992 by Routledge, Chapman and Hall, Inc. Reproduced by permission of Taylor & Francis Group.

"Trade Unionism: Illusion and Reality," in Stanley Aronowitz, *False Promises: The Shaping of American Working Class Consciousness* (Durham: Duke University Press, 1992),